Breadcrumbs

A nutritious diet of daily readings for spiritual growth

Lord, from now on give us this bread!

John ch6 v34

By

Geoff Fox

Table of Contents

Acknowledgments

To Susan, my wife, and family for the hundreds of hours each year I have spent away from them while preparing to preach God's word. Thank you for your amazing patience and valuable support.

To Phil, as well as Dave and the editorial team, who have provided helpful suggestions and corrections to the technical side of producing a manuscript. Thank you for your vigilance and assistance

To the many wonderful friends in Christian ministry who have been such a solid support and reliable sounding board over many decades. Thank you for your enduring friendship and immeasurable input.

To the members and congregation of Haven Church, Gorran Haven, who have patiently listened and absorbed my preaching. Thank you for your positive response and enormous encouragement.

About the Author

Geoff has been involved in commercial training for over half a century. From quarries to dockyards, factories to farms, construction sites to nuclear sites, from royal palaces to oil terminals, training has been personally delivered to thousands of vehicle drivers and mobile plant operators. Such training has included everything from 40t articulated lorries to 500t cranes. But Geoff's passion for training has been dominated by his passion to teach the Bible, God's word. Serving in pastoral leadership in Haven Church in Cornwall, Geoff has taught the Bible alongside his training business since 1980. His desire is that Christians would grow in their faith and in their knowledge of God through Jesus Christ, the Son of God, the only Saviour.

Note

These daily notes will be digested most beneficially when read in conjunction with the day's Bible passage. It may be necessary to read the context to each day's Bible reference before reading the notes for that day. While there are minimal abbreviations throughout this book, we have used 'ch' for 'chapter' and 'v' for 'verse'.

Preface

To my knowledge, no one had ever applied for the job of an apostle or a prophet. Each messenger had been divinely called and specially equipped. They were fallible men with profound weaknesses and sinful characteristics. Many failed miserably in their personal lives. We may quickly identify with them in this.

I preached my first sermon in 1968 at a small Methodist Chapel in West Cornwall. I had been sharing services with my father prior to that, but on this occasion I felt the enormity of the task which I faced in preaching from that most well-known of all Bible texts, John ch3 v16. On that day, if I could have done anything else other than preach, I probably would have done it.

The size and scale of the task, including the weight of responsibility, have only increased in the intervening years. To handle the word of God week by week with humility and faithfulness, wisdom and relevance, structure and sensitivity, clarity and authority is an awesome challenge. How often, as preachers and Bible teachers, preparing to minister, do we pray, 'Lord, if you don't guarantee your presence with me today, then I'm not going!'

For over half a century, I have also been involved in commercial training. The need to apply truth in an industrial context has similarities to the application of truth in a spiritual context. Delivering such lessons with passion, whether it be in the quarry, in the dockyard, on the construction site, or on the factory floor, is also the mission in the pulpit. The curriculum may be different, but the enthusiasm for proclaiming truth and the desire to see that truth in practice is the same. It has been said that an error in the pulpit is like a fire in the attic. Such fires are seen all around us in numerous churches without a Godly heritage.

The daily readings in the following pages are the product of those years since 1980 of teaching the Bible from the pulpit at Haven Church, Gorran Haven. Month after month, year after year, breadcrumb after breadcrumb, we have studied what God has to say to us through his own inerrant and authoritative word. We have worked consistently through Old Testament and New Testament books, at varying pace, but always seeking to explain what is said in all the Scriptures concerning Jesus Christ, the Son of God, our Saviour (Luke ch24 v27).

Before any message reaches a listener, it must have an impact on the messenger. Each of the following days' readings, through seventeen Bible books, has impacted this preacher before ever reaching the ears and heart of a listener. I therefore pray that these concise notes will help a wider readership, whether in personal studies and growth in grace, or in preparing to lead Bible studies, or giving structure to themes and topics for discussions, debates, and one-off events.

As you read and study the word of God, may the Lord himself help you to *'meditate on it day and night, so that you may be careful to do everything written in it'* (Joshua ch1 v8).

Geoff Fox

JANUARY 1
THE GOSPEL OF JOHN ch1 vv1-2

INTRODUCING JOHN

From around the thirteenth century, my family has been involved in the fishing industry in the Cornish village of Gorran Haven. Using trammels and seines, crab pots and long lines on the county's south coast, they eked out a living from one generation to the next.

John and his brother James were sons of Zebedee and were heavily involved in the local fishing industry on the Sea of Galilee in the first century. After their call to follow Jesus, John became one of the 'inner circle' of Jesus' twelve disciples and later became a leading apostle in the Jerusalem churchJohn wrote his Gospel in the latter part of the first century, and, while much of the narrative is a biography of Jesus, this is not the main thrust or theme of the Gospel record. John's chief objective is to exalt the Lord Jesus Christ so that his readers would believe in him (ch20 v31).

'The Word': The Old Testament informs us that it was by the word of the Lord that the heavens were made (Psalm 33 v6), as well as bringing healing and rescue (Psalm 107 v20). When the word of the Lord came to someone, it was to bring understanding, instruction, insight, and reason. John uses the term 'Word' ('logos') to describe the personalising of this divine Word. Jesus is the personification of wisdom, perception, and revelation. He is God's ultimate communication with men. He is the divine Communiqué. He is God's message in person (Hebrews ch1 vv1-2).

1 THE WORD WAS IN THE BEGINNING

Notice John isn't saying that the Word had a beginning. He is saying that, however far back you want to go (to the beginning of the universe, time, and space), the Word was already there. Even if you don't believe in an eternal Word (who always was, is, and will be), you will need to talk about 'beginnings' at some point or other. Whenever the beginning occurred, the Word was already *in the beginning*. 'There never was when he was not' (Athanasius, 4th century Church Father). In the Old Testament, God's word is seen as the expression of Himself. We view something of God's self-expression as the Word, which was active in creation, salvation, providence, and revelation. Therefore, it's perfectly right for John to apply the 'Word' to God's greatest and ultimate self-disclosure: His only Son.

2 THE WORD WAS WITH GOD IN THE BEGINNING

By stating that *'the Word was with God,'* John was not merely implying that the Word was present with God in the beginning. He meant much more than that. He is referring to the incomparable and inseparable relationship with God. The Word didn't just come from God: the Word was one with God. The preposition *'with'* implies a very close and intimate bonding. The Word is not an add-on unit to God. He is not just an extension or a development. The Word is intrinsic and indispensable to the Godhead. The Gospel tells us that the Word who was *'with God'* became the Word that is *'with us'*: Immanuel.

3 THE WORD WAS GOD IN THE BEGINNING

In these opening verses, John constructs the stage of Christ's deity upon which he builds the works and words of Jesus. If this stage of Jesus' deity is flawed, then everything else that John writes about is malicious at best and blasphemous at worst.

The First Word (Revelation ch22 v13) This is not a new concept, a new theme, or just a New Testament character.

The Last Word (Hebrews ch1 vv1-2). He will not only have the last Word, he is the last Word.

The Eternal Word He pre-dates all existence and will remain forever unchanged.

So, how must we respond to these three majestic statements that head John's Gospel?

We can trust the Word's Authority

People have often tried to trump Christianity by referring to history or science, which preceded the New Testament or pre-dated Hebrew history. The Word was before all (Job ch38 v4).

We can understand the Word's Clarity

Jesus' message is abundantly clear for all who watch and listen. He came to reveal, not to conceal. He came to be the message, not a mystery. His mission was plain.

We can know the Word's Deity

We can cling to this central plank of the Word's Godhood, despite fierce opposition.

We can believe the Word's Integrity

We can trust Jesus' truthfulness. The Word's integrity can never be impeached or tarnished. If Jesus is not a liar, a lunatic, or a libertine, then he is exactly who John declares him to be in the Gospel. There's no other possible option.

Jesus is the byword for love; the catchword for life; the watchword of faith; the password to heaven, and the crossword for Saviour.

JANUARY 2
THE GOSPEL OF JOHN ch1 vv3-5

THE GOD PARTICLES

Although there has been much speculation recently about the finding of the subatomic particle called 'The God Particle', which some believe holds the key to the origin of the universe, we can be sure that all particles are 'God Particles' since the Almighty Creator has made each one (Psalm 33 v6). This is also confirmed by John (v3).

1 JESUS CHRIST IS THE CREATOR OF ALL THINGS

Jesus is the Unbegun who began the beginning (Colossians ch1 v16; Hebrews ch1 v2). He is God's Agent in creation. He is also the incomparable Ruler and Sustainer of his creation. There is no other principle or power equal to his. Let us never lose our amazement for our Creator, nor shrink in our wonder of his handiwork displayed in the heavens and earth. We look out on a showcase of exceptional beauty, diversity, and order. We see immense complexity and mind-boggling simplicity, which are the hallmarks of divine wisdom. Everything owes its existence and endurance to Jesus, the Word. The simplest logic tells us that you can't get something out of nothing. There has to be a source, and that source is our Eternal God, our Creator Christ. True science and genuine faith harmonise at this point: *'Through him all things were made'*.

2 JESUS CHRIST IS THE GIVER OF ALL LIFE

'In him was life...' (v4) The Bible declares God to be the Origin of life (Job ch10 v12; ch33 v4; Acts ch17 v28). Many scientists utterly refute the Bible's claims and maintain that life originated by accident from amino acids in a primeval soup. Some scientists try to reconcile Biblical truth with scientific hypothesis by dismissing the Genesis account as a 'picture book story' to illustrate the teaching that God was like a 'master chef' who stirred the primeval soup and served up creation through evolution. But such a notion robs a sovereign God of the glory and majesty which belong to him as the Giver of life. Such life is described as valuable, precious, profitable, and God-given. That's why abortion, euthanasia, genetic engineering, and the demand for 'designer-babies' are repugnant to those who have a high view of life as God created it. Once we reject God as the Giver and Sustainer of life, the One who *'breathed into (man's) nostrils the breath of life'* (Genesis ch2 v7), then life becomes just another commodity which humanity can manipulate and dispose of at will.

3 JESUS CHRIST IS THE SOURCE OF ALL LIGHT

(vv4-5) God's first creative action was *'Let there be light...'* (Genesis ch1 v3). Light is essential to sight. Darkness speaks of ignorance, confusion, stunted growth, and death. But the Word is not just the Author of physical life and light in creation. He is the origin of a new creation and the source of eternal life and spiritual light.

Let's ask three questions based on the spiritual application of these statements:

Are you a new creation in Jesus?

The old creation we see around us is subject to pollution, deformation, decay, and death. Sin has spoiled God's handiwork (Genesis ch3). But the old creation is promised renewal through the cross of Christ (Romans ch8 vv20-21), and those believers who are *'in Christ'* have already become 'new creations' (2 Corinthians ch5 v17). The *'new self'* is created to be *'like God in true righteousness and holiness'* (Ephesians ch4 vv23-24). Which aspects of your attitude need to be renewed? Forgiveness? Patience? Graciousness? Generosity?

Do you have new life in Jesus?

Jesus brings spiritual and eternal life (John ch6 v35; ch10 v10; ch11 v25). He prayed in his high priestly prayer: *'Now this is eternal life: that they may know you, the only true God, and Jesus Christ, whom you have sent'* (ch17 v3).

Do you radiate the true light of Jesus?

John refers to Jesus, the Word, as *'the true light'* (v9). There has always been a search for spiritual light. Men and women have looked for that light in philosophy, wisdom, science, asceticism, monasticism, religious writings, and spiritual experiences. But the source of light in the spiritual world is the same source as in the natural world, that is, Jesus. Darkness is not only the absence of light: it is the presence of evil (John ch3 vv19-20). The followers of Jesus shine with his light in the darkness (Matthew ch5 v16; Philippians ch2 vv15-16). The blacker the backdrop, the brighter the light will seem to shine, though the darkness may not understand it or overcome it.

JANUARY 3
THE GOSPEL OF JOHN ch1 vv6-9

ARE YOU IN THE 'LIGHT BRIGADE'?

Are you related to Jesus, the Light of the World? Are you reflecting his light in your life each day?

1 THE LIGHT AND THE WITNESS

In v6, we are introduced to the witness of this Light.

The name of the witness

This witness was *'sent by God'* and *'his name was John'*. The 'John' to whom the Gospel writer refers is not himself but John Baptist. Zechariah's statement (*'His name is John'* – Luke ch1 v63) restored his speech.

The claim of the witness

John Baptist claimed that his exclusive God-given mission was to testify to Jesus (v7). His unique job was to prepare people for the coming of Jesus so that when he arrived, the people would recognise him. John's ministry was to point to Jesus. Whatever our sphere of Christian ministry, we should also be pointing to Jesus. John Baptist made his position clear in ch3 v30.

'Witness' is a key word in John's Gospel. Christian witness was so obvious, deliberate, and unshakable in the New Testament that the Greek word for *'witness'* became identified with those who were prepared to give their lives for their testimony. The Greek word gives us our English word 'martyr'. John Baptist laid down his life as a faithful witness. As Christians, our 'witness box' is the world. It's here that we take our stand for the truth. Everything we say and do is being carefully monitored. The evidence we present concerning the Light is scrutinised and analysed. What if the evidence is flawed or misleading? What if our testimony is compromised? What if our lips are inconsistent with our lives?

The aim of the witness

'...so that through him all men might believe' (v7) John's Number One objective was to exalt Jesus so that people would believe in him as their Lord and Saviour. His goal was to win men and women for the Saviour. What's our goal? The final comment on John Baptist by the people to whom he witnessed was, *'...All that John said about this man was true'* (ch10 v41).

2 THE LIGHT AND THE WORLD

Jesus is the Light of the World

Jesus declared himself to be the Light of the World (ch8 v12). Jesus is the real, genuine light. John Baptist wasn't that light. Jesus is the original, elementary, and supreme light. He is *'the true light'* of pure and holy deity, just as he is the *'true bread'* (ch6 v32) and the *'true vine'* (ch15 v1). How much are we content with copies and not the original? How much are we the *'true worshippers'* (ch4 v23) or are we just imitations at best?

Jesus is the Light for the world

Jesus is the Light for everyone, irrespective of whether they are Hindus, Buddhists, Muslims, or atheists. There is but one light: the only light for the world. Many may choose the artificial light of philosophy, science, or even religion. Others openly admit to preferring darkness. But the *'true light'* sends out a bright and constant beam, and it's thrilling to know that this light can penetrate and illuminate the darkest hearts. Even the most resistant rebel may surrender to its glare. It's Jesus or darkness: those are the stark options.

Jesus is the Light in the world

'The true light...was coming into the world' (v9). *'He was in the world'* (v10). The sun beams its light across the galaxy to Planet Earth from over ninety-three million miles away, but Jesus, the Light *of* the World, became the Light *in* the world. He brought his light to this world in person. Jesus came to our world to live our life as God in human form. His light shone in the darkness, and the darkness opposed it. His light exposed the evil of men's hearts and the sins of organised religion and man-centred theologies. His light disturbed the comfortable and the complacent. It challenged superstition and tradition. *'Christ Jesus came into the world to save sinners'* (1 Timothy ch1 v15). That's the whole purpose why Jesus, the Light, came into the world. The darkness tried to extinguish the light. Its glare not only hurt their eyes, but it also hurt their hearts and consciences. They were desperate to switch it off, and they nailed the Lord of Light and Glory to a cross. But that's the reason he came so that his light may beam into the heart of every repenting, believing sinner.

JANUARY 4
THE GOSPEL OF JOHN ch1 vv10-13

NATURAL OPPOSITION

The true Light came to where we are (v9). The Creator of the universe, the Lord of life and light, the Maker of time and space, stepped into the world he had made, but the world didn't recognise him:

1 FAILING TO RECOGNISE THE WORD OF GOD

(v10) The First World War army chaplain Studdert-Kennedy composed a poem about people's reaction to Jesus today. He entitled his poem 'Indifference'. Many claim to be entirely 'neutral' on the matter of Jesus and Christianity. Yet Jesus himself made it clear that when it comes to Christ and the Gospel there is no neutrality (Matthew ch12 v30). Some believe that taking an agnostic position on matters of religion is a superior position. Being 'non-partisan', as they see it, prevents them from being sectarian and therefore discriminatory. But John is not saying that 'the world was indifferent to him'! He says that the world failed to recognise him. They didn't recognise that Jesus was the promised Messiah, the Word of God, the one omnipotent and sovereign God who is the King of Glory. If they had recognised him as such, then they would have fallen on their faces before him. That is precisely the same failure that afflicts mankind today. People refer to Jesus as a great religious leader, or a unique example of compassion and self-sacrifice, or the founder of Christianity, but they fail to recognise Jesus as *the Word* who *was God* (v1).

2 REFUSING TO RECEIVE THE SON OF GOD

(vv11-12) Literally: 'He came to that which was his own property/place/possessions, but his own people didn't receive him'. Jesus came to his own possessions in great humility. He stooped to inhabit the planet he had made; to wear the flesh of his creatures. He came to his own place, but his own people rejected him. He surrendered himself to the curse of the cross so that those who believe in his name and receive him may discover that, first of all, Jesus has received them. The Jews were God's Old Testament people who were looking for a Messiah. But when Jesus came, they failed to recognise him and refused to receive him (ch5 vv39-40). The natural position of man towards God is enmity. He is opposed to God's law, God's standards, and God's gospel. He is entrenched in his refusal to budge. Nothing will move him, influence him, cajole him, or persuade him – except God's grace. Salvation is God's work and has been commissioned by his initiative. Without the intervention of God's Spirit, people will not receive him... *cannot* receive him! But those whose hearts God touches by his grace are those who are *'born of God'* (v13).

3 GIVING THE RIGHTS OF THE CHILDREN OF GOD

(vv12-13) We live in a world that is constantly demanding its rights. These are such 'rights' as the right to life, freedom from torture, freedom from slavery, the right to fair trial, the right to free speech, and the freedom of thought, conscience, and religion. Certainly, any society, even a global international society, can devise a framework of rights that is applicable to every member of that society. But in the wider, spiritual picture, what rights do we have as creatures who live on God's Earth? We have no rights at all, except those which God confers by his grace. There are no rights that we can earn or inherit: no rights that come to us because of *'natural descent... human decision or a husband's will'* (v13). There is only one right that God gives to all who genuinely trust in Jesus by faith and receive him: *'the right to become children of God'* (v12). Is there a greater privilege or a higher position than this? We are not God's children just because we are God's creation. Neither are we God's children just because we are children of a parent who is a child of God. God has no grandchildren. Personal repentance and faith are necessary. But once you are truly a child of God, that right cannot be forfeited. Like the prodigal son, you may drift from your Heavenly Father. You may stray from the sheep pen and even find yourself in the pig pen, but God is still your Father. The family relationship may be strained, but it cannot be broken. There is still forgiveness and restoration for those who will return.

But we must also remember that the right of being God's child is attached to responsibility. We shall miss out on the blessings of the family of God if we neglect the responsibility of caring, sharing, praying, serving, and worshipping together.

JANUARY 5
THE GOSPEL OF JOHN ch1 v14

THE CAMP SIGHT

God's servants have pitched their tents among many remote peoples and isolated tribes so that they can bring them the Good News about Jesus Christ. They all follow in the footsteps of Jesus himself, who came to 'pitch his tent' among us to become the Gospel personified. *Made his dwelling* literally means 'to pitch his tent'. Jesus came to camp here on earth: to live among us. Just as numerous missionaries have pitched their tents among pagan peoples to live in their communities, to experience their lifestyle, to eat their food and to share their difficulties, so Jesus has 'pitched his tent' among us to live in our community, to experience our lifestyle, to eat our food and to share our difficulties. Jesus took up residence on Planet Earth, which he had created (v10). The Creator camped among his creation so that his creation may be rescued and restored.

1 HAVE YOU KNOWN THE PRESENCE OF THE WORD?

This verse points especially to the incarnation of Jesus. He is 'Immanuel', 'God with us'. Deity unites with humanity in the person of Jesus. Though he did not consider equality with God something to be grasped, he was made in human likeness (Philippians ch2 vv6-7). When his time had fully come, God sent his Son to be born of a woman (Galatians ch4 v4). Here is the pinnacle of God's self-disclosure. He comes in human flesh, with skin and bones and with vital organs and blood that courses through his veins. Jesus comes to experience our limitations, to suffer our temptations, to endure our pains, and to know our weaknesses. But we must note particularly that Jesus didn't just change into a man, nor did he merely appear as a man (like an apparition). *The Word became flesh.* Without surrendering any of his Godhood, he experienced manhood to the full. He was a real person, living among real people. Sick people touched him, his parents cradled him in their arms, children nestled into his arms, disciples grasped him, and others kissed him. Tragically but graciously, his flesh was also bruised, pierced, and torn for our sin as he suffered upon the cross. Have you known the presence of this Word in your life? Has he brought you near to God as you have trusted him in repentance and faith?

2 HAVE YOU SEEN THE GLORY OF THE ONE AND ONLY?

John and the other disciples had glimpsed Jesus' glory on a few precious occasions during his earthly ministry.

They had seen His glory in His SIGNS

For example, the miracle at Cana (ch2 v11) and when Mary and Martha sent Word that their brother Lazarus was very ill (ch11 v4, v40).

They had seen His glory in His SUFFERINGS

The true followers of Jesus caught sight of his glory. Not everyone saw it, but only those who had faith (ch12 v23; ch13 vv31-32).

The reason why many people do not appreciate the beauty, majesty, and glory of Jesus today is because they have not personally trusted him as God's *'One and Only'*. They have not discovered the uniqueness of Jesus. They have never sampled the blessings of knowing him as the singularly excellent One, the ultimate 'One-of-a-kind' (for that's how *'One and Only'* may be translated).

When over two million Hebrews were camping in the Sinai desert for forty years, tents were essential to them. But there were two tents more important than the rest: the Tent of Meeting and the Tabernacle. It was in these tents that God chose to meet with his people (Exodus ch25 v22; ch33 v11). The Tabernacle was the place of sacrifice, and it is at Jesus' cross, the place of his sacrifice, that God will meet us.

3 HAVE YOU HEARD THE MESSAGE OF GRACE AND TRUTH?

The focal point of God's revelation of his presence, his glory, his grace, and his truth is in Jesus, his *'One and Only'*. Everyone is hunting for grace and truth in one form or another. The covenant love and faithfulness, which were seen in the law that Moses received on Sinai, are perfectly fulfilled in the grace and truth of Jesus. He has 'pitched his tent' here on Earth so that we may come to know his wonderful grace and truth. Doesn't it stir our souls to think that the Lord of glory should surrender his 'palace' in heaven for a 'tent' on Earth? Yet such is the magnitude of his love that he has pitched his tent among us to point out the Way and to show us the Father.

JANUARY 6
THE GOSPEL OF JOHN ch1 vv15-18

JESUS CHRIST IS THE GREATEST

There are those who are considered to be the greatest athletes, the greatest politicians, the greatest artists, the greatest scientists, the greatest pioneers. But they are all limited to a particular sphere, discipline, or profession in which they are 'great'. But Jesus Christ is the greatest, without qualification. There's no one like Jesus. He is incomparable. He is 'One-of-a-Kind'. He is *the One and Only*. Name any of history's 'greats' that you care to, and Jesus outshines them all. Jesus outmatches every religious leader. He outranks every political ruler. He outclasses every noble and royal. He outmanoeuvres every false teaching. He outlives every rival and contender. Jesus Christ is unique. Jesus Christ is God. John has already explained this in the first fourteen verses, and we can only conclude that Jesus, the Word, transcends everything and everyone.

1 JESUS' MISSION SUPERSEDES JOHN'S MINISTRY

John Baptist's ministry stirred and excited Israel. Hundreds of people came to hear this 'preaching phenomenon' called The Baptist (Mark ch1 v5). But John doesn't mince his words when he calls his hearers 'a bunch of snakes' (Luke ch3 v7), and yet they listen to his message because he was fulfilling the angel Gabriel's prophecy (Luke ch1 v17). God made John into an outstanding preacher who was *great in the sight of the Lord* (Lk ch1 v15). John was great, but not the greatest! John's ministry was to point out Jesus, the Rescuer and Messiah. John was about six months older than Jesus, yet he refers to Jesus' eternal existence (v15). Although John appeared to come first, he wasn't the first. Jesus was before John (v1) because he precedes everything. Jesus is first. He is *the First and the Last* (Revelation ch1 v17). He is *the firstfruits* (1 Corinthians ch15 v23) and he is *the firstborn* (Hebrews ch1 v6). Yet before the first second of time was created, God had already chosen a people for himself (Ephesians ch1 v4) and had chosen the sacrificial Lamb to execute that plan (1 Peter ch1 v20). Before the first man, with his first breath, his first impure thought, his first sin, God had first devised a recovery plan. Jesus' mission to seek and to save the lost superseded John's great ministry. Our ministry, too, is not an end in itself but is only significant in relation to the gospel. The success of John's ministry was because he pointed to Jesus. We should all make that our objective.

2 JESUS' GRACE AND TRUTH SUPERSEDE MOSES' LAW

The Law of Moses revealed something of God's grace and truth in his dealings with mankind. The Law is holy and good (Romans ch7 vv12,16), but it could do nothing about removing the problem of sin. The Law was pure and flawless, but it was limited. That's where Jesus' *grace and truth* come in. If we are Jesus' disciples, then our lives should demonstrate his grace and truth. There's something beautiful about displaying these qualities and virtues. *One blessing after another* suggests a waterfall of grace where there is a constant supply without interruption. Water cascades down the rock face in one unit, and yet what is happening is that water is continuously replacing water. God's grace in Moses' Law was a stream, but the grace in Jesus is a mighty torrent. How do we respond to the mighty 'Niagara' of grace and truth in Jesus?

3 JESUS' DISCLOSURE SUPERSEDES OLD TESTAMENT

PROPHECY

There was nothing wrong with Old Testament prophecies, just as there was nothing wrong with the Law. They were effective as far as they were meant to be, but they could never disclose God like Jesus could (v18). Jesus came to make God known. The phrase *'made him known'* is a Greek word from which we get 'exegesis', meaning to explain/expound/ interpret a text. Jesus is the 'Exegesis' of God. He came to reveal and to disclose God to us. He is *'the image of the invisible God'* (Colossians ch1 v15) and *'the exact representation of his being'* (Hebrews ch1 v3). Therefore, we cannot begin to understand God without knowing Jesus. As Christian believers, are we the 'exegesis' of Jesus? Are we seeking to make him known by our attitudes, our conversations, our behaviour, and our whole lives?

Jesus is indisputably the Greatest. John Baptist came to make him known, and Jesus came to make God known. Are we in turn making Jesus known by living for him?

JANUARY 7
THE GOSPEL OF JOHN ch1 vv19-28

KNOWING JESUS

John Baptist had been causing a great sensation in and around the Jordan River. This striking figure, who had qualified for the noble priesthood, was dressed in camel's hair and was living out in the desert, surviving on a diet of locusts and wild honey. But it wasn't just to *see* John *that the whole Judean countryside and all the people of Jerusalem went out to him'* (Mark ch1 v5). They came to hear his preaching and to witness his baptisms. Yet it wasn't just ordinary folk who went to see and hear (v19). Though John was *'the voice'* (v23), he didn't let this go to his head. Rather, he let it go to his heart. How much are we excited about the Lord's work and enthusiastic for his kingdom? How much passion do we have for the church, and how much love do we have for the lost? We may go through the motions because our heads tell us we must do certain things as Christians, but our hearts may be cool and lacking real zeal. John Baptist had an enthusiasm for Jesus. May God light the touchpaper of our hearts and *'kindle a flame of sacred love'* [Charles Wesley]. John was preaching and witnessing to folk who would call themselves 'religious' and 'moral'. But listen to what he tells them in v26: *'Among you stands one you do not know'*. Can that be said of us? We may know the people around us as being upright citizens and regular churchgoers, but is there One among us we do not really know?

1 DO YOU KNOW HIM AS THE HOLY ONE?

Jesus is given the title *'Lord'* (v23). The Hebrew word in Isaiah ch40 v3 is *'Jehovah'* (*'Yahweh'*) and was the name to be remembered from generation to generation (Exodus ch3 v15). Jesus is therefore *'the Holy One'*, the Lord God Almighty, the *'I AM'*, the God of the present. This is what John the Gospel writer has been saying (ref vv1-2). It was Jesus, who is God, who came to live in that small Middle Eastern region of our planet. He was *'holy, blameless, pure, set apart from sinners'* (Hebrews ch7 v26). God, the Holy One, 'pitched his tent' among unholy sinners. He stooped to the cruel death of the cross so that those who repent and believe in him may be freed from the judgement of an eternal hell. There on the cross hung the One who *'committed no sin, and no deceit was found in his mouth'* (1 Peter ch2 v22): the One whose thoughts were ever virtuous, whose motives were ever pure, whose feelings were ever undefiled, and whose actions were ever faultless. Don't you find something wonderfully attractive about the Holy One who gave his life for helpless sinners, or is it still a fact that *'among you stands one you do not know'*?

2 DO YOU KNOW HIM AS THE ANOINTED ONE?

The title *'Christ'* means 'the Anointed One'. John made it clear that he was not the Christ (v20), but his ministry was to point to Jesus, who is the Christ, the Messiah. Jesus' mission as the 'Anointed One' was to serve (Matthew ch20 v28). If we claim to be followers of Christ ('Christ-ian'), then we have been 'anointed' to serve, whatever the outcome, the trials, or the cost. We are on 24-hour active service, which is not always in pulpits, church meetings, or church missions, but in the sports centre, on the streets, and in our places of work and education.

3 DO YOU KNOW HIM AS THE COMING ONE?

John described Jesus as *'the One who comes after me'* (v27). Jesus is 'the Coming One'. His advent was soon to take place, even the very next day (v29). John's urgent mission was to prepare people for Jesus' first coming. How prepared are we for Jesus' second coming? A clue to John's readiness was in his own unworthiness: *'...the thongs of whose sandals I am not worthy to untie'* (v27). In the context of Jewish academia, a student was virtually his teacher's slave and would do everything for him, *except* take off his shoes. The line of service was drawn at untying his master's sandals. Where do you 'draw the line' of your Christian service? Is there anything that you definitely would *not* do for Jesus? John didn't have any 'lines' drawn. He just felt too unworthy to do the most menial of tasks for the Coming One. John couldn't get any lower in his attitude, yet he was urgent in making Jesus known. Do we have a similar urgency about sharing the gospel, or are we still maintaining that there are some areas of Christian service which are beneath us?

JANUARY 8
THE GOSPEL OF JOHN ch1 vv29-34

LOOK, THE LAMB!

The 'Lamb and Flag' emblem is deeply rooted in Christian history and can be dated as far back as the fifth century. The emblem's title, 'Agnus Dei', is the Latin for *'Lamb of God'*, and is indisputably associated with v29. Apart from being the name of innumerable pubs, taverns, and restaurants, 'lamb and flag' is linked to John Baptist through v29. Therefore, the 'lamb and flag' has also become the symbol for John Baptist and is the emblem owned by the College of St John Baptist. While some variations of the emblem depict a lamb with a fatal wound in its chest, it is a lamb standing in victory. The sacrificial lamb, which was *'led to the slaughter,'* is also the standing lamb of John's vision (Revelation ch5 v6). This Lamb has triumphed over death and his enemies, and he bears the ensign of the cross.

John is saying, 'Fasten your eyes upon...gaze upon...stare at the Lamb'. He is supreme and centremost. He deserves your full and undivided attention.

1 THE LAMB IS THE CENTREPOINT OF THE CROSS

In this statement (v29), we discover the fulfillment of much of the Old Testament's signposts and symbols. The sacrificial lamb was a dominant feature of Hebrew religion and culture.

Once a year, at the Passover, each family was required to prepare a lamb. Every day, two lambs were sacrificed at the temple altar. In addition, week after week, people brought lambs to the temple as personal sacrifices. The lamb was synonymous with the removal and forgiveness of sin. 'Getting right with God' meant 'the death of a lamb'. The great Bible doctrines of substitution, atonement, expiation, propitiation, and justification are all bound up in that simplest of symbols, the lamb. From Abel's offering (Genesis ch4 vv3-7), we are shown that the lamb is the right sacrifice for sin, when accompanied by faith (Hebrews ch11 v4). From Abraham's offering of his son Isaac (Gen 22), we learn that the lamb is God's appointed substitute. The instructions given to priests (Leviticus ch16) include the rigorous selection of a lamb, free from blemish or defect. The sacrificial lamb is connected to the Messiah in Isaiah ch53, where we are told that he was *'led as a lamb to the slaughter'* (v7). It was also at this very Scripture that Philip the evangelist began to preach to the Ethiopian dignitary about Jesus (Acts ch8). The teaching of the Lamb of God, *who takes away the sin of the world,* does not support universalism: the belief that everyone will be saved in the end. Why preach a gospel that demands repentance and faith if that were the case? *'World'* (v29) means 'everyone without distinction', not 'everyone without exception'. Is the Lamb of God the lamb by which you have been redeemed (1 Peter ch1 vv18-19)?

2 THE LAMB IS THE CENTREPOINT OF THE THRONE

John Baptist makes it clear that Jesus outranks him (v30). Jesus preceded John and takes precedence over John. Jesus surpasses everyone. It is this Lamb who takes the centremost position on the throne of glory (Revelation ch5 v6). He is a lamb still bearing his fatal wounds, but he is standing, ruling and reigning. If we possessed a real vision of this *'Lamb of God'*, then we should never be pessimistic or defeatist again. Every angel and archangel, cherub and seraph, worships at his feet. It is this sovereign Lamb who will always have the last word. The only inhabitants of heaven will be those whose names are in the Lamb's Book (Revelation ch21 v27).

3 THE LAMB IS THE CENTREPOINT OF THE CHURCH

Jesus, the Lamb, is identified by a dove (vv32-34). The Spirit of God rests upon Jesus, who is identified as the great Baptiser. Everyone whose name is in the Book of the Lamb will receive the Baptism of the Lamb. Pentecost (Acts ch2) was the inaugural baptism of the ChurchWhile the majority of the Lamb's disciples didn't attend the event of Pentecost, they have received the experience of Pentecost. The children of God are born into his family by the work of God's Spirit (John ch3 v6). The Church is revealed as *'the bride, the wife of the Lamb'* (Revelation ch21 v9). The Lamb must be the centre of the Church's worship and preaching. The Lamb must be the reason for the Church's witness and outreachThe Lamb must be the Church's model of meekness and self-sacrifice. The Lamb must be the example of courage and tenacity when facing the most intense pressures and persecutions. Look! The Lamb of God!

THE FORMIDABLE FORERUNNER

The next day, John saw Jesus coming towards him and said, 'Look, the Lamb of God, who takes away the sin of the world! This is the one I meant when I said,

'A man who comes after me has surpassed me because he was before me."

John ch1 vv29-30

Flocking to the Jordan valley,

like a great revival rally,

Jews came thronging in large numbers,

roused from their religious slumbers,

to attend the fiery preacher,

unlike any temple teacher.

John Baptist's condemnation

sent out shockwaves through the nation.

Sin deserved judicial sentence:

no escape but through repentance.

So they came in deep contrition

crying for divine remission.

Broken hearts, their sins confessing,

as they shared baptismal blessing.

But John's timely proclamation

pointed to a sure salvation,

as into the Baptist's vision

came the Lamb of God's provision.

Couldn't hold a myriad candles

to the One whose very sandals

were too holy for untying

by the preacher, prophesying

that the coming King's arrival

would advance a world revival.

So, for Adam's sons and daughters,

Jesus came to Jordan's waters.

People gazing, heaven rending,

voice declaring, dove descending:

since the Father's heart he pleases,

God is satisfied with Jesus.

Geoff Fox

JANUARY 9
THE GOSPEL OF JOHN ch1 vv35-42

SPENDING THE DAY WITH JESUS

If you could spend a whole day with someone, who would it be? Would it be an actor or actress, a sports personality, a pop star, a TV celebrity, a politician, a high-flying businessman, or maybe our sovereign? Would you be interested in spending a day with Jesus?

This section represents the third of three days:

Day 1 (vv19-28) John proclaims the One they DIDN'T know;

Day 2 (vv29-34) John announces the One they MUST know;

Day 3 (vv35-42) John reveals the One they WANTED to know;

- so much so, that Jesus invited them to come and see where he was staying and so they *spent that day with him'* (v39). How much would you enjoy spending the day with Jesus? How much would that single day transform your life, your thinking, and your behaviour? We may identify five things that occupied them as they spent the day with Jesus. These are the things that should occupy us if we spend every day with Jesus.

1 LOOKING AT JESUS

(vv35-36) Once again, John Baptist demonstrates the culmination of his life's unique mission, which was to herald Jesus and to turn the spotlight fully on the Lamb of God. If you are going to spend the day-every day-with Jesus, then you must first look to him in faith. *'Look to me and be saved all the ends of the earth'* (Isaiah ch45 v22). God declares: 'Look and live!' You must look to God's sacrificial Lamb, who suffered and died for sinners at the cross. Look to Jesus! Believe in him! Trust in him, and live!

2 FOLLOWING AFTER JESUS

(vv36-37) Though 'looking by faith' is the first step, there must be a continual looking to Jesus and following him. Andrew and probably John, the Gospel writer, had been followers of John Baptist. But John Baptist encourages them to become followers of Jesus. This would have meant a heavy cost to the Baptist, as there were two close and trusted disciples who were changing their allegiance to Jesus. But John knew that Jesus' ministry was to supersede his own. As preachers and soul-winners, we want men, women, and young people to become followers of Jesus. Being a 'follower' means expressing a oneness with that person. The word 'follower' is used seventy-seven times in the Gospels and suggests that a person is going 'in the same direction' and is therefore 'showing similarities to the one who is being followed'.

3 LEARNING FROM JESUS

Spending the day with Jesus will mean a complete on-the-job learning experience. The two disciples called Jesus *'Rabbi (which means 'Teacher')*' (v38). The word 'rabbi' literally means 'my great one', and it became a common address of a master by his student. It was a title of honour and distinction. But Jesus was not just another Jewish teacher. He was the Master-Teacher, the Instructor par excellence. He was the truly 'Great One'. We have so much to learn from Jesus, and he gives us the greatest invitation to learn from him (Matthew ch11 vv28-29).

4 WITNESSING FOR JESUS

(vv40-41) Note that the first thing that Andrew did was to share Jesus with his brother. We don't know of any sermons that Andrew preached, but his very life was a sermon in sandal-leather. In every encounter with Andrew in the Gospels, we discover him bringing someone to Jesus: a young boy (ch6 v8), some Greeks (ch12 vv20-22), and here (v42) it's Peter. How good are you at introducing folk to Jesus? We don't need to be an orator, or ordained, or even old! If you met with Jesus, what would be the first thing you would do following that meeting? Sign a book contract? Get onto social networking? Call a journalist? The first thing Andrew did was to find his brother. Andrew had his priorities right. Andrew had a testimony to give about Jesus.

5 CHANGING BY JESUS

Jesus saw the potential for change in Peter, which is why he changed his name (v42). Peter may have been anything but a rock during Jesus' earthly ministry (impulsive, unreliable, unstable), but Jesus would change him into a solid, rock-like foundation for the New Testament church (Ephesians ch2 v20). The Lord Jesus sees in you the potential for change but how serious are you about spending the day – every day – with Jesus?

JANUARY 10
THE GOSPEL OF JOHN ch1 vv43-51

FINDERS KEEPERS

You may have lost something valuable, and you have spent much time and effort searching for it. You will remember the euphoria and sense of relief you felt when you found it again.

There are four 'finds' revealed in these verses. Each 'find' is the culmination of a deliberate, purposeful quest. The individual was specifically targeted.

1 JESUS FOUND PHILIP (v43)

Out of all the people in Galilee, Jesus targeted Philip. Jesus fixed his sights on Philip, and he went to Bethsaida to find him. Jesus had chosen Philip to be a member of his apostolic team. This was Philip the Apostle, to be distinguished from Philip the Evangelist, whom we read about in Acts. Although it seems Philip may have been timid or reserved, Jesus had chosen him specifically. We should be encouraged that Jesus still chooses members of his team and family who are reserved, timid, slow to learn, and weak in faith (1 Corinthians ch1 vv27-29). We are not chosen because of our qualities, our virtues, or our deeds. They would only disqualify us! The Bible's great doctrine of election teaches us that God chooses to love the unlovely and to use the unusable. To believe that God saved me because of something I am, or something I have, or something I've done, is sheer arrogance. The only reason we can be saved is because God chose us for the sake of his love, his mercy, and his grace. Jesus told his disciples, including Philip: *'You did not choose me, but I chose you and appointed you to go and bear fruit – fruit that will last'* (John ch15 v16). Jesus doesn't choose his disciples, then or now, to merely sunbathe in the warmth of Christian camaraderie. He finds us so that we may follow him.

2 PHILIP FOUND NATHANAEL (vv45-46)

Notice *'the first thing'* that Philip did was to find Nathanael of Cana (ch21 v2). It's generally understood that Nathanael was the other name of Bartholomew, who is mentioned in various lists of Jesus' disciples. Although we don't know much about Nathanael, Jesus' testimony of him is worth far more than anything else (v47). He stood in sharp contrast to the Israelites of his day, especially the Pharisees, who were false and hypocritical. There may even be an indirect reference to the father of the Israelites, Jacob, whose name was changed to Israel (Genesis ch32 vv24-32). 'Jacob' means 'supplanter' or 'one who took another's place by scheming or trickery'. How much of Nathanael or Jacob is in you and me? How many of us are honest and not deceitful and false? Or are we too keen to appear to be what we know we are not?

3 JESUS FOUND NATHANAEL (v48)

Before Philip found Nathanael, and before Nathanael found Jesus, Jesus had already found Nathanael. We don't know about the incident when Jesus saw him *'under the fig-tree',* but presumably it was private, personal, and secret. Nathanael was alone, maybe in prayer or meditation. Nobody could have seen him. But Jesus had! Nothing is hidden from our Saviour's gaze. We can't keep secrets from Jesus. He knew everything about

Nathanael so that Nathanael put his faith in Jesus, whom he recognised to be a teacher (*'Rabbi'*), the promised Christ, the Anointed One (*'the King of Israel'*), and *'the Son of God'*.

4 PHILIP FOUND JESUS (v45)

Philip declared that he had found the One to whom the whole of the Old Testament points – *'Jesus of Nazareth'*. Nathanael's response indicated that the Nazarenes were regarded as being inferior: the plebs of Judea. A part of Jesus' humiliation for sinners was to be known, not as 'Jesus of royal, Davidic Bethlehem' but 'Jesus of Nazareth' (Isaiah ch53 v3). The mention of ascending and descending angels (v51) is probably a reference to Jacob's vision of a stairway from earth to heaven (Genesis ch28 v12). Jesus is the fulfillment of all the patriarchal signposts in the lives of Abraham, Isaac, and Jacob. Jesus himself is the only 'stairway' from earth to heaven (John ch14 v6). There's no other 'stairway' or access but Jesus, and heaven is only open to those who repent and believe the Good News about him. If you don't come by that way, then you are lost.

Nathanael was promised that he would see *'greater things'* (v50). Are you ready to believe that Jesus can do great things in your city, your village, your home, your heart?

JANUARY 11
THE GOSPEL OF JOHN ch2 vv1-11

DOING WHAT JESUS TELLS YOU

Most church weddings will always have some reference to this incident recorded in these verses. According to John's meticulously kept diary, it seems that this wedding took place on the seventh day. It's just as if he has mirrored the first book of the Bible. Genesis opens up with *'In the beginning God created the heavens and the earth'* and that is followed by the seven separately recorded days of creation. John opens his Gospel with *'In the beginning was the Word',* and it seems that this is followed by the first seven days of Jesus' ministry.

Jesus was included among the guest list to a wedding at Cana in Galilee. We may not know many of the details, but we do know that something distressing and embarrassing occurred. The wine ran out (v3). Apparently, at Jewish weddings, which could last for up to a week, it was customary to serve the best wine at the start of the celebrations while reserving the cheaper plonk for later when discernment had become dulled through intoxication.

But notice Mary's instructions to the servants at the wedding: *'Do whatever Jesus tells you to do'.*

Whatever circumstances, situations, or crises you may find yourself in:

1 DOING WHATEVER JESUS TELLS YOU IS THE BEST OPTION

They could have notified the guests that the wine had run out, which would probably have ruined the wedding, bringing shame and embarrassment to the bride, the groom, and their families. They could have ordered fresh wine, but that may have been an expense the bridegroom couldn't afford. They might have diluted the dregs to eke it out still further. But the best option was to do whatever Jesus said. We can guarantee that in each and every situation we are likely to encounter in life, doing whatever Jesus says will always be the best option. Jesus' Mountain Sermon is full of specific instructions (e.g. Matthew ch5 vv16,25,37,44; ch7 vv7,13,15). Jesus instructed *'Trust'* (John ch14 v1) and commanded *'Love'* (John ch15 v12). Jesus commanded 'remember' (Luke ch22 v19) and *'go and make disciples of all nations'* (Matthew ch28 vv18-20). There may be a thousand alternative options, but they will all ultimately lead to failure, loss, and judgement.

2 DOING WHATEVER JESUS TELLS YOU IS THE BEST OFFERING

Six ordinary stone water jars may not have seemed to be the best offering, but *'to obey is better than sacrifice'* (1 Samuel ch15 v22). Doing whatever Jesus tells you will always be the best offering you can make. And this begins by obeying Jesus' words to his first disciples: *'Follow me'.* How tragic it would have been if, at the end of chapter one, Andrew, Peter, Philip, and Nathanael had not obeyed Jesus' instruction to follow him. Imagine how the New Testament would have been written without the subsequent accounts of these disciples! Yet the tragedy today is that Jesus is calling folk to follow him, but they will not do what he tells them. Jesus didn't want elegant pitchers or ornate jugs or valuable goblets, but basic, unattractive jars: vessels that were offered for his filling and his use. He is still looking for vessels that are fully surrendered to him: ordinary, grey, stone jars that he can transform into valuable vessels, filled with the richest of contents, which can be such a blessing to others.

3 DOING WHATEVER JESUS TELLS YOU IS THE BEST OUTCOME

At that humble Cana wedding, with the greatest VIP guest, there could have been a different outcome which would have resulted in shame, humiliation, anger, frustration, disappointment, even argument and dispute. But because Jesus was there and because the servants did what Jesus told them, the wedding was a runaway success. Jesus' 'miracle vintage' prompted the comment from the *master of the banquet* that the best had been kept to last (v10). It was the best outcome for two defined reasons: [i] Jesus' glory, and [ii] the disciples' faith (v11).

There at Cana, the disciples glimpsed something of the glory of the Son of God (ch1 v14). Their faith, though shallow and precarious, had begun to grow. But the response to the word of Jesus must always be by faith, which comes by the word of Jesus. Indeed, *'Faith comes from hearing the message, and the message is heard through the word of Christ'* (Romans ch10 v17). Different people attended the Cana wedding, but it was only the true followers of Jesus, his disciples, who put their faith in him.

JANUARY 12
THE GOSPEL OF JOHN ch2 vv12-25

DEEP CLEANING THE TEMPLE

While we may have witnessed demonstrations in various cathedrals to do with anti-capitalism, among other things, Jesus' demonstration in the temple was primarily to do with anti-pollution. Jesus had come to deep clean the temple.

'Deep cleaning' is the expression used to describe a process by which a particular place is thoroughly purged. Kitchens, factories, apartments, and even hospitals can be thoroughly decontaminated. Deep cleaning is intrusive, invasive, and comprehensive. Jesus went to the temple to engage in deep cleaning.

1 THE TEMPLE BUILDING

The Jewish temple at Jerusalem was a masterpiece in architecture and extravagance. The main part of the temple had been completed, but the temple area and precincts had been under construction for *'forty-six years'* (v20) and wouldn't be finished for another thirty-eight years in AD64, just six years before the temple was finally destroyed in AD70. The *'temple courts'* and *'temple area'* were the only parts of the temple which was open to non-Jews (Gentiles). This was the outer court of all, which the Jews didn't even consider to be 'holy ground'. So it was in this lower, outer court, the only place that Gentiles could worship, that a market was taking place. It was into this throng of unholy trading that Jesus unleashed his holy zeal. For Jesus, his heavenly Father's honour was at stake. Jesus was consumed with a passion for God's holiness and God's glory. We may notice that although he may have been regarded as a 'religious terrorist', or a 'fundamentalist hooligan', or even a 'bigoted zealot', there was a divine authority to Jesus' actions which was not intercepted or impeded.

How much are we concerned for God's honour and glory? Or are we ready to turn a 'blind eye' to those things which would defile our worship and distract us from genuine praise? Does our worship need to be 'deep cleaned' because we are in danger of being contaminated by everyday business?

Yet the temple, with all its symbolism and ceremony, service and sacrifice, pointed ultimately to Jesus. The temple building as a place of sacrifice was made redundant by Jesus' death on the cross (Hebrews ch10 vv11-12). He achieved in his body what a thousand temples or ten thousand sacrifices could never do. He provides deep cleaning and pardon for those who repent and believe.

2 THE TEMPLE BODY

Jesus predicted his own death and resurrection (vv18-21). He referred to his own body, which, in a sense, would be destroyed and then raised again. The Jerusalem temple may have been under construction for eighty-four years, but it was fragile and flimsy. It would be destroyed and would not be rebuilt again. But Jesus' body would die and be raised to life again. Even Jesus' disciples didn't understand this until after his resurrection (v22). The Jerusalem temple was just a temporary structure, but in Jesus, we have a permanent access, an eternal sacrifice, and a never-ending refuge for every believer.

The body of every Christian is also a temple of God in which he lives by his Spirit (1 Corinthians ch6 vv19-20). Does this 'temple' need the deep cleaning process? If our worship is to be pure and unpolluted, then this temple must be thoroughly clean. Our minds, thoughts, deeds, and attitudes must all be completely purged (Romans ch12 v2).

The people believed in Jesus (v23), but he didn't believe in them (*'entrust himself to them'* v24). Their faith wasn't genuine because they only believed in *'miraculous signs'*. Believing in Jesus as a performer of miracles is one thing. Believing in Jesus as the eternal Son of God, the only Saviour of sinners, is something very different. Jesus knew their hearts because *'he knew all men...he knew what was in a man'* (v25). He knows whether we believe in him like we believe in Horatio Nelson or Winston Churchill, merely as someone who existed and whose name represents a remarkable life. He knows whether we believe in him with our whole hearts and lives (Acts ch16 v31). Jesus knows what is within our hearts, and he knows that we need to be deep-cleaned from the grime of sin and the pollution of evil. Becoming holy is not the way to Jesus, but trusting in Jesus is the way to become holy.

JANUARY 13
THE GOSPEL OF JOHN ch3 vv1-15

HAPPY BIRTHDAY TO YOU?

One song that is most recognised in the English language is the simple song that came out of Kentucky in the mid-nineteenth century, that is, *'Happy birthday to you'*. Many people like to celebrate their birthdays. We have all been born, but fewer people have been *'born again'*. The Oxford Dictionary of English states under 'born again': *'Adjective, relating to or denoting a person who has converted to a personal faith in Christ (with reference to John ch3 v3): a born again Christian'*.

1 WHEN IS YOUR BIRTHDAY? (vv1-4)

In Jesus' night-time discussion with Nicodemus, *'a member of the Jewish ruling council'* (v1), called the Sanhedrin, Jesus declared that only those who are *'born again'* will ever *'see the kingdom of God'* (v3). Like many today, Nicodemus recognised the extraordinary virtues of Jesus and the fact that he had been divinely sent. But it came as a shock to Nicodemus, as well as to others today, that religion is not enough. Jesus wasn't asking the puzzled councillor about his first birthday but his second. A Christian is one who has been born into the family of God through repentance and faith. There are no 'premature babies' in this family. Neither are there any 'stillborn babies' in this family. Though at this stage Nicodemus hadn't been 'born again', by the time of his last mention in the Gospels (ch19 v39), something had happened to him. He was prepared to stand up for Jesus and be identified with him in his death and burial.

2 WHERE IS YOUR BIRTHMARK? (vv5-8)

It may seem to be rather a personal question, but we are referring to a spiritual birthmark. Jesus stressed to Nicodemus that the second birth was not a physical birth. It was to do with the spirit, not the flesh (vv5-6). Just like Nicodemus, there are those today who believe that access to God's kingdom is because of their *physical* birth. They believe that they have been born into 'Christian Britain', or that they have been born into a family with a long Christian heritage, or that they have been born into a strong Methodist family, or a long-established Anglican family. But family heritage, ancestral tradition, godly parentage, or forefathers' faith will not give access to the kingdom of God. *'You must be born again'*. The mark of this second birth is the *'water and the spirit'* (v5). The new birth is marked by cleansing and kingship; the washing of water and the new management of the Spirit. The fruit of the Spirit (Galatians ch5 v22) is evidence of the birthmark of the *'Spirit of Christ'* (Romans ch8 v10).

3 WHICH IS YOUR BIRTHSIGN? (vv9-13)

Jesus spoke about *'heavenly things'* (v12) as opposed to zodiacal signs. The greatest sign of all is that Jesus came to earth from heaven. Jesus came down so that he might be *'lifted up'* (v14). He came to be born in a human body so that his body might be lifted up and nailed to a cross. Spiritual rebirth can only occur because Jesus suffered for our offences on the cross. This is the only birthsign that really matters. Although Nicodemus was respectful of Jesus as the performer of *'miraculous signs'* (v2), he didn't yet believe in Jesus as Saviour and

Lord. Nicodemus didn't believe in Jesus, and Jesus didn't believe in Nicodemus (as in ch2 v24). Believing Jesus to be a great man, or a special man, or even a man of God, is not enough. He needed to trust himself to Jesus for 'deep cleaning' and saving. He is the only Saviour who came from heaven to die for sinners.

4 WHAT IS YOUR BIRTHRIGHT? (vv14-15)

A birthright is a privilege or an entitlement that someone receives by virtue of being born. The birthright of everyone who has been born again is *'eternal life'*. Just as faith saved the snake-bitten rebels in the desert as they believedly looked to the bronze snake that Moses lifted up on a pole in the camp (Numbers ch21 v9), so everyone who looks to Jesus on the cross in faith will live eternally, there may have been Israelites in their desert camp who had been bitten by venomous snakes and yet who chose *not* to look at the bronze snake on the pole. They didn't have the faith to believe God's word that those who looked would live. Similarly, there are countless thousands of people today who are dying from the fatal venom of sin and yet refuse to look to Jesus and live. If you are born again, then eternal life is yours.

JANUARY 14
THE GOSPEL OF JOHN ch3 vv16-21

THE GOSPEL HEART

The one verse that is more quoted, more memorised, and more loved than any other is v16. It is often referred to as 'the gospel in a nutshell'. This is the verse that is said to lie at the heart of the gospel and is the foundational framework that underpins every Bible doctrine. Although we should guard against deciding that one part of Scripture is more powerful, more inspired, or more relevant than any other, yet it is God himself who has brought blessing to innumerable people through this single verse.

'The world' refers to a fallen universe that is hostile towards God. It encompasses an organised system of evil that is entrenched in its fierce opposition to God: his laws, his standards, his word, his people, and his Son. Therefore, it's even more astounding to read that God *so loved the world*: this cosmos of violent enmity that is directly opposed to God and all that he represents.

So, how does God deal with this *'world'* here in this passage?

1 GOD'S LOVE TO A LOST WORLD

(v16) There is no love to compare with the love of God towards the world. The little word *'so'* is an indication of size and scope. Here is a glimpse of God's heart. He has loved to such a degree that he gives freely and unconditionally. For a stinking, rotten world of loveless humanity who were united in their anger and loathing towards their divine Creator, God freely gave *'his one and only Son'* (Romans ch8 v32). Who can imagine how violently the Father's heart-strings must have been torn as he surrendered his only Son to be sacrificed in such a vile and cruel fashion? If God didn't so love the world, then none could be saved. But he loves the world to embrace those whom he would call in the gospel, *'that whoever believes in him shall not perish...'* *'Whoever'* is an all-encompassing word in which there is no restriction, no distinction, and no discrimination. Here, there is no educational pecking order, no age preferences, no colour bar, no gender prejudice, no class distinction, and no ethnic restrictions. There's a genuine equal opportunity in that word *'whoever'*. But the guarantee is not that *'whoever shall not perish'* but rather *'whoever believes in him shall not perish...'*

2 GOD'S LIFE TO A DEAD WORLD

The physical world around us is declining, decaying, and dying. Everything is spiralling downwards, not upwards. Our world is terminally ill since the Fall of Genesis ch3. Contrary to evolutionist doctrine, the second law of thermodynamics spells out the direction of the world. It's in decline. Instead of life and growth, there is decay and death. Instead of evolution, there is degeneration. This is a result of the Fall. And we don't fall *up*: we only fall *down*! Romans ch8 v21 speaks of creation in its *'bondage to decay'*. Everything is perishing because everything lies under the curse of sin (v18). Because we already stand condemned in our sin, we desperately need a Saviour (v17). Jesus' mission to save the world would be redundant if the world weren't lost. God's offer of life in the gospel would be unnecessary if the world weren't dead.

3 GOD'S LIGHT TO A DARK WORLD

(vv19-21) The distinction between life and death is further illustrated by the contrast between light and dark. Jesus is the light ('the true light' ch1 v9), but those who live in spiritual darkness *'hate the light'* (v20). The brightness of Jesus' light not only dazzles the eyes, it stings the heart. Darkened, evil hearts are convicted by the light of Jesus' holiness and truth. People don't like the light and don't want to be shamed or exposed to their evil deeds. In one hostile act, that was the culmination of conviction, they crucified the Lord of Glory in an attempt to extinguish the Light of the World. But if you have been *'born again'* (v7) and you are a believer in Jesus (vv15,16,18), then there is no more *'condemnation'* (v18). Instead, you become a light-lover and the change that occurs in your life has clearly *'been done through God'* (v21). Here's the responsibility believers face as they claim to be *'born again'*: the Light of the World must shine through them to the world around (Matthew ch5 v16). You may not be very articulate or courageous in witnessing, but if your whole life is lived in the light of truth, then your observers will note that your conversion is not man-made but God-made.

JANUARY 15
THE GOSPEL OF JOHN ch3 vv22-36

LEARNING TO BECOME LESS

Jesus said that out of everyone who has ever been born, John Baptist is the greatest. But Jesus also added that *'he who is least in the kingdom of heaven is greater than he'* (Matthew ch11 v11). In v30, John himself declares, *'(Jesus) must become greater; I must become less'*. Here is the secret to a successful Christian ministry, especially one that is public. If you read the advertising blurb for some Christian events, conferences, or seminars, you might think that the guest speakers are extraordinary examples of godly supermen. They have been exalted to the dizzy heights of glory and esteem, and yet there is none as great as he who can say: *'He must become greater; I must become less'*. The success of John Baptist's ministry hinged on that simple principle.

1 WE MUST NOT BECOME CONCEITED BY SUPPORTERS (vv22-25)

All the instruction manuals and self-help books to make better businessmen, sales staff, and marketing managers focus on teaching greater confidence, better articulation, and more assertiveness: to become more dynamic, more in control of their lives, and more prominent. This is, in fact, the very opposite of the lesson that John Baptist had been learning. John may have had every reason for thinking himself 'great' as Jesus had described him as 'the greatest' (Matthew ch11 v11). With a strong supporter base around him, he could have really thought of himself to be someone great. Such large numbers of supporters, such large congregations, so many correspondents, so many friends on Facebook can all fuel the belief that you are popular, well-liked, and important. For some people, it's the 'oxygen' that they breathe. But the believer who is progressing in godliness will desire to give to Jesus the prominence and preeminence.

2 WE MUST NOT BECOME ENVIOUS OF POPULARITY (v26)

John's disciples noticed that Jesus' ministry was becoming increasingly popular. They told John: *'everyone is going to him'* (v26). Envy can easily hijack a person's thoughts and feelings when they see a potential rival's popularity growing. How easily those seeds of envy are planted when we not only see someone doing something better than us, but that other people see that too and respond accordingly.

3 WE MUST NOT BECOME BOASTFUL OF ACHIEVEMENT (v27)

John told his disciples that a person's vocation and ministry are appointed by God. Therefore, it's not an appointment to boast about. Everything we have comes as a gift of God's grace to us and, if we must boast at all, it should only be to speak of God's kindness, justice, and righteousness (Jeremiah ch9 v24). If God's gifts to us include our career and our individual area of service, then we must guard against being tired or discontent with the ministry that the Lord has allocated to us. While we must not boast in the achievements of a successful ministry, neither must we disparage or rubbish the particular responsibilities that God has entrusted to us, even when they may appear to be unsuccessful.

4 WE MUST NOT BECOME INFLATED BY POSITION (vv28-30)

John refers to the 'best man' at a wedding. It's easy to feel rather important at being invited to take such a prominent position. The 'best man' will have control of the arrangements. He will be in the limelight and will be much at the centre of attention. But the role of the *'friend'* is to herald the arrival of the bridegroom himself. His job is to wait and listen for him so that the spotlight of joy and attention falls on the bridegroom. Believers have been appointed to be 'friends of the Bridegroom' (John ch15 v14), but it is the Bridegroom himself who must always receive the praise and glory from lives that are devoted to him.

5 WE MUST NOT BECOME DEFLECTED BY SELF (vv31-36)

Jesus is the one who must be uppermost in our thoughts and considerations. He must be foremost in our priorities. We cannot afford to be deflected by self: our needs, our comforts, our preferences, and our complaints. We must learn to make much of Jesus, for this is the key to a lifetime free from restlessness, anxiety, and despair. How much are we decreasing alongside Jesus?

JANUARY 16
THE GOSPEL OF JOHN ch4 vv1-26

A DIVINE APPOINTMENT

The shortest route between Judea and Galilee was through Samaria. But Jews despised Samaritans (v9) as they were the result of much intermarriage between Jews and Assyrians. The Hebrew blood had been diluted, and, what was even worse, the Hebrew religion had become diluted with traces of Assyrian paganism. The 'true Jews' of Judah regarded the Samaritans as half-breeds and were consequently treated with contempt. They even used the word *'Samaritan'* to insult Jesus (ch8 v48). So many Jews, travelling from Judea to Galilee, would cross the River Jordan and head up the eastern bank through the Transjordan region. However, Jesus *had to go through Samaria* (v4) because he had a divine appointment with an unknown, unnamed woman at Jacob's Well, just outside a small town called Sychar. She may remain unknown to us, but she wasn't unknown to Jesus.

1 JESUS CAME WHERE SHE WAS

She wasn't searching for Jesus in Jerusalem. Jesus came to meet her in Samaria. He came to the precise spot at just the right time (v7). The woman hadn't anticipated that in her 'ordinary circumstances' she would encounter an 'extraordinary Saviour'. If ever there was a model of personal witness, Jesus provides it here:

He spoke her language

Jesus was able to easily communicate with her. He didn't use technical or outdated words she wouldn't understand.

He understood her background

Jesus knew all about this woman's past. We should neither be lazy nor insensitive in trying to understand the background of those whom we would win for Christ.

He was friendly

Jesus began the conversation with a friendly request (v7). Here was the opening to the most important conversation this woman would ever have.

He was direct

Jesus didn't waffle or beat about the bush. He came straight to the point and spoke about 'living water' and 'eternal life'.

He was sensitive

Jesus knew that she was on her sixth man, albeit some of them could have been husbands through widowhood. Jesus exposed the truth, but he did it sensitively. He commended her for telling the truth (v18).

He was focused

Jesus wasn't deflected in his mission to tell this woman about the living water he could give her. The conversation could have gone off at a tangent when the woman referred to historical and traditional differences. How easily we become sidetracked by petty arguments or language differences, or denominational histories, or scientific debates. Keep focused on the gospel! It's through the message of Jesus and his cross that people are saved.

2 JESUS KNEW WHO SHE WAS

Jesus knew that she was an immoral Samaritan woman. She was despised and reviled. But Jesus knew all about her various heartbreaks and the mess that her life was in. He saw the shattered hopes, the raw emotions, and the failed relationships. He knows all about your deepest secrets and darkest sins, your torn emotions and your broken heart. He will bind up the hearts that are broken in repentance and contrition (Isaiah ch61 v1).

3 JESUS ADDRESSED WHAT SHE WAS

Jesus spoke to her about living water and true worship. Just as water is a fundamental necessity for physical life, so Jesus' living water is an essential requirement for eternal life (vv13-14). His well never runs dry. The believer, who has been brought into a right relationship with God, becomes a worshipper. The Christian not only drinks from the spring of living water, but he will breathe the oxygen of true worship. This kind of worship exalts God to his rightful place in our lives (Romans ch12 v1).

4 JESUS WELCOMED HER AS SHE WAS

Within the woman's softening heart, there was a desire to know more of God (v25), and here, sitting in front of her, was God himself. At that point, Jesus discloses his true identity (v26). It wasn't an issue of gender, race, religion, status, or class. The truth is that this woman needed a Saviour, and there, by the well, she had met with the only one who could satisfy her deepest longings. Be sure that Jesus welcomes us, like this woman, with all our defects, failings, inadequacies, and sins (Matthew ch9 v13).

JANUARY 17
THE GOSPEL OF JOHN ch4 vv27-42

COME AND MEET JESUS

Just as Jesus revealed his Messianic identity to the Samaritan woman, the disciples returned from their shopping expedition into the local town (ref v8). But as the disciples came out of the town, the woman went back into the town, *'leaving her water jar behind'* (v28). To abandon her pitcher meant that she was occupied with something that was more important than water from the well. It may have also indicated that she intended to return soon. But she didn't return alone! She summoned the townsfolk to come and meet Jesus (v29). Their assessment of Jesus was: *'We know that this man really is the Saviour of the world'* (v42). But *how* did they know that this man really is the Saviour of the world?

1 THE WORDS OF THE SINNER

The woman's testimony had a great impact upon her neighbours and fellow residents of Sychar (vv28-30). There was something about her witness which had stirred the townspeople to curiosity and enquiry. After all, the middle of the day (*'the sixth hour'*, 12 noon, v6) was an unusual time to draw water from a well. Most people drew water early in the morning or just before dark in the evening. So, did this woman have a poor reputation? Was she regarded as being so immoral that she couldn't draw water with everyone else? We can't be sure. However, we do know that the townspeople responded to her testimony. This woman had met with Jesus, and she wanted everyone to know about it. Jesus had exposed her sins and her failings, and, though she had felt convicted and even condemned, she must have felt loved, forgiven, and valued by the One who could give her *'living water'*. It was this lonely, lowly, despised, and unnamed woman whom God had chosen to bring the gospel to a whole town. The woman alone had been selected for this singularly important task of winning the town of Sychar for Jesus (v29). Where has Jesus chosen you to be a channel of his Good News? Your 'past' need not disqualify you if your 'present' is a testimony to God's grace. The words of this sinner were used as arrows to pierce many hearts. Jesus' last words to his disciples were, *'You will be my witnesses in Jerusalem, and in all Judea and Samaria, and to the ends of the earth'* (Acts ch1 v8). This woman at the well was already a witness in Samaria. The disciples had gone into the town to get a 'takeaway', but this woman had gone into the town to be a testimony. How much are we a testimony in the area where we live?

2 THE WORDS OF THE SOWER

Jesus speaks of sowers, reapers, and a harvest. He emphasises that they must not just think of harvest as something future. The spiritual harvest is imminent. Already the fields *are ripe for harvest'* (v35). In fact, it would only be a matter of minutes before 'many of the Samaritans from that town believed in him' (v39). But reapers and harvesters only have work if the sowers have done theirs. Out of all the preceding prophets, John Baptist was the greatest sower of them all. There's a wonderful partnership in gospel mission. The sower may be hard at work without seeing any harvest as *'one sows and another reaps'* (v37). Though if God graciously gives us the joy of reaping, then we must be aware that he has already called someone to sow that seed in the first place.

3 THE WORDS OF THE SAVIOUR

The woman's testimony was important, but it wasn't on her testimony alone that the people believed (v42). She had been the last of the sowers as she had scattered her seed of truth in her excitement. But the Samaritans didn't have a second-hand faith. They had to believe for themselves. We cannot get to heaven because of our friend's faith, or our parents' faith, or our spouse's faith, or even the preacher's faith. We must believe individually and personally. *'Because of his words, many more became believers'* (v41). The title *'saviour of the world'* may have been ascribed to other deities, but there is only one who is able to save all those who turn to him from all over the world. The Romans may have given Jesus the title 'King of the Jews', but the believing Samaritans called him *'Saviour of the world'*. Jesus was not the Saviour of the Jews or the Samaritans exclusively. He rescues everyone from around the world who truly trusts him for forgiveness and justification.

JANUARY 18
THE GOSPEL OF JOHN ch4 vv43-54

TAKING JESUS AT HIS WORD

Jesus had been staying in Sychar, Samaria, for two days. The despised Samaritans had opened their minds and hearts to Jesus, respecting and honouring him as the Christ. But Jesus' native region of Galilee was different. The locals hadn't responded to Jesus like the Samaritans, prompting Jesus' comment in v44. The Galileans had welcomed Jesus as a 'miracle-worker' for many had seen the *miraculous signs* (ch2 v23). They were ready to receive Jesus as a magician but not the Messiah; as a conjuror but not the Christ; as a sorcerer but not the Saviour. Many people continue to welcome Jesus as a historical celebrity, a religious leader, or a folk hero. But they will not welcome him as the Son of God, the Almighty Christ, and the Saviour of sinners.

A *'certain royal official'* (v46), however, had a son who was dying. He begged Jesus to go to Capernaum and heal him. He had believed that Jesus could heal his son, but thought that Jesus had to go to Capernaum to perform the healing. Jesus' response was *'You may go. Your son will live'* (v50). How did this royal official react? *'The man took Jesus at his word and departed'* (v50).

The statements that Jesus made were either powerful declarations of authority and authenticity, or they were derisory deceptions. They were either laudable or laughable. What made Jesus' words trustworthy?

1 IT'S A WELL-FOUNDED WORD

The royal official (probably an administrator in Herod's palace) had heard about Jesus and believed that he could help. There's no mention that he had tried various physicians, priests, quacks, or sorcerers that were around at the time. He went straight to Jesus. There is no limit to the crises and catastrophes that we can bring to Jesus. You cannot stretch the boundaries of God's resources. Your cheque of faith will never break the Bank of Heaven (Philippians ch4 v6). This man knew enough to trust Jesus. You may not have a great working knowledge of the Bible, or you may not do well in theological debates. You may not be able to explain fundamental doctrines of Christianity, but are you ready to trust in Jesus and take him at his word?

2 IT'S A WELL-CHOSEN WORD

Faith is not true faith when it's merely based on wonders and signs (v48). Yet this official trusted Jesus for the few well-chosen words he had spoken (vv49-50). These were the words of certainty and assurance he wanted and needed to hear. No doubt he had heard of Jesus' miraculous transformation of 150 gallons of water into the best vintage wine at a wedding in the town a few weeks earlier. But it wasn't the word 'Fill!' he wanted to hear, but the word 'Live!'

3 IT'S A WELL-AIMED WORD

The word that Jesus spoke was carefully aimed at the royal official and his dying son. His word is always personal and specific. Jesus' word of life was aimed at the son who was at death's door, twenty miles away. Yet it was not a forecast but a fact: *'Your son will live'*. The good news of the gospel comes to us individually and specifically.

Jesus does not save everyone universally. He saves all those who believe that Jesus died for them personally upon the cross. As you read the Bible in a thoughtful, prayerful, and systematic way, you will soon discover that his word is well-aimed to suit every need.

4 A WELL-TIMED WORD

Jesus' word is always perfectly timed. When the royal official met his servants on the road the next day, he discovered not only that his son had recovered but that his recovery had taken place at 1 pm: the precise time Jesus had spoken the word of life. Jesus' life-giving word wasn't late or premature. It was accurately timed so that this official could grow in faith. Time is God's creation. He is the controller of aeons and nanoseconds. He is time's potentate, and he chooses to work perfectly and punctually within the framework of time. While we may recognise that this is the case, we are often short of patience where God's timing is concerned, and woefully short of faith. Let's not be dependent on our own resources, but let's take Jesus at his word.

JANUARY 19
THE GOSPEL OF JOHN ch5 vv1-15

INDIFFERENT TO GOD'S GRACE

In this account, we are introduced to a man of whom we know nothing except that he *'had been an invalid for thirty-eight years'* (v5). We don't know his name, age, type of illness or disability, whether he had family, where he lived, how long he spent by the pool, or how he supported himself. We do know, however, that Jesus singled him out from the *'great number of disabled people'* (v3), and he comes to him personally. Jesus had travelled the seventy-mile journey from Galilee to Jerusalem for one of the many feasts (though this time John is not specific as to which feast). But not only does Jesus visit Jerusalem for the feast, but he also visits the Bethesda Pool for this invalid. What great grace and mercy to this individual! He hadn't invited Jesus to come. He hadn't made a request to Jesus' disciples. He hadn't begged Jesus to heal him. This invalid didn't even know who Jesus was. But Jesus, the Son of God, who was single-mindedly focused on his Father's plan for the cross, interrupts his supreme mission to go to the obscure north-east part of the city to find an unknown, unnamed, unhealthy nobody and give him the opportunity of eternal life. Isn't that absolutely amazing? Yet the little indications in the narrative may lead us to conclude that this man was indifferent to God's grace.

You would think that this long-term invalid would have been ecstatic about the compassion and grace shown to him. Maybe he was, but it's not reflected in John's account. Instead, he seemed to be:

1 UNENTHUSIASTIC ABOUT HEALING

When the divine Doctor of souls and bodies asked whether he wanted to get well, he didn't yell 'Yes!' (v7). Apparently, at certain times, the waters of the pool were stirred, it was believed, by an angel. Perhaps the minerals in the sediment were particularly helpful to therapeutic and healing treatment. But unlike other people whom Jesus healed in the Gospels (for example, Matthew ch8 v2; Mark ch10 v51; Luke ch5 v19; ch7 v7; ch17 v13; John ch4 v47), this man seemed indifferent to healing. Perhaps he realised that 'getting well' would mean 'getting work'. He may have relied on begging for so long that it was his way of life. Some people today realise that becoming a Christian is going to mean a huge change, and they are apprehensive of that change, even when it means spiritual healing and forgiveness. It's possible, too, for believers to lose their excitement and enthusiasm for God's grace. Prayer, Bible study, worship, and fellowship may become dry, dull, routine affairs.

2 UNGRATEFUL FOR THE OPPORTUNITY

This man didn't appear to have any friends or family. Jesus was the only one who could help him, and he was right there alongside him. But the man only thought of Jesus as someone who might haul him to the edge of the pool at the right moment. Jesus didn't come to him to be a 'care assistant' or a 'voluntary help': he came to bring life in all its fullness (John ch10 v10). Jesus hadn't gone to Bethesda Pool to chat about the weather, or to provide a shoulder to cry on, or to be a physiotherapist, or a stress counsellor. He had gone to make him better. Jesus hadn't gone to the pool to be a 'life guard', but a 'life giver'! How grateful are you for God's grace to you?

3 UNCONCERNED ABOUT JESUS

The single greatest event in this man's life had just taken place. But he knew absolutely nothing about Jesus nor, it seems, had he made any enquiries (v13). Yet it was convenient for him to blame Jesus when he was questioned about breaking Sabbath rules (v10-v11). Then, when he discovers Jesus' name, he goes straight to the Jews and reports him. How many of those within the precincts of the church have little concern or passion for Jesus? How few display Paul's yearning (Philippians ch3 v10)?

4 UNCERTAIN OF FORGIVENESS

Jesus didn't heal this man in response to his faith. Jesus didn't tell him that his sins were forgiven. Even miraculous experiences don't prove conversion. Jesus did say, however, *'Stop sinning or something worse may happen to you'* (v14). Abuse of drugs and alcohol, promiscuous living, and criminal activities can produce illness and disability. But the sickness of sin and the eternal consequences of the Fall (Genesis ch3) can only be remedied through the forgiveness of a crucified Saviour.

JANUARY 20
THE GOSPEL OF JOHN ch5 vv16-30

JESUS EQUALS GOD

The tension between Athanasius and Arius of the fourth century has continued throughout history and into the twenty-first century. The present-day Arians will try and tell us that Jesus is the greatest of men, the highest form of creation, and the chief among God's agencies, but they deny him deity. While those who follow in Athanasius' footsteps will contend unequivocally for the equality of God the Father, God the Son, and God the Holy Spirit. But Athanasius was only teaching what John had already set out in his gospel record: that Jesus is God and is equal with his Father.

The whole aim of John's Gospel is so that people may believe that Jesus is the Christ, the Son of God (ch20 v31). The two words that frequently occur together in this Gospel are 'believe' and 'life'. The acid test is who you believe Jesus to be. The Jews persecuted Jesus (v16), not only because he had healed the paralysed man on the Sabbath, but because Jesus claimed equality with his heavenly Father (v18). The fanatical hostility was such that the Jews were ready to kill Jesus for his claim. Similarly, today, you can talk about the Jesus of history, or the Jesus of Nazareth, the Jesus of the children's stories, or the Jesus of the crucifix, and it won't cause a ripple. But as soon as you assert the deity of Christ, then you may expect a storm of hostility and vitriol. Jesus' answer to the Jews (vv19-30) reveals three dimensions of his equality with God.

1 JESUS HAS EQUAL PRIVILEGE (vv19-21)

Jesus is one with the Father (ref ch10 v30). Everything his Father was doing, he was doing, and everything he was doing, his Father was doing. So if the Jews were accusing Jesus of working on the Sabbath, they were also accusing God, for Jesus is *'the true God'* (1 John ch5 v20). He had shared his Father's glory (John ch17 v5) and had confirmed that he doesn't work independently of his Father. Just in case you may have the idea that there's a kind of mechanical, clinical, impersonal relationship between God the Father and God the Son, nothing could be further from the truth. Not only should the terms 'Father' and 'Son' underscore their personal relationship, but v20 declares that *'the Father loves the Son and shows him all he does'*. That loving relationship within the Godhead is shown in the *'greater things'* (v20) of his grace to sinners. Jesus' equal privilege with the Father meant the cross (2 Corinthians ch5 v19) because the Godhead was united in its saving, redeeming, rescuing achievement.

2 JESUS HAS EQUAL HONOUR (vv22-23)

'Honour', which includes worship, adoration, and praise, is deserved equally by Jesus. No wonder the Jews, who didn't believe in his deity, were so incensed that Jesus claimed equal honour to Jehovah. But the angels and archangels, cherubim and seraphim, the very beings who spend their time in the holy presence of the Almighty, are commanded to give equal honour and worship to Jesus (Hebrews ch1 v6). God will not give away his honour to any other being (Isaiah ch42 v8), and therefore Jesus is undoubtedly God. That equality of honour

is reflected in our prayers, our remembrance at the Lord's Supper, in our hymns, and even in our benedictions where we refer to the *'name of the Father, and of the Son, and of the Holy Spirit'*.

3 JESUS HAS EQUAL AUTHORITY (vv24-30)

Jesus announced to his disciples just before his ascension that *'all authority in heaven and earth has been given to me'* (Matthew ch28 v18). The equality of Jesus' authority is the very reason that we are empowered to preach the global gospel. The word of Jesus is the word of God, and therefore, we observe Jesus' authority in:

The Word of Eternal Life

(v24) Those who hear his word and believe become the recipients of abundant, eternal life.

The Word of Resurrection

(v25, vv28-29) There is no power on earth or hell that can resist the authoritative voice of Jesus, the Son of God.

The Word of Judgement

(vv26-27, v30) Jesus is the appointed Judge of everyone (Acts ch17 v31). None will escape or be absent from his final judgement. But the Christian's future is secure because Jesus is the Lord God Almighty who reigns sovereignly. Do you know whom you have believed? (2 Timothy ch1 v12).

JANUARY 21
THE GOSPEL OF JOHN ch5 vv31-47

TESTIMONIES OF JESUS

As Christians, we should never cause confusion in the minds of those who listen to us and observe us. Our conversations, our actions, our general conduct, as well as our preaching, should ultimately point to Jesus. The last words that Jesus said to his followers were: *'You will be my witnesses'* (Acts ch1 v8). Listening to some censorious critics, you may be forgiven for thinking that Jesus had said, 'You will be my judges!' Or to read some articles and books, you might have thought that Jesus had said, 'You will be my prosecuting barristers!' But the responsibility of every believer is to bear testimony to Jesus: who he is and what he means to them individually. The word for 'testimony/witness' is used forty-seven times in John's Gospel alone. It implies a witness, whose testimony is so profoundly reliable, that they are ready to give their life in testifying to the truth (hence our English word *'martyr'*).

1 JOHN BAPTIST'S TESTIMONY (vv33-35)

Although the Jewish leaders saw John as a local celebrity, they squirmed at his message of repentance. Jesus had likened John's testimony to a lamp *'that burned and gave light'*. But John was just a reflection of *'the true light'* (ch1 v9) and he had come to be *'a witness to the light'* (ch1 v8). John Baptist was the greatest reflector of Jesus (Matthew ch11 v11), but he was still only a 'reflector'. Believers are called to be reflectors of Jesus. The light of truth, the light of God's word, the light of righteousness, the light of faithfulness, and the light of the gospel should be clearly reflected in their lives.

2 THE MIRACLES' TESTIMONY (v36)

Jesus' works, and especially his miraculous signs, were further testimony to who he was (ref ch3 v2). The kind of miracles Jesus was performing could only be done by God (ch14 v11). Jesus was a man on a mission. His mission was to finish the work that his Father had given him. The cross was the culmination of that work. His miraculous signs were an important part of his mission, and all the lines of history and prophecy, ministry, and mission converged on the cross. It was at the cross that Jesus would reveal the full extent of the miracle of God's grace to sinners. Despite all the temptations and tactics to thwart that mission and abort that work, Jesus completed every detail (ch19 v30). In that greatest event, the death of the Lord of Life (the most potent miraculous sign in history), he has triumphed over sin and death.

3 THE SCRIPTURES' TESTIMONY (vv39-40)

Although the orthodox Jews had studied the Law with zeal and diligence, they had seriously missed the fact that all the Scriptures pointed to Jesus. Though *'diligent study'* of God's word must be applauded and encouraged, it's possible to have fervour without faith. You may be able to recite the first five books of the Bible word for word, but have you listened to what the word is saying to you because faith comes by hearing (Romans ch10 v17)? Jesus' rebuke accounted for their 'diligent study' (v40).

4 MOSES' TESTIMONY (vv45-47)

If the Jewish leaders are in the dock, then Moses is the chief prosecution witness. They looked upon Moses as their advocate, but in fact, he was their accuser (Deuteronomy ch31 v26). Jesus was the complete fulfilment of Moses' Law. He kept the Law in every detail as part of a life of holiness and obedience to the divine master plan.

5 GOD THE FATHER'S TESTIMONY (vv37-38)

Jesus' mission had been approved, authorised, and anointed by God. The Father publicly endorsed the work of his Son (see Luke ch3 v22; ch9 v35; John ch12 v28). God the Father's testimony at Jesus' birth, throughout his life, and in his death confirms the unique and exclusive mission.

6 YOUR TESTIMONY?

Do you have a personal testimony of Jesus' work of salvation in your life? Are you ready to be a witness for Jesus in the things you do as much as in the things you say? Jesus doesn't need *'human testimony'* (v34), but if he were relying on you as his only 'character witness', what personal evidence would you be able to offer as to what he has done for you and what he means to you? Would he be able to say of you as he did of his Father, *'I know that his testimony is valid'* (v32)?

JANUARY 22
THE GOSPEL OF JOHN ch6 vv1-15

THE FOOD TESTS

For anyone who has followed the politics of the Middle East, the Golan Heights has been a regular feature. Situated on the eastern side of the Sea of Galilee and rising to six thousand feet (one thousand eight hundred and thirty metres), these mountains are of enormous strategic importance.

It was to the Golan Heights that Jesus went with his disciples (v3). They had crossed the Sea of Galilee (v1) and they were being hotly pursued by a huge crowd of people *'because they saw the miraculous signs he had performed on the sick.'* (v2).

If the Golan Heights was the 'place', the 'time' was early spring. *The Jewish Passover was near'* (v4), and we know that this was celebrated in March/April. Although Jesus may have been looking for some privacy as he climbed the mountains with his disciples, he did not escape the large crowd. As the Gospel writers concur that there were five thousand men, the total number could easily have been twenty thousand, with the women and children too. So many mouths to feed! And with only *'five small barley loaves and two small fish'*! If the Food Standards Agency had been there at that time, they would have had a 'field day' with their health and safety concerns. Yet on this occasion, there were three specific tests that had been conducted.

1 PHILIP'S TEST OF FAITH (vv5-7)

Jesus was conducting a test of his own. He wanted to prove Philip's faith. The word for *'test'* can also mean *'examine'*. When Jesus asked Philip where he could find bread for all these people (v5), he wasn't stumped. Jesus was not in a dilemma and needed help to get him out of this crisis. He had a plan of his own (v6). For Philip, the realisation of the enormous challenge would have stunned him. Here were 20,000 people up a mountain at the end of the day with nothing to eat, and Philip's evaluation of this predicament caused him to conclude that eight months' wages wouldn't be enough to buy bread for everyone (v7). But Philip had calculated without Jesus. Philip had done precisely what we may do so often when crises storm into our lives. We get shocked and anxious, examining all our own resources before turning to Jesus. We may think that our faith is strong and enduring when everything is going fine, but it's only when we hit a trouble-spot that the calibre of our faith is really known.

2 ANDREW'S TEST OF COMMITMENT (vv8-10)

Andrew's faith may not have been much greater than Philip's, but he did spot a lad in the crowd with his small picnic, and he brought the boy to Jesus (v9). Andrew could have seen the boy with his lunch and disregarded it altogether, but he took these meagre resources to Jesus. And that's precisely the test! You are not asked to have more than you have got. You are not required to be more gifted, more resourceful, more intelligent, or more skilled than you are. The test is whether you are prepared to bring what you have to Jesus. You may think that you have very little compared with others – just five small loaves and five small fish, with the emphasis on 'small'. But note carefully that the total commitment of that small offering, in Jesus' hands, was able to satisfy 20,000 people. Who knows what your total commitment will achieve in the hands of the Lord Jesus?

3 JESUS' TEST OF OBEDIENCE (vv14-15)

Because of this great miracle (recorded in all four Gospels), the people regarded Jesus as a great prophet, even a 'second Moses' (Deuteronomy ch18 v15). Just as Moses had liberated his people from the Egyptians, perhaps Jesus would now liberate his people from the Romans. Jesus was at the height of his popularity in Galilee, and the people were ready to compel him to be their king. But Jesus was committed to his Father's plan to rescue his people from their sin. This would not be achieved by a crown but by a cross. Jesus demonstrated total obedience. He would not be deflected from the horrors of suffering and death. If Jesus had become the 'people's King' at this point, he could never have become the 'people's Saviour'. But Jesus passed the test of obedience with the highest possible marks and has gained the highest possible place (Philippians ch2 v9-10). How often does our ego get in the way of Christian service? Are you ready to take up your cross for Jesus, who was ready to take up his cross for you (Mark ch8 v34)?

JANUARY 23
THE GOSPEL OF JOHN ch6 vv16-24

TAKING JESUS INTO THE BOAT

Storms on Lake Galilee were often strong and sudden. From six hundred and eighty-five feet (two hundred and nine metres) below the level of the Mediterranean Sea, Galilee's hot air rises to meet the cold air funnelling down from the snow-capped summit of Mount Hermon in the north. The clash of hot and cold air can produce violent squalls that even keep motorboats within the shelter of the shore today. To be in a rowing boat or a sailing boat at night could be extremely hazardous. This is where the disciples found themselves on the night following Jesus' miraculous feeding of the huge crowd of people. They were three and a half miles out into the lake when the storm erupted. Between 3 am and 6 am, in the darkest part of the night, Jesus came to them. They thought he was a ghost and *'they were terrified'* (v19). But Jesus heard their cry (Mark ch6 v49); he saw their terror; he knew their need. His response was: *'It is I; don't be afraid'* (v20). It was at that point *'they were willing to take him into the boat'* (v21). Many more are unwilling to take Jesus into their 'boat' for their voyage on the 'sea of life'. They would rather row against the waves alone. They would rather encounter scary moments alone. They would rather ride out the storm alone than take Jesus into their 'boat'.

How many professing Christians are not willing to take Jesus into their boat? They would rather he kept on 'walking on the water' outside their boat, knowing that if he came closer, it would seriously affect their lifestyle, mindset, priorities, and direction.

1 HOW DO YOU SEE JESUS?

Is he merely the phantom of your thoughts, or is he the darling of your heart? Is he a ghost or God? These verses reveal the substance of Jesus' mission and ministry:

Our Intercessor

The reason Jesus was not in the boat sailing was because he was on the mountain praying (Matthew ch14 v23; Mark ch6 vv45-46). At the end of the day, after Jesus had taken care of his disciples and 20,000 people, he found time to be alone in prayer. What was he praying about? Obviously, his relationship with his Father was paramount, but Jesus' whole purpose in being a man on earth was to do his Father's will. Every single person for whom the Saviour shed his blood is immeasurably precious to him. Jesus intercedes for them. He prays to the Father about them.

Our Creator

Jesus is the Creator of bread and fish, mountains and lakes, winds and waves. All things were made through him (ch1 v3; Colossians ch1 v16). As believers, we should never be hesitant or embarrassed about declaring that God made everything out of nothing for something. Why are we always on the back foot when it comes to affirming the truth of Christ, our Creator?

Our Saviour

Jesus stepped into their storm-tossed boat when the disciples were in their greatest need. Jesus saved Peter from drowning (Matthew ch14 vv28-31). He saved the disciples from their distress. Jesus is the only Saviour who can save from sin, death, and hell. He must come to us, not as able-seaman or oarsman, but as Pilot.

Our Comforter

The presence of Jesus made all the difference to the disciples. His presence in their frail boat brought hope, comfort, and assurance. We need reminding from time to time when the waves of life become particularly ferocious and threaten to capsize our 'little boat': *'It is I'*. Jesus is actually there in the middle of our storm. He is there in the *'all things'* of Romans ch8 v28.

2 HOW DO YOU SEARCH FOR JESUS?

The crowds expected Jesus to be still on the eastern shore of the lake (v22). The disciples expected Jesus to be up the mountain, not walking on the lake. We may have our pre-conceived ideas of those things and places we expect Jesus to be in, and those things or places in which he is not. Do we actively search for Jesus in the pages of Scripture, in our own prayer times, within the fellowship of God's family, and in the worship activities of the church? How much are we willing to take Jesus into our boat – not just for 'special fishing trips' or 'sailing excursions' – but every moment of every day? When Jesus climbed into the boat, the crew worshipped him (Matthew ch14 v33). When Peter had focused on Jesus, he walked on water, but when he doubted, he sank! The root word for 'doubt' is the word 'two'. Peter had been looking in two directions at once. Are we also afflicted by such a spiritual squint?

JANUARY 24
THE GOSPEL OF JOHN ch6 vv25-40

LONG LIFE BREAD

A bread manufacturer issued an article on the possibility of keeping bread indefinitely. He entitled the article: 'The bread that would not die'.

Here in these verses, Jesus directs the crowd's attention away from the short-lived bread, which they had eaten with the fish on the mountain, to the long-lasting bread that is only found in Jesus. But the people were more interested in the 'satisfaction of the meal' than in the 'significance of the miracle'. Spectacular miracles will always attract a following. But it is only by feeding on the bread of life that people will be prepared for eternity. Jesus said, *I am the bread of life'* (v35). This long-life bread is:

1 BREAD THAT FORTIFIES (vv27-33)

This bread doesn't spoil or disappear like manna, but it is incorruptible and everlasting. It gives strength through the spiritual nutrients it contains. Manna was a unique food sent by God to sustain the Hebrew people in the Sinai desert. They called it 'bread from heaven' because it certainly wasn't like anything on earth. But even this strange, sweet, and supernatural manna only fortified two to three million Hebrews temporarily. Jesus is the manna that fortifies eternally. Jesus is *the bread from heaven'* (v32), *the bread of God'* (v33), *the bread of life'* (v35). He is forever fresh and nutritious. Sometimes, particular food labelling will spell out the words 'genuine' or 'original'. That's what the word *true'* means in v32. Jesus is the genuine and original bread from heaven. Just as we may pray *Give us our daily bread'* (Matthew ch6 v11) with reference to our physical needs, so that should be our prayer with reference to our spiritual needs. We shouldn't fall prey to the 'quick-snack mentality'. We need a regular, healthy, nutritious diet.

2 BREAD THAT SATISFIES (vv34-35)

All breads from all over the world will eventually leave you hungry, but by feeding on Jesus, you will receive all that you need. Whatever our souls need, Jesus fully satisfies. We shouldn't be looking elsewhere. There are millions of hungry people in the world who are feeding off city rubbish tips and scrabbling for the scraps that others have thrown out. We shouldn't be feeding off spiritual scraps, but rather our hunger should be for Jesus. Paul the apostle had a great hunger: *I want to know Christ'* (Philippians ch3 v10). He yearned for a knowledge of Jesus in which he would experience something of his sympathetic sufferings and his resurrection power. How he wanted his appetite sated with Christ! Is Christ your daily delight? Is he your loaf of life?

3 BREAD THAT GLORIFIES (vv36-39)

Jesus made it crystal clear that his life's work ultimately was to glorify his heavenly Father (v38), and he would do that by keeping every single soul that the Father had given to him. None would be lost (v39). If salvation is dependent, or partly dependent upon us (our whims, thoughts, feelings, decisions), then Jesus would not be in a position to guarantee that he would lose none of those who had been given to him. But salvation is of the Lord from start to finish. As preachers, evangelists, and personal witnesses, we may invite, entreat, implore, and plead, but we cannot save! Neither can we produce a simple formula or a basic ritual that makes a person a Christian. It's a sovereign work of God, and Jesus glorified his Father by fulfilling every part of his mission statement: 'to seek and to save the lost'.

4 BREAD THAT QUALIFIES (v40)

Here is God's sovereign plan for saving his people. All whom the Father effectually calls will come, and all who come to Jesus in faith and repentance will be kept. The 'coming-calling-keeping' is the work of God. It's those who *'look to the Son and believe in him'* who shall have *'eternal life'*. There's no other qualification for eternal life and final resurrection but to look and believe in Jesus, the long-life Bread, *'the bread of life'*. And what did they say? *'Sir... from now on give us this bread'* (v34). This is the Bread that is a never-ending supply in this world and the next. This is the Bread that prepares us for the vigorous workouts of this life, and this is the Bread that entitles us to heaven.

Are you feeding on Jesus, the Bread of Life, or are you on a different diet entirely?

JANUARY 25
THE GOSPEL OF JOHN ch6 vv41-59

RESPONDING TO GRUMBLERS

Wherever a Jewish community existed, there was often a synagogue. The chief purpose of any synagogue was not public worship but instruction in the Scriptures. The synagogue was primarily an education centre where people were taught the word of God. It was in Capernaum's synagogue that Jesus taught the fundamental truths of this chapter (v59). However, there was a lot of muttering and grumbling among the crowd, especially from the religious leaders. Jesus had claimed *'I came down from heaven'* (vv38, 42), and the Jews weren't happy with that claim because they knew who his parents were (v42). They believed that Jesus had come from Nazareth in Galilee, not Bethlehem in Judea. They thought Joseph was Jesus' natural father. So they grumbled. For 2,000 years, there has been similar grumbling from those who won't accept the words of Jesus. They are prepared to believe that Jesus was the greatest of men, but not the Son of God. Jesus is very positive in his response to grumblers then and now:

1 LISTEN AND LEARN (vv43-45)

There are many important ways to learn, and one of them is to listen. What can we learn in God's academy of faith? We must know that God's teaching is:

Full of Scripture

Everything that God wants us to know and to put into practice, he has written in a Book (2 Timothy ch3 v16). Even Jesus' teaching here in these verses draws from the Jewish Bible, the Old Testament Scriptures. Jesus refers to Isaiah (v45) and Exodus (v49). If the maker's instructions are important for a tool or a machine, how much more important are the Maker's instructions for us?

Full of Structure

Listening and learning from the Father (referred to by Jesus) means a logical, structured syllabus of education and training. The Bible is a progression and development of understanding, revealing structure and design from beginning to end. Sadly, so much of our church life suffers from erratic, piecemeal teaching. We flit here and there in the Scriptures. We 'snack feed' and 'cherry pick' verses. No wonder we have a weak grasp of the Bible's history, geography, biography, and theology. Christians often don't have a joined-up understanding of the Bible because in their church's preaching, teaching, Bible studies, and youth work, they have not been taught in a structured way.

Full of the Saviour

Our listening and learning must be centred on Jesus. He must be the aim, objective, and the content of our syllabus. As we read the Bible, we should be asking, 'What does this tell me about Christ?' Jesus is the supreme theme of God's word (Hebrews ch1 vv1-4).

2 COME AND BELIEVE (vv43-47)

If we have listened to and learned from God's word, then we should pray for the faith to believe it (Romans ch10 v17). The message of the Bible is only of real and lasting benefit to us if we believe and act upon it. This is not just a general belief that Jesus is real and that Christianity is relevant to the 21st century. More than that, it must be a personal response of repentance and faith. You may even read and study the Bible, but even that in and of itself is not enough. You must come and trust in Jesus. Jesus told the Bible students of his day that their diligence in study was no substitute for obedience and faith (ch5 vv39-40).

3 FEED AND LIVE (vv50-58)

Jesus referred to feeding on the bread of life (v58). Five times in these few verses, Jesus promises that those who feed will live eternally (vv53-55). Anyone with a limited understanding of Jesus' teaching will know that he is using a metaphor in referring to his body as food. It is ridiculous to suggest he is teaching cannibalism! To suggest that Christ's body is eaten in the eucharist or communion services would be ludicrous if it were not so devilish. Yet some aspects of Christendom have built their heresies on this abhorrent teaching, which maintains that Christ is sacrificed repeatedly in the Eucharist. Instead, Jesus is teaching that we should make him our regular, nutritious, daily diet. Feeding on Jesus should not be a 'snack' or even a 'slap-up meal' every now and again. We should be feeding on him through Bible reading and through prayer so that we don't become weak, sickly, and useless.

JANUARY 26
THE GOSPEL OF JOHN ch6 vv60-71

DIFFICULT TEACHING

While the cross of Jesus continues to provoke intense curiosity and is the subject of some 'best sellers', it is frequently the object of scorn and derision. The cross remains utter foolishness to those who don't believe, even two thousand years after Paul made that statement (1 Corinthians ch1 v18). People claim to be hugely offended by the cross. The symbol of the cross has become the target for hate and violence. Men and women are scandalised by the teaching of the cross. Even before Jesus' crucifixion, his disciples had found Jesus' teachings hard to accept (v60). Jesus had responded *'Does this offend you?'* (v61). The word for *'offend'* can mean 'scandalise', that is, 'Does this scandalise you?' As long as Christian teaching is couched in terms that are neutral, lukewarm, and compromising, then they will remain inoffensive. But as soon as you proclaim the righteousness of God, the vileness of sin, the certainty of judgement, and the atoning sacrifice of the cross, then people claim to be offended.

They retaliate by calling Bible-believing Christians 'bigoted', 'fundamentalist evangelicals', and 'narrow-minded Puritans' with their uncaring message and harsh teachings. So what's changed from these verses in ch6? Very little! People still respond to such *'harsh teaching'* in various ways. It may take the form of:

1 A DEVIL (vv70-71)

We know nothing of the background of Judas Iscariot, son of Simon, but Jesus did. Jesus was betrayed by Judas, but he wasn't deceived by Judas (v64). Jesus had not been hoodwinked in choosing Judas to be one of *'the Twelve'* (v70). But Jesus identifies Judas with Satan, who was permitted to groom him so that he could manipulate and control his feelings, objectives, and actions. It should not surprise us today that much of the opposition to the church and the Gospel takes a distinctly devilish form. Satan is alive and well. Many of the atrocities and strategies that are currently being perpetrated against the people of God have the 'hallmark of hell' upon them. We see in the example of Judas that it is often a small step from Satan's 'prompting' to Satan's 'entering'. We must not let him get a foothold in our lives (Ephesians ch4 v27). We must live lives that are so godly that they are 'climb-proof' to the devil.

2 A DESERTER (vv64-67)

The outcome of Jesus' difficult message was that most of his professing disciples returned to their old way of life. They had regarded themselves as Jesus' disciples, but they were 'fair-weather sailors'. They didn't mind being on the 'light-ship', but they couldn't cope with hardship! They had struggled with Jesus' hard teaching about eating his flesh (v52), wrong motives (v30), eternal life being dependent on Jesus' death (v51), and Jesus' deity (vv58,62). But true discipleship costs, and these fair-weather followers weren't prepared for the 'discipline dimension' to discipleship.

3 A DISCIPLE (v68-69)

Most who had called themselves 'disciples' had deserted Jesus, leaving just *the Twelve'*. When asked if they wanted to desert Jesus too, Peter replied perceptively, *'Lord, to whom shall we go? You have the words of eternal life'* (v68). Peter was speaking for the other ten, if not Judas, when he said, in effect, that 'we have become believers and we are continuing in that firm conviction'. It means being faithful:

...even when the teaching is hard

Discipleship means a cross (Luke ch9 v23). There is hardship in discipleship. If religious people are looking for an easy, comfy, soft expression for their beliefs, they won't find it in being a true disciple of Jesus

...even when our numbers are small

Could the disciples have been affected by disappointment and disillusionment as they saw the followers drop away one by one? (v66). But we need to see that God always preserves a faithful, often small, nucleus.

...even when we are deceived and betrayed

The Twelve would have been affected by the extra responsibilities and workload caused by the deserters. It would be easy to feel 'let down' and even bitter. But God is sufficient for our needs.

...even when we don't see results

Salvation's work is God's, not ours (v65). We must trust God for his wisdom and mercy revealed in his prerogative to save. You may have been praying about and witnessing to an unbeliever for a long time, but keep trusting God's timing and his enabling power.

JANUARY 27
THE GOSPEL OF JOHN ch7 vv1-13

WHERE IS THAT MAN?

People seek popularity and celebrate popularity in many ways. Jesus wasn't short of those who suggested he could increase his own popularity. Satan suggested that all the kingdoms of the world could be 'transferred to him' in exchange for devil-worship (Matthew ch4 v8). The crowds in ch6 v15 were so impressed by the popularity of Jesus' miracles that they wanted to *'make him king by force'*. Here in v3-5, Jesus' own brothers thought that his popularity had been flagging and that he needed to raise his profile by a new publicity campaign in Judea. Hundreds, perhaps thousands, of disciples had abandoned Jesus (ch6 v66), and his brothers had a plan for giving him maximum publicity. But Jesus was not looking for that kind of publicity: his top priority was to do what his heavenly Father wanted. Although death by crucifixion was in his divine diary, the Jewish authorities would not be permitted to hasten that date. At the Feast of Tabernacles, these hostile leaders were already asking, *'Where is that man?'* (v11).

1 WHERE IS THAT MAN GEOGRAPHICALLY?

This is the sense in which the Jewish leaders were asking this question. They were on the lookout for Jesus, who had purposely stayed away from Judea (v1). His ministry had been conducted in Galilee and around the shores of the lake in particular. If he ventured south, then he would be a marked man.

2 WHERE IS THAT MAN PUNCTUALLY?

We ask similar questions with respect to time, for example, 'Where is that person in terms of their education, career, or family?' As far as Jesus was concerned, he was working to his Father's timetable. He was waiting for the precise time when he would attend the Feast at Jerusalem. Jesus knew there were those who wanted to kill him (v1), but the hour had not yet come (ch8 v20). Notice the exact split-second timing of Jesus' mission. In v8, it wasn't time for Jesus to go to the Feast publicly, but in v10, it was time for reference to the divine plan. We are not always so compliant when we run into situations and complain about their poor timing! Why does this happen to me *now*? If we recognise that *'my times are in your hands'* (Psalm 31 v15), then why don't we surrender to his safe, capable hands? So much of the angst and heartache we suffer is due to our failure to accept God's times and God's ways.

3 WHERE IS THAT MAN ETHICALLY?

While the authorities were demanding to know Jesus' whereabouts, there was widespread whispering among the crowds and wide-ranging views. Some considered Jesus to be *'a good man'* while others judged him to be a liar and a deceiver (v12). If the spectrum of opinion ranged from 'good man' to 'deceiver' in Jesus' day, it has hardly changed in two thousand years. There are still millions of people who will concede that Jesus was a good man, without admitting to anything more than that. Others will label Jesus 'a deceiver'. Jesus is unique because he is God. Jesus was *'holy, blameless, pure, set apart from sinners'* (Hebrews ch7 v26). No wonder the writer says:

'Such a high priest meets our need'. Jesus could never meet our needs if he were merely a good man. We need a perfect Saviour who was genuinely a man but indisputably God.

4 WHERE IS THAT MAN PUBLICLY?

Jesus' brothers wanted him to 'go public' (vv3-4). That may not have been the time, yet the time did come when he was publicly humiliated and crucified, lifted up for all the world to see and know (ch3 vv14-15; ch12 v32). There at the cross, God demonstrated publicly his supreme love to sinful humanity (Romans ch5 v8). But the greatest public display will be at the end of the age when every eye will see him, every knee will bow, and every tongue will confess that Jesus Christ is Lord.

5 WHERE IS THAT MAN PERSONALLY?

Jesus' brothers may have seen Jesus as a miracle-worker or even a prophet, but *'they did not believe in him'* as God the Son, the Christ, the Saviour of the world (v5). They were comfortable being part of a world that loves evil and loathes righteousness. If you are trying to live as Jesus did, then you will encounter hostility and hatred. But be assured that the world hated Jesus first (ch15 v18-19).

JANUARY 28
THE GOSPEL OF JOHN ch7 vv14-24

DON'T JUDGE A BOOK BY ITS COVER

Jesus rebuked the Jews (v24) *'Stop judging by mere appearances, and make a right judgement'*. They were judging Jesus on those actions that they thought they had seen and those statements that they thought they had heard. There were four matters (or 'book covers') on which they made judgements about Jesus.

1 JESUS' LEARNING

(vv14-15) Where had Jesus learned the things that he knew? It was in the middle of the Feast of Tabernacles (or booths or tents) that Jesus made his appearance, teaching in the outer courts of the temple. But there were those from Galilee who would have known about Jesus' family and upbringing. They knew that he hadn't been to a university or had studied as a pupil under one of the great rabbis/teachers of the day. The Jews were *judging by mere appearances'*. They thought that they knew where Jesus had come from, and they couldn't understand why he was so knowledgeable. If they had believed him as God, then they would have understood that his knowledge and wisdom were immeasurable (Job ch21 v22; Psalm 147 v5). Even Peter was forced to confess after Jesus' resurrection: *'Lord, you know all things...'* (John ch21 v17). As books, our 'dust jackets' may look fine and respectable, but the Lord knows our hearts (1 Samuel ch16 v7; Jeremiah ch17 v9). He knows the contents, not just the cover.

2 JESUS' TEACHING

(vv16-19) There had been serious doubts about the authenticity of Jesus' teaching. The Jews may have been puzzled about Jesus' education, but they couldn't discern whether he was really teaching the truth about God. How could they make the right judgement about Jesus' teaching? They needed a test, and Jesus provided them with one (v17). Here is the test: if you choose to do God's will and not your own, to follow his ways and to stake your faith upon Jesus' teaching, then you will prove that it comes from God. The key to proving the integrity of Jesus' teaching is faith: a personal faith in Jesus. The real moral choice is not to pick and choose which of Jesus' teachings is most appropriate for me and my situation, but rather to commit myself to all of what he teaches. The Jews represented those who pretended to keep Moses' law but didn't (v19). On the outside (the 'book cover'), they appeared to be devoted law-keepers, but their thoughts and motives were wrong. On the outside, they would boast that they kept the ten commands, and command number six, for example: *'You shall not murder'* (Exodus ch20 v13). Yet, lurking within their hearts, they wanted to kill Jesus.

3 JESUS' HEALING

(vv21-23) It seems that the miracle of healing the invalid at Bethesda's pool (ch5) provoked *'astonishment'* (v21) and *'persecution'* (ch5 v16). With their skewed vision, the Jewish critics saw Jesus as a 'Sabbath-breaker', and even a *'demon-possessed'* fanatic (v20), instead of the teaching, healing Son of God. They were quick to criticise Jesus for healing on the Sabbath while they wrestled with the choice of obeying their Sabbath Law or their

Circumcision Law. They missed the most important command to love the Lord their God (e.g., Mark ch12 v30).

4 JESUS' DYING

Jesus knew that he was a 'wanted man' (v11) and that they planned to arrest him (v45). He was already engaged in the countdown to Calvary. Jesus came to share our humanity by taking our flesh and blood. In visual terms, you couldn't tell him apart. He had no beauty or majesty to attract us to him (Isaiah ch53 vv2-3), and in his death, *'his appearance was so disfigured beyond that of any man and his form marred beyond human likeness'* (Isaiah ch52 v14). By the cross, there were those who would have only seen Jesus' disfigured, bloodied body and would have concluded that he was just another criminal executed for his crimes. They were *'judging by mere appearances'* for behind that appalling exterior was a heart beating with love for a lost world. Jesus died for sins, once for all, so that he could bring us to know God (1 Peter ch3 v18). He died to make our hearts pure and so that we may be able to make right judgements without basing them on external appearances.

JANUARY 29
THE GOSPEL OF JOHN ch7 vv25-36

LOOKING BUT NOT SEEING

Every year, it is estimated that up to one thousand five hundred motorcyclists are killed or seriously injured in the UK due to what is known as 'look-but-fail-to-see' accidents. Many of these accidents have been extremely puzzling to investigators because the driver of the offending vehicle had made eye contact with the motorcyclist just prior to the accident. There's a huge difference between 'looking' and 'seeing'. Sometimes, sadly, it's the difference between life and death. The psychologist Richard Gregory has said: 'We don't believe what we see. We see what we believe'.

In a spiritual sense, this was the problem with the majority of Jews in Jesus' day: they were looking but not seeing. They were looking for the Messiah, the Christ, but they did not see him when he appeared.

1 LOOKING AND NOT SEEING

(vv33-36) There are several reasons why a person may look and not see.

Looking in the wrong place

Many people who recognise that they have spiritual needs go to the wrong places. Some seek solace in the great religions of the world. Even primitive peoples living in small, remote communities look for spiritual help in spiritism and animism. But there is no real, lasting peace for the mind and soul outside of Jesus. In these verses, Jesus hints at the cross and the culmination of his spiritual rescue mission to save those who believe. After that, he would return bodily to heaven. Jesus was with them for a short time, and if 'looking' was important, then they had to look now, see, and believe.

Looking for the wrong person

The Jews had been attracted to Jesus because of his miracles. They wanted a leader with supernatural powers who could free them from their enemies. Many are looking for the 'wrong Jesus' today. They would prefer a 'gentle Jesus, meek and mild' who can be manipulated and adapted to suit their desires and lifestyles: an advocate but not the Judge; a servant but not the Master; a comforter but not the King; a friend but not the Lord; a counsellor but not the Saviour. But the real Jesus is the Lord God Almighty, the High and Holy One, the eternal Sovereign and Lord of all. You can't 'pick and mix' with Jesus.

Looking for the wrong purpose

The authorities were looking to arrest Jesus (v32). Some were doubtless looking for Jesus to see some spectacular miracle. Some were looking for a Messiah- Superman. But they were not looking for Jesus, the *Wonderful Counsellor, Mighty God, Everlasting Father, Prince of Peace* (Isaiah ch9 v6). Because they were looking for the wrong person, they were not seeing. What's our motive for looking for Jesus? Are we looking for the Christ of the Bible?

2 NOT LOOKING AND NOT SEEING

There were those among the Jerusalem crowds who were 'not looking' because they were ignorant of the Scriptures (v27). They had thought that the Messiah would suddenly appear from obscurity and be launched onto the world stage with power and glory. Therefore, they rejected Jesus on these grounds. They had assumed Jesus had been born in Galilee when he had been born in Bethlehem (Micah ch5 v2). Jesus claimed that the One who had sent him is *true* (v28), that is, real and genuine, not a fraud or a fake. People are still content with a fake god and a fake religion, with their short-term kicks, rather than put their faith in *'the only true God, and Jesus Christ, whom (he) has sent'* (ch17 v3).

3 LOOKING AND SEEING

Among the cynicism and scepticism of these verses, there's v31: *'Still, many of the crowd put their faith in (Jesus)'*. Just as in the first century, Jesus may still be variously described as 'mad', 'bad', or 'sad'. People deny his deity, decry his humanity, and defy his authority. But among the enmity and hostility, there are still those who *'put their faith in him'*. They look and see.

How much are we concentrating our gaze and fixing our eyes upon Jesus (Hebrews ch12 v2)? How much of our daily spiritual routines (prayer, Bible reading, church meetings) are more to do with 'looking' rather than 'seeing'?

JANUARY 30
THE GOSPEL OF JOHN ch7 vv37-44

THE DIVISIVE JESUS

When Margaret Thatcher, Britain's first woman prime minister, died, the most common comment on her policies and her personality was that she was 'divisive'. It has been said repeatedly that the nation had been divided because of Margaret Thatcher. Although she had prompted long-held and deep-seated divisions, she was not unique in dividing opinion. Throughout history, there have been many colourful and powerful personalities who have divided attitudes and opinions.

Note v43 *'Thus the people were divided because of Jesus'*. We observe that there are:

1 THOSE WHO ARE THIRSTY AND THOSE WHO ARE NOT

Everyone had been celebrating during the great Feast Week in Jerusalem. Many were camping in booths/tents, reliving the experience of the people of Israel's wanderings in the Sinai Desert. On the final feast day, a procession of priests marched from the temple to the Pool of Siloam to draw water. Led by the high priest, they would process back to the altar onto which the water would be poured. As this powerful symbol of water was used to represent God's provision for his people in the desert, so Jesus stands and announces *'in a loud voice'* (v37) that those who are thirsty should come to him and drink. There are those who thirst for truth and for understanding. Some thirst for peace and satisfaction. Others thirst for forgiveness and eternal life. Let them come to Jesus in faith and drink of him.

2 THOSE WHO BELIEVE AND THOSE WHO DO NOT

(vv38-39) This 'belief' in Jesus is more than just the belief that he exists. Millions believe in his existence. Rather, it means to personally trust in and to commit to. It means 'to have complete faith in' and 'to submit unreservedly'. Those who are genuine believers will have *'streams of living water'* flowing from within them. Jesus explained that the Holy Spirit was soon to be given after Jesus' resurrection and glorification. Pentecost and the outpouring of God's Spirit would seal the finished work of Jesus upon the cross. The unleashing of the Holy Spirit's energy into the New Testament Church would empower believers to be witnesses for Jesus all over the world (Acts ch1 v8).

3 THOSE WHO WANT TO SEIZE HIM AND THOSE WHO DO NOT

Members of the 'arresting party' had been sent to arrest Jesus (v44) but had become 'arrested' themselves. While some of the posse may still have wanted to make the arrest, the general feeling seemed to be one of awe and wonder at Jesus' teaching (v46). But if Jesus cannot be 'seized' or 'arrested' today, there is still a world that is split in its response to Jesus' followers. There are those who want to seize and arrest Jesus' disciples, to imprison them and to persecute them, while others are prepared to tolerate them, allowing them some religious liberty. As a Christian, you will meet those who are anti-God, anti-Christ, and who will not tolerate anything that opposes the secularist, humanist, and evolutionist mindset.

4 THOSE WHO THINK HE IS THE PROPHET AND THOSE WHO DO NOT

(v40) The generations of Jews had been taught to expect a prophet anticipated by Moses (Deuteronomy ch18 v15). They were on the lookout for a 'Moses Mark 2' who would lead them out of slavery and Roman rule. Just like Gandhi or Martin Luther King, people look on Jesus as a forthright religious leader who condemned social evils.

5 THOSE WHO THINK HE IS THE CHRIST AND THOSE WHO DO NOT

(vv41-43) John said that the liar is the man who denies that Jesus is the Christ (1 John ch2 v22). Divisions exist in society, in work and education, in the church, and within families because of Jesus. But Jesus himself warned of the divisive sword that he brought (Matthew ch10 vv34-36). Such divisions cut keenly and, in some cases, may result in family abandonment. We are called to live as a most attractive example of a Christian husband/wife/mother/father/son/daughter within a home where there is a division between believer and unbeliever. Such an example of Christian conduct will demonstrate compassion without compromise. Jesus should never come 'second' (Matthew ch10 vv37-38). Love, grace, patience, perseverance, tact, and wisdom will be demanded in 'bucket-loads'. Jesus knows and understands because he also had lived in a family which had been divided because of him (v5).

JANUARY 31
THE GOSPEL OF JOHN ch7 vv45-52

JESUS, THE INCOMPARABLE SPEAKER

The temple police chiefs may have listened to various reasons why their officers had failed to arrest suspects in the past. But they were surprised and angry when their officers explained their failure to arrest Jesus: *'No one ever spoke the way this man does'* (v46). We can underline four things about the way and about the words Jesus spoke:

1 HIS ACCENT REVEALED HIS HOME

Jesus was brought up in Galilee, and it would have been natural for him to have a Galilean accent. When Peter denied Jesus at his interrogation, various people accused Peter of being an accomplice to Jesus of Nazareth. *'...Those standing there went up to Peter and said, 'Surely you are one of them, for your accent gives you away'* (Matthew ch26 v73). The northern rural accents of Galilee would have been noticeable in the city of Jerusalem. The Pharisees and the religious hierarchy were quick to dismiss this Galilean yokel who was teaching in the temple courts. We should never despise accents, dialects, or languages because God uses all kinds of people with a variety of linguistic skills to share his message. Although Jesus' accent may have identified his earthly home region, his words revealed his heavenly home.

2 HIS ACKNOWLEDGEMENT REVEALED HIS HUMILITY

Jesus acknowledges that his teaching wasn't his own (v16). He submitted humbly to his Father's plan, and he knew that the Gospel Masterplan would culminate in his death. He had disclosed this to Nicodemus (ch3 vv14-15). It was by humbling himself and lowering himself that he became lifted up – on a cross (Philippians ch2 v8).

If Jesus humbled himself to a cross to become a sacrifice and a sin-bearer, should we not humble ourselves to confess our sin and to surrender to Jesus, our Lord and Saviour? For some, the only reason they haven't become a true believer is because they are not prepared to humble themselves; to bow the knee and bow the heart in repentance and faith.

3 HIS AUTHORITY REVEALED HIS HOLINESS

Even the unbelieving temple police recognised that Jesus' words were unique. Not only did Jesus have a divine mission, but he also had a divine origin. The people didn't understand that they were listening to the very words of God incarnate. These were the words of the Word made flesh (ch1 v14). Jesus' words of authority showed that he was from God: that he was God. Jesus taught with a knowledge and wisdom that was supernatural. Even the man in the street who listened to Jesus detected a unique authority. At the end of Jesus' 'mountain sermon', we read that *the crowds were amazed at his teaching, because he taught as one who had authority, and not as their teachers of the law'* (Matthew ch7 vv28-29). Another indication of Jesus' holiness, revealed in the authority of his words, is seen in Gethsemane. When the arresting posse was told by Jesus that he was the one they were looking for, *'they drew back and fell to the ground'* (ch18 v6). The awesome self-disclosure of God himself rendered them powerless before the all-powerful Christ. They were only allowed to continue with the arrest because Jesus knew that 'his time had come'. How do we respond to the living oracles of God, our Bible? Do we esteem them to be the authoritative declaration of our sovereign God to us today? Are we responsible for reading God's word, and are we accountable for what we read?

4 HIS ANNOUNCEMENT REVEALED HIS HEART

(v37) This was the climax to the Feast. As the water ceremony was being conducted in the temple, Jesus stood a few hundred yards away in the temple courts and said in a loud voice, *'If anyone is thirsty, let him come to me and drink'*. Jesus provides thirst-quenching, soul-satisfying, life-giving water. There is no 'water shortage' with Jesus. His reservoir never runs dry. Of course, like the Pharisees (v48), there are still going to be those who argue that intelligent, sensible, 'right-thinking' people are not going to fall for this evangelical message. But their ignorance is merely dressed up as intelligence. Those who have sampled the Saviour's heart by coming to him and drinking from his bottomless well of clear, pure water will never be thirsty.

Whatever Jesus says, no one ever spoke the way this man does.

FEBRUARY 1
THE GOSPEL OF JOHN ch8 vv1-11

THE TRAP

Although Bible commentators argue that the earliest and most reliable manuscripts and other ancient documents do not contain this passage, there is no reason for doubting that this event took place. The narrative ties in with the historical context of Jesus' teaching in the temple courts, and it is consistent with the Pharisees' clashes with Jesus. The account is about a carefully baited trap that the Pharisees had set for Jesus. As the Pharisees had failed to seize Jesus, they would now attempt to snare him.

With their bait in place, the Pharisees set their trap by asking the question (vv4-5). As they saw it, Jesus could answer the question in two ways. Jesus could reject the Law of Moses and therefore confirm their suspicions that he was a false teacher, or he could support the Law and the stoning of the woman, thus making him unpopular with the crowds and possibly the Roman authorities. Here was the trap! What would Jesus say? But he didn't say a word. Instead, he bent down and wrote on the ground with his finger. We recall that the Sinai Law was written with the *'finger of God'* (Exodus ch31 v18).

We don't know what Jesus wrote, but we can be sure about three things:

1 NO JUSTIFICATION OF SIN

The perpetrator had been caught red-handed. There was no excuse and no defence. Sin is a spiritual cancer that infects everyone. As far as our spiritual condition is concerned, we are 'caught in the act' (Romans ch3 v10, 23). We are all without excuse (Psalm 25 v3). We are responsible for our sinful state and the consequences of it. We are moral agents under God's law, and we are therefore accountable to the divine Law-giver. Sin is an attack on the God who made us and who has given us life. Sin is the 'weapon of mass destruction' that we use in our war against God. We bite the hand that feeds us, and we hurt the heart that loves us. There is no justification for sin, but praise God, there is justification for the sinner.

2 NO ASSERTION OF SINLESSNESS

The accusatory Pharisees may have been very self-righteous, but it became quickly apparent following Jesus' challenge that not one of them claimed to be sinless. They had been eager to interpret Mosaic Law in a way that sentenced the offender to stoning, but not one considered himself sinless enough to throw the first stone (vv7-9). The law condemned each of them, and their consciences condemned each of them. If we claim to be without sin, then we deceive ourselves: we are untruthful and we make God a liar (1 John ch1 vv8-10). If we are honest, then we know that we have a strong bias to do wrong. The temptation is there all the time, and we fall for it. When we are criticised, the anger of self-justification rises in our hearts. When someone acquires or achieves something, we may feel a surge of jealousy and covetousness. When we are put on the spot, a lie may seem the most attractive way out. If you are a believer, then you should sin less, but you are not sinless. David's prayer should be your prayer (Psalm 51 vv1-4).

3 NO CONDEMNATION OF THE SINNER

When the woman's accusers had slunk away in their guilt, the woman was left alone with Jesus. No one could condemn her, and Jesus said, *'Neither do I condemn you'* (v11). This must have been the sweetest music to her ears. Yet this is no more than for everyone who turns in repentance to Jesus. *'Therefore, there is now no condemnation for those who are in Christ Jesus'* (Romans ch8 v1). It doesn't mean that we haven't sinned. We are all guilty, as the woman was guilty. But Jesus didn't ask the woman if she was guilty. He told her to leave her life of sin. Jesus didn't say *'LOVE your life of sin'* but rather *'LEAVE your life of sin'*. The correct response to sinfulness in the past, and forgiveness in the present, is holiness in the future. The declaration of *'no condemnation'* is for those who repent and turn from their sin. Jesus didn't make excuses for the woman to make her sin appear less serious. Neither did he make it easy for the woman to continue in her sin. Jesus didn't scale down his demand or diminish the level of urgency. He said to her, and he says to us today:

'Go now and leave your life of sin.'

FEBRUARY 2
THE GOSPEL OF JOHN ch8 vv12-32

RELIABLE WITNESSES

Occasionally, we hear people make wild claims to which our natural response is 'Prove it!' As we study this Gospel, we are repeatedly introduced to Jesus' unique and mind-boggling claims, which would be fanciful at best, were he not the Christ, the Son of God. There are seven classic 'I AM' statements that Jesus makes in this Gospel. This is the second great claim of Jesus: *'I am the light of the world'* (v12).

Immediately, the Pharisees challenged the validity of Jesus' claim. In effect, they were saying, *'Prove it! Prove you are whom you claim to be.'* They knew that Jesus was not only claiming divine origin but that he was claiming to be God. By the end of the chapter, they were ready to stone him because of his claims. But as with any claim, it needs supporting evidence. They wanted reliable witnesses who would authenticate his claim. The keyword *'witness'* is used seven times in this passage, and there are four reliable witnesses who testify that Jesus is the One and Only Son of God.

1 THE FOLLOWER WHO WALKS IN THE LIGHT

The best evidence for the sun, even when you can't see it in the sky, is daylight. We enjoy regular, predictable daylight even when the sun can't be seen. On mid-summer mornings, you may walk to the bathroom in daylight. You may walk to the shops in daylight. You may walk to work or school in daylight. The evidence for the truth about the sun is when you walk in the light. The light is the best testimony to its existence. Jesus' own light was his witness. If you are a true follower of Jesus, then you must walk in his light every day (1 John ch1. vv5-7). It means acting as Jesus did, even when you may be outnumbered by hostile unbelievers in the office, the works' canteen, the local club, or the classroom. It may seem old-fashioned and weird to take a stand for the Bible, or the Lord's Day, or the life of the unborn child, or the traditional view of marriage. But walking in the light is not just about an imitation of Jesus: it's about an identity with Jesus.

2 THE FATHER WHO HAS SENT HIS SON

Four times Jesus explained that he had been *'sent'* (vv16, 18, 26, 29). If Jewish courts required two witnesses (v17), then here are two: Jesus and his Father (v18).

The Father is Personable

Jesus refers to *'the Father'* (v18), but he also refers to *'my Father'* (v19). Jesus is at one with his Father. Knowing Jesus means coming to know his Father too (v19).

The Father is Reliable

(v26) The most reliable witness of all is *'the God of truth'* (Psalm 31 v5). He speaks the truth (Isaiah 45:19).

The Father is Inseparable

(v29) Jesus is inseparable from his Father because Jesus is God. He was with God in the beginning (ch1 v2) and even upon the cross God was *'reconciling the world to himself in Christ'* (2 Corinthians ch5 v19).

3 THE FUTURE WHICH FOCUSES ON THE CROSS

(vv27-28) The lifting up of the Son of Man upon the cross would mean that he would draw people to himself (ch12 v32). Yet it's not to the image or icon of the cross to which we are drawn in a superstitious or sentimental way. It's not even being drawn to the act of crucifixion because thousands were crucified in Judea and across the Roman Empire. It's not just about the cross or crucifixion, but it's all about the Crucified. That's why *'We preach Christ crucified'* (1 Corinthians ch1 v23). Jesus' whole life and ministry were centred on his sacrificial death at Golgotha. This was the 'miracle of miracles' that proved to the centurion that *'Surely this man was the Son of God!'* (Mark ch15 v39).

4 THE FREEDOM WHICH COMES FROM KNOWING THE TRUTH

(vv31-32) The Jews may have been thinking about national freedom (freedom from Egypt or freedom from Babylon) or even political freedom (from Rome's tyranny). Many today are looking for social and moral freedom to do as they please. But the only freedom that sets people free is the freedom from sin – its grip and its guilt – by coming to know the truth of God in the gospel. Yet freedom is never the right to do as you want, but rather it is the liberty to do as you should. The consequence of those who are still shackled in sin means death in their sins (vv21, 24). True freedom from the power of sin is a living testimony to the claim that Jesus really is the Son of God, our Saviour.

FEBRUARY 3
THE GOSPEL OF JOHN ch8 vv33-47

BELONGING TO GOD

The inscription seen inside the cover of some people's books is *'This book belongs to...'* In the preface to his letter to Roman believers, Paul writes, *'You also are among those who are called to belong to Jesus Christ'* (Romans ch1 v6*).* Towards the end of his famous letter, Paul encourages Christians in Rome, who may have later suffered under Nero, saying, *'Whether we live or die, we belong to the Lord'* (Romans ch14 v8). Paul was telling believers that the external circumstances of life or death could not alter their relationship with God. Nothing could cancel the Lord's ownership of them. We could say that the inscription over each believer is *'This child belongs to Me'.*

In the middle of a world that seeks national identity, ethnic identity, cultural identity, and family identity, Jesus teaches about our identity with God's family. He speaks of:

1 LEGITIMATE CHILDREN WHO SHARE IN GOD'S FAMILY

It's always surprising how unbelief can skew a person's rationale and blind their judgement. The professing believers (v31) were not really true disciples whom Jesus described as 'holding to his teaching'. They needed to believe the truth and be freed from their slavery to sin. Their warped judgement provoked them to claim that they were *'Abraham's descendants and have never been slaves of anyone'* (v33). Had they conveniently forgotten the 430 years that they had spent in Egypt? Or the seven separate nations that subdued and enslaved Israel, as recorded in Judges? And what about their slavery to Assyria and Babylon, not to mention their present subjection to Rome's tyranny? They were liars in saying that they had never been in slavery, and this confirmed their identity as *'illegitimate children'* whose father is *'a liar and the father of lies'* (v44). As illegitimate children:

Their temporary place was Israel.

They didn't have a *'permanent place in the family'* (v35). Just because they were Jews, it didn't automatically make them belong to God (Romans ch9 v6).

Their natural behaviour was unbelief.

(v37) They were not acting as *'Abraham's descendants'*, who characteristically took God at his word and became the 'father of the faithful'. Instead, they were doing what they had heard from their father (v38), who was neither Abraham nor God.

Their father's desire was murder.

(vv40, 44) Satan brought death through sin. It's no wonder that the capacity to kill has been passed on to Satan's children.

Their native language was lies.

Instead of life and truth, Satan only offers death and lies. We may refer to Satan's contradiction of God in Genesis ch3 v4. Who was lying then?

Legitimate children would do the things Abraham did (v39), and he demonstrated obedience to God, listening intently to God's messages and believing God's word. God's sons are not slaves (v35).

2 LOVING CHILDREN WHO TRUST GOD'S SON

If God were truly their Father, then these unbelieving Jews would love Jesus (v42). They would love everything about God and would have recognised that Jesus was from God and that he was God. Love for Jesus is the motive power that enables believers to endure horrendous conditions, humiliation, suffering, sorrows, risks, and dangers. Is there anything that you wouldn't do for the 'love of Jesus'? Maybe there's some aspect of Christian service that you feel is 'beneath you'? Maybe you would prefer to do something more dignified and more glamorous? Remember that Jesus descended to the gutter of this evil world to fulfil his loving service to his Father.

3 LISTENING CHILDREN WHO HEAR GOD'S WORD

In contrast to those who don't listen (vv37, 43), those who belong to God listen carefully to what he says (v47). Such children will be keen to listen to God's word and act on the things that they hear. We should be quick to listen (James ch1 v19) and do what it says (James ch1 v22). It's Jesus' sheep who listen to his voice and who follow him (ch10 v27). The best indication that sheep belong to the Good Shepherd and that children belong to their Father is that they listen to his word. God's children will make the Bible an essential part of their daily life. They will want to 'tune in' to God's word every day so that they may hear their Father's voice.

FEBRUARY 4
THE GOSPEL OF JOHN ch8 vv48-59

WHO DO YOU THINK YOU ARE?

In everyday conversations, the question may be asked with indignation: 'Who do you think you are?' It was no doubt asked of Jesus with self-righteous anger (v53): 'Who are you making yourself out to be?' The self-appointed guardians of orthodox Judaism were determined to preserve the religious status quo in such a way that they had become blinkered to the very One of whom all their Old Testament Scriptures had spoken – the Messiah, the Christ, the Son of God. They were so locked into their bigotry and were so blinded by unbelief that they even accused Jesus of being a Samaritan and a demoniac (v48). If religious people could make such contemptible attacks on Jesus, it shouldn't surprise us that Bible-believing Christians are subjected to vicious verbal and physical attacks from so-called religious people today.

Jesus replied to his critics by showing at least four aspects of his relationship with God:

Jesus Honours God

(v49) Jesus' chief aim was to honour his Father in everything. How concerned are we about honouring our Heavenly Father in all we do and say?

Jesus is Glorified by God

(v54) The Father not only approves of his Son, but he also exalts him and glorifies him. The Father is well pleased with Jesus (Matthew ch3 v17), but can we say that we are well pleased with him too? Does he satisfy all our desires and needs, or do we want something more than Jesus?

Jesus Knows God

(v55) Jesus could say that he knew God in a unique and exclusive way. We cannot know him in the same way that Jesus does, but do we know him at all, or do we only know about him?

Jesus is God

(v58) The Jews knew exactly what Jesus was saying when he referred to himself as the *'I Am'*. Jesus was not merely claiming that he existed before Abraham. If that were the case, then he would have said, *'Before Abraham was born, I was'*. The tense is unusual and emphasises Jesus' continual existence, without beginning or ending. He applies God's exclusive title to himself.

Jesus is the Sovereign Lord. He is *'Wonderful Counsellor, Mighty God, Everlasting Father, Prince of Peace'* (Isaiah ch9 v6).

But who are you? Who do you think you are? If you are having a spiritual identity crisis, then here are four proof questions you can ask of yourself:

1 WHO'S YOUR FATHER?

Spiritually, these Jews were children of the devil (v44). Evidence of paternity can focus on behaviour patterns. The Jews were clearly showing evidence of Satan's behaviour in their lying, deceit, disobedience, blasphemy, and murder. The only way any of us could have a new father is to be born again (ch3 v7). The Jews were claiming Abraham as their father and asking Jesus if he was greater than him (v53). They were staking their spiritual security on their Hebrew heritage. They boasted that they could trace their ancestry back to Abraham. How many people continue to think that their ancestral religious connections will qualify them for heaven?

2 HOW DO YOU BEHAVE?

Jesus taught that the true children of God were those who kept his word (v51). Reading, studying, hearing, doing, and loving God's word is evidence that someone possesses eternal life.

3 WHAT'S YOUR LANGUAGE?

The native language, accent, dialect, or the use of particular words gives a clue to a person's identity. The Jews were critical, hostile, deceptive, and even blasphemous. Are our conversations constructive or destructive? Are we quick to praise or to criticise? Do we build up or pull down with our words?

4 WHAT MAKES YOU HAPPY?

The things that bring joy and pleasure contribute to who we really are. Abraham rejoiced at the thought of Jesus (v56). The patriarch looked two thousand years into the future, and the anticipation of Jesus brought him great joy. How much does Jesus bring you joy? As Christians, it should thrill our hearts to read about, hear about, and talk about Jesus.

FEBRUARY 5
THE GOSPEL OF JOHN ch9 vv1-12

'HERE'S MUD IN YOUR EYE!'

This is a toast that some people use, meaning 'I hope that any slight inconvenience or discomfort (like mud in the eye) is a sign of good fortune'. This expression may have come from World War I, when the explosion of a particular bomb left bystanders unscathed except for being showered with mud. But it's likely that the expression refers to this narrative, where 'mud in the eyes' preceded the blind beggar's healing.

Jesus was on the move from the temple courts. But as he travelled, he had time for the lowest and lowliest of society: men and women who couldn't help themselves. This blind man fell into that category. There are three key components to this passage:

1 THE MISERY OF THIS MAN'S CONDITION

(v1) There were many visually handicapped people at that time who had lost their sight through accident, violence, or disease. This man had been blind from birth and had known nothing other than his lonely world of darkness. To survive, he would have been forced to beg at sites like the entrance to the temple, where passers-by may be more likely to be charitable. The blind beggar was dependent upon the charity of others, and there could have been many days when he remained hungry and in great need. Physical blindness is a good illustration of spiritual blindness. The misery of this man's disability bears a striking resemblance to a person's miserable condition without Jesus, the Light of the World.

Humanity are fallen beings and their misery are seen in every stratum and aspect of society. *'Ruin and misery mark their ways...'* (Romans ch3 v16); *'All have sinned...'* (Romans ch3 v23). The ruin and misery of sickness, pain, disability, immobility, decline, death, bereavement, loss, and failure are never very far from every one of us. There may not always be a direct 'cause and effect' between specific sins and specific afflictions (v2), but sin is the root cause of our misery.

2 THE MYSTERY OF GOD'S METHODS

God chooses to work within this sinful, suffering world. But the way in which he works, and the timing of those works, is frequently a mystery to us. Yet we must never be tempted to think that God doesn't care or understand. His *'paths* (may be) *beyond tracing out'* (Romans ch11 vv33-34) and his thoughts and ways may not be our thoughts and ways (Isaiah ch55 v8), but we must get over the belief that God owes us an explanation for what he is doing. You may be puzzled over God's methods or perplexed about his timing. God's mysterious purposes do not always bring healing, relief from pain, or deliverance from danger. But as a Christian, you can be sure of God's personal love for you. Neither does he use the same method every time. He tailors and tempers his methods to every occasion. Two blind men had their sightless eyes touched by Jesus (Matthew ch9 vv27-31). Jesus administered spittle to one man's eyes (Mark ch8 v23). On other occasions, he healed individuals by merely speaking a word. Our experience of God's grace and love may be different, but our common testimony will be that God is gracious and loving.

3 THE MASTERY OF JESUS' HEALING

(v7) He didn't succumb to a post-operative infection. He didn't slip, trip, or fall on the way. He came home seeing. What a magnificent change had occurred! The illustration of the dramatic change between blindness and sight is a powerful metaphor of the change that occurs when a person trusts in Jesus for forgiveness and spiritual healing. We mustn't underestimate the transformation that can occur through the mastery of Jesus' healing. When the man returned from Siloam with his new twenty-twenty vision, his neighbours and friends didn't recognise him (v9). The change was so radical that they thought that he was a 'blind-man-look-alike'. How had he been healed? *The man they call Jesus...*' (v11). Of course, he had to exercise faith and obedience. The blind man had sufficient faith to tramp the streets of Jerusalem with a mudpack on his face so that he could be healed. Is it pride or the fear of indignity in submitting to Jesus that prevents people from becoming Christians today?

However much eyesight is precious to us, it's more important to see and believe with the heart than to see and believe with the eyes.

FEBRUARY 6
THE GOSPEL OF JOHN ch9 vv13-41

'I KNOW ONE THING'

It's generally understood by the man and woman in the street that we now understand how the universe works. They put their faith in scientists and 'experts', believing them to have the answers to most things. This is not the case. An honest scientist and famous inventor, Thomas Edison, declared: *We don't know a millionth of one per cent about anything'.* How often we may have floundered in a conversation, struggling to contribute something meaningful while recognising that we are totally out of our depth? David felt like that (Psalm 139 v6). Maybe the blind beggar discovered that he was out of his depth when it came to knowing what had happened to him. One moment he had been sitting begging, and the next moment he was feeling his way to Siloam with a mud-pack on his eyes. As the pool's cool waters washed his eyes, he could suddenly see. The *'night'* (v4) had been penetrated by the *'light'* (v5), giving the man sight (v7). He didn't know much about Jesus (vv17, 25, 35) or where he was (v12). He didn't know how Jesus had healed him, and he didn't know much about the theological arguments. But one thing was certain: *'One thing I know. I was blind but now I see'* (v25). There are three spiritual groups of people represented here:

1 THOSE WHO CAN'T SEE

The blind man is a powerful illustration of the disability and helplessness of those in spiritual darkness without Jesus, *the Light of the World'* (v5). Like the beggar, men and women are born spiritually blind. They are not born with a vision that deteriorates with age, but their condition has always been darkness. We are born in a state of entrenched hostility and rebellion towards God (Isaiah ch43 v8; ch56 v10). Our position is pathetic (Isaiah ch59 vv9-10) and is only compounded by the *'god of this age'* (2 Corinthians ch4 v4).

People fail to see the wonderful handiwork and craftsmanship of God in creation. They do not acknowledge the sovereign activity of God's providence in time and space, history, and politics. They fail to see the goodness of God in the daily provisions of his grace. They cannot see the love of God in the gospel and are blind to the significance of Jesus' sacrificial, substitutionary death and conquering resurrection. They are blind to their own sinfulness and the desperate need to be forgiven.

2 THOSE WHO CAN SEE

Signs of the Messiah's coming would include sight to the blind (Psalm 146 v8; Isaiah ch42 vv7, 18). Jesus has come to lift the scales from sightless eyes so that they may see and believe and be saved. In our journey of faith and conversion to Jesus, we may struggle to plot our exact course, but, with the healed man, we can say: *'One thing I know...'* You may not know the Bible very well, and you may not know how to respond in theological discussions, but the forgiven sinner can be sure of at least 'one thing.' When spiritual eyesight is received and the eyes of mind and heart are opened to the light of God's grace, then everything takes on a new perspective. *'Heaven above is softer blue, earth around is sweeter green; Something lives in every hue Christless eyes have never seen'* [GW

Robinson]. When those eyes have been opened, then a person becomes a disciple of Jesus with all the benefits and responsibilities that discipleship brings. Such discipleship will carry a cost (vv28,34).

3 THOSE WHO CLAIM TO SEE

(vv39-41) The Pharisees claimed to have the light and claimed to see, but they were religious bigots who didn't want to examine the evidence. Ignorance may have been some excuse, but the Pharisees weren't ignorant. Because they had seen and heard, their knowledge made them accountable and guilty. You may claim long associations with the church and solid friendships with Christians, even a fair knowledge of the Bible, but your spiritual eyes may still be firmly closed. Sadly, many pulpits and platforms are occupied by spiritually blind leaders who are leading blind congregations into *'a pit'* (Matthew ch15 v14).

We must faithfully proclaim the truth of the gospel. We must declare that it is only through a personal faith in Jesus, *'the Light of the World'*, that people's eyes can be opened and their sins forgiven.

John Newton, the converted slave-trader, spoke of the *'amazing grace'* that saved him: *'Once I was lost but now am found; Was blind but now I see'*.

FEBRUARY 7
THE GOSPEL OF JOHN ch10 vv1-10

'GOD'S GATE'

We use gates in every sector of industry and commerce, whether it's security gates and turnstile gates or electronic gates and metaphorical gates. The Lord Jesus declares (v9), *'I am the Gate'*. We may compare Jesus with the following gates:

1 SHEEP GATE

This is the primary illustration Jesus gives us. Jesus compares the Pharisees with *'thieves and robbers'* (vv1, 8) who try to access the sheep pen and the sheep without going through Jesus, *'the gate'* (v7). The sheep pen was often a rough enclosure made of stones or mud, and brick. It had one opening through which the sheep could enter or exit the pen. Sometimes shepherds shared a pen, and therefore several flocks could be within one enclosure. Shepherds may employ a *'watchman'* (v3) or an under-shepherd to supervise the flocks and to protect them from thieves and robbers who may try and steal the sheep by climbing over the wall (v1). The Pharisees and religious rulers are portrayed as bandits and rustlers who are guilty of plundering and injuring the flock. Jesus helps us identify our differences:

Different Access

They have got into the pen by climbing over the wall (v1). The Jewish rabbis taught that the other gates to the sheep pen of Israel included your 'family tree', or good deeds, or your law-keeping. Wannabe shepherds on the church scene today are teaching other gates apart from Jesus.

Different Voice

Sheep listen for their shepherd's voice and won't follow a stranger (vv4-5). The different voices of false shepherds may lure some away with their sweet talk and persuasive arguments. For some, it's the attraction of 'a religion without responsibility' and 'church without commitment'.

Different Motive

The motives of false shepherds are selfish. They want what they can get out of it. Their short-term profit forfeits the eternal life which the Good Shepherd offers. There's also a danger of confusing 'comfortable life' with 'fulness of life' (v10).

2 DEPARTURE GATE

The 'departure gate' is the gate that the *'watchman'* opens so that the shepherd can call out his own sheep. The sheep hear their master's voice and depart through the gate to follow their leader. Note that *'he calls his own sheep by name and leads them out'* (v3). It's not just a general call to the flock but a specific call to each individual sheep. There's a sense in which God calls everyone generally in the gospel, but there's a personal call of God's grace to the individual. God comes as the Shepherd-Saviour to effectually call his sheep by name. Jesus calls out his sheep to follow him.

3 TOLL GATE

This is a gate where a toll or payment is taken for the right to pass along a particular road. While the passage through the gate is free to the sheep, a toll has been paid and a fee has been tendered so that we can *'come in and go out'* (v9). The toll is nothing less than the death of the Good Shepherd (v11). What shepherd has ever sacrificed his own life to save a sheep? Jesus has! It's because of Jesus' unimaginable sufferings that his sheep can *'come in'* to find peace and *'go out'* to find pasture. The illustration is not to be pressed too hard, but the crucial point is that Jesus is the Gate through which the sheep have access. There are too many sickly sheep today who are not feeding on the green pastures which the Shepherd has provided through the ultimate toll he has paid.

4 LIFE GATE

Various philosophers and religious gurus have pointed to a radical way of life, but it's only in Jesus that we can know the richness, fullness, and completeness of life. It's through the Life Gate that we can live the life that God meant for us to live. People today talk about 'quality of life', but life only has 'quality' if it's the life God gives us, lived in the way God teaches us. If 'self', or 'the world', or 'pleasure' is a priority, then there's no quality. Jesus said that he is *'the life'* (ch14 v6). Having life *'to the full'* (v10) means something 'extraordinary', of a huge and unusual measure and quality.

FEBRUARY 8
GOSPEL OF JOHN ch10 vv11-21

THE GOOD SHEPHERD

For many people, including a number of unbelievers, the twenty-third Psalm is a particular favourite. They relate to the pastoral role of Jesus and derive some comfort in recognising God as the Shepherd. Jesus described himself as *'the Good Shepherd'* (v11), which is the fourth great 'I am' statement in this Gospel. Jesus is intrinsically good because Jesus is God (Mark ch10 v18). The *'thieves and robbers'* (v8) are the 'baddies' who harm the flock through subtlety and savagery. They are in complete contrast to the Shepherd and owner of the sheep, who has paid the ultimate price for them. There are five things about the Good Shepherd's relationship with his sheep:

1 HE OWNS HIS SHEEP

(v12) The *'hired hand'* is not a shepherd. He is a contract worker and cannot be relied upon. His priority is 'self', not 'sheep'. He certainly isn't going to risk his life for any sheep! David is a great example of a shepherd who looked after his father's flocks as if they were his own. When a lion and a bear attacked the flock, David went on the offensive and killed them both (1 Samuel ch17 vv34-37). Jesus will never abandon his sheep. If you belong to Jesus, are you identifiable as one of his sheep? Do you act as a member of his flock? There are those who will openly say 'The Lord is my shepherd' but of whom the Lord does not say 'He/she is my sheep'.

2 HE CARES FOR HIS SHEEP

(vv12-13) Some carers have been shown to be 'only in it for the money' and they feel no particular responsibility to those in their care. This is the same as *'the hired hand'* (v12) who is only there for 'payday'. The shepherd is the one who cares for the sheep. What a comfort it is to know that in the darkest night, when dangers lurk all around, and when the sheep may feel so vulnerable and helpless, the Good Shepherd cares. Jesus told his under-shepherd Peter to *'Take care of my sheep'* (John ch21 v16) and Peter tells all Christ's sheep to *'Cast all your anxiety upon him because he cares for you'* (1 Peter ch5 v7). Peter also encourages other under-shepherds to *'Be shepherds of God's flock, that is under your care'* (1 Peter ch5 v2).

3 HE KNOWS HIS SHEEP

(v14) The word *'know'* is not just about comprehending facts, but it's all about a relationship based upon trust and closeness. It is wonderful to be assured that as sheep of God's flock we are known and loved by a similar knowledge and love that is evident within the Godhead (ch15 vv9-10). The Good Shepherd knows every intimate detail about us. He knows us by name as well as every characteristic of our minds and hearts. Paul's lifetime quest was *'to know Christ'* (Philippians ch3 v10). Although in one sense Paul had come to know Jesus on the famous Damascus Road, he was never content with a superficial knowledge of the Saviour. He yearned to have a deeper relationship with his Shepherd. How much do you want to know the One who knows you altogether?

4 HE CALLS HIS SHEEP

(v16) Jesus calls his sheep with his unique, distinctive call. He refers to *'other sheep'* which belong to him, so that he calls both those sheep in the sheep-pen of Israel and those sheep outside that pen to make up *'one flock'* with *'one shepherd'*. Jesus' sheep are both Jews and Gentiles without any discrimination. It is Jesus who calls, and it's only when a sheep is personally and effectually called that it can come to the Shepherd.

5 HE DIES FOR HIS SHEEP

(vv11, 15, 17) Three times Jesus emphasises that he *'lays down his life for the sheep'* – his sheep. There is no suggestion that he lays down his life for any other sheep or any other flock. Jesus consciously, deliberately, and authoritatively gives his life for his own individual sheep. The cross looms large in the Masterplan of God. He proves his love for his wandering sheep by bearing their iniquity (Isaiah ch53 v6). The Bible makes it clear that we are stupid, defenceless, wayward sheep who don't have the capacity to rescue ourselves. We need the Good Shepherd. There may be other shepherds – false shepherds – but there's only one Good Shepherd.

FEBRUARY 9
THE GOSPEL OF JOHN ch10 vv22-42

THE WORLD'S GREATEST FATHER

As the winter winds whistled through the temple area, Jesus and his Jewish critics would have felt some shelter within the stone arches of Solomon's Colonnade (v22). Although there had also been an icy wind of unbelief blowing around the hearts of many Jews, it was in that particular place that *'many people believed in Jesus'* (v42).

We know that there was contention, dispute, and murderous hostility towards Jesus. *'They tried to seize him'* (v39), and some would have killed Jesus there and then as *'the Jews picked up stones to stone him'* (v31). Many hated the message that Jesus brought with vehemence and violence. But *'in that place, many believed in Jesus'.*

This should be of great encouragement to us today. While we live in a generation that is largely hostile to the gospel, there are still many who believe in Jesus.

Over the last ten chapters, John has shown that Jesus is the Son of God, the Messiah, the Christ. He is wonderfully unique and exclusively incomparable. Jesus had been very clear about who he was: in his words and his works, by his message and his miracles. But the people still asked (v24). There was a fundamental problem as to why they wouldn't accept the truth. It was unbelief. They did not believe because they were not Jesus' sheep (v26). From the human perspective, we become one of Jesus' sheep through believing and trusting in Jesus. From God's perspective, we believe and trust in Jesus because we are one of his sheep. God doesn't choose us because of our faith, but rather, he chooses us so that we might have faith.

Nine times in thirteen verses, Jesus refers to his *'Father'*. Note these important characteristics:

1 THE FATHER'S POWERFUL NAME

(vv25, 32) Jesus' work and mission were performed through the authority of the Father's name. Jesus is at one with his Father, and there is perfect unity within the Trinity (v30). Everything Jesus did, he did as a representative of his Father. The perfect unity within the Godhead is the basis on which there should be unity within the church (ch17 v23). A genuine unity between Bible-believing Christians is a true reflection of the unity between God the Father and God the Son. Sadly, Christians are often struggling for unity between churches when there isn't even unity within their church!

2 THE FATHER'S SAFE HAND

(vv27-29) Whatever a sheep may do, or whatever may be done to it, nothing can prise or pluck it from God's secure hand. There is no safer place in the whole of time or space. To those who are anxious, worried, or frightened, or to those who feel threatened and very vulnerable, there is absolute security in the Shepherdly care of our heavenly Father. *'Blessed is the man who makes the Lord his trust'* (Psalm 40 v4).

3 THE FATHER'S ONLY SON

(vv34-36) Even if modern, liberal theologians claim not to know what Jesus was saying, the Jews certainly did! They knew that Jesus was declaring that he is God. That's why they wanted to stone him for blasphemy (v33). But they were blinkered to the truth that Jesus was not merely 'making himself out to be God' but that he was God. *'He did not consider equality with God something to be grasped'* when he *'made himself nothing...'* and *'became obedient to death'* (Philippians ch2 vv6-8). He could not surrender his deity when he hung on the cross and became the appalling victim of man's sin and his Father's judgement. Jesus had been *'set apart as his very own'* (v36). The Son had been *'sent into the world'* to be *'the Saviour of the world'* (1 John ch4 v14). This is at the heart of the gospel: that the Father should give his one and only Son to save sinful, wayward sheep.

4 THE FATHER'S UNIQUE WORK

(vv37-38) The proof of Jesus' authority and accreditation is in the doing of divine works. Those works, or *'miracles'* (v38), were additional evidence of his deity. Jesus could perform the Father's unique work because he is God. He still works those miracles in people's lives today as he saves them and transforms them by his grace.

Among the community of the Isle of Lewis, new converts have been characteristically described as those 'who had begun to follow'. If you are a follower of Jesus, then there should be no mistake about which Shepherd you are following.

FEBRUARY 10
THE GOSPEL OF JOHN ch11 vv1-16

A SICK LOVED-ONE

There was a special home in Bethany, a village about two miles southeast of Jerusalem on the eastern slope of Mount Olivet. It was where sisters Mary and Martha and their brother Lazarus lived. Although we are only given tantalising glimpses of this home in the Gospels, it seemed to be the base for Jesus' southern ministry in and around Jerusalem. These siblings had a special relationship with Jesus (v5). It's obvious that Jesus loved them, and they loved him. Mary would later demonstrate her love by anointing Jesus with expensive perfume (ch12).

Many of us can readily identify with the sisters as they try to come to terms with the situation into which they had been plunged: a close relative who was dangerously ill.

What could they do? What should they do? What did they do? They took the whole situation to Jesus (v3). How often do we see prayer as a last resort when things become deadly serious? But we are slow to learn the lesson that God has his purposes, even in the sickness of a loved one.

1 GOD'S PURPOSE IN DELAYS

After Jesus had received the message that his dear friend was sick, he stayed where he was for *'two more days'* (v6). But this wasn't an indication that he didn't love them. On the contrary, they all knew that Jesus loved them. The sisters even referred to Lazarus as *'the one you love'* (v3). If you have trusted Jesus personally for the forgiveness of your sins and you are living as a disciple of his, then, like Lazarus, you are one whom Jesus loves. The proof of his love is the cross (1 John ch4 vv9-10). The size of his love is suffering and sacrifice. So what is God's purpose in delaying prayer's answers? Learning to wait and be patient may be part of the answer. It may also be to do with the development of our trust, our prayerfulness, our dependence upon God, our perseverance, and our devotion. Jesus could have healed Lazarus from a distance. He could have healed him instantly, but he had a purpose in this 'apparent delay'. The cross should always remind us that God's Loved-One died amid unimaginable suffering to secure our pardon. Relief seemed to have been delayed for twenty-four hours. The resurrection seemed to have been delayed for forty-eight hours. But God is the perfect Time-keeper, and what may seem to be 'delays' to us are in fact God's 'precise appointments'.

2 GOD'S PURPOSE IN DAYLIGHT

Jesus explains God's purpose in vv9-10. Daylight gives 2 things:

Opportunity

Daylight provides the opportunity for many people to work. Jesus is *'the light of the world'* (ch8 v12), and as Jesus goes with us, we are able to see clearly where we are to work and what the task will be.

Urgency

Darkness can halt work (ch9 v4). When it's dark, we are at risk of stumbling (v10). Let's seize the opportunity and note the urgency.

3 GOD'S PURPOSE IN DEATH

(v4, vv11-15) Notice that in v4 Jesus is not saying that Lazarus won't die, but that the ultimate outcome is not death. Lazarus would have to die and lie sealed in a tomb for four days. There was no doubt that Lazarus was dead, but Jesus explained that his death was for God's glory (v4). Jesus would show that he is Lord over death and the tomb. Death may be a fierce and fearful enemy with terrifying powers, but Jesus is death's Keyholder (Revelation ch1 v18). The Christian does not walk the *'valley of the shadow of death'* alone (Psalm 23 v4). He need not fear any evil.

4 GOD'S PURPOSE IN DISCIPLESHIP

Note that the same 'Thomas', whom Christians and the world have named 'Doubting Thomas', is ready to die with Jesus as they make their way to Jerusalem (v16). Thomas exemplified the devotion of true discipleship. Wherever Jesus was going, even into a dangerous situation, Thomas said *'Let us also go'*. The faithful disciple will also say in response to the way Jesus leads to places of hostility, challenge, opportunity, and commitment: *'Let us also go'*. It may be the way of derision and criticism (from the world and from professing Christians). It may be the way of baptism and church membership, but are you ready to declare: *'Let (me) also go'*?

FEBRUARY 11
THE GOSPEL OF JOHN ch11 vv17-37

HALFWAY FAITH

Here, in this central section of the narrative, John reveals more of the details and conversations that ensued after Jesus' arrival in Bethany. As the events unfold, we notice faith, which is reserved and conditional: a halfway kind of faith.

There was no doubt that Lazarus was well and truly dead by the time Jesus had travelled the long distance to Bethany (v17). It is encouraging to find that Mary and Martha, as well as some of the Jews, didn't doubt Jesus' power. They had witnessed Jesus' healing power, especially with the blind man (ch9). But it is not enough to believe in the power or the capacity of Jesus. We can trust Jesus' power, and we may frequently testify to Jesus' omnipotence as the sovereign ruler of the universe.

But in practical, everyday terms, we may fail to trust his wisdom.

1 WE MAY TRUST HIS POWER BUT NOT HIS PROGRAMME

In other words, we may believe in Jesus' ability, but we fail to exercise faith in his timing. Martha was very polite and respectful (v21), but in her heart of hearts, she was saying, *'Lord, why didn't you come before?'* How often have we bordered on criticising God's timing? Even if our prayers and conversations are more restrained and reserved, the anguish of our hearts may reveal our frustrations with God's timetable. We easily quote Psalm 31 v15, *'My times are in your hands'*, but in practice, we may feel very different. We must never become impatient with God's schedule. His timing is perfect and his programme never needs rewriting.

Jesus met with Martha (not Mary) on the outskirts of their village (v30). Jesus had wanted to speak to her personally, just as God wants to speak to us personally and individually through his word. Therefore, we need to take time, on the busy outskirts of our day, to be alone with Jesus. He met Martha away from the busyness and noise of everyday concerns to tell her some wonderfully good news that would bring the greatest comfort to her heart:

Jesus' Statement of Life (v25)

In the midst of sorrow, crying, loneliness, heartache, and frustration, there is the light of hope. *'The Resurrection and the Life'* was right there with them! Jesus wasn't talking about physical death because even Lazarus died and, what's more, would die again. Physical death is not the end. For the believer, spiritual death will not be the victor. Through his unstoppable resurrection, Jesus has smashed death's shackles. He has rendered death helpless, and he has triumphed over death's powers and death's claims by the cross. Because he has risen as the great 'Resurrection Pioneer', he has forged a way through death.

Martha's Statement of Faith (v27)

She is saying that she has believed and will continue to believe in Jesus' Lordship, Messiahship, and deity. Yet Martha's faith, like Mary's, was a conditional faith, for she said, '...*if you had been here'* (vv21, 32). Many of us will struggle with that same issue of our faith. We trust God's ability, but we don't always trust his wisdom with regard to timing and programming.

2 WE MAY TRUST HIS POWER BUT NOT HIS PURPOSE

There is no higher purpose for Lazarus' death than this (v4): that God should be exalted; that Jesus, the Son of God, should be honoured and adored. Lazarus' resurrection revealed God's glory, and the final resurrection of every believer will reveal the intrinsic glory of Jesus. He was outraged at the ravages of death (v33). Yet the outward, visible signs of this inward upheaval were in quiet tears over the tragedy of death and sympathy for the sorrowful. But though Jesus wept with those who wept, he had a wonderful purpose, even in the death of a loved one.

3 WE MAY TRUST HIS POWER BUT NOT HIS PERSON

Jesus had a 'miracle fan club' (v37). Some followed Jesus around because they were entranced by his supernatural works. 'Supermen' always have a following! But trusting in Jesus' miraculous powers is not the same as believing in Jesus, the Son of God, the King of Kings, the Saviour of the world, the Friend of sinners. Jesus told the gullible Galileans that they only believed because of the miracles (ch4 v48). Even our praying could be just 'faith in prayer' rather than 'faith in God'. Is your faith anchored to the shifting sands of experience and feeling, or is it anchored to the Rock of Ages?

FEBRUARY 12
THE GOSPEL OF JOHN ch11 vv38-44

DEATH'S KEYHOLDER

For all those who personally believe in and trust in Jesus Christ, death may be the end of a phase, but it is the beginning of what Paul referred to as 'absence from the body and presence with the Lord' (2 Corinthians ch5 v8). Quoting the prophet Hosea (ch13 v14), Paul asks, *'Where, O death, is your victory? Where, O death, is your sting?'* (1 Corinthians ch15 v55). There was no doubt that Lazarus had died (v14). He had been in a *'cave with a stone laid across the entrance'* (v38) for four days. But death would not be the conclusion of this episode (v4). Death would not have the final word.

We may note three instructions to warn us, challenge us, encourage us, and help us.

1 NEVER DOUBT THE FORCE OF DEATH

'...death is the destiny of every man' (Ecclesiastes ch7 v2). Death touches our lives in one way or another quite regularly. Death frequently casts its shadow over the brightest and most exciting of lives. It was 'death' that visited that spectacularly delightful home in Bethany, which Jesus had valued and used as his base. Even Jesus, who had declared himself to be *'the Resurrection and the Life'* (v25), was affected by death. He was deeply moved and troubled by the force of death (vv33, 38). That unstoppable force, with the extensive damage and destruction which it caused, provoked a violent inward response within Jesus. Did it compare with God's feelings when he surveyed his creation following sin's catastrophic pollution and corruption (Genesis ch3)?

While the secularist believes that death is 'the ultimate disaster', the believing, penitent child of God believes that death is the gateway to glory. For the believer, death is not an 'inescapable spectre' or 'the king of terrors'. Of course, death is a force to be reckoned with. But Jesus has reckoned with it and has overcome it. Through the cross, Jesus has neutralised death's force and influence.

2 NEVER SUCCUMB TO THE FEAR OF DEATH

Despite Martha's great statements of faith (vv22, 24, 27), she still protested at Jesus' order to remove the stone (v39). Martha's faith was a 'halfway faith' which crumbled at the last minute. Wholehearted faith will not respond to God's instructions or promises with *'But Lord...'* Yet too often that is our response to God's word: 'But Lord, my circumstances are different... But Lord, I don't have the finances...But Lord, I'm not so healthy or so young as I was...' How many 'But Lord's' are hindering or hampering our faith? Martha continued to fear the consequences of death. The fear of death haunts many people. As an unbeliever, who is not trusting in Jesus' grace and pardon secured at the cross, there is good reason to fear (Hebrews ch9 v27). But for the believer, who is trusting in the Good Shepherd, the evil of death need not be feared (Psalm 23 v4). Death may go through its motions, but for the believer, its venom has been removed. The Keyholder of death stood at the entrance to Lazarus' tomb, demonstrating that he has the authority and control over death, and that the timing of release is in his hands.

3 NEVER FORGET THE FREEDOM FROM DEATH

We may imagine that breathtaking moment as the stone was levered away from the mouth of the tomb. Jesus prayed with his hearers in mind (v42). The death-defying, death-defeating act of Jesus was to reveal the glory of God in him so that people may believe that he is the Son of God. Jesus freed Lazarus from death, from the tomb, and from the graveclothes. Jesus came to the door of death so that its hostage may be freed. But his authority as the Lord of Death and Life didn't end at the tomb's entrance. He could say to death itself, as well as to the mourners, *'Let him go'* (v44).

This is the consolation for each Christian. Death has been subdued and is under the authority of our risen Lord.

Jesus gives a wonderful freedom in life (ch8 v32) and a guaranteed freedom from death. *'Blessed are those who die in the Lord...'* (Revelation ch14 v13). Lazarus heard Jesus' voice but *'a time is coming when all who are in their graves will hear his voice...'* (ch5 v28). Lazarus' dramatic resurrection is just a glimpse of the triumph over death for the believer and a foretaste of that grand future resurrection.

FEBRUARY 13
THE GOSPEL OF JOHN ch11 vv45-57

ONE FOR ALL

It seems that Lazarus and his two sisters had been well known in the area, including Jerusalem. Many Jews came to visit Mary specifically in her grief. But instead of sorrowing with Mary in her bereavement, they ended up rejoicing with Mary in her joy. They became involuntary witnesses to Jesus' great miracle and Lazarus' wonderful resurrection. It may be difficult to imagine the kind of conversations that took place with Lazarus at home that evening: the many questions with which he was bombarded about his death, his dying, not to mention the four days in the tomb (v39). George Whitfield, perhaps England's greatest open-air preacher, said *Take care of your life and the Lord will take care of your death'*. The Lord is the meticulous caretaker and undertaker of every believer's death. Lazarus would have been able to testify that the Lord had taken care of him in his death (Psalm 23 v4). Are you sure that the Lord Jesus will be your careful caretaker and undertaker when it comes for you to die? Are you assured of his thoughtful preparations for you, both during and after death? (ref ch14 v2).

There were certainly two clear responses to Lazarus' unique experience:

Many Jews put their faith in Jesus

They had seen the miracle and believed in the Messiah. They couldn't dodge the incontrovertible evidence and they put their faith in Jesus.

Some reported to the Pharisees

Although some Jews may have reported to the Pharisees with sincere motives, it's likely that they reported with malicious motives.

The Sanhedrin was the highest Jewish ruling council and the final court of appeal for the lower courts. It was during the Sanhedrin's intense deliberations about Jesus that Caiaphas made his significant pronouncement about 'one for all' (vv49-50).

1 ONE FOR ALL - EXPEDIENCY

Jesus' teachings and exploits had the Sanhedrin worried. They were concerned that Jesus could cause such a revolution in Judea that the Romans would be forced to act, and that could mean that the Sanhedrin might lose its authority. Caiaphas maintained that it was much more sensible to get rid of Jesus than to plunge the whole Sanhedrin and even the nation into jeopardy (v48).

Social expediency

What was the point of 'rocking Judea's boat' and placing her at risk with the Romans if all they had to do was to stop Jesus?

Political expediency

They were ready to take Jesus out of the equation rather than risk losing their political powers. Politicians today vote against the Bible's teaching and against morality for the sake of their Parliamentary seats and political careers.

Moral expediency

They would sacrifice one life rather than risk their own skins.

Religious expediency

They were also afraid of losing their temple building (v48). Their *'place'* was more important to them than the teachings of Jesus, and, sadly, 'places of worship' are more important to many people today than the character of worship itself and the teachings of the Bible.

2 ONE FOR ALL - PROPHECY

Caiaphas prophesied (vv51, 52), but he wasn't aware of the great truth that he was describing, that is, 'one for all'. He was ignorant of the divinely prompted prophecy which concerned the giving of Jesus' 'one life' for all *'the scattered children of God, to bring them together and make them one'* (v52).

3 ONE FOR ALL - SUFFICIENCY

Jesus' death was effective and sufficient for all his people.

One Sacrifice

Jesus' single sacrifice on the cross is totally sufficient for everyone who trusts him for pardon and forgiveness. The timing of his death, however, was not in the hands of the Sanhedrin (v53) but in the hands of his heavenly Father.

One People

He would bring the scattered children of God together and *'make them one'* (v52). Through the gospel, he is effectively calling his children from all nationalities, countries, languages, and cultures.

One Way

Mary's visitors who *'put their faith in (Jesus)'* (v52) came via the only Way revealed to them. There is only one entrance to the true church of God. Jesus is the Gate, and it's through him we have access (Ephesians ch2 vv17-18).

FEBRUARY 14
THE GOSPEL OF JOHN ch12 vv1-11

DINNER PARTY FOR A CELEBRATORY GUEST

Imagine that you are fit and healthy, and yet you know that you are to die next weekend. That was the situation that Jesus was in at the start of chapter 12. Jesus knew that 'his hour' had almost come, and he was fully prepared for the sufferings of his trial and crucifixion. But the Bethany home of Lazarus, Mary, and Martha had become a place of rest and retreat for Jesus. It must have been such a loving, peaceful, Godly place in which Jesus felt comfortable and very much at home. Since Jesus had raised Lazarus from death, it was also the place of life and resurrection. So Jesus *'arrived at Bethany'* on the evening of the Saturday which preceded the first Palm Sunday and the first Good Friday. It must have been evening, after dusk, when the Sabbath had officially ended. The exact venue for this dinner party was at the home of Simon the Leper, presumably someone else whom Jesus had healed (Mark ch14 v3). Simon and Lazarus had much in common. But there are three noticeable things about Jesus' three special friends, which are for our instruction and challenge.

1 MARTHA'S FAITHFUL SERVICE

The simple statement (v2) tells us that *'Martha served'*. Those two words sum up Martha's attitude and action. She may not have been in her own home, but Martha was eagerly engaged in the hard work of entertaining guests, especially Jesus. While Lazarus was being waited upon, and Mary was preoccupied with her own dramatic act of devotion, Martha quietly and humbly served. Her service was focused on Jesus. It was all done for Jesus' honour. At that moment, six days before his great humiliation and suffering, Jesus was being honoured and celebrated. How quickly the mood changed from honour to dishonour, from welcome to rejection, and from fame to shame. Even Jesus' closest disciples, who honoured him on Saturday night in Bethany, deserted him on the following Thursday night in Gethsemane. How fickle we are! We can join together in worshipping and honouring Jesus on Sunday, giving him the place of glory and reverence as our Number One Guest, but on Monday and during the week, we can dishonour Jesus by the kind of life we live.

2 MARY'S COSTLY SACRIFICE

(v3) While the guests reclined at the banqueting table with their feet stretched out behind them, Mary approached Jesus, almost unnoticed at first. She poured a marble jar of very expensive perfume all over Jesus' feet (and his head too, according to Matthew and Mark's accounts). This valuable commodity, which cost a year's wages (v5), was extremely concentrated and sealed in the stone jar. Imagine the sudden explosion of fragrance as the seal was broken and the contents poured over Jesus. If Mary's act was unnoticed to begin with, it was unmissable now! Everyone in the whole house knew just how much Mary thought of Jesus. She had been overwhelmed with gratitude for the restoration of her brother. Here she laid everything at Jesus' feet, even her respectability and dignity (with the untying of her hair). She was saying, 'I am nothing, but you, Jesus, are everything to me!' How do we show our devotion to Jesus? Do we give him some of our valuables in a stingy way, or do we lavish them all on Jesus without counting the cost?

3 LAZARUS' DAILY WITNESS

(vv9-11) 'Lazarus the tomb-buster' had gained quite a reputation across the region. Large crowds gathered at Bethany, not only to see Jesus, but to see with their own eyes the man who had returned from the dead. Every day that Lazarus lived was a testimony to Jesus' death-defeating power. If people had asked Lazarus what had happened, he only had to say, 'Jesus!' Lazarus's death-to-life testimony can be compared to every believer's death-to-life testimony. There was always the danger of a 'Lazarus supporters' club' or even 'Lazarus' disciples', but the fact that his witness caused people to put their faith in Jesus emphasised the genuineness of the Saviour's work in him. This special dinner party publicly identified Lazarus, Mary, and Martha as devoted disciples of Jesus. This family in Bethany didn't hide their association with Jesus despite the increasing hostility and threats to kill him. They didn't shrink from being identified as his followers.

FEBRUARY 15
THE GOSPEL OF JOHN ch12 vv12-19

YOUR KING IS COMING!

Huge crowds had been converging on the city of Jerusalem for the Passover feast, which was celebrated in April each year. This feast, combined with the Feast of Unleavened Bread, made it a double festival. These feasts commemorated the deliverance of the Jews from Egypt, and all Jewish converts made every effort to attend. The Jewish historian, Flavius Josephus, estimated that over two and a half million people attended the feast just thirty years after this account.

So, we can imagine that when John writes about two crowds thronging around Jesus, the size of those crowds was not insignificant. The crowd that followed Jesus consisted of those who had witnessed the miraculous resurrection of Lazarus, as well as many in the surrounding area who had heard the news. The other *'great crowd'* (v12) had heard about Jesus and had surged out of the city to meet him. Somewhere on the outskirts of Jerusalem, these two large crowds met and merged. These 'wall-to-wall' people acclaimed and applauded Jesus as the 'coming King'.

We are told four specific things about the 'King's coming'.

1 HIS COMING PREDICTED

This was not an unexpected, unplanned event. All the lines of history had converged on this pivotal Passover period. This singular week was a prominent feature in God's calendar and had been clearly prophesied in the Old Testament. The crowds adapted part of Psalm 118 in identifying Jesus as the Messiah and as the King of Israel. The people cried *'Hosanna!'*, meaning 'Save now!' The crowds' commentary on the event unfolding before their eyes is interesting. They recognised the *'one who comes in the name of the Lord'* as the Messiah. They believed that the Messiah would be the new King of Israel, a descendant of King David. And here, on this unique occasion, they believed that Jesus was the realisation of all their hopes and anticipations, and so their united response was 'Save us now!' 'Deliver us!' 'Set us free!' 'Hosanna!' For a brief moment, they recognised Jesus as their King and their Saviour. However, the crowds may have puzzled over the prophecy (v15, Zechariah ch9 v9) which described their King riding a 'peace donkey' and not a 'war horse'.

2 HIS COMING WELCOMED

As the two huge crowds met, they were wild in their welcome. They flung their coats in front of Jesus and cut down palm branches (Mark ch11 v8). The 'palm emblem' already depicted nationalist convictions, and Jesus was being hailed as a national hero. But national fervour is no substitute for personal faith. They wanted a champion to save them from the Romans, but they didn't want a Saviour to save them from their sins. Similarly, there are plenty of people today who welcome Jesus as a sort of freedom-fighter for the oppressed, a champion for justice, a figurehead for the church, or a symbol of traditional morality, but they will not trust him personally for the forgiveness of their sin.

3 HIS COMING NOT UNDERSTOOD

(v16) The disciples witnessed Jesus' triumphal entry, but they didn't understand it. There was a vital gap in their comprehension; a gap that would only be bridged *'after Jesus was glorified'*. After Jesus had been crucified and resurrected, the jigsaw piece fell into place. It was only in the light of the cross and the empty tomb that the disciples saw clearly that the pathway to redemption and glory was through humility and suffering. If a 'King on a donkey' had seemed so outrageous, what about 'God on a cross'?

4 HIS COMING BROADCAST

(vv17-19) The second crowd had come to meet Jesus in response to the first crowd of witnesses, which had *'spread the word'* (v17). To the hostile Pharisees, it seemed that the *'whole world had gone after (Jesus)'* (v19). We may not all be evangelists, open-air preachers, field missionaries, or Bible teachers, but, as believers, we must all be involved in spreading the word (witnessing, testifying). Just as many proclaimed Jesus' first coming, so we must not be reticent in broadcasting that Jesus is coming again, when *'every eye will see him'* (Revelation ch1 v7). On this occasion, he will not return to be humiliated and killed, but he will come to rule in majesty and in power.

FEBRUARY 16
THE GOSPEL OF JOHN ch12 vv20-36

DO YOU WANT TO SEE JESUS?

Sometimes we hear mature people, who are totally immersed in some great work or project, comment, 'This is what I was born for'. They believe that they have reached the pinnacle and fulfilment of their life efforts. It's their 'raison d'être', that is, their 'reason to be'. In these verses, we note the profound words of Jesus' 'reason to be the Son of Man'. For three years of ministry, and for thirty-three years of life on earth, and for four thousand years of Old Testament history, all the prophetic signposts had been pointing to one immensely significant moment. Even Jesus, during his three years of preaching, healing, and teaching, would often say, *'My hour has not yet come'* (for example, ch2 v4). But now there is this soul-stunning announcement, *'The hour has come...'* (v23). Here, between the first Palm Sunday and Good Friday, with the cross looming into view, Jesus proclaims that his hour had come. This is the point in history at which all the lines of prophecy converge. This is the climax to the greatest mission in heaven or on earth. This is the ultimate focus of divine attention – the cross. Jesus would be glorified by being crucified (v27). Jesus' supreme objective was to bring glory to his heavenly Father by obedience to his Masterplan of salvation. The Son of Man's raison d'être was *Father, glorify your name!'* Our body, mind, and soul should constantly orbit this dazzling focal point: the glory of God. Everything we do or say should be for his glory (1 Corinthians ch10 v31; 1 Peter ch4 v11). For the third time in the Gospels, God the Father makes a public proclamation (v28). Here we see the divine blueprint, God's mission, and Jesus' ministry, woven together in seamless unity. Jesus' will was his Father's will.

It was against this background of teaching and explanation that some unknown, unnamed Greeks came to Philip expressing their desire to see Jesus (v21). We can't be sure whether they actually saw Jesus, although we know that Jesus honours any genuine enquiry. How many want to 'see Jesus' but have no desire to be changed by him? *'Sir, we want to see Jesus'.* Was this merely a polite social request, or was it an earnest personal enquiry?

What does Jesus demand of those who want to be his disciples?

1 LOVE JESUS BY PRIORITISING

Jesus spoke of priorities in v25, and he made it plain that to be self-focused would mean loss; that to be obsessed with personal achievement and personal success would mean eternal failure. Jesus tried to refocus Peter after the Resurrection by asking about his love for the Saviour (ch21 v15). If we claim to love Jesus, we shall need to prioritise. We shall learn that subtractions and losses are not the end of the road. Putting Jesus first means a whole avalanche of grace. If we really love Jesus, then obedience to his word will be our chief priority.

2 SERVE JESUS BY FOLLOWING

(v26) Being a pupil of a teacher in Greek or Roman society meant a close personal attachment. It wasn't enough for a student to turn up for a few lectures each week. Being a pupil implied discipleship. Being a disciple implied serving. Being a servant implied following. It wasn't sufficient to hear the teacher's words, but to observe the teacher's life. Serving Jesus also means serving one another in the family of God. That can often mean serving in the lowliest of tasks where there is no fame, no popularity, no honour, no glory, and often no thanks. But if *'this is the way the Master went, should not the servant tread it still?'* [Horatius Bonar, Scottish hymnwriter, preacher, and author.]

3 TRUST JESUS BY WALKING

(vv35-36) Jesus is the Light of the World, and, during the deepest, densest darkness of this world, we must learn to trust his light. A boat enters a harbour at night with the skipper trusting in the navigation lights at the port entrance, with which he aligns his course. But trust in Jesus is not just a one-off momentary decision. Rather, it implies a lifelong, consistent, persevering faith. Jesus explained the urgency of walking while they had the light (v35). The light would soon be taken away by the cross. For them, the opportunity to trust in Jesus was then and there. The darkness of men's enmity to Jesus would not make it any easier to trust in him on the other side of the cross. That may have been their last opportunity (v36).

FEBRUARY 17
THE GOSPEL OF JOHN ch12 vv37-50

BELIEVING THE MESSAGE

At the end of the Second World War, an American serviceman who had escaped Japanese soldiers by hiding in the jungle received the thrilling message that the Japanese had surrendered and that the war was over, except that he wouldn't believe the message and continued to live in the jungle in fear. He did not, he would not, he could not believe the good news that would bring him freedom, security, and a new life. One wonders what would have finally convinced this GI that the message was true. But *'even after Jesus had done all these miraculous signs in their presence, they still would not believe in him'* (v37).

1 THOSE WHO WON'T BELIEVE (vv37-41)

Out of all the wonderful and miraculous things that Jesus did, John has selected seven, in the first eleven chapters, to illustrate Jesus' divine power and to authenticate his Messiahship. What kind of miracle would really convince you that someone was a unique miracle-worker and not just a clever magician or illusionist? You may want to see him bring a dead person back to life. And the seventh of the seven miracles, which John attributes to Jesus, is just that. He brings the dead Lazarus back to life. Consequently, many Jews believed and put their faith in Jesus (ch11 v45). Although faith, because of having witnessed miracles, is not the deepest and strongest kind of faith, it is better than unbelief. But despite the amazing miracles, there were many who dug their heels in firmly and *'still would not believe in him'* (v37). But this is nothing new. The people had rejected Isaiah's message in the seventh century BC, just as they were now rejecting God's Messiah. Isaiah had asked *'Lord, who has believed our message?'* (Isaiah ch53 v1). There's almost a hint of frustration in the prophet's question. We may also feel like that at times. We talk and preach the gospel message, but it is constantly rejected. Who believes our message? But they did not believe because they *'could not believe'* (v39). This emphasises to us the desperate urgency of responding to the message when we can. We can't come to God and believe anytime we feel like it. Today is the opportunity, but tomorrow is not guaranteed (Hebrews ch3 vv7-8).

2 THOSE WHO WON'T CONFESS (vv42-46)

There was a cost to becoming a believing, confessing follower of Jesus. The cost was expulsion from the synagogue. Membership of their Jewish church was more important to them at that moment than confessing Jesus as their Lord and Saviour.

So often, the one question that prevents a person from confessing Christ is frequently, 'what will other people think?' For such, men's applause is more important than God's approval (v43). The word *'confess'* means 'to speak the same'. Paul stressed the inseparable relationship between belief and confession (Romans ch10 v9). 'Confession' or 'Confession of Faith' was the description that the Early Church gave to the testimonies of the martyrs as they were about to die. The title then became used to describe formal statements of Christian faith, especially since the time of the Reformation. Baptism has also been a clear confession of faith throughout church history. Baptism identifies Christians today who are not afraid to be known as true followers of Jesus.

3 THOSE WHO WON'T ACCEPT (vv47-50)

To believe in Jesus is to receive the light and to come out of the darkness (v46). But many will not see, will not hear, and will not accept. There may at times be a superficial 'faith' like *'the person who hears my words but does not keep them'* (v47). This may be someone who sits and listens to the Bible for an hour on Sunday but who does not obey the Bible from Monday to Saturday. They may acknowledge the Bible to be a great religious book, but would rather that it were kept in a church or a museum rather than kept in the heart. However, there's a solemn finality about God's word in these verses. Accepting Jesus' words leads to salvation, but rejecting Jesus' words leads to condemnation. The very word of salvation, if rejected, will bring its own judgement. It's exactly the same word, but it's the word of life to those who believe, confess, and accept, and it's the word of condemnation to those who refuse and reject. Let us be among those for whom the message is the word of life.

FEBRUARY 18
THE GOSPEL OF JOHN ch13 vv1-17

FOOTWASHING

The countdown to the cross is in its last stage. *'Jesus knew that the time had come for him to leave this world...'* (v1). The end of Jesus' ministry on earth was in sight. But Jesus' love for his disciples wasn't restricted to his time on earth. He didn't just love them to the end. In fact, he would demonstrate that his love was without end. His love didn't have a limit: it was immeasurable. How did Jesus reveal the greatness of his love to his disciples? He did it by submission, humility, and servitude, which was a prelude to his death the following morning. Jesus is the omnipotent King under whose power the Father had put all things (v3). But Philippians ch2 vv6-8 charts the course of Jesus' submission and humiliation right down to the cross. He took *'the very nature of a servant'* and in this footwashing action of Jesus in the upper room, he demonstrates the course of servitude to which he was committed. A host would usually instruct a servant to perform the menial task of washing the dry and dusty feet of his guests. In this case, there was no obvious host and certainly no servants. It was unthinkable that one of the disciples would volunteer to serve the others in this way, especially as they had been discussing among themselves which of them was the greatest. So Jesus shows the way yet again and teaches us about washing:

1 WASHING IS ESSENTIAL

It is only through the atoning work of the cross the following day that any sinner can be washed and made clean. It is only through the shedding of Jesus' blood that guilty, dirty sinners can be purged and made pure (Hebrews ch9 vv13-14). Peter had to learn, just as we must learn, that effective service is dependent upon essential cleansing. If a surgeon's instruments are not sterile, then his operation can be seriously compromised. If we are going to be useful and useable instruments in the divine Surgeon's hands, then we must be washed, cleansed, purified, and made fit for service. The spiritual cleansing agent is nothing less than the blood of Christ (1 John ch1 vv7-9). To have any *'part with (Jesus),'* we must be washed. For Simon Peter to be a participant in God's service, he had to be clean. In response to his protest in v8, Jesus said, *'Unless I wash you, you have no part with me'.*

2 WASHING IS EFFECTUAL

A particular pen may enjoy the status of being a personal favourite and has been chosen for a special set of tasks. However, although its ownership is not in question, its effectiveness may be influenced by its condition at any time. If the pen leaks and is not cleaned, then it may become temporarily unusable. Jesus pointed out that Peter's status was assured (v10). Peter's relationship to Jesus was different from Judas's relationship with Jesus. Judas wasn't clean (v11). But Peter belonged to God because a price had been paid for him. Though status will be unaffected, the condition may vary from day to day. This is illustrated by the washing of Peter's feet. In one sense, he didn't need a bath. The washing of salvation is historic, once-and-for-all, and never-to-be-repeated. God's eternal work in saving a soul and washing it in the blood of Jesus guarantees a believer's unalterable status. That washing is unquestionably effectual. Peter didn't need 'another bath', but he did need his feet washed. We need that daily washing from wrong desires, sinful attitudes, selfish actions, and hurtful words. We need to ensure our 'feet' are washed every day.

3 WASHING IS AN EXAMPLE

'I have set you an example that you should do as I have done for you' (v15). Jesus taught his disciples to serve and to sacrifice by being their example. It isn't specifically the example of washing people's feet that we are required to follow. It's much bigger and broader than that. It's the example of serving by humbling ourselves. Our attitude should be the same as Jesus, who took the very nature of a servant (Philippians ch2 vv5-7). He who is Lord of all became the servant of all. Jesus' display of humility, self-sacrifice, and love is the pattern to be followed by all his disciples. Humble service is at the very heart of Christian faith. Jesus told his followers, *'Whoever wants to be great among you must be your servant'* (Mark ch10 v43). Was Peter recalling this footwashing incident when he later wrote: *'All of you, clothe yourselves with humility towards one another, because, 'God opposes the proud but gives grace to the humble'. Humble yourselves, therefore, under God's mighty hand, that he may lift you up in due time'* (1 Peter ch5 vv5-6)?

FEBRUARY 19
THE GOSPEL OF JOHN ch13 vv18-30

TREACHERY AFOOT

The disciples' enjoyment of friendship at this last, intimate meal with Jesus was soon to be marred by treachery. Yet this didn't come as a surprise to Jesus (ch2 v25; ch6 vv70-71; ch12 v4; ch13 v2). The menu for Jesus and his disciples that evening included betrayal. But although Jesus hadn't been tricked, he had been troubled (v21). He was stirred up inside with grief and sorrow. The bitterness of betrayal weighed heavily on his heart. Jesus recalled David's feelings after he had been betrayed by his counsellor Ahithophel (2 Samuel chs. 15-17; Psalm 41 v9). Though Jesus had stooped to wash Judas' physical feet, Judas' metaphorical heel would be raised against him (v18). Jesus knew the intense spiritual battle which he was fighting, and he knew that his arch-enemy, Satan, was manipulating events within God's sovereign plan to concentrate the fiercest firepower upon him. What do we know about Judas, the traitor?

Judas was unsuspected

Judas was able to live and move among Jesus' closest friends without raising a hint of suspicion from any one of them. It's also possible to be among a Christian group or church, with selfish and devious motives, and to remain above suspicion. But Jesus hadn't been hoodwinked (ch6 v64). His supernatural x-ray vision saw right into Judas' heart, just as he sees right into our hearts.

Judas was unmasked

It seems that John alone knew the identity of the traitor from Jesus' revelation to him (vv23-25). He watched in stunned silence while the other disciples thought that Jesus was honouring Judas by handing him a tasty piece of bread, dripping with the juices of the cooked meat dish.

Judas was unrepentant

Here was one last opportunity to turn from his treacherous pursuit, but his cold, stony heart had not been thawed. His selfish ambitions had led to satanic control. He was now locked into devilish manipulation.

There are a number of things we must be careful about as we consider this account.

1 BE CAREFUL THAT WE DON'T SHARE JESUS' BREAD AND LIFT UP OUR HEEL

It's possible to enjoy the friendship and generosity of Jesus and yet to betray him (v18). It's possible to move within Jesus' intimate circle and yet to be responsible for the most heinous of crimes. Even though Judas had been numbered among *'the Twelve'* (ch6 v71), Jesus hadn't made a mistake.

2 BE CAREFUL THAT WE DON'T SPEND TIME WITH JESUS AND MAKE ROOM FOR SATAN

Judas entered Jesus' presence as a 'friend', but Satan entered Judas. Even Jesus offered the final piece of bread to Judas with kindness and courtesy as a final gesture of love and grace. But while Judas accepted the piece of bread, he didn't accept the peace of God. Satan, however, should not be blamed for Judas' sin any more than we should blame Satan for our own sins. Satan can only get a foothold in a person's life when there is already rebellion and disobedience (James ch1 vv14-15). The way of victory over Satan is the way of humility. Submission to God comes before success over the enemy (James ch4 vv7-10).

3 BE CAREFUL THAT WE DON'T HEAR GOD'S WORD AND REFUSE TO TRY AND UNDERSTAND IT

Judas was committed unswervingly to treachery, and Jesus urged him to get on with his dastardly business (vv27-28). But the disciples just didn't understand. All, except John, thought that Judas had been sent on an errand to purchase food or that he had been despatched on a mission to the poor (v29). We may also hear God's word today, but we don't even try to understand it: '...*ever hearing but not understanding*' (Isaiah ch6 v9). The situation is perilous when we can go through the motions of 'Bible-hearing' and 'Bible-reading' but shun 'Bible-understanding' and refuse 'Bible-applying'.

4 BE CAREFUL THAT WE DON'T LOATHE THE LIGHT AND LOVE THE NIGHT

'*And it was night*' (v30) may refer primarily to the time of Judas' exit, but it's also a summary of the state of Judas' heart (ch3 v19). How much do we love the light of truth and holiness, the light of God's word and the gospel? Or does exposure to such light make us feel uncomfortable? Loving the darkness can lead to betrayal.

FEBRUARY 20
THE GOSPEL OF JOHN ch13 vv31-38

THE DISCIPLESHIP FEATURE

We are told that in an average day, an average person can be filmed by over seventy surveillance cameras. Through facial recognition some cameras can track a person across a town or city centre. But how easy is it to spot a disciple of Jesus? Are there distinctive features that would mark someone out as a follower of Jesus? It may not be facial features, or fashion features, or movement features, but is there any way that we can identify Jesus' disciples? Jesus tells us that it is 'love' which is the single quality of genuine discipleship. In chs13-21 he uses the word 'love' forty-four times.

1 LOVE IS THE TEST OF DISCIPLESHIP

Jesus introduces this supreme quality of 'love' with a new freshness and a new impetus. It's a *'new command'* in that sense. Jesus places 'love' at the heart of true discipleship. He empowers it with a new relevance and a new significance. Jesus shows that his love is the test of what being a disciple is all about: *'As I have loved you, so you must love one another'*. The old-style, old-school-type love had become worn and threadbare. It had become intertwined with too many conditions and exceptions. Strict Pharisees had invented various clauses to excuse them from genuine love for their neighbour. So Jesus launches this foundational statement with a new authority and a new emphasis. He places love at the centre of everything that the disciples would do, and he underlines the quality of this unconditional love. It's the love that he had demonstrated to them minutes earlier when he had washed their feet. This *'full extent of his love'* (v1) was undiscriminating and unreserved. It represented humility and servanthood.

2 LOVE IS THE BADGE OF DISCIPLESHIP

(v35) Jesus made it clear that the disciples would not be known primarily for their dress sense, or their hair style, or their t-shirts with texts on them, or their lapel badges with curious quotes and symbols. The badge of their identity is love. Neither is this the passive, peaceable, non-confrontational, anything-goes kind of love that some religious people have propagated. The love Jesus was speaking about is selfless, submissive, and sacrificial. It's a divine grace conferred upon God's people.

But sadly, this 'badge of love' gets easily tarnished. Christians have so many foibles, bear so many grudges, have so many complaints and criticisms of each other, peddle so much gossip, and get jealous of each other. The standard and quality of 'discipleship love' is nothing short of *'As I have loved you'* (v34). This is not a wishy-washy, sentimental, frothy, showy love. Neither is it a love that is bound up with stiff and starchy suits, church traditions, religious ceremonies, and theoretical theology. This is the practical, everyday, selfless, costly love which comes from God, is exemplified by Jesus, and is channelled through his disciples.

3 LOVE IS THE COST OF DISCIPLESHIP

A genuine disciple of Jesus will love, even when it hurts and even when it costs. Peter thought that he loved Jesus, but he still had much to learn about his love for the other disciples (vv36-38). Peter thought that his love for Jesus was sufficient to lay down his life for him. But the disciples were in for their second shock that night. Not only was one of 'the Twelve' going to betray Jesus, but Peter would disown him. Peter's good intentions at that point were not enough. During the next thirty years, he would learn the cost of discipleship. After his post-resurrection interview with Jesus (ch21), Peter's faith didn't waver. He survived fierce opposition, imprisonment, and beatings as he faithfully proclaimed the message of Jesus. Eventually, church historians tell us, he was sentenced to death by the Roman emperor Nero. Here was a disciple who paid the supreme cost of discipleship. His love for Jesus could not be suppressed or extinguished. But Peter's love had not been refined or proof-tested at the Last Supper. Peter was more preoccupied with Jesus' words about 'leaving' rather than 'loving'. And it is still the case that Christians can be so distracted about questions of theology, church practice and criticisms of other people's behaviour, that they miss the whole point of Jesus' teaching: *love one another*. And you can't do that while 'self' is continuing to vie for attention!

FEBRUARY 21
THE GOSPEL OF JOHN ch14 vv1-4

JESUS KNOWS ALL ABOUT OUR TROUBLES

The disciples in the Upper Room had already received three pieces of 'bad news'. First, one of the Twelve would betray Jesus. Secondly, the one whom they thought to be the strongest and bravest, Peter, would disown Jesus. Thirdly, Jesus wanted them all to embark on an important mission without him. Any one of those three news items was calculated to trouble Jesus' disciples. But Jesus dealt with the concerns that they had about troubles.

1 THE TROUBLE WE CAN AVOID

Jesus said, *'Do not let your hearts be troubled'*. Although some people have suggested that Christians shouldn't experience any trouble at all, the discerning believer knows that this won't happen this side of heaven (Job ch5 v7). Notice that Jesus didn't say, 'Don't let trouble come to your home, or to your business, or to your family, or to your church, or even to your body'. He said, 'Don't let trouble come to your heart!' Yet it was understandable that his disciples should be troubled. The word for *'trouble'* is the same word that John uses to describe the pool of Bethesda when it became stirred, agitated, and disturbed (ch5 v7). We imagine waters rippling and bubbling caused by a disturbance deep below the surface. This is the agitation and anguish that a troubled heart may feel. The rippling and bubbling on the surface reveal a deeper disturbance below. Jesus knows all about these troubles. We have already seen three occasions on which Jesus' own heart or spirit was troubled (ch11 v33; ch12 v27; ch13 v21). The Lord Jesus wasn't exempt from a troubled spirit. He was deeply troubled by the consequences of Satan, sin, and death. He is not detached or aloof from our experience of trouble. But rather than being accidents of life, such troubles are appointments of God. He has also shown us that even in the middle of the fiercest hurricane of life, there is the 'eye' of peace and tranquillity. Although we may be surrounded by the spiralling winds of various troubles, it's possible to experience the 'eye of the storm' when our hearts are at peace with God.

2 THE TRUST WE CAN KNOW

In a wonderfully clear and gracious way, Jesus provides the antidote to trouble. It's trust! But it's not just 'trust', just as it's not just 'faith'. Trust is nothing without the object of that trust. You must trust in something or someone. Jesus was not asking his disciples to believe in the existence of God. Only *'a fool says in his heart 'There is no God!'* (Psalm 14 v1). Jesus was instructing his disciples to trust in him. Trusting in God and trusting in Jesus is one and the same, for Jesus is God. *'He will call upon me and I will answer him; I will be with him in trouble'* (Psalm 91 v15). Trusting in Jesus doesn't guarantee the disappearance of trouble, but it does mean, even in the middle of the fiercest fight, the hottest fire, the strongest storm, and the deepest flood, that our Lord and Saviour is right there in the middle with us (Psalm 59 v16).

3 THE TRUTH WE CAN PROVE

In three verses, Jesus points out the truth about three things:

The truth about a prepared place (v2)

Jesus has returned to heaven bodily so that he may personally prepare a place for his own people. Jesus' route to his *'Father's house'* was by way of the cross. Crucifixion and resurrection had to precede ascension. The home of his heavenly Father is going to be the home of his disciples.

No words may adequately describe the preparations that Jesus is making. But it's sufficient for us to be assured that where Jesus is, it's heaven anyway.

The truth about a guaranteed return (v3)

Jesus' return is just as real as his departure. If Jesus is preparing a home for his people, his people should be preparing their hearts for his home. We never know as believers whether at this precise moment we are standing on the very threshold of heaven.

The truth about a certain access (v4)

Years ago, someone told me about a fabulous place. It sounded so beautiful, so idyllic, and so attractive. He suggested that I go there and sample its delights. But he failed to tell me the way! Although Jesus has revealed something of the glories and good things of heaven, he has not failed to show the way. These truths should be the Christian's comfort. For every blood-bought believer, trusting the Lord Jesus Christ is the antidote to trouble.

FEBRUARY 22
THE GOSPEL OF JOHN ch14 vv5-14

ONE WAY ONLY

Jesus disclosed some of the facts concerning his relationship with his Father.

1 JESUS IS THE WAY TO THE FATHER (vv5-6)

Jesus is the Exact Way

There's nothing inaccurate or imprecise about this way. Jesus didn't come merely to blaze a trail: he is the route itself.

Jesus is the Exclusive Way

Jesus drives home the importance of his statement that no one comes to the Father except through him. Jesus is not only the way to God; he is the *only* way to God. The nauseating nonsense about 'many roads up a mountain', but all reaching the summit in the end, stands in direct opposition to Jesus' teaching (Acts ch4 v12). Jesus is the divinely prescribed way, and if you miss Jesus, you miss everything.

Jesus is the Excellent Way

Paul uses this term to introduce the method for exercising spiritual gift, which is love (1 Corinthians ch12 v31). Jesus is the 'way of love' personified. He had already demonstrated *'the full extent of his love'* (ch13 v1) with an illustration of servitude that would end with a demonstration of sacrifice (Romans ch5 v8). Jesus is the incomparable Way: the Pathway par excellence.

2 JESUS IS THE REVELATION OF THE FATHER (vv7-9)

The Old Testament is a forest of signposts pointing to the moment when God would ultimately reveal himself. It's just as if all those signposts had the name 'Jesus' printed on them. The disciples' knowledge of Jesus had been increasing each day, but they hadn't yet fully grasped that Jesus is God. Nearly thirty years later, Paul explained that Jesus *is the image of the invisible God'* (Colossians ch1 vv15-17). Jesus both reflected and revealed God the Father. Like thousands of people throughout history, Philip said that if he saw the Father, then that would be sufficient (v8). Did Philip's lack of faith add to the anguish of our Saviour's heart? For three years, Jesus had eaten with them, walked with them, talked with them, laughed with them, wept with them, prayed with them, and Philip still comes up with this request: *'Lord, show us the Father...'* How long have we been associated with Jesus and don't really know him?

3 JESUS IS ONE WITH THE FATHER (vv10-11)

There is a perfect oneness, a divine unity, in the Godhead. The coming and the appearance of Jesus doesn't make two Gods! John has already gone to great lengths in his Gospel to show that Jesus really is God: that Jesus is the revelation of God to humanity.

4 JESUS BRINGS GLORY TO THE FATHER (vv12-14)

How can a believer's works be *'greater'* than Jesus' works? Jesus is departing bodily to be with his Father, but he has promised to do whatever is requested in his name. By doing so, Jesus will bring glory to his Father. It is God's plan that through the completed work of the cross, thousands will repent and believe – even greater numbers than during Jesus' earthly ministry. As the evangelistic explosion mushroomed across the Roman Empire, Jesus equipped and empowered his disciples to do great things in his name in answer to faithful praying. The key to the *'greater things'* is faith: *'anyone who has faith'* (v12).

Do you know the Way?

It's interesting to find that Jesus' true followers were identified with *'the Way'* after Pentecost (Acts ch9 v2). They were clearly associated with the Way of Truth and the Way of Life. To be 'followers of the Way' has been costly in terms of homes, families, jobs, and even lives.

Do you have the Faith?

Far from abandoning his disciples or leaving them in the lurch, Jesus assures them that his bodily departure would not mean his spiritual absence. Jesus expects his followers to continue his work on earth while he pursues his work in heaven. Faith is the key to doing *'greater things'* for God. Paul told the believers at Colosse that he was so delighted to see just how firm their faith in Christ was (Colossians ch2 v5). Petitioning *'in my name'* means asking for those things that are directly aligned with Jesus' character, plan, and purpose. He has not promised to respond to every selfish whim or secret wish, though he guarantees to answer requests which glorify his Father.

FEBRUARY 23
THE GOSPEL OF JOHN ch14 vv15-31

ANOTHER COUNSELLOR

Jesus tempered the news of his departure with the announcement of someone who would take his place. He introduces the Personal Counsellor: the Paraclete.

Apart from 'paras' meaning 'paratroopers' (who are soldiers parachuted behind enemy lines) the prefix 'para' has two meanings, one of which is 'beside' or 'alongside', for example, 'parallel' meaning 'beside one another' or 'parable' meaning 'a story or illustration placed alongside a moral teaching or truth'.

So with the component 'clete', from a Greek word meaning 'to call', the name 'paraclete' means 'someone who is called alongside'; someone who is 'called to help'.

The word 'paraclete' today describes a counsellor or advocate, and it's this word Jesus uses to introduce the Holy Spirit (vv16, 26). He is the Intercessor, the Counsellor, and the Encourager. Jesus tells us that he is a personal Helper who is on a twenty-four-hour call-out. He is the Spirit of Jesus who takes the place of Jesus. He comes alongside us and indwells us so that we may become more like Jesus. He is *'another Counsellor'* (v16), implying that he is just like Jesus, with no discernible difference in their character because the Son and the Spirit are both God.

1 THE EVIDENCE OF HIS ROLE

We are not born in a state where we are fit for heaven (Ecclesiastes ch9 v3; Romans ch3 v10; Psalm 51 v5). We need the intervention of God the Holy Spirit. The evidence of his sovereign, saving work in a believer is love and obedience: love for God, which is also demonstrated in love for his people, and obedience to God's word (vv15, 21, 23). Jesus is the perfect example of love and obedience (v31).

2 THE RESIDENCE OF HIS PERSON

God's Spirit comes to live in the believer (v23). Isn't it amazing that just as Jesus is about to leave his people to make a home for them in heaven, he promises to come to each one of them and make his home with them (Revelation ch21 v3)? Is there anything more wonderful and more sobering than to realise that God's Spirit lives within us (1 Corinthians ch6 v19)? If the Spirit makes his home in us, should we not be all the more diligent in avoiding evil practices and unholy alliances?

3 THE PERMANENCE OF HIS PRESENCE

There's nothing temporary about the nature, work, and presence of the Divine Counsellor (v16). Even though we may hurt him, grieve him, resist him, contradict him, ignore him, and generally treat him abysmally, he never leaves us or forsakes us.

His permanent presence gives us comfort, joy, and encouragement.

4 THE IMPORTANCE OF HIS MISSION

The Spirit's counselling ministry is to teach God's word and to remind us of those things which Jesus has taught us (v26). The Holy Spirit's mission is not to bring us new revelation, or ground-breaking innovation, or even fresh declaration. The Paraclete's mission is to refresh, reinforce, and remind us concerning those things which Jesus has already spoken.

But Jesus also spoke of someone else who is coming (vv28-31). He warned that Satan would be revealed. Of course, the Evil One had no hold on Jesus, but he does have a hold on us unless we are *in Christ*. Jesus assures his followers of his legacy of peace for troubled hearts (v27). So are you ruled by the prince that is of this world, or are you ruled by the peace that is not of this world?

Men and women go to great lengths to achieve a fragile, temporary peace. They try to find peaceful locations that are far away from people and problems. They try to produce a peaceful ambience with soothing music and tranquil decor. They may even try to negotiate peace to end bitter battles and conflicts. They may induce a peaceful trance that will insulate them against stress and trouble. But the supernatural peace of Jesus is the only real answer.

In the final hours before the cross, Jesus announced to his disciples that their trouble had been taken care of. He had thought of everything. A personal Counsellor would take the Saviour's place.

FEBRUARY 24
THE GOSPEL OF JOHN ch15 vv1-17

THE DIVINE VINE

If, at the end of ch14, in response to Jesus' direction to leave, the disciples accompanied Jesus from the Upper Room, they would have been on their way to the Kidron Valley, and to the Mount of Olives and Gethsemane. And if their walk took them past the grand temple, still under construction, with its giant marble slabs and with its eastern face covered with plates of gold, they could have seen the great golden vine on the front of the sacred building. The vine had become their national emblem. It was a symbol of Israel, indicating its wealth and prosperity. The vine was featured on first-century coinage. Israel recalled their history when God had delivered them from slavery in Egypt to inhabit a land *flowing with milk and honey*. Asaph's Psalm 80 v8 begins: *'You brought a vine out of Egypt'*. So, perhaps it was that huge vine motif, sparkling in the paschal moonlight, which caught the disciples' attention as they passed. Just as the disciples may have been prompted to consider again God's love and patience with Israel throughout its chequered history, Jesus comes out with this striking statement (v1) *'I am the true Vine, and my Father is the gardener'*.

Although Jesus had used this vineyard metaphor on several occasions throughout his preaching ministry, he hadn't focused directly on the vine. Here, as the final minutes ticked past before his arrest, Jesus declares himself to be *'the true Vine'*, the last of Jesus' seven great 'I Am' statements in this Gospel. Vines were such an integral part of Hebrew life. But Israel, as a vine, had failed. Its grapes were sour, its harvests were poor, and too many of its branches had become rotten and died. But Jesus is the real, genuine Vine. He is not a fraud, and he will not fail. What does Jesus want from us?

1 JESUS WANTS US TO BE FAITHFUL

(v4) Notice the emphasis placed on *'remain'*. In just seven verses (vv4-10), Jesus uses the word no less than eleven times. The secret to a productive life is that the branch remains part of the vine. The Vine's branches have no life of themselves. They can't cut themselves off and stand alone. The usefulness and productiveness of the branches are wholly dependent upon their vital, living relationship with the Vine. If they become detached, they die. You can remain in a church, or remain as an enrolled member of a denomination, or you can remain as an active member of a Christian fellowship, but it is only if you remain in Jesus that you will be spiritually alive. And if you are indisputably attached to Jesus, then he will not allow you to become detached (ch10 vv29-30; Romans ch8 v39). But 'remaining' is not just about 'attachment': it's about 'fellowship'. It's more than just spiritual existence: it's spiritual life. Though your union with Christ is not jeopardised, your communion with him each day may be affected. Your faithful perseverance is only possible because of God's faithful preservation. Communion is conditional upon obeying Jesus' commands (v10). Joy and obedience go hand in hand. Unfaithful branches, like Judas, get lopped off (v6).

2 JESUS WANTS US TO BE FRUITFUL

There's no middle position with the divine Gardener. He only categorises two types of branches: the dead and the living, the fruitful and the unfruitful (vv2, 5, 8). A totally fruitless life is proof positive that a person is not a believer. There's a huge difference between lopping and pruning (v2). The pruning process can hurt (Hebrews ch12 v11), but the painful exercise is for a productive outcome. If we pray 'Lord, make me more fruitful,' we must realise that we are actually praying 'Lord, prune me more severely!' The Bible is not only a sedative to calm the anxious and fearful; it is a secateurs to cut away the unnecessary and unhelpful. We shall never become more fruitful if we only use the Bible as a sedative! What fruit are you bearing for Jesus?

3 JESUS WANTS US TO BE FRIENDS

(vv13-15) To be a friend of Jesus is the greatest accolade of all. But you didn't choose Jesus first to be your friend. It was, in fact, the other way round (v16). Our rotten, pre-conversion state was one of enmity with God (Philippians ch3 vv18-19). We were unlovely and unfriendly. But Jesus gave everything for his friends: those who are dearly loved and within the inner circle of his closest companions. But are we friendly towards Jesus as well as towards Jesus' friends?

GREATER LOVE

Greater love has no one than this,
than a man lay down his life for his friends.

John ch15 v13

Probing landscapes uninviting,

Bloody theatres of fighting,

Force the toughest into praying,

While their courage is displaying.

                    Greater love.

Serried ranks of snow-white crosses

Mark inestimable losses,

Testimonies to the fallen,

Who have risen to the call in.

                    Greater love.

Lyrics sung from hymn-sheet copies,

Flimsy wreaths of blood-red poppies,

Colours dipping, bugle blowing,

Names and ranks in granite showing.

                    Greater love.

Coffins shouldered by the grieving,

draped in union flags, believing,

Lives laid down for king and nation,

Proving, through the devastation,

                    Greater love.

IEDs and snipers' missions,

Suicidal expeditions,

Leaving hearts and bodies broken:

Medals speak of the unspoken

Greater love.

And to death so foul and gory

Jesus came from heaven's glory,

Gave his life in full surrender

That in dying he may tender

Greatest love

While a loveless world's rejecting,

Still the gospel is connecting,

So that penitents are kneeling,

At the cross, where God's revealing.

Greatest love.

Geoff Fox

FEBRUARY 25
THE GOSPEL OF JOHN ch15 vv18-27

TESTIMONY TESTED

Is your witness for the Lord Jesus affected by what people say or do? Is your testimony affected by the way you are treated? Christians will naturally find it easier to be good witnesses when they are respected, honoured, loved, and listened to. But how should they respond when they are reviled, despised, hated, and abused?

Jesus himself was only minutes away from being the perfect example of how to respond to the most intense hatred (v18). The Lord Jesus had just revealed himself to his disciples as *'the true Vine'* (v1). He had spoken of the necessity to have productive branches which yield *'fruit that will last'* (v16). This rich, sweet, everlasting fruit will automatically attract the hostility of the world.

1 YOUR TREATMENT

'They will treat you this way because of my name, for they do not know the One who sent me' (v21). Jesus gives two fundamental reasons why his disciples are hated by the world with such vigorous hatred:

His Choice

(v19) In God's great kindness and grace, he has chosen his people. There's an unfathomable mystery about his choice since he certainly didn't choose us on the basis of what he saw in us (v16). Instead, he chose us to *'bear fruit'*, including the spiritual fruit of Galatians ch5 v22. It's the Holy Spirit, living in the believer, who produces and develops this fruit of Christian character, but it's frequently these virtues and graces that the world hates. It pokes fun at those who are patient, kind, and who do good. It ridicules faithfulness and, instead, we are encouraged to live for ourselves. It despises gentleness when we are expected to be assertive and insensitive. It minimises the importance of self-control by excusing those who don't possess it, and by giving labels to those who display anger, hostility, and temper tantrums. These may even be medical labels to conveniently hide behind, as if the perpetrators are not to blame. But 'love' must be the characteristic of the church, just as 'hatred' can be the characteristic of the world. We are called to be distinctive as Christians. If you always try to blend in with the world, like a chameleon, then you will escape hostility.

His Name

(v21) The world of the twenty-first century is no different from the world of the first century. They would still crucify Jesus. Every day, hundreds of professing Christians are killed, and thousands of Christians are abused and imprisoned, because of Jesus' name. If we identify ourselves with the name of Jesus, then we must expect to be bullied, harassed, and victimised. How must we respond to such hatred and ill-treatment? *'Rejoice and be glad'* (Matthew ch5 vv11-12); *'Do not be ashamed'* (1 Peter ch4 v16); *'Commit...'* to God and *'continue to do good'* (1 Peter ch4 v19). The Christian church is a history of men and women responding to evil with goodness; reacting to brutality with meekness and replying to malice with kindness.

2 YOUR TESTIMONY

(vv26-27) Jesus encourages his followers to be faithful in their testimony. Jesus spoke to Peter (ch21 v18) and revealed that he would suffer for his testimony. It's through the faithful, and often painful, testimony of Jesus' followers that he chooses to build his churchSevere trials prove sincere testimony. What should our testimony be like?

Spirit-filled

We must have Jesus' Spirit, the Counsellor, whom he sends to us (v26). In whatever form we need a counsellor in today's context, he or she is expected to 'come alongside'. How much more, then, in a spiritual sense, Jesus' Spirit-Counsellor (the Paraclete) comes alongside us in a way that's like no one else?

Truly-spoken

Jesus said that it's *'the Spirit of Truth who goes out from the Father'* (v26). Any witness that the Spirit gives is incontrovertibly truthful. As 'children of light', our testimony must never be inaccurate or false. There should never be any suggestion of being 'economical with the truth'.

Jesus-centred

The 'hot topic' proclaimed by the Counsellor, and which should also be upon our lips, is Jesus. Our experience of Jesus, within the pages of the Bible and within the moments of our lives, should enable us to testify about how he has saved us and how he is keeping us by his grace. God has called us to be living, daily witnesses.

FEBRUARY 26
THE GOSPEL OF JOHN ch16 vv1-15

DEPARTURE AND ARRIVAL

If you have had the unusual experience of being at an airport or railway station to say farewell to someone who is leaving and, at the same time, to greet someone who is arriving, you will understand the mixture of emotions. Often it will mean a dash between 'departures' and 'arrivals' at an airport, or a race between platforms at a station. You will have experienced the 'pendulum swing' of emotions. For Jesus' disciples, they were being prepared for such an experience. In forty-three days, they would witness Jesus' departure, and in fifty-three days, they would experience the Holy Spirit's arrival. Both events are not only extremely emotional, but both events are also momentous milestones in the history of Christianity and the founding of the New Testament churchThe stunned disciples were catapulted from 'departures' to 'arrivals' in such a short space of time that they couldn't take in all that was happening to them.

But in his own kind and compassionate way, Jesus prepares his disciples for their rollercoaster experience and their see-saw emotions.

Here are four outcomes of the divine departure and arrival that we may notice:

1 OUR GRIEF (vv5-6)

Someone once defined a railway station as 'a place of tears'. It's either tears of rejoicing at someone's arrival or tears of sorrow at someone's departure. Jesus had forewarned his disciples that his departure would bring sorrow. He had already spelled out to them the hatred that would be unleashed upon them by the world. Jesus specified that persecution would come from religious people, including the Jews, who would evict them from their synagogues (v2). Certain religious people will believe they are carrying out God's will by destroying Christians (for example, ch12 v10; Acts ch8 v3). Among those who have suffered much *for* Jesus, there are those who have realised that they have suffered much *with* Jesus. He is with his people in the severest of trials and the greatest of tribulations (Isaiah ch43 vv2-3).

2 OUR GUILT (vv8-11)

The Holy Spirit's ministry includes conviction of guilt. The world continues to believe that there is nothing wrong with its sinfulness until the Spirit convicts and exposes individuals to the guilt of their sin. As the Holy Spirit makes his presence known, there is an acute awareness of the awesome holiness of Almighty God. It's that power of purity that exposes the slightest flaws and the smallest sins. We need to be convicted of our sin, and the sin of unbelief is the greatest sin of all (v9). God is not primarily concerned with our happiness but with our holiness. While we may be obsessed with our own personal comforts and peace, God's aim is our holiness, which may mean trouble, pain, distress, and heartache. The Spirit's arrival would also mean the conviction of self-righteousness. Our pretended righteousness will be exposed as hollow, superficial, and false.

Jesus also said that we would be shamed as to the guilt of our judgement. *The prince of this world* (v11) has always provoked erroneous judgements and wrong decisions since his first successful temptation (Genesis ch3).

3 OUR GOOD (v7)

Jesus' departure and the Spirit's arrival is for our good. Jesus' departure from his disciples would be in their best interest as the omnipresent Spirit's power would be with all God's people, in every place, and all at the same time. The *'all things'* of Romans ch8 v28 includes Jesus' departure. We can be sure that because of the arrival of God's Spirit-Counsellor that we shall never be deprived of Jesus' presence with us.

4 OUR GUIDE (vv12-16)

The very special sense in which the Spirit was a Guide to the apostles included the founding of the New Testament church and the writing of the New Testament scriptures. The Spirit's teaching was not contradictory to or independent of what Jesus had given them. Rather, it complemented what they had already received (v13). We can check out the integrity and veracity of our guidance today by asking: 'Does it agree with the Bible?' and 'Does it bring glory to Jesus?' The Spirit's guidance will never contradict God's word and will always make much of Jesus. The Counsellor's aim is always to exalt the Lord Jesus, the One whom we should earnestly desire to know.

FEBRUARY 27
THE GOSPEL OF JOHN ch16 vv16-33

DRECKLY

In the Cornish dialect, there's a word which can be the answer to many questions beginning 'When?' It's the word 'dreckly'. This word is defined as 'a universally known dialect word, which could mean a lot longer than later' ('Cornish Dialect' by Les Merton). This indeterminate and somewhat cryptic expression is like the expression *'in a little while',* which Jesus uses seven times in four verses. Remembering that in just a few hours Jesus would be crucified and then, on the third day, would rise again, this helps to explain Jesus' predictions in v16. The faithful few didn't comprehend that 'in a little while' ('dreckly') Jesus would rise again, even though Jesus had told them plainly. *'In a little while,'* Jesus would emerge from the tomb resplendent in his resurrection glory. This phrase *'in a little while'* may have been a puzzle to Jesus' disciples, just as 'dreckly' may sometimes be a puzzle to us. But there are certainties which give us great assurance and a reason for optimism:

1 JOY FOLLOWS GRIEF (vv20-24)

Jesus promises that *'your grief will turn to joy'* (v20), and the illustration he gives is of a woman giving birth to a child. During labour, the mother experiences discomfort and anguish. There is joy and pain, and for a little while, the pain may be dominant. But soon the pain is eclipsed by the birth. We don't minimise the pain or discount the distress, but the anguish is not the end of the story. The normal process of giving birth means that grief is transformed into rejoicing. So if we may be experiencing suffering and anguish, there is the eternal hope that, even if there is no end to grief in this life, there is no end to joy in the next. Joy comes in the morning. Paul asked the Galatian Christians *What has happened to all your joy?'* (Galatians ch4 v15). These believers were so caught up in criticisms and accusations concerning rites and ceremonies that they appeared miserable and joyless. But Jesus promises his disciples that their joy will be complete as they come to understand the benefits of prayer (v24).

2 PRAYER REPLACES PRESENCE (vv25-28)

In a few hours, Jesus would be crucified. In a few days, Jesus would rise again. In a few weeks, Jesus would ascend into heaven. Jesus would no longer be bodily present with his people because he would be bodily present in heaven. With the help of the Spirit, Jesus encourages his disciples to pray:

Prayer is by Jesus' Instruction

Jesus wants us to pray. He commands us to pray. How can we expect to achieve anything worthwhile unless we pray? The Spirit helps us in our weaknesses (Romans ch8 vv26-27), including the weaknesses of prayer. While we may be preoccupied with 'better methods', God wants us to be better men and women: people of purity and prayer.

Prayer is through Jesus' Work

Jesus came from the Father with a mission that would culminate in the cross (v28). The torn temple curtain when Jesus died signifies the 'Way In' to the Father. We have direct access to God through prayer.

Prayer is in Jesus' Name

Praying 'in Jesus' name' is not some magic formula or incantation that we can attach to our prayers to guarantee their success. Praying in Jesus' name is a humble recognition of the authority that we claim and the sovereignty to which we yield in our prayers.

3 FAITH CONQUERS UNBELIEF (vv29-32)

While the disciples' faith would ultimately triumph, in the meantime, there would be desertion and scattering (v32). Their present faith would crumble under pressure. It was not fit for purpose. It was not robust enough to face the demands of the hour. How strong is our faith? Is it fit for the purpose God intends?

4 PEACE SURPASSES TROUBLE (v33)

Jesus underlines the great contrast between *'trouble'*, which exists *'in this world'*, and *'peace'*, which is found *'in me'*. When the world seems ever more powerful in its influence, its hostility, and its devilish ingenuity, we can be comforted that Jesus has overcome the world. *'In this world you will have trouble'* – that's Jesus' guarantee. But it's only half the guarantee: *'But take heart! I have overcome the world'*. If we are in Jesus, then we shall always be on the victory side. Jesus has disarmed our most troublesome enemy, and therefore we can know his peace.

FEBRUARY 28
THE GOSPEL OF JOHN ch17 vv1-5

THE NUMBER ONE PRIORITY OF KNOWING GOD

Whether Jesus is still in the Upper Room or is already on his way to Gethsemane, he shares some intimate moments with his heavenly Father. This chapter is Jesus' longest recorded prayer and has been variously described as 'The Prayer of Consecration', 'Jesus' Farewell Prayer', and, since the 16th century, 'Jesus' High Priestly Prayer'. It is in fact 'The Lord's Prayer', in contrast with the pattern-prayer that Jesus' taught his disciples (Matthew ch6 vv9-13), which could be called 'The Disciples' Prayer'. Here, Jesus is praying to his Father, heart to heart.

We may risk being over-simplistic in daring to analyse Jesus' prayer, but there are three clear sections: Jesus prays for himself (vv1-5), for his disciples (vv6-19), and for all believers (vv20-26). Three words help to summarise Jesus' petitions in these sections: Glorify (vv1-5); Sanctify (vv6-19); Unify (vv20-26).

The red-letter day had arrived on the divine calendar. The clock couldn't be wound back. God the Father would be glorified by the Son's obedience, even to the cross (Philippians ch2 v8). Jesus' complete obedience in his life culminated in his unswerving obedience in his death. God's grant of authority to his Son was so that he could effectually *save his people from their sins* (Matthew ch1 v21).

'Knowing God' is not 'knowing about God'. Neither an acquaintance with God nor an acknowledgement of God comes anywhere near to knowing God. However, we were created to know God (Jeremiah ch9 vv23-24). But what is 'knowing God'?

1 KNOWING GOD IS TRUSTING HIS WORK

(v4) Jesus wasn't deflected in his mission, nor did he abort his mission at the last moment. He completed all the work the Father had given him to do. He declared in his final moments on the cross, *'It is finished'*. The debt had been paid in full. But not everyone trusts in Jesus or believes in him. They don't love the Lord with all their heart, soul, strength, and mind. They won't repent of their sin and cry out to God for mercy. The Jews refused to come to Jesus, even in the face of Biblical testimony (ch5 vv39-40). How can we refuse to come to the very One who has completed the mission to bring life, hope, and salvation to undeserving sinners?

2 KNOWING GOD IS BEING HIS GIFT

(v2) Jesus speaks of those whom the Father had given to him. If you are a believer, then you are a love-gift from the Father to the Son. The price tag you wear is 'the blood of Jesus' (1 Peter ch1 vv18-19). If you really know God, then you know that you are redeemed. You know that the highest price has been paid to save you. But do we live and act as those for whom an inestimable price has been paid? Do we dignify our calling by our conversations and our language, or do we promote the kind of unacceptable talk that is vulgar, frivolous, and coarse? Are our conversations full of complaints and criticisms, accusations and slander? Do we radiate the characteristics of God's Spirit, if we are God's gift to Jesus? (Galatians ch5 v22). If so, our love will not be discriminatory; our joy will not be a shallow feeling of happiness; our peace will not be affected by storms; our patience will not have a short fuse; our kindness will not be conditional; our goodness will not show favouritism; our faithfulness will not be temporary; our gentleness will not have 'strings attached'; our self-control will not fluctuate. To be more like Jesus is to become the best gift that the Son could receive.

3 KNOWING GOD IS HAVING HIS LIFE

(vv2-3) Eternal life is not just a life that is everlasting, but fundamentally and exclusively it's a personal relationship with the living God. Paul's top priority was to know God. He said that he considered *'everything a loss compared to the surpassing greatness of knowing Christ Jesus my Lord. I consider them rubbish that I may gain Christ...'* (Philippians ch3 vv8-10). We must learn to think of God and to acquaint ourselves with him in a much loftier way than we think of or acquaint ourselves with one another. Jesus assures us that the one, true and living God can be known, and that knowing him is eternal life. This is the relationship that has been forged through the completed work of the Saviour.

FEBRUARY 29
THE GOSPEL OF JOHN ch17 vv6-19

CALLED TO LIVE DIFFERENTLY

This section of Jesus' prayer, specifically for his apostles, could be summed up by the word 'sanctify' (vv17, 19). 'Sanctify' is to do with 'separating' or 'setting apart'. It's closely connected to the word 'holy', that is, 'to make holy'. It means to dedicate or to consecrate to God. In trying to appear 'cool' in the eyes of the world, Christians today want to blend in with the world and not to stand out as being 'weird' or 'wacky'. These disciples are *'out of the world'* (v6), but they are *'still in the world'* (v11) because that's where they live and that's where Jesus wants them to serve him. They haven't yet been taken to heaven. Yet they are called to be different and distinctive. We may work overtime trying not to become the world's caricature of a Christian. Yet the bottom line is that we are sanctified and therefore called to live differently.

Jesus' disciples had been different in that the Father had given them to Jesus (v6); that Jesus revealed God the Father to them (v6); that they had obeyed God's word (v6); that they had accepted Jesus' teaching (v8) and that they had believed that Jesus had been sent by his Father (v8). We may think of Jesus' disciples as twelve 'problem cases'. They argued, doubted, contradicted, and vied for prominence. They were also weak and shallow at times. But Jesus credits them with understanding, believing, and accepting his teaching. Even though in a few moments they would disown him and desert him, Jesus makes this amazing comment about them: *'All glory has come to me through them'* (v10). It's extremely humbling to learn that Jesus is glorified by our lives of faithfulness. His disciples would be known by their love (ch13 v35) and the Father would be glorified by their *'much fruit'* (ch15 v8). Certainly, this truth should encourage our hearts and not swell our heads!

So Jesus petitions three things for each of his disciples:

1 MAKE THEM SAFE (vv11, 15)

We live in a dangerous world. At one level, we see the outward dangers to Christians by pernicious persecution and vicious assaults, and, at another level, we may experience personal threats and discrimination. There's a prowling lion trying to devour Jesus' disciples, and we are told to stand firm in the faith (1 Peter ch5 vv8-9). We may not be immune to physical pain and spiritual heartache. That will only happen when we are taken out of the world. But Jesus didn't pray for that: only that they would be protected from the Evil One (v15). Our most intense battle is often against the Unseen (Ephesians ch6 v12), but protection is in God's powerful name (v11). The name by which we are saved is the name by which we are kept safe. Jesus prays for their protection on the basis of God's holy character, and he uses that divinely exclusive title *'Holy Father'* (v11). It's this name that offers his people one hundred per cent cover.

2 MAKE THEM ONE (v11)

Jesus also prays for a unity that is not imposed by regulation or policy. He's not speaking about a unity that's manufactured by 'Truth and Reconciliation' inquiries, during which truth is sacrificed in favour of reconciliation. The secret of true unity with one another is embedded in our relationship with God. How can we expect to be united in our hearts, one for the other, if our hearts are estranged from God? Judas didn't have a living relationship with God. He serves as a reminder that we can be part of the 'church scene' without knowing 'Christ's salvation'.

3 MAKE THEM HOLY (vv17, 19)

We return to this truth that those who are set apart for God must be free from contamination and pollution. Truth must purge and purify the soul. The agencies for this deep-cleaning process are God's word, which is truth (v17), and God's Spirit, who is Truth (ch16 v13). We can never be cleansed by error or falsehood. It is only the truth that can clean us so that we are set apart and useable for God. Hearers and believers of God's word are important, but we shall only be made holy by becoming the doers of the word. We must let the Bible spotlight our sin and provide us with the remedy for that sin.

If we are truly sanctified, then there will be:

Cuts

There will be severances from the world's priorities, values, attitudes, ambitions, and treasures.

Costs

Consecration means that a price will be paid, possibly in terms of jobs, careers, rewards, and relationships.

Crosses

We are called to complete self-crucifixion for the sake of Jesus and his gospel.

MARCH 1
THE GOSPEL OF JOHN ch17 vv20-26

ONE FOR ALL AND ALL FOR ONE

You will notice that Jesus' prayer is fundamentally practical. It's not theoretical or abstract. It's a down-to-earth, up-to-heaven prayer. It's relevant, relational, and real. In this third part of his prayer, Jesus includes the wider company of believers and followers. He prays for all those who believe in him, and the burden of his prayer is 'unify', 'unite'. It is one for all and all for one. There are four strands to this unity:

1 A GOSPEL UNITY

Here is the basis for true unity among Christians. It is founded upon and rooted in the gospel of Jesus (v20). The message of the gospel, which Jesus preached and his disciples proclaimed, is the unifying bond that binds his people together. First of all, they have a common experience of the gospel. This is the message that has saved them and that is transforming them. The message has not had its power diluted or neutralised (Romans ch1 v16). In response to Jesus' commission (Mark ch16 v15), his followers for two thousand years have been trying to communicate this 'good news message' in the world's 13,500 languages and 30,000 dialects. It was Paul's ambition (Romans ch15 v20). But it is one Gospel, one message, and one Saviour.

2 A GODLIKE UNITY

(v21) It's an amazing thought that the unity within the Godhead, between Father, Son, and Spirit, is the same unity that should be reflected among believers. Notice that Jesus doesn't pray for uniformity, but for unity. He doesn't plead that we are all the same, just as God the Son is not the same as God the Father and God the Spirit. But while Jesus doesn't pray that we should all be the same, he does pray that we should all be one. And if Jesus' prayer is for unity, then it must be the work of Satan to cause disunity. If Jesus prays for oneness, then it must be Satan's mission to instigate division. Who knows what a powerful influence there is upon society when Jesus' prayer is answered and all of his people are united. This is not a unity which is achieved at any cost, but rather it's a unity which is Godlike because it reflects the unity that exists within the Godhead. If we were more concerned about living Godly lives, then unity would be automatic.

3 A GLORIFYING UNITY

(vv22, 24) While Jesus expresses the desire that his people should one day *see* his glory, he also wants his people to *show* his glory here in the present. One of the clearest ways in which the revelation of Jesus' glory can be seen is in their unity. Such a unity must be clearly recognisable and identifiable to the world. The unity of the church proclaims to the world that Jesus' mission to save his people by going to the cross has been effective. Anything less than their unity is not glorifying. The love of Jesus is both the 'glory' and the 'glue' that binds believers together. And that leads us to:

4 A GRACIOUS UNITY

(vv25-26) The titles which Jesus uses to address his Father (*'Holy Father'; 'Righteous Father'*) are unique and exclusive to his prayer. Jesus reveals the intimacy of his relationship with his heavenly Father, and he prays that the love which binds Father and Son may be the same divine love which binds believer and believer. This genuine love of God will prove that they really are Jesus' disciples. It's an observable unity. Jesus' mission of love to a lost world would be continued in the lives of his disciples (*'...that I myself may be in them'*). And just as Jesus' glory is associated with his humility and service, so Jesus' followers should display similar characteristics. There are always going to be things that Christians don't like about each other, just as there may be habits and traits of character that family members don't like about each other. But just as it's a powerful love which binds a family together, despite the frictions, so it should be love which binds God's family together. Instead of asserting our rights, we shall be promoting the rights of our King and Saviour. Instead of a preoccupation with happiness, we shall be concerned about holiness. Instead of complaining that we are not being loved, we shall show love to others. Jesus' burden of his prayer is so that each believer is united to him for the combined blessing of the church (one for all), with our focus on Jesus (all for one).

MARCH 2
THE GOSPEL OF JOHN ch18 vv1-11

DASTARDLY ASSAULTS

The Last Supper had ended. Jesus' final discourse had finished, and v1 tells us that now *'he had finished praying'* the Lord's Prayer of ch17. Jerusalem would have been crammed to capacity with thousands of pilgrims who had come for the Passover Feast. As Jesus and his disciples passed homes in which the Passover was being celebrated, none of the occupants realised that the following morning Jesus, God's Passover Lamb, would be sacrificed. But Jesus knew all that was going to happen to him (v4). Jesus led his disciples out of the city and to the garden on the Mount of Olives, which he had regularly used to meet, to talk, to pray, and to rest. Here, where the olives were pressed to produce their valuable oil, Jesus was being spiritually pressed so that he may obtain our precious redemption. The other Gospel writers inform us of Jesus' agony of spirit as he contemplated the vicious assault that Satan would make upon his soul (for example, Luke ch22 v42). Judas knew about this secluded spot, and he arrived with a posse to arrest Jesus. He was a pawn in the hands of Jesus' enemies and a tool in the hands of Satan (ch13 v27). We should be prepared for such dastardly assaults.

1 WE MUST KNOW SATAN FOR HIS SUBTLE TACTICS

Paul refers to *'the serpent's cunning'* and he warns that *'Satan himself masquerades as an angel of light'* (2 Corinthians ch11 v3; 14). It seems that his guise can fool the unwary. Even believers fall for his ruse. Those who may give the appearance of being so close to Jesus and to Jesus' friends, allow themselves, like Judas, to become instruments in Satan's hand. Satan's subtle tactics included using a close friend to whom Jesus had only shown compassion and friendship. Judas was Satan's 'fifth columnist' working from the inside to overthrow Jesus' government. Subtlety has been the mark of his trade since the beginning of time (Genesis ch3 v1).

2 WE MUST EXPECT SATAN IN UNGUARDED PLACES

Judas came to the most secluded, private, and personal of places to betray Jesus. He *'knew the place'* (v2). They could have arrested Jesus at any time as he moved around Jerusalem in daylight and in open view (Luke ch22 vv52-53), but his enemy chose the most unguarded of places at the most unexpected of moments. This was certainly the case for the disciples, but not for Jesus, who was thoroughly prepared. Jesus' close friends failed to *'watch and pray'* (Mark ch14 vv37-38). This is the answer to Satan's attacks. We shall always be in great danger if we spiritually slumber (1 Thessalonians ch5 vv5-6). We may think that our daily times of prayer and Bible study are 'safe,' but Satan will do all he can to intercept those times. He will also do his best to prevent us from worshipping on the Lord's Day. Quality family time can become disrupted when he interferes with the dynamics of relationships and causes unnecessary heartache.

3 WE MUST FIGHT SATAN WITH THE RIGHT WEAPONS

Peter was determined to defend Jesus against Satan's agents who were at work in the gloomy darkness of Kidron's garden. As Peter sliced the right ear of Malchus, Jesus rebukes him (Luke ch22 v51) and heals the high priest's servant. How did Malchus regard this unusual event in his life? What did he think of Jesus? Peter's surge of passion and impulse was misguided at best. Jesus could have summoned sixty thousand angels (Matthew ch26 v53), but he had to drink the cup of suffering and sacrifice (v11). Peter was using the wrong weapon against a spiritual enemy (Ecclesiastes ch9 v18; 2 Corinthians ch6 v7). We cannot overcome Satan with the weapons of the world (2 Corinthians ch10 vv3-4). Though spiritual conflicts may manifest themselves in physical strife and bloodshed, the real battle is with an unseen, devilish enemy (Ephesians ch6 v12). Our spiritual arsenal should be filled with faith, the word of God, righteousness, truth, prayer, and vigilance.

4 WE MUST DENY SATAN ANY FOOTHOLD IN OUR LIVES

Despite Peter's initial outburst of courage, Satan had managed to get a foothold in his life (vv15-27). Paul referred to personal sins such as anger and lying, and he warned *'Do not give the devil a foothold'* (Ephesians ch4 v27). Sometimes even feelings of indignation, superiority, hurt, or self-pity can be used by Satan. He works away at those feelings, beginning with a toe-hold, then a foot-hold and, if we're not vigilant, a spiritual strangle-hold. But if we are truly one of his sheep, then the lion can prowl and growl and scowl, but it will not completely devour one of the Lord's own (v9).

MARCH 3
THE GOSPEL OF JOHN ch18 vv12-27

THINGS MAY NOT ALWAYS BE AS THEY SEEM

As we read the narrative of Jesus' arrest and trial, we may need to bear in mind that, on the surface, things may not always be as they appear:

1 FETTERED NEED NOT BE FEEBLE

The arresting posse of soldiers and officials bound Jesus. They tied him up. He was fettered. He could have defeated all of their puny forces with a single thought, but he voluntarily surrendered to the authorities. Jesus was handed over to them by *'God's set purpose and foreknowledge'* (Acts ch2 v23). God's design for salvation came before God's design for the universe. In that sense, the cross preceded creation. To *'save his people from their sins'* (Matthew ch1 v21). Jesus couldn't circumvent the cross.

2 FORMALITY NEED NOT BE FAIR

Jesus allowed himself to be subjected to a trial that involved the most powerful people in Judea at that time. Annas was the high priest who had been in office before his son-in-law, Caiaphas. The Roman governor, Pontius Pilate, and Herod (Luke ch23 v8) also provided further stages in this judiciary process, which was anything but fair. It didn't even meet the Jews' own standards of justice and equity. At every stage, the trial should have collapsed because it was unjust and unfair. There are ten examples of injustice:

- A defendant must always be tried in daylight, but Jesus was tried at night.

- A trial must be conducted under public scrutiny, but Jesus was tried in secret.

- A trial couldn't be conducted on a feast day, but this was the Passover.

- The Jewish Supreme Court, the Sanhedrin, could only try cases; they couldn't prosecute.

- A 'guilty' verdict must be made on the day following the trial, not the same day.

- The Sanhedrin was not permitted to sit in the high priest's house.

- The trial had to begin with the explanation of the defendant's innocence.

- Evidence had to be guaranteed by at least two witnesses (Mark ch14 vv55-56).

- False witnesses were punishable by death, but in Jesus' case, this was encouraged.

- A defendant was guaranteed freedom from abuse while being tried (v22).

At every level, it was a sham of a trial, a complete travesty of justice. The formality of a judicial system doesn't always equate to equity. We must recognise that as believers, we will not always be treated fairly, evenly, and without discrimination. We should be wonderfully encouraged that, when we become the target of men's spite, and the victim of men's discrimination, and the butt of men's jokes, Jesus is being honoured by our faithful stand for him.

3 FOLLOWING NEED NOT BE FAITHFULNESS

(v15) Peter plus an unnamed disciple were following Jesus. Peter had boasted that he would be the only one left standing when all the others fell away (Matthew ch26 vv33, 35; Mark ch14 v29), yet here he clearly and deliberately denies Jesus before three different people on three separate occasions. We may appear to follow Jesus and be among the crowd of Jesus' associates, but our hearts may reveal a different story. Jesus looked straight into Peter's heart (Luke ch22 vv61, 62) and this provoked regret and remorse. But faithful following will also mean true repentance, and this may be costly.

4 FAILURE NEED NOT BE FINAL

Peter failed 'big time'. When he had the opportunity to stand up for Jesus, he failed. The Teacher and personal Friend, with whom Peter had spent the last three years, had just been snatched away from him, and when the crunch came, Peter crumbled. This was the lowest ebb of his life. But if Peter had abandoned Jesus, Jesus had not abandoned Peter. Though Peter had stooped to commit such a despicable and reprehensible sin, Jesus had stooped much lower for him! He had stooped to the cross where he would become the Sin-bearer. God had a great plan in which he would take this abject failure and transform him into a useful instrument of blessing. You may have many unmentionable regrets. You may have made several irreparable mistakes. You may wish you could turn the clock back and 'stop the cockerel crowing'. Failure can mean 'delay' but it need not mean 'defeat'. There is merciful forgiveness for the penitent failure (Micah ch7 vv18-19). If you have blundered, flunked, and messed up, be sure that there is pardon and renewal in the cross of Jesus.

MARCH 4
THE GOSPEL OF JOHN ch18 vv28-40

BEHOLD, YOUR KING

It has been said that *'hypocrisy is the loudest lie'*. Certainly, that 'lie' was 'deafening' on the night of Jesus' trial. After only a feeble pretence at justice, the Jewish Supreme Court ordered that Jesus be taken to the Roman governor's palace. But the Jewish officials refused to enter Pilate's house because it was a Gentile residence and therefore it would make them 'ceremonially unclean', prohibiting them from participating in the Passover Feast (v28). Though they were guilty and unclean by condemning the sinless Jesus, they wanted to be clean enough to celebrate the Feast! Though they had plotted to destroy the Lamb of God, they wanted to eat the Passover lamb (which pointed to Jesus).

There is a glaring contrast between this selfish Roman ruler and the selfless King of kings. Pilate thought he was in control, but it was Jesus who had the real authority. What do we learn about this King from these verses?

1 THE AUTHORITY OF THIS KINGSHIP

Pilate was puzzled at the prisoner standing before him. He was not just another criminal who was a pretender to the throne. Pilate was probably deeply affected by the serene majesty of Jesus in all his interrogations and hostile treatment. Pilate referred to Jesus as 'king' on four separate occasions and eventually used this title for the notice he fixed to the cross. What Pilate didn't comprehend was that his 'prisoner' was the Son of God, the King who upholds and sustains everything by his power (Deuteronomy ch10 v14; Psalm 95 vv3-5; Matthew ch28 v18; Ephesians ch1 v21). Jesus is the supreme Ruler of time and space. He has been given a *'name which is above every other name'*, before which all creation will bow (Philippians ch2 vv9-11). His sovereignty is absolute. He is not subject to anything or anyone. He does all that he pleases, without limit and without restraint. He is the only all-powerful, almighty Being (1 Timothy ch6 v15). Although Jesus, as 'the Accused', is paraded before five separate judiciaries, we perceive that it's not really these who are examining Jesus, but Jesus who is examining them. He is the One who sees our hearts and our motives.

2 THE NATURE OF THIS KINGDOM

Jesus gives a brief insight into his kingdom (v36). Jesus defines his kingdom as having its origin from outside the world. If it were a territorial kingdom of this world, then he would have marshalled his armies to prevent his arrest and to assert his rulership. But Jesus' kingdom has no armies to fight for it; no tanks to defend it; no fighter jets to preserve its airspace. Jesus frequently refers to this kingdom as *'the kingdom of God'* and *'the kingdom of heaven'* interchangeably. The heart of Jesus' teaching had centred on the theme of his kingdom (referred to specifically eighty-five times in the Gospels). There is both a future dimension (Matthew ch7 vv21-23; Mark ch14 v25; Luke ch11 v2) and a present dimension (Luke ch11 v20; ch17 v20). There is a present, spiritual, internal character to this kingdom as well as a future, physical, external character. Jesus has revealed the access to this kingdom (John ch3 vv3, 5). This kingdom is eternal (Revelation ch11 v15) and as citizens of this 'unshakeable kingdom' we are encouraged to be thankful and worshipful (Hebrews ch12 vv28-29).

3 THE TRUTH OF THIS KING

(v37) Pilate couldn't get his head around Jesus' claim to kingship. But Jesus confirmed that he had been born to be a king. He had come to disclose the truth about God and the truth about his kingdom. Pilate asked the same question that has been asked for two thousand years: *'What is truth?'* The pivotal truth of eternity is revealed in these last four verses. The King of Glory, who is born to be King of his kingdom, had to die a self-sacrificing, substitutional death on a cross. The Jews wanted a prisoner exchange: Jesus for Barabbas. So Jesus, the Son of his Father, takes the place of Barabbas (whose name means 'son of the father'). The One who is accused of rebellion (ch19 v12) takes the place of the rebel (v40). Jesus died to save rebel hearts which continue to cry *'No, not him!'* (v40). May God free us from rebellious hearts so that we shall find great joy in bowing to his sovereign will. This is the King who demands and deserves our unswerving allegiance and undivided love.

MARCH 5
THE GOSPEL OF JOHN ch19 vv1-16

HERE IS THE MAN

All the gruesome relics of religion, including what is purported to be 'the barbs from the crown of thorns'; 'splinters from the cross'; the reed, the spear, the purple robe, even drops of Christ's blood, have been Satanic sideshows to divert attention from the true wonder of the cross. The facts of Jesus' death point to that pivotal day in history when the power of sin was neutralised and when the forces of hell were overthrown. After Pilate had ordered Jesus to be flogged (v1), a punishment that on its own had caused the death of many victims, the soldiers created a crown of vicious thorns which was pressed onto Jesus' head. They mocked him, dressing him in a purple robe and ridiculing him as a king. Then Pilate paraded his blood-spattered prisoner in front of the Jews, claiming that there was no basis for any charge (v4), and declaring, *'Here is the man!'*

Like Caiaphas before him (ch18 v14), Pilate had unwittingly pronounced a fundamental theological truth. This is the *'Word made flesh'* (ch1 v14). This is the One who was *'made in human likeness'* and *'being found in appearance as a man'* (Philippians ch2 vv6-7). This is Jesus, the Son of God and Son of Man, whose appearance was *'so disfigured beyond that of any man and his form beyond human likeness'* (Isaiah ch52 v14)

Notice four things about this Man as he endures inhuman suffering:

1 THE PATIENT MAN

In vv1-3 Jesus' patience was tried and tested. He is the Creator who suffered abuse at the hands of his creation. He is the sovereign Lord who endured the maltreatment of his subjects. He is the King of glory who was mocked as a king and who was made the plaything of hardened soldiers. When our Saviour could have annihilated all his enemies with a single thought, in the flash of a nanosecond, his patience overrules. Was there ever such patience displayed as in this Man of Calvary? This supremely patient Man from heaven is our example, and we must try and mirror him by being patient (2 Corinthians ch6 v6; James ch5 vv7-9). If you are suffering, or if your Christian service appears to be hard, painful, dry, and barren, then be patient.

2 THE INNOCENT MAN

(v4) Even the guilty governor proclaimed Jesus' innocence. His wife, too, had referred to Jesus as *'that innocent man'* (Matthew ch27 v19). Although the Bible teaches the true humanity of Jesus, there is a singular distinction: Jesus was without sin (2 Corinthians ch5 v21; Hebrews ch7 v26; 1 Peter ch1 v19; 1 John ch3 v5). The writer to the Hebrews encourages us that, as a result of our sinless High Priest, we can confidently approach the throne of grace in time of need (Hebrews ch4 vv15-16). Jesus' sinlessness is our warranty to direct access. God's gracious throne is open to us because of our Saviour's prevailing innocence. If he had just one stain or one sin, then heaven's door would be slammed shut to us.

3 THE PRUDENT MAN

As we re-read vv8-11 we are in awe of the prudence with which Jesus responded to Pilate. Both Jesus' statement and his silence unsettled the governor. He shows us that there is a time to speak and a time to remain silent (Ecclesiastes ch3 v7). He exemplifies a courageous testimony, standing up for truth, whatever the consequences. But Jesus also demonstrates that silence can be just as powerful when used correctly.

4 THE OBEDIENT MAN

Jesus' obedience, like everything else about him, was faultless. He had been obedient to his earthly father (Luke ch2 v51), and he was obedient to his heavenly Father. He was also *'obedient to death'* (Philippians ch2 v8). Jesus would not be deflected in his divine commission. The cross was the only possible route for the obedient Son of God. As children of God, we are called to a life of obedience. Like small children, we often ask 'Why?' when our heavenly Father is not duty-bound to explain. He doesn't need to provide us with a raft of reasons, even if we could understand. Obedience is all about following his instructions and directions, not because we understand why, but because we trust him.

This patient, innocent, prudent, and obedient Man has left us an unbeatable example that we should follow in his steps (1 Peter ch2 v21). *Here is the Man!'* – the Man of Calvary, the Man of Sorrows, the Man of Glory, the Son of Man.

MARCH 6
THE GOSPEL OF JOHN ch19 vv17-27

GOD AT GOLGOTHA

Several memorable adventure stories feature maps showing the locations where, it is believed, treasure is buried. It is usual for a large 'X' to mark the spot! And on the heavenly treasure map, which discloses a little about the divine plan in which God's immeasurable treasures are hidden, 'X' marks the spot. The cross of Jesus is the starting point for unearthing heavenly treasure. This unlikely spot – 'Skull Place' – is where Paul declares that we have *redemption...the forgiveness of sins, in accordance with the riches of God's grace that he lavished on us...* (Ephesians ch1 vv7-8). Of course, the wooden cross is only a potent symbol. It's Jesus who is the treasure.

Here is the Creator upon a cross. No one could have ever imagined seeing the Person of the Son at the place of the Skull! This is God at Golgotha.

How is it possible to grasp the enormity of this greatest wonder of the world: *'The immortal God for me hath died'* [Charles Wesley]? How can the eternal One be compressed into time? How can the sinless One be made sin? How can the immortal One die? Here in vv17-27, we have three separate 'jig saw pieces' which could symbolise three different perspectives of what happened on the day that Jesus, the immortal God, died. Some see the events as:

1 DETERMINED BY LAW

The basic perspective of Jesus' crucifixion is that it was the outcome of a judicial process, though it was anything but just. The Romans were in firm control of Judea, and, although it was in their interest for the Jews to conduct their own judicial system, capital punishment had to be sanctioned by the Roman governor. Pilate governed with a mixture of tolerance and brutality. His cruelty is seen in the way he ordered Jesus to be flogged (v1) and then to become the plaything of hardened soldiers (v2). They would enjoy being given permission to vent all their anger and frustration on a Jew. It was Pilate's law that sentenced Jesus to be crucified (vv17-18). The simple statement - *'Here they crucified him'* (v18) – sums up the process which inflicted the most unimaginable horrors and excruciating suffering. *'Christ suffered in his body'* (1 Peter ch4 v1). Pilate probably took great delight in winding up the Jewish officials by proclaiming on his notice that Jesus was *'the King of the Jews'* (v19). He also made sure that the cosmopolitan crowds could read it in *'Aramaic, Latin and Greek'* (v20). Although the chief priests protested loudly, Pilate wouldn't be swayed. Too many Roman and Jewish laws combined to put Christ on the cross.

2 DECIDED BY LOT

Others believe that Jesus' circumstances, just like everyone's, were decided by fate and only the outcome of fortune, good or bad. The four soldiers, who made up the execution squad, shared four items of Jesus' clothing, but ownership of the seamless undergarment was decided by lot (v24; Psalm 22 v18). Just as the soldier who won that item of clothing would have attributed it to 'good luck', so people regard Jesus' suffering and death as 'bad luck' for him. But Jesus is the Maker and Master of his own destiny. His death on the cross was neither an accident of fate nor the consequence of luck. Jesus himself is the Ruler of all, and he never abdicated his rulership at Calvary. Although he allows men to perpetrate their evil against him, he is still Lord of all. Jesus is nothing less than the King upon his cross.

3 DEMONSTRATED BY LOVE

In his dying, agonising moments, the Saviour's love is clearly demonstrated as he commends John and Mary to each other as mother and son. When all the other disciples were noticeable by their absence, four women stood with John *'near the cross of Jesus'*. The monumental demonstration of unfathomable love, which Jesus demonstrates in surrendering himself to the awfulness of the cross, is illustrated in his love and compassion for his mother and for John. Jesus put others first. Jesus' immeasurable love meant sacrifice, and frequently our expressions of God's love to others will mean the sacrifice of time, energy, rest, finances, possessions, and peace. Our demonstration of compassion may mean great patience, wisdom, and humility as we reach out to fellow pilgrims with the love of Jesus.

MARCH 7
THE GOSPEL OF JOHN ch19 vv28-42

MISSION ACCOMPLISHED

An American War Office information film, about the success of the B-17 heavy bomber called 'Flying Fortress', gave the world the expression 'Mission Accomplished'. Verse 28 could be paraphrased in the same way.

Jesus had not deviated from the divine plan. He had already anticipated the completing of the mission in ch17 v4. Our Lord's 'earth mission' was at an end. He had nothing remaining to 'mop up'. He had nothing outstanding to cater for. He had no 'to do' list left.

1 FULFILLED SCRIPTURE

(vv28, 36, 37) There is a majestic cohesiveness in the way that all the various scriptures, written by numerous authors spread over a thousand years, harmonise beautifully in Jesus.

Thirst – Psalm 22 v15; 69 v21. A raging thirst was one of the characteristics of crucifixion. Jesus refused to take the myrrh wine to deaden pain (Mark ch15 v23), but he took the cheap wine in a sponge, extending life and prolonging agony.

No Broken Bones – Exodus ch12 v46; Numbers ch9 v12. Breaking victims' legs accelerated death as they could no longer push up to allow them to breathe. None of the bones of this Passover Lamb would be broken. He met the criteria prescribed by Mosaic Law.

Pierced – v34; Zechariah ch12 v10. Over four hundred years earlier, Zechariah referred to a 'pierced Messiah'. The fulfilled Scriptures, directly relating to the death of Jesus, attest to this undiluted truth that the Bible is the inspired, infallible, and unshakeably trustworthy word of God.

2 FINISHED WORK

(v30) Jesus triumphantly announces that his mission is accomplished. Notice that Jesus is in full control right up to the final second of his life. His head doesn't flop in death. Jesus deliberately *'bowed his head'* and consciously *'gave up his spirit'* as he says his final words from the cross, as recorded by Luke (ch23 v46). Jesus' work is complete and sufficient. Just as Jesus implied that his everyday sustenance (*'my food'* he says)...*' is to do the will of him who sent me and to finish his work'* (John ch4 v34) – so our everyday sustenance, our 'bread and butter', is to serve our God and to finish what he has given us to do. God is looking for 'starters', but he also wants 'finishers' who have perseverance, commitment, and 'stickability'. Paul was also a 'finisher' (2 Timothy ch4 v7).

3 FINAL VIEW

There are two final views:

Jews' Final View

v37 is a quote from Zechariah, which reveals that the final view that unbelieving Jews will have of Jesus is as the One they have pierced. They killed the Messiah for whom they had been eagerly waiting.

John's Final View

John is not an unreliable witness. He was there and witnessed the *'flow of blood and water with his own eyes'*. John's testimony is for one all-important reason: *'so that you also may believe'* (v35).

4 FAITHFUL SERVICE

Two secret disciples came out into the open at Jesus' death (vv38-42). Notice:

They had their Principles in Place

The faith of Joseph and Nicodemus had matured. They were men of principle who now wanted to put Jesus first. Their daring and audacity moved them to seek Pilate's permission for Jesus' proper burial.

They had their Preparations all Done

This was *'the Jewish Day of Preparation'* before the Passover, but it was more important for his followers to be prepared to serve Jesus. It's obvious that seventy-five pounds of mixed spices couldn't have been produced without planning and expense. A genuine workman for God will be *'prepared to do any good work'* (2 Timothy ch2 v21).

They had their Priorities in Order

Joseph and Nicodemus would have both been disqualified from joining the Passover celebrations because they had handled Jesus' dead body. They may have been latecomers to faithful service, but their mission was accomplished because they did their best for Jesus.

What is the best that you can do for Jesus today?

I SAW IT ALL

The man who saw it has given testimony, and his testimony is true.

He knows that he tells the truth, and he testifies so that you also may believe.

John ch19 v35

The sun was red hot and had now climbed quite high,

As we arrived at the top of the hill,

No storm clouds were gliding across the blue sky,

As we heard the command to stand still.

The day was just great to be lived, though for some,

Today is declared as their last,

For to Golgotha's hill the procession has come,

To approve of the sentence just passed.

They say that his crimes are as long as your arm

and they tell me he's worthy to die;

He had given a nobleman's daughter her life

and had answered a poor blind man's cry.

To a widow, he lovingly gave back her son

and the man in the tombs he set free;

With sick and with poor, he left nothing undone

and the children he sat on his knee.

His care for the body was also displayed

when a feast for five thousand he spread.

His followers state that a tempest obeyed

the words of command which he said.

A leper has proved the return of his skin,

And a woman who fell at his feet

gives witness to power and healing within,

His great love and compassion repeat.

They've made him to lie on a cross on the ground,

The blood from his back wets the grass;

His face bears the blood from the head that's been crowned,

The crown undeserved by his class.

His body, distorted, is stretched to its full,

The nails are plunged deep in his hands;

The cross is put upright with one savage pull

in fulfilling those cruel demands.

That pain-twisted body, his family said,

Once lay where the animals feed;

his eyes, which are set in his blood-spattered head,

Once saw every deepest-felt need.

His feet, which are pinned in such anger and hate,

once walked on the crest of the waves;

his hands, now restricted in bearing his weight,

embraces the world that he saves.

I can but repent of this terrible crime

in destroying this innocent man:

I fear that perhaps this is really God's Son,

That perhaps this is part of his plan –

To die here in torment, without any guilt,

without any sin of his own;

the one who the bricks of the universe built

Now suffers the sentence alone.

Why should he? How could he? Why did he, for me,

Deliver the ransom in blood?

What right does he own, Satan's captives to free

from their sinful estate in the mud?

He is Christ the Creator, the Saviour, the Lord:

It is he who the freedom decrees.

Trust in Jesus and new life with him be assured –

God stands with eternity's keys.

Geoff Fox

MARCH 8
THE GOSPEL OF JOHN ch20 vv1-18

I HAVE SEEN THE LORD

This chapter is yet another unique hallmark of this extraordinary biography. Although biographies generally conclude with the death and burial of their subjects, in Jesus' case, chapter 19 is far from being the end of the story. If Christ has not been raised, then our preaching is useless, our faith is futile, and we are still in our sins (1 Corinthians ch15, vv14, 17). While the believer's experience is knowing the living Christ personally, the Bible must always be the authoritative answer to scepticism and unbelief.

This narrative centres on the empty tomb and Mary's statement in v18, *'I have seen the Lord'*. A personal appreciation of Jesus' resurrection will include:

1 KNOWING WHERE HE'S GONE (vv1-2)

Mary had left her accommodation in the darkness to go to the tomb (vv1-2). By the time she got there, the sun had risen (Mark ch16 v2). Mary discovered that the tomb was empty, and she ran to Peter and John, telling them that someone had snatched her Lord and that she didn't know where they had put him. Mary's distress at seeing her Lord so brutally killed was intensified when she thought that his body had been stolen. But she needn't have worried. Jesus had risen as he had promised, and he will one day take his people home to be with him (ch 14 vv1-3)

2 BELIEVING WHAT HE SAYS (vv3-9)

John was convinced of Jesus' resurrection by the absence of his body, though for most of the witnesses to his resurrection, it was the presence of Jesus' body that persuaded them. Though John believed, it was not because he had understood the Old Testament scriptures. Nevertheless, he had believed what Jesus had taught (for example, Mark ch8 v31). At that moment, John was in the smallest of minorities, but he believed. Majorities don't have a monopoly on being right! If you are in a minority at home, school, college, or work, be encouraged that the early New Testament church was in a small minority too because they believed what Jesus had said.

3 RECOGNISING HOW HE APPEARS (vv10-14)

Mary didn't recognise Jesus' appearance, although she did eventually recognise his voice. Paul refers to the resurrection body as having a distinctive heavenly splendour, different from our present natural bodies (1 Corinthians ch15 v40). Jesus' body could be touched and handled, but it rose through the grave clothes. Jesus' body could cook and eat fish, but it could also enter a locked room. Jesus comes to each of us in different ways to bring us to himself. Do we recognise his voice when he is speaking to us through the Bible and through his messengers?

4 UNDERSTANDING WHAT HE DOES (vv15-16)

Mary, who had once been bound by seven demons (Luke ch8 v2), was brokenhearted on that Sunday morning and was also blind to Jesus initially. But Jesus had come to heal the brokenhearted, to free the captive and to open blind eyes (Isaiah ch61 v1). It was in the personal way that Jesus spoke her name that Mary recognised him. Jesus comes to each of his sheep and calls them by name, *'and his sheep follow him because they know his voice'* (ch10 vv3-4). Whether bound by addictions, superstitions, or traditions; whether brokenhearted by tragedy or loss; whether blinded by ignorance, scepticism, or unbelief, there is good news in Jesus for those who turn from sin and turn to him.

5 OBEYING WHAT HE COMMANDS (vv17-18)

Jesus said to Mary: *'Go...and tell'*. This became the mission of every believer following Jesus' resurrection: Go and tell! Our task is not to win debates but to make disciples (Matthew ch28 v19), and part of that will mean living in such a way that it makes it easier for others to believe in God. How consistently Christlike are we in seeking to live for Jesus? We will find it difficult to describe a 'welcoming Saviour' if our attitude is distinctly stand-offish and unwelcoming. We shall be compromised in sharing Jesus if we also share smutty jokes and sick humour. We shall struggle in testifying of a Saviour who engages with needy sinners if we remain remote, isolated, and insular. *'I have seen the Lord'* was Mary's clear testimony. What is our testimony?

MARCH 9
THE GOSPEL OF JOHN ch20 vv19-31

STOP DOUBTING AND BELIEVE

Some people decide to be undecided regarding God's existence. They are 'respectable doubters' and call themselves 'sceptics'. But scepticism and doubt are often a cop-out by those who cannot be bothered to assess the evidence, examine the facts, and discover the truth. *It is the pert superficial thinker who is generally strongest in every kind of unbelief* [Sir Humphrey Davey, chemist and inventor]. In this section, we are confronted with the hard-core scepticism of Thomas Didymus. He wanted concrete proof of Jesus' resurrection. Thomas has given his name to myriad doubters who, for two thousand years, will not believe in the resurrection of Jesus. They may refer to themselves as 'rationalists', but their logic is often irrational. 'Thomas' and 'Didymus' are the Aramaic and Greek words for 'twin' respectively. Although we don't know who Thomas's twin was, there are many who are twinned with him in their scepticism.

1 DOUBTING BRINGS FEAR: BELIEVING BRINGS PEACE

Verse 19 puts the disciples behind locked doors, cowering with fear of the Jews. Jesus appears with the assurance they desperately needed. He brought calm to their troubled hearts. Scepticism will always create insecurity and instability because there is no solid anchor for the soul in unbelief. *You will keep in perfect peace him whose mind is steadfast, because he trusts in you* (Isaiah ch26 v3).

2 DOUBTING BRINGS SADNESS: BELIEVING BRINGS JOY

The disciples had been grief-stricken over Jesus' crucifixion. To them, it seemed that the light had gone out, that the Light of the World had been extinguished. But they were overjoyed at his appearance (v20). One of the tests of true discipleship is in how much joy you get from Jesus' presence – in his word; through the messages of his servant-preachers; in prayer; in dedicated service; and among God's people.

3 DOUBTING BRINGS POWERLESSNESS: BELIEVING BRINGS THE SPIRIT

(vv21-22) Jesus was sending out his disciples to represent him in the world while he was bodily absent. If they went alone, then they would fail miserably because they lacked power. So Jesus empowers them by equipping them with his Spirit. Our mission for Jesus will only ever be successful when we are Spirit-filled and Spirit-directed. Jesus still says, *I am sending you* (v21), and he equips us with all we need through his Spirit. He assures us of his presence *even to the end of the age* (Matthew ch28 v20).

4 DOUBTING BRINGS GUILT: BELIEVING BRINGS FORGIVENESS

Verse 23 becomes much clearer in the context of the gospel and the evangelistic mission on which Jesus sends his disciples. As the Good News is preached and people respond with faith, so they are forgiven. If hearers reject that message, then they remain unforgiven. It is belief in Jesus, the Son of God, which brings divine forgiveness. Doubt and unbelief imprison sceptics in their guilt. God's forgiveness of people's sins doesn't depend on whether we forgive their sins.

5 DOUBTING BRINGS LOSS: BELIEVING BRINGS BLESSING

This beatitude (v29) is for us today, if we believe. 'Seeing is believing' was the experience of each of those early resurrection witnesses. The sceptics were disarmed by Jesus' personal appearances to them, including Thomas. Yet none of them were saved merely because they had 'seen'. Salvation is only ever by faith, and that opportunity still exists today (Romans ch10 v17). For us, it is not seeing the work of Christ but believing the word of Christ which saves.

6 DOUBTING BRINGS DEATH: BELIEVING BRINGS LIFE

(vv30-31) John reveals the stark contrast between doubting and believing as the difference between life and death. Those who remain unsaved and unbelieving are not merely 'sick' or 'dying'. The Bible certifies them 'dead' (John ch3 v36; Ephesians ch2 v1). John's selection of Jesus' *'miraculous signs'* in his Gospel is not exhaustive. Many others remain unrecorded. But the testimony to the few is provided so that sinners may believe and receive eternal life.

Are you twinned with Thomas in his scepticism? Do you still doubt, or do you believe?

MARCH 10
THE GOSPEL OF JOHN ch21.1-14

FISHING ON THE RIGHT SIDE

There are always many criticisms and judgements when a fishing trip turns into a disaster. But someone has commented that there has never been a fishing trip so severely judged as this expedition in these verses. Many critics have judged the disciples' fishing as a return to their old ways in contradiction of Jesus' commission to evangelise. But there's no criticism of their trip in this passage. Indeed, Jesus seemed to endorse their fishing expedition with a bumper harvest.

There's a lot of discussion today in the fishing industry about tracking the fish from sea to plate. So let's track the 153 fish in this narrative:

1 RECEIVING OF WHAT GOD GIVES

God graciously gave the seven disciples success in their fishing because they obeyed Jesus' instructions, even without knowing who he was at that point. They may have failed to recognise the risen Jesus initially, perhaps due to the morning darkness, but there was something engaging and compelling about him that made them obey. How did the disciples respond to and receive of what God had given to them?

i] Without any Debate

They could have argued realistically with the 'stranger on the shore', but they didn't. We must learn to receive what God gives us, whether blessings or lessons, without debate or argument. Instead of being blinded by impatience, we should learn to accept various circumstances, challenges, and resources as coming from God. We may fail to recognise Jesus in these situations.

ii] Without any Destruction

The boat didn't sink, and the nets weren't torn (v11). We may not see the blessings because we are more concerned about our comforts. Even though we may suffer the hottest fires and darkest trials, God will not allow his people to be destroyed because they are immensely precious to him.

iii] Without any Distance

The disciples didn't go very far to receive God's enormous blessing. Just a hundred yards from shore! (v8). God's blessings are not limited by geography or location. He can come to us right where we are. He can save us, send us, and supply us wherever we may be.

2 GIVING OF WHAT WE RECEIVE

The disciples had just been given 'the catch of their lives' and then Jesus invited them to bring some to him. It's important for us to understand our responsibility to give to God a proportion of what he gives to us. If *every good and every perfect gift is from above* (James ch1 v17), what percentage of our homes, our food, our possessions, our income do we willingly give back to God? If the disciples worked by Old Testament Law, then they would have offered a tithe of their catch, and ten percent would have been sixteen fish. In the New Testament church age, we may believe that we are no longer bound by such restrictions, and therefore our starting point may be the legal ten percent (2 Corinthians ch9 v7). The disciples in Galilee that morning gave according to their income. How would we feel if God brought our income in line with our giving?

3 RECEIVING OF WHAT WE HAVE GIVEN

God gives freely and graciously to us, out of which we freely and cheerfully give back to him, and in that sacrificial giving, we receive God's richest blessing. The fish went from sea to net, net to shore, shore to barbecue, and back to the disciples again (v13). Without fanciful speculations about the number, John recorded the fact that there were 153 large fish and that the net wasn't torn. Out of that catch, the disciples brought *some of the fish* (v10) to Jesus. Everyone who has given freely to Jesus can confirm that he is no one's debtor. His grace far exceeds our gifts. Jesus gave himself sacrificially at the cross so that we may become rich (2 Corinthians ch8 v9). We should never be concerned that we shall lose out if we give generously to God. We can be sure that our loving and gracious God is not inconsiderate or dismissive of our giving to him. He will never be in the debt of any one of us who gives sacrificially to him. God gave the disciples the 'catch of their lives' and of that gift, the disciples willingly gave a percentage to Jesus, and he returned a much-needed blessing to his obedient followers. Real spiritual quality and maturity are directly related to our capacity to give selflessly in response to the grace we have received.

MARCH 11
THE GOSPEL OF JOHN ch21.15-25

DO YOU TRULY LOVE ME?

A black cloud had hung over Peter's relationship with Jesus. Even during Jesus' many resurrection appearances, this cloud hung dark and heavy. It was the 'cloud' of Peter's public denial of his loving Master and best Friend (ch18 vv15-27), how that unequivocal denial must have plagued Peter's mind and heart in the following hours and days! How Peter must have yearned to be able to turn the clock back, be given another opportunity, start again! Maybe we have experienced a similar situation in which we have let the Lord down, and we would love to be able to wipe the slate clean and start again. If Peter had longed to tell and demonstrate to Jesus just how he really felt about him, he was given the opportunity at the beach barbecue that morning. Three times Peter had denied Jesus, and three times he was given the chance to profess his love for Jesus. The Saviour wants to know from us, as well as Peter, *'Do you truly love me?'* God's people are known as those who 'love the Lord' (Psalm 97 v10; Ephesians ch6 v24). Jesus' tête à tête with Peter on the seashore provides us with a checklist for confirming our true love for Jesus:

1 KEEP FEEDING THE FLOCK

Three times Jesus responds to Peter's three affirmations by instructing care for his flock (vv15-17). We cannot truly love Jesus without taking responsibility for Jesus' people, the flock of God. Though there are specific responsibilities for pastors, preachers, elders, and teachers, every believer has a responsibility to feed and to care for the flock. Jesus instructs each believer to look out for each other. This is the essence of true church fellowship. He's not promoting Peter to governance or rulership, let alone appointing him to become the First Pontiff, as Romanists claim. Instead, Jesus shows us all what some of the humble tasks of servanthood entail: feed, tend, care for, look out for, serve. Some pastors and ministers have boastfully referred to their church members as 'my flock' or 'my sheep'. But notice whose lambs and sheep Peter is told to feed (vv15, 17). We are to shepherd the *'church of God, which he bought with his own blood'* (Acts ch20 v28). These are Jesus' sheep. He is the Good Shepherd. They belong to him (ch 10 v3).

2 KEEP FOLLOWING THE SAVIOUR

Jesus was instructing Peter to do more than just follow him along the seashore (vv19, 22). You must follow Jesus, keeping to his pathway:

i] Even when work occupies you

Jesus didn't criticise their fishing. 'Fishing' and 'following' need not be mutually exclusive. We can follow Jesus in our legitimate work.

ii] Even when age weakens you

(v18) Age takes its toll with regards to strength and health, but lack of activity, and even mobility, must not interfere with our following of Jesus. Old age may require humility and submission. The active and energetic Peter would be tested to the limits, but he still followed Jesus.

iii] Even when persecution threatens you

In Peter's case, old age would mean increased persecution and ultimate martyrdom (v19). Peter would follow Jesus in the shadow of the cross. Our test of loyalty may not be as severe as Peter's, but we are called to follow Jesus despite the opposition, ridicule, and pressures we may face.

3 KEEP FOCUSING ON THE MISSION

Even while Jesus was speaking with Peter about the importance and the consequence of following him, Peter still showed he could be distracted (vv20-23). Peter took his eyes off Jesus to ask about John. Often, we may be keen to make judgements about other people: what about him or her? We are apt to lose sight of the individual mission to which Jesus has called us individually. Notice how damaging Peter's lack of focus could be:

i] Distracted by Wrong Talk

Peter wanted to talk about someone else. How easily gossip can distract us from our calling and our mission.

ii] Deflected by Wrong Teaching

Rumour can develop into tradition; tradition can become principle; principle can become doctrine. We must guard against heresy built on hearsay. But John's Gospel is totally reliable, even if it doesn't record everything Jesus did (vv24, 25). John's own focus and mission were clear (ch20 vv30-31).

MARCH 12
EXODUS ch1 vv1-22

THE DUEL BETWEEN KINGS AND THE KING OF KINGS

Departure, embarkation, exit, going out, going away, setting off, taking off – all are synonyms for 'Exodus'. This second book of the Bible, which is a continuation of the Genesis narrative, takes its title from the embarkation/departure of the Hebrews from Egypt. God had called Abram from Ur in Babylon to Canaan, fifteen hundred miles away. But the account of Joseph shows that his family relocated to Rameses, Goshen, around Egypt's Nile delta. For 430 years, Abram's descendants prospered and expanded. The family grew from seventy (Genesis ch46 v27) to possibly two to three million.

But the Hebrew demographics were clear to the Egyptians. They feared the growing numbers and a possible takeover by the Israelites. The *'new king'* voiced their concern and decreed the Hebrew enslavement. We should not lose sight of the spiritual duel which occupies a third of this book: a contest between the king of Egypt and the King of Glory. It's a duel that Pharaoh lost!

But this duel is played out today between the authorities of this world and the authority of Almighty God. His laws and commands are being constantly challenged and countermanded.

Take a look at Egypt's *'new king'* while thinking about the 'Pharaohs' of the twenty-first century:

1 HE DIDN'T KNOW ABOUT THEIR PAST

(v8) This new king (probably Thutmose I, who reigned from about 1539-1514BC) was ignorant of Egypt's history and the significant role which Joseph had played in Egypt's survival. What an indictment of any royal, political, or military leader to be ignorant of the past! Such ignorance condemns them to repeat history's follies. Under God, Joseph was the 'saviour of the world' in providing famine relief. Joseph's actions will remind us of a greater 'Saviour of the world' (1 John ch4 v14). As men came to Joseph in humility, seeking the resources to live, so sinners must come to Jesus in humility, seeking forgiveness and eternal life. Today, our modern 'Pharaohs' are ignorant of our nation's rich Christian heritage and the gracious way in which God has provided wealth, protection, wisdom, deliverance, and countless blessings and privileges.

2 HE DIDN'T TALK ABOUT THEIR FAITH

The king forced the Hebrews into hard labour, making them build great cities (v11). But the oppression didn't reduce the number of Hebrews. On the contrary! (v12). He ordered the midwives to operate on 'gender selection'. But they feared God more than they feared Pharaoh (v17). Similarly, our 'new kings' have ridden roughshod over the principles and beliefs of godly people. Doctors and nurses have been ordered to kill unborn children. The next stage is to produce genetically modified babies. Our leaders have no room for ethics based on faith. The issues facing Shiprah and Puah have not gone away.

3 HE DIDN'T CARE ABOUT THEIR LIVES

(vv16,22) Pharaoh was capricious and malicious. Both the Egyptians and the Hebrews were forced to throw infants into the crocodile-infested Nile (Acts ch7 v19). To Pharaoh, the lives of the Hebrews were cheap and expendable. The 'Pharaohs' of our day continue to order death and destruction, for if you reject God as the Creator and Giver of life, then you are free to kill unborn babies, or terminally ill patients, or the elderly. This is the natural outcome of Evolutionism – the survival of the fittest, healthiest, and strongest. If you don't believe that ultimately you are accountable to God, then you are not restricted by any moral compass. Contrary to this, Christians believe that they have a duty of care to the poor, the homeless, the vulnerable, the hungry, the orphaned, and the persecuted. They care about them because they believe in the sanctity and dignity of life itself. We believe that everyone has been created in God's image. But Pharaoh was on a collision course with God for daring to hurt his chosen people.

4 HE DIDN'T THINK ABOUT THEIR GOD

Pharaoh and the Egyptians believed in gods that actually lived in images carved out of wood and stone. They also believed that, because the whole of Egypt depended on the life-giving waters of the Nile, the river itself was a god to whom they offered sacrifices, such as the Hebrew baby boys. They didn't believe in the God of Israel, the one, true and living God. Pharaoh didn't realise that God was being kind and gracious to the Hebrew midwives because of the stand that they had taken (vv20-21). The 'new kings' of politics, media, science, and entertainment do not think about the God of creation, the God of redemption, the God of the Bible. They treat him with ignorance and contempt, even loathing and hatred. Our sovereign God holds in his hands the very breath that his scoffers breathe (Daniel ch5 v23): the breath which they use to mock his name and his being. We are amazed at the grace and patience of our God. He still tolerates even those who are scientifically and ideologically opposed to him, so that they may come to repentance.

MARCH 13
EXODUS ch2 vv1-25

WATER BABY

The history and general circumstances of the Hebrew people in Egypt, as outlined in ch1, provide the perfect backdrop to the personal story of one Jewish family as described in ch2. This chapter neatly splits into two sections, which are divided by forty years.

1 DRAWN FROM THE WATER

This title, 'drawn from the water', is the meaning of the name 'Moses', which the daughter of Pharaoh gave to the baby boy she had discovered. Her father had been operating his 'Gender Selection Plan' – his Final Solution – to limit the Hebrew 'population explosion'. It seems that little has changed from Pharaoh to Hitler. The evil hearts of mankind continue to plot to destroy the descendants of Jacob. But God always has his man or the woman for the moment. Three hundred and fifty years earlier, that man had been Joseph. Now it was to be Moses. Moses' parents tried to conceal their baby from those who would kill it. For three months, Moses' mother succeeded, but it became very difficult as the baby grew. Not to be beaten, she built a vessel for him so that he could float among the reeds of the Nile. The vessel was a *'papyrus basket...coated...with tar and pitch'* (v3). Between verses one and two, there are about fifteen years to allow for the birth and growth of Miriam. She was sent to keep watch on the 'Moses basket' from a distance. It was here that she spotted Pharaoh's daughter, who had also spotted the floating basket. When a *'slave girl'* had fetched it (v5), the crying baby tugged at the princess' heartstrings (v6). But Miriam, with wisdom beyond her years, offered to find a nanny for the baby: his mother, of course! Talk about 'Child Benefit'! Moses' Mum was to receive a royal allowance for bringing up her own son. God's wonderful ways never cease to surprise us. What can we learn from this first section to help us?

i] God's Timing is Perfect

Of all the four thousand miles of the River Nile, it was precisely then and there that the princess came to bathe. It was where Pharaoh's daughter met God's servant-to-be. God never makes a mistake with his timing. He is always perfectly punctual with his planning. We may frequently become frustrated because our timing is not God's timing. Not only are all the events and circumstances in the hands of God (*'my times'* Psalm 31 v15), but also the precise chronology and nanosecond-accuracy (my timings) are in God's perfect control.

ii] God's Rescue is Complete

Think of the tender love and meticulous care that was used to construct the baby's 'lifeboat'. It had to be the right size and shape. It could not capsize or sink. It had to be covered to protect the baby from the sun as well as from bugs and predators. This floating vessel preserved life for the eventual fulfilling of God's purpose. It's no wonder that the same word is used to describe the vessel that Noah built. Moses' basket was a miniature version of Noah's ark. In each case, God rescued a minority from the majority that was under threat of death.

The name 'Moses' would forever remind him of his unique rescue. He was a fine child (v2), an extraordinary child (Acts ch7 v20), and a saved child. We must never forget our salvation.

iii] God's Arrangement is Best

Despite Miriam's anguish, God had arranged for her baby brother to be found by the Egyptian princess. He arranged for the baby to cry at that moment and for the princess' maternal emotions to overwhelm her (v6). We couldn't have scripted a set of circumstances so uniquely wonderful. Like Miriam, we must be wise, brave, and prayerful.

2 DRAWN TO THE WELL

Moses seemed to have 'jumped the gun' with regard to leading and delivering his people (Acts ch7 v25). While the consequences of Moses' action made him a fugitive, we may learn three things:

i] God's Continuing Control

Despite Moses' rash action to accelerate God's plan for his life, God was in control, though Moses had to wait another forty years in a foreign land (vv15-22). Due to his impetuosity, Moses was forced to learn the lesson of humility and patience after rescuing Jethro's daughters at the well. Though he had been *'educated in all the wisdom of the Egyptians'* (Acts ch7 v22), it was time to be educated in the wisdom of God. Moses learned the values of eternity in the context of time. His growing faith foresaw the coming of Christ (Hebrews ch11 vv25-27).

ii] God's Enduring Covenant

God hadn't forgotten that he had promised a homeland for his Old Testament people (v24; Psalm 105 vv8-11) and in the New Covenant, which Jesus has made with his Church and has ratified with his blood, he promises a permanent home for his believing people (John ch14 v2).

iii] God's Loving Concern

(v25) God's concern was evident in his knowledge about the plight of the Israelites and in the revelation of himself to them through his mercy, power, and grace. Realising God's concern for us should always allay our anxiety about other things. Jesus said that we shouldn't be anxious about food, drink, clothes, and life in general (Matthew ch6 v26). The Israelites were valuable to God, and we are valuable to him as well.

MARCH 14
EXODUS ch3 vv1-22

WHAT DOES GOD HAVE TO DO TO GRAB OUR ATTENTION?

The 'wanted' posters of the Wild West films are still being used in their updated versions. The FBI publishes its 'FBI's Most Wanted List' and the BBC TV Crimewatch has its 'most wanted' persons.

Moses was on the King of Egypt's 'wanted list'. Moses was a fugitive: a man on the run. After killing an Egyptian slavemaster (ch2 v12), he had to flee when he realised that his actions had become public knowledge. He fled to Midian, to the east of the Sinai desert. It was there that Moses intervened to rescue the seven daughters of a Midian priest called Reuel Jethro after they were prevented from drawing water from a well used by shepherds. Moses was invited to stay with Jethro and married Zipporah, one of Jethro's daughters. Moses was made very welcome, but he couldn't forget his Hebrew roots and so named his first son 'Gershom', meaning 'a foreigner here'. The birth of his son only confirmed Moses' 'immigrant status'. But Moses spent forty years learning in the 'Academy of Human Experience' so that he could graduate as the chosen leader of God's people, who were suffering increasingly in Egypt. But God had to speak to Moses first.

1 GOD'S PROCESS TO REVEAL HIMSELF

Moses was shepherding his father-in-law's flocks on the Sinai Peninsula in the area around Horeb. A burning unburnt bush made Moses curious, and he went to investigate (vv2-3). Once God had grabbed Moses' attention, he could speak to him, and Moses would listen. What does it take to grab our attention? Our daily routines and patterns, doing the same things with the same attitudes, may be just like Moses' flock-watching in the desert. But God may want to speak to you clearly about something. Will your 'burning bush' be a sudden and unexpected change in circumstances? A health scare, perhaps? A near-miss? An unusual event? What does it take to grab our attention and for us to take him seriously? God's process to reveal himself included the fire and the angel, his voice and his name (vv13-14). *'I Am Who I Am'* is the name God discloses for himself. It may seem very enigmatic, but God is stating something wonderfully profound about his Being. The first person singular of the verb 'to be' is 'I am'. We expect some qualification when we use this verb, for example, 'I am hungry'. But when God says, 'I Am', no qualification is necessary. God is, and he continues to be. He *is* the God of Abraham, Isaac, and Jacob, not *was*. Jesus likewise declared his own deity (John ch8 v58). Jesus is the God of the eternal present, and he is unchangeably the same.

2 GOD'S PLAN TO RESCUE HIS PEOPLE

(vv7-10) God says: I have seen, I have heard, I am concerned, I have come down, I am sending. If these statements apply to the rescue of God's people from Egypt, how much more do they apply to the rescue of sinners from their sins? Jesus came down to raise us up. He descended into the deep pit with its mire and filth so that he may save us and take us out. But that's not the final chapter! God had a uniquely special mission for Moses in sending him to Pharaoh, and he has a special mission for every rescued child of God. God said, *'I am sending you'* and Moses responded, *'Who am I?'* (v11). But God answers us just as he answered Moses: *'I will be with you'*. The authentic record of the rest of the Book of Exodus (and Leviticus, Numbers, Deuteronomy) is that God never reneged on his promise. Jesus endorsed the promise of his presence with those whom he sends (Matthew ch28 v20). Do we question God's commission like Moses did (*Who am I?*) or do we respond like Isaiah: *'Here I am. Send me!'* (Isaiah ch6 v8)?

3 GOD'S PROMISES TO REASSURE HIS SERVANT

If Moses needed a sign of God's presence and confirmation of his commission (v12), then God said that when the people are rescued from Egypt, they will worship God on the same mountain, Horeb (which is identified with Mt Sinai). If Moses is still apprehensive about the details of this daunting task, God reinforces his assurance with additional promises: a promise to end misery (v17), a promise that the elders will listen (v18), a promise to strike the Egyptians (v20), and a promise to plunder them (vv21-22). God graciously provides us with his promises like immovable pitons in our climb to the summit. We can hang our faith on the secure pegs within his word. Moses could have spent the rest of his life in a desert, tending sheep, but God had to stir him to send him. What does God have to do to stir us and to grab our attention? Which particular 'bush' is burning in your 'desert' just at the moment? Notice the three hands:

v8: The painful hand of the Egyptians – from which God came to rescue his people.

v20: The powerful hand of God – which would effect that rescue (ch6.vv1, 6; ch7 vv4, 5; ch13 vv3, 9, 14, 16; ch15 v6).

v21: The prosperous hand of God's people – filled with the riches of his grace (Genesis ch15 v14).

MARCH 15
EXODUS ch4 vv1-31

EXCUSE ME!

We have all been creative with our excuses at one time or another. We discover in this chapter that Moses is no exception. In ch3 vv14-22 God provided Moses with an authoritative mandate and a powerful commission, backed up with the promise of supernatural resources. We might have thought that Moses, this man of faith, would have been all too ready to advance in the confidence that God had underwritten for him. But we observe that this great patriarch is really no different from us in some respects. He is quick to excuse himself from doing what God tells him to do. We shall see from these three excuses that much hasn't changed in three and a half thousand years. God had promised Moses that *the elders of Israel will listen to you* (ch3 v18) and that the Egyptians would eventually become *favourably disposed towards this people* (ch3 v21). Yet Moses' first excuse was:

1 THEY WON'T LISTEN TO ME

Moses could have been stalling for time, just as we may stall for time when we are convinced of a particular course of action, but we are reluctant to take it. We don't refuse point blank, but we may procrastinate, hoping that, as we employ 'delay tactics', the issue may resolve itself. Yet God is patient with the 'What If…?' game that Moses is playing. Moses could have had an 'off day' with his faith. There is no doubt that Moses had huge faith. He is not listed in that champion chapter of faith for nothing (Hebrews ch11 vv24-26). Such was the calibre of Moses' faith that he saw the Messiah fifteen hundred years into the future. He believed that ultimately God would send 'the Christ'. So if Moses had such a rock-solid faith and an unshakable belief in God's promises, we may be surprised to hear him stalling for time and making excuses to God. But God was faithful to Moses, even if his faith had taken a temporary nose-dive. God showed Moses three clear signs:

i] Staff-Snake (vv3-5) Moses' shepherd stick transformed to a snake and back again;

ii] Hand-Leprosy (vv6-7) Moses' healthy hand became leprous and back again;

iii] Water-Blood (vv8-9) The water from the Nile became blood when it was poured out.

We may think that when we preach, or witness, or give young people's talks, or talks at other events, that folk won't listen to us and they won't believe. But God still has his way of making people listen, even if he doesn't always use snakes, diseases, or blood! The power of God's word is the chosen way to make people listen.

2 I HAVE NEVER BEEN ELOQUENT

(v10) Moses is saying that he has never been a man of words. He has never been a public speaker or debater – not now and not ever! It wasn't that he had a speech impediment because Stephen described Moses' speech as powerful (Acts ch7 v22). The trouble with Moses was that he felt that he wasn't wise enough, or fluent enough, or quick-witted enough to take on Pharaoh. He said, *I am slow of speech and tongue'* (v10). But once again, Moses was calculating without God. He was making these excuses to the one Being who can meet all our needs and our deficiencies. It is the Lord Almighty who gives the gifts of speech, sight, and hearing. Just as the Lord can open people's ears to hear the word, so he can open his people's mouths to speak his word. God not only promised to help Moses to speak, but he would also teach him what to say. But it's not necessarily oratory or verbosity that God is looking for. Even Paul's critics compared his speaking with other orators of the day and commented, *'...his speaking amounts to nothing'* (2 Corinthians ch10 v10). Yet God used Paul's preaching in a powerful way to take the gospel around the world. It's not always the skills in oratory or speech-making that God seeks, but rather the willingness to be his mouthpiece.

3 SEND SOMEONE ELSE

(vv11-13) After dealing with all of Moses' feeble excuses, the real reason comes to the surface. Basically, Moses didn't want to go! His words, in Hebrew, could be translated: *'Choose anyone else, but not me.'* We may also recognise that kind of response to a task or mission that is presented to us. In our heart of hearts, we don't want to get involved. Here is an all-knowing, all-present, all-powerful God, promising to be with his servant, to embolden him, empower him, and encourage him, and his servant says: 'Not me!' In effect, Moses was saying, 'I know better than you, God'. We don't know all the facts concerning the short but difficult narrative in vv24-26. Maybe Moses had given in to his wife's demands to not have their son circumcised. Zipporah realised that she had put her husband's life in jeopardy and submitted her son to the rite. Though she complied, she seemed to find God's demands repulsive. It's not enough to comply with God's requirements. We must want to obey him, whatever is required, and without excuses.

MARCH 16
EXODUS ch5 vv1-23

IN BIG TROUBLE

For the Jews in big trouble in Egypt, there was the light of hope because of God's covenant promise to them. He would rescue his people and deliver them eventually to the Promised Land. But for Moses, v22 was an *'I told you so'* moment! Moses had already protested to God that Pharaoh wouldn't listen; that the Israelites and their elders wouldn't listen; that Moses himself wasn't articulate enough; that God ought to send someone else. After Moses had secured an audience with Pharaoh and had asked for the release of the Israelites, the labour regime only intensified *'that same day'* (v6). Let's analyse this 'big trouble':

1 POWER WITHOUT GOD (vv1-5)

Pharaoh, the king of Egypt, was possibly the most powerful man in the world at that time, but he openly confronted the Lord Almighty (v2). We may be shocked at the audacity of Pharaoh's refusal to know God and to obey his command. Yet this is probably the same language that we hear and the attitude that we see displayed by powerful people today, including celebrities and superstars.

2 BRICKS WITHOUT STRAW (vv6-10)

Up until that point, the Egyptians had supplied the straw to mix with the Nile clay to make bricks. But Pharaoh probably thought that if the Israelites had enough time on their hands to want to hold a festival in the desert (v1), then they had the time to collect their own straw. They would have to scour the land looking for straw to be chopped up for their bricks. But there was worse:

3 QUOTA WITHOUT REDUCTION (vv8-14)

There was no allowance for the additional requirement to find straw. The quota of bricks remained the same. *'Your work will not be reduced at all,'* said the slavedrivers (v11). Such was the pressure that the Israeli foremen appealed directly to Pharaoh and complained that they were being beaten for not meeting the targets. They even blamed the Egyptians (v16). But Pharaoh maintained that the slaves were just plain lazy (v17). So the Israelites vented their anger on Moses and Aaron (v21).

4 CRITICISM WITHOUT UNDERSTANDING (vv20-21)

The Israeli foremen were quick to dump the blame on their new leaders (v21). Sometimes we can be perplexed in our service for God, so that we resort to criticising God's servants just because we dare not blame God for the way things work out. This 'blame game' is nothing new. When trouble happens, we look around for people to blame, rather than to examine our own hearts. Christians, as much as anybody, can be embroiled in criticising to make up for their own failures and deficiencies.

5 HARDSHIP WITHOUT RESCUE (vv22-23)

But if the Israeli foremen stopped short of blaming God, Moses didn't! Moses laid the blame for the Hebrews' troubles and hardships at God's door (v22). We may still ask the same kind of question that Moses asked: 'Why?' Misery and trouble are not the results of God's plan, but man's sin. Jesus came to experience the trouble of sin firsthand so that he could provide a way of escape through his sufferings. Therefore, whatever constitutes trouble for us, Jesus is fully qualified and fully equipped to lead us through those troubles and eventually to bring us out safely on the other side. That's what God would do for the Israelites, if only they would trust him. We must learn three responses and lessons if we are going to trust God in our troubles:

i] Patience without Complaining

Moses was short on patience even though God had forewarned him (ch3 vv19-20). He wanted God to work to his own timetable and 'now' would be 'a good time to act', he must have thought. We may wonder why God doesn't intervene to save his people from misery. God has set a day to deal with the ungodly (Acts 17. v31), but do we patiently wait for the day of liberation (Romans ch8 v25)?

ii] Obedience without Questioning

To God's simple instruction *'Go'* (ch3 vv10,16), Moses had replied with a volley of questions (ch3 vv11,13; ch4 v1; ch5 v22). Parents may have their patience tested when children respond to their commands with questions. But it seems that we respond to the commands of God's word in much the same way.

iii] Faith without Wavering

Abraham's faith didn't weaken or waver (Romans ch4 vv19-20), but God would give this octogenarian, Moses, another forty years to develop his faith. Without it, pleasing God is impossible (Hebrews ch11 v6).

Like a plant, our faith is strengthened as our roots grow deeper in God.

MARCH 17
EXODUS ch6 vv1-30

PRESENT TO ACT

It shouldn't surprise us to learn that the names which God uses for himself are super-significant. God already called himself *'I am who I am'* (ch3 v14). In the following verse, he calls himself *'the Lord, the God of your fathers'*. It is this name for *'Lord'* (usually written in large and small capitals in our Bibles) which is the most frequent name for God in the Old Testament. In the original, it's a four-letter name without any vowels (YHWH). Just to pronounce it, we need to insert a couple of vowels (YAHWEH). Although there is still something of a mystery surrounding this name, its revelation may be summarised best as meaning 'present to act'. It wasn't that the patriarchs Abraham, Isaac, and Jacob didn't know this name for God. They did! But read vv2-3. Although the patriarchs knew the name of God (YAHWEH - the Lord), God hadn't yet revealed himself to them regarding the significance of his name, that is, 'present to act'. In fact, it was to Moses that the Lord was going to reveal the significance of his name, especially 'present to act in saving them from the Egyptians' (vv6-8). This is how Moses and all the Hebrew people would witness and experience the full-blown significance of God, the Lord's mysterious name. Here was a wonderful revelation to Moses and the Israelites that God is present to act. He is not a remote God who is disinterested in his people. The living, powerful, active presence of God would be revealed so that his people would know, as never before, that the Lord was with them to help them and to save them. God's covenant with his people (v4), reinforced to Moses, provided them with the unbreakable, unshakeable promises, which are so certain that they have been written in the past tense. But Moses was agitated and lacking faith at this point. We may also identify with the spiritual afflictions highlighted in this chapter:

1 DOUBT CAN MAKE US BLIND

God said that Moses would *'see'* the results of his power (v1). But had he not already seen a sample of God's great power in the signs that he had been given (ch4): the staff and the snake; the hand and the leprosy; the water and the blood? These weren't God's entertaining illusions or party tricks. Moses had seen a demonstration of God's power close-up and firsthand. But still he doubted. Moses had recently seen the burning, unburnt bush and had listened to God speaking to him from the bush. But still he doubted. How often are we led into a cul-de-sac of doubt when we listen to the media, or listen to popular notions, or listen to modern science, or the perversion of our own hearts? The evidence of God's glory and handiwork is all around for eyes to see. Jesus' order to Thomas is still applicable to all doubting hearts: *'Stop doubting and believe'* (John ch20 v27).

2 DISCOURAGEMENT CAN MAKE US DEAF

Although the creating, redeeming, covenant-keeping God had spoken with such unbreakable guarantees, the Israelites wouldn't listen *'because of their discouragement and cruel bondage'* (v9). How often are we just as fickle? Despite our all-powerful, unchangeable God, who promises to be with us and never let us down, we easily become discouraged by issues, circumstances, and situations. How often do we mope and only see the bleakness of our own personal lives when we become disappointed by people and disheartened by things that happen? And such discouragement can make us deaf to God's word. We become deaf to his guarantees and deaf to his promises. Jesus spelt out to his disciples (John ch16 v33) *'In this world you will have trouble...'* But somehow we expect everything to be rosy and plain sailing. Becoming a Christian doesn't mean that all your troubles are over! We often quote Hebrews ch12 v2 but we don't always quote the following verse: *'Consider him who endured such opposition from sinful men so that you will not grow weary and lose heart'*. The antidote to discouragement is to consider Jesus and the opposition he received. When troubles lurk, consider him who endured the cross.

3 FEAR CAN MAKE US DUMB

(vv10-12; 28-30) There he goes again! Moses is worrying about his *'faltering lips'* (ref ch4 v10). Moses was complaining yet again that he was not eloquent or quick-witted enough to say the right things, especially to Pharaoh. We may often fail to think straight or to string our words together effectively, because of fear or apprehension. Jesus encouraged his disciples that if they were faithful, the Holy Spirit would provide help with words (Luke ch12 vv11-12). The faithful and eloquent speeches of humble men and women through church history, facing extreme trials and even death, are testimony to the truth of Jesus' promise. But the genealogy (vv14-25) emphasises that Moses and Aaron were not chosen for the task because of their credibility, nobility, or ability. They were chosen according to God's wisdom and God's grace. He doesn't call the equipped, but he does equip the called.

MARCH 18
EXOUS ch7 vv1-24

THE BATTLE OF THE WILLS

When a ship enters certain harbours at night, the pilot will ensure that he aligns three lights so that they appear as one. When this happens, he can be certain that he is entering the harbour in the right channel. The aligning of our will with the will of God is the sure guarantee of our security and our safe arrival at the 'heavenly harbour'. However, the sad reality is that so often our own will is not at one with God's will. Like the harbour lights, our will may remain stubbornly separate from God's will, which can take us on a course that results in collision or disaster.

There is the 'main harbour beacon', which is the will of God. His will is the one, fixed, unalterable point by which we must plot our course. If only we realised that the many knocks, scrapes, and sinkings that we experience on the approach to God's heavenly harbour are because our will is not being aligned with his will. In these early chapters of Exodus, we are spectators to the fierce battle of wills that is taking place. We have observed Moses' entrenched position in opposing God's plan, trotting out excuses such as 'they won't listen' and 'I'm not eloquent enough'. But here in this chapter, we notice a mellowing in Moses' position.

1 A YIELDED HEART

Moses listened to the Lord's gracious explanation in answer to his question *'Why...?'* (v1).

i] Attentive

He listens carefully to the details which the Lord provides. It has taken eighty years (v7), but Moses is now prepared for the mission God has reserved for him. How long does it take for us to yield our hearts so that we listen carefully to what the Lord has to say to us? Moses learned that they were to be a uniquely powerful team. Moses and Aaron were going to act with divine authority, exercising divine powers and speaking divine words. At last, Moses was attentive to God (vv2-5).

ii] Obedient

Listening to particular words is not the same as obeying those words. But Moses and Aaron *'did just as the Lord commanded them'* (vv6, 10, 20). In one sense, it didn't matter about the consequences as long as they were obedient. Pharaoh's 'magic men' tried to copy Moses and Aaron's powers, but they were outclassed and outmanoeuvred. The supreme example is Jesus, who was *'obedient to death'* (Philippians ch2 v8). God looks for an unswerving obedience that will not crumble under the burden of hard work or capitulate under the threat of suffering.

iii] Reverent

Moses and Aaron had learned from their early years to respect the Lord with awe and wonder. We must also learn this aspect of a yielded heart: *Be still, for the presence of the Lord, the Holy One, is near. Come, bow before him now with reverence and fear'* [David J Evans]. While we can know God as our Father and Friend, he is still the awesome, majestic, and righteous Lord. We must never trivialise our relationship with him or treat it casually and with carelessness (Deuteronomy ch13 v4).

2 AN UNYIELDED HEART

Contrasted with Moses, Pharaoh, King of Egypt, demonstrates that he is:

i] Inattentive

There is no doubt about the hardening of the King's heart (vv3-4a; 13; 22). Although Pharaoh is responsible for his own inattentiveness and the hardening of his heart, we also notice that the Lord is hardening his heart too (v3). But Pharaoh's hard heart will also be for God's greater glory as he displays his *'miraculous signs and wonders in Egypt'* (v3) and then rescues his people. He calls them *'my divisions'* (v4), which is a military term referring to God's armies. He is the Commander of divisions; the Yahweh of armies; the Lord of hosts. The Holy Spirit's warning in Psalm 95 vv7-8, echoed in Hebrews ch3 v15, is: *'Today, if you hear his voice, do not harden your hearts'.*

ii] Disobedient

Pharaoh persisted doggedly in his resistance, and the Lord turned Egypt's water sources into blood. It's difficult to imagine the severity of the consequences. We visualise the Egyptians' desperation in scrabbling for drinking water (v24).

iii] Irreverent

Pharaoh had no time for the Lord. He tried to pit his demonic resources against the Lord, but they were far inferior (v12). Pharaoh's leading 'magic men' were Jannes and Jambres, who were *'men of depraved minds'* and *'opposed the truth'* (2 Timothy ch3 v8). Their spiritual descendants are just the same today. In the 'Battle of the Wills', we are called to surrender like Jesus did (Matthew ch26 v39; Hebrews ch10 v7). Let's pray with David: *'Teach me to do your will'* (Psalm 143 v10) and align our light with God's light.

MARCH 19
EXODUS ch8 vv1-32

GOD'S CREEPY-CRAWLY AGENTS

Imagine the impact felt upon England and the South East in particular if 215 miles of the River Thames, with its 5,000 square miles of river basin, turned into blood! How would MPs and the lords react to the vast volume of blood flowing past their beloved Houses of Parliament? All the fish and wildlife would die. Drinking water would be an instant problem. Laundry and washing would cease. Contamination, pollution, and disease would be an immediate risk, and the stench would be unbearable. So now imagine the scene in Egypt with its 200,000 square miles of Nile basin swamped in blood! And all of this because Pharaoh refused to let God's people leave the country. This was the first of ten awesome plagues that the Lord would inflict upon Egypt until Pharaoh gave the Israelites an 'exit visa'.

Plague No 2

Frogs everywhere! They hopped into Pharaoh's palace, into his bedroom, and onto his bed. They got into kitchens, and there were so many that they hopped into the mixing bowls and ovens (v3). Pharaoh's 'magic men', not to be outdone, added to the infestation (v7). When Pharaoh temporarily relented and asked for the frogs to be removed, they didn't just hop away into the distance. They all died! There were piles of stinking frogs everywhere (v14).

Plague No3+

When Pharaoh went back on his word, Egypt's dust turned into gnats (v17). When the 'magic men' tried to copy this phenomenon, they failed (v18) and were forced to admit that it was the work of Yahweh, the Lord God (v19).

Plague No4

This fog of flies was the 'mother of all infestations' (v24). It affected all the land of Egypt, except Goshen, where the Israelites lived (v22). These creatures, like horse flies, bit the Egyptians and their livestock (Psalm 78 v45). The Lord uses the same verb twice in v20, viz *Let loose my people or I will let loose swarms of flies*. These creepy-crawly agents were sent so that people would come to know the one, true, and living God. What can we learn from this?

1 KNOW THE UNIQUENESS OF THE LORD

(vv9-10) Moses was courteous to Pharaoh and gave him the option of when he wanted the frogs removed. Pharaoh could choose the day of God's demonstration of power to end the plague *'so that you may know there is no one like the Lord our God'* (v10). Egypt may have been full of false deities, but Pharaoh had to learn that the Lord is unique. He is unique in his independence, his unrivalled wisdom, his unimaginable power, his incomparable holiness, his unerring justice, his infinite grace, and his uncompromising truth. *'O the depths of the riches of the wisdom and knowledge of God!'* (Romans ch11 vv33-36). It's therefore not surprising that God can answer the most demanding or the most outrageous of our prayers. The surprising thing is that God condescends to answer at all. In the middle of his frog-infested home, Pharaoh cries in desperation, *'Pray to the Lord to take the frogs away...'* (v18). He had finally been forced to acknowledge that the Lord could do what none of his Egyptians could do. So why are we so reluctant to pray?

2 KNOW THE FINGER OF THE LORD

Pharaoh's 'magic men', including Jannes and Jambres (2 Timothy ch3 v8), were compelled to acknowledge God's power (v19). God would write his law in stone by his finger (ch31 v18), and he is said to have formed the heavens by his *'fingers'* (Psalm 8 v3). Demons are driven out by his finger (Luke ch11 v20). Such is his immense and incalculable power that he can perform feats of breathtaking wonder with just a word; just a thought; just a finger. It's that power that we must know in our lives: to save us (Romans ch1 v16), to transform us, and to preserve us. We need to pray for the power that will change us, move us, and energise us so that, as a church, we may be a living, active, dynamic organism within our community (Ephesians ch3 vv16-17).

3 KNOW THE PRESENCE OF THE LORD

God promised that they would know that he is in this land (v22). Not only would the Israelites know that God was with them (evidenced by their fly-free zone), but also all the Egyptians would know God's presence with his people. There was no getting away from the facts. Here was the great land of Egypt (386,000 square miles of it), blackened completely with flies (v24). But there was the region of Goshen (just 900 square miles) completely fly-free. Not a buzzing bluebottle anywhere! It was as if an invisible cordon had been placed around the Israelites so that not a single fly had permission to enter Goshen airspace. Now, if that didn't alert the Egyptians to the power of an awesome God, then what would? Yahweh is demonstrating that he is 'present to act' for his people. He wasn't like one of the pathetic, impotent Egyptian deities. In answer to prayer, every last fly was removed (v31). Let's not doubt the power of God or the effectiveness of prayer.

MARCH 20
EXODUS ch9.1-35

ACTING WITH DISTINCTION

Pharaoh was in a 'head-to-head' with God. The most powerful ruler on earth stood opposed to the all-powerful Lord of heaven and earth: the Egyptian king versus the King of Kings. It was a 'no-brainer'! Pharaoh was going to lose! The only question was: 'By how much?' Pharaoh's obsession with holding on to the Israelites had become psycho-spiritual. His hard heart was becoming harder as he resisted God's word. The same happens today when the good news about Jesus is preached. Some resist the gospel invitation, refusing to respond. Gradually, the hardening of the heart takes place so that it becomes possible to hear God's word, but, like Pharaoh, it may no longer have any influence. What a dreadful state, to have resisted God's word so much and so often that the heart becomes calloused, stubborn, and unyielding. As the gospel is preached, it's possible for two people sitting side by side to react differently. One person's heart becomes softened and responsive, while the other person's heart may become more resistant to that word. Pharaoh was becoming further entrenched in his obstinacy.

Plague No. 5: All the Egyptian livestock was struck by a fatal disease.

Plague No. 6: Festering boils and painful abscesses covered the Egyptians from head to toe.

Plague No. 7: A violent hailstorm (v18) stripped trees, flattened crops, and killed men and livestock who had stayed out in the fields (v25). But the moment the hailstorm stopped, Pharaoh's heart became harder (v34). Pharaoh wouldn't budge. He wouldn't give in – yet!

It's clear that God was acting differently towards the Egyptians and the Israelites. He had made a distinction with the plague of flies (ch8 vv22-23) and now with the livestock (vv6-7). The boils only seemed to affect the Egyptians (v11), and the hailstorm didn't affect Goshen (v26). The plague of locusts only affected the Egyptians (ch10 v6), and the plague of darkness descended on the Egyptians while the Israelites had light (ch10 v23). There would be wailing across Egypt as each firstborn son died, but *'Among the Israelites not a dog will bark at any man or animal. Then you will know that the Lord makes a distinction between Egypt and Israel'* (ch11 v7).

We are assured that the gospel makes no distinctions. *'Everyone who calls on the name of the Lord will be saved'* (Romans ch10 v13). The gospel has the power to save anyone and everyone who believes (Romans ch1 v16). But God does act with distinction:

1 GOD DISTINGUISHES ACCORDING TO HIS SOVEREIGNTY

Romans ch9 vv17-21 is a commentary on God's dealings with Pharaoh. God makes choices according to his sovereign wisdom and will. Nobody is chosen because they are good, generous, or religious. Our sin disqualifies every one of us. God's choosing is to do with his mercy and grace. No one seeks after God (Romans ch3 v11) without God seeking them first.

2 GOD DISTINGUISHES ACCORDING TO OUR LOYALTY

Throughout the Bible, God rewards those who are loyal and faithful to him (Psalm 37 v28; 97 v10; Revelation ch2 v10). Even v19 demonstrates that those who listened and took God's word seriously escaped death in the hailstorm. Those *'who feared the word of the Lord'* lived (v20).

3 GOD DISTINGUISHES ACCORDING TO OUR GENEROSITY

Jesus underlined this truth (Matthew ch6 v4; Luke ch6 v38). God sees the generosity of those who give freely to him: to his people and his work. Jesus saw the woman place her gift in one of the thirteen trumpet-like collection boxes at the temple treasury (Luke ch21 v2). It may have only been *'two very small copper coins',* but Jesus knew that it represented a huge percentage of her finances. He made the distinction between those who give out of their wealth and those who give sacrificially out of their poverty. God loves those who give cheerfully (2 Corinthians ch9 v7).

4 GOD DISTINGUISHES ACCORDING TO OUR HUMILITY

We have already noticed Pharaoh's pride contrasted with Moses' humility. The Lord gives grace to the humble (Proverbs ch3 v34). If you want more grace, then you must pray for more humility. God deals specifically with the humble: he saves them (Psalm 18 v27); he guides them (Psalm 25 v9), and he crowns them (Psalm 149 v4). We are promised that if we humble ourselves under God's hand, then he will lift us up in his time (1 Peter ch5 v6).

The family of God comprises folk from all over the world without discrimination or distinction. Peter addressed a meeting of apostles and elders over the question of 'equal rights' for Christian Jews and Gentiles. He said, (Acts ch15 vv9, 11) *'(God) made no distinction between us and them, for he purified their hearts by faith...We believe it is through the grace of our Lord Jesus that we are saved, just as they are'.*

MARCH 21
EXODUS ch10 .1-29

HOW LONG?

Plague No. 8: The media has regularly carried reports of crops being eaten by huge swarms of locusts, plunging poorer countries into famine. But even these destructive swarms don't compare with the mega-swarm that descended on Egypt (vv5-6). It was unlike anything before or since (v14). The Lord did this in response to Pharaoh's unyielding heart.

Plague No. 9: An unnatural, supernatural darkness enveloped the whole land of Egypt for three days. The Egyptians were completely imprisoned in their own homes. The only exception to this divinely sent phenomenon was in the region of Goshen, where the Israelites lived.

The king of Egypt, or any other power-hungry ruler, can strut the world stage at various times and in different forms, but the very breath they breathe is in the omnipotent hand of God. Believers around the world are experiencing all kinds of life-changing, even life-ending, situations. But their God omnipotent reigns! He holds in his hand their sighs, their tears, their life-blood, and their very breath. You may be suffering particular struggles, heartfelt agonies, and life-changing crises at the moment, but if your trust is in God, he never fails. Our God is a God of order and structure. We may take time for granted, but time is God's creation. *There is a time for everything, and a season for every activity under heaven'* (Ecclesiastes ch3 v1). God, the Lord, directed the precise timing of these devastating plagues, and there are two questions in this chapter that were asked of Pharaoh and which should have alerted him to the fact that he was subject to God's timing:

1 HOW LONG WILL YOU REFUSE TO HUMBLE YOURSELF

BEFORE ME? (v3)

Even Pharaoh, his family, his palace, and his officials had not escaped the plagues. Pharaoh's words of confession (ch9 v27) were just empty words. God patiently waited for Pharaoh's genuine humility and repentance, asking *'How long...?'* His act of contrition had just been an act. His show of softening had only been a show. Deep down, Pharaoh's heart remained hard.

Time to Give In

The opportunity to surrender before God had not been taken. God requires us to humble ourselves before him (1 Peter ch5 vv5-6). Like Pharaoh, we may be on a collision course with God. We may remain proud, and *'God opposes the proud'*. We are often too stubborn to give in to God and to confess our sin and to repent of our transgressions. We may have a lot going on in our lives: a lot to live for and many issues and concerns that take priority over the things of God.

Time to Decide

It seemed that, after each of the plagues, Pharaoh had made his mind up to obey the Lord. But as soon as each plague had been removed, he retracted his decision. How often do people make vows and promises when they are in deep trouble, but when the trouble passes, they revert to their old ways? *'Be not deceived. God cannot be mocked. A man reaps what he sows'* (Galatians ch6 v7).

Time to Die

We don't like to be reminded of the inevitable. Ecclesiastes ch3 v2 speaks of *'a time to be born and a time to die'*. It was Pharaoh who broached the subject anyway (v28)! Pharaoh may have thought that he had power over whether Moses should live or die, but Pharaoh was not the keyholder of death. Jesus is! (Revelation ch1 v18). The Lord of life is also the Lord over death. Jesus has been to the cross and has died in the place of sinners to set them free from the condemnation of their sins and the judgement of hell.

2 HOW LONG WILL THIS MAN BE A SNARE TO US (v7)

This was the question that Pharaoh's officials bravely asked their king. It was:

Time to Recognise God's Power

Pharaoh and the Egyptians were not in a confrontation with one of their petty pagan deities. They had clashed with the omnipotence of Almighty God, the Creator of the universe, and the One who held their breath in his hand. God will never be deflected by inferior powers or idle threats, even though the nations may conspire against him (Psalm 2). Various men and women of faith have been perceived to be a *'snare'* by the ungodly, and they have tried to stifle them by imprisonment or silence them by execution. This is the question that is asked in as many words by prosecutors and government officials who have opposed the clear Christian testimonies of believers who have remained firm in their allegiance to Biblical precepts and Godly principles. But a day will come when every knee will bow before King Jesus and every tongue will confess his name.

Time to Go

Even the Egyptians could see that it was time for the Israelites to 'go'. But notice Moses' priority. It wasn't that they should go on a pilgrimage, or go on a holiday, or go and make money. They wanted to go and worship. Let us be ready to go, pray, worship, and serve.

MARCH 22
EXODUS ch11.1-10

HIGHLY REGARDED

Egypt must have been in a mess. Even the king's officials declared that it had been *'ruined'* (ch10 v7). Nine calamities had already 'exploded' upon Egypt in just a few weeks. Any single one of these plagues would have brought havoc of cataclysmic proportions upon the country. But to suffer nine in succession would have spelt utter doom and destruction. But there was worse to come! There was still a tenth plague which the Lord would send upon Egypt, and, again, a distinction would be made between the people of Egypt and the people of Israel.

Plague No 10

Every firstborn Egyptian son would die, along with the firstborn of all the Egyptian cattle (that had managed to survive plagues five and seven). This ultimate plague had been threatened as far back as ch4 v23. Pharaoh had been given notice, but even this wasn't enough to shock his stubborn, evil heart into submission before God. But as Pharaoh had become increasingly entrenched in his opposition to God, Moses' character was developing in godliness. In fact, *'Moses himself was highly regarded in Egypt by Pharaoh's officials and by the people'* (v3). This lofty esteem for Moses resulted in the Egyptians being *'favourably disposed'* towards their Hebrew slaves. What can we learn from Moses' developing character as he spent time with God and learned how to conduct himself as God's servant and God's mouthpiece? Here are seven characteristics:

1 DIGNITY

In all Moses' conversations with the king and his officials, Moses maintained a dignified approach. Just because Pharaoh was truculent, abusive, and threatening, it didn't mean that God's servant could act in the same way. This is an important lesson for believers to learn. In all their conversations, negotiations, and debates with unbelievers, they must not ape their attitudes or mirror their emotions. Like Moses, we may suffer deep provocation at times, but we must ask for the Lord's grace for each of those situations. We may face various attacks, abuse, criticism, and lies, but we should never stoop to losing our patience, or our dignity, let alone our temper!

2 CONSISTENCY

The snapshot we have of Moses' life and testimony, especially in his audiences with Pharaoh, is in marked contrast to the conduct and attitude of the king. Pharaoh was inconsistent. One minute, he was all for releasing the Israelites; the next minute, he had refused permission. One minute he was admitting his own sinfulness and asking for forgiveness (ch10 vv16-17), and the next minute he was ordering Moses out of his sight and threatening him with death (ch10 vv28-29). Pharaoh was unpredictable, inconsistent, and unreliable. Believers must be consistent and reliable. What message does it send to unbelievers if we pick and choose the sections of God's word that we are going to obey? We can't make up our own standards and be selective about God's standards.

3 FAITHFULNESS

Moses was learning to be loyal to God, and his faithfulness was going to be seriously tested over the next forty years. But the New Testament records his triumph in faithfulness (Hebrews ch11 vv24-28). Moses pleased God by his faithfulness (Hebrews ch11 v6). Exercising faith and being faithful go hand in hand.

4 AUTHORITY

If Moses spoke with power and authority, it wasn't because of any personal charisma or dynamism but rather because he spoke the words of God. This should confirm to us that, although we may be weak and timid, when we use the word of God, there is an authority that is conferred upon us. As we read, learn, preach, and quote the Bible, the Spirit wields his *'sword'* (Ephesians ch6 v17).

5 COURAGE

Whatever we may have thought about Moses' earlier hesitancy and reservations, he repeatedly marches into Pharaoh's palace to confront him with the word of God. The word 'courage' is derived from the Latin term meaning 'heart'. When a person's heart is right before God, he imbues them with courage to stand out and to stand up for him.

6 ANGER

After Pharaoh's persistent intransigence and the looming judgement upon all Egypt's firstborn, Moses was overwhelmed with a righteous anger (v8). This wasn't a temper-tantrum, nor was it the anger of sin, but it was the anger at sin's consequences. There is something seriously wrong when we are no longer affected by evil and the sinfulness of human hearts, including our own.

7 HUMILITY

In humility, Moses disassociated himself from royalty and all the attendant privileges (Hebrews ch11 v24), putting Jesus first (Hebrews ch11 v26). Even Moses' enemies respected him for his characteristics.

MARCH 23
EXODUS ch12.1-30

GETTING IT RIGHT

This would be a momentous turning point for the Israelites, who had been 430 years living in Egypt. They would be suddenly and spectacularly freed from their slavery. They could never have imagined the scale and the success of their rescue. In fact, it was to be so significant that God changed their calendar to make this date the beginning of their New Year. It was one way in which the Israelites couldn't forget the magnitude of their deliverance. The double feast of Passover and Unleavened Bread would be celebrated during the first month of their New Year. The divine act of the Passover represented a fundamental Biblical teaching, which is often ignored or misunderstood today. We know from v12 that the Lord entered Egypt that night to bring judgement. Every firstborn in every house would die. The only way that God's judgement could be deflected was if you were sheltering in a house that was covered by the blood of the lamb. Because a sacrifice had been made, and faith was being applied (if you were sheltering in a house smeared with the lamb's blood), then the judgement would have been averted. This is what is known as 'propitiation'. An atoning sacrifice had been offered and accepted. The New Testament confirms that God sent his Son to be the propitiation/atoning sacrifice (1 John ch4 v10). Everyone who is sheltering in Jesus by faith, through repenting of their sin, can be assured that God's righteous judgement has been deflected. God's anger and judgement have 'passed over'. God can never 'pass over' sin, as in turning a blind eye to it. He can only pass over because a sacrifice has been offered and a penalty paid. Everything had to be in place. Everything had to be right for the Passover to be effective:

1 THE RIGHT SELECTION OF THE LAMB

The Israelites couldn't use any lamb for sacrifice. It couldn't be sick or unhealthy. It couldn't be undernourished or unusually skinny. Neither could it be an injured lamb or a maimed lamb (v5). The lamb could be from the sheep or goats, but it had to be male, one year old, and without defect. This sacrifice of the lamb clearly points to the future and the provision of God's Lamb, meeting the stringent criteria (1 Peter ch1 vv18-20). There was only one Lamb which ticked all the boxes; only one Lamb which could be the propitiation and the atoning sacrifice for our sins.

2 THE RIGHT PREPARATION FOR THE DEPARTURE

The food to be eaten at the Passover, along with the lamb, was very symbolic (v8):

Bitter herbs

Herbs such as endive, wild lettuce, and chicory were included in the meal to remind them of the bitterness of their slavery in Egypt and of what they had been rescued from.

Yeast-less bread (unleavened bread)

(vv15-20) Yeast was a symbol of sin. A little yeast would affect the whole batch of dough (1 Corinthians ch5 vv6-8). So the Israelites performed the ritual of cleaning their houses from top to bottom, removing the yeast, so that they were ready for departure. The people had to be ready to leave at a moment's notice (v11). God wants holy and disciplined lives that are yielded to him. Our hearts should be swept clean of sin's yeast so that we are ready to go for God. Are there crumbs of yeast lying around in our lives that contaminate our usefulness for God? Maybe it's the yeast of selfish motives or a critical spirit, bitterness, moodiness, deviousness, or insincerity?

3 THE RIGHT APPLICATION OF THE BLOOD

Precise instructions were given as to what should be done with the lambs and kids (vv6-7; vv22-23). The blood of the lamb could only save those who actually applied the blood personally. Personal faith and obedience were vital. Jesus is the perfect Lamb and his blood is thoroughly effective and efficacious (Ephesians ch1 v7; Colossians ch1 v20; 1 John ch1 v7; Revelation ch5 v9). Jesus' death is sufficient for all, but it is only efficient for some – for those who take the hyssop branch of faith and apply it to the door frames of their hearts. But we can never boast in our choice of a 'hyssop branch', or our dexterity in applying the blood. It is by grace that we are saved through faith, *'and this not of yourselves, it is the gift of God'* (Ephesians ch2 vv8-9).

4 THE RIGHT COMMEMORATION OF THE DELIVERANCE

God introduced the Feast of Passover so that the Israelites would never forget how the Lord had passed over them in judgement and had rescued them from Egypt. At midnight, on that first Passover, a terrible wailing could be heard right across the country, from palace to prison (v29) as the firstborn died (v30). But Jesus introduced a simple feast to commemorate our deliverance through his own death (1 Corinthians ch11 vv24-25). The Breaking of Bread/Communion/Lord's Supper is our opportunity to express gratitude for God's wonderful Lamb and the forgiveness which he brings.

MARCH 24
EXODUS ch12.31-13.22

THE TABLES TURNED

The Israelites were about to leave Egypt. After severe trials and hardships as Pharaoh's slaves, and after witnessing ten catastrophic, divinely sent plagues, it is 430 years *'to the very day'* (v41) that they exited Egypt. We may note five things in these verses that happened to God's people:

1 RESCUED BY THE LORD

Pharaoh may have done his worst, but he was just a puny pawn in the plan of God. The execution and timing of God's rescue plan were perfect. He would save a precise number, on a precise day, using a precise method. The tables had turned completely. It was now Pharaoh, his officials, and all the Egyptians who were desperately urging Moses and the Israelites to leave their country. Pharaoh even had the audacity to ask for a blessing (v32)! It is very difficult to imagine the enormous scale of this rescue. Here were 603,550 men alone (ch38 v26), rounded down to *'about 600,000 men'* (here in v37). Adding in the women and children, we can realistically estimate the number to be between two and three million Israelites. There were also other non-Israelis with them (v38). This is equivalent to mobilising the whole population of Cornwall, Devon, and Dorset to leave the South West overnight and cross over the Bristol Channel into Wales! Imagine the leadership and the logistics involved to make a coordinated exodus, taking livestock and food with them. But it was the Lord who rescued them. God is never responsible for a half-hearted or partial rescue. He is thorough, comprehensive, and complete. The Divine Watchkeeper kept vigil on the night that they left Egypt (v42). God watches for us, and we must watch for him (Mark ch13 vv35, 37).

2 REGULATED BY THE LAW

(v43) The Passover was not just a party. It was a commemoration, a memorial feast, and therefore, there were strict rules to be observed. But just because it was tightly regulated, it didn't mean that there couldn't be great excitement and joy. Some people identify regulation with oppression, but God's laws provide protection and freedom.

3 REMINDED BY THE LIPS

(ch13 vv1-10) The two key commands in these verses are 'Consecrate' (v1) and 'Commemorate' (v3).

It was vitally important that the New Year's feasts would be perpetual reminders of the dramatic deliverance (v9). The forehead represented their thinking. The hand represented their offering. Their lips represented their speaking. The thinking and offering would naturally lead to speaking about the law of the Lord. Orthodox Jews have used leather pouches strapped to their foreheads and left arms to contain portions of Scripture. They have interpreted v9 literally. Jesus condemned their show (Matthew ch23 v3). We, too, can make a show of being a Christian without God's word on our lips and in our hearts. Our church attendance, Bible-carrying, stickers in our houses and on our cars will all be hollow practices unless we live faithful and sacrificial lives that are devoted to God's law.

4 REDEEMED BY THE LAMB

Firstborn males of the livestock were to be sacrificed to the Lord. The one exception was for donkeys, which were extremely important for transportation. The Israelites could avoid breaking the donkey's neck by redeeming it with a lamb (v13). A sacrifice could be offered on its behalf. A substitute would be provided. A price had to be paid. Here is yet another clear signpost pointing to the coming of Jesus, God's Messiah – *'the lamb without blemish or defect'* (1 Peter ch1 v19). Jesus is the Lamb-Substitute. We have redemption through his blood (Ephesians ch1 vv7-8). According to Titus ch2 vv13-14, two of the purposes of our redemption are (1) to make us good and (2) to make us eager to do what is good. It's one thing knowing what is good; it's another thing to be eager to do what is good. We should not be passive or indifferent about 'doing good'. While we know what will be helpful, supportive, encouraging, load-sharing, and load-bearing, we may not always be inclined, let alone *eagerly* inclined, to be proactive in doing good. We must not forget to do good (Hebrews ch13 v16) because failing to do it is sin (James ch4 v17).

5 ROUTED BY THE LIGHT

God was the Route-Planner for the Israelites. He knew that the shortest route to Canaan (northeast through Philistia) would not be the best route. We may think that the shortest route for us in life is the best route, but our gracious and faithful Route-Planner may take us on a circuitous route, avoiding hazards and dangers of which we know nothing. He knows our frailties and our strengths. He forges ahead with the cloudy and fiery pillar of his presence to lead us (Psalm 23 vv2-3). His presence is continual, consistent, and constant. Why would we seek another guide or leader when we have Jesus?

MARCH 25
EXODUS ch14.1-31

THE LORD'S GREAT POWER

The whole company of Israelites had travelled south east from Goshen, towards the Red Sea, following the divine pillars of cloud and fire. But the Lord told Moses to *'turn back'* (v2) and take a route north, camping between *'Migdol and the sea'*. Do you ever question what God is doing in your life when sometimes it seems that you are going backwards rather than forwards? Even if you don't actually think that God got it wrong, you may question whether you have misunderstood his leading or misread his directions. Pharaoh thought that the Israelites were trapped when, in fact, he himself was trapped. Both the Israelites and the Egyptians were to witness the might and majesty of the one true God (v31).

1 THE LORD'S GREAT POWER TO DEFEND

The Israelites were under the Lord's watchful eye (ch12 v42). But he not only watched for Israel: he fought for Israel (vv13-14). Is there any greater encouragement for us when we are facing the worst of adversaries: *The Lord will fight for you*? God jealously defends his people. Even when the Israelites appeared trapped between the charging Egyptians and the Red Sea, God's defence never faltered (vv19-20). *We rest on thee: our Shield and our Defender. We go not forth alone against the foe'* [Edith Cherry]. If you are trusting in Jesus to save and to keep you; if you are secure in the certainty of his salvation, because you have been redeemed by his blood and forgiven by his grace, then you can be sure that you won't be *'alone against the foe'* – whoever or whatever that foe may be.

2 THE LORD'S GREAT POWER TO DEFEAT

There may have been a lot of sabre-rattling by Pharaoh and his army, but they were all destined for defeat and the complete annihilation of their forces. The king's mind was so overwhelmed with evil that it seemed he had forgotten the ten catastrophic plagues which had shaken his country. He personally took charge of his army (v6) and the sight of his war machine, bearing down on the Israelites, terrified them. So much so that they turned on Moses with cutting sarcasm (vv11-12). These were fickle people, influenced by God's power one moment and terrified by Pharaoh's power the next. Yet we may also be intimidated by the powers of this world and those who threaten God's work, God's word, and God's people. But God's almighty power can paralyse all opposition. *'If God is for us, who can be against us?'* (Romans ch8 v31). Trapped between the Egyptians and the Red Sea, the Israelites had once again calculated without God. They were told to *'stand firm'* in their hearts (v13) but to *'move'* forward on their feet (v15). What an overwhelming defeat (v13). The Israelites would never see the Egyptian threat again. They would only see their bodies *'dead on the shore'* after the Red Sea closed over them. We can also be assured of Jesus' power to defeat sin (Colossians ch2 v15), Satan (Hebrews ch2 vv14-15), death (2 Timothy ch1 v10), and hell. The Lamb wins! Jesus is forever the Lamb upon his throne. He never has to retreat, and he never suffers defeat. *This is the victory that overcomes the world, even our faith'* (1 John ch5 vv4-5). It's faith that spells victory. But it's not just 'faith'. Faith is nothing without the object of that faith. Personal faith in Jesus ensures that his victory over sin, death, and hell also becomes our victory. See how Moses triumphantly stretches out his hand over the sea in response to the Lord's command (v21). God continues to open a way for his people through the middle of impossible obstacles.

3 THE LORD'S GREAT POWER TO DELIVER

(v22) Crossing on the dry sea bed at a rate of 200,000 persons per hour, and allowing for livestock, possessions, and treasures, the pathway would need to be about half a mile wide. This was a mammoth mobilisation of people, and their deliverance was so complete that they didn't even get their feet wet! (v29). Even the doubting Israelites who had once wished that they could have remained as slaves (v12) witnessed their own *'deliverance'* (v13). The floating corpses of their enemies on the shoreline reinforced the scale of their rescue (v30). God's justice is unerring. Those who had drowned the newborn Hebrew babies in the River Nile were themselves drowned in the Red Sea. The greatest deliverance of all was made by Jesus, who came to save sinners (1 Timothy ch1 v15). Jesus saves completely (Hebrews ch7 v25). How did the Israelites respond to their deliverance? With fear and faith (v31). With renewed respect and reverence, they saw God glorified (v4), and they put their trust in him. God's power is not diminished. Whether it's the Red Sea, the Yellow River, or the 'black abyss', which is facing you and which you need to cross, you can trust in the Lord's great power. The requirements are still the same: fear and faith.

MARCH 26
EXODUS ch15.1-27

THE SONG OF THE SEA

The 2015 Eurovision Song Contest was won for the sixth time by Sweden with a song called 'Heroes'. It seems that the author of that song had written about those who stood up for him when he had been bullied as a child in school. Moses wrote and sang a song about the God who stood up for his people when they were bullied and threatened by the Egyptians. This song, composed and sung on the eastern shore of the Red Sea, may be described as a:

1 PRAISE SONG

(vv1-2) Moses may not have been such a prolific hymnwriter as King David, Charles Wesley, or Isaac Watts, but he has written three hymns which are recorded for us, viz Deuteronomy ch31 v22; Psalm 90, and here in Exodus ch 15. The song is a hymn of praise to Yahweh, whose name is mentioned ten times. Moses begins with a personal confession, which is then accompanied by all the Israelites. Moses testifies that the Lord is *'my strength', 'my song', 'my God',* and *'my father's God'.* We don't know how two million Israelites learned the words or the music, but, as they joined in the chorus, the singers would be personalising what they were singing. It prompts the question as to whether we are singing the truth when we adopt the lyrics of our hymns and we sing about 'my God', 'my Lord', 'my Saviour', and 'my Friend'. While we may sing with gusto and a good feeling, we should quiz ourselves as to whether we are singing the truth about our personal experience. We may sing heartily, but do we sing truthfully? We may tell the Lord in our songs that we are happy when really we are sad. We may tell the Lord that we are strong and bold when, in fact, we are weak and fearful. There is also a danger of singing and talking about 'praise' and 'worship' but never actually praising or worshipping. To praise anyone, we shall need to know that person, and to praise God with depth and richness, we shall need to know him.

2 VICTORY SONG

In vv3-12 Moses praises the scale of the Lord's victory. All Pharaoh's gigantic war machine had been annihilated. Six hundred prized chariots were no more. Egypt's top army officers had been wiped out in one stroke, and thousands of Egyptian soldiers had drowned. In their arrogance, the Egyptians had boasted about how they would pursue the Israelites and destroy them (v9). But God had other plans. He had a victory plan. The Bible reveals the Lord variously as a Shepherd or as a Potter, but here we see him as a *'warrior'* (v3), defending and fighting for his people. The Lord's victory at the Red Sea would be forever remembered at the Passover. God's *'right hand'* of omnipotence (v6) *'shattered the enemy'.* Jesus has triumphed through his finished work on the cross. We can look to the cross and say, in the words of v11, *Who among the gods is like you, O Lord? Who is like you – majestic in holiness, awesome in glory, working wonders?'*

3 LOVE SONG

(vv13-18) Moses is smitten with love: with the Lord's *'unfailing love'* (v13). What other reason can we give for why a righteous and holy God should redeem complaining, obstinate, arrogant, disobedient, and faithless sinners, other than his immeasurable and unfailing love? If human love in all its shades and dimensions is the perpetual theme of popular music, then should not the Lord's unfailing love be the perpetual theme of the Christians' songs? We might be more sophisticated, more knowledgeable, and more affluent than the Israelites of Moses' day, but we're certainly no better! We deserve God's judgement and punishment. We deserve hell in all its unimaginable intensity and everlastingness. We have no good qualities to plead (Romans ch3 vv10, 23). This situation would be desperately hopeless and irreversible, except for God's *'unfailing love'* (Psalm 32 v10; Romans ch5 v8). This is the love which unites a holy God and unholy sinners. It's the love that intervened at the cross. It's thoroughly dependable because it never fails.

4 POP SONG

(vv19-21) The song of Moses was most definitely a 'popular' song with all the Israelite women. They sang, they danced, and they played tambourines. Moses was the first 'pop singer', perhaps! His big sister, Miriam, who had kept watch from a distance when her baby brother had been hidden in his 'Moses basket' on the Nile, now leads the women in a chorus (v21). Together, they could praise God's greatness and celebrate his mighty victory. But triumph and testing go hand in hand. God's test is about trust (v25). How quickly rejoicing can turn into grumbling! They had only just complained about too much water at the Red Sea; now they were complaining about not enough water! The God who saves us can keep us and provide for us. But we must *'listen carefully'* and *'do what is right'* so that we shall know God's joy and not God's judgement.

MARCH 27
EXODUS ch16.1-36

THE TRUST TEST

One clergyman, in talking about the body of Christ, likened some people to the appendix: 'We didn't notice they were there until they started grumbling!' The Israelites were the archetypal grumblers (ch14 vv11-12; ch15 v24; ch16 vv1-3; ch17 v3). It seemed that they grumbled about everything. The eternal Provider of infinite resources was personally identified with them, and yet they still grumbled! The Lord's visible presence in cloud and fire was with them day and night, but they still grumbled! Only a month earlier, the Lord had unlocked the mighty Red Sea to provide them with an evacuation route out of Egypt, but they still grumbled! Did they think that God had supernaturally delivered them from the Egyptians only to let two to three million of them starve to death in the desert? Yes! Obviously, they did think that! (v3). Sometimes our thinking is equally perverse and confused. We grumble about our situations and circumstances, forgetting that a sovereign God has his plans, even in adversity. While we pray to the Lord, asking for things which he is happy to give to us, we grumble about the way, the method, and the timing of those gifts. Our response should be grace, not grumbling; faith, not fretting.

We may not always like the idea of being tested, and yet our whole lives are structured around tests. Certain common elements may appear in such tests:

1 INSTRUCTIONS TO FOLLOW

God said: *'I will test them and see whether they will follow my instructions'* (v4). How many times have candidates failed tests because they didn't follow the instructions? The Israelites were hungry, and their loving God would not allow them to starve in the desert despite what they may have thought (v3). He graciously provided special *'bread from heaven'* (v4), but the moaning migrants were tested as to whether they could follow the Lord's specific instructions. First, they had to *'come before the Lord'* (v9). Second, they had to look out across the desert and be reminded of God's presence with them (v10). Third, they had to gather quail, which arrived in the evening (v13), and the flaky, bread-like food in the morning (v14). Three instructions: Go; Gaze; Gather. Go to the Lord. Gaze on his glory and be reminded of what he can do. Then gather because there's work to do. God could have put meat straight into their larders or onto their dinner tables, but he taught them, and he teaches us, to follow instructions. We have God's complete instruction manual in his word. We are given special instructions for home and family, business and employment, rule and government, law and order, health and education, church and worship. What disasters come upon those who dispense with God's instruction manual?

2 FACTS TO REMEMBER

It was a fact that they had to gather meat and bread each day. They had to perform this daily routine so that they would remember this fact above all facts (v12): *'...you will know that I am the Lord your God'*. Yahweh has unlimited powers and immeasurable resources. The people asked, *'Can God spread a table in the desert?'* (Psalm 78 v19). Yes, he can! Every morning, he spread a table of sweet bread for the Israelites, which equated to about four thousand tons of food every day for forty years!

How big is *your* God? We must remember the fact that God can meet all our needs through his invested riches in Jesus (Philippians ch4 v19).

3 TIMESCALES TO KEEP

There aren't many tests that you can take any time that you like and take as long as you like. The 'trust test' had particular timings. They had to gather food every morning and every evening. The only exception was the sixth day, when they had to gather twice the amount so that they didn't need to gather on the seventh day, the Sabbath. If they had forgotten to prepare for the Sabbath, then they wouldn't find any food, and they would have to go hungry that day. The seventh day was God's special rest day. It was an arrangement that God made at the beginning of time for the physical, mental, and spiritual well-being of humanity. The Sabbath was God's love-gift to the world. In his generosity, he has provided one day in seven for our benefit. But just like God's gift of his Son, so God's gift of his Sabbath has been spurned, ignored, and abused.

4 STANDARDS TO ACHIEVE

The name for the unusual food was 'manna', that is, *What is it?'* (vv15, 31). God wanted future generations to achieve the highest standards of faithfulness and obedience, and so some manna was sealed in a golden jar (Hebrews ch9 v4) and preserved as a reminder. God is not satisfied with less than holiness. He wants us to achieve and to live by the highest standards, not least for the generations to come. To succeed in this test, we must trust in the Lord.

MARCH 28
EXODUS ch17.1-15

IS THE LORD AMONG US OR NOT?

If in ch16 God had tested the Israelites, here in ch17 the Israelites were unwittingly testing God. They were quarrelling and grumbling again because they had no water. Do we similarly 'test' the Lord when we grumble about circumstances and situations which God has brought us into? Our discontentment and frustrations may be testing God, who has sent them to us for a purpose. In ch14, with the impassable Red Sea stretched out before them, the Israelites had complained about too much water! Now, in chapters 15 and 17, the people complained that there was not enough water! But God was still with his people. His pillars of cloud and fire were constant testimonies that he hadn't deserted his people then, and he won't desert his people today. Notice God's patience and grace in dealing with these testing and trying people. Moses named the place 'Massah' ('testing') and 'Meribah' ('quarrelling') as permanent reminders of the Israelites' sin and folly in asking the question (v7): *'Is the Lord among us or not?'*

The overwhelming evidence of the Lord's presence with his people makes this question so contemptible and ungrateful. But there are five supplementary questions that we could ask ourselves in a self-analysis:

1 IS THE LORD OUR REDEEMER?

For the Israelites, the most significant event that had occurred in the previous two months, and indeed their whole lives, had been their redemption from Egypt by God (ch6 v6; Psalm 78 v35). We may be totally bewildered as to how the Hebrew people could so easily forget their great redemption from the bondage of Egypt. The historical account of the Red Sea redemption signposts an even greater redemption which God performed in Jesus (Colossians ch1 vv13-14). Can you say with Job, *'I know that my Redeemer lives'*? (Job ch19 v25).

2 IS THE LORD OUR PROVIDER?

The Lord patiently provides yet again for these moaning migrants (vv5-7). Every single day, the Lord provided the equivalent of four Olympic-sized swimming pools of water in the middle of a desert! Could the people point to any time that the Lord had not provided for them? No! If God had so miraculously provided for his people at the Red Sea, would he not continue to provide for them in the desert? Moses took his problem to the Lord (v4). Do you have a problem that threatens your mental composure and your spiritual stability? *Is there trouble anywhere? We should never be discouraged - take it to the Lord in prayer.* [Joseph M Scriven]. God provided food and drink for their bodies, and he provided spiritual food and drink for their souls. Paul refers to this divine provision in Jesus (1 Corinthians ch10 vv3-4) *'...that Rock was Christ'.* When the people dared to ask, *'Is the Lord among us or not?'* Christ the Rock was standing with Moses at Horeb (v6).

3 IS THE LORD OUR LEADER?

The Lord dwelt with his people in the most prominent place. His presence was represented by the towering pillars of cloud and fire in front of the people. Everyone could see the colossal columns indicating the Lord's presence, directing and leading them. What position does Jesus take in our lives? The positions that are rightfully his are lordship and leadership.

4 IS THE LORD OUR CONQUEROR?

In vv8-14 we are told about the Amalekites' attack on the Israelites. Joshua and some hand-picked men fought the enemy while Moses stood on top of a nearby hill. Joshua had a sword, and Moses had a staff. While Moses' arms were raised, the Israelites were winning, but when he lowered his arms, the Amalekites prevailed. As Moses' arms grew tired, he sat on a stone with Aaron and Hur on each side of him to prop up his arms. There should have been no doubt that the Lord conquered. Moses was tenacious; he didn't give up even though this octogenarian grew tired. He was humble enough to accept help and support. He didn't muddle on his weakness, shunning assistance. He was certain of victory because he trusted implicitly in the Lord.

5 IS THE LORD OUR BANNER?

(vv15-16) Victors today often run up a flag. They will hoist their colours - an ensign – indicating victory over the territory secured. Moses did a similar thing in building an altar and proclaiming 'The Lord is our Banner': the Lord is our Flag, our Ensign. We rally under his colours and we identify with the One who is *'high and exalted'* (Isaiah ch6 v1). Though at times we may falter and fail, we may become weak and discouraged, and the battle may seem to go against us, we should want to testify that Jesus is our Lord and our Banner. As the flag flutters triumphantly from the masthead, so we proclaim for all to see that our allegiance is to Jesus and to Jesus alone.

MARCH 29
EXODUS ch18.1-27

IN-LAWS NEEDN'T BE OUTLAWS

In this chapter, Moses' father-in-law had a name for excellence. His name means 'excellence'! Jethro's other name – Reuel – means 'friend of God'. That would be a wonderful testimony to have: to be known for excellence and to be known as a friend of God.

When Moses had become a fugitive in his earlier years, fleeing from Pharaoh, he had been welcomed into Jethro's home after he had shown kindness to Jethro's daughters by helping them to fetch water for their flocks. Eventually, Moses married one of those daughters, called Zipporah, with whom he had two sons: Gershom (meaning *'I have become an alien in a foreign land'* v3) and Eliezer (meaning *'My father's God was my helper; he saved me from the sword of Pharaoh'* v4). We learn from v2 that Moses had previously sent Zipporah and his two sons to Jethro's home in Midian. In v6 Jethro brings Moses' wife and family back to meet him.

Contrary to all those mother-in-law and father-in-law jokes, which announce the arrival of in-laws with horror and dismay, Moses warmly welcomes his father-in-law (v7). Moses had his own recipe for defusing any potential conflict with his father-in-law. He didn't talk to him about his wife or about himself. Instead, he told him *'everything the Lord had done...for Israel's sake...how the Lord had saved them'* (v8). Jethro was delighted to hear it (v9). Jethro learned that by following the Lord and by obedience to him, they had avoided destruction. This is the first of three lessons:

1 DEVOTION: THE ANSWER TO WIPEOUT

The Israelites had not been wiped out on the western shores of the Red Sea by Pharaoh's armies because Moses had led the people to trust in the Lord's deliverance. As they devoted themselves to trust in God's word to them (albeit reluctantly at first), they experienced God's supernatural rescue. The Lord had preserved them when they had faced a formidable foe. To the Israelites, trapped between a 'black sea' of soldiers and the Red Sea, it looked as if it was going to be a total wipeout. In fact, according to Moses' song (ch15 v9), Pharaoh had boasted, *'I will pursue them, I will overtake them. I will divide the spoils; I will gorge myself on them. I will draw my sword and my hand will destroy them'*. But Moses had instructed his people (ch14 v13), *'Stand firm and you will see the deliverance the Lord will bring you today'*. Reluctantly and hesitantly, the Israelites trusted in the Lord to deliver them from annihilation. They could so easily have been wiped off the face of the earth at that point, but for God! The Lord intervened to protect his people and to deliver them to safety. When he heard about their divine rescue, Jethro was full of praise (vv10-11). Faith in Jesus will prevent eternal destruction (John ch3 v36). The believer, who is trusting unswervingly in God's Son, is delivered from the power of Satan and the terror of hell itself.

2 DISCERNMENT: THE SOLUTION TO FALLOUT

(vv13-16) You may well imagine that if the Israeli people regularly grumbled against God and their leader Moses, then it was certain that they would quarrel and complain among themselves. There would be disputes happening all the time in a community of over two million people. You can easily imagine the endless questions that Moses had to deal with all day, every day, *'from morning till evening'* (vv13-14). Moses' discernment and wisdom were essential to mend the fallouts, which were the everyday occurrences in the Israelite community. Nothing changes! How many fallouts occur in our churches over songs and hymns, Bible versions, decor, seating, heating, alcoholic wine or non-alcoholic wine, and many other issues which seem to be so fundamentally important to some people? But we need more discernment in seeking God's will and in desiring to live mature Christian lives. Moses' answer to Jethro's question (v15) emphasises that many of our disputes are about 'our will' rather than 'God's will'. We need to be equipped with *'everything good for doing his will'* (Hebrews ch13 v21).

3 DELEGATION: THE ANTIDOTE TO BURNOUT

Moses' father-in-law could see what Moses couldn't see (vv17-19). Jethro's antidote was to delegate all *'the simple cases'* to hand-picked judges who were God-fearing, trustworthy, and conscientious. They formed a system of tiered courts with Moses himself being the final Court of Appeal (v22). Moses listened to this wise advice and recognised this as God's word to him. Sometimes God's will may be made clear to us from the most unexpected places or people. A sign of Moses' greatness was that he was humble enough to listen (v24). Paul wrote (Philippians ch2 vv5, 8) that *'our attitude should be the same as that of Christ Jesus'* who *'humbled himself...'*. His duty to the will of his Father resulted in making himself as nothing so that his Father's plan could be accomplished. God expects every child of his to do his duty, with humility and grace.

MARCH 30
EXODUS ch19.1-25

FIT TO MEET GOD

God lovingly and graciously provided for his people while they were camping in the Sinai Desert:

(v4) The Care Shown

Just as an adult eagle will carry its fledglings on its wings, powerfully supporting them as they flutter and fall from the safety of their eyrie, so the Lord reminds Israel of his strength, protection, and watchfulness.

(v5) The Cost Paid

They are referred to as God's *'treasured possession'*. They are valuable because of the price paid to redeem them (Titus ch2 vv13-14). As Christians, we ought to remember that our 'price tag' is 'the blood of Jesus'.

(v6) The Confirmation Given

Israel was to be special, separate, and distinct. She would be a holy nation among the unholy nations of the world. God continues to call his people to holiness and distinctiveness as his children. What was the people's response, and how should we prepare to meet God?

1 ONWARD AGREEMENT

There was a united response to the Lord's message – v8: *The people all responded together, "We will do everything the Lord has said".'* God had inserted conditions into the guarantee that they would be his *'treasured possession'*. Obedience and compliance were the conditions of this covenant. The 'onward agreement', with which over two million people responded together, would count for nothing unless it was evidenced by obeying God's instructions and complying with his directions. God's message in the gospel to us – the Good News of forgiveness and the rescue from sin and hell through Jesus – demands our response of obedience and compliance, faith and repentance. Access to the kingdom of God is conditional upon new birth (John ch3 vv3, 7).

2 OUTWARD ARRANGEMENT

The Lord announces his intention to come to his people (v9). The Israelites had to prepare themselves for God's arrival. How ready are you to meet God? The people had three days to prepare (v11) by washing their clothes, keeping off the mountain, and abstaining from marital relations. Mount Sinai would be the place of God's holy arrival, and to trespass on the mountain would be a flagrant disregard for God's holiness and would result in death (vv12-13). It would be easy to dismiss such outward arrangements as being part of the Old Covenant with Israel. Christians argue, using the words of 1 Samuel ch16 v7, that *'man looks on the outward appearance, but the Lord looks on the heart'*. But as he looked on the hearts in David's day, so he also looked on the hearts in Moses' day. The Lord *always* looks on the heart. But he also knows that our practical preparations are frequently a sign of our spiritual preparations: that if our preparation for worship is casual, careless, and unpunctual, then this may reflect the state of our hearts. 1 Samuel ch16 v7 is not an excuse to be casual, dilatory, and unprepared. We cannot have a casual attitude to God's holiness. We often think that heaven is the place of wall-to-wall happiness. But we should remember that, first of all, heaven is the place of wall-to-wall holiness.

3 INWARD COMMITMENT

God's holiness demands our holiness. 'To consecrate' (vv10, 14, 22) means 'to make holy'. The people's outward cleansing and purifying had to reflect an inward cleansing and purifying. Clean bodies should reflect clean hearts. Our fitness to meet God includes clean hands and pure hearts (Psalm 24 vv3-5). Right attitudes and right motives will be evidenced by outward actions. Yet it's possible to conform to a ritual, perform a ceremony, and go through the motions without having our hearts fit to meet God. What will we have done today that only a Christian would do? Do we speak out for Biblical truth? Do we swim against the flow in a morally corrupt society? Are we distinctive in a world that tries to make everyone conform to its secular, humanistic, politically correct rules? Do we stand against institutional deceit and injustice? Do we stand up for the dignity of life and the primacy of families? Are we fit to meet God?

4 UPWARD MOVEMENT

Moses was summoned to a summit meeting with God. Violent trembling, fire, and smoke on Sinai announced God's holy presence. The church awaits the arrival of Jesus, the King of kings (1 Thessalonians ch4 v17). Our upward movement in anticipation of his second coming should prompt us to be increasingly ready for that momentous day. We are not called to be 'Sunday Christians', or 'part-time Christians', or 'fair-weather Christians'. We are called to full consecration and commitment, indicated by Israel's profession: *We will do everything the Lord has said'*.

MARCH 31
EXODUS ch20.1-26

THE LAW OF LOVE

What does it take to make people keep to the rules? Some people may argue that if there is sufficient love for other people, then we don't need endless laws. Of all the expressions of human love, there is probably no more pure and beautiful love than that of a parent for a child. Yet when a child's safety is at stake, it seems that a parent's love is not enough. Who would argue that before September 2006, parents loved their children less than since that date? Yet before 2006, many children were seriously hurt each year because they were not secured safely when travelling in a car. The law was introduced to enable parents to demonstrate love for their children by providing more effective safety measures for them. The law insists on the correct restraints for children in cars. Those restraints are applied with law and love.

God provides restraints as a combination of law and love. Here are ten statements to be obeyed. In Hebrew, they are called, literally, 'ten words' from which we get our term 'decalogue'. The fundamental principle on which this law was established was love. God had redeemed his people because he loved them. In turn, the covenant demanded that Israel must love the Lord their God, which is also expressed in their love for one another. Generally, God's law is divided into:

Civil Law - which was to do with Israel functioning as a state, with courts and penalties;

Ceremonial Law - providing regulations for worship and sacrifice under the Old Covenant;

Moral Law - which provides foundational rules for living holy lives.

It is this moral law that transcends time and doesn't change. Jesus taught this moral law in the Gospels (for example, Matthew ch22 vv36-40). Jesus showed that the keeping of the Decalogue is not only everyone's duty and obligation; it is also the expression of the Christian's love for God (John ch14 v15). God's law here in this chapter has never needed to be revised or edited, annulled or amended.

1 EXALTING GOD FIRST

For holy living, God must be first in our lives.

No. 1 God's Uniqueness - this is the principle of monotheism. The Lord God is not just the first among gods, or even the best among gods: he is the only, true and living God (Isaiah ch40 v25).

No. 2 God's Glory - God demands exclusive devotion (Isaiah ch42 v8). He will not share his glory with the trashy trinkets and sham shrines that are manufactured in his name.

No. 3 God's Name - The name of the Lord must always be honoured, revered, respected, and treated as holy, with heartfelt sincerity. We dare not treat his name frivolously or flippantly.

No 4 God's Day- The Sabbath as a day of rest had existed since creation (Genesis ch2 vv2-3). The fourth command reinforces this creation principle. God values both work and rest. 'Sabbath' means 'restfulness'. One day in seven is to be devoted to the Lord for spiritual rest and worship. It's the day of the week designated as 'the Lord's Day' (Acts ch20 v7; 1 Corinthians ch16 v2; Revelation ch1 v10). It's a day that should be different and distinctive for believers. The way in which Christians observe the Lord's Day indicates the seriousness with which they regard God's great Law of Love.

2 HONOURING PARENTS SECOND

No 5 Honouring Parents - 'Honour' means 'to prize highly'; 'to respect intensely'; 'to value exceptionally'; 'to care for devotedly'. While we are commanded to honour our parents, their word and their will can never trump God's word and God's will. Ephesians ch6 vv1-3 repeats this command emphasising that obedience to parents is conditional on obeying the Lord.

3 ESTEEMING OTHERS THIRD

No. 6 No Murdering - Because we're created in God's image, the deliberate killing of a person is violence against God. This also applies to the murder of those who don't want to live (euthanasia), the murder of infants in the womb (abortion), and the murder of oneself (suicide).

No. 7 No Cheating - Marriage and the bond between spouses is another creation principle. 'Troth', used in some marriage ceremonies, refers to faithfulness and is connected to 'truth'.

No. 8 No Stealing - This forbids the seizure of anything to which a person has no right.

No. 9 No Lying - This protects a person's name and reputation. The sins of the tongue (such as slander, flattery, and gossip) are all condemned by this one command.

No. 10 No Coveting - This means 'desiring earnestly' and thus revealing a general dissatisfaction and discontentment. The desire to gain and to acquire is satisfied by godly contentment, which, in itself, is *great gain* (1 Timothy ch6 v6). Love is the method for fulfilling these commands (Romans ch13 vv8-10).

Yet none of this perfect Law can save us. We don't need a lawyer: we need a Saviour. We are already lawbreakers, and we need a Mediator to bring us to God (1 Peter ch3 v18).

APRIL 1
EXODUS ch21.1-36

BE RESPONSIBLE

In the middle of the desert in Kenya, there was a place with a population the size of Manchester, called Dadaab. It's no ordinary city. In 2019, this was one of the largest refugee camps in the world and was home to half a million people. Most came from Somalia to escape the civil war, which began in the early 1990s. But there was structure and organisation in the camp, with the principal concern of getting enough for everyone to eat. Laws and regulations are necessary to avoid chaos, disorder, and anarchy. But if that refugee camp in the Kenyan desert was one of the world's largest, then compare a camp over four times that size in the Sinai Desert. In God's grace, he provided a framework of civil law for his Hebrew people: clear principles upon which we can still build today.

While aspects of family and community life in Sinai were culturally, circumstantially, and technically very different from our own, nevertheless, there are definite areas of responsibility which we must emphasise. It's easy to view these practices, principles, and procedures through the lens of our politically correct democratic society with all its equality and diversity constraints. The majority of people today would think that they could take the moral high ground and look down their noses at what they consider to be a primitive and male-dominated society. But even if our twenty-first-century society is different from this Hebrew society of 1500BC, we cannot claim necessarily to be a better society and nor can we claim to be morally superior. We must not forget that these regulations were for a particular people, in a particular condition, in a particular place, and at a particular time. Nor should we forget that these were God's laws and were imposed upon his people by his divine wisdom. While politically correct critics may savage the plans and works of the divine Architect, he is not obliged to disclose his purposes or to divulge his reasoning. What can we learn about principles of responsibility that are applicable to us?

1 RESPONSIBILITY FOR SERVANTS (vv2-11)

The word for 'servant' or 'slave' can mean someone who had either been pressed into service or someone who had entered service voluntary. There was a limited contract (v2) from which the slave could be released at the end of the term (v3). If a slave didn't want to leave and could make a declaration of commitment (v5), then his ear was pierced as a sign of consecration (v6). A Christian believer is freed from enslavement to sin and death when they commit to Jesus. The ear may symbolise the hearing of the gospel message (Romans ch10 v17) and it is metaphorically pierced as a sign of consecration to Jesus. Some believers want the benefits without the sacrifice. Some want to be 'free agents' without the identity and responsibility of a 'pierced ear'.

2 RESPONSIBILITY FOR HOMICIDE (vv12-21)

The death penalty was imposed for murder, kidnapping, and for striking, or even cursing, one's parents. The principle of Genesis ch9 v6 underpins the sanctity and dignity of life, which is God-given. That is why the theft of another human being (kidnap) is included in the list (v16). The fabric of any society depends on how much value is placed on life (whether it's life in the womb or life in old age) and how respect is shown to parents. There's a correlation between the breakdown of respect for the value of life and the breakdown of society. There's a direct link between the erosion of parental authority and the erosion of values and standards within a community.

3 RESPONSIBILITY FOR INJURY (vv22-27)

God values unborn infants (vv22-23). The penalty of retribution was set out as a guideline for the courts' judges, and not to be executed by any private retaliation. Even in the case of slaves, there was a system of compensation. God is just and righteous (Deuteronomy ch32 v4; Psalm 89 v14; Zephaniah ch3 v5). The greatest display of justice was seen at the cross (2 Thessalonians ch1 vv6, 8-9). God punishes his own Son so that the believing penitent may be forgiven and acquitted (Isaiah ch53 v5; Romans ch3 vv25-26).

4 RESPONSIBILITY FOR ANIMALS (vv28-32)

Death by animals is always a calculated risk for livestock workers. There are extreme penalties for those who are criminally negligent, as well as compensation for the victim. The death of a slave was fixed at thirty pieces of silver: the price for which Judas agreed to betray Jesus (Matthew ch26 vv14-15). Here is a signpost pointing to the Master who became a slave to bring us to God.

5 RESPONSIBILITY FOR HAZARDS (vv33-36)

The 'pit-bull' terror (vv33-35) is an example of hazards for which we are responsible. Loving our neighbour means not being reckless in exposing others to the consequences of our negligence. We must show love to the helpless, the faithless, and even the loveless. This is how the disciples of Jesus will be recognised (John ch13 vv34-35), even by their thoughtfulness and their consideration.

APRIL 2
EXODUS ch22.1-31

THE IMPORTANCE OF RESTITUTION

Chapters 21, 22, and part of chapter 23 are to do with principles and precedents which God imposed for the equitable management of his covenant people in a Hebrew society. In this chapter, we are provided with a scale of restitution for crimes and claims.

1 RESTITUTION IS ABOUT PRIORITY

The Hebrews could neither excuse themselves nor exempt themselves from restitution just because they couldn't afford to pay (for example, v3). The thief would lose his status as a freeman. He would become a slave to his master for six years or until the year of jubilee (ch21 vv2-6). It's rare to find imprisonment as a punishment in the Old Testament. Neither were there fines to swell the coffers of the state or to finance local authorities. Restitution, however, restores what has been lost to the owner and may encourage an improved relationship between the offender and the offended, between the criminal and the victim.

2 RESTITUTION IS ABOUT PENALTY

In vv1-24 there is a range of penalties to be imposed, which is weighted towards restoration and restitution. Those who are criminally-minded or criminally-negligent are to be penalised according to the severity of their offences. They are held accountable both for their actions and inactions. It's a constructive contribution to any society where an offender is not merely locked away or made to pay fines to the state but is compelled to make meaningful restitution to his victims. The Law of God does not make restitution a soft option. It was a penalty, though a constructive penalty. It penalised the offender but went some way to compensate the victim.

3 RESTITUTION IS ABOUT PLENTY

Restitution had to be generous. Some compensation, which is awarded to victims and casualties today, can be derisory and does little to help those who have been disadvantaged. But in God's Law, restitution had to be plentiful. One stolen ox had to be paid back with five oxen. An ox represented a man's livelihood. Imagine a similar court-imposed restitution today, where a tractor thief must pay the victim five new tractors or be contracted to work for the farmer until the debt is paid! Restitution is also about quality and not just quantity. You couldn't use injured or unhealthy animals to recompense a victim. Neither could you make repayments from your poorest crops (v5). Restitution is not just replacement. It is not replacing like-for-like. There is also compensation for the time wasted and the distress caused.

But this chapter about restitution also tells us something about the flawless nature and dazzling character of our God:

1 God's Guardianship

(vv22-23) God is jealously protective of those who are weak or disadvantaged. Any maltreatment of them would incur the Lord's anger. It should help us to put into perspective the vulnerable and disadvantaged in our society, particularly those who are in reduced circumstances through no fault of their own. God cares about our vulnerability. He says: *'I will certainly hear their cry'* (v23). Jesus sympathises with our weaknesses (Hebrews ch4 v15). We can call upon our Guardian God in faith, believing that he provides strength in all our adversities and protection from our worst adversaries.

2 God's Compassion

He understands the heartaches and distresses that afflict us at times. God's compassion (v27) is his mercy extended to the miserable. He intervenes with his kindness to support those in pitiful conditions. He is the Father of compassion (2 Corinthians ch1 vv3-4). The practical outworking of God's compassion to us is in our compassion for those in trouble. We must not ration compassion!

3 God's Holiness

God's appointed representatives should be respected (v28). He demands the firstfruits and the firstborn to be consecrated to him for his service (vv29-30). The Hebrew people had to remember that the Lord was their holy God and they were to be his holy people (v31; Leviticus ch11 v44).

In Conclusion:

When Zacchaeus encountered Jesus (Luke ch19 vv1-10), his salvation was evidenced by restitution. His confession and testimony proved costly. He promised to *'pay back four times the amount'* (v8) to his victims. If we have cheated, defrauded, or misappropriated in any way, the solution is in restitution. This is one of the evidences of God's Spirit at work in a believer's life.

APRIL 3
EXODUS ch23.1-33

CLOSE ENCOUNTERS OF THE DIVINE KIND

This first part of the chapter concludes the section on Civil Law, which began in ch 21. We have a list of very practical laws which was to be the framework for guiding the Hebrew magistrates.

vv1-9: Show justice and impartiality among the people. We can learn much from these precedents. Spreading false reports (v1) is destructive to society and the church. Going along with the crowd (v2), because people are afraid to champion truth, means that the majority could be in error. Kindness to enemies and defending the poor and the alien is encouraged.

vv10-13: The fourth command of God's moral law (ch20 vv8-11) is emphasised. The seventh day is to be devoted to the Lord, and in the seventh year the farmer is to rest his ground (lie fallow)

vv14-19: Three annual festivals are mentioned in which no one should appear before the Lord empty-handed (v15). We must offer the best of our lives and the first of our gifts to the Lord (v19).

If the film 'Close Encounters of the Third Kind' gripped sci-fi students, 'Close Encounters of the Divine Kind' should grip Bible students.

Note that this angel is not an 'ordinary' angel (v20). His description is too lofty. If he is able to forgive at all (v21), then we are reminded that no one can forgive sins but God alone (Mark ch2 v7). He also bears the name of the Lord Almighty. He is unique and incomparable. He is vested with the power and authority of the Godhead. This is the divine being who is elsewhere described as *'the Angel of the Covenant'* (Isaiah ch63 v9; Malachi ch3 v1). This is therefore none other than the second Person of the Trinity, the pre-incarnate Son of God. His presence is promised to his people, and his role is:

To Guard: *'See, I am sending an Angel ahead of you to guard you along the way...'*

To Guide: *'...to bring you to the place I have prepared'*

The Lord Jesus Christ is the Guard and Guide for all of his faithful followers in every generation. But there are certain obligations on the part of his holy people:

1 WE MUST LISTEN CAREFULLY (vv21-23)

'Pay attention'... 'Listen to what he says' (v21). *'Listen carefully...'* (v22).

Failing to listen carefully is called *'rebellion'* (v21). The word 'rebellion' is one of three primary words for sin in the Old Testament. Every refusal to obey God's word and every non-compliant action is sin. It's about going our own way (Isaiah ch53 v6). We are not sinners because we sin, but we sin because we are sinners. We are born that way (Romans ch3 v23), and no psychological influence, or social conditioning, or moral instruction, or religious doctrine can change our birth state. We must be born again. God's Spirit must come to unblock our ears and to soften our hearts. He makes us pay attention. Sometimes he needs to do it dramatically as he did to Saul on the Damascus Road. He effects the change by giving faith. But where does that faith come from? *'From hearing the message'* (Romans ch10 v17). Not everyone hears, and not everyone who hears believes (Romans ch10 v16). Those Israelites who failed to obey also failed to receive the blessing of God's promise (vv22-23). If folk will not pay attention to the gospel message, then they remain unsaved and lost (Hebrews ch4 v2). We must not harden our hearts to his voice (Hebrews ch4 v7).

2 WE MUST WORSHIP DUTIFULLY (vv24-30)

The Israelites must not worship the Canaanite deities. Instead, they were to smash the sacred stones of the idolatrous shrines (v25). Worshipping the Lord exclusively had divine promises attached to it. It was a 'no-brainer'! For faithful Hebrews, it meant 'win, win'! But the Lord had to remain number one in their lives. Their duty was to worship him. The whole of a Christian's life should be lived to the glory of God. Worship (worth-ship) is not limited to singing a few songs, or a time of prayer, or a 'worship spot' in a service. Worship is the giving to God the worth of which he is worthy. 'Sacred stones' have also been erected in our pagan land, such as the untouchable stones of equality and diversity, atheistic evolution, death on demand for unborn infants, human rights, and freedom of expression. But our sovereign God still can employ agents to execute his plans (v28). His timing is perfect (v29) and we must learn to be patient with his programme (v30). Sometimes he does things *'little by little'* to increase our faith, our patience, and our perseverance.

3 WE MUST RESIST POWERFULLY (vv31-33)

The Israelites were commanded to resist Canaanite influence. They were not to become corrupted by their culture, their lifestyle, and, in particular, their religion. Such heathen practices would be a *'snare'* (v33) like those which can entrap the unwary believer today. We must not live by the world's standards, values, and lifestyles. We must not allow Christians' distinctiveness to become blurred. We are called to be separate and free from pollution (James ch1 v27).

APRIL 4
EXODUS ch24.1-18

COME NEAR TO GOD

Despite Russian cosmonauts returning from their space explorations in the 1960s and arrogantly declaring, 'We have flown around the earth and we didn't see God!', it is obvious that they were not *'pure in heart'*, since only such *'will see God'* (Matthew ch5 v8). Yet v11 provides us with one of the most striking verses and one of the most amazing statements of all Scripture: *'they saw God'*. Throughout history, people have wanted to see God. If, however, someone did see God, you would think that it would revolutionise their life. But this experience of seeing God didn't prevent the Israelites from engaging in pagan acts in less than six weeks. So much for their encounter with God! There are those who walk out of God's presence weekly, after engaging in public worship and listening to God's word, and yet who seemingly remain unaffected. But these leading Hebrews saw God – and lived (ref ch33 v20). While no one has ever seen God (John ch1 v18: 1 Timothy ch6 v16) for God is Spirit (John ch4 v24), yet men have looked upon God in the Person of Christ. It wasn't an ethereal spirit that the elders saw, but a divine Being with feet (v10) and hands (v11). We were introduced to the divine Representative (ch23), who is elsewhere referred to as *'the Angel of the Covenant'* and the divine Messenger (Malachi ch3 v1). This can be none other than the pre-incarnate Christ, God's Son. The summons issued to Moses and the leaders was *'Come up to the Lord'* (v1). We are also urged to come near to God (Hebrews ch10 v22).

Five elements enabled the Hebrews to draw near to God. How can we come near to him today?

1 THROUGH THE MEDIATOR OF THE COVENANT

Moses was God's chosen man to be the mediator of the covenant (vv2-3). But this covenant of Law is superseded by God's new covenant of love, and he has graciously provided a perfect Mediator (Hebrews ch9 v15; ch12 vv23-24). There is no one to rival Jesus in this office. He is greater than Moses (Hebrews ch3 v3). He is the God-Man who mediates between God and men (1 Timothy ch2 v5). Because Jesus is our great High Priest, we are encouraged to come near to God with sincere hearts and certain faith (Hebrews ch10 vv19-22).

2 THROUGH THE OFFERING OF SACRIFICE

(vv4-6) Moses was up and ready at the crack of dawn to build an altar, erect twelve stone pillars, and to offer sacrifices as *'fellowship* (or *'peace') offerings'* (v5). Peace between God and men can only be achieved through the blood of a sacrifice. Through the Old Testament, it was the blood of sacrificial animals such as bulls, goats, and sheep. But these offerings were merely signposts pointing to the ultimate sacrifice of Jesus, which is eternal. He has made *'peace through his blood, shed on the cross'* (Colossians ch1 v20). Hearts and consciences can be made spotlessly clean (Psalm 51 v7) through the blood of Jesus (Hebrews ch9 v13; 1 John ch1 v7).

3 THROUGH THE WORD OF GOD

(v7) The *'Book of the Covenant'* was probably the scroll on which Moses had recorded God's commands and judgements (chs20-23). It was God's laws for God's people and formed the basis of the covenant relationship between God and man. But notice that the *'Book of the Covenant'* (v7) had to be ratified by the *'blood of the Covenant'* (v8). God's word is the foundation for his covenant. We cannot hope to come near to God if we don't comply with our Maker's instructions. Our Bible reading and study must be an intrinsic part of our daily walk with God.

4 THROUGH THE OBEDIENCE OF HEART

(vv3, 7) While their motives and intentions may have been genuine at the time, words without actions are meaningless. If we read the Bible without seeking to comply with what we read or to apply what we read, then it is little more than an academic exercise or, worse, a charade. We can't draw near to God with hearts full of hypocrisy and pretence. We must say honestly and meaningfully: *'We will do everything the Lord has said; we will obey'* (v7)

5 THROUGH THE MEAL OF FELLOWSHIP

(vv9-11) Moses and the Hebrew leaders saw God on a platform of clear blue sapphire. They glimpsed a little of divine glory – and lived! Here was a very special time of fellowship. Because a sacrifice had been offered, with bloodshed, they came to know God and to commune with him in a deeply special way in this Old Covenant fellowship meal. Jesus introduced the fellowship meal of the New Covenant (Luke ch22 vv19-20) that would become an essential part of the disciples' devotion (Acts ch2 v42). This communion of believers is at the heart of our covenant relationship with God through the sacrifice of his only Son. Jesus' disciples today won't miss any opportunities to *'devote themselves'* and to come ever nearer to God, our Saviour.

APRIL 5
EXODUS ch25.1-40

THE PATTERN

There was one special building in HM Naval Dockyard at Devonport, Plymouth, which raised great interest and even excitement when the opportunity arose to visit it. In this building were full-scale replicas of various vessels' compartments (for example, the bridge, control centre, conning tower, torpedo bay, etc.). They were all constructed in detail, but from wood! This was where new equipment could be checked for any problems with space and manoeuvrability on installation, thus avoiding the need to have a ship alongside for weeks at a time. For this was the pattern shop. Now God had planned to live among his people – not in a warship, or even a palace, but in a tabernacle. Moses was instructed to build the sanctuary according to the divinely given pattern (vv8-9).

The tabernacle, the earthly dwelling place of Almighty God, was to be a pattern of the heavenly reality. Moses was warned: *'See to it that you make everything according to the pattern shown you on the mountain'* (Hebrews ch8 v5). Unlike the pattern shop in Devonport, where everything was made of wood, the materials God required for his pattern are listed in vv1-7. Nothing was too good for this pattern. No sacrifice that the Israelis made was too great. Here in this chapter, there are the first three items of furniture for the tabernacle, and, because they are part of God's pattern, you would expect them to have spiritual significance relevant to us today.

1 THE ARK: MEETING WITH GOD

(vv10-22) It's significant that out of all the detailed furniture and furnishings, God works from the inside outwards. He begins with the most important detail of all: the Ark of the Covenant (or the Ark of the Testimony). 'Ark' (Latin: 'arca') means 'a chest or box'. The Ark of the Covenant was a wooden chest of precise dimensions, overlaid with pure gold. Because it was a holy chest, which no one should touch, provision was made for it to be lifted and carried using two wooden poles threaded through four gold rings. It would contain the Law of God (*'Testimony'* v16), which formed the basic contractual obligations of the Covenant, of which the Ten Commandments (ch20) were at the heart. The Ark had a lid of pure gold with two gold cherubim at each end of the lid facing each other (v20). It was upon this *'atonement cover'* that the high priest would sprinkle the blood of the sacrificial lamb once a year. It was there and then that God said, *'I will meet with you'* (v22). Note that the only place that God would meet with sinful, rebellious mankind was at the place of atonement, where a sacrifice had been offered for sin. This Old Testament signpost points straight to Jesus (John ch1 v29). It's at the cross of Jesus and his atoning sacrifice that God says he will meet with us (Romans ch3 vv23-25). It's at this rendezvous and none other that we can have our sins forgiven because God's judicial anger has been unleashed upon his sacrificial Lamb. Have you met him there?

2 THE TABLE: OFFERING TO GOD

(vv23-30) This special table, made from acacia wood and overlaid with gold, also had two poles for transportation. The plates and pots on the table were to be made from pure gold, reminding us that only the best is good enough for God. We should be offering him the best of our time, the first of our finances, the best of our skills, and the best of our energy. The Biblical principle of giving the 'first' to the Lord (such as firstfruits, firstborn) contrasts with some people's idea of Christianity, where they are content to give the second-rate, second-class, the tag end, and leftovers to God. But the most significant thing about the table was the twelve loaves that were placed on it. This 'Presence Bread' represented God's presence with his people, the twelve tribes. Bread signifies our basic daily needs. Jesus declared that he is *'the Bread of Life'* (John ch6 v35). As the twelve loaves were reminders of God's presence 24/7, so we are assured of God's presence with his faithful followers (Joshua ch1 v5; Psalm 89 v15; Matthew ch28 v20).

3 THE LAMPSTAND: GUIDING BY GOD

(vv31-40) The lampstand was an enormously valuable and intricate work of art. The six branches and central column supported seven *'flower-like cups'* (v31) fashioned to look like the buds and blossoms of the almond tree. This stand, bearing seven lamps, was to be located on the south side of the tabernacle's Holy Place next to the Most Holy Place. This was the only light to illuminate the pitch darkness. It represents the glory and guidance of God. It emphasises to us the principal method by which God guides his people today: through his word (Ps 119 v105). The single light of God's word is our thoroughly reliable guide. Some people will look for supernatural guidance in superstition, rituals, transcendental meditation, astrology, mystic gurus, and false teachers, but we must not take our eyes off the guiding light of the Bible. If we are careless about its guidance, then we shall tragically lose our way. God's word must be both prominent and preeminent in our lives.

APRIL 6
EXODUS ch26.1-37

THE WAY IN

Between two and three million Hebrew campers in the Sinai Desert had learned to live in tabernacles or tents. Therefore, it's not surprising that God would choose a similar structure to represent his presence camping among his wandering people. This divine tent would show that God was among his people, but at the same time separate from them. It reminds us of Jesus' life on earth. *'The Word became flesh and made his dwelling* (camped/tabernacled/pitched his tent) *among us'* (John ch1 v14). He lived among us but was separate from us (*'set apart from sinners'* Hebrews ch7 v26). Though there were similarities with God's dwelling in a tent, there was separation. The Hebrew people had to learn about the awesome and majestic holiness of God. Hence, the specific materials, the accurate measurements, the exact methods of construction, not to mention the precise procedures for transportation, location, sacrifice, offering, and worship. Moses had to work according to God's plan (v30). Moses couldn't alter God's gospel plan, and neither can we.

This two-roomed tent (13.5m x 4.5m) had an inner lining of beautifully embroidered linen and an exterior layer of goat hair and leather. The larger of the two rooms was called the Holy Place, which contained the Table of the Presence and the golden lampstand. The second room was about half that size and only accessed through the Holy Place. The smaller room was probably a cube (signifying completeness and perfection), with its length, height, and width being about 4.5m. This was called the Most Holy Place (or the Holiest, or the Holy of Holies). The Ark of the Covenant was situated in this inner room. This was the place where God chose to meet with his people, who were represented by the high priest.

So how were these two rooms divided? They were divided by a very special curtain or 'veil' (vv31-33). It had to be made from blue, purple, and scarlet yarn with images of cherubim woven into the fabric (v31). The curtain was a barrier between a holy God and sinful humanity. This curtain was all that separated God's holiness from man's unholiness. The curtain blocked man's access to God. The later temples were modelled on the tabernacle and, by the time Herod's Temple was built, it is estimated that the curtain was over 20m in height and probably up to 100mm thick. It was as massive and as immovable as a wall. But one day this mega-curtain was torn top to bottom. It was on the exact day that Jesus died (Mark ch15 v38). The priests who ministered in the temple on that day saw something staggeringly significant. No wonder many of them were converted and *'became obedient to the faith'* (Acts ch6 v7). The torn curtain now represented the Way In.

1 THE WAY IN TO THE THRONE ROOM

The purple of the embroidered linen and the pure gold of the Ark spoke of royalty. But the 'throne room' reveals the character of the throne to those who are saved. It's the *'throne of grace'* (Hebrews ch4 vv15-16). It's not a throne of domination to receive humiliation, nor is it just a throne of judgement to receive sentencing. It's a throne of grace to receive mercy. In stark contrast to the high priest who ventured timidly behind the curtain once a year, we are urged to approach with confidence and frequently. We can have complete confidence through the blood of Jesus (Hebrews ch10 vv19-22), but we need sincere hearts: hearts which are neither critical nor hypocritical.

2 THE WAY IN TO THE SUPREME COURT

Within the Ark, within the Most Holy Place, was the Testimony, the Law. Everything that God does, he does judicially because of his holiness. But the Law within the Ark had already been broken by sinful man. Yet above the Law was the Lid – the Atonement Cover - on which the sacrificial blood was sprinkled. This pointed to Jesus, who fully satisfied all God's judicial requirements in his atoning death. The believer can boldly enter this Supreme Court because he has been acquitted on all charges. There is now no condemnation for the believer (Romans ch8 vv1-2).

3 THE WAY IN TO THE ANCHORAGE

The security for the soul is a firm and certain hope which is anchored within *'the inner sanctuary behind the curtain, where Jesus who went before us, has entered on our behalf'* (Hebrews ch6 vv19-20). Any ship has to have confidence in its anchor and the ground on which the anchor is embedded. The Christian's hope is in the presence of God. This is the anchor that is firmly embedded in the enthronement and atonement of Jesus behind the torn curtain. It is futile to anchor among the cares and concerns, the priorities and preoccupations of this life. The storms of life will rock our boat, but that boat is going nowhere if our anchorage is secure in Jesus, behind the torn curtain.

APRIL 7
EXODUS ch27.1-21

THE UNALTERABLE ALTAR

In CS Lewis' popular book, 'The Lion, the Witch and the Wardrobe', Aslan the lion allows himself to be humiliated by the white witch and tied to the stone table where he is ceremonially killed. Countless religions and superstitions have involved such an altar on which various sacrifices have been made. Even as God was instructing Moses about worship and sacrifice on Sinai, there were pagan perversions being conducted in Egypt (from where the Israelites had left) to Canaan (where the Israelites were heading). God's design programme for his place of residence, the Tabernacle, included the outer courtyard (about a quarter of the size of a football pitch). This provided:

Identity: A particular plot was marked out and reserved for God. It was within the camp but separate.

Privacy: Curtains were high enough to screen the priests' work as well as keep animals out.

Sanctity: The courtyard, and everything in it, was sacred and set apart for God.

The Altar of Burnt Offering in the courtyard was distinguished from the Altar of Incense, which was located in the Holy Place of the Tabernacle. Like other Tabernacle furniture, the Altar was made of acacia wood but overlaid with bronze. It was to be a square with a side of about 2.3m (7 6"). It was to be about 1.4m (4' 6") high. It had rings on each side so that poles could be inserted for transportation. Each of the four corners had a horn which symbolised power, help, and safety. The Altar had a grating halfway up (v4), and there were various bronze utensils and pots to be used in servicing the Altar. Yet all these Tabernacle details are pictures of the New Testament reality, fulfilled in Jesus and his 'Earth Mission'. *We have an altar from which those who minister at the Tabernacle have no right to eat'* (Hebrews ch13 v10). We note the contrast between the Old Testament pattern and the altar of Jesus and his New Testament sacrifice:

1 A DEEPER SIGNIFICANCE

The death of Jesus and his sacrifice eclipse and nullifies all other altars. The transient man-made altars are wholly ineffective. By persisting in using altars of wood and stone, we are refusing to believe in the once-and-for-all, never-to-be-repeated sacrifice for sin which God has provided.

2 A BETTER SACRIFICE

Leviticus ch4 explains the rituals to be observed when using the Altar for burnt offerings. The animal had to be *'without defect'* (v3) and some of its blood had to be poured on the four bronze horns. The parts of the animal which were not burnt on the Altar had to be taken *'outside the camp'* (v12) and burnt there. These rituals, introduced at Sinai, were practised for about five hundred years, until the first temple was built, and then practised for nearly another thousand years in the temple. Then came Jesus (Hebrews ch10 vv8-12). He is the perfect sacrifice, without defect. Jesus' blood is sufficiently powerful to bring us the help of salvation and the hope of security. Jesus suffered *'outside the city gate to make the people holy through his own blood'* (Hebrews ch13 vv11-12).

3 A HIGHER SATISFACTION

The believer can be fully satisfied with Jesus' sacrifice. It is acceptable to us in every way. But, even more importantly, God the Father is fully satisfied with the atoning work of his Son upon the cross. *Jesus has become the guarantee of a better covenant'* (Hebrews ch7 v22). God was certainly not pleased with the annual slaughter of sacrificial animals, which was only an interim measure. His 'gospel plan' centred on sending Jesus to be the permanent offering. *'After the suffering of his soul, he will see the light of life and be satisfied'* (Isaiah ch53 v11).

4 A WIDER SCOPE

Leviticus ch1 v2 implies that anyone could bring an offering to the entrance of the Tabernacle, which the priests would then sacrifice on the Altar. Anyone, that is, from the twelve Hebrew tribes. But the altar of Jesus and his cross is not restricted to the Israelites. Peter proclaimed to the cosmopolitan crowd on the Day of Pentecost: *'Everyone who calls on the name of the Lord will be saved'* (Acts ch2 v21). 'There's a wideness in God's mercy like the wideness of the sea; there's a kindness in his justice which is more than liberty' [FW Faber]

5 A GREATER SALVATION

There was only one Altar of Burnt Offering, which was in the courtyard of the Tabernacle. There was only one entrance to the Tabernacle, and if you entered, you had to pass the Altar. There's still no other route to God except by way of his Son and the altar of his sacrifice ('*...the Way'* John ch14 v6). The Altar's horns provided asylum: a place of refuge to grip and to shelter (Exodus ch21 vv12-14). The 'horns' of Jesus' altar are a powerful, permanent refuge where we may find stability, reliability, safety, and protection. Let us continue to grip him by faith, knowing that God's grip of us is infinitely greater.

APRIL 8
EXODUS ch28.1-43

THE HIGH PRIEST'S ENSEMBLE

We may balk at the extravagance of an actress who recently attended an Oscars Academy Awards' ceremony wearing an ensemble valued at £12.3m. Here in this chapter, we are presented with the details of a unique ensemble exclusively designed for Aaron and the succession of high priests. There is a striking symbolism in every part of these sacred garments. Such priests were given great privileges, but they also carried enormous responsibilities. They couldn't afford to have anything out of place in their dress. They couldn't fail to prepare themselves with bathing and sacrificing. They had to follow every procedure of every ritual in their service to their holy and mighty God. The seriousness of their service was reinforced to the Levites (Leviticus ch10 vv1-2) when two of Aaron's sons carried out an unauthorised procedure contrary to God's commands. Fire from heaven consumed them where they stood. While we may no longer have to abide by these strict ceremonial procedures or precise conformity to a dress code, we mustn't forget that God hasn't changed. He hasn't relaxed his standards. He hasn't learned to turn a 'blind eye'. God is still majestic in his righteousness and awesome in his holiness. We must never treat him with less than the awe and esteem which he deserves.

1 The Ephod: (vv6-14) This was like a waistcoat woven out of gold, blue, and scarlet thread. It hung from straps that had two onyx stones set in gold, one on each shoulder. Engravers inscribed the names of the six younger sons of Israel on one stone and the names of the six older sons on the other stone (vv9-10). The high priest bore on his shoulders the heavy burden of representing the twelve tribes in the presence of God. No one was excluded from his representation.

2 The Breastpiece: (vv15-30) This was a 225mm (9") square piece of cloth and was attached to the ephod with gold rings and chains. Most importantly, the breastpiece carried twelve precious stones in four rows, with each stone bearing the name of one of the tribes. So all Israel was doubly represented before the Lord. Those twelve names were dear to God: engraved on jewels and carried over the high priest's heart. It symbolises the value that each believer is to God (1 Peter ch2 v4). Our great High Priest, the Lord Jesus, bears each believer's name on his heart as he enters the presence of God, behind the curtain, having made atonement for us. The breastpiece also contained the *'Urim and Thummim'* (v30), which were used to discern God's will.

3 The Robe: (vv31-35) This long, blue, sleeveless garment was woven in one piece without a seam. Such seamlessness reminds us of Jesus' own garment while here on earth, and also the completeness of his high priestly ministry. The pomegranates may speak of Jesus' fruitfulness, and the golden bells on the hem proclaim the good news, announcing that Jesus has triumphed over death and is able to save all those who come to him in repentance and faith.

4 The Turban: (vv36-39) This headdress featured a *'plate of pure gold'* on the forehead (v36), engraved with the inscription, *'Holy to the Lord'*. This was a powerful, unequivocal reminder that God is unalterably holy and his plan is to make his people holy through Jesus' atoning work at the cross.

5 The Woven Tunic: (v39) This was a white inner garment, worn over the undergarments.

6 The Sash: (v39) This was to be the work of a skilled embroiderer.

1 SERVING FOR THE RIGHT REASONS

There should be no ulterior motives for serving God other than for his honour. Dignity (vv2, 40) and humility are combined in our service. The priestly duties could have been lowly, repetitive, even monotonous, but they were done for the Lord and his glory (Colossians ch3 vv23-24). May we be given priestly hearts to minister with grace and gentleness.

2 PRAYING WITH THE RIGHT CONCERNS

Aaron was so concerned for the people that he wore their names over his heart when he met with God (v29). How concerned are we for Jesus' honour and the salvation of our friends, families, and communities? Jesus' exemplary high priesthood teaches us to be sympathetic with the weak (Hebrews ch4 v15) and to deal gently with the wayward (Hebrews ch5 v2). What concerns are on our hearts?

3 DECIDING WITH THE RIGHT GUIDANCE

While the *'Urim and Thummim'* (v30) may be a bit of a mystery, they represented making the right decisions with the right guidance (Proverbs ch16 v33). God, in his grace, has given us the Bible. There is no guidance equal to that of Scripture. Providentially, the Lord may use issues, circumstances, and people to guide us in a particular direction, but nothing is a substitute for the word of God. That word needs to be hidden in our hearts as a sin-repelling agent (Psalm 119 v11) and a prompt to obedience (Psalm 119 v112), as well as being a lamp to direct us in our Christian walk (Psalm 119 v105)

APRIL 9
EXODUS ch29.1-46

CONSECRATION

Everything about the tabernacle and the priesthood had to be set apart (made holy) for God. In case anyone should forget the reason for all the most expensive materials, the most skilled craftsmanship, the most unusual furnishings, the most detailed garments, and the most elaborate rituals, the reason was plain to read. It was emblazoned on the high priest's forehead, written on a plate of pure gold: *'Holy to the Lord'* (ch28 v36). All that has been considered in the last four chapters is because of the Lord's holiness. This chapter is about 'consecration'.

The verb meaning 'to make holy' is 'to consecrate'. It can also mean 'to devote to'; 'to dedicate to'; 'to separate for'; 'to set apart for'. Anything that is holy is set apart. It is no longer a common item: it is a sacred item. Persons, places, times, and objects were considered 'holy' when they were deliberately and specifically consecrated to God. The seventh day was holy: reserved for God and the worship of him. Mount Sinai was holy because God came down in fire to give the Law. The priests of Israel were holy, and everything connected with the tabernacle, the sacrifices, the ceremonies, and the priesthood had to be set apart for God. Also, in a particular sense, Israel was regarded as 'set apart' for God as his own special possession.

When someone or something was set apart for God, there had to be a clear distinction. There couldn't be any confusion between that which is secular and that which is sacred. Israel had to fiercely guard its distinctiveness from other cultic, pagan influences all around (Leviticus ch19 v2).

This chapter focuses on the elaborate cleansing and sacrificial ceremonies that were performed to separate the high priest, the priests, and their garments for the service of God. Once consecrated, Aaron and the priests were anointed with oil, marking them out for divine service (vv7-9). The priests were only sinners themselves, and they had to be forgiven. A bull was sacrificed as a sin offering (vv10-14) and a ram was sacrificed as a burnt offering (vv15-18). The *'entire ram'* had to be burned on the altar (v18) symbolising the completeness of dedication to God. The priests also received from the 'food basket' (vv2-3) and from the altar (vv22-28). The food was taken in the priests' hands and waved before the Lord in what was called a *'wave offering'* (v24), indicating dedication to God. Then the priests were permitted to eat this food as part of a fellowship meal (vv31-34), which was their entitlement as a share from the people for their priestly service. There was a schedule of daily offerings (vv38-46) which continued every day of the year and for the succeeding generations. This emphasises that the Lord's service is truly 'full-time'. If we are the Lord's servants, because we have been consecrated to the Lord through Jesus' atoning work, then we don't have holidays from being his servants!

How much are we consecrated (set apart) for God? God told Moses (v20) to take some of the blood of the sacrificial lamb and to sprinkle it on the priests' ears, hands, and feet.

1 CONSECRATED EARS

It is easy to be distracted by all the sounds and voices which clamour for our attention. It seems today that everyone has a point to make, an opinion to express, an issue to publicise, an argument to articulate or a brand to advertise. But the faithful servant of God, whose ears are consecrated to him, will be careful to listen for the voice of God. Moses had to listen attentively to God's voice (vv1, 35). He couldn't pick and choose which instructions to obey. *'Everything'* (v35) means that nothing can be exempted, excluded or excused.

2 CONSECRATED HANDS

Our 'hands' represent what we do for the Lord. Whatever it is, we are to do it with all our might (Ecclesiastes ch9 v10). We must not be idle or neglectful. Instead, we must *'work with our hands'* (1 Thessalonians ch4 v11) in such a way that will serve the Lord and make a difference to others.

3 CONSECRATED FEET

As with the ears and hands, it is the *'right'* foot. *'Right'* symbolises power, dignity, influence and productiveness. We are to give our best when we walk or travel for Jesus. We can criss-cross the world today with comparative ease on holidays or business, but where are we prepared to go for God? Those who bring the good news of the Gospel are said to have *'beautiful'* feet (Isaiah ch52 v7).

The Lord has saved us and called us to live a *'holy life'* (2 Timothy ch1 vv8-9). Some people have misinterpreted a holy life to mean 'isolation from people' rather than 'separation for God'. They have shut themselves away in remote monasteries or hermitages. But separation is not isolation. *'Holiness'* is being set apart for the Lord's service right in the middle of the world in which we live. The supreme example of such 'consecration' is Jesus himself and his life on earth.

APRIL 10
EXODUS ch30.1-38

APPROACH WITH CARE

The words which challenged the American preacher DL Moody when he was visiting the NE of England, and which revolutionised his ministry, were: 'God has yet to see what God will do with a man who is fully consecrated to him'. In this chapter, we have additional instructions on consecration, particularly with respect to the Altar of Incense, the Tabernacle's Wash Basin, and the Anointing Oil. The symbolism has a distinct message for the keen and diligent Bible student:

1 THE CAREFULNESS OF PRAYERFULNESS

Having already considered one altar (the Altar of Burnt Offering, situated in the courtyard between the entrance and the Tabernacle), the second altar is the Altar of Incense and was to be located within the Holy Place, right next to the curtain which separated it from the Most Holy Place. This was the third item of furniture within the Holy Place, alongside the Table of the Bread of the Presence and the Golden Lampstand. It wasn't a large altar: about 500mm (18") square and 1000mm (3') high. It was to be made of acacia wood and, like the other furniture, overlaid with pure gold, including the horns on the corners (vv1-3). Gold rings were fitted for wooden poles to be inserted for transportation. On this altar, the high priest (Aaron) was required to burn incense twice a day. In the Bible, incense is frequently associated with prayer (Psalm 141 v2; Revelation ch5 v8; ch8 vv3-4). Every detail of the offering of incense had to be carefully observed, and, while we are encouraged to come boldly to *'the throne of grace'* in our prayers, we must always guard against casualness and flippancy. We can learn four features of genuine prayerfulness:

Regular Prayer (vv7-8): Incense had to be offered regularly, twice a day. The priests couldn't afford to miss a day if they were tired, or too busy, or just 'didn't feel like it'. There was a discipline in burning incense and there should be a discipline to our praying. We are not limited to specific times or locations but certain times and locations each day help us to ensure that these sacred occasions are not missed.

Pure Prayer (v9): The altar was not to be misused. It couldn't be used for any mixture of spices: only those prescribed (vv34-35) and this formula was declared to be *'holy to the Lord'* (v37). Our prayers must never become contaminated by the wrong motives, attitudes or priorities.

Valuable Prayer (v10): The place of prayer is so valuable because Jesus, our Great High Priest, has bought us access into the presence of God through his death. The sprinkling of the blood on the altar (v10) as an *'annual atonement'* is a reminder of the enormous cost which has been paid.

Fragrant Prayer (v7): The pungent aroma which filled the Holy Place and the Most Holy Place was the *'fragrant incense'* offered on the altar every morning and evening. We are so privileged that our prayers of praise and adoration form the fragrance of heaven itself (Revelation ch5 v8).

2 THE CLEANLINESS OF GODLINESS

Moses is instructed to make a bronze basin (vv17-21) for washing Aaron and the priests. They had to wash their hands and feet whenever they entered the Tabernacle. Failure to be clean meant death (v21). The washing of the priests was a sign that they were properly prepared and cleansed from all impurity before serving the Lord. The basins were made from the bronze of ladies' mirrors (ch38 v8). Women were required to sacrifice the one item they used to make themselves presentable to each other so that the priests could make themselves presentable to God. Do we spend a disproportionate amount of time on external appearance while neglecting the state of our hearts before God? Clean hands and pure hearts are necessary for approaching God (Psalm 24 vv3-4). Jesus' blood is able to purify us thoroughly (1 John ch1 v7).

3 THE COSTLINESS OF HOLINESS

Procedures are laid down when Moses conducted a census of the Israelites from time to time (vv11-16). So that those over the age of twenty should not forget their redemption from Egypt, they had to pay a *'ransom'* (v12). The amount of *'half a shekel'* was levied on everyone irrespective of wealth, rank or skill. The perfect atonement of Jesus is a one-fit-all redemption for everyone who genuinely repents and believes. In vv22-29 Moses is provided with the formula for making the *'sacred anointing oil'*. Expense is no object in the worship of God. The costly ingredients and materials represented the people's commitment and devotion to the Lord. The most prominent material used in the Tabernacle was gold. The dominant fragrant spice mixed into the incense was frankincense and the major spice used in the anointing oil was myrrh. These were the gifts that the wise men brought to the infant Jesus. Whatever they may or may not represent, with ch30 before us, gold may speak of Jesus' atonement; myrrh, the anointing of his ministry and frankincense, a ministry that was fragrantly pleasing to his Heavenly Father.

APRIL 11
EXODUS ch31.1-18

GOD'S MASTERFUL DESIGN

From knitting to sewing, typing to texting we all have the potential to be extremely dexterous with our fingers. God's wise design is evident in all creation, though his pièce de resistance in the natural world is humanity itself. It's not surprising that divine characteristics can be seen replicated, in a limited way, in creation. The design and dexterity capabilities of humanity are two of those characteristics. In chapters 25-30 we have marvelled at God's design for the Tabernacle and all its features and furnishings. Every aspect of the priests' ministries and sacrifices underlines repeatedly the uncompromising holiness of God. Every delicate detail and every elaborate ritual points forward to Jesus who fulfils the symbolism completely by becoming the perfect High Priest, the perfect Altar and the perfect Sacrifice. Until Jesus came and 'pitched his tabernacle among us' (John ch1 v14) Israel had to ensure that the symbolism followed God's design. Notice how it was revealed.

1 REVEALED IN HIS CRAFTSMEN

(vv1-11) Bezalel and his assistant Oholiab were appointed to oversee the construction project (v5). Bezalel's skills were God-given, and his artistry was exercised within God's artistry. He was:

i] Hand-picked: *'See I have chosen Bezalel...'* (v2). His name means 'in the shadow of God's protection'. The Lord had earmarked Bezalel for a particular task and had equipped him to do that work. Not everyone is called to such a uniquely responsible role, but all of God's workmen and women are hand-picked for the task. You may feel that others could do it much better than you, but you must not concern yourself with that. If God has hand-picked you to serve him in a particular way, then he will provide all the necessary skills, materials, and wisdom to do that job.

ii] Spirit-filled: Bezalel has the distinction of being the first person in the Bible to be described in this way (v3), although it doesn't necessarily mean that others weren't filled at some point with God's Spirit. It's mentioned specifically in Bezalel's case so that we don't run away with the notion that only leaders like Moses and Aaron are filled with God's Spirit. Sometimes we are apt to believe that only pastors, preachers, missionaries and 'super-pious' people are filled with the Spirit. We desperately need the Spirit's filling: his influence, power and motivation (Ephesians ch5 v18).

iii] Multi-gifted: Sometimes it can be both dazzling and daunting to meet people who are gifted in many ways. We can almost feel intimidated and, like the guy in Matthew ch25 v18, who only had one talent, we go and bury it. Our reasoning may be that there are many others who can do the same job – and better! Doubtless, Bezalel was a multi-gifted individual and his artistic talents qualified him to oversee the sacred construction programme. But imagine the man or the woman who was only good at sewing ram's skins. They had done it successfully before and now Bezalel invites them onto the 'tab building team'. With all their experience and knowledge, they stitch together the ram's skins for the tent covering, yet when the Tabernacle was erected, their workmanship couldn't be seen. Inside there was a linen lining hiding it from view and outside a further covering of hides concealed the rams' skins. All the dedicated, meticulous craftsmanship was obscured to human gaze but, nevertheless, was seen by heaven. We should be encouraged that, though much of our Christian service will never be noticed by folk around us, it is observed by God and it is for his praise and glory.

2 REVEALED IN HIS COVENANT

(vv12-17) The word 'covenant' (appearing about 280 times in the Old Testament) refers to the contractual relationship God had with his people, by his grace (v16). The keeping of the 'Sabbath' (vv13, 17) was a sign of this. It's one of the marks of the identity of God's people. The New Covenant, which Jesus inaugurated at the Last Supper (Luke ch22 v20), points to the cross as the power and proof of its effectiveness in securing our right relationship with God (Hebrews ch8 v8; ch9 v15). How distinctive are we in keeping one day in seven for God? We need to stand out rather than blend in!

3 REVEALED IN HIS CREATION

The 'Sabbath principle' is a 'creation principle', not merely Mosaic Law (v17). Every facet of creation from the gigantic to the microscopic reflects the power, wisdom and glory of God. God's masterful design of our time, using fifty-two sections, each with seven divisions, divided into twenty-four units is God's loving provision for our health and rest. How should we respond to the message of God's design?

i] **Praise God's Grace:** Both the Old and New Covenants have been given by God's grace.

ii] **Live God's Word:** We must live according to our Divine Designer's instructions.

iii] **Use God's Gift:** Like Bezalel, we must use our gifts and abilities for God's glory and purposes.

iv] **Know God's Truth:** To know God we must begin by knowing his holiness (v12).

APRIL 12
EXODUS ch32.1-35

THE GOLDEN CALF

Have you ever witnessed something spectacular which has changed your thinking completely? When the Hebrews were held captive in Egypt, they had witnessed God's awesome power in unleashing ten devastating plagues on the nation, one after another. Any one of those mega-plagues should have confirmed not only the existence but the omnipotence of the one, true and living God. Then they witnessed God's power at the Red Sea when they were all safely delivered in one night. The following morning they saw the complete destruction of their enemies as Egyptian corpses floated onto the shore. But neither had God abandoned his people in the Sinai Desert as they needed huge supplies of food and water every single day. Then God had a 'summit meeting' with Moses on the mountain. The people knew where Moses had gone but, after less than six weeks' absence, what happened (v1)? We may query as to whether we have read this right! The Lord Almighty had been before his people in the plagues, the Red Sea deliverance, the provisions of the desert and was now before them on the mountain. Yet in the valley below this ignorant and rebellious people were saying, *'Come, make us gods who will go before us'*. Is it not that same sentiment which our own nation has been expressing so vehemently in recent years? Our nation, which has enjoyed the blessings and privileges of God's grace through Christianity over hundreds of years, is making for themselves 'golden calves' of modernism, secularism, evolutionism, sentimentalism, sacramentalism, diversity and equality.

1 SEPARATED FROM THE LORD

As the Israelites had deliberately separated themselves from the Lord, so our nation is doing precisely the same today:

i] The Iniquity of Religious Lawlessness: The Law of God was 'hot off the press'. Moses was already descending the mountain with his two precious stones containing God's covenant law, which the people were already breaking in the valley below. They brought their gold to make their god. They would rather worship at the hooves of their calf than at the feet of their Creator.

ii] The Audacity of Religious Lies: Any false religion has to be propped up with lies. They actually said that the calf was the god that had delivered them from Egypt (vv4, 8)! Even Aaron had the audacity to say to his brother Moses, when challenged about the golden calf, *'I threw (the gold) into the fire, and out came this calf'* (v24). Really? The one clear way of not being deceived by religious lies is to read and digest God's word. We must even test our preachers and Bible teachers by the Bible just as the Bereans did (Acts ch17 v11).

iii] The Futility of Religious Leadership: The first newly appointed religious leader of God's people was Aaron. What a disappointment he was when faced with his first test of leadership. He may have tried to back-pedal a little by announcing a *'festival to the Lord'* (v5) and by offering sacrifices but all of this was in front of the golden calf. This was followed by the *'revelry'* of a pagan orgy (v6). They were *'running wild'* (v25). Where are the church leaders today who provide clear, strong instruction and example? Where are those with spiritual backbone who fear nothing but God and teach nothing but the Bible: leaders who are credible and Christ-like?

iv] The Depravity of Religious Liberty: The people who were *'prone...to evil'* (v22) were *'quick to turn away'* (v8) from God's holy law and standards. They became 'freethinkers' and threw off all restraints and accountability. They were *'out of control'* (v25) and so became *'a laughing stock to their enemies'* (v25). How many professing Christians today have become laughing stocks to the enemies of Christ because of their careless lifestyle or their thoughtless words?

2 SEPARATED BY THE LORD

Moses had been specifically chosen by the Lord to be a mediator. He was the go-between between God and the Israelites (vv11-14). Although he was their mediator he couldn't be their redeemer. Despite being willing to die in their place (v32) he couldn't *'make atonement for...sin'* (v30). Only the One *'found worthy of greater honour than Moses'* (Hebrews ch3 v3) can *'make atonement for the sins of the people'* (Hebrews ch2 v17) and bring forgiveness and fellowship with God.

3 SEPARATED FOR THE LORD

After Moses had made the Israelites drink the 'gold paste', he declared *'Whoever is for the Lord, come to me'* (v26). Jesus our perfect Redeemer summons sinners to himself (John ch7 v37). We must come in humility, faith and repentance. The Levites were separated for the Lord and his service. Let us be decisive and distinctive in serving the Lord so that we may be preserved from becoming a dishonourable laughingstock among those opposed to Christ and his church.

APRIL 13
EXODUS ch33.1-23

LIVING IN GOD'S PRESENCE

There's a day in September which is often a life-changing day for young children. It's the day that they start school. Before the advent of playgroups and pre-school nurseries, the first day of school was often the first day that a child had been away from its mother. More than one little child, kitted out in their brand-new oversized uniform, has been told that their older brother or sister would take them to school, and more than one child has stood on the doorstep of their home and has announced defiantly to their mother, 'If you don't go with me, then I'm not going!'

In this chapter Moses may be compared to that child on the first day of school. The Lord has said to him (v1) *'Leave this place'*...take the Israelites up to the land that has been promised to them. The Lord adds *'I will send an angel before you'* (v2) and Moses replies, *'If your presence does not go with us, do not send us up from here'* (v15) or, perhaps, like the child on its first day at school, *'If you don't go with me, I'm not going!'*

There comes a point in our lives when we realise that we can only really move forward with the personal presence of Almighty God. Unbelievers, on a collision-course with hell and destruction need the presence of a competent Saviour to rescue them. Christians who are facing enormous trials and hardships are dependent upon God's presence in a huge way. Believers in the twilight years of their lives, facing the final frontier of death, need the powerful, assuring presence of God to face eternity with the absolute confidence of his presence with them (Psalm 23 v4).

From these verses we can notice that God's presence with believers is:

1 THE MARK OF GOD'S PEOPLE

The fact that God is with his people in a special way marks them out as the people of God. Moses argues the point that it is God's presence that is the distinguishing feature of those who are the children of God (vv15-16). He has the audacity to tell the Lord, *'Remember that this nation is your people'* (v13). God was pleased with Moses because he was able to argue from the position of faith in God's covenant promises. We can know about God's promise of his presence, but we must also act upon it. The real mark of God's people is when they take him at his word and move forward in faith.

2 THE SIGN OF GOD'S SATISFACTION

Moses asks the Lord how anyone is going to know that he is pleased with them unless he goes with them (v16). Certainly the Lord had not been pleased with the Israelites (v3). The people were prone to sin (ref ch32) and they were at risk from divine destruction should such sin occur when God was with them. They were an obstinate people (vv3, 5) which we see represented in our society today. But God is wonderfully patient (Isaiah ch65 v2) and to those who surrender unconditionally to him, he promises his presence to bless, because he is satisfied.

3 THE PROMISE OF GOD'S REST

'Rest' in the Bible is not 'inactivity'. Obviously we all need the 'rest' of sleep but though the Sabbath rest may be a cessation from normal six-day activities, it is not 'one long snooze'! 'Rest' (v14) refers to Canaan, the Promised Land, where there would be cities to seize, battles to fight, homes to build and businesses to establish. But a whole generation of Israelites would not enter that rest due to faithlessness and disobedience (Numbers ch14 vv21-35). The warning is emphasised in Hebrews ch4 where disobedience to the Gospel is compared to the Israelites' disobedience.

4 THE REALITY OF GOD'S FRIENDSHIP

Moses knew God's friendship in a special way (v11; Numbers ch12 vv6-8) and Moses' faith is a clue to that friendship just as Abraham's faith was implicit in his friendship with God (James ch2 v23). The greatest accolade of all is to be known as 'God's friend' (John ch15 v14).

5 THE PLACE OF GOD'S SECURITY

Moses' faith had allowed him to be bold and adventurous with God (vv12-17). Moses took God at his word and asked for the ultimate prize: to be shown God's glory (v18). It wasn't possible for a sinful, finite being, even one as godly as Moses, to look upon the awesome splendour of God's dazzling glory and live! Moses would be in danger. He could die from exposure! Although God is Spirit, he reveals himself to Moses in human terms: hands, feet, back (v23) and he tells him that he will be safely held in *'a cleft in the rock'* and covered with his hand (v22). We can be sure that whichever unfriendly powers we may be facing at present (threats, intimidations, hostility from unbelievers, bureaucracy, laws curtailing our freedom, ill health) there is no safer place in the whole of the universe than sheltering under the mighty hand of our omnipotent God.

APRIL 14
EXODUS ch34.1-35

HOW SHOULD DAILY TIME WITH GOD AFFECT US?

The BBC's Antiques Roadshow programme has revealed some pieces which have been declared 'priceless' by the experts. At least one of those pieces has been broken subsequently! Moses was given charge of two matching stone plaques which were unique and of crucial national importance. They had been personally engraved by God. They were priceless. There was nothing which came close to the value of those awesome stones. But what happened? Moses breaks them – and deliberately too! But while Moses may have been the first to 'break' all Ten Commandments at once, history has proved that the sin within us creates the bias which makes us prone to regularly breaking God's moral law. This law was so important that Moses was summoned to spend almost another six weeks (v28) alone with God on the mountain. That mountain was a strict 'exclusion zone' (v3) to which only Moses had a permit to enter. You may ask why, if God could create the universe in six days, he should need six weeks to inscribe ten commands! But the Lord knew that Moses needed forty days and forty nights of uninterrupted communion with God. He wouldn't even be distracted by the bleating of a sheep (v3), let alone the bleating of the Israelites. Moses was totally occupied with God. Do you spend 'Quality Time' with God every day? Is it an 'exclusion zone' where just you and the Lord can meet without interruption? What is there in your day that is more important than spending time with God?

Part of the answer to this question may be found within this chapter.

1 DEEPER KNOWLEDGE OF GOD'S BEING

(vv1-9) Just like Moses chiselling out two new stone tablets, we may find some things that are mundane and repetitive hard work, which may even be the consequences of our mistakes, just like Moses. But if we are faithful in the rudimentary, the repetitive and the routine, then God can meet with us and bring us into a deeper knowledge of himself. God's faithful octogenarian climbed the mountain *'early in the morning'* (v4) and the Lord met him there (v5). The Lord proclaims his name, and therefore his character, twice (v6). We are reminded just how loving, gracious and merciful this great God is. He is holy and righteous, and the guilty cannot escape justice. Nevertheless, he provides rescue and redemption through Jesus, God's Son. If we really love someone then we shall be eager to know all there is to know about that person. Even after twenty-five years since his Damascus encounter with Jesus, Paul still yearned: *'I want to know Christ'* (Philippians ch3 v10)

2 BETTER VISION OF GOD'S POWER

(v10) In mercy God renewed the covenant with Moses and the people, despite the Israelites' idolatry with the golden calf. The Lord promises to show unique wonders. This should be the catalyst and the encouragement for our prayers if our daily time with God is going to affect us. We want to see the Lord at work in our nation, our community and our church. May the people, whom we live among, see the awesome work that the Lord will do among us. So then, what is the burden of our prayers? What awesome work do we really want to see? Do we want to see conversions, repentance, renewal and spiritual awakening?

3 CLEARER DISTINCTIVENESS OF GOD'S PEOPLE

(vv11-16) God warned the Israelites that the pagan idolaters living in Canaan could become a dangerous *'snare'* (v12). The Israelites could be seduced into making a peace treaty with the Canaanites and that would lead to recognising pagan gods and even offering sacrifices to them (v15). God's people must separate and be distinctive. They must not compromise with worldly beliefs and values. They must not become tainted by the prevailing world mindset. Daily time with God will not make us more camouflaged with the world but contrasted with it.

4 GREATER OBEDIENCE TO GOD'S WORD

'Obey what I command you today' (v11). In vv17-28 God emphasises the sections of the covenant which identify God's people. If they were obedient in keeping the feasts, then God would protect them (v24). Understanding God's word may take time but obedience to it shouldn't take time.

5 CLOSER LIKENESS TO GOD'S SON

(v29) Moses had been in the presence of God for almost six weeks and he radiated God's glory unconsciously. But that brightness would fade. In 2 Corinthians ch3 vv7-18 Paul contrasts Moses' ever-decreasing glory with the ever-increasing glory of knowing the Mediator of the New Covenant. The progressive transformation of the Christian's character is produced by the Spirit. The more time we spend in the presence of our Saviour, the more we shall reflect him. Thirty years after Lelia Naylor's conversion, she wrote the hymn: *'Nearer, still nearer, close to thy heart. Draw me...'*

APRIL 15
EXODUS ch35.1-35

SPIRITUAL ECONOMICS

We all have a part to play in 'social economics', whether consciously or unconsciously. Economists use the letters WTA (willing to accept) and WTP (willing to pay). The price of any goods' transaction will be at a point between the buyer's willingness to pay and the vendor's willingness to accept. While we have frequently considered criticism of the Israelites who were obstinate, ungrateful, faithless, and disobedient, here in this chapter, we see a different side to them. We view something of their social and spiritual economics, that is, what they were willing to pay and what God was willing to accept. God had already made it clear that in establishing the Old Covenant atonement, he was only willing to accept the finest, the costliest, and the best.

God's WTA: God's holiness demanded the best materials and the best skills.

Israel's WTP: The Israelites responded to God's demands with willingness. Note the word *'willing'* in vv5, 21, 22, 26, 29. We cannot escape the essential requirement of willingness. In case we may be sceptical as to the reason why the Israelites were so willing, v21 tells us that *'everyone who was willing and whose heart moved him...'* This was not merely an academic willingness where they felt pressured into conforming to a request. They were moved by their hearts, not just their heads. How much of what we do is heart-driven? How much is it motivated by our love for Jesus? The Saviour reminded people of their greatest obligation to *'love the Lord your God with all your heart...'* (Matthew ch22 vv37-39). Real, deep-down, life-changing love for God will make us willing. How willing? How willing were the Israelites?

1 WILLING TO GIVE

(v5) What do we give to a God who has everything (Psalm 50 vv9-12)? We must give our love, our devotion, our consecration and every practical expression of that love. Love for God caused the Israelites to obey (here in ch35 at least). They gave liberally and sacrificially: about one ton of gold, four tons of silver and three tons of copper (ch38). Everyone should give as decided in their heart, *'not reluctantly nor under compulsion, for God loves a cheerful giver'* (2 Corinthians ch9 v7). When God told King David to build an altar upon Araunah's threshing-floor, Araunah willingly offered his property to David as well as oxen and wood for the sacrifice. Araunah's open-heartedness was so refreshing. But it was David who refused the offer, saying *'...I insist on paying you for it. I will not sacrifice to the Lord my God burnt offerings that cost me nothing'* (2 Samuel ch24 v24). There will be a cost to our giving. That gift to the Lord should be a sacrifice, accompanied by willingness.

2 WILLING TO MAKE

(v10) An inventory is provided of the fixtures, fittings and furnishings to be assembled for the tabernacle and its atoning purposes (vv11-19), What a range of skills was required! Carpenters, blacksmiths, metal-workers, embroiderers, seamstresses, engravers, jewellers, riggers, potters, artists, dressmakers, leatherworkers, leaders, supervisors, administrators, accountants, and other skilled workers too. The Israelites were willing to make their best and finest for the Lord, to use for the good of the community. What can we make? Where does our skill lie? We may not be able to make music, but we can make tea. We may not be able to make a speech, but we can make a bed. We are unable to make Christians, but we can help *'make disciples'* (Matthew ch28 v19)?

3 WILLING TO USE

Some people had valuable assets to bring to the Lord, but others may have only owned wood – acacia wood – which they brought (v24). We may imagine that some had tools and facilities which they willingly offered for use in the construction programme. While we may feel that our craftsmanship is minimal or non-existent, we all have facilities and resources which may be used for the glory of God and for the good of his church.

4 WILLING TO BE

Bezalel was *'chosen'* for his task, as is every believer. He was willing to be *'filled with the Spirit'*, committed to the people and sent on a mission *'to make artistic designs'* (v32) and *'to teach others'* (v34). Not everyone's mission involves a career change or learning a foreign language, or travelling to another country.

Finally, the Gospel is a lesson in spiritual economics. God's WTA is holiness and sinlessness, but his WTP was his Son, whom he gave to the cross (1 John ch4 v10). He is willing to save all who are called to repentance and faith (2 Peter ch3 v9). Jesus willingly took the sinner's place and willingly completed the mission upon which he had been sent.

APRIL 16
EXODUS ch36.1-38

WORKING FOR THE LORD

A significant section of the Israelite community had shown their diligence, faithfulness, and self-sacrificing generosity in contributing to the work of building the tabernacle and its accessories. They were men and women who had been touched by the Spirit of God to give of their linen and wool, precious stones and gems, oils and spices, artistic skills and craftsmanship. Chapter 36 is almost a copy of ch26. In ch26 we have God's instructions, which were given to Moses, and in ch36 we are provided with the account of how these instructions were carried out. These passages may remind us of a theme text from Colossians ch3 v23: *'Whatever you do, work at it with all your heart, as working for the Lord, not for men'*.

1 Whatever you do – WHOLESALE WORK

There's no limit to the type of work or the scope of work. The word *'whatever'* covers everything, however extensive or indiscriminate. Whether it's surgery or carpentry, in a factory or a laboratory, frequently or infrequently, the Lord's people should regard it as *'working for the Lord'*. Moses summons the artistic directors (v2) along with all those with ability and willingness. There is a wide diversity of tasks and an extensive range of abilities that are employed in the work of God. Apart from the artists and artisans who worked on the tabernacle construction programme, there was a whole army, possibly up to 200,000 Levites, whose job was to manage, supervise, transport, rig, de-rig, pack, and prepare all the fixtures, fittings, and furnishings throughout the wilderness wanderings. They may not have had prominent roles like the priests, but their work was no less important because it was 'the Lord's work'. Their skills may have been diverse, but the construction showed that all those skills could be employed (v8). Our work in contributing to the building of God's spiritual house may be just as diverse. There is a whole spectrum of abilities to be utilised in this wholesale work.

2 Work at it with all your heart – WHOLEHEARTED WORK

The word *'wholehearted'* refers to something that comes from deep within the soul. Work, even hard work, may be only superficial. Wholehearted work is prompted by a sincere desire, a genuine earnestness, and a real commitment. The work, in which Bezalel, Oholiab, and their large team of skilled craftsmen were engaged, was a work that demanded full, wholehearted involvement. Our Christian service must be wholehearted. There's no such thing as part-time, hobby Christians. If Jesus had not been wholehearted in his unswerving devotion to his Father's rescue plan, then there would be no hope, no help, and no heaven. But *'as the time approached for him to be taken up to heaven, Jesus resolutely set out for Jerusalem'* (Luke ch9 v51). Literally, Jesus set his face. We may look at the expressions on the faces of Olympian athletes just before their event. The look of determination, concentration, and single-minded focus sums up years of rigorous preparation and steely commitment. Jesus 'set his face' towards Jerusalem, towards the cross, towards becoming the one once-and-for-all-and-forever sacrifice for sins. Nothing could deter or distract him from his mission. By becoming a disciple of Jesus, you will be directed by what pleases him in your life. You will want to be wholehearted in everything you do

(Ecclesiastes ch9 v10). However, we must be clear in asserting that we cannot rely on wholehearted service as justification before God. We are not saved by our works but by grace (Ephesians ch2 v8). None of the *'freewill offerings morning after morning'* (v3) could bring the people into a living relationship with God. Like them, we need to be justified by faith.

3 As working for the Lord, not men – WHOLESOME WORK

Whether you are making curtain loops (v12) or gold clasps (v13) or staining the crossbars (v31) or fixing hooks on top of posts (v38), then you are working for the Lord. It means too that whether you are sweeping streets or vacuuming the church, or whether you are baking, building, making, buying, selling, teaching, accounting, driving, negotiating, managing, emailing, or whatever you are doing as a believer, you are working for the Lord, not for people. Therefore, that work is wholesome. If we see that work in the context of serving the Lord, it is given great dignity, however menial or humble that work may appear to be. The tabernacle workmen were reminded that their individual task, whatever it was, was *'the work the Lord commanded to be done'* (v5). It may not be a glamorous work, or a popular work, or an attractive work, but it will be a wholesome work if it's the Lord's work (1 Corinthians ch12 vv4-6). Jesus is no longer building a tabernacle but a church, and he's still looking for the equivalent of carpenters, metalworkers, dressmakers, leatherworkers, jewellers, and weavers to serve him in the work of the kingdom. It's not the particular job we do, or even how long we live to do it: it's how well we live that matters.

APRIL 17
EXODUS ch37.1-29

GOING FOR GOLD

Bezalel was the craftsman in charge (v1), and he ensured that God's plan for the tabernacle was fulfilled down to every last detail. As listed before, we are provided with the four items of tabernacle furniture which have now been constructed according to plan.

THE ARK OF THE COVENANT: This was the divinely ordained meeting place between God and men. It's at the cross of Jesus that God says to us today, *'There I will meet with you'* (ch25 v22).

THE TABLE: This was the table on which the twelve loaves of 'Presence Bread' were placed, representing God's presence with his people, the twelve tribes.

THE LAMPSTAND: The only light in the tabernacle was provided by this lampstand, which was tended by the priests daily. God provides one genuine light in the Bible, which we must not ignore.

THE ALTAR OF INCENSE: The high priest burned incense on this altar twice a day. Incense throughout the Bible is connected with prayer. We may therefore glean from the incense picture that prayer is to be regular, pure, and fragrant.

The word *'gold'* is used in this chapter no less than twenty times. While studying the Bible, we discover that gold is compared to the value of:

OUR FOUNDATION: *The ordinances of the Lord are sure and altogether righteous. They are more precious than gold, than much pure gold'* (Psalm 19 vv9-10).

OUR FUTURE: In John's vision, he saw heaven opened and *'the city of pure gold'* (Revelation ch21 v18)

OUR FAITH: Peter refers to the believer's sufferings in the Christian life and he says: *'These have come so that your faith – of greater worth than gold...may be proved genuine and may result in praise, glory and honour when Jesus Christ is revealed'* (1 Peter ch1 v7).

So what can we notice about the significance of gold? Why was it the predominant material used in the construction of the tabernacle? Why is it the material to which the Bible, the new creation, and our faith are compared?

1 GOLD IS VALUABLE

While silver, platinum, and palladium are employed internationally as commodities and currencies, gold is the rarest of them all. Yet in God's accountancy, your faith in Jesus Christ for salvation and your faith to trust his word and his plan for your life is inestimably more precious than gold.

2 GOLD IS PLEASURABLE

There's something aesthetically pleasing about gold, which doesn't tarnish or lose its lustre. There's a universal attractiveness and beauty in gold. Its appearance, not only its value, gives pleasure. It must always be a source of wonder that our weakest faith brings pleasure to God. He delights in our faith and is willing to answer our prayer when we pray: *'Lord, increase our faith'.*

3 GOLD IS DURABLE

Gold doesn't decay or tarnish like other materials. There is an expiry date or finite life for nearly everything we consume, but gold endures. It is this enduring quality that makes faith so attractive. Real faith doesn't buckle under pressure or weaken through heat. Genuine faith in God is durable. Faith may waver at times, and it may be dented occasionally, but it endures.

4 GOLD IS INCORRUPTIBLE

One of the great characteristics of gold is that there is very little that can corrupt or compromise its purity. It is not subject to rot, rust, or ruin as other minerals are. Our faith, which *'is of greater worth than gold'*, should not become tarnished or corrupted by the secular values and religious standards of our age. It will become increasingly difficult to stand firm for Jesus and his gospel in the future. Our faith will always be under attack, and the world's corrosive powers will do their utmost to dissolve or destroy our faith. But real faith in God will not be corrupted.

5 GOLD IS ADAPTABLE

Though unchanging in its purity, gold is extremely malleable. It was this characteristic that made it a prime choice for all the delicate ornamentation of the tabernacle. Everything from moulding to lamp holders, rings to pole sleeves, plates and dishes, bowls and pitchers, wick trimmers and trays – all were fashioned out of hammered gold. The Lord calls us to adapt our faith to needs and circumstances without it becoming tarnished or corrupted. It's faith that is to be used every day, in every kind of situation. We may suffer from discrimination and victimisation, criticism and malicious gossip, but our faith is of *'greater worth than gold'* and results in the honour and praise of Jesus. Faith is the currency of the Christian, and it's this 'gold', exchanged for the trials and hardships of life, which is warmly appreciated and valued in heaven.

APRIL 18
EXODUS ch38.1-31

VALUABLE SERVICE

The tabernacle was furnished with very valuable items, worth millions of pounds in today's money, and costing tens of thousands of man-hours. These were holy items which had been consecrated to the exclusive use and for the glory of God. They couldn't be misconstructed, misused, misplaced, or mishandled. These details remind us that every detail of our worship is important to God. He is not only interested in the 'partitioned area' of our lives, with its linen curtains of praise, which we set aside for worship. He is also mindful of the *'hooks and bands'* of our thoughts and attitudes, for these *'hooks and bands'* hold everything together. Every single fastening in the tabernacle was accounted for. The chief rigger was one of Aaron's four sons, Ithamar. He had a responsible task in supervising the Gershonites and the Merarites who were charged with the rigging, de-rigging, and transportation of the tabernacle throughout the period of the wilderness wanderings (Numbers ch4). Ithamar was diligent about detail. Neither should we, who serve the Lord, be careless, thoughtless, or disorganised. Nothing was missed by Ithamar's 'checkers and tickers' as they measured and recorded the value of the materials used in the tabernacle's construction (v21). The value was staggering. But the immense value of the tabernacle's components must point us to the inestimable cost of our atonement. Jesus, the Son of God, paid the greatest price and made the greatest sacrifice for our redemption. The punishment for sin was deflected upon Jesus. He took the full impact of God's judgement against sin so that everyone who truly believes in him may escape the judgement and horror of an everlasting hell. These verses also challenge us about the value of Christian lives, which are lived for Christ and his church.

1 THE VALUE OF GIVING EXTENSIVELY

Although Ithamar and his 'checkers and tickers' were able to put a monetary value on the materials used in the tabernacle construction, all those materials had been donated freely by the Israelites. They donated as much as their hearts prompted them to give (ch25 v2). Some hearts may have been prompted to give only a few sticks of acacia wood, while other hearts prompted the giving of gold jewellery (2 Corinthians ch9 v7). The Israelites responded with *'freewill offerings morning after morning'* (ch36 v3) until Moses had to call a halt, for they had *'more than enough to do all the work'* (ch36 vv6-7).

Imagine a charity, church, or mission announcing that they have received enough donations! But how much do our hearts prompt us to give to the building of the Lord's spiritual church and the work of extending the church family through the preaching of the gospel? We are to give from the bottom of our hearts, not from the top of our purses. If we want to gain, we must learn to give. It's possible to give without loving, but it's impossible to love without giving.

2 THE VALUE OF FOLLOWING SUBMISSIVELY

Bezalel and his craftsmen *'made everything the Lord commanded Moses'* (v22). Bezalel and his highly skilled artists and artisans complied with the Lord's directions precisely. We should not wonder that marriages, homes, and families are so dysfunctional when the Maker's instructions have been abandoned. Why are there huge problems on our streets, in industry, in hospitals, in schools, among our judiciary, and in Parliament? Is it not because they have torn up the Maker's instructions and directions? Neither is the church immune from conflicts which threaten to split it or paralyse it when its leaders and its members want to edit and redefine the directions of its divine Designer. Jesus himself is the best example of following submissively. He came to do his Father's will (Hebrews ch10 v7). If Jesus followed his Father's will submissively, with all the hellish horrors of the cross staring him in the face, then should we not be compliant with God's will and God's word?

3 THE VALUE OF WORKING CO-OPERATIVELY

The tabernacle construction programme was completed accurately and on time because every worker worked in unity and humility for the common goal. They weren't pulling in all directions, asserting their self-interests and promoting their individual abilities. Neither are we told that they only worked in family groups, nor that there was any inter-tribal rivalry. They worked as one unit, with one standard and with one purpose. Jesus is the Head of the church, and it is from him that the whole church body grows and builds in love *'as each part does its work'* (Ephesians ch4 v16). Unity is dependent upon maturity and stability, held together by love. Sadly, there is much evidence today of an absence of love, leading to instability, immaturity, and, ultimately, disunity.

Let's strive to draw closer to Jesus so that we may draw closer to one another in the body of Christ.

APRIL 19
EXODUS ch39.1-43

THE FINAL INSPECTION

Every soldier's nightmare for a thousand years or more has been the regular kit inspection. The effectiveness of a soldier in an efficient, disciplined army is reflected in the way in which they look after their equipment. They must ensure that nothing goes missing; that every piece is maintained in working order; that every item of equipment can be presented neatly for inspection.

In vv42-43 we are told that Moses' army of tabernacle construction workers presented all the fixtures and fittings for inspection. In vv2-31 we are provided with another list of the *'sacred garments'* which were made for Aaron, the high priest. This is a copy of the account in ch28:

Ephod – A waistcoat that hung from the shoulders on two straps, each containing an onyx stone on which the names of Israel's sons were inscribed;

Breastpiece – Bearing twelve precious stones, each inscribed with the name of Israel's tribes;

Robe – Sleeveless, seamless garment with embroidered pomegranates and gold bells;

Tunic – White, an inner garment worn over undergarments and stretching down to the ankles;

Turban – Made of fine linen and with a pure, gold plate inscribed with the words 'Holy to the Lord';

Sash – Embroidered with finely twisted linen and blue, purple, and scarlet yarn.

Everything had been completed (v32) and *'the tent and all its furnishings'* (v33) were presented to Moses for his final inspection. This included the frames and fixings, posts and bases, curtains and coverings, ark, table, lampstand, altars, ropes and tent pegs, as well as each of the priestly garments. There are three things to note from vv42-43:

1 THE COMPLETION OF ALL THE WORK

Everything in the making of the tabernacle's equipment was complete. There was nothing to finish off at a later date. There was no 'snagging list' to be addressed. Some of the tasks had been extremely detailed and precise. Other tasks had been very repetitive, and some had been dirty (for example, the preparing and curing of the rams' skins and the dugongs' hides used for the tent).

Some of the work would always be on view (for example, the lampstand, altars, table, and ark), and other work would always be concealed (for example, the carpentry under the hammered gold, the middle coverings of the tent). But all of the work had been done. We, too, should aim to finish everything well. We live in an age when variety and change are the order of the day. People don't stick with a task if it's too difficult. They try something else. This spills over into the life of our churches, too. If the work is too hard, then give up, try something else, move on, we're told. But the Bible consistently teaches commitment, perseverance, and persistence. God is looking for those who will complete the task he has given to them, however challenging, testing, unpleasant, or hazardous that task may be. Our greatest example is Jesus (John ch17 v4). We praise God that Jesus was a Finisher! *'Tis finished! The Messiah dies! Cut off for sins, but not his own. Accomplished is the sacrifice: the great redeeming work is done'.* [Charles Wesley]

2 THE COMPLIANCE OF ALL THE WORKMANSHIP

The one thing, emphasised repeatedly in these chapters, is that the Israelites' workmanship was 'divinely compliant'. *Just as the Lord commanded Moses'* (vv1, 5, 7, 21, 26, 29, 31, 42, 43). Everything complied perfectly with God's design. His plan and schedule were complied with meticulously. Our lives must be 'heaven-compliant'. Are we striving to listen, not to the various voices of men, but to the voice of God? It's one thing to be defiant of the Bible's critics, but are we compliant with the Bible's teachings?

3 THE COMPLIMENT OF ALL THE WORKERS

The four telling words at the end of the chapter were *'So Moses blessed them'.* They had passed the kit inspection with flying colours. Moses' blessing was a fitting tribute to the thousands of hours of devoted work that the Israelites had expended in the building of the tabernacle. This would have been one of the most momentous days in Israel's history. The result of their united service and sacrifice was a blessing. We should learn that a church will also experience great blessings when it is united in service and sacrifice. We don't all have the same skills, nor can we all exert equal effort. We don't all have the same resources. But we should all be united in our commitment to the Lord's work in the building up of his spiritual church, and we should be equally committed to one another if we are a part of that church. 'Blessing' comes from the word translated 'eulogy', that is, to speak well of someone. As Christians, we should speak well of each other. We must try to build each other up, to support, to encourage, and to bless. Moses could have criticised his people for many things, but he blessed them. God blesses his faithful servants still.

APRIL 20
EXODUS ch40.1-38

TRAVELLING WITH GOD

It seems that, after all the component parts of the tabernacle had been completed, the structure was erected in a single day (v17). The Israelites had entered the Sinai desert exactly three months after leaving Egypt (ch19 v1), so the tabernacle was set up within nine months from that date. The first Passover took place in the first month of the Hebrew calendar (Abib/Nisan), corresponding with our March/April. It was precisely on the fourteenth day of the first month that the lamb was sacrificed and the Passover meal eaten. So the tabernacle was set up just two weeks short of that great anniversary when the Israelites would celebrate their mighty deliverance. In vv1-33 the tabernacle was erected carefully with nothing missing or out of place. Everything was fit for God's holy visitation. If the Israelites had completed all their work (ch39 v42), we are now informed that Moses' work was completed too (v33). This reminds us:

1 Our Assignment needs to be Finished: As Christians, we are assigned particular tasks. These may be short-term assignments, such as the faithful witness to an unbelieving friend or the practical help for someone in special need. Although we find ourselves in a 'give up and throw away' society, we must finish each God-given assignment meticulously. Some of our assignments may be long-term, even lifelong, as we represent Jesus wherever he places us.

2 Our Atonement needs to be Finished: The whole of the tabernacle is an ornate symbol of the atoning work of Jesus. Every feature is a demonstration of how reconciliation with God is achieved through sacrifice. We are brought near to God, and God's presence dwells with us. The perfect, never-to-be-repeated sacrifice is Jesus (Hebrews ch10 v14). While we are pleased that Moses *finished the work* (v33), we are eternally pleased that Jesus finished his work (John ch19 v30). Regarding the tabernacle, eventually its gold would tarnish, its wood would rot, its animal hides would decay, its bread would go mouldy, its priestly garments would become threadbare, and all its priests would die. The tabernacle was necessary, but it was transient (Hebrews ch10 vv1-4). The priests always performed their ministry standing; they never sat down. There were no seats in the tabernacle because their work was never finished! By contrast, after Jesus had made his perfect sacrifice, he sat down, signifying eternal completion (Hebrews ch10 v12). For the moment, however, God's temporary dwelling place was finished, and his glory took up residence (v34). God had come to camp among his people, pointing to the day when he would 'pitch his tent' ('tabernacle') among his people in the person of his Son (John ch1 v14).

1 TRAVELLING WITH GOD'S PRESENCE

(v34) God approved of the construction, and his glorious presence was a sign of that approval. The Israelites could count on 'God with them' as we can count on 'God with us' (Immanuel). We are the temple of God and his Spirit lives in us (1 Corinthians ch3 v16; ch6 vv19-20; 2 Corinthians ch6 v16). We must therefore be careful to behave accordingly.

2 TRAVELLING TO GOD'S STANDARDS

(v35) God's uncompromising standard is holiness (Hebews ch12 v14). Even God's chosen servant couldn't enter because he was unholy. While God will never become corrupted by our presence, we can be transformed and made holy by his presence. Holiness, unlike salvation, demands hard work, perseverance, and tenacity. Holiness should permeate every fibre of our being and every sphere of our lives. We must live holy and godly lives (2 Peter ch3 vv11-12).

3 TRAVELLING IN GOD'S TIME

(vv36-37) The Israelites only moved forward when God's glorious cloud moved. If they set out prematurely, then they would forfeit God's providing and protecting presence. We all share the common urge to hurry God. While the Israelites had to be ready to move, they also had to be prepared to wait. That should be the state of our lives in the light of Jesus' promised return: 'Ready to go: prepared to wait'. But it should also be the attitude of our hearts daily in response to circumstances and challenges we encounter: 'Ready to go: prepared to wait'.

4 TRAVELLING BY GOD'S DIRECTION

(v38) The pillars of fire and cloud were used to lead the Israelites in the right direction. We can be confident that God's wisdom ensures that he always takes us in the right direction, even when we think that the shortest route between two points is a straight line. Navigating a mine field or a marsh will teach us otherwise. The importance of following a guide cannot be overstated. Jesus leads the way (John ch8 v12) and he guarantees his company (Matthew ch28 v20) right to our ultimate 'Exodus' and our arrival in the Promised Land of our wonderful Saviour.

APRIL 21
HEBREWS ch1.1-2

JESUS CHRIST IS THE GREATEST

This fifty-eighth book of the Bible, and nineteenth of the New Testament, is described as being a 'great commentary on the Old Testament' and 'the greatest commentary on the Book of Leviticus'. We don't know much about the background to this epistle.

AUTHORSHIP: The balance of evidence is in favour of someone other than Paul. Some argue for potential candidates including Luke, Barnabas, Apollos, Philip, Priscilla/Clement of Rome, and Silas. We don't know, and we're not meant to know.

READERSHIP: Hebrews – converted Jews who were familiar with the Old Testament, though we can't be sure which group of Hebrews. It was possibly those living in Jerusalem, or Alexandria, or Italy (and particularly, Rome), although ch13 v24 doesn't necessarily prove that the letter was written *from* Italy or *to* Italy.

DATE: Various ideas range from AD50 to AD100.

Although the authorship, readership, and date of Hebrews may be shrouded in mystery, the motive of this anonymous author is unmistakable. There are two strands to the theme:

1 The Person of Christ: We're left in no doubt as to the supremacy and sufficiency of Jesus Christ. He is prominent and pre-eminent throughout the letter. There's nothing or no one like Jesus! You can parade all the greatest men from among the patriarchs, prophets, and priests. You may choose whichever king you like. You can pick on feast days, holy days, holy systems, holy vessels, and holy places. You may select anyone you care to, or select everyone, all together, and the conclusion is just the same: Jesus Christ is the greatest!

2 The Progress of Christians: Hebrews is more than just a letter: it's a written word of exhortation. There are challenges, warnings, and encouragements throughout (ref ch13 v22). This book has been written not to intimidate, but to invigorate; not to frighten, but to strengthen; not to pull down, but to build up.

Immediately, we are introduced to God's unique Son, the One and Only (John ch1 v14). The writer is in complete accord with all the New Testament authors that 'God' is the true title of Jesus.

1 HIS SON – BY WHOM HE HAS SPOKEN ALL THINGS

Down through the avenues of time, God has raised up spokesmen, prophets, and messengers to voice his message. '...*But in these last days he has spoken to us by his Son*' (v2). The 'message of Jesus' is that 'Jesus is the message'. He's not just another religious radical or a 'fanatical faith merchant': he's the Prophet par excellence.

2 HIS SON – TO WHOM HE HAS GIVEN ALL THINGS

Jesus is God's Son and Heir. This is not a heirdom triggered by his Father's death, since he is immortal and eternal. Jesus has entitlement to the ownership of all things since he is the Son and *'firstborn over all creation'* (Colossians ch1 v15). The privileges and rights of sonship are all conferred upon Jesus. He is not only the appointed head over all things (Ephesians ch1 v22); he is the appointed heir of all things. Believers are *'co-heirs with Christ'*. If you are an heir, then you are being prepared for heirdom, and that means suffering (Romans ch8 v17). Adoption means adaption, with all the attendant suffering of a long, painful process of preparing you for glory. The right attitude, the right behaviour, the right language, the right characteristics all need developing, and your present trials are preparing you for heirdom.

3 HIS SON – THROUGH WHOM HE HAS MADE ALL THINGS

The appointed heir of all things is also the appointed Creator of all things. The Son of God is the mighty Maker. *'Universe'* (or *'worlds'*) is not limited to the physical cosmos but embraces all of time and space. To deny the creation of the universe is to reject its Creator. To attack the six-day creation of the universe is not only to challenge the authority of the Bible as God's infallible word, but it also challenges the authority of Christ as God's incomparable Creator. God has created all things through his Son. The Bible reveals who it was who put life into our universe, and who it was who built the universe in which he installed life: it's God's Son, *'the appointed heir of all things'*, the One through whom *'he made the universe'*. Don't you want to magnify him and glorify him; to praise him and love him?

APRIL 22
HEBREWS ch1.3

THE FLAWLESS IMPRESS

The Lord Jesus is the focus of God's attention and the centre of his affection – and he should be OURS too! The writer to the Hebrews is constantly stimulating, comforting, and exhorting his fellow believers by drawing their attention to the Person of Christ:

1 HE REPRESENTS GOD'S BEING CEASELESSLY

- SO THAT WE MAY KNOW HIM

'The Son is the radiance of God's glory and the exact representation of his being'. The word for *'radiance'* does not imply a 'reflected brightness', like the moon reflects the sun. Jesus is not just 'bouncing' the light of God onto us. It may be said that the Old Testament messengers, whom God used *'at many times and in various ways'* (v1), reflected God's glory to a small degree. But Jesus comes, not to merely reflect God's glory, but to radiate God's glory himself. The 'Tent of Meeting' was the place where God dwelt with his people in a visible way (Exodus ch40 v34). In John ch1 v14 we are informed that in Jesus Christ, *'the Word became flesh and made his dwelling (tabernacled, encamped) among us'.* Just as the cloud of God's glory encamped among God's people, so the Christ of God's glory has encamped among us. Jesus came and 'pitched his tent among us' in the body of his flesh. In Jesus Christ, God was made man.

Jesus also came to reveal and to represent God's being. The word for *'representation'* gives us our words 'character' and 'characteristic'. The Greek word refers to a tool for cutting or embossing. Jesus is the perfect impress of God's being. He is the flawless stamp of God's essence and substance (John ch1 v18; ch14 v9; Colossians ch1 v15; 2 Corinthians ch4 v6). Jesus represents God so that we may know him. The popular notion, that it's possible to know God through a variety of means and mediators, runs contrary to the revealed truth of Scripture. It's Jesus, the unique One, the One and Only, who represents God exactly.

2 HE SUSTAINS GOD'S CREATION CONTINUOUSLY - SO THAT WE MAY TRUST HIM

He has created all things (v2), and he sustains all things (v3). But any idea that Christ upholds the universe as some kind of 'Atlas' is nonsense. He sustains *'all things by his powerful word'.* Some religious philosophers and teachers have a vested interest in persuading us that God started the universe, but he doesn't sustain it. That suits the evolution theory of many professing Christians, because a 'sustaining God' would threaten their interpretations. It also suits the kind of Pelagianism that asserts man's control of his own destiny, denying God's sovereignty. But Jesus Christ is the Master Controller of time and space, geography and history, thrones and dominions, life and purpose. And if he actively sustains all things, should we not trust him?

3 HE FULFILS GOD'S MISSION COMPLETELY - SO THAT WE MAY APPROACH HIM

Which mission? His mission is to provide *'purification for sins'*. There are two aspects of this mission:

JESUS' ATONEMENT: A treatment or medication that purges us is known as 'catharsis' (from the Greek word for *'purification'*). Although Christ's representing role and sustaining role is continuous, his purifying work is once and for all. The very point about Christ's atoning work is that it's *not* continuous or repeated (John ch17 v4).

JESUS' ENTHRONEMENT: The permanent once-and-for-all nature of Christ's atonement is emphasised by his enthronement. The high priest's duties in the Old Testament were always temporary. The work was incomplete. There were no chairs or pews in the tabernacle, and so the high priest couldn't sit down. But through Jesus, the work is finished! He has done it all to the full satisfaction of his Father, and he never has to make a re-run.

These opening verses introduce us to Jesus, our Prophet (*'...He has spoken to us by his Son'*), our Priest (providing *'purification for sins'*), and our King (*'...sat down at the right hand of the majesty in heaven'*). For the child of God, communing with God, it's open access'. The veil is torn down, and the 'way in' is clear.

How much of a priority is it for us to spend time in God's presence, enjoying the freedom and privilege of approaching him because of Christ's unique work and role?

APRIL 23
HEBREWS ch1.4-14

JESUS CHRIST IS GREATER THAN ANGELS

The famous heavyweight boxer of the twentieth century was Muhammed Ali. His own claim, which became the catchphrase throughout his boxing career, was *'I am the greatest!'* However true Ali's claim may have been in the world of boxing, the writer to the Hebrews makes it crystal clear in asserting the truth that 'Jesus Christ is the greatest'. There's no one like Jesus. He is incomparable!

In continuing the staggering list of comparisons, this section declares that Jesus Christ is greater than angels.

To Jewish thinking, angels were holy, heavenly beings only second to God himself. Consequently, angels were honoured, reverenced, exalted, and worshipped. Like agents on secret service, angels were believed to hold great sway over the forces of Satan and sin. But reading v4 in isolation has spawned heresy in the Church. Christ has not become superior to the angels by some recent promotion. He has not been given a new name, or a new status, or a new title as a reward for successfully completing his Father's mission. Jesus Christ has been forever the Son of God. He has been forever superior to angels, and forever he has had a superior name to theirs. Jesus is the eternal Son of God.

1 JESUS CHRIST IS GREATER THAN ANGELS IN HIS SONSHIP (v5)

Some acknowledge that Jesus is more than a man, but not quite God! The 'compromise Christ' of some religious thinkers is not the Christ of the Bible. If he is not God over all and God altogether, he is certainly not the God of Scripture. Jesus deserves all honour as God (John ch5 vv22-23). Jesus is not just another angel, or even the greatest among angels: he is God the Son.

2 JESUS CHRIST IS GREATER THAN ANGELS IN HIS WORSHIP (vv6-7)

Jesus is God's Son and heir. He is the Firstborn (Colossians ch1 vv15, 18; Romans ch8 v29). And if there's any shadow of doubt about Christ's deity, the author quotes the Hebrew Bible: *'Let all God's angels worship him'*. Could you imagine that all the hosts of holy angels were mistaken in giving worship to Jesus? Of course not! It was the angel Gabriel who said to Mary (Luke ch1 v35) *'...the Holy One to be born will be called the Son of God'*. Gabriel and all the angelic battalions are members of God's Special Service. Just as *'wind'* and the *'flames of fire'* (v7) are God's created servants, so too are angels. Their 'design-purpose' is to worship God – God the Father, God the SON, and God the Holy Spirit. If God's angels worship Jesus ceaselessly, shouldn't God's people do so too?

3 JESUS CHRIST IS GREATER THAN ANGELS IN HIS KINGSHIP (v8)

All are subject to heaven's superior Sovereign. This verse crushes any opposition to the deity of Christ. Here are two powerful symbols of Christ's kingship:

His Throne of Everlastingness: The one place where believers may find security and stability is in *'the glorious throne exalted from the beginning'* which is *'the place of our sanctuary'* (Jeremiah ch17 v12). But it's not too lofty and aloof to approach it. The throne of greatness is also the throne of grace (ch4 v16).

His Sceptre of Righteousness: Not only is a sceptre an emblem of authority, but it also conveys the character of that authority. Christ's loyal subjects will be characterised by righteousness too (Matthew ch5 vv6, 10, ch6 v33; Philippians ch1 v11; 1 Timothy ch6 v11)

4 JESUS CHRIST IS GREATER THAN ANGELS IN HIS COMPANIONSHIP (v9)

Angels are God's appointed messengers, but they are our appointed ministers. Yet they do not provide the companionship of Jesus. He is the Friend of sinners (Matthew ch11 v19). And he rejoices (*'oil of joy'*) in our friendship. Believers are called his *'friends'* (John ch15 v13).

5 JESUS CHRIST IS GREATER THAN ANGELS IN HIS CRAFTSMANSHIP (vv10-12)

Christ is the Creator, and angels are the creatures.

He's Timeless: – Jesus transcends time, but *'My times are in your hands'* (Psalm 31 v15).

He's Changeless: – Everything changes except Jesus. *'You remain the same'*.

He's Endless – *'...Your years will never end'*. He is the eternal Son of God.

6 JESUS CHRIST IS GREATER THAN ANGELS IN HIS LORDSHIP (v13)

This quote begins, *'The LORD says to my LORD...'* (Psalm 110 v1). All the enemies of Christ and his people will be made his footstools. If you're on Jesus' side, then be comforted to know that every adversary of yours will ultimately become his footstool.

APRIL 24
HEBREWS ch2.1-4

PAYING MORE CAREFUL ATTENTION

Following on from the clear reminders of ch1 – the exaltation of the Lord Jesus Christ, God's Son and Heir, as God's Final Word to humanity – *'we must pay more careful attention'*.

In the past, God had sent many messages through the prophets. Even angels had been dispatched from the throne room of heaven to bring God's word to God's people. But the ultimate divine communiqué has come through no one less than God's Son. This is Jesus, whom all God's angels worship (ch1 v6); whose throne is everlasting (ch1 v8); who is immortal (ch1 v8), unchangeable and eternal (ch1 v12); the undisputed, unconquerable King of Glory (ch1 v13). This is Jesus, the unique Son, the One and Only, through whom God has chosen to speak personally – *'Therefore'* says the writer, *'we must pay more careful attention'*.

But why should we pay more careful attention?

1 SO THAT WE DON'T DRIFT AWAY FROM WHAT WE HEAR (v1)

The Cornish coastline, in particular, has been the backdrop to a huge catalogue of terrible shipwrecks. But other maritime calamities can occur much more slowly and gently. Vessels have drifted from their anchorage – slowly, quietly, almost indiscernibly – and people have only noticed when it has been too late. Frequently, this is because crews have not been *'paying more careful attention'*. Many Christian casualties occur, like many maritime casualties, not through the violence of the conditions, but merely through not paying more careful attention. The result is drifting. It can happen very slowly at first! We must pay more careful attention, or we shall become careless in our Christianity.

We become careless about our prayer life

Why is it that, for many believers, prayer is a chore? Is it because their love for Christ is not very deep?

We become careless about God's word

As with prayer, the daily reading of the Bible becomes neglected, and we start to drift.

We become careless about church services

You know you're drifting when you calculate the minimum attendance necessary to remain respectable in the view of most church members.

We become careless about our responsibilities

Relinquishing responsibilities and duties in God's service to spend more time on oneself can be an indication of drifting.

We become careless about our relationships with the world

The New Testament emphasises the importance of believers being different from the world. But the church today seems to be doing the opposite by making believers more like the world. It's not long before Christians can be caught up in risqué entertainment, social drinking, fashion addiction, and then they're drifting–drifting from the fixed bearing of God's word; from personal holiness and a stand for truth

2 SO THAT WE DON'T DISOBEY WHAT WE KNOW (v2)

If the law that was mediated by angels (Deuteronomy ch33 v2; Acts ch7 vv38, 53; Galatians ch3 v19) is so binding and carries with it such dire consequences for disobedience (Leviticus ch24 vv10-16; Numbers ch15 vv32-36), then how much more the word and the gospel that is mediated through Jesus? We must heed and obey the commands of Jesus if we truly love him (Proverbs ch19 v16; John ch14 v21; 1 John ch2 v5). The close relationship between love and obedience is obvious.

3 SO THAT WE DON'T IGNORE WHAT WE NEED (vv3-4)

We dare not treat God's great salvation lightly. It's not to be ignored or neglected.

An Immeasurable Salvation

It's *'great'* in every sense. Immeasurable are its depths (Romans ch11 v33); height (Ephesians ch4 v10); fulness (Ephesians ch4 v13); completeness (Hebrews ch7 v25)

An Inescapable Condemnation

This is implied by the text *'How shall we escape...?'* (See Matthew ch23 v33).

An Unanswerable Question

The 'narrow escape lane' of *'such a great salvation'* has been clearly signposted in the gospel. To miss this saving message of Christ will result in plunging headlong into destruction.

If you know in your heart that you have become a spiritual drifter, then resolve to make Jesus the Lord of your priorities, values, energies, career, and aspirations.

APRIL 25
HEBREWS ch2.5-9

WHO DO WE SEE?

It appears that vv1-4 are in parenthesis. It's not that these verses are less important. On the contrary! It's because they are so important that they have been included in the text. But after the solemn warning and the challenging question of vv1-4, verse 5 continues with the princely theme of 'Jesus Christ - greater than angels'. We are provided with two subjects to survey, each of which we may view from different perspectives.

1 WE SEE MAN

Lower than the angels

Psalm 8 is the great Song of Creation, which is quoted. In the midst of God's pristine creatorial handiwork, he positions mankind. He is crowned higher than any earthly creature but lower than the heavenly beings: *'lower than the angels'*. He is instated as ruler over the works of God's hands, as God's vice-regent on earth (Genesis ch1 vv26-27). Mankind is the pièce de résistance of God's workmanship, the crowning glory of his creation. Yet his vice-regency has been challenged and compromised by sin. He has limited rule on earth, and he struggles, for example, with containing disease, making contingencies for famine and drought, and is helpless in the face of tsunamis and hurricanes.

Higher than the angels

For the moment, we are caught up with this present evil world, but there is *'the world to come'* (v5). Rulership in that world will be assigned to the children of God (1 Corinthians ch6 v3). Angels are special agents in the present world. In the new world of a renewed creation, redeemed man will have his 'crown of glory and honour' restored.

Greater than the angels

Men and women are only greater than the angels because of the dignity and honour that God has conferred upon them, making them in his own likeness; redeeming them; indwelling them by his Spirit; restoring them to the likeness of Jesus. Angels are exempted from these privileges. God didn't spare angels who sinned (2 Peter ch2 v4; Jude 6). The Good News of salvation is foreign to angels' experience (1 Peter ch1 v12). The view of man, promulgated by an atheistic world, reveals him to be 'just a higher form of evolution', whereas the Bible reveals him to be just *'a little lower than the angels'*.

Your view of man will determine your views on such ethical issues as abortion, contraception, euthanasia, reproductive technologies, genetic engineering and stem cell research. If you have the view that we are only frogs that have changed into princes, then there is no special value, worth, dignity or uniqueness in humanity. As a consequence, our society has few qualms about murdering babies in the womb, producing foetuses with which to experiment and killing the old, the sick and the disabled. The Bible teaches that God created man to rule over creation; to bring him glory and to be enjoyed forever.

2 WE SEE JESUS

Psalm 8 is perfectly fulfilled in Jesus. He applies Psalm 8 v2 to himself in Matthew ch21 v16. Paul quotes Psalm 8 v6 in 1 Corinthians ch15 v27.

Lower than the angels

This Jesus, with a superior position and a superior name to angels (ch1 v4) *'was made a little lower than the angels'* (v9). Jesus, the model Man of Psalm 8, was exposed to all the frailties and frustrations of human life and human death. He came to experience first-hand the suffering within a fallen world. Isaiah ch53 v7 reveals something of his patience, obedience and silence in his sufferings for sin upon the cross.

Higher than the angels

'now crowned with glory and honour'. It's precisely because Jesus endured the cross that he now wears the crown. The fathomless depths to which the Saviour descended is only matched by the dazzling heights to which he ascended.

Greater than the angels

This is the author's grand theme for these first twenty-three verses. Jesus is unique in every way and especially in the way that *'by the grace of God he might taste death for everyone'*. Every son (v10), every brother (v11) every child (v13) – everyone for whom Jesus tasted death will be brought to glory. Every saved person is only saved because Jesus has tasted death for him or her individually. *'We see Jesus'* – do you SEE Jesus?

And if you have seen him by faith, is Jesus now seen in you?

APRIL 26
HEBREWS ch2.10-13

OUR TRAILBLAZER

The word that describes Jesus in v10 is variously translated *'Author'*, *'Captain'*, *'Prince'* or *'Leader'*. The title proclaims 'one who takes precedence', 'one who leads the way' or 'one who blazes a trail for all to follow'. Jesus is the Trailblazer of our salvation. He has opened up *'a new and living way'* (ch10 v20), blazing a trail from earth to heaven, from the cross to the throne. Jesus has gone where no one else has ever been: to the cross of humiliation, degradation and sacrifice. It's clear that Jesus didn't become an angel to rescue fallen man. He stooped lower than that! He came to earth as man in order to blaze a trail of salvation for the redeemed. Why? To *'bring many sons to glory'* and so that Jesus might be made *'perfect through suffering'* (v10).

Certainly Jesus was not being made perfect in the sense that he had some deficiency or defect that needed addressing. But *'it was fitting'* that Jesus should endure unique suffering to become perfectly qualified as the Saviour of his people. It was suitable/appropriate/fitting, in the 'personal saving plan' of God, that Jesus should qualify as the trailblazing Saviour. But what kind of trail has Christ blazed for his people?

1 HE HAS BLAZED A TRAIL TO BRING THEM HOME (v10)

We may view our champion Christ descending from glory to do battle with his fiercest enemies. He conquers sin, death and Satan at the cross and he returns in the splendour of his triumph. But he doesn't return alone! He brings with him all the *'many sons'* whom he has liberated from their captivity. *'God exalted him to his own right hand as Prince (or Trailblazer) and Saviour that he might give repentance and forgiveness of sins to Israel'* (Acts ch5 v31).

How do you look upon your earthly journey? Do you look upon your life as a daily encampment… *'a day's march nearer home'* [J. Montgomery]? Or have you already come to regard this world as your home? Where's your permanent address? Is it earth or heaven? If you're not sure, then where are your valuables (Matthew ch6 v21)?

2 HE HAS BLAZED A TRAIL TO MAKE THEM HOLY (v11)

There is an inseparable relationship between the Sanctifier and the sanctified; between the One who sets apart and those who are set apart. The process, to bring outsiders into the family of God, means giving to them the new nature of Jesus. You don't drift into the family of God in the way that a stray cat drifts into a family home!

Those who are given *'the right to become children of God'* are those *who received him...who believe on his name'* (John ch1 vv11-13).

And every single believer, who has turned to Christ for his forgiveness and salvation, is set apart: identified in the family of God. But the kind of lifestyle that they lead will be the proof that they are *'of the same family'* as Jesus, our perfect Pioneer.

3 HE HAS BLAZED A TRAIL TO DECLARE THEIR HONOUR (vv12-13)

'So Jesus is not ashamed to call them brothers'. Jesus declares their honour in two ways:

i] He proclaims their name, and ii] He sings their praise.

The quotation from the Psalm of the Sufferer concerns the desolation and distress that Jesus endured during the agonies of his atonement. It's in this context that the suffering Messiah makes his announcement (Psalm 22 v22). Jesus provides access to the grace in which all believers stand. And he calls them *'brothers'*. But he doesn't keep this relationship secret. He doesn't hide the truth that those who were once sin-loving, heaven-hating, God-rejecting rebels are now in the same family.

After all that Joseph's brothers had done to him by despising him, ill-treating him and selling him into slavery, Joseph forgave them all. But Joseph didn't hide his relationship with these foreign shepherds who bowed and grovelled in his presence. Instead, he openly rejoiced over his brothers so that everyone, including Pharaoh himself, was informed of their family relationship. Joseph was not ashamed to call them 'brothers'.

But if Jesus is not ashamed to declare that you are his brother, are you ever ashamed to declare that he is your Brother, Saviour, Shepherd, and Friend (Mark ch8 v38)?

Christ, our triumphant Trailblazer, has left a clear trail for us to follow (1 Peter ch2 v21).

APRIL 27
HEBREWS ch2.14-18

DEALING WITH THE ENEMY

Jesus came into the world to *'share in (our) humanity'* (v14). It was imperative that Jesus became a man so that he could be appointed as a High Priest on behalf of men. He had to become a tempted Man so that he could help tempted man (v18). Jesus Christ had to die man's death so that man could live Christ's life.

Therefore, Jesus didn't stoop to become an angel. He stooped even *'lower than the angels'* to become a member of humanity. Jesus became the perfect pattern of mankind – the One who left faultless footprints on earth for all to follow.

But it's not enough to have an example: mankind needs a Saviour. *'Sharing in humanity';* partaking of flesh and blood; exhibiting a flawless example – cannot save on its own. Jesus not only lived a human life, but he died a human death. He suffered all the horrors and terrors of death upon a cross to become, not only the example to the faithful, but also the Saviour of his people. But what has Christ's death achieved? The conquering power of Christ's atoning death has dealt with four enemy powers:

1 CHRIST'S DEATH NEUTRALISES THE POWER OF DEATH (v14)

Any power that the devil possesses is only under the whole over-arching sovereignty of God. But Satan has been permitted to wield the power of death. The devil is the prince and protagonist of sin, and the consequences of sin are death. Jesus declared that *'the devil...was a murderer from the beginning'* (John ch8 v44). The Lord Jesus came into the world, assuming the frailty of humanity, to disarm this 'serial killer'. Death is not destroyed completely for the moment. But its potency has been neutralised for the believer. Death still goes through the motions but it has no sting for the Christian (1 Corinthians ch15 vv54-57). It was at the cross, where the devil directed all his venom, that death stung itself to death.

2 CHRIST'S DEATH REMOVES THE POWER OF FEAR (v15)

If death cannot harm the believer, we must acknowledge that the fear of death can sometimes paralyse usefulness. There are slaves to the fear of death. But Jesus came as our Trailblazer to live our life, to die our death, so that all terrors may be removed. If you are trusting in the cross of Jesus, you are safe and secure (Psalm 23 v4).

3 CHRIST'S DEATH CANCELS THE POWER OF SIN (vv16-17)

Jesus had to be made like his brothers *'in every way'*, except for sin. He did this to qualify as an effective High Priest. How could he do this? By turning aside God's wrath; by wiping out sin; by annulling the power of sin that creates a barrier between God and man. Although the death of Jesus was both atoning and reconciling, the word *'propitiation'* (v17) more accurately describes the turning away of God's judicial anger by providing an offering. God graciously provides the means of removing and deflecting his own wrath. Jesus is the High Priest who is *'merciful'* to sinners and *'faithful'* in his service to God.

4 CHRIST'S DEATH CONQUERS THE POWER OF TEMPTATION (v18)

Just as Jesus was made like us *'in every way'* (v17), so he was tempted like us *'in every way'* (ref ch4 v15). Jesus was tested at specific times throughout his earthly life, but ultimately his greatest test, his fiercest trial, was in his suffering and death on the cross. But it is because of this that Jesus *'is able to help those who are being tempted'*. A fellow Man has encountered the same temptations that you and I face, and he has triumphed. He has passed the test at every point.

God has appointed 'help' within the church through fellow members, encouragers, elders, deacons, and pastors. But there's no one who helps like Jesus.

If you are suffering from recurring temptations and your power of resistance is weakened, then rush to Jesus, our ever-present Help in time of need. How can we know his help in our personal and particular temptations?

Tell Jesus about them. Be specific. Tell him all the details.

Confess your own inadequacy at coping with temptation. Confess your sin and how prone you are to giving in to temptation. Seek his power to resist.

Read God's Word. Be assured of his direct help. Be encouraged by the many accounts in Scripture of those who overcame by God's grace and help.

Don't deliberately court temptation. Avoid its lure and influence.

APRIL 28
HEBREWS ch3.1-6

JESUS CHRIST IS GREATER THAN MOSES

The writer enjoins the *'holy brothers'* (who are set apart by God through receiving the *'heavenly calling'*) to concentrate on Christ. This is One who is greater than all the prophets and greater than all the angels. Our own response to these six verses may take the form of two words:

1 FOCUS

'Fix your thoughts on Jesus'...*'consider Jesus'*...think about him... meditate on him. Jesus deserves our thorough consideration and complete concentration. In comparing Jesus with Moses, the author is driving at the heart of Old Testament Jewish religion.

- Moses is regarded as the great national hero – the champion and saviour of the Israelis, delivering them from slavery in Egypt.

- There's no other Old Testament figure who compares with Moses. He was the servant of the Lord (Numbers ch12 v7) and enjoyed a special relationship with the Lord.

- God declared Moses to be *'faithful in all (his) house'* (Numbers ch12 v7) and the one with whom he spoke *'face to face'* (Numbers ch12 v8).

- Moses is also described as being *'more humble than anyone else on the face of the earth'* (Numbers ch12 v3).

- Moses had a great zeal and enthusiasm for God. He was the lawgiver under God, so that the Pentateuch is described as the 'Books of Moses' and the 'Law of Moses'.

- Moses was the leader of his people: their intercessor; their patriarch; their prophet; their 'father' and the mediator of the covenant.

Moses was great! Moses was greater than all other leaders and mediators. But Jesus Christ is the greatest. How was Jesus greater than Moses?

Jesus is appointed to Greater Office: (v1) *'Apostle'* (meaning 'one who is sent') identifies Jesus as the One who had been sent by his Father (John ch10 v36; ch20 v21; Romans ch8 v3). Jesus had been sent to the poor, the prisoners, the blind, and the oppressed (Luke ch4 v18). Jesus is also our *'High Priest'* (of which the author has much to say later in the epistle).

Jesus is worthy of Greater Honour: (v3) God honoured Moses in many ways throughout his life by revealing, empowering, entrusting, equipping, and inspiring. But Jesus is worthy of greater honour.

Jesus is faithful in Greater Service: Moses' service was uniquely special and singularly important in the founding of the Israeli nation. But there are four contrasts we can make between Moses' service to God and Jesus' service to God:

i] Moses was *in* God's house: Jesus was *over* God's house (vv5-6).

ii] Moses had honour as a member: Jesus had honour as the Builder

(vv3-4).

iii] Moses was faithful as a servant: Jesus was faithful as a Son (vv5-6a).

iv] Moses was the witness of God: Jesus was the Word of God (v5; ref

ch1 vv1-2).

All the Mosaic signposts pointed to Jesus. There's no one like him. Therefore, Jesus must be the focus of our meditation and contemplation; our reading; our Christian service and our conversations.

2 FASTEN

The condition that we are members of *'his house'* is that we hold on/hold firmly/fasten to *'our courage and the hope of which we boast'* (v6). This does not assert that salvation is dependent upon our efforts or achievements. Christ is essential to our salvation. We cannot save ourselves either by giving our cash to the church or by giving our hearts to Jesus. Salvation is God's work from start to finish. But what is the evidence of God's gracious saving work? It's just this: *'if we hold on (fasten onto) our courage and the hope of which we boast'*. Perseverance is the identity tag of the true believer (Matthew ch10 v22; ch24 v13). If a person claims to be a believer but there is no evidence of their perseverance, endurance, tenacity, or faithfulness, then their claim is hollow and false. Live confidently for the Lord. Fasten onto *'courage'* and *'hope'* as you focus clearly upon Jesus.

APRIL 29
HEBREWS ch3.7-19

THE DESPERATE DANGER OF UNBELIEF

Some people claim to believe only what they can see, that is, the visible and the tangible. That, of course, is nonsense! When asked whether they believe in gravity, electricity, or the wind, they are forced to backtrack and explain that they can see the effects of each of those phenomena. When you point to the effects of the grace of God upon those who have been miraculously transformed, they don't want to know. They prefer to remain entrenched in unbelief.

Behind the obvious human authorship of the Scriptures, there is a divine momentum. Peter reminds us that *'men spoke from God as they were carried along by the Holy Spirit'* (2 Peter ch1 vv20-21). The anonymous author is just the penman. It is God the Spirit who speaks these solemn words (v7). What are the dangers of unbelief?

1 UNBELIEF HARDENS HEARTS

(vv8, 13, 15). In medical terms, the prefix 'scler' refers to something 'dry' or 'hard' (for example, scleritis, scleroma, sclerosis). It frequently refers to a condition that progressively deteriorates. There is an increasing dryness or hardness with time. Unless there is drastic intervention, tissues and membranes will become completely insensitive. It's precisely this word that is used three times in this chapter. There is grave danger in leaving the hardening process untreated. The hardening of the heart must be our chief concern. In hearing the message of God's word, everyone responds in one of two ways. They either receive that word (apply, submit to, obey) or they resist. Each time they resist, the hardening intensifies; the calluses become thicker. Moses' era is a case in point. The period of forty years in the desert is described as *'the rebellion'* (vv8, 15).

2 UNBELIEF LEADS ASTRAY

(vv10, 12) It's the *'sinful, unbelieving heart'* that rejects the truth about God. The point at which a person *'turns away from the living God'* is almost always the point at which they have a deficient view of God: a view that is incompatible with Scripture. The original for *'turn away'* or *'departs'* gives us our word 'apostasy', meaning rebellion, defection, and the abandonment of the truth. Those who have professed faith in Christ, but who have later rejected and abandoned their position, prove the falseness of their earlier claims. It's only if we *'hold firmly to the end the confidence we had at first'*, which is the irrefutable evidence that *'we have come to share in Christ'* (v14)

3 UNBELIEF PROHIBITS ENTRY

(vv17-19) The Israelites, who had witnessed God's delivering and preserving power, reacted adversely to the reports from those who had been sent to explore Canaan (Numbers chs13-14). They were bitter towards God and their leaders. Because of their unbelief, the Lord sentenced them to wander in the desert for forty years. All those who were twenty years old and above, who had rebelled against God, would die in the desert. All the unbelievers were barred from entry to the Promised Land (v19). The great spiritual picture is clear (John ch3 v36).

Urgent action is required today! This action may take three forms.

Today is for hearing clearly:

There's an urgency about teaching the Bible and preaching the Gospel. There's also an urgency to hear and to respond to the message (John ch5 v24; Romans ch10 v17). We need to hear God speaking to our hearts – convicting, warning, instructing, encouraging, convincing – and we must not delay our response.

Today is for helping personally:

v13. Encourage/exhort each other. Be of mutual help to each other. This is our daily duty. Don't get a reputation for being a cynic and a critic. Ensure that others don't learn to associate your name with discouragement and despondency. Be a source of help to your fellow believer. Begin today!

Today is for holding firmly:

If you are a genuine *'sharer/partaker in Christ'* then you will *'hold firmly'* to your initial faith in Christ (v14). Those who don't 'remain' prove that they 'don't belong' (1 John ch2 v19).

Today is the day of action. We must not be guilty of procrastinating. If you do not act today, then it may be too late!

APRIL 30
HEBREWS ch4. 1-13

THE GOSPEL OF REST

For many people today, rest is denied, and for others, rest is elusive. Though we live in a 'playtime society' that is obsessed with games, sport, leisure, and holidays, yet there are many to whom real rest is a myth or a dream. But in the Lord Jesus Christ, there is genuine, lasting, refreshing, heavenly rest (Matthew ch11 v28). These first thirteen verses proclaim a 'gospel of rest'. We may identify three kinds of 'rest' here:

Creation Rest – the Sabbath rest God took at the end of the first week (vv3, 4, 10).

Canaan Rest – the Promised Land into which Joshua led the obedient (vv5-8).

Conversion Rest – the rest that comes through faith in Jesus (v11).

But how can we define the word 'rest'? It's not the rest of inactivity. It's not about 'doing nothing'.

'Rest' can be described by three different words.

Cessation

The Greek word for 'rest' gives us our English word *pause*. It's a cessation from what has preceded. God ceased from his six-day work of creation. The Israelis ceased their forty-year struggle in the desert. The believer ceases from his own efforts to save himself when he is converted, and he will ultimately cease from the burdens and battles of this life when he enters heaven's rest.

Completion

Wherever the word 'rest' is used, there's an indication that something has been completed. In God's plan, 'rest' is the signal of fulfilment. God's programme comes to fruition.

Communion

In the context of mankind enjoying 'rest', it's always about a right relationship with God, whether it's Canaan or heaven, the life of sanctification, or the daily, uninterrupted walk with God. Jesus explained that divine rest for burdened souls can only be found in being yoked to him (Matthew ch11 v28). The secret of a soul at rest is a soul at peace with God, through Christ's reconciling work.

What can we learn from these verses about the 'gospel of rest'?

1 NO HEARING WITHOUT PREACHING (vv1-2)

Christendom's media moguls may have designed alternative communication packages, but the divinely appointed means of publishing the gospel is through the preaching of the word of God (Romans ch10 v14). The Good News of redemption, atonement, reconciliation, and substitution was preached repeatedly to the Israelis in the desert. Reinforced by the signs, symbols, and ceremonies of the Passover, the tabernacle, the priesthood, and the sacrificial systems, the Good News about Christ was preached.

2 NO VALUE WITHOUT FAITH (v2)

Hearing the message is of no value without the faith to believe and act upon it. The Israelis heard the word preached to them about the Promised Land, but they rejected it. They didn't combine hearing with faith. You can't expect to know about resting unless you know something about trusting.

3 NO ENTRY WITHOUT OBEDIENCE (vv3-6)

Due to their disobedience, the Israelis were barred from Canaan. They had been disqualified from admission on the grounds of their disobedience. The pattern that God introduced for one day's rest in seven was established in the creation week (Exodus ch20 vv8-11). Rest is an essential ingredient of creation, and it is an essential ingredient of redemption. The Christ of the cosmos is the Christ of the cross. The *'Sabbath rest for the people of God'* (v9) is enduring, eternal, and reserved for every child of God.

4 NO CONVICTION WITHOUT SCRIPTURE (vv12-13)

v12 doesn't stand in isolation from the preceding verses. We may not be able to confidently discern between a professor and a possessor of faith, but the Bible has no such difficulty. The X-ray capability of God's word cannot be thwarted. It pries, probes, and penetrates. Faithful Bible preaching disturbs. It makes us feel uncomfortable. We may writhe and squirm as the *'double-edged sword'* probes our motives, attitudes, aspirations, and consciences. So how must we respond to this gospel of rest?

Let us be Careful (v1)

We must be seriously concerned that we don't become like the disobedient, missing the opportunity this gospel gives to us.

Let us make every Effort (v11)

Persistence and perseverance, steadfastness and single-mindedness are encouraged each and every day.

MAY 1
HEBREWS ch4.14-ch5.10

JESUS CHRIST IS GREATER THAN AARON

For fourteen centuries a civil leader in the form of a patriarch, judge, king or governor administered the Jewish people. During that period they were also administered by a religious leader. From Aaron to Phannias there were over eighty high priests that held this superior office and who were directly responsible to Almighty God.

In Hebrew the 'high priest' is referred to as '*the* priest' (sometimes 'great priest', 'head priest' or 'chief priest'). He was set apart from all other priests. He alone was anointed with holy oil (Leviticus ch21 v12) and appointed to wear the high priestly garments.

But here the writer shows that the highest 'high priest', and the greatest 'Great Priest' is *Jesus the Son of God* (v14). If Aaron was considered to be the first and foremost of high priests, in Jesus we have a greater than Aaron.

1 OUR GREAT HIGH PRIEST

There are five personal characteristics and priestly qualifications to note.

His Selection

Just as the high priests were divinely appointed, so Jesus meets that specific criterion. He is selected by God and *'designated by God to be high priest in the order of Melchizedek'* (v10). Jesus was *'called by God, just as Aaron was'* (v4) The 'selection' of Jesus doesn't imply that there were any other suitable candidates. There were none! The Son's equality with the Father is not in doubt, but Jesus the Son assumes the role of man, servant and priest to fulfil the redemptive plan.

His Sympathy

Jesus has compassion for us because he has a fellow feeling for our condition (ch4 v15). He has experienced humanity firsthand, and he is therefore able to sympathise with us in all our weaknesses and temptations. Though our High Priest is ascended and *'has gone through the heavens'* (v14) out of sight for the moment, yet he continues to be sympathetic to our circumstances.

His Sinlessness

Jesus was a sinless man living among sinful men. He was *'without sin'* (ch4 v15) and he *'did no sin'* (1 Peter ch2 v22). Jesus as High Priest had no need to offer sacrifices for his own sins, as all other priests did (ch5 v3). But if Jesus could not sin by virtue of his deity, how is it possible for him to *'sympathise with our weaknesses'* and to be *'tempted in every way just as we are'* (v15)? Yet Jesus did suffer all the agony of temptation even though he could never be defeated by it. Jesus has endured the vicious cuts and thrusts of the battle, even though the ultimate victory was never in doubt. If Jesus could have sinned it would have shown that he was not God, for God cannot sin.

His Submission

The obvious example of this in Jesus' life was his trial in Gethsemane. But Jesus submitted to his Father's will (Matthew ch26 vv38-42). Jesus *'was heard because of his reverent submission'* (v7).

His Suffering

There's no suggestion that Christ was not obedient before his suffering (v8). But his life of obedience prepared him and qualified him as our Great High Priest. It's in this sense that Jesus was *'made perfect'* through his suffering. 'Perfect' means 'complete'. His work was 'complete' and Jesus is our 'complete Saviour' who is superlatively qualified to intercede for us.

2 OUR GREAT RESPONSIBILITIES

'Let us hold firmly to the faith we profess' (v14).

This has been a matter of concern in the preceding passages (ch2 v1; ch3 v6; ch3 v14). *'Hold firmly'* means to seize and not let go. It's the same word used for holding onto a sheep so that it would not be dropped or released (Matthew ch12 v11). The believer must not be enticed to release his grip on the fundamentals of faith by the philosophies of our age, by political correctness, by social pressures or by intimidation from family, neighbours, employers and others.

'Let us approach the throne of grace with confidence' (v16).

There's no sin too great for God's mercy and no need too great for God's grace. It's possible to tell when a believer has not recently approached the throne with confidence. It's when they are overwhelmed with guilt and everything seems so bleak and desperate. It's when God seems so remote and when they are doubting God's provision. It's when they are wallowing in self-pity and when prayer and Bible study is such a chore. Don't delay in approaching God's gracious throne with confidence.

MAY 2
HEBREWS ch5.11-ch6.12

MOVING FORWARD IN YOUR FAITH

Progress is not only the assumed characteristic of mankind; it is the vital trait of a Christian. The author is concerned that his readers move forward in their faith, consolidating their previous position, but progressing to a greater knowledge, a better understanding, a wider experience and a stronger faith. If it's possible to summarise the passage in a so-called soundbite, the author might have said: 'Be mature! Be genuine! Be diligent!'

1 BE MATURE! (ch5 v11-ch6 v3)

There is much to be said about Christ's high priestly ministry, especially in relation to the enigmatic figure Melchizedek. But the author is afraid that his readers will not be able to grasp the significance because they are *'slow to learn'* (v11). They hadn't progressed as they should have. These Hebrews had been Christians for a long time. They should have been able to teach others. But they still needed the *'elementary truths of God's word'* taught to them *'all over again'* (v12). Are you like that? You've been a Christian for many years. You should have a good grasp of God's word and be able to teach others. But you're still struggling with the ABC of Biblical truth and consequently still playing in the 'nursery' of the church. You need:

The Right Food

If milk is your only diet, then you are either immature or sick. Feeding on the 'milk' of Sunday School stories and sipping at sweet homely homilies is not enough. Don't be a newborn Christian all your life! Grow up! Feed on the *'solid food'* of Scripture. One of the indicators of a nutritious diet is:

The Right Discernment

Christ-centred, Bible-focused thinking will enable us *'to distinguish good from evil'* and truth from error.

The Right Experience

(ch6 vv1-3) Although we may have differing experiences, they should all lead to maturity (*'leave'...'go on'*). Passing through childhood and adolescence to adulthood gives the right experience for development (1 Corinthians ch13 v11). The six examples given are foundational teachings. They are not to be dispensed with, as we don't dispense with the foundations of a building. They are essential. But when you fit a new kitchen or a bathroom, you don't have to dig up and re-lay the foundations. Rely on them. Build on them. Move on. Be mature!

2 BE GENUINE! (ch6 vv4-8)

The centre of the controversy that has provoked endless debate and divisions is to do with the meanings of the words *'enlightened'; 'tasted'; 'shared'* (vv4, 5). If you believe that these describe conversion and being saved, then you either need to conclude that it is hypothetical and cannot happen (that is, *'it is impossible'*), or you'll argue that it's possible to be saved and lost again. This latter position militates against the whole tenor of the New Testament. A believer's security is only ever in doubt if it's left to him. If left with Christ, he is unquestionably safe and secure (John ch10 vv27-29). No-one can prise God's sheep from the Good Shepherd's hand. So vv4-8 must speak about those who are not genuine: those who are frauds, impostors or counterfeit disciples. They may have even spent time with Christians, testifying before congregations and preaching from pulpits, but who have never experienced salvation. They have *'shared in the Holy Spirit'* to the extent of being present when the Spirit has moved in regenerating and reviving power. They have witnessed the Bible's impact upon others and will have derived temporary benefit for themselves, but they have *'fallen away'*. Such apostates are guilty of trampling underfoot the blood of Christ and despising his sacrifice, just as if they are re-crucifying Him. They may have been at the hub of church life: active, prominent and witnessing answers to others' prayers. But by turning their backs on Jesus and his cross they have proved that they are not genuine believers at all. Their hatred for Jesus has not replaced love for him, since they never really loved him in the first place. They choose darkness to *enlightening*; they spit out what they have *tasted*; they sever themselves from what they have *shared*. The author is confident though that his Hebrew readers are not apostates (v9).

3 BE DILIGENT! (ch6. vv9-12)

There's no room for laziness or slothfulness in God's family. Be diligent in:

Helping (v10) We show love to God in the way we help his people;

Persevering (v11) Being patient and faithful to the end will confirm *'our hope';*

Imitating (v12) Copy those who are holy role models of faith (Romans ch12 v11).

MAY 3
HEBREWS ch6.13-20

SAFELY ANCHORED

Abraham's elderly wife Sarah thought that having a child at ninety years of age was impossible. In fact she laughed at the very thought that her tired and wrinkly body could produce a vibrant infant. The God who specialises in 'impossibilities' asked Abraham *'Is anything too hard for the Lord?'* (Genesis ch18 v14). God had promised that Abraham's offspring would be as numerous as the stars, and this promise would be fulfilled in Isaac. But then came the great blow a few years later (Genesis ch22 v2): *'Take your son, your only son Isaac, whom you love'* (the son on whom all the Abramic future family rests; the son in whom you have vested all your hopes for your descendants; the son of divine promise) *'and sacrifice him...as a burnt offering'*. When they got to Moriah, Isaac surrendered to Abraham, and Abraham surrendered to God. With Isaac on the altar and the knife in his hand, poised to take his son's life, what was going through Abraham's mind? 'Perhaps I've got this all wrong? Maybe I've misheard God's voice? Perhaps I'm all mixed up and need psychiatric counselling!?' No! Abraham was not thinking like that. Here was a man who lived close to God and Abraham knew that God kept his promises. *'Abraham reasoned that God could raise the dead'* (Hebrews ch11 v19). How's that for faith in God's word! And what was God's response? A promise and an oath (Genesis ch22 vv15-18).

Every child of God is now an *'heir of what was promised'* (v17), so there are two great and glorious guarantees that every believer can fasten onto:

1 AN UNCHANGEABLE AFFIRMATION

'two unchangeable things' (v18) – God's promise and his oath. God didn't *need* to confirm his promise with an oath. The word of God is enough. So what was the purpose of his dual affirmation? He wanted to make it abundantly clear that he would never go back on his word to redeem guilty sinners. This is *'the unchanging nature of his purpose'* (v17). His plan to redeem a people for himself meant the 'unthinkable' – God on a cross. But however unimaginable the details of the divine plan would be, God would not be deflected in his purpose. And he doesn't want us to think that he may one day amend or update his plan. The Greek word for *'unchanging'* is only used here in the Bible (vv17, 18). It's probably a technical word used in connection with making a will. God wants to make it absolutely clear to his true children that he will never cut them out of his will.

2 AN IMMOVABLE ANCHOR

If you were concerned about the security of a mooring, you may ask certain questions:

What is the anchor made of?

'hope' (vv18, 19). 'Hope' in Scripture never suggests uncertainty. It's always associated with confidence, faith and certainty. What is this particular 'hope'? It's hope in Jesus.

What vessel is it anchoring?

'the soul' (v19). It's the individual believer: his life and his being. The storms of life and death will sweep away every vessel that's not securely anchored in Christ.

Where is the anchor embedded?

It's not clinging precariously to time's shifting shingle, or the world's swirling sands, or the moving mud of philosophy or religion. Instead, it is secured in *'the inner sanctuary behind the curtain'* (v19). The high priest, once a year on the Day of Atonement, entered the Holiest Place under cover of blood. The Israelis pinned their hopes on God accepting the high priest and the sacrifice he offered. And *'(our) hope is built on nothing less than Jesus' blood and righteousness'* [Edward Mote]. Jesus the Great High Priest has entered the inner sanctuary through his death. He is accepted at the throne of God. That's where our 'anchor' must be embedded.

What is your anchor's condition?

'firm and secure' (v19). If you are anchored in Jesus, then you may be *'greatly encouraged'* (v18). Take a close look at the Lord Jesus. The more you examine him, the more you will be able to trust him. Everything and everyone else in time and space changes and deteriorates. But Jesus is the one, fixed, constant point. Let us continually inspect the matchless wonders of the Lord Jesus, not because he is subject to change, but so that we can be more encouraged in our faith and more convinced of his unchangeable, immovable security.

MAY 4

HEBREWS ch7.1-28

JESUS CHRIST IS GREATER THAN MELCHIZEDEK

In vv1-10 we have a commentary on the incident recorded in Genesis ch14 vv18-20. The Old Testament character Melchizedek prefigures Jesus. Just as an image is formed by using the impress of a seal, so we may talk of events and characters in the Old Testament as being 'types' of New Testament truths. There are Old Testament characters, like Melchizedek, who are types of Christ. Although some commentators have referred to Melchizedek as a prototype of Christ, in fact Jesus is the original, the model and the seal. Jesus is the divine die from whom all the types are stamped. In what way is Melchizedek a type of Christ?

His Name

v2 *First, his name means 'King of Righteousness.'* We see how that this great name, however much it may have represented Melchizedek, is perfectly suited to Christ. He is our great King of Righteousness (2 Timothy ch4 v8; 1 John ch2 v1)

His City

'King of Salem'. Although maybe just a small, fortified city in Melchizedek's day, it is believed to be the beginning of 'Jeru-salem' – the foundations of 'peace'. Psalm 110 connects Zion and Melchizedek.

His Background

v3. Some believe this enigmatic Old Testament king to be a theophany: a pre-incarnate manifestation of Christ (although *'like the Son of God'* seems to suggest that he was not the Son of God). Neither Melchizedek nor Jesus had the fundamental qualification for Jewish high priesthood, that is, descent from Aaron (Melchizedek preceded Aaron). Jesus came from Judah, not Levi (vv14-16).

His Offices

Both Jesus and Salem's king held dual offices of king and priest (v1). This ancient king-priest is a unique signpost pointing directly to Christ.

His Superiority

Consider his greatness (v4). Abraham stood at the pinnacle of the patriarchal pyramid. Abraham is indisputably great, but the point is made that the mysterious king must be greater than even Abraham since it was Abraham who brought tithes to him (v7). Melchizedek's priesthood is greater than Aaron's, just as Levi was a descendant of Abraham, who was inferior to Melchizedek. (v10)

Yet the point is this: if Melchizedek was regarded as being so great, Jesus is greater!

There are three features of the 'Melchizedek Order' of Jesus' high priestly office. It is:

1 FOR GOD

v1 declares Melchizedek to be *'priest of God Most High'*. Jesus, the greatest and dearest priest of God Most High, came to do all that his Father gave him to do (ch10 v7). His principal concern was the glory of God in everything. The overarching purpose of the cross and the purpose of Jesus' death was 'the glory of God' (John ch17 v4)

2 FOREVER

Made a Priest for ever (vv3, 17, 21) The great truth, eloquently asserted in this chapter, is that Christ's priesthood is permanent and eternal. The priesthood of Aaron was fine while it lasted, but it was transient and temporary. Jesus does not hold the office of High Priest 'for the time', but *'for ever'*.

Made Perfect for ever (v28) Even the great and the good among the priestly succession were sinners with weaknesses and sins. The best among human priests were human priests at best. But Jesus, the Son of God and Son of Man, has been *'appointed'* and *'made perfect'*. Jesus was, is and always will be blemishless and blameless. *'Perfect'* implies 'finished', 'completed' and 'mission accomplished'.

3 FOR US

Christ's Abilities (v25)

He is able to save completely (or *'save forever'*). Christ's salvation will never wear out. We can trust his ability to save us comprehensively.

He is able to intercede continually. As we are frequently in need, are we freely availing ourselves of his intercessory ministry?

Christ's Qualities (v26)

We desperately need a priest that is *'holy, blameless, pure, set apart from sinners and exalted above the heavens'*. Jesus is the only One who possesses these superlative qualities. Therefore he is dependable and One to whom we should venture regularly. Unbelievers need to *'come to God through him'* and believers need to constantly *'come to God through him'* because Jesus meets our every need totally.

MAY 5
HEBREWS ch8.1-13

THE REAL THING

The writer has been pointing out that, such is man's desperate condition, he needs something better than the inferior copy of the tabernacle, ceremony, sacrifice, hope, priest, and covenant that the Old Testament provided. His need is so great that the stopgap measures of the Old Testament systems and ceremonies could not last for long. He needed a better hope, a better promise, a better sacrifice, and a better high priest. In fact, he needs a better covenant altogether. He reaffirms that *'we do have such a High Priest...'* (v1) *'Jesus has become the guarantee of a better covenant'* (ch7 v22). Jesus' sinless and timeless priesthood is the guarantee that sinners need. The copies of the Old Covenant were just that – replicas. The ministry of Jesus is 'the real thing'! (v6)

1 JESUS IS THE MINISTER OF A SUPERIOR COVENANT

His Superior Seat

Our High Priest has *'sat down'* (v1) at the powerful and privileged position at the right hand of the Father. One item of furniture never found in the tabernacle was a chair. A seat represented a work finished. The Old Covenant always represented unfinished business. Nothing was complete from one year to the next. But Jesus completed everything for salvation.

His Superior Service

v2 refers to Jesus' service in the sanctuary. Earthly priests only serve in the *'copy and shadow'* (v5). Jesus' ministry is in heaven.

His Superior Sacrifice

v3. Jesus offered himself (ch7 v27).

His Superior Sanctuary

v2. The Greek word for *'sanctuary'* comes from the word for 'holy'. Moses had been given clear instructions as to how to assemble a model of the heavenly sanctuary where God dwells. He couldn't afford to get it wrong (v5). The 'Sinai instructions' were a *'pattern'* (Greek word: 'type') of *'what is in heaven'*. However good Moses' craftsmanship was, it was only a model or copy.

2 JESUS IS THE MEDIATOR OF A SUPERIOR COVENANT

'Mediator' is formed from two words: *'to go'* and *'middle'*, that is, a 'go-between'. Jesus is the 'Go-between' who brings a holy God and unholy sinners together. Jesus is able to guarantee the better terms of a New Covenant.

A New Foundation to Build on (v6)

v6 *'it is founded on better promises'*. The words of vv8-12 come from Jeremiah's prophecy. The Old Covenant is past its 'expiry date' (*'obsolete'* v13), but God designed it with 'built-in obsolescence' to point to its fulfilment in the New Covenant. What's different? v6 *'But...Jesus'* – that's the glorious and eternal difference! It's through Christ's ministry and sacrifice that God's *'better promises'* can be made. Note each reference to *'I will'* (vv8-12). You would think, by the way that some believers behave, that the New Covenant is ageing and decaying. They become disillusioned with God's work, impatient with God's timing, dissatisfied with God's arrangements, and critical of God's people. The building work may be long and hard, year after year, just one brick on another. All our 'bricks' may be laid 'out of sight', 'below ground level'. But the immovable foundation of Christ and the New Covenant should encourage us in the work

A New Fellowship to Learn from (vv7-11)

This New Covenant is all to do with an intimate and mutual fellowship with God. There's no class distinction: *'They will all know me'* (v11). The majority of Old Testament Israel didn't have a personal relationship with the living God. Only a remnant had faith and knew God. Yet in the New Covenant all will know God *'from the least of them to the greatest'*. Jesus prayed that they may know the Father (John ch17 v3). Our desire should be to know God more (Philippians ch3 v10), both personally and experientially. We must not depend on a 'second-hand experience'. His laws must be on our *'minds'* and written on our *'hearts'* (v10)

A New Forgiveness to Trust in (v12)

Here is a 'forgiveness' that is complete. God has deliberately chosen to *'remember their sins no more'*. Under the Old Covenant, with the regular round of sacrifices and offerings, there was constant reminder of sins. But in Jesus there is total cleansing and full forgiveness (1 John ch1 v7). Sin always mars fellowship with God, keeping us from prayer and from reading the Bible and from being obedient. But if sin has been truly forsaken, then don't let it continue to haunt you and stalk you.

Cling to v12 and don't remember what the Lord doesn't remember!

MAY 6
HEBREWS ch9.1-15

HOW MUCH MORE

In these verses, we are provided with a 'guided tour' of the tabernacle. As with any conducted tour of a site or a building, there are two main parts:

The Fixtures and Fittings (vv1-5)

There are two rooms to the tabernacle: the 'Holy Place' and the 'Most Holy Place'.

The Holy Place

In this room you would notice the lampstand with its seven golden branches; the table made of acacia wood and overlaid with gold. There were gold plates and dishes, pitchers and bowls set out upon it. The consecrated bread (literally 'bread of the face') consisting of twelve loaves was set out before the face and the presence of God. Because it was displayed (or 'shown') it is often referred to as 'showbread'.

As we pass through this first room we come to a *'second curtain'* (or 'veil') which divided the Holy Place from the Most Holy Place (or the 'Holiest', or 'Holy of Holies'). Just as you were about to venture into the Most Holy Place, you would see the golden altar of incense, which was associated directly with the inner room. Although located in the Holy Place, the writer connects it to the 'Most Holy Place' (v4) because, on the annual Day of Atonement, the High Priest would take coals from this altar and blood from the offering, carrying them into the Most Holy Place.

The Most Holy Place

This is half the size of the Holy Place. The one item of furniture here was the Ark of the Covenant, which was a box or chest. Inside, there were three significant contents (v4):

- gold jar of manna, reminding the people of the Lord's provision (Exodus

  ch16 v33);

- Aaron's staff that budded, showing Aaron was the Lord's priest

  (Numbers chs16-17);

- the stone tablets of the covenant, emphasising the Lord's precepts.

The Comings and Goings (vv6-10)

The Outer Court of the tabernacle was for Israelis only. The Holy Place was restricted to priests alone (v6). The Most Holy Place was reserved exclusively for the High Priest (v7). All of this is a powerful indicator of the New Covenant to come. The Holy Spirit was showing (v8) that as long as the 'comings and goings' of the old order had to be followed, the new order was yet to be disclosed with its eternal 'Way In', even Jesus (vv 8, 10). Everything pointed to one Mediator, one High Priest and one Sacrifice. We are directed to the monumental contrast: *'how much more'* (Luke ch11 v13; ch12 v24). The fixtures and furnishings, comings and goings of the tabernacle, and later the temple, were only temporary and incomplete. If the blood of *'goats and bulls'* was able to provide some short-term part-cover, then *'how much more'* will be achieved by the precious, atoning blood of Christ!

1 CHRIST'S BLOOD CAN MAKE YOU INTERNALLY CLEAN

Observing ceremonies shows a measure of conformance and obedience, but it doesn't clean hearts. How much of our religion is just a ceremony? We 'go through the motions' but our show of being a Christian may be just a sham. Christ's blood purifies from all unrighteousness for all those who confess and repent (1 John ch1 v7).

2 CHRIST'S BLOOD CAN MAKE YOU ETERNALLY BLESSED

The 'prefab' tabernacle had an expiry date. Animals' blood had no lasting value. But notice:

'eternal redemption' (v12) Christ's ransom will never become dated or devalued.

'eternal Spirit' (v14) The Godhead is involved inseparably in the atonement.

'eternal inheritance' (v15) Christ's death guarantees this inheritance to his 'born again' beneficiaries. What an inheritance! (1 Peter ch1 v4).

3 CHRIST'S BLOOD CAN MAKE YOU LEGALLY FREE

The Old Covenant of tabernacle and priesthood could never perform a legal transaction and set the sinner free. He was forever entangled by the law and had the 'death sentence' hanging over him. But in the Supreme Court of the universe God has declared the sinner 'not guilty' because Jesus our Advocate and Mediator has shed his blood to pay the penalty in full. We can do nothing to 'save the dying soul', but we can do everything to *'serve the living God'* (v14). This is the grand purpose for which we have been made internally clean, eternally blessed and legally free. It is to *'serve the living God'*. 'How much more' should we be serving Him?

MAY 7
HEBREWS ch9.16-28

JESUS CHRIST IS GREATER THAN SACRIFICES

People ask questions about Jesus' death. They may consider that Jesus was a young man in the prime of life – capable, healthy and active. He was physically strong, mentally alert and socially interactive. He was at the height of his career with everything to live for. What possible reason can there be for such a tragic loss, such an abrupt end to life? Why did Jesus die?

Any comprehensive answer to this question must begin with heaven. The principal purpose for the suffering and death of the Saviour was the glory of God (John ch13 vv31-32). Jesus delighted in doing his Father's will, and the glorious objective in his sacrificial life and death was to bring glory to God. But there are four other purposes in these verses:

1 HE DIED TO EFFECT THE WILL (vv16-18)

The 'contract' or 'covenant' referred to here is a *'will'*. A will may only be made during a person's life and it can be added to or amended right up to the moment of the person's death. That's why the executors of any will need to be sure that the will that they execute is the very 'last will and testament'. It's no good executing a will that has been superseded by another because the 'last will and testament' makes all other wills null and void. But though the will can only be established when the one who made it is alive, the will can only be executed when the one who made it is dead.

Therefore it is only the death of Jesus that activates the will of God, and the children of God, who are the beneficiaries of that will, are guaranteed to receive the eternal inheritance. God the Father declares his irrevocable will. God the Son dies the death of the cross to make that will effective. God the Spirit is a deposit or a downpayment of what is to come (2 Corinthians ch1 v22; ch5 v5).

2 HE DIED TO BRING FORGIVENESS (vv19-22)

The ceremony that Moses performed in Exodus ch24 involved the sprinkling of sacrificial blood upon the altar and people. The writer to the Hebrews adds the detail that even the *'scroll'* (v19) and *'the tabernacle and everything used in its ceremonies'* (v21) was, in fact, sprinkled with blood. The law required cleansing (v22) and the sprinkling of animals' blood was a temporary measure. This was another signpost pointing to the lasting forgiveness that has been procured through the blood of Christ. If ever you doubt that Christ's forgiveness is free, total and unreserved, remember that it is his blood alone that was shed at the cross to deal with 'the enormous load of human guilt' [William Williams' hymn]. Is there anything greater that could guarantee forgiveness to the penitent?

3 HE DIED TO REPRESENT SINNERS (vv23-24)

You may have noted three 'appearances' in this chapter:

v26 Christ appears *to* us (meaning to reveal/manifest his true identity).

v28 Christ appears *with* us (meaning 'to be seen with').

v24 Christ appears *for* us (meaning 'to make known' as in the giving of a testimony).

Jesus has died in the place of sinners so that he can speak and act for them *'in God's presence'*. He appears for us as One who has experienced our life and our death first-hand. Jesus has experienced all our experiences (apart from sinning).

4 HE DIED TO REMOVE SIN (vv25-28)

The root of every problem, heartache, defeat, sickness, conflict, confrontation, and temptation is sin. The consequences of sin are death. Death is unavoidable and judgement is inescapable (v27). Without Christ, the judgement means everlasting terrors and torments with no reprieve, no relief, and no release. But in the gospel, there is hope instead of hell for those who believe. A sacrifice has been offered for sin:

- **Personal Sacrifice:** *'HE has appeared'*: Jesus has come into the world personally;

- **Single Sacrifice:** *'once for all'*: Unlike the Old Testament sacrifices, Jesus is enough;

- **Punctual Sacrifice:** *'At the end of the ages'*: Jesus' sacrifice was at exactly the right moment (Galatians ch4 v4). The cross stands at the pivotal point in history. We must never undermine or diminish the place that the cross occupies in Biblical theology;

- **Total Sacrifice:** *'Himself'*: He gives himself unstintingly and unconditionally.

We are told that the Lord's people are *'those who are waiting for him'*. Are we on the 'tiptoe of expectation', waiting eagerly for the glorious appearance of our Saviour?

MAY 8
HEBREWS ch10.1-18

JESUS PLEASED HIS FATHER

The Hebrews' author continues to show that the detailed prophecies and prefigurements of the Old Testament were all pointing to Jesus. He is 'the Father's chief delight'. Jesus is the Son of God who came to please his Father perfectly. All the ceremonies and sacrifices, rites and rituals were just an ineffective, temporary measure. Almighty God derived no satisfaction from them. None of the Old Testament systems could deal eternally with the monstrous problem of sin. They only pointed to the reality that is in Christ.

The Father had no pleasure in the perpetual slaughter of animals because they were not effective in removing sin. But Jesus came to do the Father's will. In what specific ways did he please his Father?

1 BY GOING WHERE HE WANTED HIM TO GO

v5: *'Therefore, when Christ came into the world...'* It was God's eternal plan that Christ should enter the realm of time and space, geography and history, flesh and blood. The shadows of the Old Testament had given way to the presence of the Son of God. *'Christ Jesus came into the world to save sinners'* (1 Timothy ch1 v15). His readiness to go where he was sent brought pure pleasure to his Father's heart. If we are disciples of Jesus Christ, are we prepared to go for God? Wherever? It may mean going across the seas, or across the town, or maybe across the road!

2 BY BEING WHAT HE WANTED HIM TO BE

'Coming into the world' meant becoming a man – becoming incarnate, taking on human likeness, and knowing all the humility and indignity of human flesh. *'...a body you prepared for me'* (v5). A close comparison with the Hebrew of the Old Testament passage quoted (Psalm 40 vv6-8) shows a slight difference ('ears pierced' and 'body prepared'). The 'ear piercing' is to do with the relationship between a slave and his master (Exodus ch21 vv1-6). A Hebrew slave had to be freed from his service obligations after six years. But if his master had been good to him and had treated him well, then he could opt to remain in his service. To make this legal, a servant would allow his ear to be pierced with an awl, signifying his willingness to serve. The 'pierced ear' indicated complete devotion to the master. The slave loved his master and was in service because he wanted to be. It represented the complete consecration of his body and therefore unswerving and unconditional service. No one was more consecrated than Jesus, for whom humanity and humility went together (Philippians ch2 vv7-8). Jesus became what his Father wanted him to be.

Are we becoming what our Heavenly Father wants us to be? Are we growing more like Jesus: more humble, more obedient, more willing, more devoted?

3 BY SAYING WHAT HE WANTED HIM TO SAY

'Then I said...' (v7). Jesus made this dynamic declaration. What a glorious expression of commitment that brought joy and pleasure to the Father. All the words of Jesus caused his Father to be pleased. Because he was pleased with his Son, he wanted his disciples to *'listen to him'* (Matthew ch17 v5). Are we guilty of idle words, unprofitable gossip and wasted conversations that do not please our Heavenly Father?

4 BY DOING WHAT HE WANTED HIM TO DO

'I have come to do your will, O God' (v7). We recall the intense moments that the Saviour suffered in Gethsemane (Matthew ch26 vv39, 42) and his commitment to doing his Father's will. He was ready to do all the things that had been *'written about (him) in the scroll'* (v7). But Jesus came to do God's will for the eternal benefit of his people. It's by God's will that we are made holy (v10), made perfect (v14), made secure (v16), acquitted (v17) and forgiven (v18). In everything that Jesus did, his Father openly declared that he was *'well pleased'*.

But can *our* 'going/being/saying/doing' bring pleasure and satisfaction to God? It can, if we have been forgiven. If Christ has dealt with your *'sins and lawless acts'* at the cross, then God announces, *'I will remember (them) no more'* (v17). *'And where these have been forgiven, there is no longer any sacrifice for sin'* (v18). The Old Testament sacrifices are dispensed with and Christ's one sacrifice will never need to be repeated. God is very pleased with those who by faith say: *'Here I am...I have come to do your will'*.

MAY 9
HEBREWS ch10.9-31

NO TRIFLING

There's a real danger in reading about Christ's dealings with sin, to underestimate the destructive nature and power of sin. Nothing short of Christ's cross could effectively put paid to sin. Yet it's possible to think of sin lightly and casually because we know the efficacy of Christ's one supreme sacrifice. We cannot afford to 'pet' or 'play with' sin! Sin is everything that is opposed to God: everything that God loathes. For those who have learned about God's truth and who have professed allegiance to Christ, and then to turn their backs on his love, his grace, his cross, and his sacrifice, then v26 warns that there is no other sacrifice for sins. There's only judgement (v27). This kind of apostasy is described in v29 as:

- Trampling the Son of God – like pigs trampling pearls in the mud (Matthew ch7 v6).

- Despising the blood of the covenant – defying the means of claimed sanctification.

- Insulting the Spirit of Grace – denying the Spirit's exclusive work is diabolical.

Men cannot trifle with the precious truths and glories of the Godhead and expect to get away with it. *'It is a dreadful thing to fall into the hands of the living God'* (v31).

So what are we exhorted to do?

1 LET US DRAW NEAR SINCERELY (v22)

The previous verses have spoken about the tabernacle in which the visible presence of God resided. There is reference to the dividing curtain between the Holy Place and the Most Holy Place. The high priest entered once a year, after he had thoroughly washed himself, and under cover of sacrificial blood. Now we are encouraged to enter *'the Most Holy Place'* of continual fellowship with God. *'A new and living way'* has been opened for us. On the day that Jesus died, the huge temple curtain was torn in two (Matthew ch27 v51). This signified that through Jesus' one sacrifice, a way has been opened into God's presence. Therefore we should have confidence in drawing near to God: not with deceptive, hypocritical hearts but with *'sincere hearts'*; not with a vain, shallow hope but with *'full assurance of faith'*.

2 LET US HOLD UNSWERVINGLY (v23)

We can have a secure hope because the One who made the promises is entirely trustworthy. We must not cling to the homemade security of a man-made religion. God's inestimable promises (regarding the New Covenant, a once-and-for-all sacrifice, redeeming blood, forgiveness of sin, Christ's wonderful reappearance for his people) are an integral part of the *'hope we profess'*. We must hold immovably to that.

3 LET US CONSIDER LOVINGLY (v24)

To *'consider'* means 'to think carefully and perceptively' and 'to give time to weighing up' the best way in which we may motivate fellow-believers to love and to good deeds.

We should be asking the question: 'How can I motivate and stimulate my brother or sister *'towards love and good deeds'*? What means can I use to propel them or stir them?

4 LET US MEET REGULARLY (v25)

If we have a genuine love for God, his word and his people, then there will be no 'avoidable absences' in our weekly routines. The telling commentary on the three thousand who had just been saved at Pentecost, shows that *'they devoted themselves to the apostles' teaching and to the fellowship, to the breaking of bread and to prayer'* (Acts ch2 v42). They were committed to every opportunity to assemble for teaching, fellowship, breaking bread and prayer. By comparison, we, who have so much in terms of facility and opportunity, have become casual and negligent about 'meeting together'.

5 LET US ENCOURAGE INCREASINGLY (v25)

Within the context of the first part of the verse, mutual encouragement is essential. Christians are not 'born again' to live in isolation. Every believer *needs* encouragement and every believer should be *giving* encouragement. Nothing succeeds like encouragement. The references to Barnabas (*'Son of Encouragement'* in Acts ch4 v36) seem to exemplify what a life of encouragement should be. We must do it *'all the more as (we) see the Day approaching'*. Prior to Christ's Second Coming we may expect increasing hardships, pressures, disappointments and persecutions. But all of this should prompt increasing encouragement from fellow-believers, and not the negativity and discouragement for which Christians are frequently responsible.

How can I be an encouragement to a fellow believer today?

MAY 10
HEBREWS ch10.32-39

A GREAT CONTEST

With the exception of just a few countries, the majority of believers throughout the world are suffering the whole spectrum of hardships and persecutions. Genuine Christians are not a part of the 'picnicking, partying church' (that is portrayed by some religious leaders). Instead, the true Church is engaged in a great fight, a great struggle.

The word for *'remember'* ('recall') is only used here in Hebrews, but it implies the requirement to apply effort in remembering. Immediately that a person becomes a believer through repentance of sin and faith in Jesus Christ, they are plunged into a great war. Their citizenship has changed and they soon come to realise that there are many adversaries that would attack them in many subtle and not-so-subtle ways.

But what part do we play in this contest? How should we respond to the persecutions that our fellow-soldiers are experiencing in other parts of the world?

1 SUFFERING FACE TO FACE (v32)

Two particular examples of suffering face-to-face are cited:

Publicly exposed to insult and persecution (v33)

'publicly exposed' is taken from a Greek word which gives us our word 'theatre'. They had been made a public target and the focus of attack. We don't need to travel to China or Indonesia or Iraq to hear the vitriolic vilification of believers. Our media is full of insult and ridicule aimed disproportionately at Christians, rather than at other religions. This is 'natural' since the 'nature' of an unbelieving world is at enmity with God's people.

Confiscation of property (v34)

How heartbreaking it must be to have all your treasured possessions stolen or trashed. What if that happens with the sanction of the very authorities that should be protecting property? This happens in many lands where Christians have had their homes demolished and their ancestral lands seized. Yet many rejoice, even in this trial (Matthew ch6 vv19-20). Even if 'suffering for Christ's sake' is not our daily experience, we must be quick to identify ourselves with those for whom intense suffering is their way of life.

2 STANDING SIDE BY SIDE (v33)

The writer to the Hebrews commended his readers for providing public support to those who were ill-treated for their faith in Christ. This can be very costly, as it is today. The New Testament concept of fellowship contains the idea of 'partnership in suffering'. Fellowship for these believers was not the superficial chitchat accompanied by tea and biscuits at the church hall after a service. Fellowship was all about standing side by side with them in their suffering. We may take regular mission magazines and pray for the persecuted church on

Sundays, but how much are we committed to praying for them every day. How much do we personally support them with our gifts and finances? How often do we contact them and demonstrate practical love to them?

3 SYMPATHISING HEART TO HEART (v34)

The word *'sympathy'* literally means 'to suffer with'. The Hebrew believers displayed courageous solidarity. They were ready to identify themselves with those who were imprisoned for their faith. Does our sympathy cost us anything? True believers are characterised by perseverance and faith (vv36-39). Biblical Christianity is neither about faith in monuments or buildings, nor faith in services or ceremonies, nor faith in preachers or priests. Rather it is faith in the eternal Son of God, Jesus Christ the only Saviour of sinners. You must persevere:

To achieve God's will

This may be in the face of pain or persecution because even in this, the will of God is achieved (1 Peter ch4 v14).

To receive God's promise

(v36) The afflictions of this life will soon pass, and there are *'better and lasting possessions'* (v34) in Christ. Endure for a short while. Jesus is coming again!

To believe God's salvation

Are you among those who *'shrink back'*, or are you saved? Notice that this faith is not only the faith to be *saved* by, but it's also the faith to *live* by (v38).

MAY 11
HEBREWS ch11.1-7

GRANITE FAITH

At times we may stand in front of a granite monument that is situated in many of our town and village squares. We may read the names of those courageous servicemen who gave their lives in defence of our realm; heroes and heroines whose names are now written in stone. This chapter may be viewed as such a monument – a testimony to the heroes and heroines of faith who have stood firm and unmoved in their trust of God. Their names have been etched into the indestructible stone of God's word. Just as monuments and memorials have an inscription over them, so there is a profound title to this 'memorial' in v1.

Here is a description (some would argue, 'a definition') of 'faith': *'Faith is the essence of things hoped for, the evidence of things not seen'*. It has been suggested that 'faith is the title-deed of things hoped for'.

These great pioneers and pillars of faith demonstrate that their rock-solid faith in the 'unseen' produces the reward that is 'seen'. But God is the unstated Object of their faith. What do we know about faith?

1 FAITH MAKES CREATION CREDIBLE (v3)

There may be rational and logical arguments for a created universe, but we accept the Creator by faith. Any grasp that we may have of the invisible coming from the visible, or the tangible coming from the intangible, is by faith. It's by faith that we believe in the powerful word of God forming the universe *ex nihilo* ('from nothing').

But this faith is more than a 'bottomless bin' into which we can dump all those things for which we have no answers. 'Faith' is not just a convenient solution for those things that we cannot explain. Of course, we cannot explain everything and, yes, we believe in God's ways, works and words, even when all human explanation stands opposed to him. But v3 states that it is *'by faith'* that *'we understand that the universe was formed at God's command'*. There can be understanding: an understanding that flows from a knowledge of God and who he is. If we believe in the God of the Bible - almighty, immense, omniscient, eternal, all-wise, unbegun – then it's possible to *'understand'* that everything came into being by his word. Therefore, it's not 'blind faith' but faith that has the one true and living God as its objective. Faith in God, the Creator of the universe, is not the same as logic and reason. But faith in an eternally existent and almighty Creator is neither illogical nor unreasonable.

2 FAITH MAKES SACRIFICE ACCEPTABLE (v4)

A murder occurred in the first family of Adam and Eve. Cain killed Abel because God had accepted his sacrifice but had rejected Cain's. Abel had been the first to offer a blood sacrifice. His sacrifice of a lamb looked forward to the Lamb of God who would take away the sin of the world. Abel lived the life of faith and was commended for it. Even the costly sacrifices of people like Cain are not acceptable to God without faith. Although Abel has been dead for a few thousand years, his faith continues to shout aloud.

3 FAITH MAKES PLEASING POSSIBLE (vv5-6)

Pleasing God, that is! Enoch's great commendation was that he was *one who pleased God*. To please God requires a life of devotion and righteousness, like Enoch's. Although the world around him was spiralling downward in a vortex of evil and godlessness, Enoch rose above it by faith. He walked with God each and every day. To walk with God is the highest commendation.

4 FAITH MAKES OBEDIENCE INDISPENSABLE (v7)

Noah had never seen a flood, had never seen a ship, had never seen God's global judgement, but he believed. He didn't have years of historical documents, biographies or testimonies. He didn't have a Bible! But his faithfulness condemned a world of faithlessness. He believed in God and obeyed by building an ark and preaching righteousness. Belief in God and obedience are inseparable.

How can we therefore profess faith in God and not live a life of obedience to him? What 'ark' have we been called upon to 'build' for him? Our 'ark' may seem illogical, unnecessary, and difficult. There may only be a handful of helpers, and the details may appear impossible, but are we prepared to trust and obey like Noah?

MAY 12
HEBREWS ch11.8-19

ABRAHAM'S MONUMENTAL FAITH

The Christian believes in one God, the Lord God Almighty, the Creator of the universe. Judaism and Islam also claim to be monotheistic, but the rest of the world's religions are almost all polytheistic, believing in a multitude of different deities. For example, there is Hinduism, Confucianism, Taoism, Shintoism, as well as various African and South American tribal religions. In the ancient world, it was polytheism that characterised the religions of the Assyrians, Egyptians, Babylonians, Greeks, and Romans. It was from a polytheistic society that God called a believer, that great patriarch of faith, Abraham (see Joshua ch24 vv2-3). God called Abraham, and Abraham followed by faith (v8). All these 'giants of Scripture' died in their faith, and many died for their faith. But they all provide a pattern for us in showing that *'the righteous shall live by faith'*. We may underline four characteristics of Abraham's faith:

1 A FAITH THAT'S NOT RESTRICTED BY 'WHERE' (vv8-10)

Abraham was called to go to a place *'even though he did not know where he was going'* (v8). Abraham was prepared to leave the known for the unknown. Yet it wasn't an incentive that made him move. The promise of receiving the land of Canaan as an inheritance only came after he had moved there. But Abraham's faith was such that he had a more permanent home, a greater city, a better country in view. It would be five hundred years before Canaan would become the recognised and established dwelling-place for Abraham's descendants, but the patriarch was looking much further ahead than that (v10). This is the strength of Abraham's faith. He was looking beyond Canaan's horizons, and even beyond the building of Jerusalem. Abraham was completely focused on the New Jerusalem, which he *'only saw...and welcomed from a distance'* (v13). His sights were firmly set on the eternal city of God's glory and his presence (v16). How much are we preoccupied with heaven?

This world is not our permanent home, although we often live and act as if it is. We're only backpackers here! Have we forgotten that our citizenship is not of this world (Philippians ch3 v20)? Are we in danger of becoming too tied to our present comforts and earthly securities?

2 A FAITH THAT'S NOT HAMPERED BY 'WHEN' (vv11-16)

For Sarah, Abraham's ninety-year-old wife, it seemed to be the wrong time for thinking about starting a family. Abraham was also *'as good as dead'* at one hundred years old! We may sympathise with Sarah's response when she was told that she would become a 'ninety-year-old expectant mum'. She laughed (Genesis ch18 v12). But God replied, *'Is anything too hard for the Lord?'* (Genesis ch18 v14). That's the question that should come to our minds when our faith is challenged by an impossible timetable. Is our God limited to dates and deadlines? Is he constrained by calendars and clocks? Abraham's faith didn't weaken (Romans ch4 v19). Humanly speaking, we may be inclined to think that God has 'run out of time' in a particular situation. A dead daughter in bed (Mark ch5 v35)? A dead boy in a coffin (Luke ch7 v15)? A dead man in the ground (John ch11 v37)? But nothing is too late for the Potentate of time, the Controller of the cosmos, the God of the 'when'.

3 A FAITH THAT'S NOT CHALLENGED BY 'WHAT' (vv17-18)

The most difficult thing that Abraham ever did is recorded in vv17-18. God had told him that all his descendants would come through Isaac, and now he was telling Abraham to sacrifice his son. His faith didn't buckle under the challenge. He took God at his word. As far as Abraham was concerned, God had everything in hand. It wasn't that Abraham didn't care – on the contrary! He cared so much that he was ready to trust God with every inexplicable and incomprehensible detail.

4 A FAITH THAT'S NOT DISTRACTED BY 'WHY' (v19)

We don't read of Abraham getting into a heated debate with God over the importance of Isaac's life and Israel's future. Such was Abraham's faith, he calculated that because God had promised to feature Isaac in his plans, then he must raise him from death. Is that faith, or what? He told his servants that they would both come back (Genesis ch22 v5), even if it meant that Isaac would have to die in between. Do we desire that kind of faith? How can it be obtained (Romans ch10 v17)? Without faith, it's impossible to please God (v6), but with faith, nothing is impossible with God.

MAY 13
HEBREWS ch11.20-31

THE ENDLESS POSSIBILITIES OF FAITH

We may meet a doctor, solicitor, dentist, or financial adviser, and, after our first appointment, we may comment, 'I don't have much faith in him/her'. Yet as we continue to meet them over a series of appointments, we may come to learn more about their character, their knowledge, their experience, their skills, and their successes. Our faith in them increases steadily. If that happens at a human level, we can be assured that it happens in respect to God. Why are we so slow to trust in a sovereign and omnipotent God? God doesn't develop or change, but our faith does. The more we get to know him, the more we should trust him. The apostles said to the Lord, *'Increase our faith'* (Luke ch17 v5). What does faith do for us?

1 FAITH OPENS HEARTS

When we first believe in the Lord Jesus Christ for salvation, there is a wonderful opening of the heart – our intellect, our will, and our emotions (Romans ch10 vv8-10). As Lydia listened attentively to Paul's preaching, *'The Lord opened her heart to respond to Paul's message'* (Acts ch16 v14). Each of the spiritual giants in the 'Faith List' of Hebrews ch11 first exercised faith for salvation and justification. But faith continues to open a believer's heart:

To Choose

Our whole lives are a series of choices. The heart that has been opened by faith is moved to make the right choices (vv24-26). For Moses, he could have stayed in Egypt with all the trappings of wealth, status, title, and power. He could have enjoyed all the temporary comforts of life in Pharaoh's palaces, but instead, Moses chose to be identified with the ill-treated people of God. We, too, are confronted with important choices every day. We can choose the ways of comfort, popularity, and success. Or we can choose to identify with the true people of God and suffer hassle, heartache, confrontation, and discrimination. It will soon cost so much more to be identified with God's people in the British Isles. Humanists, feminists, evolutionists, Islamists, homosexuals, and politically correct fanatics have hijacked the law-making process. But faith opens a believer's heart to make the right choices before God.

To Change

The change in Moses' life couldn't have been more pronounced. The change in Rahab's heart (v31) meant a clear change of allegiance. Where's the evidence of our hearts opened by faith?

2 FAITH OPENS EYES

To Look Up

(v27) Moses' faith caused him to bow to the invisible King of glory rather than the visible king of Egypt. Faith enables the believer to look up and to see the Unseeable, and to love him (1 Peter ch1 vv8-9).

To Look Ahead

(v26) Moses made a correct evaluation because his eyes were firmly fixed on Christ. In the hazy distance, along the corridors of fifteen hundred years, Moses could make out the shape of a Saviour. He was ready to surrender all for Christ. Don't underestimate the size of Moses' faith!

To Look Into

(v28) Moses could see (perceive, discern, recognise) that the shedding of sacrificial blood was a potent symbol. Through blood there would be deliverance and life. Christ's blood provides eternal freedom (Hebrews ch2 vv14-15).

3 FAITH OPENS DOORS

Opportunities and possibilities are all opened by faith:

Through Deep Seas

(v29) The Sea of Reeds opened up in response to a combination of God's sovereignty, an east wind and Moses' faith (Exodus ch14 vv21-22).

Through Thick Walls

(v30) Jericho's walls crumbled and collapsed in such a way that every Israeli soldier (wherever he was standing around the circumference of the city) was able to charge straight in without having to clear away rubble or fallen stones.

How much faith do we have in a God who is able to make paths through the seas or ways through the walls? Sometimes we become so fixated on the problem (our 'Red Sea' or our 'Jericho's walls') that we forget that Moses' God and Joshua's God is our God too. What hinders God's people like you and me from trusting in God's provision of an 'open door', however deep the 'sea' or however thick the 'wall'?

MAY 14
HEBREWS ch11.32-40

HOW DOES MY FAITH RELATE TO OUR WORLD?

Heroes come in all shapes and sizes, but frequently they may be unnamed, unsung, and unknown. Moses' humble parents are included in v23 as well as the Gentile prostitute, Rahab, in v31. But the author has a problem since there are many that he could have included in this list, but he doesn't have *'time to tell'* (v32). Yet these concluding verses drive home to us the all-important truth concerning the results of faith. In response to the question, 'How does this faith relate to the world?' we can make three statements:

1 FAITH PROVIDES THE VICTORY THAT OVERCOMES THE WORLD (vv32-35a)

Gideon, Barak, Samson, Jephthah, David and Samuel were all different people from different backgrounds. They all had their flaws and weaknesses, but they have all been united in this Bible text by their herculean faith. All their stirring achievements were accomplished by faith (vv33-34). It's faith that guarantees the victory over this sinfully powerful world (1 John ch5 vv3-5). A victorious Christian life must be founded upon the bedrock of this immortal truth: the deity of Christ. Jesus is the Son of God. What were those victories?

'Conquered kingdoms' (v33) We recall Moses defeating the Egyptians, Joshua conquering the Canaanites, Samson and David subduing the Philistines, and Gideon overcoming the Midianites. We are reminded too of the great kingdoms of Antiochus, Herod, Caesar, Mary I, Hitler, and Stalin, who were all opposed to Jesus and his faithful followers. But where are those kingdoms and empires today? The faith of God's people has triumphed.

'Administered justice' (v33). They wouldn't be compromised. They championed the cause of righteousness in society even when the cost was great.

'Gained what was promised' (v33). Their victory of faith ensured that the promises of God were claimed.

'Shut the mouths of lions' (v33). Even ferocious beasts were not outside the scope of faith's conquest.

'Quenched the fury of flames' (v34). We naturally think of Shadrach, Meshach, and Abednego in Nebuchadnezzar's super-heated furnace (Daniel ch3).

'Escaped the edge of the sword' (v34) David escaped Goliath's sword and Saul's spear. David, as the shepherd youth, epitomises the statement: *'whose weakness was turned into strength'*. Paul knew all about Christ's *'power is made perfect in weakness'* (2 Corinthians ch12 v10). But all these heroes have not been listed primarily for their holiness but for their faith. We may notice their weaknesses: Gideon wasn't very brave to begin with. Barak refused to fight without the prophetess Deborah accompanying him. Samson lacked stability and self-control in his life. Jephthah made a stupid promise. David had domestic problems. Samuel failed to keep his sons under control.

But they all appear in God's 'Portrait Gallery of Faith' and therefore there's hope for believers who are constantly hounded by sins that dog their footsteps.

2 FAITH PROVOKES THE VIOLENCE THAT COMES FROM THE WORLD (vv35b-38)

The most outstanding feats of endurance are only performed by faith. Repeatedly, the bloodstained ensign of faith's victory is seen flying majestically over the broken and burnt bodies of the martyrs. The Lord's superlative comment on his faithful people is: *'the world was not worthy of them'* (v38). None of the biggest, the bravest or the best whom the world honours, compare to those whom God honours. They may be regarded as unfit for the world, but the truth is that the world is unfit for them. If you are concerned that you would buckle under the same pains and privations, remember that God always supplies sufficient strength and courage for the moment (1 Corinthians ch10 v13).

3 FAITH PROCLAIMS THE VALUE OF THE SAVIOUR OF THE WORLD (vv39-40)

All these giants of faith have earned the Lord's commendation, yet there was something missing. The declaration that *'God had planned something better'* reminds us of the dominant theme of Hebrews that Jesus Christ is the greatest. Jesus is the only One through whom the Old Testament heroes of faith and the New Testament champions of faith, and those of us who consider ourselves to be pygmies of faith, can be *'made perfect'* (v40). There's no exclusive method for those with great faith and another method for those with little faith. God unites his people through the same faith in Jesus, the Saviour of the world.

MAY 15
HEBREWS ch12.1-3

COMPLETING NOT COMPETING

So intense were the ancient Olympic Games, with all their physical exertions and mental anguish, that the Greek word for *'race'* (v1) gives us our English word 'agony'. It suggests a fierce contest in which the competitors committed everything. Each born-again Bible-believing Christian is in a race. It's not that they are competing against each other: the aim is to finish the race. We are called to complete, not to compete! The Hebrews' author refers to the *'great cloud of witnesses'* who surround the racers. They're not spectators who are there to be entertained, or to be regaled by the spectacle of Christians at various stages of the race. They are *'witnesses'* – the giants of faith – who are there for a purpose. They are our:

Examples - who show the way through all the agonies of the race;

Inspirers - who instil within us the desire to reach the finishing line;

Encouragers - who support us and spur us on when we are tempted to flag.

Although our eyes are not on them, nevertheless we must not forget them. They are those who *'were all commended for their faith'* (ch11 v39). But faith is not past tense: it's always present tense. You and I cannot run the race that is marked out for us by using 'someone else's faith' or 'yesterday's faith'.

1 LET US THROW OFF (v1)

There are two descriptions of the things that we must 'throw off':

i] Weights that Hinder

The word for *'hinder'* implies a 'bulk' or a 'mass', even a 'weight'. This Greek word supplies the prefix for our word 'oncology', meaning 'the study and treatment of tumours'. A tumour is a mass/swelling/abnormality/hindrance that shouldn't be there. We are prompted to *'throw off everything that hinders'*, that is, everything that shouldn't be there. It's possible to make a distinction between 'weights' that may not be sinful in themselves and the sins that entangle. The 'weight' is a personal hindrance that holds us back and impedes our progress. It could be:

Wealth - unnecessary concern with accumulating wealth can be a severe hindrance.

Ambition – aspirations and ambitions can interfere with the Christian life when there is an imbalance in priorities and the wrong weights get jettisoned.

Popularity – some are always concerned about their image and their 'street cred'.

Sport/Leisure – anything that demands a disproportionate amount of time, commitment, or finance and which interferes with the Lord's work;

Comfortable Lifestyle – our hindrance could be our own personal circumstances such as our cosy houses, familiar routines, easy-going lifestyle, home comforts and pleasures.

These may be like weights around our necks and hinder us in the race.

ii] Sins that Entangle

We are called upon to take positive action against those things that would enmesh us or ensnare us. Put them aside; cast them off (Romans ch13 v12).

2 LET US RUN (v1)

What should we run?

'The race marked out for us' (v1). It's a pre-determined course. Every detail is controlled by a caring, sovereign God who has lovingly prepared the route and who has wisely determined the distance for each one of us (Proverbs ch16 v9).

How should we run?

'With perseverance' (see *'endurance'* vv2, 3). These 'runners' should be reliable and faithful, through good times and the bad, and who never give up, whatever happens.

3 LET US FIX (vv2,3)

Jesus is the 'Model Runner'. He is not only the classic Example of faith, he is also *'the Author and Perfecter of faith'*. Jesus has blazed a trail of unwavering faith. He is faith's Pioneer and its Pathfinder. Jesus opened up a path from the cross to the throne (v3) and from endurance to enthronement. It's Jesus on whom our eyes must be focused. We must *'consider* (make a careful judgement about) *him'* so that we don't *'grow weary or lose heart'*. Our race, however energy-sapping and time-consuming it may be, can only be seen in its true perspective when viewed alongside Jesus. If you only look at your own hardships, you won't want to cast off the weights. Fix your eyes on Jesus!

MAY 16
HEBREWS ch12.4-17

THE LORD'S LOVING DISCIPLINE

It is true that, for the Christian, learning obedience needs to frequently take place in the classroom of suffering. These verses tell us something about discipline. Not any discipline, but the Lord's discipline. Although the word *'discipline'* (vv6, 7, 10) applies specifically to parental discipline, in the widest sense it means 'the education of children', which is an education that involves guidance, training, instruction, and correction. A variety of methods may be employed to train children to become mature and competent members of society, for example, encouragement, reproof, example, and correction. These verses provide two important aspects of the Lord's discipline:

1 THE HARDSHIP OF DISCIPLINE (v7)

v7 *Endure hardship as discipline...'* In the context of the running race (vv1-2), there is great discipline – either a discipline that's imposed upon the athlete by the trainer, or a self-imposed discipline. Serious athletes may shed blood, sweat, and tears to achieve their goal, although the writer says that they *'have not yet resisted to the point of shedding (their) blood'* (v4). In the *'struggle against sin,'* considerable effort is called for. Sin is never going to be a pushover. The word for *'struggle'/ 'striving'* gives us our English word 'antagonism'. In our fight against our arch-antagonist, sin, we may need to resort to drastic action that may cost us bloodshed! If we continue to view our tension with sin as 'just a little juvenile scuffle in the park', then we shall never overcome our adversary. The Lord's discipline is designed to keep us on track.

The Lord's Treatment:

How does God treat his own people in the process of discipline? *'...God is treating you as sons'* (v7). This relationship is emphasised in vv5-6. The Lord disciplines those *'he loves'.* The strength of the father and son relationship is seen in discipline. If the father didn't care about his son, he would let him live any way he pleased. But the concerned and caring father delivers a rigorous training programme. The treatment may be painful but it proves that God loves us. The hardship of the Lord's discipline is not to crush, but to create; not for our grief, but for our good.

The Lord's Encouragement:

'...you have forgotten that word of encouragement...' (v5). The Lord's discipline is inextricably linked to his love. None of his discipline is ever unhelpful. The Lord never uses discipline to express retaliation or vindictiveness, but as a means of expressing and proving his love.

2 THE HARVEST OF DISCIPLINE (v11)

This *'harvest of righteousness and peace'* (or *'the peaceable fruit of righteousness'*) is the outcome of discipline. Discipline is a fruit-bearing tree. Sometimes that fruit may take several years to develop and ripen, but eventually it produces according to the investment that has been placed in it. Such fruit will include:

Peace

Instead of becoming bitter, discipline can bring a contented peace.

Righteousness

A life of distinctiveness and difference (Genesis ch9 v6; Job ch1 v8).

Faith

The 'giants' of ch11 had their faith forged in the crucible of discipline.

Patience

This 'flower' will blossom and its sweet fruit appear. It's *'in all things'* that *'God works for the good of those who love Him...'* (Romans ch8 v28) and it's in the hardships of life that God works *'for our good'* (v10).

For the sons of God, there's a four-point Action Plan:

i] Strengthen the weak (v12) Be Strong!

Don't let despondency, despair and self-pity get the better of you.

ii] Level the rough places (v13) Be Straight!

Potholes and debris on the track can be a serious hazard to runners. But we are called to keep our eyes on Jesus and to run straight.

iii] Be holy (v14) Be Separate!

True unity cannot be achieved without holiness. Any external harmony will be fragile without internal holiness. Separation from the world is essential.

iv] No bitter root (v15) Be Sweet!

This is not the sickly, sentimental sweetness of an artificial Christianity, but the sweetness of Christ's character that eradicates all *'bitter roots'* of poison.

MAY 17
HEBREWS ch12.18-24

MAKING COMPARISONS

Subconsciously we make comparisons all the time. Appearances, possessions, health, ability, ages, skills – we are always placing one thing alongside another for the purpose of comparing. It's what Jesus does in the Gospels and the word that the Greeks used for *'placing one thing alongside another for the purpose of comparing'* gives us our word 'parable'. In this epistle, the writer's structure can be seen in a succession of comparisons. He compares Jesus to angels, prophets, Moses, Aaron, Melchizedek, sacrifices, and each time his conclusion is indisputable – Jesus Christ is the greatest! Now, in these verses, we are shown a final list of comparisons.

1 TWO MOUNTAINS

The description of Mount Sinai (vv18-21) reveals the phenomena that occurred during the giving of the Law.

- *'burning with fire'* – the mountain was engulfed with a huge blaze (Exodus ch19; Deuteronomy ch4).

- *'darkness, gloom and storm'* – smoke, thunder and lightning (Exodus ch19 vv16-18).

- *'trumpet blast'* – so loud that everyone in the camp trembled (Exodus ch19 v16).

- *'a voice speaking words'* that overwhelmed the listening Israelites (Exodus ch19 vv19-20).

The presence of God was revealed in a tangible way. All five senses could detect his presence. But the physical mountain of Sinai is compared to the spiritual mountain of Zion. Though Sinai was a mountain *'that can be touched'* (v18), yet it must not be touched. Zion, the mountain that cannot be touched, can be approached as it signifies our fellowship and communion with God. God is present among his people. Between the peaks of Mount Sinai's' Law and Mount Zion's Life there is the plateau of grace where we have been saved and transformed into *'the church of the firstborn...'* (v23).

2 TWO CITIES

The narrative of two mountains leads to the tale of two cities. It's not the earthly Jerusalem referred to, but the *'heavenly Jerusalem, the city of the living God'*. The believer is a citizen of that heavenly city, *'the city that is to come'* (ch13 v12). Paul answered the question about whether he was a terrorist with the testimony, *'I am a Jew, from Tarsus in Cilicia, a citizen of no ordinary city'* (Acts ch21 v39). Like Paul, we are also members of 'no ordinary city' – Zion's City, the city of God.

3 TWO COVENANTS

Righteousness and perfection were the standards of the Old Covenant. But the Old Covenant had no inherent ability or power to make anyone righteous or perfect. Enter Jesus. He mediates the New Covenant (1 Timothy ch2 vv5-6). For what the Old Covenant couldn't do, Jesus did in the New Covenant.

4 TWO DEATHS

Abel died and Jesus died. Abel shed his blood and Jesus shed his blood. Abel's blood was shed as a martyr; Jesus' blood was shed as a mediator. Abel is listed at the head of faith's patriarchs (ch11 v4) and is proclaimed as *'a righteous man'*. He received the divine commendation and, though dead, *'by faith he still speaks'*.

But though Abel's sacrifice of his lamb and the sacrifice of his own life continues to speak, it can never save. Only Jesus' blood can save.

5 TWO KINGDOMS

Shakeable Kingdom

Exodus ch19 v18 tells of *'the whole mountain trembl(ing) violently'*. Earthly kingdoms can be shaken irreparably by earthquakes, volcanoes, tsunamis and wars. None can resist the divine shaking (Haggai ch2 v6).

Unshakeable Kingdom

Christ's kingdom is unshakeable, and as King, he is unconquerable. What should be our response?

Let us be thankful

God is on the throne and we're in his kingdom (Colossians ch1 vv13-14).

Let us be worshipful

He deserves our acceptable, reverent worship (vv28-29).

6 TWO WARNINGS

God spoke on earth through Moses and the Law. But *'in these last days he has spoken to us by his Son'* (ch1 v2). Through Jesus (who came to us from heaven and continues to speak in heaven, by his Spirit, through the Scriptures) God's word comes to us today. There are two warnings but the same warning: *'...don't refuse him who speaks'* (v25).

How much do we listen to God speaking, yet refuse to heed His words?

IS YOUR NAME WRITTEN IN HEAVEN?

You have come to thousands upon thousands of angels in joyful assembly, to the church of the firstborn, whose names are written in heaven.

Hebrews ch12 vv22-23

Your name may be stylishly rare or unique,

May be hard just to spell or pronounce.

It may be the name that the VIPs speak,

But it's where your name's written that counts.

Your name may be etched on a doorplate of brass,

To which titles and letters are given.

Your name may be written in granite or glass,

But has your name been written in heaven?

Your name may be known within Parliament's walls

or at galleries of art be on view.

It may be displayed in some grand stately halls,

But in heaven is your name written too?

Your name may be spoken on everyone's tongue,

And be known across Cornwall and Devon.

Your name may be shouted or whispered or sung,

But has your name been written in heaven?

Your name may be listed with Burke's noble peers,

Or given the 'Hollywood look'.

It may be remembered for hundreds of years,

But is your name inscribed in God's book?

The name of Messiah the Scriptures agreed,

Is this the Jesus the angel proclaims?

The baby who lay where the animals feed,

Has the name above all other names.

That name means salvation for all who believe,

And to whom the Redeemer is given.

To all who his grace and forgiveness receive,

And whose names have been written in heaven.

Geoff Fox

MAY 18
HEBREWS ch13.1-8

DOING OUR DUTY

To do anything important it is necessary to have a solid foundation. The epistle's author has been explaining in chs1-12 about the solid foundation that the believer has in Jesus Christ. Jesus is infinitely superior to all the other heroes, leaders, examples and patriarchs who have been an integral part of Judaism. Jesus outshines and outranks them all. The teachings concerning Christ are the pivotal planks of faith. It would be heresy to 'doctor these doctrines'. But doctrine always goes hand in hand with duty. This final chapter concentrates on our duty in response to the doctrine that has been expounded in the first twelve chapters.

We could summarise our obligations in these eight verses under six instructions:

1 BE LOVING (v1)

Where else would you find such a mishmash of members as in the Church of Christ? But the cohesive force is love (1 John ch3 vv16-17). This love is not some 'pious sentiment' or 'nice warm feeling'. It's an active, practical love. Such 'heavenly love' is 'down to earth'. It's a love that not only recognises someone's need but addresses that need. It not only sees someone's burden but shares that burden (John ch13 v35).

2 BE HOSPITABLE (v2)

Hospitality is one of the clearest evidences of love (Genesis chs18-19 may be in mind). The principle we may infer is that whichever strangers we may show hospitality towards, we should treat them with the same respect and generosity that we would show to angels. For such strangers could be angels in disguise. There is a difference between 'entertaining' (which shows off the house, decor, garden, food, etc) and 'hospitality' that puts people before possessions.

3 BE SYMPATHETIC (v3)

This draws attention to believers, in particular, who are imprisoned and suffering ill treatment because of their faith. We must not only remember them 'from a distance' but we must sympathise with them by identifying ourselves with them. We should help them, support them, pray for them and comfort them with the same intensity as if we were in the prison with them.

4 BE FAITHFUL (v4)

The institution of marriage has always been under attack. Not only is it undermined by unfaithfulness at a personal level, but also it is constantly opposed and threatened by liberal pressure groups, secular dogma, arts and the media, entertainment and even government legislation. This 'honourable estate' is being dishonoured.

5 BE CONTENT (v5)

We can remain content in the knowledge of God's presence (Deuteronomy ch31 v6) and his provision (Psalm 118 vv6-7). If the Lord is always with us and never deserts us, and if he is our Helper, our Defender and our Provider, then what else do we want? Our total sufficiency is in Christ. Everything we need or want is in Christ.

6 BE IMITATORS (v7)

The Hebrew readers were encouraged to remember their former church leaders:

i] Consider them: The word *'consider'* is only used here and in Acts ch17 v23. Such foundational fathers of the faith should be examined, studied, and considered.

ii] Copy them: *'Imitate their faith'*. Follow their example of faith and courage.

If you merely copy a copy, then it doesn't yield the best results. It's important that we don't lose sight of the Master, the Original, our unchanging, contemporary Christ (v8).

- The authority of Christ's name doesn't change – it still strikes terror into the hearts of every demonic agency and will cause every knee to bow one day.

- The power of Christ's gospel doesn't change – this Good News still transforms lives and prepares sinners for heaven (Romans ch1 v16).

- The security of Christ's church doesn't change – Jesus promised that all the pent-up power of the pit of Hades will never prevail against the Rock-solid Church of Jesus Christ (Matthew ch16 v18).

- The truth of Christ's word doesn't change – Truth is truth. Jesus is the Truth (John ch14 v6) and the basic message of Christianity is 'truth' (1 John ch2 v21).

- The promise of Christ's return doesn't change – He will come back (John ch14 v3).

MAY 19
HEBREWS ch13.9-14

INSIDE AND OUTSIDE

It has been said that the most dangerous of all false doctrines is the one that is seasoned with a little truth.

The prefix 'xeno' (as in 'xenophobe') is the Greek word used here in describing *'teachings'*. It means 'foreign', 'strange' or 'alien'. The author warns about the distinct possibility of being *'carried away'* (enticed, lured) by false doctrine. The *'strange teachings'* that threaten to infiltrate the church today are the recycled heresies of the past two thousand years: New Ageism, Neo-Evangelicalism, Charismatic Phenomena, Health and Wealth theology, Church Growth Movement, which all attract many followers, but do not necessarily produce disciples of Jesus Christ.

The spiritual strength we depend upon doesn't come from false doctrine. Neither does it come from eating the *'ceremonial foods'* and the rituals of religion (Judaism was in mind). We don't derive spiritual power by keeping to some mystical diet.

True believers distance themselves from the various heresies and blasphemies which have become associated with holy water, holy wafers, consecrated bread and wine and the 'host'. How we need to be purged from the *'strange teachings'* that have hijacked churches and denominations that were once 'Bible believing'.

In vv10-14 the writer recalls the Israeli camp in the desert and the tabernacle within that camp. Inside the camp there was acceptance and belonging, sacrifice and worship, atonement and forgiveness.

But the writer contrasts that with what is outside.

1 OUTSIDE TO DESTRUCTION (v11)

The 'red letter day' in the Hebrew calendar was the Day of Atonement. Unlike the cooked meat of other sacrifices which the priests were permitted to eat, the carcasses of the bulls and goats on the Day of Atonement were destroyed outside the camp. There was no place inside the camp for the bodies of animal sacrifices symbolically polluted by sin. The only place for contaminated carcasses was outside the camp.

All of Aaron's priesthood, which has been graciously dismantled in the earlier chapters, has been replaced with Christ's superior priesthood. Our altar is Christ and his cross (v10) – nothing less, nothing other! Man-made altars have no place in his priesthood.

2 OUTSIDE TO DEATH (v12)

In an amazing way, Jesus' death *'outside the city gate'* is compared to the animals' bodies which were *'burned outside the camp'*. The sin-contaminated carcasses prefigured the sin-bearing body of Jesus who died *'outside the city gate'*. The beloved Son of God became a curse, an outcast, like the rejected carcass of an animal, outside the camp, that he may redeem his people (Matthew ch1 v21; 2 Corinthians ch5 v21; Galatians ch3 v13).

Jesus died in separation from all that was heavenly, holy, and wholesome.

Jesus came to the world to be separate from his Father so that we may come to the Father and be separate from the world.

Jesus died in such unholy circumstances as to make his people holy.

3 OUTSIDE TO DISGRACE (v13)

Jesus suffered disgrace outside, and here we are being encouraged to go outside to him *'bearing the disgrace he bore'*. We cannot participate in his atoning sufferings, but we can be identified with Jesus in his death. Such identification with him will mean disgrace and suffering. It's easy to 'stay safe' in our Christianity and not to 'go outside'. We can remain comfortable and cosy in our warm Christian environment, the fellowship of believers and the internal work of the church. But we are called to venture out from our isolated, insulated 'comfort zones' and to go outside to Christ: outside in his rejection, ill treatment and disgrace. Moses regarded *'disgrace for the sake of Christ as of greater value than the treasures of Egypt'* (ch11 vv25-26).

Isn't Jesus worth all the disgrace? Is there anyone who means so much as Jesus?

He became a curse so that we may be freed from the curse. He was made sin so that we may be made righteous. He experienced disgrace so that we may experience his grace. He was taken outside so that we may be brought inside.

MAY 20
HEBREWS ch13.15-25

SUITABLY EQUIPPED

The striking, stirring theme of 'Hebrews' has been 'Jesus Christ is the greatest'. There's no one like Jesus. He is the greatest, the loveliest and the best. But the Bible believer knows that Christ is the dominant theme of *all* Scripture. Wherever we may turn the pages of the Bible there are direct or indirect references to Christ. It is therefore in the Lord Jesus that all sacrifices and offerings are pulled sharply into focus (v15). Jesus is the One through whom all the Old Testament crystallises. He is the divine 'master key' to unlocking the mysteries of Old Testament types, shadows and prefigurements. It is also *'through Jesus'*, our great High Priest, that we can perform our own priestly duties of sacrifice and worship. What are we exhorted to do?

1 TO OFFER CONTINUALLY (vv15-16)

What kind of sacrifices should we be offering?

i] Unceasing: *'continually'*. Our whole lives should be one continual offering.

ii] Unsilenced: Our *'sacrifice of praise'* should be *'the fruit of lips that confess his name'*. It's a fruit that proves the real nature of a tree or plant. We must not be silent in our witness and worship.

iii] Unspoiled: Just as the Old Testament offerings had to be unsullied and unspoilt, so our offerings should come from pure motives and clean hearts.

iv] Unstinting: Our offering to God must always be the best. Just as the firstling, firstborn and firstfruit were demanded in the Old Testament, so we should offer the first of our time, talents and tithes to God.

v] Unselfish: Our sacrifices of praising must also be sacrifices of sharing. God is pleased with the sacrifices that are made in doing good to others.

2 TO OBEY WILLINGLY (v17)

The local church is a group of God's people who are covenanted together in their representation of Christ in the world. There must be order, structure, and coordination.

Two important things may be noted about church leadership:

i] Authority: This does not mean 'authoritarian'. It implies the ability to lead, teach, and direct. Any church leader (whether overseer, elder, deacon, bishop, or presbyter) will need a degree of authority to fulfil their ministry effectively. Such authority must never be exercised manipulatively or dictatorially, but always lovingly and graciously.

ii] Accountability: They are accountable to God for 'keeping watch'. We are all called to be diligent and obedient in our various roles within the church. Any leadership will be a joy when there is co-operation and positive support in that ministry. This is a long way from either a dictatorial or a subservient attitude.

3 TO LIVE HONOURABLY (v18)

'Honourable living' should be the Christian's 'badge'. When Paul had been seized by a mob in Jerusalem (Acts ch21) he was rescued by the Roman commander. The following day it was arranged for Paul to testify before the *'chief priests and all the Sanhedrin'* (v30). Paul declared that he had been living honourably *'in all good conscience'* (Acts ch24 v16). His life as an 'open book' was honourable and faithful to God. In a sense, God's reputation in the world is in our hands. Should that not make a difference to the way we live?

4 TO PRAY EARNESTLY (vv18-19)

Even the respected writer of this letter needed prayer. How should we pray?

i] Faithfully: We may not always 'feel' like praying. But we have a duty to pray, and setting aside a time and place each day ensures it is not neglected.

ii] Personally: *'Pray for US'*. We are able to 'name names' before the 'throne of grace' in our private prayers.

iii] Specifically: The writer had a particular request in mind: that they might meet soon. There may have been more important matters to pray about as well, but this was his burden at this time.

The *'word of exhortation'* (v22) may have been brief, but what a profound letter!

God wants to *'equip'* us with *'everything good for doing His will'* (vv20-21). The same word is used for the preparing or mending of nets (Mark ch1 v19). Like nets, we are not so useful if we are broken, damaged, holed or incomplete!

'God of Peace, equip me with everything good for doing your will and work in me what is pleasing to you, through Jesus Christ'.

MAY 21
JUDGES ch1.1-36

THE DANGERS OF COMPROMISE

The judges who ruled over Israel following the death of Joshua didn't wear black gowns, scarlet robes or a full-bottomed wig! These judges, who included a woman, were fighters, adventurers and heroes who became military deliverers under the hand of God. They were raised up to save the Hebrews from their enemies. It has to be said that some of the narratives of the Book of Judges are brutal, barbarous and bloodthirsty. Not all their characters or actions can be condoned.

WHO

Although some identify the author of this book as Samuel, there is no proof. The judges are deliverers or saviours who had been sent to save Israel from being completely oppressed by their pagan enemies in Canaan.

WHEN

'Judges' covers the period between Joshua and Samuel, between the patriarchs and the kings. It's a period accurately summed up in ch21 v25. It's estimated as being about four hundred years, roughly between 1500-1000BC.

WHERE

The theatre in which these colourful scenes are acted out is Canaan. It's the Promised Land (Joshua ch1 vv3-4).

WHAT

Israel had descended into great moral and spiritual decay. They were in danger of losing their identity as they wallowed in the pagan practices of Canaan's inhabitants instead of driving them out, as they had been instructed to do. It's said that that the spiritual climate of Canaan can be summed up by 'apathy, anarchy and apostasy'.

WHY

Why has God in his sovereign purposes allowed this period of darkness in Israel's history? Why has he permitted the shame and disgrace that his degenerate people have produced? It is so that they may learn the bitter lesson of God's judgement and so that his people may be ultimately restored to him.

It was Joshua who had been Israel's great leader, governor, statesman and saviour. Therefore it's strikingly significant that the opening words of 'Judges' marks this next turbulent period in their history: *'After the death of Joshua...'* Be warned about the dangers of compromise.

The Lord had given clear instructions to possess the land of Canaan. It rightfully belonged to Israel. God had said so. The Canaanites were now 'trespassing' as 'squatters' and God had given Israel the permission and the power to evict them. But Israel acted like a landlord who had given his tenants notice to quit, had broken down the front door, yet chose to live alongside them in his own house by sharing the wardrobe, the toothpaste and the fridge. It's a recipe for disaster! What a compromise!

1 THE RISK OF COPYING THE WORLD'S PRACTICES (vv5-7)

The mutilator Adoni-Bezek became the mutilated (vv6-7). There's no particular condemnation of the Israeli treatment of this pagan leader but it's easy to be sucked in by the same practices, customs and procedures that are acceptable among the pagan peoples of our own society. Jesus said that his people must be different from the pagans (Matthew ch5 vv44-47; ch6 v7; v32). We must not rush to copy them in their behaviour.

2 THE RISK OF FOLLOWING THE WORLD'S TRADITIONS (vv12-13)

Marriage is portrayed in the Bible as a covenant of beauty and dignity, love and commitment. Marriage is not the 'star prize' for the capture of an enemy city! As Christians, we must be vigilant in upholding the high ideals of marriage, family, truthfulness of speech, honouring promises and commitments. We are to be the saltiness in society.

3 THE RISK OF APPLYING THE WORLD'S STANDARDS (vv22-26)

The pact between the spies and this Bethel traitor was honoured (as with Rahab in Jericho). But if *the Lord was with them*' (v22) was it necessary to negotiate a deal with the enemy? Bethel had its name changed from Luz by Jacob who met God there. And what does this informer do after he had been spared? He goes to the land of the Hittites and builds another city, defiantly calling it 'Luz'. We compromise our position, our testimony and our influence when we apply the world's standards. Is it to be Luz or Bethel?

4 THE RISK OF ACCOMMODATING THE WORLD'S DEMANDS (vv27-36)

The problem of the book is summed up in v28. They had failed to take drastic action. Have we entered into an 'agreement' with sin in our lives? Have we ejected sin with God's power, or does it continue to live in our lives as a 'tenant under notice to quit'?

May it never be said of us that we had failed to drive out the enemy completely!

MAY 22
JUDGES ch2.1-23

A GENERATION IGNORANT OF GOD

'Out of Africa' may be the name of a popular film, as well as the title to an attractive hypothesis on human origin, but *'Out of Egypt'* is the theme of God's Masterplan to save the Hebrews from slavery and deliver them safely to Canaan. God reminds Israel frequently that he brought them *'out of Egypt'* (vv1,12, also see Exodus ch3 v11; Numbers ch24 v8; Hosea ch11 v1). For Israel, *'out of Egypt'* meant rescue under cover of blood. It meant grace, hope, new life, a new walk with God and the prospect of entering a new home, no longer despised or displaced. For every child of God there has been an *'out of Egypt'* experience.

But the period of the judges is full of problems that are summed up in v10: *'another generation grew up, who knew neither the Lord nor what he had done for Israel'.*

It may help us to think of four generations in Israel's history at this point:

Generation 1 - would be the last generation to experience life in Egypt. This was the generation that had experienced the suffering and had witnessed the plagues in Egypt. They had also been brought through the Red Sea but they forfeited entry to Canaan because of their complaints (Numbers ch14 vv29-31).

Generation 2 – had entered Canaan under Joshua's leadership. They had seen the River Jordan open up to allow them passage. They had witnessed the total collapse and defeat of Jericho. This is the generation referred to in vv6-7.

Generation 3 – didn't know about the Lord and what he had done for Israel (vv10-14).

Generation 4 – is also identified with the succeeding generations who became *'even more corrupt than those of their fathers, following other gods and serving and worshipping them'* (v19).

It's 'Generation 3' that's especially described in v10. But why was this generation so ignorant? Why didn't they know about their history and how great was their ignorance?

1 THEY WERE IGNORANT OF GOD'S COVENANT

(vv1, 20) God's people were bound to him by a covenant that he had established with Abraham and had reaffirmed to Isaac and Jacob. It was a treaty (a contract, an agreement) which provided the Hebrews with identity and security. The Lord had faithfully fulfilled every detail that he had promised. But it was not an unconditional covenant. Israel was required to be loyal and loving towards God (Deuteronomy ch30 vv15-18). Now, if these conditions formed part of the title deed to Canaan, would you not think that this generation would have been taught their covenantal obligations by their parents, priests, and leaders?

Although Britain has never been a 'covenant people' in the same way that Israel were, nevertheless this nation has a history in which the mercy and faithfulness of God has been witnessed clearly. Yet a generation has sprung up who has not been taught the account of God's faithful dealings with our nation.

2 THEY WERE IGNORANT OF GOD'S COMMANDS

(vv16-17) This Israeli generation chose not to know or to follow God's commands, and it was disobedience that precipitated their downfall. As parents, church leaders, educationalists, and legislators, we have abdicated our responsibility for training our children properly. How are children in our land today going to know about God's commands (his standards, his laws, and his requirements) unless those children are being taught the word of God? We can bemoan the deplorable standards of morality and behaviour, of respect and decency that are endemic in our society, but which generation has failed to lead by example?

3 THEY WERE IGNORANT OF GOD'S COMPASSION

(vv18-19) Israel had repeatedly despised God's compassion and grace. Throughout Israel's history, and here in Judges especially, this cycle is repeated ad nauseam. We read of disobedience, defeat, distress, and deliverance (for example, vv12-16). God remains compassionate, but Israel doesn't want to know. God continues to show compassion (Psalm 145 v9; Matthew ch5 v45), but this generation doesn't want to know either. This is the message that we should be teaching our children. This generation needs to hear of the wonderful grace of God in the gospel. They need to know that he *pardons sin and forgives the transgression* (Micah ch7 vv18-19). But who will tell them?

MAY 23
JUDGES ch3.1-31

RESTING AND TESTING

Israel had dreamt of their own home in Canaan. The thought of a long uninterrupted rest from war and enemies was attractive (Deuteronomy ch12 v10). But whatever their dreams of 'rest' consisted of, the reality would be quite different. Certainly they would experience periods of peace (such as vv11, 30) but the resting went hand in hand with the testing (vv1, 4). Israel's experience in Canaan teaches us that our Christian lives are a process of a resting and testing.

We know the wonderful 'rest' there is in the gospel of Christ (Matthew ch11 v28). We also know the rigorous campaign of testing and constant warfare. But all the most precious metals and all the most dependable of materials are subjected to the severest of tests.

In this chapter we are introduced to the first three of twelve judges. Each was a champion that God raised up to deliver his people. God is able to use every one, with their peculiarities and weaknesses, for the glory of his name and for the good of his people.

1 OTHNIEL: GOD CAN USE YOUR UNORTHODOX BACKGROUND (vv7-11)

Othniel had won the 'star prize' (ch1 vv12-13). He had been given Caleb's daughter Acsah as his bride. Othniel was not only Caleb's son-in-law but he was also his brother, half-brother or nephew. Othniel and Caleb were Kenizzites (Joshua ch14 vv6, 14). Othniel is said to be a *'son of Kenaz'* (v9). The Kenizzites had probably descended from Esau (Genesis ch36 v15) and were one of ten tribes that were firmly established in Canaan. Othniel's ancestors were therefore the sons of Esau and not the sons of Jacob (the sons of Israel). It seems though that this Kenizzite ethnic group had been proselytised (converted to Judaism and counted among the tribes of Judah). Othniel had been called to deliver Israel following a sickening cycle of disobedience (v7), defeat (v8), distress (v9) and deliverance (v9).

There may have been those in Israel who questioned Othniel's right to lead them. After all, he came from a family of 'outsiders". He couldn't trace his ancestry through Jacob. There may be some believers who feel like 'outsiders' in the church. They don't have the same background in church, Sunday School, upbringing or Bible training. But the significant factor in Othniel's experience was that *'the Spirit of the Lord came upon him'* (v10). We need men and women today who are empowered by God's Spirit.

2 EHUD: GOD CAN USE YOUR PECULIAR ABILITIES (vv12-30)

Once again we observe this cycle of disobedience (v12), defeat (v13), distress (v15) and deliverance (v15). Just as God raised up Eglon as judgement for Israel (v12) so he raised up Ehud as a judge for Israel (v15). God uses those with peculiar abilities and disabilities. Ehud may have been left-handed because he was handicapped in his right hand. After dismissing the porters who carried the tax/tribute to Eglon, Ehud returns to have a private audience with the king. It was too late for the unsuspecting Eglon when Ehud reached for his homemade sword on his right side and plunged it into the king's corpulent body. The trumpet signal rallied the Israeli troops to dispose of ten thousand *'vigorous and strong'* Moabites (v29).

Our 'hand' may be weak, small or unskilled. It may be a metaphorical 'left hand', but we're to use it energetically and wholeheartedly for God (Ecclesiastes ch9 v10).

3 SHAMGAR – GOD CAN USE YOUR LIMITED RESOURCES (v31)

Little is known of Shamgar, except that he may have been another Canaanite converted to Judaism (*'Anath'*: ref 'Beth-Anath', the Canaanite goddess of war). The Philistine enemy may have already monopolised iron production (1 Samuel ch13 v19), depriving Israel of weapons. But Shamgar's limited resources of an ox-goad (a two to three metre pointed pole) didn't stop him from killing six hundred Philistines. Shamgar didn't give up because he felt that he didn't have the right tools or equipment. Referring to the lad's limited resources (loaves and fish) in Matthew ch14 v18, Jesus said: *'Bring them here to me'*. He was able to make a feast for thousands from those 'limited resources'.

You may often feel that your limited resources are just as rough and basic as Shamgar's 'pointed pole'. But don't be discouraged! God can use them (1 Corinthians ch1 vv26-28)! They may be small, limited and insignificant, but in God's hand they can achieve his purposes. Jesus said, *'Bring them here to me'*.

MAY 24
JUDGES ch4.1-24

A FALTERING FAITH OR A TRIUMPHANT FAITH?

At this period in history, the 'Bronze Age' was giving way to the 'Iron Age' during which iron was found to be more productive and creative. Iron-working technology was perfected by the Hittites and by about 1340BC the Hittites had emerged as a major power. The famous treaty between the Egyptians and the Hittites brought a period of stability in the Middle East that, some people think, is consistent with the eighty years of peace that Israel enjoyed under Ehud (ch3 v30). But the Hittite influence at the dawn of the 'Iron Age' is seen particularly in the manufacturing of agricultural implements and weapons. Sisera's *'nine hundred iron chariots'* (v13) reveal the extent of technological developments. Here was a formidable 'war machine' that Jabin of Hazor had created, together with his field commander, Sisera.

Again, we notice the cycle of disobedience (v1), defeat (v2), distress (v3), and deliverance (v4). But here are two considerations:

1 WHEN FAITH FALTERS

The following factors contribute to a faltering faith.

i] Surprise at Enemy Success

We recall the comprehensive victory that Joshua and the Israelites secured at Jericho. The crumbled, empty ruins of Jericho would have stood as a memorial to that great victory. But for how long? (Note ch3 v13) Jericho had been reclaimed. Israel's enemies were allowed successes too. Joshua had captured Hazor and had annihilated all its inhabitants (Joshua ch11 vv1-11).

What a thorough victory! So v2 may surprise us. Even allowing for the possibility that 'Jabin' could have been the name of a royal dynasty, nevertheless that dynasty is enjoying success again – and based in Hazor!

David frequently complained about his enemies' successes (for example, Psalm 10 vv2, 5). Jeremiah couldn't understand the progress and prosperity of his enemies either (Jeremiah ch12 vv1-2). But the Lord assures that he had not abdicated his sovereign control. Our faith must not falter when we see God's enemies prospering. It's only short-term.

ii] Fear of Man's Strength

Nine hundred iron chariots must have seemed formidable (vv3, 13). Yet at nearly every point in history God's people have encountered a 'Jabin'. Their 'war machines' have been used to attack and destroy God's people. But we are encouraged to stand firm. Remember Moses' words when Pharaoh's armies were bearing down (Exodus ch14 vv13-14).

iii] Rejection of Moral Values

Israel's track record wasn't good. They were still guilty of doing *'evil in the eyes of the Lord'* (v1). They had been 'taken in' by the false Canaanite gods of the Baals and the Asherahs, and ch3 v7 reveals that, amazingly, *'they forgot the Lord their God'*.

iv] Neglect of Spiritual Responsibilities

This chapter promotes the achievements of two women in particular:

Deborah (a prophetess and judge) and Jael (*'the wife of Heber the Kenite'* v17).

Without subtracting anything from the character and faithfulness of these Biblical heroines, where were the men? Where are the men of faithfulness, courage, godliness and authority today who should be taking the initiative and positions of leadership?

v] Doubt in God's Power

Does the man who would be remembered for his faith (Hebrews ch11 v32) have a 'faltering moment' in v8? Do we doubt God's power to save us or preserve us?

2 WHEN FAITH TRIUMPHS

i] Trust in God's Plan

Barak may not have known how he was going to cope against Sisera's chariots, but he trusted God's word through Deborah, and he obeyed in faith (v14). When he took the first step of faith, the Lord responded victoriously (v15).

ii] Believe in God's Promise

God had promised to *'hand Sisera over to a woman'* (v9). Sisera was lulled into a false sense of security (v19) and he didn't see the tent-peg coming! (vv21-22). Sisera thought he had escaped but no one escapes God's judgement (Romans ch2 v3). The only escape is in Jesus. Faith comes by hearing and believing God's word (Romans ch10 v17).

Let's see our faith in God triumph!

MAY 25
JUDGES Ch5.1-31

WHEN THE PEOPLE WILLINGLY OFFER THEMSELVES (v2)

In 1888 Hudson Taylor, founder of the China Inland Mission, wrote *'We are manning our station with ladies'*. The two prominent ladies in this hymn of praise are Deborah, the prophetess and judge, and Jael, the wife of Heber the Kenite, whom God used to defeat Sisera, the commander of Israel's enemies. Barak was also appointed by God to lead an army of ten thousand Israelis. Although at first glance someone may think that this hymn is a celebration of women's achievements, there is unequivocal praise to Almighty God. It's the Lord who has worked mightily on Israel's behalf. It's the Lord who has appointed these women to serve him. God continues to appoint godly, consecrated women to serve him in both prominent and less prominent ways. Great things can happen when *'the people willingly offer themselves'* (v2).

1 AM I WILLING TO LEARN?

To date, our reading of Judges only underlines the apparent unwillingness of the Israelis to learn. Over and over again, God had taught them a lesson, but they had refused to learn that lesson or to remember it. What memorable lessons they should have learned about their mighty God? Who could ever forget the dynamic displays of divine sovereignty in their history? Well, it seems, Israel could! How slow are we to learn about God's might and strength, his grace and mercy, his justice and holiness? It's true that sometimes the lessons are learned the hard way. The Academy of Adversity produces a constant trickle of graduates with great potential. Are we willing to learn from history, from experience, from others' testimonies and from God's word?

Jesus said, *'Take my yoke upon you and <u>learn</u> from me...'* (Matthew ch11 v29) just as a young novice animal would be yoked to a mature, experienced animal for training purposes, so the believer is yoked to Christ.

2 AM I WILLING TO LEAD?

The world is full of people who want to be leaders but who are unsuitable and unqualified. But true leaders should lead. When good leadership is given, then there is blessing – *'When the princes in Israel take the lead...'* (v2). Sadly, for Israel, they hadn't always enjoyed honourable and faithful leadership. As in our own times, weak leadership can produce 'no go areas' in our land (v7). Barak too may have been a reluctant leader initially (see ch4 v8).

What position of leadership or responsibility is God calling you to just now, and you are less than willing? Like Moses, you may be saying 'Not that! Not here! Not now! Not me!' Deborah may have hoped that the princes of Israel would have been better rulers who were more faithful, more godly and more authoritative. But God had bypassed these men to appoint this woman. Deborah would live to do God's will and to praise his glory (v3).

3 AM I WILLING TO LOSE?

In vv13-18 we are provided with a list of the willing and the unwilling: the tribes that were ready to *'(risk) their very lives'* (as Zebulun and Naphtali v18) and those who refused. Some gave the matter great consideration (v16) but in the end they were unwilling to commit themselves to fight. Perhaps they believed they had too much to lose! Perhaps, like Gilead, we may prefer to *'(stay) beyond the Jordan'* (v17), just 'keeping our heads down'. We may be nominally supportive of our brothers on the front line, but 'east of the Jordan' is more comfortable for us as there's less pressure, no great risks and not too much to lose! Are we frightened of Paul's challenging 'profit and loss account' for the sake of Christ and knowing him (Philippians ch3 vv7-8)?

4 AM I WILLING TO LOVE?

v31. The final refrain of Deborah's song is a petition for God's people to be like the blazing sun. Do you really love the Lord with heart, soul, mind and strength?

Light: We should shine brightly like the noon sun (Matthew ch5 vv14, 16). Are we guilty of putting up the 'black out curtains' and preventing the light from shining through?

Warmth: A cold, piercing light, without warmth, may be compared to teaching truth without love and grace.

The warning to the unwilling Meroz (v23) stands in contrast to the willing Deborah, Barak and Jael. There's no room for neutrality with Christ (Matthew ch12 v30).

MAY 26
JUDGES Ch6.1-40

THE LORD IS WITH YOU, MIGHTY WARRIOR

Now we're introduced to the fifth judge and the one with the longest narrative. All the judges are very different people, emphasising that the Lord calls and uses all kinds of individuals in his service. They are not equal in terms of ability, availability or suitability, but God shapes and sharpens his instruments for his work.

The cycle of disobedience (v1), defeat (v1), distress (v6) and deliverance (v14) seems tiresome and nauseous. After sending the unnamed prophet (v7), the Lord appears to Gideon in the form of an angel (v12). His first words were, *'The Lord is with you, mighty warrior'.*

The Lord may call us, using the same words. Our response may be much like Gideon's. *'Me? A mighty warrior? You must be joking!'*

1 HE NEEDED TO BE STRONG (vv11-24)

Gideon was full of doubts, even though the Lord himself was personally visiting him and calling him.

i] He had doubts about his circumstances (vv12-13)

Gideon could point to the Midianites who had been the scourge of Israel for seven years. The Midianites were also descendants of Abraham by his wife Keturah (Genesis ch25 v1). But these nomads were engaged in a campaign to destroy Israel's prosperity (v4) and the Israelites had been forced to hide in the mountains (v2). When the *'angel of the Lord appeared to Gideon'* and said, *'The Lord is with you, mighty warrior'* (v12), Gideon replies *'If the Lord is here with us, why has all this happened to us?'* (v13).

Isn't this the question that we sometimes ask today, in our hearts if not audibly? Why this accident? This disability? This loss of jobs? This hostility from neighbours or family?

ii] He had doubts about his qualifications (v15)

Do you feel like that? 'There's no one more unsuitable than me? There's no one less able or less qualified than me'. But it's not ability but availability that the Lord looks for. The Lord responded to Gideon's complaint of weakness (v16). Is there anything that can trump God's promise *'I will be with you'*? No, there's nothing!

iii] He had doubts about his call (vv17-18)

God appearing in person didn't seem enough convincing for Gideon! God graciously confirms his call to each of his servants today through prayer and the reading of his word.

2 HE HOPED TO BE SAFE (vv25-32)

If anything was calculated to provoke hostile reaction from pagan worshippers, it was Gideon's first mission (v25). God had promised his presence but Gideon wanted extra insurance. He took ten of his servants and he went at night (v27). We're not very good at trusting God *completely*, are we? That's not to say that we shouldn't use our common sense. But if the Lord says, *'I will be with you'*, you can count your life and destiny upon it. Gideon was on the Baal worshippers' 'hit list' for destroying their altar and Asherah pole. But Gideon's father said that *'if Baal really is a god, he can defend himself'* (v31). So Gideon was nicknamed 'Jerub-Baal', meaning *'Let Baal contend'* (or, we might say, 'It's Baal's quarrel'!).

3 HE WANTED TO BE SURE (vv33-40)

'Putting out the fleece' is a well-known expression in some Christian circles. It refers to a method of confirming what some would believe God is telling them. Gideon devised a 'signal system' for God to use. God was gracious and patient with Gideon in his devising of these tests, but that shouldn't be seen as approval of the method. If 'putting out the fleece' is God's 'preferred method of discernment', why is the rest of Scripture, and especially the New Testament, silent about such a system? We should be very careful about playing mind games with God:

i] Because it's evidence of our arrogance. In effect, we're saying to the Lord, 'You do what I'm telling you to do and then I'll do what you're telling me to do';

ii] Because it assumes that God will work within our time frame. We think that he will provide a 'quick fix' solution instead of developing our patience and perseverance in prayer;

iii] Because we are provided with another method: Colossians ch3 vv15-16 provides two sure guides for discerning God's will: the peace of Christ ruling (acting as an umpire) in our hearts and the word of Christ dwelling in us richly. What more do we need for our assurance?

MAY 27
JUDGES Ch7.1-25

ARE YOU AMONG THE THREE HUNDRED?

There is a dramatic change in Gideon since chapter six. Gideon seems to have 'grown up' spiritually. His confidence in God has been developed and he is learning to trust in God and his word. Are we more like the 'Gideon' of ch6 (doubtful, timid, apprehensive, uncertain of God's word and unsure of his calling) or are we like the 'Gideon' of ch7 (trusting God, placing complete confidence in his word and assured that his planning and organisation is always best)? Ch7 is like a 'breath of fresh air'. Gideon is no longer devising his petty 'hoops and hurdles' that he expects Almighty God to 'jump through' and 'jump over'. Instead, he is developing the character of a *'mighty warrior'*, a valiant man of faith who qualifies for inclusion in 'Faith's Hall of Fame' (Hebrews ch11 v32).

But what is the evidence of Gideon's faith?

1 HE TRUSTED THE LORD'S ENLISTMENT OF HIS PEOPLE

In vv2-8 the Lord sifts and separates the men he will use. We mustn't forget the scale of Midian's forces and resources (v12). It may have seemed such a crazy thing to reduce the size of Israel's army (v2). Even thirty-two thousand would seem to be less than required. But the Lord prunes the army to ten thousand, allowing those who *'trembled with fear'* to be excused (v3). If Israel had beaten the Midianites with thirty-two thousand they would have boasted that they were the architects of their own success. But even ten thousand were too many. Using the 'water test', nine thousand seven hundred of them were sent home. Gideon trusted the Lord's enlistment of his special army. They weren't Gideon's selection: the Lord had called each and every one. But a small band in the service of a great God can achieve mighty things, then and now. God may continue to prune and trim his team of workers so that they may prove his all-sufficiency. It seems that everyone is obsessed with numbers today, even in our churches! Of course, we long for people to be saved. We want those who will respond to the gospel. We pray for the Lord's 'addition', as in Acts (for example, ch2 v47). But sometimes, in God's mathematics, there is subtraction before addition, and division before multiplication. We mustn't always be discouraged when the Lord reduces the number of workers before he pours out a blessing.

Are you among the twenty-two thousand who left because their hearts weren't really in it? Are you among the nine thousand seven hundred who were not trusting God for his daily provision?

Are you among the three hundred who will serve God, whatever the conditions or the cost?

2 HE TRUSTED THE LORD'S ENCOURAGEMENT OF HIS PEOPLE

(vv9-15) It was during the night that God instructed Gideon to spy out the enemy camp: *'Listen to what they are saying, you will be encouraged to attack the camp'* (v11). Gideon and Purah overheard a man talking about his dream (v14).

i] Encouragement often comes at an unexpected moment

They were all ready to attack when this encouragement came. The 'unexpected moment' is usually the 'right moment'.

ii] Encouragement often comes from an unexpected source

The middle of the enemy camp may have seemed the last place that Gideon expected to receive any encouragement. But the Lord surprises us! (compare Paul's experience in 2 Corinthians ch7). Often it is the short letter, the card, the e-mail, or the visit that comes when it's most needed. Are we known as Christians of 'encouragement' or 'discouragement'?

3 HE TRUSTED THE LORD'S EQUIPMENT FOR HIS PEOPLE

Torches, trumpets, and jars are not the usual weapons of war. We can trust God that:

i] Our basic tools are effective

The Lord's implements must never be despised. Our tools and weapons may not be the result of the latest technological advances, but they are the equipment that has been divinely provided (2 Corinthians ch10 vv3-5).

ii] Our simple abilities are useful

The men that 'made it through' to the last three hundred were not necessarily known for their firing accuracy or swordsmanship, but they could blow a trumpet, break a jar, wave a torch, and could shout. Don't despise the simple skills or abilities you have been given.

iii] Our formidable enemies are confused

Even our most powerful spiritual foes may be conquered by simple tools, solid faith, ordinary abilities and an extraordinary God.

MAY 28
JUDGES Ch8.1-35

BEWARE OF THE SNARE

We've all suffered from illogical or unjustifiable criticism. Although Gideon had secured a great victory over the huge Midianite army, he was not immune from sharp criticism. How often do we feel the barbs of criticism right after a particular spiritual success? The advance on the Midianite camp (ch7 vv22-23) was just the beginning of their defeat. Over the next two days, and for about seventy miles, the Israelites left a trail of 135,000 Midianite corpses (vv10-12). Although Gideon's small detachment of three hundred had been used by God to gain the initial victory, Gideon had sought the help of men from Naphtali, Asher, Manasseh and Ephraim to complete their enemies' destruction. This is where the criticism came from. God's servants frequently receive similar criticisms today.

i] Criticism from those who want to do a different job

The men of Ephraim were churlish because they had wanted to be among that elite company that had surrounded the camp (v1). The people of Ephraim were 'touchy' and 'prickly'. Like many in the church today they wanted to pick a quarrel over who does what! They wanted a job that was more glamorous, more prestigious and less onerous. Gideon could have justifiably attacked Ephraim for their pride and selfishness (two of the most common causes of criticism) but instead he gives compliments (vv2-3: Proverbs ch15 v1).

ii] Criticism from those who want to do nothing

The *'officials of Succoth'* (v6) and *'the men of Peniel'* (v9) wouldn't lend support. What a great discouragement! These 'armchair critics' didn't want to get involved. They represent those who want to criticise from the sidelines without an ounce of support or encouragement. Through Gideon, the Lord dealt severely with them. Don't be among those who are frugal with their support but free with their censure.

But there was weakness in the life of Gideon. There was a gap in his spiritual defences, which became a snare to Gideon and his family (v27).

The word for *'snare'* means a kind of 'gin trap'. As a vicious trap with a pair of jaws on a strong spring, it can hold its victim in its vice-like grip (see Proverbs ch29 v6, Isaiah ch28 v13).

The *'ephod'*, which Gideon made from donations of gold, warns us of four dangerous snares.

1 THE SNARE OF POPULARITY

(vv22-23) Gideon seemed to resist public opinion, which sought to crown him king. He pointed out that Israel's government was theocratic, not democratic. Yet how much did he secretly hanker after power, prestige, and royalty? The kings of Midian admitted that Gideon appeared and acted as royalty (v18). There's a reference to Gideon's harem, a badge of royalty (vv30-31). There's also the expectation of family succession (ch9 v2) and

Abimelech's own name means *'my father- a king'*. Look out for the trap of popularity that continually ensnares preachers, pastors, authors, musicians, and others.

2 THE SNARE OF AUTHORITY

It's a small step from being popular to becoming powerful. Kingship was within Gideon's grasp, but he refused (v23). Yet he still exercised influence in securing a donation from everyone. Authority is not wrong per se, but it can easily ensnare. The Early Church Father, John Chrysostom, warned: *'Nothing will so avail to divide the church as love of power'*.

3 THE SNARE OF PROSPERITY

Gideon may have rejected the call to reign as a king, but he lived like a king. He seemed to enjoy the royal treatment. It's true that Gideon may have deserved it for the many *'good things'* he had done (v35). But the pursuit of wealth has snared believers who have forfeited lives of useful service in the process (reference Luke ch18 vv22-23). For many Western Christians, their possessions, acquisitions, investments, and money in the bank have become a hindrance – a snare – to effective ministry in the Lord's name.

4 THE SNARE OF IDOLATRY

In ch6 Gideon tears down his father's idols but in ch8 he makes his own (v27). Whatever Gideon originally intended for this ephod (possibly a memorial or a monument) it became an idol (Exodus ch23 v33). Which objects have we invested with special status in our lives that are in danger of becoming idols, detracting from the true worship of God? Which snares keep us from prayer and from God's word? Which 'gin trap' snaps shut on our feet to prevent us from helping someone, from doing God's work, from attending church or from going where God wants us to go? Beware of the snare!

MAY 29
JUDGES Ch9.1-57

GOD REPAYS WICKEDNESS

This is the longest and darkest chapter in Judges. We may be shocked at the evil and depravity of man as we read this account of Abimelech. But whatever we learn here about the scale of evil and the depths of depravity, we should know that God repays wickedness.

There are three simple questions that can be asked under this title.

1 WHAT IS WICKEDNESS?

Every daily newspaper reports the horrific details of wickedness that have been perpetrated over the previous twenty-four hours. The daily diet of wickedness and evil continues unabated. Terrorist attacks, assassinations, multiple shootings, hijacks, kidnaps, infanticide, family murders, depraved immorality, not to mention the endless line of Christians brutally persecuted for their faith.

Ophrah and Shechem became associated with wickedness on a grand scale. Abimelech was the only one of Gideon's seventy sons who didn't have an Israelite mother. In returning to his 'roots', Abimelech persuaded the people of his mother's town, Shechem, that he would make the best king. With a donation from the pagan temple funds, Abimelech hired a gang of *'reckless adventurers'* (v4) to slaughter his brothers. All except one – Jotham – were murdered like sacrificial animals on a stone. Such wicked acts have been employed by many other historical figures in the name of 'political expediency'. So how might we define 'wickedness' from these verses?

i] Breaking God's Laws

The law of God brings sin into sharp focus (Romans ch7 v7). It has the purpose of showing sin for what it really is – ugly, destructive, and opposed to God. Abimelech had broken the first, second, fifth, sixth, eighth, and tenth commandments repeatedly.

ii] Rejecting God's Purposes

Abimelech wanted to be crowned king and to spearhead a Canaanite revival. He was the 'thornbush king' of whom Jotham spoke (vv8-15). He had nothing to offer in terms of benefits, fruit, value, or usefulness. He was only a liability and a curse.

iii] Despising God's Character

The Bible consistently declares the holiness of God. He is light and there's neither darkness (1 John ch1 v5) nor wickedness (Psalm 92 v15) in him. Sin is an affront to God's nature and an attack on his Being.

2 HOW DOES GOD REPAY WICKEDNESS?

i] An Unprofitable Life

The fable of the trees proclaims Abimelech's life to be unprofitable and unproductive. There was no redeeming feature, no usefulness or profit. How productive is your life (Titus ch3 v14)?

ii} An Undignified Death

He was killed by a woman with a millstone (v56). By contrast, the deaths of the Lord's people are dignified and *'precious'* (Psalm 116 v15).

iii] An Unenviable Memorial

The memory of Abimelech would only ever be associated with evil. Men and women of infamy are the architects of their own disreputable memorials. It's better not to have lived than to have lived and died in wickedness.

iv] An Unavoidable Destiny

The wicked are already walking down the broad highway to destruction. It's a one-way street to hell. Unless they leave the broad road and join the narrow road to life, their inescapable destination is eternal death.

3 HOW CAN WE BE SAVED FROM WICKEDNESS?

We are all wicked and sinful by God's standards (Romans ch3 v23). But there is a Saviour who *'gave himself for us to redeem us from all wickedness'* (Titus ch2 v14). Jesus came to live with wicked people; to die by the hands of wicked people (Acts ch2 v23) and to be buried with wicked people (Isaiah ch53 v9). Yet he remained perfectly untainted by sin and wickedness. Jesus has provided the means for our redemption. But how can that affect us, and how can that be transmitted to us personally?

We must be active in seeking him. We must be fervent and genuine in calling on him by faith. What's more, *'let the wicked forsake his way and the evil man his thoughts. Let him return to the Lord and he will have mercy on him, and to our God, for he will freely pardon''* (Isaiah ch55 v7). The Israelites of Jeremiah ch14 v20 confessed: *'O Lord, we acknowledge our wickedness ... we have indeed sinned against you'.*

MAY 30
JUDGES Ch10.1-18

WHERE DO YOU TURN IN A CRISIS?

This chapter tells us of three more judges or deliverers. These were Tola (vv1-2), Jair (vv3-5), and Jephthah (his account begins in v6). Three years of unrest were followed by forty-five years of peace. Jair seems to have had a tight control over Gilead as his thirty sons ruled a town each. They had their own personal transport too!

But v6 repeats the whole sorry cycle again. Israel had forgotten and forsaken its God. Each time Israel had been plunged into a crisis (sometimes on the verge of annihilation), God had come to their rescue when they had eventually made their 'distress call'.

We often hear the cry from some distressed person, 'I don't know where to turn'. Those who have proved the Lord God Almighty to be an unchanging, unending supply of strength, help, comfort, guidance, and assurance can only wonder at those who put their trust in inferior and useless deities. But this is precisely what Israel did (v6). They had fallen under the spell of pagan deities. How could they be so stupid? Is it any surprise that the Lord said, *'Go and cry out to the gods you have chosen. Let them save you when you are in trouble!'* (v14) The gods of the Canaanites (listed in v6) seem remarkably similar to the gods that continue to be worshipped by our pagan society. Although our world claims to be superior in its sophistication, its 'pet gods', which are worshipped, honoured, and sacrificed to, are much the same.

1 THE GOD OF SEX AND IMMORALITY

Baal became the greatest contender for the hearts and minds of the Israeli people. The worship of this most prominent of Canaanite deities was marked by various obscene fertility rites. We are bombarded by images, graphics, articles, advertisements, and storylines that reverence such a god today. Everything seems to conspire to seduce ordinary people to worship at the shrine of this 'modern-day Baal'. Paul uses the illustration of a sentry standing guard. He says that the *'peace of God'* should be the sentry that stands guard at the door of a believer's heart and mind (Philippians ch4 v7) to keep from sin. We need the peace of God's pardon, power, and assurance.

2 THE GOD OF VIOLENCE AND BLOODSHED

One of *'the gods of the Ammonites'* was Molech, who was worshipped by gruesome orgies of child sacrifice. Unborn children are still sacrificed on the altar of choice, independence, and prosperity. This 'god', whether called 'Molech', 'Feminist Freedom', or 'Mothers' Rights', continues to demand oblations from its worshippers.

3 THE GOD OF RELIGION AND SUPERSTITION

The gods of the Philistines' (v6) included Baal-Zebub (same as Beelzebub), the prince of demons (Matthew ch12 v24, Mark ch3 v22, Luke ch11 v18). This god has a strong grip on the way people behave and conduct their lives today. For many, their brand of religion includes faith in humanity, the world, science, nature, the cosmos, evolution, spirit powers – even faith in a church or denomination, but not faith in Christ as Lord.

4 THE GOD OF HEALTH AND WEALTH

Another of *'the gods of the Philistines'* was Dagon. The name comes from either the word for 'fish' or 'grain'. This chief god represents material prosperity and promotes greed and materialism in the hearts of its worshippers. Not only is this the religion of those who claim 'not to have a religion', but it has also been adopted by some significant sections of Christendom (variously called 'prosperity teaching', 'health and wealth gospel', 'word-faith system'). Men have corrupted Scripture in a bid to satisfy their own greed and materialistic ambitions (see the letter of Jude vv11, 12, 16).

So which god can we turn to in a crisis? There's only One who is real, reliable, powerful, and accessible. He is the Lord God, the Rock, the Fortress, the Creator and Redeemer of his people (Isaiah ch40 v18; ch42 v8; ch44 v6). So how must we turn to him?

i] Confession: v15 *'We have sinned'.*

This is the first and greatest hurdle for many.

ii] Submission: v15 *'Do with us whatever you think best'.*

It has to be total surrender with nothing held back.

iii] Petition: v15 *'Please rescue us now'*

In faith, we must call upon Jesus Christ for rescue and redemption.

iv] Conversion: v16 *'They got rid of the foreign gods...'*

They took drastic action and forsook their sin, making a complete break with the past to serve the Lord.

MAY 31
JUDGES Ch11.1-40

HOW GOOD IS YOUR WORD?

The 'word', given at its face value, implies truth. When someone is found to have broken their word, it is difficult to trust them ever again. People are identified with their words. Politicians are notoriously slippery with their words, and therefore, it may be hard to 'take their word for it'.

Are you known as a man or woman of your word? Can you always be trusted in what you say? This chapter about Jephthah has lessons to teach us about our 'word'.

What do we know about Jephthah?

He came from Mizpah (meaning 'watchtower') in Gilead on the eastern side of the River Jordan. Gilead shared a border with Ammon. Jephthah was *'a mighty warrior'* (v1), but he had been thrown out of the family because, unlike his half-brothers, his mother had been a social outcast. Again, we see how God raises up the disowned, the rejected, and society's outcasts so that he may use them for his purposes. Jephthah became the eighth judge or deliverer of Israel. His portrait hangs in 'Faith's Hall of Fame' (in Hebrew ch11), located between Samson and David (v32)! Jephthah wanted to know if these elders were genuine and trustworthy in their request.

1 THE IMPORTANCE OF KEEPING YOUR WORD

The elders called upon God as their witness (vv10-11). They entered into a pact before the Lord. They didn't have a sheaf of legal documents to sign. They simply recognised the veracity and integrity of the spoken word. We hear some people attempting to make their 'word' more authentic and more believable by saying 'I swear on my mother's grave' or 'cross my heart and hope to die'. But Jesus condemned such evil practices (Matthew ch5 vv34-37). James also condemns the flippant, casual use of oaths to make the word more truthful (James ch5 v12). The Christian must ensure above everything that his word is pure and uncorrupted. His word must be truthful, and his promises must be kept. There is no excuse for broken vows or 'going back on one's word'.

2 THE CONFIDENCE IN TAKING YOUR WORD

We frequently hear a statement made with the attachment *'Take my word for it!'* How much confidence can a person have in your word? After Jephthah had been appointed commander over the Israelites, he confronted the enemy. The Ammonites accuse the Israelites of land-stealing. Such a response invited a 'history lesson' from Jephthah (vv14-27). He reminded the Ammonite king of the Exodus and how they had sought permission to cross the Amorites' territory (Numbers ch21 v22). The Israelites gave their word that if they were allowed to pass through the Amorite land that they wouldn't touch any of the Amorites' fruit, veg, water, or livestock. They gave their word that they would keep to the main road. But Sihon *'did not trust Israel to pass through'* (v20). The king had no confidence in their truthful word. So God gave victory over the Amorites. The King of Ammon later took over the land of the Amorites that God had given to Israel. Our 'oath-taking' and 'vow-making' today are because of man's innate dishonesty. But the Christian, converted by God's grace, should be trusted in every word. There shouldn't be any reason to emphasise that we are telling the truth because all our words should always be pure, unadulterated truth.

3 THE CONSEQUENCE OF GIVING YOUR WORD

Jephthah's rush into a rash commitment resulted in sin. His vow to sacrifice to the Lord the first thing that greeted him on his return home after conquering the Ammonites led him to sacrifice his only daughter. Jephthah kept his word, though it meant the greatest cost. Once again, we are confronted with the folly of making bargains with God, that is, 'You do what I want you to do and I'll do what you want me to do'. We are reminded of Abraham's sacrifice, where God intervened to stop Isaac from being offered. But God didn't intervene in Jephthah's case. There were consequences in giving his word.

But Jesus has not only given his word, he has given his life to make his word possible (John ch6 v37; ch8 v12; ch11 v25). Have you taken Jesus at his word?

A Final Point

The tragedy of the ending of a life is compounded by the ending of an 'unfulfilled' life. How fulfilled is our life for Christ? What if we knew we only had two months left (v38)? How profitable and useful is our life being lived for God?

JUNE 1
JUDGES Ch12.1-15

HARD TO PRONOUNCE?

The Ephraimites were known to have held a grudge (see ch8.1-3). In vv1-3, we discover that the same prickly Ephraimites were challenging Jephthah because they hadn't been included in the victorious army that had defeated the Ammonites. The Ephraimites were 'glory-seekers'. They would have loved to be included in the victory celebrations, but they weren't prepared to risk themselves in battle. Yet now they were ready to turn on their own people for the sake of a grudge! How much 'in-fighting' has erupted within churches and denominations as a result of some petty, long-standing grudge? The battle between Gilead and Ephraim has been re-enacted regularly in the history of the church. But Jephthah and the Gileadites gained the advantage and captured the fords that led back to Ephraim.

It was difficult to spot the Ephraimites when they came to cross the fords. A simple test was devised to identify the retreating Ephraimites from other Israelis crossing the river. They were asked to say *'Shibboleth'*. Apparently, Ephraimites could only pronounce it as *'Sibboleth'* (vv5-6).

'Shibboleth' became a distinguishing feature of 'life and death importance' for the people of Ephraim. This word is still used to distinguish a group of people by habit, custom, dress, principle, or belief. Especially, it refers to a long-standing distinguishing feature, often regarded as outmoded or no longer important. Here are seven 'shibboleths' that distinguish the beliefs of true disciples of the Lord Jesus Christ from those who merely profess to be 'religious', or 'church-going', or 'Christian'.

SHIBBOLETH 1 – THE DEITY OF CHRIST

Jesus Christ is not a 'superman' or 'cosmic hero'. He is God who was revealed in human flesh (John ch1 vv1, 14). Millions of people are content to accept a Christ that's anything less than God because it releases them from any personal obligations to conform to his teachings; to obey his commands; to believe his promises; to proclaim his truth; to live his life; to serve his will and to worship his majesty.

SHIBBOLETH 2 – THE AUTHENTICITY OF THE RESURRECTION

The resurrection is not an 'optional extra' as far as Christian teaching is concerned (1 Corinthians ch15 vv14-15). If Christ did not rise from the dead, our witness is false and our faith is futile. It is through the resurrection of Jesus that the believing sinner is justified (Romans ch4 v25) and released from the power of sin (Romans ch6 v14); is regenerated (1 Peter ch1 v3) and is guaranteed a similar resurrection (2 Corinthians ch4 v14). If you *'have been raised with Christ'* then you are under obligation to *'set your hearts on things above'* (Colossians ch3 v1).

SHIBBOLETH 3 – THE AUTHORITY OF THE BIBLE

It is either trustworthy in every part or trustworthy in no part. If this is the living, dynamic, probing, personal word of the living God, then why aren't we taking it seriously?

SHIBBOLETH 4 – THE REALITY OF CREATION

We must listen carefully to the many religious people who are talking about a 'Creator' and 'creation' today. How are they pronouncing this 'Shibboleth'? They may use the same terms, but may not be saying the same thing. They may be pronouncing 'Creation' as 'Evolution' and 'Creator' as 'Intelligent Being'!

SHIBBOLETH 5 – THE MORALITY OF THE CHURCH

The decline in moral standards and decency is sadly reflected in the church. Once unacceptable practices are now openly encouraged to keep pace with trends, fashions, and styles. But sin is still loathsome and abhorrent to God. Time doesn't alter that!

SHIBBOLETH 6 – THE CENTRALITY OF THE GOSPEL

The good news of Christ coming into the world to save sinners must be pivotal to our message. Yet on any day of the week, you will find marriage services and funeral services being conducted in the name of Christ, in which the Biblical gospel is being denied: that everyone is alright and they will all be received at the Final Resurrection.

The gospel of God's grace and the words of our precious Saviour are rejected.

SHIBBOLETH 7 – THE CERTAINTY OF CHRIST'S RETURN

Jesus is coming again (John ch14 v3, 1 Thessalonians ch4 v16) to take his waiting people home.

Is the 'shibboleth' of authentic Biblical Christianity hard for you to 'pronounce'?

JUNE 2
JUDGES Ch13.1-25

A HUMBLE HOME FOR GODLY PEOPLE

How predictable are you? We may be more predictable than we think in our choices, our routines, our pet phrases, and clichés. Israel was certainly predictable in their cycle of sin and disobedience. The opening words of this chapter shouldn't surprise us now. But how predictable is our own cycle of temptation, sin, regret, repentance, and confession?

We have read previously of Israel's suffering under the oppression of powerful enemies such as the Moabites, Canaanites, Midianites, and Ammonites. But the Philistines were different. They continued to make their incursions, gaining greater power and influence in the land. But Israel seemed to become accustomed to Philistine domination. Perhaps the Philistines had not been as aggressive as other enemies had been, and Israel had become lulled into accepting the status quo. They didn't even cry out to the Lord in distress, as previously. We may even get the impression later that they didn't want Samson to 'rock the boat'. How easily we are lulled into accepting our sinful surroundings and spiritual compromises.

But God was about to raise up another champion, a strong judge. It wasn't an accident that Samson was born into a humble home with godly parents. Samson's home was:

1 A GOD-HONOURING HOME

This humble Jewish family loved God, honoured his laws, and exercised faithfulness. It is often among such homes that God prepares his great men and women of faith. It may not always be a home of academia, or prosperity, or great awareness, in terms of fashion, technology, and culture, but it will be a home of great love for the Lord and his honour. There's never any substitute for a home in which God is honoured, his name revered, his truth loved, and his commands taught.

2 A PRAYER-CENTRED HOME

When told that she would have a son, the childless, sterile wife of Manoah didn't laugh as Sarah (Genesis ch18 v12), or doubt as Zechariah (Luke ch1 v20), or even get troubled as Mary (Luke ch1 v29). Instead, she simply explained to her husband (v6) without any over-dramatisation, under-estimation, or 'spin'. What was Manoah's response? He prayed (v8). Did he argue, complain, or doubt? Was he upset that the angel had appeared first to his wife and not to him? Not a bit of it! He prayed sincerely, not that God would take away their heavy responsibility in bringing up a Nazarite, but that God would teach them how to do it. Remember how the disciples didn't ask Jesus to teach them to preach, but to teach them to pray (Luke ch11 v1).

3 A CHRIST-LOVING HOME

The 'angel of the Lord' in the Old Testament is regularly used to denote the revelation of the Lord himself. There's good reason to believe that the pre-incarnate Christ visited the home of Samson's parents. Christ is *'the image of the invisible God'* (Colossians ch1 v15). Manoah wanted to know the visitor's name so that he could honour him. The word used for his answer (that is, *'It's beyond understanding'* or *'Wonderful'*) is the same word used in Isaiah ch9 v6 to identify the child to be born (*'He will be called Wonderful...'*).

How much do our homes smell of the fragrance of Christ's presence?

4 A BIBLE-BELIEVING HOME

It's clear that Manoah believed God's word. He didn't doubt the Lord's message (*'WHEN your words are fulfilled'* vv12, 17). The word of God should be the divine document that's central in our homes, because we believe in its authenticity, we submit to its authority, and we're in love with its Author.

5 A SELF-SACRIFICING HOME

We can notice three ways in which Manoah and his wife *didn't* put themselves first:

i] Welcome

Even before Manoah knew the uniqueness of his visitor, he wanted to be hospitable towards him (v15).

ii] Work

From Manoah's prayer, we know that they weren't looking to abdicate responsibility for their son. His birth may turn their lives upside down, but they were committed to effort, dedication, perseverance, and self-sacrifice.

iii] Worship

The sacrifices of a goat and grain may be costly, but they are accepted by the Lord. True worship is always costly. Such a home that puts Jesus first, 'Others' second, and 'Yourself' last will be a home of real JOY.

JUNE 3
JUDGES Ch14.1-20

A RIDDLE WRAPPED IN A MYSTERY INSIDE AN ENIGMA

Every age and society has its riddles and puzzles. It seems that at ancient Jewish weddings, guests enjoyed being entertained by getting their heads around a good teaser! It's not surprising then that Samson comes up with this memorable riddle (v14) that has adorned Tate and Lyle's syrup tins and jars for decades.

But here are three more riddles or questions while considering Samson in the light of ch14.

1 WHO'S A MAN OF FAITH WHO NEEDED TO BE FAITHFUL?

Whatever we may think of Samson, we mustn't forget that he is listed among six named heroes who are remembered for their faith (Hebrews ch11 vv33-34). He has gone down in history as a champion of faith. Yet at the same time, we cannot ignore his faults because there are lessons for us to learn. We may imagine the heartbreak that Samson caused his parents when he announced that he wanted to marry a Philistine girl. He would have known, along with his parents, that God had prohibited treaties, covenants, and especially marriages with the Canaanite peoples (ch3 vv5-7; Deuteronomy ch7 v3; Joshua ch23 vv9-13). Although his parents tried to get him to change his mind, Samson would not be dissuaded (v3). Irrespective of whether this was God's 'right one' for Samson, he declared, *'she's the right one for me'*.

We may also get it into our heads that a particular course of action, a desire, or a situation is 'right for us'. It's exactly suited to 'our perceived need'. No amount of chiding, warning, counselling, teaching, or preaching will deflect us in our chosen course. We may even abandon logic, defy reason, and reject God's word in our consuming quest to obtain what we believe is right for us. Like Samson, we may say adamantly, 'It's right for me'. That's the thinking that dominates our society and culture today. People are encouraged to ignore what others say or think about their behaviour, lifestyle, attitude, or preferences, and to do what's 'right for them'. The closing comment of Judges (ch21 v25) emphasises that everyone did what they thought was right for them, and what a disastrous time it turned out to be!

2 WHO'S A MAN OF STRENGTH WHO NEEDED TO BE STRONG?

We can't be sure why Samson's parents didn't know what he had done with the lion (v6) since all three had been on their way to Timnah (v5). Maybe like a sulking teenager, Samson had been walking on ahead or lagging behind! His parents didn't know where the honey had come from. His Nazarite vows had been broken. Samson had been contaminated by a dead body. He was not strong in this, nor was he strong in resisting the Philistine girl. Samson may have been strong in the arms when it came to a lion, but he was weak in the knees when it came to a girl! In three chapters, Samson's weakness is seen with three different women. This strongest of men, physically, was the weakest of men morally. Each of us has a weakness that requires special vigilance.

God's Sovereignty in Samson's Susceptibility

God is never dictated to by our sins and weaknesses. He doesn't make contingencies to accommodate our failures. His plans are never thwarted or put 'on hold'. What an encouraging thought! Even in the middle of Samson's self-willed determination to marry outside of God's covenant people, God was in control (v4). That doesn't excuse Samson's sins or our sins, for which there may be consequences. But he weaves our errors and transgressions into his own sovereign programme.

3 WHO'S A MAN OF THE SPIRIT WHO NEEDED TO BE SPIRITUAL?

Samson was a man marked out by God and who experienced the power of his Spirit. The Spirit stirred him (ch13 v25) and strengthened him (ch14 vv6, 19; ch15 v14).

Stirring Us

The Spirit stirs us with the life and power of God. As spiritual corpses, we cannot self-resuscitate. It's the Spirit who animates and regenerates (John ch3 v6). But we need a constant stirring to spend more time with God, to live a life of holiness, and to become more like Jesus.

Strengthening Us

He enables us to defeat spiritual enemies and to resist the *'roaring lion'* of 1 Peter ch5 v8.

Samson's wedding went from bad to worse! Certainly, the Lord may act graciously and patiently in his sovereignty to bring fruit out of folly and good out of bad. But we must never presume upon his purposes.

JUNE 4
JUDGES Ch15.1-20

TIED UP WITH NEW ROPES

The phrase 'tit for tat' (meaning 'blow for blow' or 'like for like') accurately describes the persistent exchanges between Samson and the Philistines (chs14-16). Samson had stormed out of his own wedding, but now he appears at the home of his 'in-laws' expecting to carry on from where he left off. He didn't know that his wife had been given to his 'best man'. Samson declined the offer of the 'more attractive' younger sister and stormed off again to 'get even'. Once again, Samson asserts his 'rights' (reference ch14 v3) – the *'right to get even with the Philistines'* (v3). How often do we hear people bleating about 'their rights'! What rights does anyone have?

Although societies and governments may confer rights upon their citizens, the Bible teaches that we have no inherent rights before God. Any rights have been forfeited by sin and the Fall (Romans ch3 vv10, 12, 23). It's only because of God's incomprehensible grace that we have not been hurled into hell (2 Peter ch3 v9). The Lord Jesus voluntarily surrendered his riches and rights so that sinners may receive the *'right to become children of God'* (John ch1 vv11-13).

So Samson destroys the Philistines' harvest. Then we have the sad spectacle of this fearless champion of Israel being handed over to his enemies by his own people. This may be a legitimate illustration of what Christendom and nominal Christianity is doing to faithful, Bible-believing Christians today. They are attempting to 'bind them' with 'new ropes' and hand them over to their enemies. We might describe the 'ropes' as:

1 THE ROPE OF A 'NEW UNITY' – WHATEVER THE COST

Although there is true and genuine unity among those who have been saved by God's grace, religious groups strive for a wider unity that is not founded upon Christ or his word – inter-denominationalism, ecumenicism, multi-faithism. Contentious issues have been removed, and the main issues of contention for a man-made unity are those truths that are fundamentally important to Bible-believing Christians. Samson represented discomfort and discord for Israel, and his people wanted him removed. They wanted to live harmoniously with their 'enemies'. Evangelical Christians are blamed for discomfort and discord on the religious scene today. The nominal Church wants a harmonious relationship with the world and its paganism. Instead of professing Christians retaining their distinctiveness, they are doing their best to remove their differences and become identified with the world around them. Bible-believing Christians make others feel uncomfortable. Bible-believing Christians 'rock the boat' and stand out. But Jesus was accused of 'rocking the boat'. His own people betrayed him, bound him, and handed him over to their enemies to kill him.

2 THE ROPE OF A 'NEW MORALITY' – WHATEVER THE CONSEQUENCES

How can the Church have any influence when it's adopting the 'new morality' (or should that be 'immorality'?) of a liberal, politically correct, anti-Bible society? Such 'New Age morality' champions the rights of homosexuals, relaxes the rules on divorce and marriage, remains strangely silent about infanticide, criticises those who promote chastity, condones cohabiting, violates the sanctity of the Lord's Day, and advocates leniency for offenders while ignoring the victims of crime. God's law is being systematically outlawed. Christendom, like the *'men of Judah'*, is trying to bind Bible-believing Christians, to disassociate from them, to identify them as troublemakers, and to hand them over to their enemies.

So how can we be freed from these 'ropes' of 'New Unity' and 'New Morality'?

We need the two things that Samson experienced:

i] God's Power to Release us (vv14-16)

The new ropes of pseudo-Christianity will make us more like the world. The animating, liberating power of God's Spirit will make us more like Jesus. We need the Spirit to strengthen us (Romans ch8 v26; Ephesians ch3 v16) and set us free from the ropes that bind us.

ii] God's Water to Revive us (vv18-19)

Jesus provides the cool, refreshing water that we desperately need (John ch7 vv37-38) for our tired, difficult, painful lives of service. Pray that the ropes that men would restrain us with *'become as charred flax and the bindings (will drop) from (our) hands'* (v14).

JUNE 5
JUDGES Ch16.1-31

IMPRISONED IN THE DUNGEON OF HIMSELF

'Imprisoned in the dungeon of himself' is the seventeenth-century poet John Milton's apt description of the strongest of men, Samson. New ropes, city gates, fresh thongs, or even an army of soldiers couldn't restrain him. Yet he was overpowered by his own disobedience and selfishness.

1 HE WAS UNCONCERNED ABOUT THE LORD'S LAW

We have every reason to believe that Samson had been brought up in a godly home where he had been taught the law of God. This would have included sound moral instruction as well as the requirements to keep himself separate from the pagan Canaanites. But we see Samson persisting in relationships with three Philistine women (if Delilah was a Philistine). Samson hankered after forbidden fruits. Delilah's name has always been associated with seduction and betrayal. He may have been too strong for new ropes and city gates, but he was overpowered by the disarming tones of women. The Philistine rulers (ch3 v3) knew that what they couldn't achieve by strength they could achieve by stealth, and so they bribed Delilah to discover *the secret of his great strength'* (v5). Because Samson was unconcerned about the Lord's law, he was already on the slippery slope to defeat.

2 HE WAS UNAFFECTED BY THE LORD'S LESSONS

How loudly does the Lord need to speak to Samson (or us) to get attention? We may wonder why Samson was so gullible and why he was so easily caught in Delilah's honeytrap. But it's the case that sin makes people single-minded. They become blind to danger and deaf to warnings because they have become obsessed with one objective. We may ignore the lessons God is teaching us in our obsession with pursuing the path of sin. Israel was the same. However many times they were taught a lesson, they didn't learn their lesson.

How insensible may we become to the Lord's easy, basic lessons? We ignore his frequent reminders and resist his gentle prodding. We cry out with David, *'Teach me to do your will'* (Psalm 143 v10), but the truth is that we don't like the lessons and we really don't want to be taught.

3 HE WAS UNAWARE OF THE LORD'S LEAVING

We are given one of the most solemn and most tragic comments in the Old Testament (v20): *'He did not know that the Lord had left him'*. Here was God's champion, Israel's leader, one of the 'Hebrews heroes', who had enjoyed the supernatural power upon him on three recorded occasions. But now he was helpless and alone. Not only had God left him, but he also didn't *know* that God had left him! He couldn't presume upon God's Spirit to empower him whenever he demanded. Samson wasn't a 'superman' who could rush in and out of a 'telephone kiosk' anytime he wanted, recharged with superhuman powers and 'fly away to take on the world'!

Samson was totally dependent upon the Spirit of God. And he had left him!

It's possible to experience God's power in your life – saving, equipping, anointing, and blessing – but then for that power to be withdrawn on account of sin and disobedience. Samson had treated his consecration to the Lord with contempt. Do we need reminding of those things that we have affirmed and avowed to the Lord at our conversion, baptism, call to service, in the singing of hymns, as well as at other times?

May the Lord awaken us before he withdraws the anointing of the Spirit's power upon our lives, our churches, our services, and our ministries.

4 HE WAS UNSEPARATED FROM THE LORD'S LOVE

All is not over as we view Samson in the Gaza prison. The Lord had promised that he would be a Nazarite to death (ch13 v7). God still mercifully regarded him as 'set apart for the Lord'. He was still embraced by the wonderful, inseparable love of God (Romans ch8 vv38-39). Samson may have been separated from God's power for a time, but he was never separated from his love. What's interfering with your 'power supply'? However great the sin, however regrettable the failing – there is forgiveness for those who humbly seek reconciliation with the Lord. The Lord's love for his own people never diminishes. Be vigilant! Keep awake!

Don't be like Samson, who woke up, only to find his power gone!

JUNE 6
JUDGES Ch17.1-13

A D-I-Y RELIGION

While Bible scholars and commentators agree that these last chapters are an appendix to the Book of Judges, we dare not dismiss them as being irrelevant or unpalatable. The dominant theme of the book, and especially the last chapters, is highlighted in v6: *'In those days Israel had no king; everyone did as he saw fit* (or *'everyone did as he pleased'* or *'everyone did what was right in his own eyes'*). There was no central authority or strong religious leadership to provide moral guidance and stable government. Everyone was doing what they *thought* was right. Although they were attempting to conduct themselves according to their conscience and their limited spiritual knowledge, their standards were low and their beliefs were seriously warped.

Israel was practising a 'Do-It-Yourself Religion', which had developed through the abandoning of God's standards, God's laws, God's requirements, and God's word.

1 CORRUPTED MORALS

Micah had stolen about 28lbs (13kg) of silver from his own mother. 1100 shekels represented a huge amount, particularly as the priest's annual salary was going to be just ten shekels (v10). The woman's powerful curse triggered Micah's confession. Beginning with Micah's one immoral act, the first, second, fifth, eighth, and tenth commandments were broken. The corrupting influence of sin is powerful and far-reaching. How quickly the silk threads of sin can bind its helpless victim like the spider's prey (Proverbs ch5 vv22-23). Sin *'so easily entangles'* (Hebrews ch12 v1). Drastic action is called for in order to be released from sin's snares. Jesus compared such action with self-mutilation (Matthew ch5 v30).

2 PERVERTED CONSECRATION

The sincerity of Micah's mother is in doubt. Although her cursing quickly changes to blessing, she professes to consecrate the 1100 shekels to God (v3). Yet when Micah returns the treasure to his mother, she only sets aside 200 shekels (18%). Of course, 18% is above the tithe (10%), but she had not honoured her initial consecration (see Ananias and Sapphira – Acts ch5 vv1-2). How many promises do we make to the Lord that we fail to keep? How solemn and serious! Often it's in the hymns that we sing that such vows of consecration are made (for example, *'Take my life and let it be consecrated, Lord, to thee'* – FR Havergal). We may sing such a hymn when we have no intention of being *fully* consecrated to God. Throughout Christendom today, we are suffering from 18% commitment, not 100%. ' 18-per-cent-ers' are not committed to prayer, to Bible study, to church duties and responsibilities, to helping those in need, to mission, and to the publishing of the gospel. Are you just an '18-per-cent-er'?

3 POLLUTED WORSHIP

The second great command of the Decalogue (Exodus ch20 v4) prohibits the making of idols. The actions of Micah's mother may surprise us (vv4-5), but Israelite worship had become contaminated by the religions of the Canaanites. Instead of ruthlessly driving the Canaanites from the land as God had instructed, Israel were now suffering the consequences (Joshua ch23 vv12-13). Polluted worship still infects a Church in which pagan rites and superstitions have been imported. From the lighting of candles to the use of sacred vessels and furniture, from wearing religious vestments to observing religious diets, from the raising of crosses and crucifixes to the touching of statues and relics, so-called worship is conditional upon special performances, special postures, and special places. Jesus spoke to a woman whose religious people had rejected much of God's revelation about true worship (John ch4 vv23-24). Genuine worship is where God is given his rightful place, when he is loved, honoured and adored *in spirit*, from a heart and lips that have been set on fire by the Spirit of God. True worship is rooted in truth.

4 DISTORTED REASONING

Following the installation of his son as his priest, Micah then finds a more qualified personal priest: Jonathan, the Levite (ch18 v30). Micah's religion consisted of superstition (v13). His basic formula amounted to 'shrine + ephod + idols + priest = God's goodness'. He omitted the vital ingredients of obedience, humility, repentance, and faith. Micah was clinging to his possessions, contacts, rituals, and superstitions. God's goodness is to those who *'love him'* and who are *'called'* by him (Romans ch8 v28).

JUNE 7
JUDGES Ch18.1-31

WHAT ELSE DO I HAVE?

The fifth son of Jacob (Israel) was Dan. In four hundred and thirty years, Dan's tribe had increased to 62,700 (Numbers ch1 v39). When Dan's tribe, with the others, eventually entered Canaan under Joshua's leadership, they began conquering the land. This included the five kings of the Amorites who ruled over five of the major cities of the Southern Mountains (Joshua ch10). The Amorites were defeated and routed. The land was seized as Israel's promised possession. It was this particular territory that formed the seventh lot when the land was apportioned to the tribes, and it was the tribe of Dan that received the seventh lot. But the Danites had allowed the Amorites to creep back into the region and regroup (Joshua ch19 v47). Consequently, the Amorites became stronger so that they restricted the Danites' movements (ch1 vv34-36). So much so that the Danites were dispossessed of the land allotted to them because they hadn't been serious enough or strong enough to suppress the Amorites.

So ch18 traces the movement of a group of the Danites, which travelled northwards to Laish ('*Leshem*' ch1), looking for a land to call their own. The advance party of five spies encountered Micah and his priest, Jonathan (ch17). With the priest's blessing, the spies continued on their mission and discovered a peace-loving people who were easy to defeat. When the spies reported back, the Danite soldiers marched north and seized the land mercilessly. On the way north, the Danites called in on Micah and offered Jonathan a job with them. He agreed and took Micah's idols and images with him. When Micah found out, he chased after the Danites, who warned him that he could get killed if he pursued his claim. Micah's pathetic question (v24) summed up the state of pagan Israel and sums up the pitiful state of many religious people today: *'What else do I have?'*

In other words, if you take away my powerless gods, my helpless priest, and my hopeless religion, what else do I have? Stripped of all the props and paraphernalia of a belief system founded upon superstition and sentiment, what else do I have?

1 HOME-MADE GODS

These were useless, impotent, hand-crafted gods (ch17 v4). Micah failed to see the ridiculousness of his bizarre attempts to 'rescue' his captured gods! How could he put his trust in a god that couldn't help itself? Yet many are living in the same way today, placing their hopes in, and stacking their eternity upon, home-made gods which cannot help themselves. They are trusting in untrustworthy devices.

2 SELF-INSTALLED PRIEST

Just as it's trendy for people to have personal trainers, personal assistants, and personal analysts today, Micah had his own personal priest. But Jonathan was a priest without any loyalty to Micah. He was easily attracted by promotion, and he was complicit in the robbery of Micah's images and idols. In vain, Micah had put his confidence in this corrupt and undependable priest.

3 EMPTY RELIGION

Micah was left with nothing. If we were stripped of all the props and trappings of our religion, what would we be left with? If our hymnbooks, Bibles, commentaries, musical instruments, church buildings, and Christian organisations were all seized from us, what would we have left? Is our religion a real religion of the heart that cannot be snatched away? In stark contrast, those who believe the gospel of Christ possess:

i] A Saving Faith

This is the right belief about God, which involves trusting his word, trusting his Son, and trusting in his grace to save personally. This is not from *'yourselves'* (Ephesians ch2 vv8-9).

ii] A Living God

We don't trust in an inanimate, impotent god that is dependent upon *our* craftsmanship, *our* imaginations, and *our* help. *'We put our hope in the living God...'* (1 Timothy ch4 v10). The world needs to hear that our God is alive. He is exalted, and he reigns supreme.

iii] An Atoning Priest

God's designated priest is Christ (Hebrews ch5 v10). He has not been appointed on the whim of an Ephraimite or by the tribe of Dan. Jesus is the perfect Priest who is also the only sacrifice for sin (Hebrews ch9 v26). What else do I have? What else do I need but Christ?

JUNE 8
JUDGES Ch19.1-30

GOD REIGNS EVEN IN THE DARKNESS

In the darkest days of Church history, when the spectre of evil loomed large in the world, God's power had not diminished and his kingdom had not declined. Neither does he need human authorities by which to govern, just because *'In those days Israel had no king'* (v1). In every area of godlessness and in every arena of evil, we can be assured of this all-encompassing truth that 'our God reigns'.

Therefore, even the deepest depths of depravity to which Israel had sunk in the days of the Judges were controlled by God.

The unnamed Levite had a callous disregard for God's law, for marriage, even for life itself. After fetching his concubine from her father's house, they journeyed to Gibeah. Only one old man took pity on them and persuaded them to receive his hospitality.

We cannot understand, on the one hand, the host's revulsion at the abhorrent and disgraceful behaviour of *'the wicked men of the city'* and, on the other hand, his willingness to sacrifice his daughter to the mob (v24). When the thugs wouldn't listen, the Levite pushed his wife outside to be pounced on by the brutal and bestial mob.

After abusing her all night, they released her to struggle back to the house with her last ounce of strength. When her husband opened the door to continue his journey in the morning, he almost tripped over his wife, who lay with her hands on the threshold (v27).

The Spiritual Night is Very Dark

This Levite, from the priestly tribe with its star status and privileges, takes a concubine. He seems to be a 'party animal' (vv4, 6, 8, 22) who was more interested in a good time than in his marriage (Note that it was four months before attempting reconciliation – vv2-3). He was quick to save his own skin by sacrificing his wife. It seems that he was able to sleep on that fateful night when his wife was being abused. His callousness is also seen in the way he treated her in the morning and his disrespect in dismembering her body (v29).

The Spiritual Pit is Very Deep

To what abhorrent depths of depravity had the men of Gibeah fallen? This loathsome incident has many comparisons to Lot's experience with the Sodomites in Genesis ch19. Yet God's view of merciless violence and depraved sodomy has not changed. Such sin is still abhorrent in his sight. So what can we learn from this grisly account?

1 OUR HIGH MORALS MAY BE PERVERTED

The Levite thought he was 'doing right in his own eyes' when he recovered his unfaithful concubine from her father's house (v3). But it seems that there was no real love or forgiveness in his heart. How could he treat her as he did if he really loved her? The old Jew's morals were corrupted, too. He was right to condemn the demands of the mob as *'vile'* and *'disgraceful'* (v23), but he was ready to surrender the women to their perversions. Sometimes we may profess high morals over certain matters while retaining a 'blind spot' to other matters. We may be quick to condemn blasphemy, pornography, and gratuitous violence, and yet we are happy to be entertained by these on our TVs, DVDs, and in our books. How easily we become accustomed to the appalling standards of morality around us.

2 OUR GOOD DEEDS MAY BE LIMITED

The old man may have been generous with his hospitality (v20), but we notice that he also referred to the depraved mob as his *'friends'* (v23). His provision for his guests didn't extend to their protection. Instead of curtailing our good deeds, we should be encouraging one another to flourish with them (Proverbs ch3 v27; Galatians ch6 vv9-10, Hebrews ch10 v24).

3 OUR BEST INTENTIONS MAY BE INTERRUPTED

The Levite explained that they were on their way to *'the house of the Lord'* (v18). The house of God was in Shiloh (ch18 v31). 'Shiloh' represented worship, communion, sacrifice, and consecration, but sadly, it was not a priority for this Levite. How easily do we become distracted from our best intentions? 'Shiloh' means 'whose it is' or 'to whom it belongs'. Does the Lord receive from us all that is rightfully his?

In Genesis ch49 v10, *'Shiloh'* refers to the One who will ultimately take rightful possession of his own. Jesus was never deflected in his purposes. He was not distracted from his priority to go to the cross. Thank God that our Saviour's determination wasn't diluted nor his intentions interrupted.

JUNE 9
JUDGES Ch20.1-48

UNITED AGAINST EVIL

People go to extraordinary lengths of endurance and self-sacrifice to call attention to a perceived injustice or victimisation. For the unnamed Levite (ch19), his gruesome publicity stunt was to chop his wife's body into twelve parts and to send them to each of the twelve tribes of Israel. The whole of Israel was shocked by this grisly tactic. He had calculated on attracting Israel's attention, and it had worked. Israel united *'as one man'* (vv1, 8, 11) in their determination to make the *'wicked men of Gibeah'* pay for their vile and disgraceful actions. Although Israel is portrayed as being disunited and fragmented elsewhere in Judges, she is united over this incident. Christians, too, should be united in their campaigns against evil and immorality. There may be many differences that divide believers, but in support for God's moral law and in opposition to depravity and corruption, the Church of Jesus Christ should be *'as one man'*. If sections of the Church not only fail to condemn immorality, but are also seen to condone it, then what hope is there for unity, let alone purity? Solidarity is achieved when unity is firmly embedded in God's word and the pure gospel of Christ.

1 THE LORD'S WISDOM PROVIDES DIRECTION

The tribes sought the Lord's direction as they prepared to purge the evil from their midst. They *'enquired of God'* (vv18, 23, 27). In the first two attacks, the Israelites suffered humiliating defeats, losing thirty thousand of their soldiers. They couldn't understand what was happening. How easily we may think that we have mistaken God's guidance and direction when everything goes against us. Since engaging in a particular work, we may have experienced more defeats than victories, more sorrows than joys, more discouragement than encouragement. But we must trust the wisdom and leading of our loving God. He is too wise to be mistaken and too good to be unkind. We may have to learn the hard way that walking with God means humility, penitence, and submission (v26). Victory was assured on the third day (v27). In the Lord's wisdom, he may allow several defeats before we taste victory. We shouldn't always presume that all the 'right doors' will swing open just as we expect them, and that we shall always avoid delays, sickness, accusation, suffering, and loss.

2 THE LORD'S HOLINESS DEMANDS REPENTANCE

Israel may have thought that victory over the Benjamites was a foregone conclusion. After all, the Israelites outnumbered the Benjamites fifteen to one. But God's holy presence was represented by *'the ark of the covenant of God'* (v27), and they had to approach him with true repentance (v26). The ark demonstrated the only way that an absolutely holy God and thoroughly wretched sinners can be brought together. The lid of the ark was the place where sacrificial blood was spilt. In the cross of Christ and the blood shed there, a way back to God has been opened up for those who repent and believe.

3 THE LORD'S LAW ENFORCES JUSTICE

The tribe of Benjamin may have thought that they had evaded judgement when they defeated Israel on the first two occasions, but God's timing is perfect (v28). The Lord dealt his crushing blow (v35). It was a wipeout. Like the Benjamites who defended the *'awful crime'* (v12), who supported the monstrous depravity of the Canaanites, there are many whose shocking behaviour is equivalent to shaking a provocative fist in the face of the Almighty. But there will always be accountability for none can escape God's sovereign justice (Psalm 9 vv7-8; 45 v6; 97 v2). The signature of the Lord's rule upon the earth is his justice. The Lord has *'a day of vengeance'* (Isaiah ch34 v8).

4 THE LORD'S WORD REQUIRES OBEDIENCE

To the Israelites' question (v28), the Lord responded *'Go'*. Victory came to Israel because they obeyed the Lord (vv35, 41). If we truly love God and love his word, then it will be an easy thing to obey him. Jesus emphasised to his closest followers, *'If you love me, you will obey what I command'* (John ch14 v15). Obedience will keep you close to the one you love. In that great alphabetic acrostic of Psalm 119, the psalmist repeatedly reveals his devotion to the word of God by his obedience (for example, vv17, 34, 57, 100, 129, 167). The Lord Jesus, our great example, was wholly obedient to his Father's will and purpose (Philippians ch2 v8; Hebrews ch5 v7). But we can't *go* for Jesus in obedience until we have first *come* to Jesus in repentance.

JUNE 10
JUDGES Ch21.1-25

EVERYONE DID AS HE SAW FIT

Many politicians, civil servants, councillors, teachers, doctors, servicemen, and charity workers, among others, are committed to doing the things they believe to be right. Although their standards of rightness may vary, they have clear objectives and principles to which they conform. Everyone does as he sees fit. This also sums up the Book of Judges. Though there are glimmers of light in the book, where men and women do 'as God sees fit', we conclude from the closing comment of v25: *'Everyone did as he saw fit'*.

There hadn't been clear, national leadership in Israel for some time. No one had been able to unite the twelve tribes by their authoritative rule, powerful words, or godly life.

1 MAKING PROMISES AS THEY SAW FIT

The eleven tribes had wanted nothing more to do with Benjamin, the guilty section of their community. They had been ostracised, defeated, and regarded as being 'non-Jew', to the extent that the rest of Israel had sworn never to allow marriage to a Benjamite (v1).

However, they quickly regretted this extreme action. They realised that, with 97% of Benjamin's tribe annihilated and only six hundred men surviving, the tribe would soon become extinct. The oath, which the Israelites had taken, prevented them from allowing any of their girls to marry men from Benjamin. This situation was further complicated by a second oath (v5). We have already witnessed in this book how people can become easily trapped by their oaths and promises (for example, Jephthah in ch11).

There is great danger in making rash promises in the emotion of the moment, for example:

In Grief: Irrational promises may be made when racked with sorrow or distress;

In Joy: impulsive promises may be made during great pleasure (see Mark ch6 vv22-23);

In Fear: Bargaining promises may be made to secure freedom, health, or comfort;

In Excitement: Sudden promises may be made in the flush of excitement. Was it excitement that prompted the teacher of the law to promise to Jesus, *'Teacher, I'll follow you wherever you go'* (Matthew ch8 v19), or Peter, when he promised *'Even if all fall away on account of you, I never will'* (Matthew ch26 v33)? We are not asked to make oaths of allegiance, or vows of consecration, or promises of dedication. The reality is in the action. Allegiance, consecration, and dedication are not in the finely crafted words of a witness statement, but in the faithfulness of a life lived for the Lord.

2 OFFERING PEACE AS THEY SAW FIT

Having almost wiped out the tribe of Benjamin, Israel now had feelings of grief and guilt. They reflected on the scale of the calamity (v6). The remnant of six hundred survivors, sheltering at *'the rock of Rimmon'*, would have been an easy target for Israel's soldiers, as they were just as guilty as their fellow Benjamites who had been slaughtered.

But now they were being offered unconditional peace. There was no requirement that they should be penitent. It was to be peace at any price.

By contrast, the peace with God that sinners can know has been secured through Christ's reconciling work (Colossians ch1 vv19-20). The sweet words of peace, forgiveness, and reconciliation are made real to the penitent sinner because of the cross. Here is not 'peace at any price' but 'peace at an incomprehensible price': the death of the Son of God, the Prince of Peace.

3 SOLVING PROBLEMS AS THEY SAW FIT

The problem was that there were not enough wives to go round for the Benjamites (vv7-8). Four hundred wives were found among the survivors of Jabesh Gilead. But there was still a problem (vv15-18). How could it be solved? The Israelites were interested in the 'letter' of their promise, not the 'spirit'. They found a legal loophole that would get them off the hook. The remaining two hundred Benjamites would ambush the dancing girls of Shiloh. The elders worked out the response they would give to any complaining father or brother (v22). Problem solved – as they saw fit! How often do we look for loopholes to satisfy our consciences? But Christians are called to live as God sees fit: to do everything that is right in his eyes. They are required to stand out as those who live the alternative lifestyle in a world that has abandoned moral absolutes and discarded Biblical standards. Christians are bound by the constraints of different laws and the merits and virtues of a different King, *'one called Jesus'* (Acts ch17 v7).

JUNE 11
1 JOHN Ch1.1

WHAT'S YOUR PERSONAL TESTIMONY OF JESUS?

If you take a visit to Ephesus in Turkey, you may also be persuaded to travel up a nearby mountain where you will find a few ancient buildings nestling among trees near the summit. Many believe that this is where John the apostle spent his final years while pastoring the congregation in Ephesus and the six other churches referred to in Revelation chs2-3.

THE AUTHOR:

While John doesn't divulge his authorship, there is evidence from the second-generation church leaders that the correspondent was John, brother to James, son of Zebedee, a former fisherman and disciple of Jesus. Compare the letter with John's Gospel and you will discover that the style, language, and many of the themes are identical. John doesn't write in shades of grey. It's either light or darkness, love or hate, life or death, truth or falsehood. John is the elder, and he regards his Christian readers as his *'children'*.

THE RECIPIENTS:

The letter has been written in a pastoral way to Christians for whom John has assumed spiritual responsibility. Persecution was a constant threat, and John warns of controversy, heresy, and apostasy. He teaches them to be alert, discerning, and loving.

THE DATE:

Generally reckoned to be in the 80s or 90s of the first century

THE REASON:

John's letter contains a blend of advice, warning, challenge, encouragement, instruction, and information. One of the most dangerous heresies at that time was the claim that salvation could only be obtained by a special or secret knowledge outside of the Bible and the apostles' writings. This type of heresy, in its many forms, has continued to plague the church for two thousand years. It is generally referred to as 'gnosticism' (Greek word for 'knowledge'). Gnosticism asserts that we can be saved by special knowledge rather than by faith in Jesus. Modern-day gnostics claim to have received special revelations through visions, supernatural encounters, or the discovery of golden plates with cryptic messages. John writes to Christians reasserting the fundamental that the truth has come through Jesus, who is God the Son. Jesus is the eternal Word of life who has always existed. He was there when the beginning began (John ch1 v1). Jesus is the Unbegun who began the beginning. You can have all the special visions, secret revelations, mystical golden plates, dodgy translations, and theatrical manifestations, but the only revelation that matters is Jesus Christ. God reveals himself in Jesus (John ch1 v18). Jesus is *'the image of the invisible God'* (Colossians ch1 v15). John records Jesus' words to Philip: *'Anyone who has seen me has seen the Father'* (John ch14 v9). He is *'the exact representation of his being'* (Hebrews ch1 v3). The key to Christianity is a right understanding of Jesus. John gives his testimony about the Word of life.

Hearsay may be interesting. To listen to or to read other people's testimony of Jesus should be greatly encouraging. But what testimony can you provide as to your personal encounter with Jesus? What evidence would confirm your salvation and your developing relationship with God? John gives a unique testimony of his involvement with Jesus.

1 JOHN HAS HEARD THE WORD OF LIFE

John would have recalled the first day that he heard Jesus calling him (Matthew ch4 v21) when he immediately responded. Jesus' words continued to have a great impact on John's life. No one spoke like Jesus (John ch7 v46). John could describe Jesus' style, assess his pronunciation, evaluate his vocabulary, pinpoint his accent and dialect, but, more than that, he learned his message of truth and life.

2 JOHN HAS SEEN THE WORD OF LIFE

Jesus wasn't an invisible spirit or phantom as some gnostics wanted to portray him. John speaks of Jesus' real humanity. John saw Jesus up close, including at the cross and the resurrection. One day, *'every eye will see him'* (Revelation ch1 v7), but many will only see him as Judge and King. We need the confidence of Job to know that we shall see our personal Redeemer (Job ch19 vv25-27).

3 JOHN HAS TOUCHED THE WORD OF LIFE

Even a phantom may be seen and heard, but not touched! Yet John and the disciples could confirm that Jesus was flesh and bones (Luke ch24 v39). This must be the message that *'we proclaim concerning the Word of life'*. Jesus is fully God and became fully human. We must proclaim this truth by the way we follow him – in our faithful, sincere words that Jesus has saved us; by our loving actions to folk inside and outside the church; by our gracious, patient attitude to others, and by our reaction to adversity and hostility which may strike at any time. Let's proclaim Jesus, the Word of life.

JUNE 12
1 JOHN Ch1.2-4

LIFE WITH A CAPITAL 'L'

Jesus became like us. The Incarnation of Jesus proves that God understands us. Yet Jesus came not merely to provide sympathy or even empathy: Jesus came to bring us life. Jesus is the Life: He is *'the Word of life'* (v1); *'In him was life...'* (John ch1 v4). He revealed himself to John on Patmos as *'the Living One...'* (Revelation ch1 v18). Jesus told Thomas, *'I am...the Life'* (John ch14 v6). Jesus also responds to Martha's grief-fuelled comments at the mouth of her brother's tomb: *'I am the Resurrection and the Life...'* (John ch11 v25).

1 THE LIFE REVEALED

(v2) As a child, you may have enjoyed a puppet show as glove-puppets became animated in a simple production. It's possible to become engrossed in the performance as the puppets act out their roles. Eventually, the show ends, and you are transported back to reality by the applause of the audience. The puppet characters take their bow. Then the animator appears. The puppeteer stands up and reveals himself. The one who has given 'life' to his creations is manifested. In the Incarnation, the Animator and Life-Giver is manifested. Jesus appears in human flesh so that John and others can hear, see, and touch (v1). *'The life appeared; we have seen it and testify to it...'* (v2). Just as children could testify to their parents that they had seen the puppeteer – the 'life-giver' – the one around whom the whole universe of the puppet theatre revolves, so John says of Jesus that *'through him all things were made; without him nothing was made that has been made'* (John ch1 v3). The fundamental reason for Jesus' coming was to give eternal life (John ch10 v10; ch17 vv1-3). The evidence for this eternal life should be seen in all those whom the Father has given to the Son, to quote Jesus' prayer. Each believer should be displaying the characteristics of eternal life.

2 THE LIFE PROCLAIMED

(vv2-3a) While we may have received this life as it has appeared to us, so now we must proclaim it. There's nobody like Jesus. Each day's new experiences and new discoveries about Jesus should give us an increasing amount of personal testimony to proclaim about him. It's vitally important for us to *be* a witness before we *bear* witness. We must first receive the new life in Jesus before we proclaim the new life in Jesus. If we are to proclaim this Life Personified, then we must be:

i] Clear: We can't afford to be muddled or confused in our proclamation. We must be clear in the language and terms we use. We must not 'fuzz the edges' of this all-important message.

ii] Confident: After Peter and John had spent a night in gaol for proclaiming the Word of life, they prayed that they might give a bold statement (Acts ch4 v29). Just as we expect a bona fide witness in a court to be confident and unshakeable in their testimony, so we must be confident in God's word of truth and God's Word of life.

iii] Consistent: Just as a barrister will point out any inconsistencies in a witness's testimony, so the world around us is watching for any inconsistencies in a believer's words and deeds.

3 THE LIFE SHARED

The goal in proclaiming the Word of life is so that others will become part of the fellowship of the family of God (v3). We have a horizontal fellowship with all true believers, and we have a vertical fellowship with God the Father and God the Son, through God the Spirit. The reference to the Father and the Son drives home their unity and their equality. If we have fellowship with someone, it means that there is commonality. With regard to Christian fellowship, it means that each believer has a common experience of Jesus (the Word of life) and a common faith in the Bible (the word of God). While we may easily understand this in relation to the fellowship of believers, how can there be commonality in our fellowship with God? Surely these are two poles, infinitely apart? But the common ground is in Jesus, the God-Man. When did you last thank him for the fellowship we have with him? Our fellowship with one another is so valuable that we must always seek to protect it. How easily it can become damaged by our sinfulness – pride, greed, resentment, slander, deceit, self-assertion, lovelessness, and carelessness. The closer we live to Jesus, the closer we shall live to one another.

4 THE LIFE ENJOYED

Why is John writing these verses about fellowship? Answer: verse 4. The mathematics of God-given joy is that it is multiplied when it is divided among one another. Fellowship with God and fellowship with each believer is the source of real joy. Our joy is easily disturbed by strained or broken fellowship. We are upset and in danger of being destabilised when there are fractured relationships. John is so passionate about underlining the importance of Christian fellowship within a church family. God wants our joy to be filled to the full (John ch15 v11; Acts ch13 v52). The two things that are high risks to joy are sin and self. When there's a breakdown in our communion with God, or a fractured relationship develops between believers, then it will be sin or self, or both, which are responsible.

JUNE 13
1 JOHN Ch1.5-7

WALKING IN THE LIGHT

How do you respond when someone asks you 'What, or who, is God?' Of all the Bible authors, John, under the inspiration of the Holy Spirit, provides the clearest and simplest definitions of God: *'God is spirit'* (John ch4 v24); *'God is love'* (ch4 v16), and here, *'God is light'* (v5). Notice that John uses neither a definite nor an indefinite article. John is revealing something of God's nature by using the words *'spirit'*, *'love'*, and *'light'*. I can refer to the sun in the sky as 'a light', or even 'the light', referring to its position, purpose, and function in the universe. But by declaring 'the sun is light' (without a definite or indefinite article), I am referring to the sun's intrinsic nature. So, in a simple yet profound way, we glimpse a deeper understanding of God when we declare with John that *'God is light'*. We are not merely describing his position or function: we are describing the knowable, yet unknowable, nature of God. The spiritual and moral perfection of a holy God proclaims that he is light...*'in him there is no darkness at all'* (v5). In the gospel, we must continue to preach the absolute moral perfection and purity of Almighty God. Nothing can taint his character or tarnish his nature. His name is holy (Isaiah ch57 v15). *'Holy, holy, holy is the Lord Almighty'* (Isaiah ch6 v3). But if this is the reality, then what's our responsibility? We must live in the light: *'walk in the light'*.

We have a natural affinity for darkness. It is only when, by God's grace, his work of salvation is performed in our lives, that our inclination is towards the light. There are three challenges we should take on board:

1 BEWARE: A FALSE CLAIM (v6)

This is the first of three false claims made in the next five verses: claims which heretics and hypocrites make. They claim that they know God, but their conduct doesn't match their claim. Their way of life is still sinful. They walk in darkness. There are some who think that they fellowship with God because they get a buzz out of coming to church meetings and events. Jesus made it clear in his mountain sermon that folk can be under a terrible illusion (Matthew ch7 vv21-23). Some may claim to have conducted great religious feats, yet they remain in darkness. One noted atheist uttered these dying words: 'I am taking a leap in the dark'. Indeed, without Jesus, the Light of Life, as his Saviour, it was a leap into darkness that Jesus referred to as *'outside...darkness where there will be weeping and gnashing of teeth'* (Matthew ch8 v12). For such, their false claim becomes their true judgement.

2 BELONG: A FELLOWSHIP CLOSENESS (v7)

'Walking in the light' is the key criterion for fellowship *'with one another'*. When this fellowship between two believers becomes disrupted or damaged, you can guarantee that one or other, or both are not walking in the light. This fellowship of God's people is a communion that is forged through participation, because there is commonality. Philippians ch3 v10 speaks of the *'fellowship'* (or 'participation') of *'sharing in (Christ's) sufferings'*. Such sufferings are an indicator of our belonging to him. 1 Corinthians ch10 vv16-17 refers to the communion at the Lord's Supper, which is called a *'participation in the blood of Christ'* and a *'participation in the body of Christ'*. Within that fellowship, there can be no hint of elitism or hierarchy. There is no elevated status for anyone who is older, or more gifted, or who has been a Christian the longest, or who is a church leader. All such distinctions and barriers must be removed for true fellowship to be enjoyed by God's people. The church of Jesus is the only real classless society. The closeness of this fellowship will not only confirm our belonging to God, but it will confirm our belonging to one another. If we are walking in the light, then we shall be participants in and a contributor to the 'community of encouragement'. We should be forever striving to nurture and build each other up in every way.

3 BELIEVE: A FULL CLEANSING (v7)

John refers to 'sin' nine times in just seven verses. The child of God who is walking in the light can have the great assurance that all their sin is covered by the blood of Jesus: *'all sin'* – a full and complete cleansing. There's no limit to the power of Jesus' blood: it covers *all* sin. There's no restriction on the type of sin: it covers *all* sin. There's no limit to the period of sinning: it spans *all* sin. What a joy to know the deep and lasting forgiveness of God, which is made possible because the *'blood of Jesus'* eternally erases that sin. In the context of our fellowship with God and our fellowship with one another, we must be constantly reminded that the one thing which threatens to mar or break our fellowship (that is, sin) has been covered by Jesus' blood. Of course, that doesn't mean that we can sin carelessly and still expect our fellowship to be unaffected. It does mean, though, that if we are genuinely contrite, then the blood of Jesus will guarantee a restoration of fellowship – with God and with one another. It's the sin of pride and superiority that needs purifying. It's this sin that can fracture our fellowship and damage relationships. Living the life of holiness is one of continual *'downward growth'* where the pronouns of 'I', 'me', and 'my' are reclassified in Jesus. *'He must become greater: I must become less'* (John ch3 v30).

We need each other, and to that end, we need to ensure that our fellowship remains intact.

JUNE 14
1 JOHN Ch1.8-10

OUR CLAIM OR OUR CONFESSION?

If only we could see the real filthiness and evil of our sin, we would not be attracted to it. The truth of God's word proclaims that we are all sinners. David admitted the plight of all humanity in his psalm of confession: *'Surely I was sinful at birth, sinful from the time my mother conceived me'* (Psalm 51 v5). Paul the apostle reveals that we are all contaminated by sin: it's part of our spiritual DNA (Romans ch3 vv11, 12, 23). None are exempt. The one thing that every single human has in common at birth is that they are a sinner. We may think that it's an 'old-fashioned, non-PC, medieval term', but the Bible makes it clear that we are all guilty of sin and that makes us 'sinners'. In vv8-10 we are confronted with two types of persons. One type refuses to accept that they are a sinner, and the other type is ready to confess their sin.

1 'I'M NOT A SINNER' – OUR CLAIM

(v8) There are some people who really believe that they have never done anything wrong and have no guilt for which they should be ashamed. Others will admit to making mistakes but refuse to be labelled 'sinful'. So what are the consequences of making a false claim?

i] We Deceive Ourselves: By claiming that we are without any trace of sin in us, we may fool some people but not all people. Neither do we fool God. In the main, we are fooling ourselves and lulling ourselves into a false state of complacency. It's part of the Freudian philosophy, which declares that we should have no feelings of guilt or that we are to blame in any way. So our society reclassifies sin with all kinds of terminology to make sin seem more acceptable and excusable. In doing so, we contradict God and we deceive ourselves.

ii] We Reject God's Word: From Genesis ch3 to Revelation ch22, the unavoidable truth of God's word is that we are all sinners. If we reject God's word, then v8 states that *'the truth is not in us'*. Similarly, we may reject the honest diagnosis that *'the heart is deceitful above all things and beyond cure'* (Jeremiah ch17 v9). Just as a patient may refuse the life-giving treatment of a physician, so there are multitudes who are refusing the life-giving prescription of God's word – that *'the blood of Jesus, (God's) Son, purifies us from all sin'* (v7). Is there some other secret cure for the terminal condition of sin? Is there some other 'fantasy remedy', contrasted with the real cure proclaimed in the gospel?

iii] We Attack God's Integrity: (v10) In the same breath that we call ourselves a 'non-sinner', we are calling God a liar. Following Satan's egregious contradiction of God (Genesis ch3 v4), attacks on God's integrity have spiralled. The thinking of our age makes out that God didn't create the universe; that God's standards of morality and decency don't apply to our society; that the gospel is just a placebo for those who are unstable, and that the church is irrelevant to today's world. Contradiction of God is nothing new! When we begin to tamper with God's word: re-editing huge chunks of Scripture to avoid its convicting message; rebranding immorality to make it socially acceptable; reclassifying evil to excuse the human bias to sin – then we are making a full-on assault on God's integrity.

2 'I'M A SINNER' – OUR CONFESSION

(v9) Paul confesses that he is *'the worst of sinners'* (1 Timothy ch1 vv15-16). While Paul's self-description may be vigorously contested by those of us who know our own hearts, we can be thrilled with God's gracious intervention in providing a rescue. When we're honest with God about our sinnership, then:

i] We Learn God's Faithfulness: God remains unwaveringly faithful to his character and to his word (2 Timothy ch2 v13). There is never a 'last straw' that will break his faithfulness. His faithfulness reaches to the skies (Psalm 36 v5). He invites us to reason with him about our salvation (Isaiah ch1 v18).

ii] We Prove God's Righteousness: *'...he is faithful and just...'* The justice of God is clearly revealed in the way in which he deals with our confessed sin. The only action that could save guilty sinners and, at the same time, satisfy God's uncompromising justice was through a sacrifice of atonement. God wouldn't be God if he could ignore his righteous standards any time he felt like it. Justice had to be done. The perfect sacrifice of Jesus on the cross paid the full debt of sin for every believing, confessing sinner (Romans ch3 vv25-26). It's wonderful to know that we can be forgiven by God's grace, but it's eternally reassuring to know that we can be forgiven through God's justice. God will not require the debt of sin to be paid twice: *'Payment God cannot twice demand, first at my bleeding Surety's hand, and then again at mine'* [Augustus Toplady]. In God's accountancy, the death of Jesus has wiped out the debt of sin completely for those who repent and believe.

iii] We Know God's Forgiveness: We can be 'forgiven' and 'purified' through the blood of Jesus. All our unrighteousness can be removed, and we can stand freed and forgiven.

So, are we sticking to our claim, or are we making our confession and trusting in Jesus to deal with our sin?

JUNE 15
1 JOHN Ch2.1-2

WAR AGAINST SIN

The story is told of a businessman who advertised for a chauffeur. Three applicants responded, and they were each asked the same questions. They were asked how close they thought they could drive to a cliff edge without losing control. One of the applicants said that he could drive a yard from the cliff edge, and another applicant reckoned that he could drive as close as twelve inches. The third applicant admitted that he would always keep as far away as possible. He got the job! Sin is not to be played with. We must not risk getting as close as we can. We must keep as wide a margin as possible from all sin. John is emphasising that, for the Christian, sin is not inevitable. There are three things that we need in our personal war against sin.

1 WE NEED THE RIGHT ATTITUDE (v1a)

John addresses his readers as an affectionate father who is concerned about the well-being of his children. He loves them so much and, as an experienced, understanding older man, he writes to prevent them from falling into sin's snares. If we are to avoid the clutches of sin, in all its guises, then we must be prepared to take decisive action. We are in danger of treating sin far too lightly. We can become so familiar with it that we overlook its deadly nature. How dangerous it is to make a pet out of some sin or other. It need not be very big to begin with – a lie, a grudge, jealousy, greed, anger, impatience, deceit, bad language, or pornography. It may seem so petty and controllable at first. But we feed it, fondle it, pet it, and we allow it to coil around us until it constricts us irresistibly like some lethal python (Romans ch7 v11). It's God's law which accurately identifies sin as 'God's would-be killer'. It enslaves humanity and leads to spiritual death. If we are nurturing the seeds of sin in our hearts and minds, then we must take instant, drastic action. We must have the right attitude towards sin (Ephesians ch4 vv23-24). We must reject sin in all its guises and forms. We cannot be 'Mr Nice-Guy' where sin is concerned. Shun it, repel it, eject it! We must not tolerate it, let alone entertain it.

2 WE NEED THE BEST ATTORNEY (v1)

God supplies the best defence possible if we are accused of sin. He provides a divine Advocate in Jesus, our free 'Legal Aid'. He is our intercessor, our mediator, and one who is called alongside us. This is a Defence Counsel who is perfectly qualified to speak on our behalf. Jesus' supreme qualification is that he is fully God and fully man, and therefore the perfect Go-Between. He represents deity and humanity, and therefore, he can act for the Christian who is found guilty of sin. There is no intercessor like him (Romans ch8 vv33-34). But Jesus is not limited to merely hearing our confession. He is able to plead our case on the basis that our sin is forgiven (ch1 v7). This is not a 'guilty one' whose case is being pleaded by another 'guilty one'. This is a 'guilty one' whose case is being pleaded by *Jesus Christ, the Righteous One'* (v1) and he pleads, not to a condemning Judge, but to a forgiving Father so that we may be reconciled to him (1 Peter ch3 v18). While many human attorneys are very credible people, none is completely righteous. Some may offer their advocacy out of genuine concern for the defendant, but there are also those who see it as a means to make money, or to improve their influence, or to further their career. Jesus doesn't lose cases! Every penitent believer is successfully represented.

3 WE NEED THE PERFECT ATONEMENT (v2)

Our Advocate is even more than just an advocate. He is our *'righteous'* Advocate. Yet, even more than our 'righteous Advocate', he is our *'atoning sacrifice'*. But why couldn't God just forgive all our sins, wipe out the past, and 'let bygones be bygones'? Because of that four-letter word in ch1 v9: *just*! God is perfectly just and righteous. To be true to his nature, he cannot sweep everything under the proverbial carpet and forget about it. His law can't be transgressed, and for everyone to get away 'scot-free'! God is still angry about sin and is committed to judging it. But here is the good news – the best news! When God's law demanded a sacrifice, God's love provided that sacrifice. It's Jesus and his cross. *'He is the atoning sacrifice for our sins…'* The basic idea of Jesus' sacrifice is propitiation, which means 'appeasing' or 'satisfying'. God is offended by sin, and his anger and judgement are provoked. But Jesus took the full force of God's judgement upon sin. In his supremely loving and selfless death on the cross, he put himself between God's justice and the penitent sinner. He bore the full weight of judgement so that the debt of sin may be paid. He is the *'atoning sacrifice'* for every Christian believer in the Asian churches to which John was writing, but he adds, *'and not only for ours but also for the sins of the whole world'*. John is not suddenly teaching some new doctrine of 'universalism' where everyone gets saved. He is referring to those anywhere in the world who walk in the light (ch1 v7); who have been purified by the blood of Jesus (ch1 v7); who have confessed their sin (ch1 v9), and who have come to know Jesus (ch2 v3). Shouldn't such a truth fill us with awe, wonder, joy, and eternal gratitude?

JUNE 16
1 JOHN Ch2.3-11

BE YOUR OWN CLAIMS' ASSESSOR

Her Majesty Queen Elizabeth was a remarkable woman, and during her long reign, there were thousands of people who were photographed with her. To substantiate the claim of those world leaders, celebrities, and politicians who have met the Queen, they will have framed photographs hanging in their homes or offices. However many people may claim to have met the Queen, there is only a handful of folk who can claim to know her. And out of the millions of people who claim to know God, there is only a comparative handful who really know him in a personal, relational way. The church of John's day had only been a few decades post-Pentecost when it came under serious attack from a hotchpotch of heresies generally known as 'gnosticism'. One of the gnostics' ploys, then and now, is to rebrand sin. So 'blasphemy' becomes 'creative expression'; 'living in sin' becomes 'cohabiting'; 'infanticide' becomes 'abortion' or 'the woman's right'; 'sodomy' becomes 'gay marriage'; 'idolatry' becomes 'individual faith choice' and 'adultery' becomes 'an affair'. But John says that claiming not to sin makes God a liar (ch1 v10). We can rebrand a lion and call it 'a big cuddly pussycat,' but it still has the nature and character of a vicious predator. Just so with sin! False gnostic teachers can rebrand sin and even claim to know God, but they have no intention of conforming to his word and to his commands. Such a person *is a liar, and the truth is not in him'* (vv3-4). 'Knowing God' cannot therefore be separated from 'obeying God'. In the world of faith and religion, spurious claims are being made constantly.

1 A PRACTICAL CLAIM TO GOD'S LIFE (v6)

This is the claim that we have eternal life. *'In him'* (vv5, 6) describes our communion with God, our heavenly Father. Some will claim to have all kinds of emotional and spiritual experiences when they believe that they are in close company with God. But John is not easily persuaded by such unverifiable claims. He wants clear, hard evidence of God's life in an individual. So he writes: *'Whoever claims to live in him must walk as Jesus did'* (v6). This is the 'crunch test'. This is where the evidence lies. Our airy-fairy claims must be backed up with solid, measurable proof. That proof is directly allied to the life which Jesus lived here on earth. The evidence is fully observable. We should be walking as Jesus walked. So how did Jesus walk?

In Humility: Jesus' life was one of humility, and we are told that we should be like-minded. Our attitude should be the same as Jesus' (Philippians ch2 v5). What attitude was that? He made himself *'nothing'* and humbled himself to the cross (Philippians ch2 vv7-8). How deep was Jesus' humility and humiliation? The cross! Is our attitude such that God is put first and self is put last, behind everyone else?

In Holiness: Peter stated that Christians will suffer for doing good. He calls it *'commendable'* (1 Peter ch2 v20). Jesus is our example (1 Peter ch2 v21). What a high expectation that we should walk in the holy steps of Jesus! That is God's great design, and that should be our great desire.

With Wholeheartedness: Jesus' life was lived in wholehearted commitment to his Father's will. He was wholly devoted to pleasing his Father. It's in these footsteps that we are called to walk.

2 A MORAL CLAIM TO GOD'S LIGHT (vv7-9)

To claim that you are *'in the light'* is to claim that you are regenerate and saved. The gnostics' lives are a testament to the darkness in which they walk. There is little humility and little love shown for God's people. Any claim to living in God's light must be observable (Matthew ch5 v16). What's the point of hiding a light under a bowl? Light is for vision. If this dark world is going to see the light of God, then it must see it reflected in the lives of God's children. This world needs the light of Jesus, who said, *'I am the Light of the world'* (John ch8 v12). Christians have a responsibility to shine out the gospel light and the moral light. The powers of darkness are desperately trying to overwhelm this light. We have seen it in so many different ways where the State seeks to curtail or undermine the standards of morality and decency taught in God's word.

3 A SOCIAL CLAIM TO GOD'S LOVE (vv9-11)

One of the earliest evidences of living in the light is by loving in the church. Not that 'love' is a new command or a new policy. In fact, it's an *'old one'* which they had *'since the beginning'* (v7). Loving God and loving your neighbour is as old as the Old Testament (Leviticus ch19 v18; Deuteronomy ch6 v5). But there was something 'new' in the way Jesus taught this command. Jesus taught that there must be:

i] No Discrimination: Women, Gentiles, and the disabled were not to be despised or marginalised.

ii] No Distinction: The truth must be seen in us as it was in Jesus (v8). His love was sacrificial (John ch15 vv12-13).

iii] No Disruption: No simmering dislikes or gnawing hatred, lingering in our hearts, should cause us to *'stumble'* or fall apart. Real Biblical, Christ-like love is the only answer. But love is very costly. If we are to assess our claim to God's love, then we must assess how much our love for one another costs us.

JUNE 17
1 JOHN Ch2.12-14

ENCOURAGEMENTS FOR BELIEVERS

When only twelve years old, the Archbishop of York (1983-95), John Habgood, wrote a letter to God offering him accommodation in their home. He had sent it through the post, addressed to 'Our Father which art in heaven'. Instead of marking the envelope 'Gone away' or 'Unknown at this address', the Post Office returned the letter marked 'Return to sender'! Young John Habgood had written his letter in good faith and with a loving concern. John the apostle, too, is writing this letter in good faith and with a large dose of loving concern. His reason for writing was a combination of rebuke, challenge, and encouragement. Here in this passage, he addresses his readers using three terms, viz, *'dear children'*, *'fathers'*, and *'young men'*. The term *'dear children'* is used elsewhere in the letter and refers to believers generally. However, here it may refer to young believers in particular. *'Fathers'* could refer to mature Christians, and *'young men'* could refer to those who are taking on duties and responsibilities within the church. Whichever way we may view this, John's writings are relevant to all of us as believers. Indeed, there are five encouragements for those walking in the footsteps of Jesus.

1 YOU HAVE BEEN FORGIVEN (v12)

There is little joy that can be compared to the pronouncement: 'You have been forgiven!' Imagine the euphoria and the relief to know that past transgressions have all been forgiven. When one believes in Jesus to save and to change a life, there is nothing quite like the assurance of being forgiven. We may recall the furore that was caused in one house in which Jesus was preaching to a packed audience. As he preached, bits of the roof floated down, and then a hole appeared, followed by faces. It wasn't long before a paralysed man was lowered right in front of Jesus. *When Jesus saw their faith, he said, 'Friend, your sins are forgiven'* (Luke ch5 v20). Yet the critical Pharisees and teachers of the law who were present believed that Jesus was blaspheming, as no one can forgive sins but God himself. But Jesus knew what they were thinking, and he asked them: *Which is easier: to say 'Your sins are forgiven', or to say, 'Get up and walk'? But that you may know that the Son of Man has authority on earth to forgive sins...'* (Luke ch5 vv23-24). Not only did Jesus free the man from his sins, but he also freed him from his paralysis. Jesus provides forgiveness in response to faith. There is wonderful forgiveness through the power of Jesus' name (Acts ch10 v43).

2 YOU HAVE KNOWN GOD (vv13,14)

'Knowing God' is much more than 'knowing about God'. When a person is saved, then they come to know God's salvation, strength, help, faithfulness, care, and provision, as well as many of his glorious attributes. But the great fact which underpins the confession that 'I know him' is the stunning truth that 'he knows me'. Everything that I know about God is dependent upon his knowledge of me. This should give unspeakable comfort and reassurance that, while my knowledge of God is irregular, erratic, and incomplete, his knowledge of me is constant, consistent, and complete. Wonder of wonders: God knows everything there is to know about me, and he loves me just the same. That I should ever come to love God as my Friend is amazing indeed. But that he should love me as his friend, one who was once hostile to God and all he represents, is too amazing for words. It has been said that God's love for me is like the mighty Amazon River flowing down to water just one daisy.

3 YOU HAVE BEEN STRONG (v14)

It's not easy to hold your own as a Christian. The temptation to give in is ever-present. 'Sunday Christians' are prepared to compromise with the world from Monday through to Saturday. But the *young men* here were of sterner stuff than that. They had already developed a spiritual backbone. They were resisting the gnostic teachings, which had threatened to infiltrate Christian congregations.

4 YOU HAVE LIVED GOD'S WORD (v14)

Looking at God's word and learning God's word are wonderful. But living God's word is the evidence that the word of God has not only been believed but it has been adopted (Psalm 119 v9). What we learn from God's word in our own private readings, as well as from the preaching in church, must be acted upon. Is there a greater compliment that someone could pay another believer: 'That person lives God's word!'?

5 YOU HAVE OVERCOME THE EVIL ONE (vv 13,14)

The *young men* had matured sufficiently in their faith that they were enjoying victory over Satan and his nefarious tactics. The secret of their conquest was that they were living in God's word, and God's word was living in them. But lest some complacency should creep in, note that the 'overcoming' refers to past conquests. They were required to face new conflicts each day and, while it's the old strategy that's successful (living God's word), they needed new strength. Like Christian's conquest over Apollyon in *Pilgrim's Progress*, we need the '*double-edged sword*' and its Master Swordsman, the Spirit of God (Ephesians ch6 v17; Hebrews ch4 v12).

JUNE 18
1 JOHN Ch2.15-17

LOVING THE WORLD v. LOVING THE FATHER

When you study maps of the world over the last five hundred years, it is amazing that even the earliest maps have a semblance of accuracy, having been compiled without modern equipment and the technology available to us today. Joel Gascoyne produced the first 'inch-to-the-mile' map of Britain in 1699, and Cornwall was the first county to be mapped. But the world that can be mapped was not necessarily the 'world' that John was thinking about in his gospel and epistles. Yet John refers to *'the world'* more than any other New Testament writer. He uses the term seventy-nine times in his Gospel and twenty-three times in this letter.

He refers to *'the world'* in three different ways:

[1] God's creation: the physical earth, with all its beauty and wonder (see John ch1 v10; 1 John ch4 v17). [2] Sinful humanity who are the objects of God's love (see John ch3 v16). [3] Everything that is opposed to God: all that is evil, anti-God, anti-Christ; everything which is rebellious, godless, and pagan. This is the world that is at war with God and the world to which John is referring in these verses. This leads us to conclude that:

1 THE WORLD IS TEMPESTUOUS

The world that God made has changed radically since its creation. Genesis ch3 identifies some of the effects of humanity's first sins and the consequences of what we often refer to as 'the Fall'. Sin spoiled God's perfect handiwork and introduced the tensions that exist within nature and the natural disasters that continually rock our global habitat. We see a tempestuous world of earthquakes, hurricanes, tsunamis, floods, drought, famine, and disease. Through the media, we witness a world of conflict, war, ethnic cleansing, genocide, homicide, suicide, muggings, child abuse, torture, theft, rape, drug abuse, blackmail, and internet scams, among others. We live in a turbulent, tempestuous world which is characterised by sin and hostility to God's laws. God's arch-enemy is determined to keep unbelievers enslaved in their unbelief (2 Corinthians ch4 v4), and so there is a constant spiritual struggle (Ephesians ch6 v12). The rebellion against God, which took place in a pre-cosmic universe, when certain created beings attempted a coup against God's sovereign government, resulted in their condemnation and ejection (2 Peter ch2 v4). While awaiting final judgement, they have been allowed to regroup into a 'kingdom of evil' and continue in their intense hatred of God and violent opposition to his kingdom. Satan's objective is to destroy God's works and to produce chaos by whichever means he can, including violent assault or the seeds and subtleties of doubt, deceit, and heresy.

2 THE WORLD IS TEMPTING

John points out that if we dare to love the world (that is, the realm of evil which is anti-God), then *'the love of the Father is not in (us)'* (v15). We cannot love the Father and at the same time love this evil, hostile world. But the world is very alluring, and its united strategy is to put 'self' on the throne of your life instead of God, just like Satan's earliest attempt before creation. John summaries the 'kingdom of self' (v16):

i] Self-Indulgent: (*'the cravings of sinful man'*) This is a life governed by senses – sensual. The only thing that matters is to satisfy base appetites and ignore any moral compass in their self-indulgence.

ii] Self-Advancement: (*'the lust of his eyes'*) Whatever they see, they want. It's a materialistic mindset called 'covetousness'. They want better cars, better homes, better holidays, a better lifestyle in order to 'keep up with the Joneses'.

iii] Self-Sufficient: (*'the boasting of what he has and does'*) This is the arrogance of 'self-made' people who brag about what they believe to be their 'maker' – themselves. They boast about what they have achieved, what they possess, where they have been, and what they can do. Social media helps to normalise and glamorise such boasting. We are encouraged to boast about our successes and publicise our achievements. The world is very powerful in the hold that it can have upon us. But if risks to our spiritual welfare seem high, be assured that:

3 THE WORLD IS TEMPORARY

(v17) The whole pagan, anti-God, anti-Christian world system has been 'given notice' along with its evil architect. 'Time has been called' on all organised hostility towards Jesus and his people. The rock-solid guarantee that *'the world and its desires (are passing) away'* is the unconquerable power of the cross and Jesus' resurrection. We should also be encouraged that the kingdom of God is being extended and expanded. His kingdom is being populated by those who *'do the will of God'* (v17). These are the ones who are members of Jesus' family (Mark ch3 v35). 'Doing God's will' means that first of all we have come to know him as our Saviour by repenting of our sin and trusting in Jesus by faith to rescue us. So how do we 'do the will of God'? Generally, by 'doing the word of God'! It means 'having the word of God live in you' (v14). 'Doing God's will' is not receiving a list of twenty instructions from which you choose five! 'Doing God's will' requires humble, wholesale obedience and devotion to God. The Christian life is no place for a rebel!

JUNE 19
1 JOHN Ch2.18-23

THE LAST HOUR

If you know anything about Biblical history, you will know that between the Old and New Testaments there is a period of about four hundred years, which is called the 'The Intertestamental Years' or 'The Silent Years'. But this interval was anything but silent. Alexander the Great had seized Palestine and had sought to force the Greek language and Greek culture upon the Jews. This was fiercely resisted. One of Alexander's successors was Antiochus Epiphanes (ruling from 175-164BC). With a title meaning 'God made manifest', Antiochus proceeded to inflict terrible atrocities upon the Jews in an attempt to eradicate their religion. His violent massacres of Jewish priests, even forcing the sacrifice of swine in the temple, identified Antiochus with God's arch-opponent as described in Daniel ch8. Although in the second century BC the Messiah (the Christ) had not yet been revealed, Antiochus became the epitome of opposition to God and therefore opposition to his kingdom plans, including the coming of Christ.

So now, wind the clock forward a couple of centuries, after Jesus' life, death, resurrection, and ascension, and there had arisen *'many'* who had set themselves against God and against Christ ('against' = anti, therefore *'antichrists'* v18). With so many opposing Christ and the Gospel kingdom, John says that this is an indicator that *'this is the last hour'* (v18). John announces that his believing readers were in *'the last hour'* of God's gospel timetable. The countdown had begun. This *'last hour'* will culminate with the glorious return of Jesus.

John has already said that *'the world and its desires pass away'* (v17). The final period of human history began with the first coming of Christ and will end with the second coming of Christ. We are still in *'the last hour'*. Elsewhere, this period is referred to as *'the last times'* or *'the last days'*. In every age, believers have expected Jesus' coming to take place at any second, particularly as they have witnessed the atrocities by the antichrists. There are places all around the world today where there are enemies who are vehemently opposed to Christ and his followers. *'...The whole world is under the control of the evil one'* (ch5 v19).

1 LIES FROM THE EVIL ONE

Those who are antichrists are full of lies. They may be clever, cunning, convincing lies, but they are lies nonetheless. How do we spot an antichrist?

i] They Don't Belong: (v19) Many who oppose the church have spent some time in the company of the church. Some have had a Christian upbringing but have later defected and have sought to undermine and attack the church. This emphasises the truth that *'he who stands firm to the end will be saved'* (Mark ch13 v13). This doesn't mean that salvation is a reward for endurance, but it does mean that endurance is the characteristic and the hallmark of those who are truly saved.

ii] They Don't Believe: Lies come from the evil one. Jesus spoke of him as *'the father of lies'* (John ch8 v44). John asks, *'Who is the liar?'* His answer tells us that at the heart of antichristian unbelief is the refusal to accept the truth about God the Father and God the Son. The heresy, which is spawned by the evil one, who has a vested interest in pernicious propaganda, is that Jesus is not who he says he is. They deny that Jesus is the Word who became flesh. They deny that he is one with the Father. They refuse to accept that he is the Way, the Truth, and the Life. They will not acknowledge that he is the Living One who was dead and is alive forevermore. Satan is the master of misrepresentation. So how can we counter the evil one's devilish devices? We can't! He's much too powerful for us! But we can proclaim:

2 TRUTH FROM THE HOLY ONE

(v20) The best way to show the lies of the evil one, for what they are, is to teach the truth about the Holy One. The antichrists are only interested in perpetrating deception and untruth. But the Bible-believing Christian has a mandate for declaring the truth of God's word and the truth of the gospel. It's the Bible, through the power of the Holy Spirit, which changes lives. We must persevere in declaring the truth about God the Father and God the Son because there are all sorts of antichrists, intoxicated by the power of the evil one, who would try and prise them apart. The *'anointing'* is the great difference and significant advantage that Christ's followers have over the antichrists. The Greek word for *'anointing'* is only used in this one verse in the New Testament. Here is the distinctive for a believer – the Holy Spirit (Romans ch8 vv9, 16). Antichrists cannot belong to us, as Christians, if they do not belong to Christ. We need the Spirit's guidance in speaking the truth about God (John ch16 vv12-14). How is it possible to check out the veracity of the 'guidance' we are offered today? We can ask certain questions:

Does it agree with the Bible? The Spirit's guidance will never contradict the Bible.

Does it bring glory to Jesus? The Spirit's ministry is to make much of Jesus. Jesus came to bring glory to his Father. The Counsellor is sent to bring glory to Jesus. May *'all of you'* have this anointing (v20).

The last seconds may be ticking away in *'the last hour'*, but beware of those who don't belong and don't believe.

JUNE 20
1 JOHN Ch2.24-27

LEAVERS AND REMAINERS

23rd June 2016 was a historic day for the UK when 51.9% of the participating UK electorate voted to leave the EU. Without making any political points, this historic Referendum divided the country into two distinct camps: the 'leavers' and the 'remainers'.

In a wholly different situation, John writes about two distinct groups of people in these verses: the 'leavers' and the 'remainers'. He has already referred to those who *'went out from us'* (v19) because they didn't belong to the Christian congregation. Those who abandoned the church were not merely the curious or the critical. They are identified as *'antichrists'* (v18) who were opponents of Christ and his people. They had attempted to hijack the church by peddling their false teachings. But if these are the 'leavers', John now turns his attention to the 'remainers'. He uses the word *'remain'* four times in vv24-27. In the context of 'The Final Hour', the 'remainers' are those who belong to God's family. As well as *'remain'*, the word has been translated 'abide', 'continue', and 'dwell'. John doesn't want them to leave, as the antichrists had left. He wants the flock of God to remain in the fold of God. John encourages his readers to *'remain'* in three ways:

1 MAY THE TRUTH REMAIN IN YOU

(v24) This *'truth'* is the basic, original, apostolic teaching. This is the orthodox theology of the apostles. Some people always want new ideas, new styles, new teachings, and even new theologies. They are addicted to trends, fashions, and vogues. They need a regular 'fix' of new philosophies, new morality, even a 'new Christianity'! Over the centuries, the false teachers and antichrists have been ready to oblige. But it's love for the Lord Jesus that should spur his people to teach his truth with uncompromising accuracy. They should be striving to have a right view of Jesus and a right understanding of his teaching and the teaching of his apostles. One of the significant challenges to Jesus' teaching occurred in the fourth century when Constantine, the Christian emperor, became world ruler. A popular preacher from Libya, called Arius, began to teach that the Father alone was God and that God's Son had been created by the Father. Arius, the elderly, cultured church leader, denied the deity of Christ in trying to defend the fundamental truth of 'one God'. The controversy spread and threatened to divide the church. Constantine called a world council of bishops, which assembled in Nicaea in AD 325. The lengthy debates finally produced a Confession of faith designed to assert the deity of Christ and the equality of God the Son with God the Father. This Confession, used by Christians for over seventeen hundred years, is known as The Nicene Creed.

2 MAY THE ANOINTING REMAIN IN YOU

(v27) The two clear advantages which Christians have over the antichrists are God's word and God's Spirit. Perfect harmony exists between the truth of God's word and the teaching of God's Spirit. A Christian who is committed to God's word and submitted to God's Spirit doesn't need human agency to discern the truth (although pastors, elders, and teachers may be helpfully provided). This is the great doctrine of 'the priesthood of all believers' which was rediscovered at the time of the Reformation. Christians are *'a holy priesthood'* (1 Peter ch2 v5) whose duties include offering sacrifices of praise (Hebrews ch13 v15).

What does John tell us about the Teacher-Spirit's curriculum?

i] It is Comprehensive: He teaches us *'about all things'* (v27). We are trained in everything we need to know about life and death, time and eternity, heaven and earth, sin and salvation, faith and practice. The curriculum is extensive and all-inclusive.

ii] It is Genuine: *'real, not counterfeit'* or 'truth, not lies'. The Spirit's teaching is always thoroughly truthful and accurate, as well as being strikingly relevant.

3 MAY YOU REMAIN IN JESUS

(v24) This speaks of a continual communion with God, and God has promised *'eternal life'*.

i] Quantity: 'Eternal' is 'forever'. It is never-ending, everlasting. God will never retract his gift or curtail his promise. He will never have a change of mind and decide to terminate *'eternal life'*. Jesus promises the security of eternal life (John ch3 v16, ch10 v28).

ii] Quality: A synonym for *'eternal life'* is 'remaining in the Son and the Father' (v24). Eternal life is not merely a life that begins at death and continues through eternity. Eternal life begins at conversion. While remaining in him assures us of our security in Jesus, we have obligations because of our identity with Jesus. So we must:

Cling to Jesus: 'Remain in him', in the sense that we shall derive strength, confidence, hope, and the assurance of close fellowship with him every day. The climber climbing a rock face may know that he is ultimately secured by his safety rope. Nevertheless, he still strives to improve his technique so that he may cling to the rock face more tenaciously, using the best hand-holds and foot-holds.

Walk with Jesus: (v6) Does our Christlike walk make it easier for others to believe and trust in Jesus?

JUNE 21
1 JOHN Ch2.28-ch3.3

CHILD BENEFITS

While most people associate the name of Christopher Columbus with the discovery of the Americas, many will not know him as a self-styled prophet. Columbus wrote a volume called 'The Book of Prophecies' in which he prophesied that the world would end in 1656. He was taken seriously by a considerable number of people, as, indeed, with others who have similarly predicted 'end of the world' dates. But John still speaks of *the final hour'* commencing with the first coming of Jesus and ending with his second coming. Yet it is within this crucial hour that we are called to spot antichrists and their destructive, antichristian strategies.

However, John now reminds his readers of the wonderful benefits that we enjoy if we belong to God's family.

The elderly apostle looked upon his scattered flocks with great affection, addressing them as *'dear children'* or *'little children'* seven times in this epistle. John looked upon believers as 'his' children, though they are first and foremost 'God's' children (ch3 v1). The benefits of being children of God are too numerous to list, even if there were a defined list! But three particular benefits arise from these verses:

1 OUR UNSHAKEABLE CONFIDENCE

(v28) *'The last hour'* (v18) will end with the *'appearing'* and *'coming'* of Jesus Christ. The precise time and date are not for us to know. We can neither delay nor hasten that moment. John emphasises that the children of God who *'remain in the Son'* (v24) and who *'continue in him'* (v28) are those who will be unshakeably *'confident'* when he comes again. Such confidence is not in a particular interpretation of Biblical history or Biblical prophecy. This confidence is only derived from a living, personal relationship with Jesus. Our hope in Jesus should be preparing us to meet Jesus (v3). How well is your relationship developing? Which new aspects of Jesus' character and personality are you discovering as you spend quality time with him every day? How much more do you know God's word this year compared with last year, or this month compared with last month? John is not preoccupied with our interpretation of prophecy, but he is preoccupied with our application of purity. He wants us to be living holy lives so that we shall be more ready to meet Jesus at his appearing.

2 OUR UNSURPASSABLE CALLING

If our passion is for Godly righteousness (v29), then this demonstrates that we are members of God's family and that we have been born again. This refers to our calling as children of God (v1). It is not just that Christians are now regarded and even recognised as God's children: they really are God's children! It's not merely a concept, a designation, or even a title. It's a reality! John says: *'And that is what we are!'* How great is this wonderful divine love! It's not just referring to quantity (though there is no love which is so immeasurably vast as God's love), but it's speaking especially of quality. How majestic is the surpassing excellence of this love! How can we measure the quality of this love? We can only do it by the cross on which the Saviour suffered and died (Romans ch5 v8). Here is the 'quality assurance'. The hallmark of the cross is the guarantee of genuine divine love. The enemies of Christianity won't recognise our relationship or our title (children of God) because they don't recognise our heavenly Father (ch2 v22; ch3 v1). Which features, characteristics, or mannerisms identify us as children of God? One day we are going to be like him, but what about today? (v2)

3 OUR UNMISTAKEABLE CONFORMITY

While the Christian believer can be unshakeably confident in the security of being in God's family, the future grace and glory of that family relationship have not yet been fully disclosed. *'Now if we are children, then we are heirs – heirs of God and co-heirs with Christ, if indeed we share in his sufferings in order that we may also share in his glory'* (Romans ch8 v17). The future inheritance is described in that tantalising phrase: *'share in his glory'*. While Paul the apostle reveals in his epistles that the Christian's destiny is 'with Jesus', John the apostle reveals here that the Christian's destiny is also to be 'like Jesus'. The believer is going to see him in all his unveiled glory and, what's more, the believer is going to be like him in that glory (Philippians ch3 vv20-21). The believer is going to be like Jesus! But if we're going to be like Jesus, *then* we should be striving to be like Jesus *now*. We're not called to be cold, lifeless 'waxworks' of outward conformity but warm, living likenesses of inward beauty.

Are you doing what is right? (v29) We should be doing right in every area of our lives

Are you showing what is your hope? (v3) Your hope in the hereafter will be shown in what you're after here! Our personal morality and conformity, as well as our individual accountability, will be determined by just how much we really want to be like Jesus.

JUNE 22
1 JOHN Ch3.4-10

WHY DID JESUS COME?

We may be able to think of certain dates and certain events that have introduced new eras. The year 2000 is one that we are familiar with. We know that the time and the event of Jesus' coming into the world signalled the greatest era in human history. Questions such as when, where, and how Jesus came/appeared can be answered clearly and Biblically. But the question that we focus on in this passage is:

Why did the Son of God appear in human flesh? Why did Jesus enter our time and our world? Why was he *'found in appearance as a man'*? (Philippians ch2 v8). Why did God send his Son to be *'born of a woman, born under law'* (Galatians ch4 v4)? Answers can be provided in a number of ways, but principally Jesus came to do his Father's will (Hebrews ch10 vv5-7) and he came to bring glory to his Father (John ch17 v4). The overarching reason that Jesus came to live our life, walk our road, breathe our air, feel our pain, and bear our sins is so that he could bring glory to his Father by completing his mission.

1 JESUS CAME TO REMOVE THE SINNER'S SINS (v5)

Jesus' mission was to remove all traces of sin in our lives.

i] Definition of Sin: (v4) *'Lawlessness'* is not just the flouting of the law, or even the breaking of many laws. *'Lawlessness'* refers to the spirit and the attitude that defiantly refuses to keep God's laws. 'Missing the mark' is the basic definition of sin. Sin is like shaking a defiant fist in God's face.

ii] Confirmation of Sinfulness: (v6) The Christian and sin should have nothing to do with each other. If believers are to *'remain'* (abide/dwell/continue) in the sinless Son of God, then it follows that they should live sinlessly too. It also follows that those who are characterised by consistent, deliberate sin are not God's children.

iii] Ambition of Sinlessness: (v7) If the heretics had been teaching that it's possible to be made righteous, without the necessity of living righteously, then John denies this. While he has spoken of the root of lawlessness producing the bad fruit of sins, he now shows that the root of righteousness will always bear the good fruit of right living. While absolute sinlessness is unachievable this side of Glory, this should be our constant aim and ambition. We cannot *'go on sinning'* (v9) as if nothing has changed.

iv] Qualification of the Sin-Bearer: (v5) What a glorious announcement! Christ has appeared *'so that he might take away our sins'*. How this should thrill the soul of each one who confesses their own sinnership and recognises that they are dead in their transgressions! Jesus (*'in him is no sin'*) took our sins away, *'nailing it to the cross'* (Colossians ch1 vv13-14). The atoning sacrifice of Jesus upon the cross is sufficiently powerful and effective to jettison the sin and to justify the sinner. Only a sinless Saviour is qualified to do that (1 Peter ch2 v22). He is *'the Lamb of God, who takes away the sin of the world'* (John ch1 v29).

358

2 JESUS CAME TO DESTROY THE DEVIL'S WORK (v8)

The devil's work is sin. Sin has a diabolical origin. It began with the principal lawbreaker himself – the devil. Satan's work (or *'works'*) is diverse and comprehensive. His devilish devices have infected every corner of our universe. Planet Earth is the theatre for his malicious and malevolent activity. Every human being is assaulted constantly, in mind, body, and soul, by both the temptation to sin and the consequences of sin. In response to the frequently asked question: 'Can a Christian sin?' John has made it clear that sin is out of place in a Christian's life. For sin to be lurking in the mind, body, and soul of a believer, it is incompatible with the Holy Spirit in a Christian and the Christian remaining in Christ.

(v6) The person who is walking with Jesus will not deliberately, continuously, or recklessly sin against God. But, as Christians, we do sin! But if we sin, we have a heavenly Advocate (ch2 v1) and our confessed sin is forgiven (ch1 v9). Jesus came to destroy the devil's work, especially in the life of a believer. 'Continuing to sin' is not an option for the true believer. The reason? *'Because God's seed remains in him...because he has been born of God'* (v9). So how should we act?

i] Act Lively: (v7) We are called to be alert and vigilant so that no one leads us astray. There are many who would lure us by some attractive bait, and any lack of discernment could easily get us disastrously hooked.

ii] Act Lawfully: (vv4, 10) Acting lawfully, in essence, means doing the things, saying the things, and being the person that God wants us to be. We are not our own person: we are bought with a price. Keeping God's laws and commands is the privilege and joy of the believer.

iii] Act Lovingly: (v10) If God's great love has been lavished upon his children (v1), then they must love their brothers and sisters. This love is not abstract or passive: it's active and practical. We need Jesus' love to flow in us and through us to those who are the children of God.

JUNE 23
1 JOHN Ch3.11-15

MURDER HE WROTE

Whereas at one time a murder would always attract headline news, today it sometimes attracts only a passing reference. In 1960, before capital punishment was repealed, there were less than three hundred murders each year in the UK. Since then, the annual number of murders has been steadily climbing, reaching an all-time high in 2002/03 of 1,047. Murder is as old as time itself. The first family was not exempt from the crime of murder, even before any homicide laws had been introduced. In Genesis ch4 we have the first recorded killing. Adam and Eve's firstborn, Cain, killed his younger brother, Abel. John has been showing that true love is the character of God's children, upon whom God's own love has been lavished (v1). Contrasted with this, hate is the character of the devil's children who have not come to know the love of God in Jesus. If we continue to hate our spiritual brothers and sisters, then we are no different from Cain, who hated his brother Abel and killed him. The first murder is John's illustration of a lawless and hateful heart.

'Lawlessness' (v4) is to do with the lawless spirit and lawless attitude from which the sinful act is spawned. Jesus said that we are answerable for the murder that is committed in our hearts (Matthew ch5 vv21-22). Jesus told his own would-be murderers that they belonged to their father, the devil, who *'was a murderer from the beginning'* (John ch8 v44).

1 THE MURDERER'S MOTIVES (v12)

Cain had been angry because the Lord had accepted Abel's sacrifice of a lamb but had rejected Cain's offering of the fruit of the ground (Genesis ch4 vv1-8). Whatever we bring to the Lord must be with the right attitude and with pure motives. It's not so much about the kind of offering, but everything to do with the character of the offeror. Hebrews ch11 v4 tells us that the critical difference between Abel and his brother Cain was faith. Abel had faith in God and trusted God while seeking to live righteously. Cain, on the other hand, went through a form of worship, without real faith, and without any desire to live righteously for God. It is Cain's posterity that continues to hate true believers today, even resulting in their persecution and murder (John ch3 vv19-20). The love of darkness, which is exhibited in greed, jealousy, anger, hatred, and murder, is referred to as *'the way of Cain'* (Jude 11). Murder in the heart can quickly become murder with the hand. Similarly, jealousy, greed, and anger can quickly erupt like a volcano, causing great destruction. We are instructed not to give the devil a foothold by being angry, which leads to sin (Ephesians ch4 vv26-27).

2 THE MURDERER'S ACCOMPLICES (vv12-13)

'The way of Cain' is the way of the world. The ugliness of humanity is clearly visible in the painful sufferings which it inflicts upon the children of God. Peter urges us to rejoice in suffering (1 Peter ch4 vv12-14). How often do we see the hatred of the world boiling against those in whom it sees goodness and righteousness? How often do we see anger being vented against those who live moral and upright lives? Abel was murdered because he was faithful and righteous. He didn't speak out against Cain. He didn't argue with Cain. He didn't react

violently towards Cain. Abel lived out a righteous life in front of Cain, and for that, he paid with his life. Cain's accomplices are still alive and very active in their hatred against believers today.

3 THE MURDERER'S SENTENCE (v15)

One of John's great themes, both in his Gospel and in this epistle, is 'eternal life'. The contrast couldn't be greater. The 'divide' couldn't be wider. John isn't into 'shades of grey', which blur the gospel. John's writings are all about 'black and white' (see ch5 v12). We talk about 'matters of life and death,' and knowing Jesus is an eternal matter of life and death. God's children have eternal life. It therefore follows that those who won't believe in Jesus as their Lord and Saviour, who have hatred in their hearts, do not have eternal life. Their end is eternal death. Hell is the reality for those who remain estranged from God. Cain pleaded that his estrangement was more than he could bear (Genesis ch4 v13). His punishment consisted of alienation from God (Genesis ch4 v16). Cain and all his murderous accomplices, who have rejected God's word and have refused to surrender to Jesus Christ, remain condemned in their sin. *'Anyone who does not love remains in death'* (v14) and *'No murderer has eternal life in him'* (v15).

4 THE MURDERER'S PARDON (v14)

One of the evidences of God's saving, justifying work in the life of a believer is in their love for their brothers and sisters. It's the love of Jesus that he showed at the cross. The proof of the believers' pardon is that they will be following 'the way of Christ', not 'the way of Cain'. That means they will be ready and quick to forgive, just as they have been divinely forgiven. Jesus showed us the way (Luke ch23 v34). It tests the genuineness of our Christianity to the extreme when we are called to forgive those who have treated us harmfully, unfairly, and unjustly. *'We should love one another'*. This is the age-old message! (v11)

JUNE 24
1 JOHN Ch3.16-20

LOVE IS...

In the 1960s, a New Zealand cartoonist called Kim Casali produced a series of cartoon love notes for her husband Roberto, which were later published in booklets. Then the cartoons began to appear as a regular feature in a newspaper under the title 'Love is...' They have sought to depict and define love in thousands of different ways. But two thousand years before Kim Casali came on the scene, John wrote his own 'Love is…'

V16 begins: *'This is how we know what love is...'* Immediately, our attention is heightened. We are 'all ears'! Love is...what? How does John define love? He cannot explain love without reference to the Author of love and the greatest demonstration of all: *'This is how we know what love is: Jesus Christ laid down his life for us. And we ought to lay down our lives for our brothers'* (v16). In the first place, then:

1 LOVE IS... SACRIFICIAL NOT SELFISH

Most of us are familiar with John ch3 v16. But if John ch3 v16 tells us about the scope of God's love, 1 John ch3 v16 tells us about the scale of our love, as Christians. Because of Jesus' sacrifice, we should be ready to sacrifice for one another. Sacrifice must be the calibre of Christian love. It's essentially 'sacrificial'. Whenever the New Testament speaks of God's love to us, it is almost always with reference to the cross. Of course, Jesus' death was undoubtedly unique. No other death could procure redemption for the sinner. John is saying that just as Jesus sacrificed his life for us *'we ought to lay down our lives for our brothers'* (v16). The word *'ought'* is a significantly strong word meaning to be indebted or obligated. We are called to show love to our Christian brothers and sisters. This is not just any kind of love. We are called to demonstrate a love which costs us, not merely something, but everything. This love may mean that we shall go without – even without life itself.

2 LOVE IS...KIND NOT CALLOUS

(v17) A person who shuts their eyes and shuts their hearts to a believer's basic material needs reveals that they don't possess the love of God. In fact, worse than that, they display the callousness of Cain, who killed his brother (v12). The distance between murder in the heart and murder with the hands is only eighteen inches! (ch4 v20). Christian believers are not saved by 'doing good', but they have an obligation to 'do good'. They will want to show the love of God by being kind. Paul urges Celtic Christians to *'do good to all people, especially to those who belong to the family of believers'* (Galatians ch6 v10). How good are we at showing the love of Jesus to those whom we meet? Many people may be just 'one act of genuine kindness' from meeting a true Christian.

3 LOVE IS... PRACTICAL NOT THEORETICAL

(v18) Love is much more than words, however or whatever is said. Love is active, not passive. Love is not a theory or just a set of principles. Love is always totally practical (James ch2 v15). God's love for sinners didn't merely flow from his emotions, but from his will. Jesus came to demonstrate his Father's love by performing his Father's will (Hebrews ch10 v7). Practical love has to manifest itself. By its very nature, it will be demonstrated just as *'God demonstrated his love for us in this...'* (Romans ch5 v8). The church today may be compared to those four lepers who were cowering in the misery and poverty at Samaria's city gates (2 Kings ch7). Added to the misery of their illness and disability was the dreadful famine that had paralysed the city due to the King of Syria besieging the city. Some had resorted to cannibalism. The lepers reasoned that they had nothing to lose if they ventured outside the city and made their way to the Syrian camp. They crossed 'no man's land' at dusk and arrived at the enemy camp. But there were no guards or sentries. They discovered that the camp had been suddenly evacuated. There was food, drink, clothing, gold, and silver all over the camp. The Lord had caused the Syrian army to hear the sound of chariots and horses, as from a huge army. The Syrians left quickly in fear. So the four lepers were rummaging and plundering the camp on their own, gorging themselves on the food and stashing away the valuables. Then they stopped and said: *'We're not doing right. This is a day of good news, and we're keeping it to ourselves'* (2 Kings ch7 v9). So they shared the news and blessings with the rest of the city. Real, practical love is to be shown and shared. It must be truthful, genuine, and 24-carat.

4 LOVE IS...CONFIRMING NOT CONDEMNING

(vv19-20) Some commentators have suggested that these verses are the most difficult to understand in this letter. John is saying that the expression of our Christian love is acceptable and approved by God. It demonstrates pure, unadulterated motives. The evidence of this quality of love confirms that we belong to God, who is the source of this love. Christian love confirms that we are in God's family, and the expression of that love will not condemn us or afflict our conscience. The response of Cain was to take the life of his brother. The response of love is to give one's life for one's brother. How do we show our sacrificial love?

JUNE 25
1 JOHN Ch3.21-24

HOW CAN WE PLEASE GOD?

Judy Garland, who died in 1969, was a successful actress of stage and screen who had a compulsive desire to please other people. She had a deep yearning to be accepted. Most of us like to please. But how much of a desire do we have to please God? A celebrity may want to please fans; a chef will want to please diners; a beautician will want to please clients; and a doctor will want to please patients. But how much do we want to please our Lord, our Creator, our King, and our Saviour?

There's a sense in which it is right to please other people and not to be offensive. However, we all know that it's impossible to please everyone all the time. Indeed, it's right that we shouldn't please everyone or try to conform to their particular ideas and philosophies. It means inevitably that we shall displease people who displease God. We should not be able to please people who are opposed to God. Our priority must be to please him. These verses guide us in how we can please him.

1 OBEYING HIS COMMANDS (vv21-22)

Jesus emphasised the two greatest commands (Mark ch12 vv30-31). Loving God will mean obeying his commands (John ch14 v15; ch15 v10). Obedience is evidence of knowing God (ch2 v3). 'Trust and obey' was the theme of Rev John Sammis' popular Gospel song. Trusting is vitally important to obedience. We must trust God, even when we think he has made a mistake in the circumstances or the timing of those circumstances. We must trust and obey, even when it's obvious that we shall suffer some kind of adversity or hardship. We need faith to please God (Hebrews ch11 v6).

2 RECEIVING HIS ANSWERS (vv21-22)

The confidence that we can have *'before God'* is the assurance that we have been justified and pardoned because of Jesus' sacrifice for us. To *'receive from him anything we ask'* is a guaranteed benefit if we are in the right relationship with God our Father. 'Anything' we ask? If we are obedient and do the things that please God, and therefore ask for the things that please God, then we shall receive those things for which we ask. Even when earthly children ask their father for those things that they know he is pleased about, and approves of, and is able to do, then they receive. Jesus encourages faith and trust in asking for those things which God is pleased about (John ch16 vv23-24).

3 BELIEVING HIS SON (v23)

Many people genuinely believe that they are engaged in doing God's work, however perverse, corrupt, and foolish that work may be. God's work is *'to believe in the one he has sent'* (John ch6 v29). To believe in Jesus means to believe all the things that he said of himself (such as John ch6 v48; ch8 v12; ch10 v11; ch11 vv25-26). Martha's great response (John ch11 v27) was: *'I believe that you are the Christ, the Son of God, who was come into the world'*. In one short, profound statement, she declared her belief in Jesus' authority, deity, and humanity. Is that our personal confession of faith?

4 LOVING HIS PEOPLE (v23)

Though love is important, love is not in isolation. This verse conjoins faith and love: believing in Jesus and loving his people. We're not going to please God unless practical love is demonstrated. When faced with the needs of our brothers and sisters in Christ, do we long for a greater capacity to meet those needs? But, at the same time, do we use all our capacity and ability to do whatever we can, with God's help?

5 LIVING HIS LIFE (v24)

How could John ever forget Jesus' words about the vine and the branches (John ch15 vv1-4)? Our fruitfulness will depend on our 'mutual abiding', that is, I am living in Jesus and Jesus is living in me. But we shouldn't regard this day-to-day relationship as some kind of mystical airy-fairy kind of experience that is spiritually subjective. This is everyday, feet-on-the-ground Christianity. This is fellowship with God as a 'walking, talking, living...child of his'. Here is the wonderful blessing of becoming a child of God through faith in Jesus. We not only have Jesus' leadership, but we have Jesus' companionship too. The stunning Old Testament example is Enoch (Hebrews ch11 vv5-6), who pleased God. The words *'earnestly seek'* translates the image of 'beating a path underfoot'. A well-worn path to a neighbour will ensure that the grass would not grow. We should seek God so frequently that we beat a path to him. Our daily times of fellowship with him will keep the path well-worn. That was what pleased God so much with Enoch that he took him straight home to be with himself, without the intervention of death.

6 KNOWING HIS SPIRIT (v24)

The internal evidence of God dwelling in us is God's life through his Spirit. The external evidence of God's life dwelling in us is God's love through his Spirit (Romans ch5 v5). Love is not always the 'Gorilla glue' applied with a distemper brush. Often, it's the tiny, spontaneous, single drops of super glue applied accurately and timely.

JUNE 26
1 JOHN Ch4.1-6

SPOTTING THE FAKE

In 1950, a Dutch fisherman called Louwrens van Voorthuizen declared that he was God. Gathering a small but dedicated group of followers around him, he explained that his role was similar to that of Jesus, but greater! He rejected historic Christianity as outdated and irrelevant. He declared that now that he – 'God' – was here on earth, the Bible was superseded. All his claims lost credibility when Lou died in 1968, and his followers fizzled out. We might wonder how such a person had become so seriously deluded and arrogantly blasphemous. We may also wonder how so many people are gullible and easily seduced by such teachings. But nothing is new here. John issues a serious warning in the first century (v1) about spotting fakes.

There have always been things that are counterfeit and pretence. The trademark of Satan's activity is deceit. He is the 'father of lies' and is a liar from the beginning. Just as he once aspired to be 'God', we can therefore recognise his disciples, such as Lou, the Dutchman. Satan is an imitator and has been extremely busy devising and creating huge scams. Trading Standards will tell you that, over the years, the manufacturers of the Far East have been flooding the world with imitations. John is telling you that over the years, Satan and his manufacturing spirits have been flooding the world with imitations. We must have the wisdom and insight to discern the genuine from the fake; the true from the false. That calls for a test which avoids, on the one hand, superstitiously believing everything and, on the other hand, suspiciously believing nothing. Behind every spiritual speaker, there is either the Holy Spirit of God or there is the *spirit of antichrist'* (v3), deceiving and undermining. So what tests can we apply to the 'spirits'? How can we spot the fake? We can ask four probing questions in testing which 'spirit' it is:

1 WHERE DOES HE COME FROM?

Does the spirit come from God or not? Those two words *'from God'* are used seven times in these seven verses. A preacher, teacher, or prayer leader may be particularly powerful and convincing, but where does their power come from? Are these speakers the mouthpiece of God, or are they the mouthpiece of something devious and antichristian? We must check out what is being said (Acts ch17 v11), not with a cynical or critical spirit which constantly looks at the preacher's style, vocabulary, appearance, or whatever, but we should be discerning in assessing the tenor and substance of the message. Systematic expository preaching from the Biblical text helps the preacher and the listener to anchor their thoughts, understanding, and application in God's word.

2 WHOM DOES HE ACKNOWLEDGE?

(v2) John's test, to distinguish whether the Spirit of God or the spirit of antichrist is behind the preacher, is to discover what they believe about Jesus (1 Corinthians ch12 v3). Here then is the pivotal truth: the rejection or acceptance of Jesus as the incarnate Son of God. *The Word became flesh'* (John ch1 v14) reveals that Jesus didn't originate with Bethlehem, or even nine months before. Jesus is the pre-existent, pre-incarnate Son of

God. He *'became'* man. He came to wear our humanity and to bear our iniquity. The correct view of Jesus, by believing what Jesus said about himself, is the acid test.

3 WHAT DOES HE SAY?

(v5) The spirit of error and falsehood will be speaking from the viewpoint of God's objectors and opponents. The spirit has nothing in common with the Spirit of Truth. Their world views are fundamentally different. The *'viewpoint of the world'* does not acknowledge the divine Lordship of Jesus Christ. If the spirit cannot speak endearingly of Jesus as their glorious God, their sovereign Lord, the precious Redeemer and personal Saviour, then it begs the question, 'What spirit is it?' There is so much fudge and mush in Christendom today that people don't know what they really believe, and therefore, they are unable to discern between the Spirit of Truth and the spirit of antichrist.

4 HOW DOES HE BEHAVE?

(v6) John, as an apostle, has been invested with special authority as a teacher who speaks *'from God'* and who is *'carried along by the Holy Spirit'* (2 Peter ch1 v21). Christians should also be able to identify the person who has no time for the incisive truth of Scripture and who *'does not listen to us'*. The spirit of falsehood will not be comfortable when the truth of God's word is expounded. Instead, it will wriggle and wrestle and resist. John is declaring something startling by stating (v4) that if the Spirit of Truth is our possession, and the Scriptures of truth are our confession, then we have *already* overcome the spirits of falsehood and antichrist.

With the Bible in our hands and the Spirit of God in our hearts, we shall be able to spot the fake. Let's learn to check out what is being said by comparing it with Scripture. Much damage is being done to congregations and churches because *'false prophets'* have not been identified and removed. Unitarianism has been welcomed in by the back door, and naive, undiscerning believers have been beguiled by friendship and commitment without applying the spirit-test.

JUNE 27
1 JOHN Ch4.7-12

LOVE DIVINE, ALL LOVES EXCELLING

John has not been writing about the mechanics of romantic love. He is teaching the true meaning of Christian love, which comes from the believer's new nature. We love in a Godly way if we are in the right relationship with God. The source of that love is God himself: *'love comes from God'* (v7). The love, which is radiated through the lives of Christian believers, who seek to live for Jesus, has its origin with God for *'God is love'* (v8). This is the excellent, divine love which is on view in John's letter.

1 THE FULL EXTENT OF GOD'S LOVE (vv9-10)

John tells us that there are two parts to the 'full extent' of divine love; two parts which are inextricably linked:

i] His Sending of His Son: Through the Old Testament, we read of God who sent great leaders, great champions, great kings, great priests, and great prophets. He even sent angels and archangels. But every 'sending' is eclipsed by the sending of his Son. The Old Testament forms the preparations and the preliminaries for the sending of Jesus.

ii] His Sacrifice of His Son: (v10) The ultimate purpose for sending Jesus into the world was to become a sacrifice for sin. But this wasn't just any sacrifice! Unlike the Old Testament sacrifices, Jesus' sacrifice was to be unique, permanent, and totally effective. God's *'one and only Son'* had been sent as an *'atoning sacrifice'*. The atonement is a direct reference to the Old Testament system. God is perfectly just and holy. He cannot set aside his holiness or overlook it so that he can forgive sinners. His holiness and justice demand punishment for sin. Here then is the huge dilemma. How can God satisfy his holy character while at the same time provide pardon for every repentant sinner? Humanly speaking, it can't be done! Divinely speaking, it can be done! Jesus' atoning death is the answer. Jesus died to propitiate for our sins – to avert God's judgement upon sin. Jesus took the full impact of the death sentence to satisfy God's justice and to justify every believing sinner.

2 THE FULL EXPERIENCE OF GOD'S LOVE (vv7, 9, 12)

When we become true followers of Jesus (not merely religious, charitable, or church-going), then we experience God's love in:

i] New Birth: (v7) Knowing God means that we have been re-born; born into God's family; *'born of the Spirit'* (John ch3 v8). This is the new birth that we desperately need to enter into a right relationship with God. Jesus urged *'You must be born again'* (John ch3 v7).

ii] New Life: We *'live through him'* (v9) and *'God lives in us'* (v12). When we are born again, then the unseen God comes to live and dwell in his people. John is not saying that if we love one another, then God will live in us. Rather, he's saying that if God is living within us because we have been born into his family, then the evidence of that will be our love for one another. Love is not conditional upon whether the other person is lovable, lovely, polite, clean, generous, or agrees with us about everything! Love is all-encompassing and all-embracing. It's easier to be loving to the lovable but not so easy to be loving to the unlovely. Jesus told us to love even our enemies (Matthew ch5 v44).

3 THE FULL EXPRESSION OF GOD'S LOVE (v12)

While God is an invisible Spirit and Jesus has ascended bodily into heaven, God cannot be seen at the moment. But while the world cannot see God, it can see God in us, if we are true Christians living the Christian life as we should be doing. People should be able to glimpse something of God's holiness, God's kindness, God's grace, and especially God's love in the lives of those who profess to be his children. This is profoundly astonishing that God should choose to live in his weak, deficient, sinful people! What's more, he is saying that the full expression of God's love can be seen in his children: *'his love is made complete in us'*. How can this be? This love, which originated with God and was demonstrated in Jesus at the cross, is actually completed in the people whom he saves. Here is the full expression of God's love and the ultimate extent of his marvellous plan: that those who have come to know the love of God in salvation should now become the channels for the love of God in its completion. This is the final purpose for the wonderful love of God: that it should be expressed in the lives of those who have been saved by God's grace. When we look into the clear sky, we may spot a vapour trail. We may not see the jet plane, but we can see where it has been. John says that we cannot see God, but we should be able to see the 'vapour trails' of God's love criss-crossing our world. Every child of God is called to make such a vapour trail, showing God's love in our speech, actions, and attitudes. Does the 'vapour trail' that we create spell out to others that God's love has crossed their 'sky'?

Nobody will understand us when we say that 'God is love' unless that love is visible in us.

JUNE 28
1 JOHN Ch4.13-21

WHAT KIND OF LOVE IS THIS?

We may feel unqualified to minister in many ways. We may not even know what to say to needy people at times. But if we are believers, then we can begin by showing the love of God to those we meet. Learn to show the love of Jesus in a practical way. You may not believe that you are very eloquent in theology, but you can be eloquent in love – God's love. John continues to tell us about God's love, emphasising things he has already taught, but confirming the wonderful character of this 'Love divine, all loves excelling'. There are five more things that we can learn about God's love and how those characteristics relate to us:

1 GOD'S LOVE IS KNOWABLE (vv13-15)

These verses continue to drive home the message to every Christian that the nature of their relationship with God is fundamentally a relationship of love. The residence of God's Spirit in the life of the believer (v13) confirms that Jesus is their *'atoning sacrifice'* (v10) and that they have come to know the love of God in salvation. It's an astonishing truth to recognise that it's possible for a flawed, rebel sinner to know God. How can an unloving, unlovely person come to know God, for God is love (v16)? John himself has defined God in three simple but profound ways: *God is spirit* (John ch4 v24); *God is light* (ch 1 v5); *God is love* (ch4 v16).

The nature and character of God's being may seem to be a billion miles from our own nature and character, yet God has initiated a way in which we can know him and know his love (v14). The fourth-century BC Greek philosopher, Plato, said that even if one were to find God, it would be impossible to express him in terms that all could understand. Impossible? John writes, *'God is love'*. God welcomes us into a living, dynamic relationship with himself through Jesus Christ our Saviour.

2 GOD'S LOVE IS RELIABLE (v16)

The word *'rely'* in this verse translates to such belief and confidence that we can stake everything, including our lives, upon it. God's love is 100% reliable. The love of God, which is majestic in its greatness and awesome in its scope, has been proof-tested at the cross (v10). Only the atoning death of Jesus could achieve a lasting relationship between our heavenly Father and his believing children. Just as God himself is invariable and unchangeable, so his love is similarly immutable. Therefore, it's totally reliable, in this world and the next.

3 GOD'S LOVE IS IDENTIFIABLE (v16, vv20-21)

One of the great wonders of God's amazing love is that he chooses to express that love through his people who have been saved by his grace. The hallmark of genuine, twenty-four-carat Christianity is the love of God. John is saying that the evidence of God's life in a believer is God's love through a believer. We can't claim to be a Christian and at the same time harbour grudges and hatred against a fellow believer. We can't profess to know God's love in salvation if we are not prepared to demonstrate God's love in service and sacrifice. We can't testify to God living within us if we are ignoring the gaping needs and aching hearts of brothers and sisters in Christ. The love of God is a badge of discipleship.

4 GOD'S LOVE IS VERIFIABLE (v17)

When the final Day of Judgement arrives, the Christian can be certain and confident that God lives within, and that they have become more like Jesus, because God's love is *'poured out'* into their hearts *'by the Holy Spirit whom he has given'* (Romans ch5 v5). No one will escape the judgement of God unless they have demonstrated the love of God. No one can demonstrate the love of God unless they possess the life of God. There may be many likenesses to the love of God in charitable works, acts of self-sacrifice, personal commitment, generous deeds, neighbourhood kindnesses, acts of mercy, and selfless giving. But the genuine love of God will be the fruit of a heart that knows Jesus as Saviour and has been cleansed from its sin by the blood of Jesus, God's Son. A passport proclaims who we say we are, and the genuine original is thoroughly verifiable. A copy, however good the copy, will not do! Someone else's passport won't do either. Our confidence on Judgement Day will be founded upon God's love, revealed supremely in Jesus' atoning death on the cross and *'made complete among us'* (v17). It will be verifiable if we are a believing Christian, because it will proclaim that we are who we say we are – a sinner saved by God's superlative, sovereign grace.

5 GOD'S LOVE IS UNCONQUERABLE (v18)

Love is incompatible with fear. As believers, we have nothing to fear from the past, present, or future. While there are those who genuinely fear each new day as it dawns, those who are fully trusting in God's love can be certain that each new day is in his safe hands. God's children are identified, not by their fear, but by their love. *'Perfect love drives out fear'*. This is the character and the calibre of a love that is unconquerable. Nothing can subdue it or bind it. *'We are more than conquerors through him who loved us'* (Romans ch8 v37). This love is both unconquerable and inseparable (Romans ch8 vv38-39).

JUNE 29
1 JOHN Ch5.1-5

WINNING THE WAR

Where cynics and sceptics may view the Christians' heartache, loss, sickness, and death as 'defeat', John writes: *'This is the victory that has overcome the world, even our faith'* (v4). The core belief of the church is that Jesus Christ, God the Son, is our Lord and Saviour (v5). John's message is not merely for those who engage in 'great' works of Christian service, but for each and every believer. There is no distinction here! The victory is past, present, and future:

i] Past: There is victory when we first believed and trusted in Jesus to save us. The world's grasp was broken, and we were freed from the chains of sin and the claims of Satan.

ii] Present: Our day-by-day encounters and skirmishes with the world are won by faith. They may take the form of moral temptations and pressures, intellectual arguments, or contemporary cultural philosophies. They may confront us with psychological and emotional pressures from unbelieving families and friends. They may appear as heartbreak, loss, anguish, grief, physical pain, or weakness.

iii] Future: We shall never need a new super nuclear weapon to replace faith. Faith is guaranteed to subdue all the powers and conquer all the enemies that the world can stand against us. The world can produce no power that faith cannot overcome. How can we be an 'overcomer'? How can we experience victory? John emphasises three things. We need to be:

1 BORN RIGHT (vv1, 4)

The tense of the word *'born'* indicates a past event that affects our present circumstances. Our natural birth occurred on a day that determined the family into which we entered. Our spiritual birth determines that we have become *'children of God'* (v2). This is conferred on all who receive Jesus and believe in his name (John ch1 vv12-13). Membership in God's family is only because God lovingly and graciously calls us in the gospel. The 'believing' and 'receiving' is not determined by human achievement, but it is determined by divine atonement. In order for us to win the war as an 'overcomer', Jesus had to achieve that decisive victory over Satan, sin, and death at the cross. Calvary was the battleground on which the foes of the world and the powers of hell united in an 'axis of evil', attempting to defeat and eliminate Jesus, God the Son. But with all their combined hellish fury, they only contributed to their own momentous downfall and subjugation (Hebrews ch2 vv14-15). Jesus' triumph is unprecedented. He is the Supreme Overcomer. There's no conqueror like Jesus. Paradoxically, it was through death that he defeated death and disarmed all his enemies (Colossians ch1 vv13-15).

2 BELIEVE RIGHT (vv1,5)

Later (v13) John says that he is writing these things to those who *'believe in the name of the Son of God'*. Belief in Jesus and who he says he is is fundamental to our Christian faith. Many people will believe in a percentage of what the Bible teaches about Jesus. Some may believe that Jesus is a historical person (maybe 2% belief). Some may even believe that God sent him into the world on a saving mission (say 60% belief). But the crux of our message, the core of our faith, and 100% of which John is writing, is that the Lord Jesus Christ is God the Son. You will encounter all kinds of people who profess to be Christians and who refer to themselves as followers of Jesus, but they refuse to follow him or believe him for what he says about himself. The Pharisees were in no doubt that Jesus referred to himself as the Lord God when he quoted Psalm 110 v1 (in Matthew ch22 v44). Jesus identified himself to his Jewish enemies in precisely the same way that God the Father identified himself to Moses (Exodus ch3 v14; John ch8 v58). Jesus is the eternal God. Winning the war and overcoming the world depends on a rock-solid faith in Jesus Christ, who is God (Colossians ch1 v19; ch2 v9). Faith is necessary to overcome. This is not the airy-fairy, wish-washy message of the mystics and sentimentalists who tell us that as long as we have faith, we shall be alright. Faith is nothing without the object of faith. It's faith in Jesus and who he is that provides the victory over the world.

3 BEHAVE RIGHT (vv2-3)

If we are going to experience anything of an 'overcoming life', then we must show our love for God and for his children by obeying his commands. The convoluted regulations of the Pharisees and teachers of the law were heavy burdens. By comparison, the yoke of Jesus is easy and his burden is light (Matthew ch11 v30). God's commands are neither a chore nor *'burdensome'* (v3). To some Christians who are not walking with Jesus daily, the obligations and instructions of the Bible may seem irksome and burdensome. How much of a priority and a delight is it to worship God with his people or to pray with our fellow believers? Do family or friends, fishing or football, business or travel, TV or social media take priority over the things of God? If God is less than our Number One priority, then our love for him has cooled, and we shall not be winning the war.

JUNE 30
1 JOHN Ch5.6-12

THE THREE WITNESSES

In the second century, a man from Smyrna, called Irenaeus, had spent time being taught by the city's famous bishop, Polycarp. Polycarp himself had been a keen student of John the apostle, the author of this letter. So Irenaeus was just one generation removed from John. Irenaeus moved to Rome, and perhaps, due to the persecution of Christians in the capital, he later moved to Lyons, where he became an elder in the church. When the Bishop of Lyons died in prison, Irenaeus was chosen to take his place and position. Irenaeus devoted much of his ministry to defending the church against heresy. It was the same kind of heresy that John had exposed and refuted in his writings. Gnosticism was, and is, a mixture of Christianity and pagan philosophy. Gnostics claim that you can know salvation through 'special knowledge'. Not only did Irenaeus write an authoritative work entitled 'Against Heresies', but he also set out a 'Rule of Faith', which was a simple statement summarising the fundamental doctrines and Christian beliefs. Today, the 'gnostic monster' has many heads. Recycled gnosticism appears in so-called 'gay marriage'. It also appears in transsexualism and is at the root of unitarianism. It surfaces in some aspects of feminism, new ageism, and libertarianism. So how does John deal with the gnostic heresy? He does it in the best possible way. He reasserts the truth. In the 'Supreme Court of Enquiry' he calls three irreproachable, irrefutable, infallible witnesses (v7): *'the Spirit, the water and the blood'.*

1 CALL WITNESS No1: THE SPIRIT

The Spirit gives evidence of Jesus (v6; John ch15 v26; ch16 v13). He is the principal witness since he is *'the Spirit of Truth'.* As the divine witness, he will only speak *'the truth, the whole truth and nothing but the truth'.* The Spirit's role includes opening minds and unlocking understanding of the truth of God and the truth of God's word. Opinions alter, civilisations fluctuate, policies need adjusting, manifestos appear fluid, but the truth is forever unchangeably true. We need the Spirit to show us:

i] The Truth about God: There is one God, uniquely and incomparably holy, just and true. He is eternal and completely independent. He is all-knowing, all-powerful, and ever-present. God is good, gracious, merciful, loving, faithful, and patient. God is our Creator and Sustainer, our Protector and Provider, our Rock and our Refuge, our Hope and our Peace.

ii] The Truth about Ourselves: Though created in God's image, we have basically rejected God in favour of our own ways. We have chosen the ways of sin, folly, rebellion, and death (Proverbs ch14 v12). The Spirit of Truth confirms through the apostle that *'there is no one righteous, not even one...All have turned away'* (Romans ch3 vv10, 12). We have all sinned (Romans ch3 v23). Our relationship with God has been shattered, and there's no way that we can mend it. Left to us, that relationship is irretrievable and irrecoverable.

iii] The Truth about Jesus: A restored relationship must be God's initiative. He both instigated and implemented the reconciliation plan through Jesus our Saviour. God has given us life in his Son (v11). Unless the Son is God, then he could never have achieved the redemptive mission. Any attempt to undermine Jesus' deity undermines the very rescue plan on which humanity depends.

2 CALL WITNESS No2: THE WATER

John has narrowed down the key fundamental doctrine to the true Christian faith, that is, believing in Jesus for who he says he is. The 'overcomer' of v5 is *he who believes that Jesus is the Son of God*. The Jesus of history has a ministry which can be defined by two historical events – Jordan and Calvary; his baptism and his crucifixion; the water and the blood. The whole of Jesus' ministry on earth is embraced by these two historical events, which, among other things, are used as evidence to refute the heresies that John the apostle, Irenaeus, and many other believers have encountered. Jesus' baptism declares his humility and his authority; his humanity and his deity. He is God the Son, as his baptism witnesses (Matthew ch3 v17).

3 CALL WITNESS No3: THE BLOOD

The witness of the blood refers to Jesus' death on the cross: *He did not come by water only, but by water and blood* (v6). Jesus' baptism, though significant, was not sufficient. To achieve the redemptive goal, Jesus had to suffer on the cross as our atoning sacrifice (ch2 vv1-2; ch4 v10). Jesus not only took the curse of sin and took the punishment of sinners who believe, but he also took their place. Jesus is our perfect Substitute. Human testimony is always fallible, but divine testimony from one witness, let alone three, is infallible. The right response is to repent, believe, and receive eternal life. The wrong response is scepticism and unbelief (v10). Eternal life is the free gift which God gives to those who believe in his Son and trust him for his salvation (v11). Eternal life is found nowhere else! There's no alternative supplier of eternal life. If you won't believe God's Son, you won't receive God's life. It is with your heart that you believe and are justified (Romans ch10 v10). As the pastor and poet John Newton wrote in his poem: 'What think you of Christ? is the test...'

JULY 1
1 JOHN Ch5.13-17

HOW CAN I BE CONFIDENT IN PRAYER?

In contrast with the doubts which may be sown with the seeds of gnostic heresies, John asserts that there are truths which every believer can know. At least forty times in this letter, including seven times in these concluding verses, John uses the word *'know'*. We may talk with some people whose testimony is less than positive. They may say that they 'hope' that they are a Christian and that they 'hope' that they have been saved. They may 'hope' to receive eternal life and 'hope' that God will one day accept them in the end. But John is not content that the Christian believer should be wallowing in doubt, hesitation, or uncertainty. He wants them to *'know'*, without reservation or suspicion (v13), and to be convinced and assured. Is our final destination and our present possession eternal life, rather than eternal death? If we know these things, then *'this is the confidence we have in approaching God...'*

One preacher referred to prayer as 'a summit meeting in the throne-room of the universe'. Most believers struggle with prayer. It may be a somewhat sweeping and even surprising statement but if you took time to conduct a survey of Christians and their prayer life, we should discover that prayer is a constant struggle and battle with time, with quietness, with distractions, with priorities, with words and even with sleep! Helpfully, these verses provide us with an answer to this question:

1 BY APPROACHING IN JESUS' NAME

Of course, this has to be more than merely using the name 'Jesus' somewhere in our prayers. We're talking about believing, trusting and depending upon Jesus for who he says he is: God the Son, our Lord, our Sovereign and our Saviour. The Lord Jesus is the only access to the Father for both Jew and Gentile (Ephesians ch2 v18). Jesus emphasised that his name was the key to bringing answers to prayer and bringing glory to the Father (John ch14 vv13-14). We can be bold in asking if we are abiding (John ch15 v7). Jesus' name is the guarantee (John ch15 v16). Believing in Jesus and who he says he is, as God the Son, becomes the key to accessing the will of God. Praying in the name of Jesus means praying with the authority of Jesus. How much authority is that? Romans ch10 v9 and v13 remind us that the name of Jesus the Lord is paramount in our salvation. Those who humble themselves, calling on Jesus as Lord, are promised his salvation. We dare not come to God in any other name than the name of Jesus. The same is true for prayer as it is for salvation. It's Jesus' authority as 'Lord of all' that we need. Our invoking of the name of Jesus is not some trite phrase that we tag onto our prayers. It's not the same as invoking some magic spell like 'Open Sesame!' or 'Shazam!'. It's a firm belief in Jesus, the Lord, the sovereign ruler over time and space, who is almighty God.

2 BY ASKING IN GOD'S WILL

(vv14-15) Does prayer seem rather complicated sometimes? Does prayer seem very mysterious, with some prayers getting answered and others not being answered? If God is sovereign and acts out his will according to his wisdom, does it really make a difference whether we pray or not? In fact, if God is Lord and sovereign, are our prayers ever going to change his mind or influence his heart anyway? Fundamentally, prayer is communion with God. Each prayer should be entitled *'Your will be done!'*, just as Jesus taught in the Disciples' Prayer (Matthew ch6 v10). What's more, Jesus not only gave us the exhortation, he gave us the example (Matthew ch26 v39). Our motive for asking should be the same as his motive for answering. When we both want the same thing, then we can say that 'prayer changes things'. Our boldness in approaching God should include wanting the very thing that he wants. That may mean a serious alignment of our will to God's will. But, think about it, would we really want anything that God didn't want? Would we want to depend on our limited wisdom for the right answer to prayer? Yet 'wanting what God wants' should never be looked upon as a reduction of our freedom, but rather a safeguard to that freedom.

3 BY PRAYING FOR OTHERS' NEEDS

One of the great privileges of being a Christian is intercession: praying on behalf of others. Practical love, which has been highlighted so often in this epistle, includes bringing our concerns about others to God. These concerns include sins and failings (v16). The gnostic denial of Jesus' deity, authority and salvation is damning indeed. This *'sin leads to death'* - eternal death, in contrast to eternal life. While we are not expressly forbidden to pray about such heretics, our normal intercession embraces needy brothers and sisters in Christ. Jesus prayed specifically for Simon Peter (Luke ch22 v31). We are encouraged to continue praying for all the saints (Ephesians ch6 v18). How can we prevent our praying from becoming stale, lethargic and mechanical? Ring-fence a regular, uninterrupted daily time. Keep the routine fresh and alive. Use a psalm each day to prompt praise. Keep a prayer diary to remember current concerns in the church family and further afield. Use the prayer diaries of our missions and missionaries. Keep a simple world map with your diary so that you can pray intelligently about situations around the world. Always be thankful! Approach with confidence (Hebrews ch4 v16).

JULY 2
1 JOHN Ch5.18-21

TO TELL YOU THE TRUTH

It is said of many of us that we like to be sure of everything. If the weight of our brain is equivalent to an average apple pie, then it is said that we use only about one slice! With that 'one slice' there are many who would like to plumb the infinite, unravel all mysteries of time and decipher all the intricate codes of science, while simultaneously dispensing with God's moral blueprint for living life on Planet Earth. Most people would rather trust the 'slice' of 'apple pie brain' of the creature rather than trust the eternal, infallible word of the Creator. All the way through John's epistle, he has been asserting the truth in response to the fake teachings of gnosticism. With all the doubts that gnostic doctrines have sown, in relation to the Christian and sin, the deity and authority of Jesus, the true church and salvation by grace through faith, John concludes this letter by underlining three things that we can really know, and he has written to tell us the truth.

1 WE KNOW VICTORY WITH GOD'S POWER

(v18) John declares that a true believer does not habitually and deliberately sin. Because that person is *'born of God'*, they are under new management, they have new life, they display new behaviour, they are in a new family and they enjoy new victories. While each Christian is certainly not sinless (ch1 v8), sin is not their normal behaviour. While they may fall into sin, the person who is truly *'born of God'* cannot *'continue to sin'* deliberately. So why does John make this great assertion? He gives two parts to his reasoning:

i] The Believer is kept free from Sin: With Jesus providing life and a new way of living, that life is no longer characterised by sin. No one who is born of God will continue to sin habitually (ch3 v9). When a person becomes a genuine believer, the ruling principle is no longer sin but holiness. If a person is truly saved, then would they want to continue to sin against God and offend him? Because of Jesus' victory at the cross, the believer can experience victory over sin. Confessed sin is forgiven (ch1 v9).

ii] The Believer is kept free from Harm: Satan and his minions cannot deprive a believer of their security in Jesus. He may try! He desperately tried with Job, but God only allowed Satan to torment him up to a divinely appointed limit. God watches closely the temperature of our trials (1 Corinthians ch10 v13). He provides the *'way out,'* and he knows just when we need it. 'Kept free from harm' means that Satan can't touch you without God's permission. Jesus prayed for his followers and demonstrated that his power is adequate for every need (John ch17 vv12, 15). We may suffer hurt (whether physically, mentally, emotionally or spiritually) but we may not suffer harm if we are protected by Jesus

2 WE KNOW LIFE WITH GOD'S FAMILY

(v19) This is no mere boast or idle claim. John is not intending that every believer should be arrogant. But every believer can be assured. You may have had some 'spiritual experience' many years ago, but what is your testimony of faith today? Is there evidence of the Holy Spirit's transforming, regenerating work in your life? Is the fruit of the Spirit (Galatians ch5 v22) growing in your life for others to notice? Do you love the fellowship of God's people and hunger for the ministry of God's word and for the sound teaching of the church (ch2 v24; ch4 v6)? We may like the fun and chit-chat of the church community's friendship, but we may not be so keen on the commitment and perseverance of the church family's fellowship. If we prefer the 'tea and biscuits' of friendship to the 'prayer and ministry' of fellowship, then that should alert us to our own lack of genuineness and effectiveness.

3 WE KNOW TRUTH WITH GOD'S SON

(v20) This verse sums up the whole of John's letter. Jesus Christ is not only true: he is truth. His coming into the world made it possible for us to *'know the only true God'* as we come to know Jesus. Therefore we must shun and reject anything that is spurious or false. We must not be taken in by 'counterfeit Christianity'. John urges his *'dear friends'* to *'keep themselves from idols'* (v21) Those idols don't always take the form of carved images and sculpted figures. *'Idols'* represents all that is false and fake, even within the realm of the church and Christendom. We should be careful to purge from our praying, Bible reading, singing, worship and fellowship all that is sham and pretence. How much of these things is open and honest, and how much is hypocritical?

John has encouraged the children of God, who know the truth, to persevere in the face of those who make counterfeit claims. There will always be those who try and foist their religious hoax upon undiscerning people. Let us be men and women of truth. Let us retain a right view of Jesus, our God and Saviour.

JULY 3
2 JOHN vv1-13

CHRISTIAN TRAVELODGES

During the thirty-one occasions that John Wesley visited Cornwall, there were several generous hosts who provided hospitality. Some went even further and built extensions on their homes to accommodate Wesley and other Methodist itinerant preachers on their travels. John the apostle, 1700 years earlier, had been concerned that Christian hosts in the first century could be exploited by false itinerant teachers who were travelling around the continent propagating their counterfeit Christianity. So John writes to a particular hostess (or to a church or churches) which host travelling preachers. He has the same themes which he had previously used in his first letter: truth, love, Jesus' incarnation, sound teaching and warnings about deceivers.

John's concerns in this letter may be summarised as:

1 WALK WELL! (vv4-6)

Following the greeting (vv1-3), John expresses concern that his recipients walk faithfully:

i] Walk in Truth: (v4) With so much that is false and heretical, we need John's passion for the truth. He refers to 'truth' four times in his greeting. Truth is indestructible. It may be hidden; it may be compromised; it may be misrepresented. But truth is truth, and it does not alter or erode.

ii] Walk in Obedience: (vv5-6) Law and love are not mutually exclusive. Law and love are inextricably bound up in each other. Jesus said that all *'the Law and the Prophets'* hinge on the first and second great commandments (Matthew ch22 vv37-40), which demand love for God and for each other. Therefore, we must also:

iii] Walk in Love: (v6) Expressions of love with words can easily be counterfeit, but expressions of love in practice are more difficult to replicate consistently. The mark of 'obedience to God's commands' is love, and the mark of 'love for God' is obedience to his commands. People may talk about love without showing it. Genuine love requires demonstration. For Christian hosts of the first century, this was one of the ways they could assess a potential guest. Was he a genuine Christian or was he an imposter, masquerading as a teacher of the truth?

2 WATCH OUT! (vv7-9)

John warns about prowling deceivers. They are false teachers who deny Jesus' authority and Jesus' deity. They refuse to accept that God the Son appeared *'in the flesh'* and have separated themselves from the community of God's people and *'have gone out into the world'* (v7) These scam merchants were not just a few: there were *'many deceivers'* (v7) National Trading Standards frequently warn us to look out for counterfeit goods' fraud. This involves passing goods off as originals when they are actually fakes. We are encouraged to test the quality of the goods, check out the integrity of the trader, and enquire about a guarantee.

i] Test the Quality: Does the teaching tally with Scripture? Like fake 'designer label' goods, they may appear genuine on first inspection. The attractiveness of the product may blind us to detecting the fake. John urged in his first letter to determine what the suspect teacher/preacher thought of Jesus. If Jesus is proclaimed to be anything less than God the Son, the Sovereign King, Creator of all things and the Redeemer and Saviour of his people, then the message is sham and not to be trusted.

ii] Check the Integrity of the Teacher: (v7; ch4 v1; Mark ch13 vv22-23) We must learn to watch their lives as well as their lips. Do they practise what they preach? Is Jesus really Number One in their lives, or does he get demoted when their business, family, health, finance, home, or holiday vie for top spot? The false teachers believed themselves to be gospel preachers and Christian missionaries deserving of hospitality, but their credentials were fake, their message was false, and their ministry was counterfeit.

iii] Enquire about the Guarantee: What assurance can we have that the message they preach is not only 'good news' for today, but also 'good news' for tomorrow and for all eternity? Why would anyone want to stake their eternal future on a perversion of the truth or a poor imitation of what is real?

3 WELCOME WISELY! (vv10-11)

While we are encouraged to welcome friends and strangers, we must show discernment. The 'Christian travelodges' of believers' homes must not serve to promote those who are 'antichrist'. It's not right that these homes, which God has graciously given to his children, are used for denying and opposing his Son. John is stating that to give such an antichrist hospitality is to become complicit in *'his wicked work'* (v11) It's God's true servants who deserve hospitality. Up to the age of eighty-six, John Wesley visited Cornwall where he had been welcomed into the homes of wise people who, though not hearing such powerful, Biblical preaching previously, discerned that it was the word of God. Their wise welcoming helped promote the gospel throughout the county, which was the seed sown for the great 19th century Cornish Revival. We are called to have open hearts and open homes as we encourage and support God's true gospel preachers.

JULY 4
3 JOHN vv1-8

CHURCHES (REALLY) TOGETHER

As you read the New Testament, have you ever thought that it would be a good idea to collate all the various instructions given to the church into one manual of Church Practices and Procedures? Some churches and denominations have tried to do just that in their Constitutions and Statements of Faith. The oldest surviving manual like that dates from around the first century and is entitled 'The Teaching of the Lord to the Gentiles through the Twelve Apostles', frequently referred to as 'The Didachē'. This is not Scripture, but it does give an insight into the early believers' understanding of church practices, especially in relation to providing support and accommodation for travelling Christian workers. But potential Christian hosts had to be alert to the deceptions of false teachers with ulterior motives.

In this letter, John commends his dear friend Gaius for his discernment in providing hospitality for Christian workers. In this first section of his letter, we realise the importance of churches together. But this is not any grouping of churches, but only those that have the same foundations of truth and love. In the New Testament, 'churches together' meant that churches were bound together by the truth of God's word.

We may notice that they:

1 CARE TOGETHER (vv1-2)

The twin themes of John's first letter were 'love' and 'truth'. The apostle emphasised in his second letter that his correspondent was walking in truth and walking in love. Here in his third letter, John begins by telling Gaius that he loves him in the truth (v1) before making reference to the characteristics of love and truth. There are at least three people named 'Gaius' in the New Testament and we can't be sure who this Gaius is. It seems that this Gaius was a church leader in one of the Asian churches and that he was a *'dear friend'* of John's. John cared about Gaius as he did for all believers under his pastoral charge. He knew too that Gaius cared for other travelling ministers, even though they had been *'strangers'* (v5). We, too, must be caring in our speech, actions, and attitudes. We must learn to serve Jesus by serving others: caring about them and showing concern for them.

2 WALK TOGETHER (vv3-4)

Churches have true fellowship when they love the truth and walk together in the truth. The church is not a religious social club: it is an organism, a body, and a family. We cannot afford to pare away the truth because some so-called churches don't agree with certain teachings. We can't take away or discard some component of the truth because it is 'unattractive' or 'unpalatable'. Some have tried to remove the deity of Jesus as being unnecessary for the church's unity. Some have argued for dispensing with the substitutionary, atoning work of Jesus on the cross as being unattractive to twenty-first-century Christianity. Others insist that belief in hell and judgement is inconvenient to modern theology. Others will tell us that the truths of creation, resurrection, Biblical authority, and the sanctity of life are all indispensable in bringing churches together. But if we are to walk together, we must walk in truth as well as in love. John was overjoyed to hear that his spiritual children were walking in the truth (v3). Two can only walk together if there is agreement (Amos ch3 v3).

3 SHARE TOGETHER (vv5-6)

The travelling gospel preachers had reported back to John and the churches that Gaius had been generous in his hospitality, even though the travellers had been strangers to him. Sometimes, itinerant preachers that we meet may refer to a particular host's extensive experience in Christian ministry, or their wide knowledge of churches and church leaders, or even their theological acumen, or sometimes the size of their library. But John's itinerant preachers mentioned none of those things in complimenting Gaius. So what did they say? *'They have told the church about your love'* (v6). As Christians we are called to be loving and hospitable (Romans ch12 v13; Hebrews ch13 vv1-2; 1 Peter ch4 vv8-9). Gaius was ready to share his own home and even to *'entertain strangers'*, but it was not done without discernment. We must do it *'in a manner worthy of God'* (v6).

4 WORK TOGETHER (vv7-8)

The itinerant preachers went out *'for the sake of the name'*, revealing their missionary hearts. But they couldn't do it without the partnership of hospitable supporters. The best examples of *'working together'* should be in the local churches where we are called, among other things, to support and supply the travelling ministers and missionaries. *'Working together'* may mean working in some mundane, unglamorous job, earning money to finance the mission. It will mean wholehearted commitment to prayer and taking an interest in their reports. It can mean providing meals and accommodation, or to stand with these Christian workers against their critics. It will mean encouraging them when they feel downhearted and anxious, or uncertain. Sometimes we resign ourselves to what we can't do rather than to actively look for areas of ministry that we can do in working together.

JULY 5
3 JOHN vv9-14

LOVED TO BE FIRST AND FIRST TO BE LOVED

The twin themes of truth and love are applied to three individuals: John's *'dear friend'* Gaius (v1) who had been consistently *'(faithful) to the truth'* (v3); a prominent church leader or pastor called Diotrephes, who certainly lacked love; Demetrius who was highly commended by everyone for his truth and love. Perhaps this third letter of John's didn't get any further than Diotrephes who was incensed at its content.

We learn lessons from both Diotrephes and Demetrius:

1 DIOTREPHES – LOVED TO BE FIRST

The description by John the apostle, which has defined this otherwise unknown church leader, is that he *'loves to be first'* (v9). Diotrephes is interested in 'number one'. He is full of himself and not filled with the Spirit. Diotrephes wanted to be prominent and preeminent in the church. He exercised his leadership in a unilateral and dictatorial way. This should alert us to the importance of following the Biblical teaching on the plurality of church leadership and the dangers of giving one man too much power and authority in the church. The practice of Paul and Barnabas was to appoint elders in *'each church'* (Acts ch14 v23). Each of those elders had to meet the criteria that Paul lists for Timothy (1 Timothy ch3) and for Titus (Titus ch1). This included self-control, peace-loving, good reputation, not overbearing, not quick-tempered, loving what is good, upright, holy, disciplined, temperate, and respectable. Therefore, it is hard to see that Diotrephes, or anyone like him, is qualified to be an elder or overseer in the church. The Diotrephes of today still loves to be prominent, holding power over their churches and beyond; flaunting their own names and publishing their own achievements. They become greatly irked by those who challenge what they say. John was ready to *'call attention'* (v10) to what Diotrephes was doing and, in particular, John identified his:

i] Malicious Gossip: It seems that Diotrephes had been bad-mouthing believers with whom he didn't agree. Every community has its gossip, and, sadly, the church community is not exempt. Some feel inebriated by the power of having knowledge about something or someone. But the content of the gossip is frequently privileged, personal, and confidential information which should not be shared (Proverbs ch11 v13; ch16 v28). The one who *'loved to be first'* had slandered the particular apostle whom Jesus loved (John ch13 v23; ch19 v26; ch20 v2; ch21 vv7, 20).

ii] Ungracious Attitude: He refused to welcome believers. It's so important for us as churches to be warm, winsome and welcoming. Ignoring or cold-shouldering visiting believers is alien to the kingdom of God. We should be alert to the needy and to the newcomer.

iii] Petty Interference: Diotrephes was not content with refusing to welcome believers: he stopped others from doing so as well. Here was a 'control freak' who wanted to exert power over every part of his church members' lives.

iv] Unjustified Excommunication: Diotrephes had expelled from his church those members who had followed John's recommendation to entertain and support travelling gospel preachers. While discipline is necessary and Biblical, it should never be exercised in a loveless, insensitive, and arbitrary way – and certainly not by a self-appointed 'dictator'! Diotrephes stands as a timeless warning against the pride of a heart that craves to be first.

2 DEMETRIUS – FIRST TO BE LOVED

Gaius is counselled to only imitate *'what is good'* (v11). We know nothing about Demetrius other than what we read in v12, but we know that he is *'good'*. Look at his credentials and his commendations:

i] Commended by the Believers: No one had a bad word to say about Demetrius (v12). Here was a man in tune with truth because he was in touch with God. There is hardly anything more characteristic of genuine Christian love than hospitality. It may not always be a bed for the night but sometimes just a coffee and a chat. 'Being hospitable' is one of the marks of a believer. Hospitality may be precisely what a person needs to be encouraged, helped, and strengthened. Sometimes, hospitality shown to an unbeliever may be just the stepping stone that brings them into a saving relationship with Jesus. Demetrius clearly showed that characteristic and he was commended by his brothers and sisters.

ii] Commended by the Truth: This is a lovely commendation which means exactly what John has been referring to previously (v3; 2 John ch4; 1 John ch2 v6) when he speaks of walking in the truth and walking as Jesus walked. The heroes of Hebrews ch11 were all *'commended for their faith'* (v39). Demetrius lived out what he believed. His life harmonised with truth and love.

iii] Commended by the Apostle: To have apostolic endorsement for the way in which Demetrius conducted his life was the highest human commendation. Even Demetrius' enemies would have struggled to find fault with him. He was first to be loved. Let us not be like Diotrephes, who loved to be first, but let us be like Demetrius, who loved to be last, because he put Jesus first.

JULY 6
1 SAMUEL Ch1 vv1-28

DON'T GET WOUND UP!

Originally, in the Hebrew Scriptures, the First and Second Books of Samuel were just one book. When these Scriptures were translated into the Greek around 150BC, the books of Samuel and Kings were joined together to provide a complete history of the Israeli kingdoms. This one book then had four sections. Sometime later Samuel and Kings were separated again with two sections each.

Author: We can't be sure who wrote these historical books. Jewish tradition points to Samuel as the author of the first part of the book (chs 1-24) and the prophets Nathan and Gad had a hand in writing the rest.

Date: The lives of Samuel, Saul, and David were intertwined roughly around the turn of the first millennium BC.

Theme: The dominant theme in First Samuel is the transition from judgeship to kingship as the Kingdom of Israel became established. Old Testament history is a consistent series of signposts pointing to the Lord Jesus Christ. All the Old Testament lines of monarchy, priesthood and prophecy converge in him.

To date, Israel has been without solid leadership. God had raised up various champions and leaders through the time of the Judges as Israel staggered from one calamity to the next. With a lack of consistent leadership and with a polluted priesthood, and by ignoring God's word and disregarding his laws, the nation had plunged deeper into godlessness. But there was one family, and one woman in particular, who marked the turning point for Israel. Enter Hannah. It was to be her son, the prophet Samuel, who became God's chosen representative at the beginning of this new age. Samuel may not have been king, but he was the kingpin in this transition from anarchy to monarchy. Hannah was God's woman for that time but there was trouble, and we may learn this truth from the narrative: 'Don't get wound up!'

1 DON'T GET WOUND UP BY OTHERS' TAUNTS

Peninnah had been deliberately taunting Hannah about her incapacity to have children. Childlessness was viewed as a disgrace, and Elkanah's other wife caused hurtful provocation and irritation. We notice the hurt Hannah suffered, and we may identify with the sarcasm and caustic gibes, the relentless criticism and unjustified provocation, which are sometimes aimed at us. Yet Jesus knows all about it because he suffered it firsthand (1 Peter ch2 vv23-24). He died to become the Saviour of those who trust in him.

2 DON'T GET WOUND UP BY CHURCH TENSIONS

It's a sad fact that the deepest wounds can be sustained in the context of the church. Eli the priest misunderstood and jumped to wrong conclusions (v14). Eli represents many religious people who condemn others' weaknesses while turning a blind eye to glaring sins in their own lives. They point out misconduct in other families when there are huge problems in their own. Eli was a weak, over-indulgent office-holder with poor judgement and who represents similar weak, self-indulgent, self-righteous, undiscerning, religious people today. Hannah however was learning to be in tune with God's will.

3 DON'T GET WOUND UP BY GOD'S TIMING

The Lord had closed Hannah's womb (v5), but the Lord opened it in his time. God works to a different timetable than us and he sets his programme by a different timepiece than us. He chose the right time to answer Hannah's request (v19). The fact that *'the Lord remembered her'* doesn't mean that he had ever forgotten her. *'In the course of time'* – God's time - he answered (v20).

How can we avoid getting wound up in our Christian walk?

i] Be Patient: Nurture it and cultivate it as a part of the Spirit's fruit (Galatians ch5 v22).

ii] Be Prayerful: Though her heart was breaking, Hannah turned to God.

iii] Be Committed: Nothing was too great a sacrifice for her God, even her own son.

iv] Be Gracious: Hannah's name means 'woman of grace'. She had shown non-retaliation when provoked and had shown great grace in handling the situations at home and at Shiloh. God gives his grace to the humble (Proverbs ch3 v34).

Brokenness is frequently followed by fragrance. Let it be the fragrance of godliness.

JULY 7
1 SAMUEL Ch2.1-10

A SONG OF THE HEART

The Lord had been gracious to Hannah in providing her with a son – Samuel – meaning, 'heard of God' but sounding much like 'asked of God' (v20). In the person of Samuel Hannah's prayers and God's provision came together. Hannah's asking and God's answering found their fulfilment in the birth of Samuel. Samuel, the last of the judges and the first of the Major Prophets, was to be the God-appointed link between anarchy and monarchy. Hannah knew firsthand the power of prayer. So, if in ch1 Hannah had felt like screaming, by ch2 she felt like singing. Her heartfelt prayer is also a beautiful song. What type of song is it? Well, we could say it's a:

Classical Song: It covers some of the great themes that the songs of David, Zechariah, and Mary include, for example, God's greatness and grace.

Folk Song: Since it's rooted in Jewish culture, it would have probably been transmitted orally through the generations.

'Pop'ular Song: It deals with issues that the popular majority identify with, for example, hunger, poverty, need, loss, and even death.

Rock Song: In v2, Hannah proclaims, *'there is no Rock like our God'.*

Gospel Song: It looks forward to the good news of the coming king, the Lord's Anointed.

But Christians should also be able to sing Hannah's song as a:

1 FREEDOM SONG

Hannah's 'freedom song' expresses her great *'delight in (God's) deliverance'* (v1). These themes of freedom, deliverance, and salvation can also be observed in the Song of David (2 Samuel ch22 vv2, 3, 20), the Song of Mary (Luke ch1 vv47, 52), and the Song of Zechariah (Luke ch1 vv68, 69, 74). Mary's song, in particular, has several comparisons with Hannah's song so that this song of ch2 is sometimes referred to as 'The Magnificat of the Old Testament'. The Lord had visited Hannah in his saving power and had set her free. Jesus sacrificed freedom so that his believing people may have true freedom (John ch8 vv34-36).

Hannah is full of praise to the Lord for his gracious rescue. He is:

Our God: v2 *To whom will you compare Me?* (Isaiah ch40 v25);

Our Deliverer: v1. Charles Wesley (in his hymn beginning 'And can it be...') likens his conversion to Peter's escape from prison (Acts ch12): *'I rose, went forth, and followed thee'*;

Our Rock: Even Earth's greatest rocks are prone to cracking, crumbling, and erosion. But *'there is no Rock like our God'* (v2) who is everlasting and unaffected by the ravages of time and space.

We are reminded that he is all-knowing (v3), all-powerful (v4), and ever-faithful (v5) – he endures forever. He is also:

Our Sovereign (vv6-8), **Our Creator (**v8), and **Our Protector (**v9). What a great God he is!

2 WISDOM SONG

The Lord knows precisely what is best for his people. God's thoughts are greater than our thoughts. *'The Lord Almighty (is) wonderful in counsel and magnificent in wisdom'* (Isaiah ch28 v29). He is *'the only wise God'* (Romans ch16 v27). Hannah had confidence in God, knowing that he can make victors out of the defeated and winners out of losers. Notice the great contrasts in these verses: weak and strong, hungry and full, infertile and fertile, dead and alive, sick and well, poor and wealthy, humble and exalted. In God's wisdom, he effects radical changes: he brings about complete opposites. Perhaps you can identify with Hannah in the misery and disgrace of her victimisation (ch1). Praise God for the wisdom that directs our paths and guards our feet (v9).

3 KINGDOM SONG

Hannah's first son became a 'kingmaker'. Physical strength and military might, though, were not the secrets of victory (vv9-10). God will give strength to his king. Horns are symbols of strength and status (vv1, 10). In the immediate future, God's king would be David. But David would look forward to a King from his own line. He was inspired to compose psalms, which depict the deity of God's anointed Son (Psalm 2), his atoning death (Psalm 22), together with his resurrection, ascension, and future kingdom (Psalm 16, Psalm 24, Psalm 68). The word for *'anointed'* in Hebrew is *'Messiah'* and the Greek form is *'Christ'*, the Son of David (Isaiah ch9 v7). So in Hannah's song, there is already a hint of the coming Messiah, her Lord and her King.

JULY 8
1 SAMUEL Ch2.11-36

FIRST OR SECOND?

Like the large and ancient sequoia trees, that have become big and strong through enduring hundreds of storms and fires, great believers have developed deep roots through suffering. Hannah's faith in God and her love for his law had increased because of the storms of provocation and misjudgement that she had endured. She had become stronger and more immovable in her faith.

Hannah's family is contrasted with Eli's family in these verses. The growth and godliness of Hannah's young son Samuel is in stark contrast to the greed and godlessness of Eli's sons, Hophni and Phineas.

1 ELI PUT GOD SECOND

Eli was God's priest who ministered at the national worship centre in Shiloh. We know that Eli was an old man whose eyesight would fail (ch4 v15), but, more notably, his spiritual eyesight had failed. He had turned a blind eye to the wickedness of his sons, who were allowed to perform priestly duties at Shiloh (vv12, 17). The strict regulations governing the offering of sacrifices (for example, Leviticus ch7 vv28-34; Deuteronomy ch18 vv1-5) permitted priests to take a specific part of the boiled sacrifice as food. This was because the priestly tribe of Levi had no lands or livestock of their own, like the other tribes. This was God's way of providing for the priests whose exclusive duty was to serve God in the tabernacle. But Eli's sons preferred roasted meat and demanded a portion of it before it was properly sacrificed. They wanted the best share of the meat for themselves, hence the greatness of their sin (v17). Eli had put God second (v29) behind his sons, who had:

i] No Ministry: They went through the motions of a priesthood but they were alien to God. They went through the performance of acting like God's servants but they didn't know the Lord. The 'Hophni and Phineas syndrome' is perpetuated within Christendom today by its 'ministers without portfolio'. They show contempt for Christ's sacrifice on the cross by preaching a universalist gospel. They make sacrifices out of bread and wine. They turn the cross into a superstition. They accept the things that God rejects. They appoint women clergy to their ranks, ordain homosexuals and heretics, and are always plunging their *'three-pronged fork'* (v13) into the pot to try and serve the best for themselves. By asserting personal 'rights', they wrong God.

ii] No Morality: It was common knowledge that Eli's sons were guilty of *'wicked deeds'* (v23). Everyone knew about their unrepentant corruption.

iii] No Mediator: Hophni and Phineas had rejected God's Law, God's truth, God's requirements, and God's priest (in the form of Eli, their father). As they had disregarded the Lord, there could be no further hope for them. If men reject God's mercy and grace, then judgement is the only outcome. There was no confession, no repentance, and therefore no mediator. There is no hope for those who reject Christ, the one Mediator between God and men (1 Timothy ch2 v5).

2 HANNAH PUT GOD FIRST

Interlinked with the disturbing account of Eli's family's wickedness there was the quiet confirmation that God was working out his great plan in the life of Hannah and her young son, Samuel.

i] Samuel ministered before the Lord (v18)

Wearing the priestly garment, Samuel was trained to perform everyday menial duties. How much do we disdain the routine, behind-the-scenes, non-glamorous tasks of Christian service?

ii] Samuel grew up in the presence of the Lord (v21)

Could Hannah have wanted anything better for her son? As Christian parents, could we want anything more than children who are separated to God and consecrated to his service?

iii] Samuel grew in stature and favour with the Lord and men (v26)

Hannah didn't ask God for a son who would be clever, powerful, great or attractive. She wanted a son whose whole life would be given to the Lord (ch1 v28). Growth is not about healthiness but about holiness. Many want to grow in favour with men, but do not want to grow in *'stature and favour with the Lord'*. Self-pleasers and men-pleasers swell the ranks of pretend priests today, but few want to please God by performing his service humbly, sacrificially and with wholehearted obedience to his word.

JULY 9
1 SAMUEL Ch3.1-21

SPEAK, LORD, FOR YOUR SERVANT IS LISTENING

'Listening carefully', it would seem, is almost a dying art. The account of the boy Samuel, lying on his bed at night in the tabernacle at Shiloh, listening carefully to God's voice, has captured the imagination of numerous poets and artists. Probably the most memorable statement of the chapter is, *'Speak, Lord, for your servant is listening'*.

Observant students will notice the one-word difference between what Samuel was told to say and what he actually said. Samuel was no longer the toddler or the young child: he was probably a youth in his early teens. Eli, the old priest, had one final important lesson for Samuel to learn: to recognise the word of God and to submit to it.

But what does this account tell us about the word of God at that time?

1 THE WORD OF THE LORD WAS RARE (v1)

This represents the greatest tragedy of all in respect to Israel's condition at this time: God remained silent. He hadn't spoken to his people because they were under his judgement due to their spiritual lethargy and corrupt leadership. They had disregarded God's word, and that word was no longer communicated to the people. We may also say of our own nation: *'In these days the word of the Lord is rare'*. Of course, we don't mean that we don't have copies of God's word, the Bible. We have more copies than ever before. But while we may be encouraged to hear about the Bible's publication and its popularity, we are more interested in its power: the power that comes through God speaking. When God doesn't speak, there is great trouble. God's judgement is synonymous with his silence (see Amos ch8 vv11-12). If God's voice is rarely heard and obeyed in our nation, what about our individual hearts? Is God's word rare in our studies, our meditations, and our personal experience?

2 THE WORD OF THE LORD WAS REVEALED (vv7, 11-14, 21)

For Samuel, lying in his bed within the holy precincts, it was just another night, or so he thought! Probably towards the end of the night and just before dawn, while *'the lamp of God had not yet gone out'* (v3), Samuel encounters the Lord personally. He had been brought up in a godly home; he had been taught the Scriptures from infancy and he had spent years in the 'church'. Samuel knew many religious people and knew all about religious routines, but the sobering fact remains (v7): *'Samuel did not yet know the Lord'*. However, in standing at the boy's bedside, the Lord reveals his word to him, and in so doing, he graciously reveals himself. Verses 11-14 show that it was a massive, meaty message that the Lord gave the young boy. It was a solemn declaration of rebuke and judgement for Israel, and particularly for Samuel's master and mentor Eli and his family. God is not thwarted in his work. He prepares a young lad to be his mouthpiece. Samuel had come to know a lot that night, but, most significantly, he had come to know the Lord.

Notice how that understanding God's word and 'knowing the Lord' doesn't always mean that we move on to new, exciting, more glamorous ministries. Samuel continued with his daily tasks (v15). There were still the routine jobs to be done.

3 THE WORD OF THE LORD WAS RECOGNISED (vv16-18)

Eli recognised clearly that this was God's word to Samuel and through Samuel. There doesn't seem to be much to commend this old priest, but he still recognised the word of the Lord. Eli was ready to submit to God's will (v18), and he was ready to hand over to a younger worker without reluctance or jealousy. Not only did Eli recognise the word of the Lord, but all Israel did too (vv19-21). They later came to recognise that Samuel had become a tried and tested prophet of the Lord. They understood that the Lord *revealed himself to Samuel through his word* (v21). This continues to be the proof test of preachers and teachers today. The proof test is not in dreams, visions, innovative thoughts, inspirational ideas, theological qualifications, or academic successes. It's not whether they can make people laugh or whether they can draw large crowds and fill churches. The proof test is whether they are faithful servants of God telling forth the word of God without fear or favour.

In the final analysis it will depend on whether such a servant is able to say humbly and genuinely, *'Speak, Lord, for your servant is listening'.*

JULY 10
1 SAMUEL Ch4.1-22

ASKING THE RIGHT QUESTION

The Philistines had been the traditional enemies of Israel, probably arriving from the Aegean region in the twelfth or thirteenth centuries BC. They were wealthier and more advanced in technology than their Hebrew neighbours. They certainly were not the 'uncultured' and 'smugly conventional' people that the word 'Philistine' often describes today. The Philistines' technological superiority ensured that their migration to Canaan was not transient. They had come to stay. This chapter details a major conflict between the Israelites camped at Ebenezer and the Philistines camped at Aphek (v1):

i] God's People were Defeated

The elders recognised that this was more to do with the hand of God than the hand of the Philistines. They hadn't learned that disobedience to God equals defeat (Leviticus ch26 vv14, 17; Deuteronomy ch28 vv15, 25). Thirty-four thousand Israeli soldiers perished.

ii] God's Ark was Displaced

The Ark of the Covenant had been seized from the Most Holy Place at Shiloh and taken away by the Philistines. It was unthinkable that the Ark, which represented the presence and power of Jehovah, could be displaced and held in heathen hands (vv11, 17, 19, 21, 22). But it had become just a sign of superstition, a talisman, a lucky charm. The symbol had become the most important thing in Hebrew thinking. Superstition and idolatry have polluted Christianity and its teaching for hundreds of years. For many people, the cross is a similar 'lucky charm' to be worn as an amulet. 'Magic powers' are believed to be invested in other Christian emblems too, like so-called 'holy water', 'holy vestments', crosiers, sacraments of bread and wine, various statues, murals and relics, as well as the perceived powers of numerous 'saints'. Reverence for the symbol is no more than superstition.

iii] God's Glory had Departed

Eli's daughter-in-law, in her dying moments, had a keener perception than most (v22). The glory was not contained in the Ark, but both the Ark and glory had departed from Israel because God's people had rejected their God.

If ever Israel needed a 'reality check', it was now. Although they may not have got the answer right, they did ask the right question (v3): *'Why did the Lord bring defeat on us today?'*

In the sovereign purposes of God, there are many cases where Christians suffer apparent defeats, oppressions, humiliations, and losses. There are several reasons why we may face such calamities today:

1 TO FACE OUR SIN

Defeat may be a sign of God's judgement on our sin. Samson was defeated for not giving God his rightful place in his life (Judges ch16). Joshua's men were defeated at Ai (Joshua ch7) because they had been unfaithful and had violated God's covenant.

2 TO DEEPEN OUR HUMILITY

We may be brought low so that we repent and cast ourselves upon God. It has been said that the loveliest Christian is the lowliest Christian.

3 TO TEST OUR PATIENCE

'Patient endurance' (Revelation ch13 v10) is required in the face of death and defeat. Paul didn't give up or look for a quick-fix, easy-fit solution when he was faced with the experiences of 2 Corinthians ch11. God teaches patience and endurance in our trials, troubles, and tragedies.

4 TO INCREASE OUR PRAYING

Believers testify that they pray harder and more frequently when they are suffering. Their prayer life increases in tandem with distresses and defeats.

5 TO STRENGTHEN OUR FAITH

How much are we prone to trying to live our lives independent from God? Defeats often cause us to throw ourselves upon God. Joshua's soldiers experienced temporary defeat (Exodus ch17) when Moses' hands, holding the staff of God, drooped. The victorious Christian life is lived through a practical, everyday faith in Jesus Christ, our Saviour and our Champion. Trying to live a passive Christian life will spell defeat in spiritual terms. If you have suffered apparent defeat, get close to Jesus, who is the Mighty Victor.

JULY 11
1 SAMUEL Ch5.1-12

MORE THAN A HOT POTATO

The pagan Philistines had captured the *'Ark of the Lord's covenant'*. Worse than that, the light had gone out in Israel for the glory of God had departed. This chapter directs our attention to the contrast between the impotence of the Philistine god Dagon and the almighty strength of the one true and living God.

1 THE POWERLESS HANDS OF DAGON

Dagon was the chief god of the Philistines, although the Canaanites had been worshipping such a god before the Philistines arrived in the area. Dagon was believed to be the father of the other popular deity, Baal. The Ark was taken into the heathen temple at Ashdod and placed next to Dagon's image. Alongside the holy vessel, of which the Lord was rightly jealous, Dagon's image didn't stand a chance. By morning the image had been thrown on its face, symbolising the superior power of Jehovah.

Observe this pathetic but significant picture of the Philistines picking up their god from the floor and manhandling it back to its place again. How ridiculous can you get? Men and women are prepared to submit to a god of their own making, a god which is powerless to help itself. The following morning, the chief god was totally humiliated, lying smashed on the threshold. Dagon's contemporary cronies, whether Krishna, Allah, Sun Myung Moon, Baha'ullah, or whichever deity man can dream up, are powerless before Almighty God. The 'pick 'n' mix' assortment of faiths and religions today may temporarily satisfy certain needs for inner calm or social wellbeing, but they are powerless to provide forgiveness of sin and eternal life. In that sense, the images of Buddhism, Sikhism, Hinduism, Confucianism, Taoism, Shintoism, Zoroastrianism, New Ageism, and hundreds more - all lie prostrate with broken heads and hands.

2 THE POWERFUL HAND OF GOD

The Lord's hand was heavy upon Dagon and the Philistines (vv6, 7, 9, 11). The Ark of the Covenant had become more than a hot potato: it represented God's burning anger. The plague of tumours wasn't a coincidence. Throughout Scripture we observe God's powerful hand at work:

i] His Creating Hand: (Isaiah ch40 v12; ch48 vv12-13) Only the most ignorant or insensitive person could not be in awe of the power of a hurricane or a tornado, or the illuminations of an electrical storm, or the invincible force of a tsunami or volcanic eruption. The believer can say to the Lord, *We are all the work of your hand'* (Isaiah ch64 v8).

ii] His Providing Hand: (Psalm 145 v16) Whereas the closed fist is a sign of selfishness and anger, even violence, the open hand is a symbol of selflessness and generosity. We give with open hands, so how much more does God give out of his grace (Matthew ch7 v11)? Even the best that we give to God has been given by him first of all (1 Chronicles ch29 v16).

iii] His Guiding Hand: (Psalm 139 v10) David wasn't talking about the mystical 'guidance' that people claim today – the strange feelings, inner voices, subjective sensations, and compulsions. Such statements as 'God told me to do so and so' have been used to justify all kinds of questionable actions and activities. There is no guidance equal to the authority of Scripture.

iv] His Conquering Hand: Even the Philistines acknowledge that Israel's God had secured a great victory for them over the Egyptians (ch4 v8). Moses and Miriam sang a victory song about the power of the Lord's *'right hand'* (Exodus ch15 v6). Sometimes the nature of our 'victory' may not be too apparent. Locked in a gaol, evicted from your home, struggling to make ends meet, harassed at work, weakened through illness – may not always seem like being a conqueror. But it's precisely on those battlefields that the victorious life of a believer is observed (Romans ch8 v37).

v] His Saving Hand: (Exodus ch13 v3, Psalm 17 v7) Jesus reached out his hand to save Peter on the stormy lake (Matthew ch14 v31). In grace and love, the Lord continues to stretch out his powerful hand to save those who repent and believe.

vi] His Preserving Hand: (John ch10 v28) Jesus, the Good Shepherd, explained just how safe and secure his sheep were. Just in case anyone may be in doubt as to which are Christ's sheep, he says that they are the ones who listen to his voice and follow him. Is there anything that can ever prise the believer from the great grip of God's love (Romans ch8 vv38-39)? The broken hands of false deities provide no shelter or salvation. Only God!

JULY 12
1 SAMUEL Ch6.1-21

HOLINESS IS NOT HALOS

The Philistines were in the grip of an epidemic that affected the whole of their territory. *'The Lord's hand was heavy upon (them)'* because they had seized *'the Ark of the Covenant'* from the Israelites (v5). The plague, apparently carried by rats, produced tumours just like the Bubonic Plague, which afflicted Europe throughout the Middle Ages and caused the Black Death of 1348.

The Philistines were now desperate to get rid of the Ark and so consulted their own religious gurus (v2). Although Israel's exodus from Egypt had occurred four to five hundred years earlier, that mighty deliverance was still talked about (v6). Moses and Miriam had sung about Philistia's fear (Exodus ch15 vv13-14).

The gurus came up with a simple but ingenious plan to dispose of the Ark. Hitched up to a brand-new cart were two cows, patently unsuitable for pulling it as they had never been trained. Significantly, the cows were suckling calves and so their strong maternal instincts wouldn't normally allow separation from them. If God was responsible for the plague, then he would cause the cows to return to Israel with the Ark on the cart, and, it was reasoned, the golden models of tumours and rats might appease him. If the plague was just a coincidence, then the cows wouldn't leave their penned-up calves, let alone pull the cart in a straight line. The gold would remain with the Philistines.

The cows took the Ark straight to Beth Shemesh, and the Israelites rejoiced at the Ark's return. They sacrificed the cows and cart to God. But we must not overlook one striking truth: God's holiness doesn't fluctuate. He doesn't have one standard for one group of people and another standard for others. The men of Beth Shemesh tampered with the Ark and were struck down. The survivors cried out (v20), *'Who can stand in the presence of the Lord, this holy God?'*

God's holiness has often been referred to as 'God's central and supreme attribute'. This transcendent characteristic reveals conclusively that the Lord is the one true and living God. While mankind may attempt to copy other divine attributes in his invention of false gods, 'holiness' is never replicated. Who can stand before this holy God (Psalm 24 vv3-4; Psalm 76 v7; Malachi ch3 v2)? So how should we respond to his majestic holiness?

1 REVERE HIS HOLY NAME

The Philistines' bodies, gods and cities were under God's judgement. They tried to *'pay honour to Israel's God'* (v5) whose name is *'holy and awesome'* (Psalm 99 vv1-3; Psalm 111 v9). The world despises and blasphemes the Lord's holy name, which, to believers, is so precious. Isaiah confessed that he was *'a man of unclean lips'* (Isaiah ch6 v5) when confronted with a dazzling vision of God's glory and the seraphs calling to each other *'Holy, holy, holy is the Lord Almighty'*. Holiness pervades every facet of God's greatness and glory. He is exclusively and uniquely holy, unlike even the worshipping beings in his holy presence (Revelation ch15 v4). Let us revere his name in our worship and our conversations. Let us hallow his name in our prayers (Matthew ch6 v9).

2 RESPECT HIS HOLY LAW

The Philistines had learned the hard way to respect those things that belong to Almighty God, like the Ark of the Covenant with the Ten Commands inside. But the Israelites, too, had to re-learn the important lesson of respecting God's holy law. They were prohibited from seeing the Ark, let alone touching it. God had made his law very clear. But the men of Beth Shemesh had disregarded God's law and were suffering the consequences. What about us and our own land and people? How do we treat God's solemn commands (Exodus ch20 vv1-17)? How do we respect his word?

3 REFLECT HIS HOLY WILL

A life reflecting God's 'holy will' may be summarised in one word: 'holiness' (2 Timothy ch1 vv8-9). The life of holiness is not a life of quiet inactivity in which people wear halos and speak in hushed tones! 'Being holy' is simply 'being Godly'. God's holy will for our lives is that we become more like him. The dominant theme of the Book of Leviticus is 'holiness'. Israel's consecration to God was to be demonstrated in every microscopic detail of life (Leviticus ch11 v44). An unholy Christian is a contradiction in terms.

May we live to be holy, knowing that it's only the holy, pure in heart, who will see God (Matthew ch5 v8; Hebrews ch12 v14).

JULY 13
1 SAMUEL Ch7.1-17

THUS FAR HAS THE LORD HELPED US

Samuel led the Israelites to look away from themselves and look to God, who had helped them. He erected a monument of testimony – *'a stone set up between Mizpah and Shen'* (v12) – which Samuel called *'Ebenezer'* (literally, 'a stone of help'). Countless numbers of people have been able to testify to divine help (Psalm 118 vv6, 7; Psalm 121 v2). The stone which Samuel set up represented God's help to date. It reminded the Israelites that their resources were not restricted to earth. Israel's history had been one of God's gracious help.

1 UNEXPECTED HELP

'All the people of Israel mourned and sought after the Lord' (v2). That's certainly the right place to begin – a sorrow for sin and a search for God. People will insist on trying to 'find God' in their own way, using their own self-appointed methods. But God prescribes the way that any sinner should approach him (Psalm 51 v17). There's no room for haughtiness, only humility.

Samuel was Israel's intercessor (v5), leader (v6), and judge (vv15-17), and he laid down the conditions that would bring divine help (v3). Note that these were the conditions, not the causes. We are not provided with a formula, like some magic spell, where a few phrases can be uttered, or a few gesticulations demonstrated, and, hey presto, God brings his help like a genie out of a bottle. Yet to the people of God, who are described in Isaiah ch41 v8 as his servants, his chosen ones and his friends, the Lord says, *'I will strengthen you and help you'* (Isaiah ch41 v10).

Even as Samuel was still sacrificing, the Philistines prepared to attack (v10). But the Lord suddenly intervened as his voice boomed from the heavens (Psalm 29 vv3-9).

As the Lord's thunderous voice splits the heavens, the balance of power changes on a knife-edge. One minute the Israelites were scared to death (v7); the next minute the Philistines were panicking and running away (vv10-11). The Lord brings help to his people in unexpected ways, and yet in ways that are so appropriate and timely.

2 UNLIMITED HELP

Just as we cannot place a time on God's provision of help, we cannot place a limit on it either. Believers have continually derived great comfort from Paul's word to Philippian Christians (Philippians ch4 v19). The measure of those *'glorious riches'* is that they are *'in Christ Jesus'* – and that is immeasurable! All the resources to help us are vested in the Lord Jesus, whom God has exalted (Ephesians ch1 vv20-21) and *'appointed him to be head over everything for the church...'* (Ephesians ch1 v22). Jesus is head over everything, he has power over everything, and he has control over everything. His resources are inestimable and incomparable. What's more, they are for his church, his people. We have everything we need in Christ. He is the dearest treasure and in him is unlimited help.

One of the greatest demonstrations of supernatural help was at the tomb of Lazarus. Martha knew that nothing is too hard for God and she trusted in Jesus (John ch11 vv21-22). Even some of the crowd believed that Jesus could have helped (v37) but their faith stopped short of believing that he could provide unlimited help. Jesus is *'the resurrection and the life'* and he is the One who can call corpses from their tombs.

Jesus' help may be unlimited, but if there's any limit at all, it's in the size of our faith and the earnestness of our prayers. How much do we restrict God's help (James ch4 v2)?

3 UNMERITED HELP

Any help that Israel received from the Lord was undeserved and unmerited. God's people are always thoroughly indebted to his grace. Samuel and the Israelites continued to experience God's grace (v13) as his divine hand was against the Philistines. All the towns and territory, which the Philistines had seized from Israel, were returned. There was even peace between Israel and the Amorites (v14).

In an age of monuments, memorials, and memorabilia, where plaques, honours, and trophies abound, we should not forget to mark every stage of our lives with an 'Ebenezer'. Such a milestone should cause us to offer gratitude, praise, and worship. We should also look for an increase in our love and faith, as well as spurring us on to greater prayerfulness, consecration, and zeal for God, knowing that up to this precise point, he has helped us.

JULY 14
1 SAMUEL Ch8.1-22

WE WANT TO BE LIKE EVERYONE ELSE

The Israelites living in Canaan around 1000BC had been looking at their pagan neighbours (most of whom were their enemies) and they felt inferior! These very special people (whose God was the one, true and living God, who had routed the Philistines in ch7.10) wanted to be like the pagan Philistines, Moabites, Ammonites, Edomites, and Midianites, whose gods are of wood and stone. In what way did Israel want 'to keep up with the Joneses'? All the other nations were led by kings. Yet in wanting a king they were rejecting the Lord God who was Israel's mighty King (v7).

The Case for a King:

The elders had made three points:

1] They felt that Samuel (probably in his sixties) was too old to lead Israel. They wanted someone more youthful, dynamic, and contemporary. Samuel was a reminder of a previous generation. But things had moved on. Canaan was entering the new technological age of a new millennium. Already, the Philistines were well ahead in the Iron Age, and there was a very real danger of Israel lagging behind. They needed to 'keep in step with the times'. The spiritual leadership of the former generation wasn't suited to the New Age. Samuel just wasn't funky enough! They needed to be contemporary in their society, their government and their religion.

2] Samuel's sons were not godly men. Gold had come before God in their priorities.

3] Israel wanted to be like the other nations with a king to lead them and to fight for them. They wanted a hero, a champion, a celebrity before whom all the people could applaud and follow.

The Cost of a King:

The Israelites were left under no illusion as to what a monarchy would inflict upon them. Samuel spelt it out in terms of servants, property, produce, and livestock. A king would make a huge impact on everyone's life, and each person must contribute to bearing the cost. But the people refused to listen (v19). They wanted a king just like everyone else.

From an early age, people are conditioned to follow fashion and to conform to popular trends, views, and activities. Non-conformists are regarded as odd, maverick, or even eccentric. It's just so much easier to be like everyone else. Yet from the days of Abraham, God wanted a distinctive people: one that was unique, separate, set apart, and holy. God's people must recognise that they are different from the world:

1 THE LORD IS THEIR KING

Israel wanted a man from their own number who would be king rather than he who is the King of Heaven and Earth (ch12 v12). Do we forget that Jesus Christ is our King (John ch1 v49; Revelation ch17 v14)? The reign of Christ is a distinctive feature in the life of a believer. Such a testimony can be costly when we show disregard for the world's idols and deities, its priorities and its values.

2 THE BIBLE IS THEIR AUTHORITY

The people of Israel were given God's word as their authority. It came in the form of the Law of Moses and also through the teachings and prophecies of men like Samuel. Samuel spoke on behalf of the Lord (v10) and was ranked alongside Moses as the Lord's authoritative mouthpiece (Psalm 99 v6). Israel was very different from the world because they were bound by God's word. Christians today are similarly under the authority of the Bible, which is the final arbiter of truth and the mandate for Christian living. Sadly, too many professing Christians want to be like everyone else and be influenced by friends, fashion, philosophy, and feelings rather than submit to the word of God.

3 THE CHURCH IS THEIR FAMILY

Israel, as God's Old Testament family, had family commitments, family duties, and family responsibilities. Believers today have similar obligations. For some, the church family is a convenience where they thrive on its benefits, make the most of its privileges, and use its many resources. But they don't want to contribute. They want to be like everyone else – without obligations and commitments. A Christian's service and individual ministry within the church may take various forms – from public to personal, from practical to spiritual – but there is no opt-out clause for a true disciple of Jesus.

Such a follower should be like Jesus and not like everyone else.

JULY 15
1 SAMUEL Ch9.1-27

THE TALE OF THE LOST DONKEYS

We are introduced to a powerful and influential family from the tribe of Benjamin. The Benjamites were one of the twelve Israeli tribes settling in the land of Canaan. We know from the second census recorded in Numbers ch1 v37 and ch26 v41 that there were in excess of forty-five thousand Benjamites, which would have increased in the three hundred years or so following the census. Donkeys represented a chunk of Kish's business (compare Job ch1 v3), but they had disappeared. Kish's son, Saul, and a servant were sent to find them. But Saul wasn't just another donkey-herder:

Saul was Israel's Distinguished: He was physically impressive and unequalled (v2). Saul stood out in a crowd, quite literally.

Saul was Israel's Deliverer: Samuel had already been primed by God regarding Saul's visit. The young man had been earmarked by God to *'deliver'* (v16) his people.

Saul was Israel's Desire: (v20) Israel was eagerly awaiting Saul's appointment as their king. They desired a monarch, and they had made it clear that God's Kingship wasn't enough. They wanted a king like everyone else but, by desiring Saul, Israel had revealed her disaffection for the Lord.

For Kish and Saul and their family, the loss of the donkeys could have been a huge setback. However, we notice that 'the tale of the lost donkeys' features within God's providential plan. Saul is on a journey: a journey of life, whose Route Planner is God.

1 FROM LOSS TO GAIN

Saul is taken from the loss of donkeys to the gain of God's blessing. Not only did Samuel tell Saul that the donkeys had been found (v20), but that Saul would become *'leader over (God's) inheritance'* (ch10 v1). Even though the loss of a donkey herd was a big thing at the time, the gain of God's purpose far outweighs any loss. We often mourn losses without rejoicing in the blessings of God's grace.

- Abraham lost his home to gain God's promised land.

- Joseph lost his family comforts to gain rulership in Egypt.

- Job lost his sons, daughters, and livestock to eventually gain double prosperity.

- Matthew lost a lucrative tax collecting business to be one of Jesus' Twelve.

- A boy lost five loaves and two fish to gain Jesus' material and spiritual provision.

Paul once considered his Jewish privileges and pedigree to be of great value (Philippians ch3 vv5-6), but he considered everything a loss compared to gaining Christ (Philippians ch3 vv7-8).

The lost donkeys may represent for us a lost opportunity, a lost business, a lost job, a lost income, lost home, lost friends and even lost health. But the believer can never lose Christ and, praise God, he can never lose us.

Is there anything to compare to gaining Jesus as Friend, Saviour, Advocate and King?

2 FROM DISAPPOINTMENT TO APPOINTMENT

Saul and his servant were obviously disappointed at not finding the donkeys (v5). But the servant remembered that a *'man of God'* (v6), a *'prophet'*, a *'seer'* (v9) lived nearby. Samuel would be able to tell them where their donkeys were. They met him coming towards them as they entered Ramah. Samuel had been prepared for this divine appointment twenty-four hours earlier (vv15-17). God's providence would lead Saul from disappointment to appointment. If we are truly trusting God's ways, then we shall not be disappointed (Psalm 22 v5). Disappointment overwhelms us when we are expecting God to work out his purposes in *our* way. Perhaps we had expected God to bless in a particular way (conversions, baptisms, memberships, ministries or leadership) and we are racked with disappointment. Yet in the middle of Saul's disappointment, God had already prepared Saul's appointment. While we wallow in our disappointment, God is sovereignly at work fulfilling his promises and purposes.

3 FROM LEAST TO GREATEST

Saul's meteoric rise from relative obscurity to the throne of Israel is announced. God specialises in taking the weakest, smallest, and lowliest and transforming them into powerful instruments (1 Corinthians ch1 vv27-29). Saul may have come from the humblest of origins, but he was destined for God's use. Prosperity is preceded by humility.

JULY 16
1 SAMUEL Ch10.1-27

GOD CHANGES HEARTS

The phrase *'life-changing experience'* is sometimes overused, but it's not overused in respect to a person who becomes a believer through faith in the Lord Jesus Christ. A tremendous change occurs, and that change should be noticeable.

Saul, the young donkey-herder from the smallest tribe and the least clan, had been chosen by God to be Israel's first king. In ch9 we read of Saul's appointing, and in ch10 we read of his anointing.

Samuel said, *'You will be changed into a different person'* (v6).

'As Saul turned to leave Samuel, God changed Saul's heart' (v9).

Whatever the 'change' represented, it had been a sovereign work of God. It was God who had effected the change by his Spirit. Certainly, it wasn't to do with Saul's own efforts or initiative. God stepped into Saul's life and found him when he wasn't even looking for God. As we look at Saul after his 'change of heart', we note some of the things which he experienced, and we may make a comparison with the new things that a believer experiences following conversion.

1 NEW ABILITIES

When the Spirit of God came upon Saul as he joined a *'procession of prophets'* (v10), he worshipped and prophesied with them. Such was this unnatural, unexpected phenomenon that Saul's friends and acquaintances were asking what had happened to him (v11). Is this anything different from the questions that friends, family, and acquaintances ask today when a person becomes a Christian?

Saul was Israel's first appointed king, and God would provide him with all the abilities necessary to fulfil that office. A new believer doesn't always immediately become an accomplished preacher or public speaker. He doesn't transform instantly into a competent Bible teacher, linguist, musician, or author. But God does provide all the ability necessary to do the tasks that he assigns. Our new abilities should begin with usability, followed by capability, closely succeeded by stability and availability.

2 NEW PRIORITIES

Up until now, the place of God and the people of God hadn't featured much in Saul's life. It seemed that Saul didn't know that Israel's great spiritual leader, Samuel, lived reasonably close. Saul also wanted to go to *'the high place'* (v13) which had become the place of worship between the days of the tabernacle and the building of the temple.

Although 'high places' were frequently used for pagan worship, Samuel and other godly people had commandeered certain such places for the worship of the Lord. One of the great indicators that a person has become a true believer is that they will want to be with the Lord's people and at the places of worship.

3 NEW OPPORTUNITIES

In Service:

Saul was God's chosen man for the ministry of leading Israel (v24). God provides each of his people – those whose hearts he has changed – with opportunities to serve him. 'To serve' is 'to minister' and each believer has a ministry to perform for the glory of God (1 Corinthians ch10 v31). Saul had been appointed to the highest office in Israel so that he may serve Israel – to lead her, defend her, care for her, and provide for her.

In Fellowship:

What a great encouragement these men must have been to Saul (v26). They were united in a common desire and common purpose because they had received this common experience – God had touched their hearts. The quality of our horizontal relationships is dependent upon the quality of our vertical relationships. We cannot have real fellowship with one another if our communion with God is marred.

4 NEW DIFFICULTIES

When God changes hearts, there will always be opposition and hostility (v27). Man is fundamentally at war with God, and any work of God's grace is viewed as 'fair game' for God's adversaries. Even families are divided over the Person of Jesus Christ (Luke ch12 vv49-53). By being born into God's heavenly family, we are often divided from members of our own earthly families. The division is like a sword (Matthew ch10 v34). Jesus' reaction to ridicule (1 Peter ch2 v23) and Saul's reaction to the troublemakers' despising (v27) may help us in our response to similar hostility and insults.

JULY 17
1 SAMUEL Ch11.1-15

SIGNIFICANT DAYS

The tribal territory, which stretched across the middle of the land of Canaan, from the Mediterranean coast in the west and across the River Jordan and out to the east, was Manasseh. Located within Manasseh, about ten miles east of Jordan and twenty-five miles south of Galilee, was the city of Jabesh Gilead. Not far to the south of this city was a small territory possessed by the Ammonites, who were distantly related to Israel. The Ammonites were mainly a nomadic people with 'itchy feet' and 'green eyes'. They always wanted what didn't belong to them. They were also very aggressive and hostile. Except for one brief period during David's reign, their relationship with Israel was usually associated with brutality and aggression.

Nahash had besieged Jabesh Gilead, giving the Israelites two stark options: to surrender and have their right eyes removed, or to be killed. The elders of the city wanted to buy some time, and the Ammonites, confident of their superiority, granted a seven-day waiting period. But the next seven days included two important and highly significant days for Israel.

1 MAYDAY – THE DAY OF DISTRESS

'Mayday' is the universally recognised distress call (from *'M'aidez'*: 'Come, help me'). It's an urgent call for immediate assistance. That was the call that went out from Jabesh Gilead. The people of Gibeah were grieved over the helpless plight of their desperate Jewish brothers (v4). What could they do? There was a feeling of complete helplessness in which they were overcome by fear or sorrow, or both.

Israel was no stranger to distress over the centuries, which had been compounded by their obstinacy and their refusal of God's rescuers – his prophets, priests and, later, kings (Matthew ch23 v34).

In the New Testament, Jesus was overwhelmed with concern about the imminent danger that Israel was in (Matthew ch23 v37). Jesus could save Israel from the gathering storm of God's judgement, but they were *'not willing'*. They would not listen to him and repent. *'Unless you repent, you too will all perish'* (Luke ch13 v5). Just like stubborn Jerusalem, which rejected and crucified God's Son, people today continue to resist and reject the good news about Jesus.

Many may seek refuge and help for their distressed souls in relationships and religions, or in therapies and theologies. But complete satisfaction and salvation are only found in Jesus.

Those who recognise their helplessness, like the citizens of Jabesh Gilead, should turn to Christ in repentance and faith. Call on him, believing. 'Save our souls' should be the 'Mayday' of everyone who is distressed.

2 D-DAY – THE DAY OF DELIVERANCE

Saul had returned to his work in the fields after the life-changing experience of ch10 when he had been anointed first king of Israel. But even when Saul had been chosen, he went into hiding and they needed the Lord's help to locate him again (ch10 v22). Now he's back on the farm when there was a nation to lead. When he was told the news about Jabesh Gilead, Saul was consumed with a righteous anger (v6). The threat of losing their livelihoods forced three hundred and thirty thousand men to muster against Jabesh Gilead. There would be a rescue at high noon (v9).

Israel might have claimed the victory except that Saul demonstrated maturity and wisdom by giving God the glory (v13). He wanted everyone to know that 'D-Day' belonged to God. He was the Deliverer who had sprung to Israel's aid. If we marvel at the grace that God exercised towards Israel, how much greater is the grace that he lavishes upon each and every one he saves (Ephesians ch2 vv4-5).

Saul later became disobedient and discredited, but at this point he illustrates grace is sparing those Israelites who had opposed him (v13).

In the context of grace, the word 'deserve' is out of place. None of us deserves anything from God. We are completely undeserving.

Verses 14-15 conclude the chapter with Saul's coronation. Sadly, it wasn't the Lord's kingship that they were affirming. They had wanted a king like their pagan neighbours, and God had acceded to their request. But the path of Saul's kingship would not run smooth. Submission to Jesus Christ the King is demanded of all who follow him.

JULY 18
1 SAMUEL Ch12.1-25

CONSIDER THE GREAT THINGS HE HAS DONE FOR YOU

If you were asked to produce a list of the four greatest things in the world, it might be interesting to know what would be on your list.

In this chapter there are listed at least four great things that the Lord has done for Israel (v24). Saul had just been crowned first king of Israel, and it was at this high point in Israel's chequered history that Samuel underlines God's faithfulness towards Israel and the great things he has done for them.

1 HE HAD SENT GREAT LEADERS

Samuel is not boasting about his own integrity as God's chosen leader, but he wants Israel to affirm that he is not guilty of any wrongdoing. In vv1-5 we are provided with the image of a courtroom scene and a legal inquiry in which Samuel takes the stand. Samuel's behaviour has been above reproach. His life is open to public scrutiny, and he has nothing to fear. As Christians, our public conduct should be exemplary and we should have nothing to fear from our critics' pointing fingers or accusatory lips. Israel had not only been provided with a great leader in Samuel, but also in:

Moses and Aaron: (v8) Just in case Israel might boast in *their* appointing of Moses and Aaron to lead them, Samuel emphasises that *'the Lord sent'* them. They were quite literally 'Godsends'.

Gideon: (v11) The Lord sent Gideon too (or 'Jerub-Baal', which was the name he had been given after he had opposed the pagan god Baal in Judges ch6 vv28-32). Here was a man whom God had called from obscurity to become a great champion over the Midianites.

Barak: Barak raised an army of a hundred thousand men, who had been disarmed by the Canaanites, to rout the enemy's nine hundred iron chariots and heavily armed troops. Sisera was finally 'nailed' by a woman (Judges ch4). Barak's name is listed among those who achieved great things by faith (Hebrews ch11).

Jephthah: Here is another name that appears on the 'Hebrews 11' list of the faithful. Though he had been an outcast, he was appointed to secure a great victory over the Ammonites (Judges chs10-12).

2 HE HAD PROVIDED GREAT DELIVERANCE

From the Egyptians: (v8) God's rescue of Israel from the Egyptians has entered Hebrew history as the greatest of all deliverances. Nothing compares with the 'Great Escape' when probably upwards of two million Hebrews exited Egypt overnight through the Red Sea. God was the Architect of that 'Great Escape'. His planning and power created the Exodus, which illustrates so graphically every believer's deliverance from Satan and sin through the light of the gospel and the power of the cross.

410

From the Canaanites: (vv9-11) The Philistines and Moabites represent the heathen enemies that Israel constantly encountered, and which were never fully subdued.

From the Ammonites: (vv12-13) Saul's first victory was against the Ammonites (ch11).

Each believer can testify to the greatest deliverance of all. God not only delivers from the sentence of sin but the stranglehold of sin as well.

3 HE HAD DEMONSTRATED GREAT POWER

(vv16-18) To see a thunderstorm in the dry months of harvest was something unique and awesome: a clear sign from God. *'Stand still and see this great thing...'* Maybe we don't recognise the great things that God is doing in his world today because we don't stand still and contemplate. Note how he continues to build his church, even in the middle of terrible suffering and persecution. Daily, he is saving his people.

4 HE HAD GIVEN GREAT ASSURANCE

(vv20-22) The Lord will not forsake those who truly belong to him. God's electing love doesn't depend on his people's merits. The security of God's people is not dependent on their efforts. The honour of God's own name is at stake (v22). Therefore, if you belong to him:

Be Prayerful: (v23) For God's people. It's a sin not to pray for others.

Be Fearful: (v24) Put God first in everything – honour him, revere him, obey him.

Be Faithful: (v24) Genuine fearfulness will automatically produce faithfulness.

Be Thoughtful: (v24) Meditate, consider, contemplate, and reflect on the great things that God has done for you.

THIS IS PRAYER... NOT!

As for me, far be it from me that I should sin against the Lord

by failing to pray for you.

1 Samuel ch12 v23

When we pause with heads bowed, to start praying out loud,

And our thoughts and opinions we air;

Clever points that we make, for our own ego's sake,

Maybe politics, yes, but not prayer.

When attempting to pray, and the words that we say,

Are but eulogies fine and so fair;

To the friends we impress by the praise we express

May be flattery, yes, but not prayer.

Is it prayer that we use just to broadcast some news,

Or an urgent announcement to share?

Yet the lists we compose and the things we disclose,

Maybe bulletins, yes, but not prayer.

If the prayer meeting's threat is the trite sermonette,

Or the lesson we proudly prepare;

Though it's truth that we teach, through our eloquent speech -

Timely homily, yes, but not prayer.

Even lines we rehearse, while excelling in verse,

May have little with which to compare;

If our greatest concern is the lyrics we learn,

Then it's poetry, yes, but not prayer.

Meeting with the church folk, as we seek to invoke,

And a fault is rebuked without care;

While pretending to pray, we go out of our way

To give reprimand, yes, but not prayer.

So when marching apace to the throne of God's grace,

And petitions and praises declare.

Let's be sure that his name is our singular aim

And we've no other motive but prayer.

Geoff Fox

JULY 19
1 SAMUEL Ch13.1-23

A MAN AFTER GOD'S OWN HEART

One can easily imagine how that Jewish mothers, three thousand years ago, would have shared fears for their sons serving with Saul in his army because they were so ill-equipped. The reason for their lack of proper army equipment was that the Philistines had forcibly deprived them of the military advantages of the new technological Iron Age. Hebrews even had to pay a heavy tax just to get their farm implements sharpened (v21).

Saul's army had been reduced from three thousand to six hundred (v15), and they only had two spears and swords among all of them (v22)! God's people were once more humiliated by their enemies because Israel's first king had not obeyed the Lord. Samuel came with a pronouncement of judgement upon Israel's premier, which included the announcement that God had *'sought out a man after his own heart'* (v13).

God had already chosen a boy with desires, priorities, and preferences like his own. This boy was to be a man after God's own heart. From the negative things we observe about Saul in this chapter, we may conclude three things about a heart that is like God's.

1 A HEART THAT LOVES GOD'S WORD

Sadly, Saul had grown cold towards God's word. He didn't love it any longer. God's word, at that time, came via God's prophets. Samuel was such a messenger (ch3 v20) but Saul had reached the stage where he couldn't wait for God's word through Samuel.

When the 'chips are down' God's word is often disregarded. For Saul's weaponless army that were in hiding from the advancing Philistines, the prospect was imminent doom (v5). Samuel had explained to Saul (ch10 v8) that he would come to Gilgal and offer the burnt offerings and fellowship offerings. Saul was to wait until Samuel came, who would then tell him what to do. But Saul was impatient and acted in disobedience. Although Samuel's arrival had been delayed, there was no justification for disobeying God's word. Like Saul, there are those who continue to show contempt and disregard for the Bible. Even in so-called evangelical churches the Bible is often deliberately misquoted out of context or quoted in a joke! How can we claim to be men and women after God's own heart if we treat God's word in such a casual and cavalier fashion?

For Saul at Gilgal, times had changed. He was prepared to disregard God's word in an effort to be contemporary and relevant (v14). He was ready to reinterpret it according to his own superstitious faith. Do we love God's word because it's the word of our loving God and Father, or do we regard the Bible as being manipulated and reinterpreted for our times?

2 A HEART THAT EXALTS GOD'S NAME

'Blowing one's own trumpet' is an expression that we use to describe someone who is full of pride and boasting. Saul had a trumpet blown throughout the land proclaiming that he had attacked the Philistine outpost (v4), although it was in fact Jonathan's achievement. Jonathan's success was showing up his father's failure, even though the royal press release gave the king the credit. A heart that is attuned to God's heart will love to make much of the Lord's great name as Saul's successor did (Psalm 5 v11; Psalm 34 vv1-3). One of the most wonderful things that we can do in our worship is to exalt the name of God's one and only Son, and to make much of him. Christ is the radiance of God's glory and represents him exactly (Hebrews ch1 v3). Jesus Christ is the ultimate revelation of God (John ch1 v18). He is the Bible's glorious theme. He is the Axis of Creation; the Alpha and Omega of eternity; the Focal Point of all our worship. Let his name be magnified!

3 A HEART THAT HONOURS GOD'S TRUTH

Saul was full of excuses (v11) and he was prepared to compromise the truth to justify his own actions. Saul's successor would say that God desires *'truth in the inward parts'* (Psalm 51 v6). If our hearts are not like God's heart in respect to truthfulness and integrity, then we are in danger of spawning all kinds of deceptions, distortions, and duplicity. Believers who walk in the light have their lives characterised by truth (John ch3 v21) and that truth is completely revealed in Jesus (John ch1 v17). A person, whose heart is compared to God's heart, will have a passion for living according to the truth. Let us be those who tell the truth about God by reflecting his likeness and by sharing his heart.

JULY 20
1 SAMUEL Ch14.1-52

NOTHING CAN HINDER THE LORD

Julia Howes's famous *'Battle Hymn of the Republic'* conveys the powerful message that *'our God is marching on'*; that he strides ahead with his divine plans without shortening a step or missing a beat. God will not be deflected in his movements or judgements. He will never be forced to amend his promises or adjust his purposes. He marches through the corridors of history, across the battlefields of continents, and through the governments of nations, totally unchecked and unimpeded. Our God is marching on! That may well be the thought that is in Jonathan's mind when he summoned his young armour-bearer to accompany him on his daring mission to attack the Philistine outpost (v6).

God will not be influenced by spurious philosophies, or persuaded by powerful arguments, or intimidated by vicious threats, or halted by superior forces. Nothing can hinder him in his sovereign movements. This is the truth that we need to be reassured about today. If we listen to various broadcasts, speeches, articles, and even some preaching, we are apt to think that God is some kind of pawn or puppet to be manipulated by mankind. Nothing can be further from the truth. Nothing can ever deflect him from his mission. Our Almighty God is absolutely unstoppable.

1 FEARFULNESS CANNOT HINDER THE LORD

Israel had been terrorised by Philistia's military capability and superior strength. Two thousand four hundred troops had deserted Saul's army, leaving him with only six hundred soldiers quaking in their boots (ch13 v7). We may all experience fear at some point. But fear can paralyse a believer's ministry and deny a particular blessing. Fear can hinder prayerfulness and restrict usefulness, but it doesn't stop God.

2 FEWNESS CANNOT HINDER THE LORD

Saul was worried about his depleted army, but Jonathan showed that God could overthrow vast numbers through just two men who trusted in the Lord. God honoured the courage and faith that trusted in his covenantal promises (for example, Leviticus ch26 vv6-8). God frequently accomplishes his purposes through 'the few' so that men will not boast in their own resources. Think of God's global purposes achieved through just eight people (Genesis ch6 vv17-18). The fewness of Noah's family didn't hinder the Lord. Remember Gideon whose forces were deliberately cut from thirty-two thousand to three hundred in order to defeat the numberless Midianites (Judges ch7). Nebuchadnezzar and his government were challenged by the faith of just three brave men (Daniel ch3 v12) and Elisha told his servant, when surrounded by a great army, that *'those who are with us are more than those who are with them'* (2 Kings ch6 v16).

We may bemoan the fact that there are never enough helpers in the Lord's work, but his work in our church and nation is ultimately not hindered because of few numbers. He never has to postpone or cancel his plans.

You may feel at times that you are in the smallest of minorities, but do you think that hinders God (Joshua ch23 v10; Romans ch8 v31)?

3 FOOLISHNESS CANNOT HINDER THE LORD

Have you heard those who say foolish things just to try and impress people with their 'spirituality'? Saul seemed to have attempted to make up for his deficiencies by pronouncing a daring oath (v24). Such a statement may have sounded impressive, but the imposed fast on his troops and the calling for the Ark of God (v18) was more superstition than religion. Saul was a 'control freak' like those today who get their kicks out of trying to dominate and manipulate people's families, careers, finances, time, marriages and even churches. Jonathan showed how to deal with such 'control freaks'.

1) Don't compromise your faith! He wasn't going to humour Saul by giving in to him.

2) Don't put God second! He was ready to jeopardise everything to put God first.

4 FAITHLESSNESS CANNOT HINDER THE LORD

We may be surprised to read of Saul's achievements (vv47-48), but God accomplished his purposes for Israel despite Saul's lack of faith and obedience. Saul displeased the Lord because he lacked faith (Hebrews ch11 v6). God works today to build his church, to equip his people, to defend his testimony, to provide for his children, to spread his word and to reveal his Son. Faith may be thin on the ground, but nothing can hinder the Lord.

JULY 21
1 SAMUEL Ch15.1-35

WHAT GOD WANTS

'Beware of the sheep!' may have been a good warning to those who had tried to maltreat God's flock, the people of Israel. God had exercised special care and supervision over his people as their Shepherd (Genesis ch48 v15; ch49 v24, Psalm 80 v1, Isaiah ch40 v11). God led his flock out of Egypt and through the desert, where they had been attacked by the Amalekites in Rephidim (Exodus ch17). These predators had been particularly cruel in attacking the weak and vulnerable (Deuteronomy ch25 vv17-19). The Amalekites picked off the stragglers as a lion picks off its prey. So God issued a decree that these enemies of Israel would be annihilated, and in this chapter, the 'judgement day' arrives (vv2-3). The Lord is compassionate, gracious, loving, and slow to anger, but *'he does not leave the guilty unpunished'* (Exodus ch34 vv6-7). If anyone dares to charge God with being intolerant, unforgiving, spiteful, and sadistic, then they haven't read the Bible (see Romans ch5 v8; 2 Corinthians ch5 v21; Isaiah ch53 vv3-5; 2 Peter ch3 v9).

For the Amalekites, God had shown four hundred years of patience, but they had not turned to him in repentance and faith. God then sent Saul on a mission to execute divine vengeance on the Amalekites. God told Saul to *'totally destroy everything'* (v3) but Saul conducted a partial destruction. We are faced with these three words as we contemplate God's instructions and Saul's actions: 'What God wants'.

These three words should dominate our lives.

1 GOD WANTS HUMILITY NOT NOBILITY

In Saul's eyes and in the eyes of the people, Saul was a total success, but in God's eyes, he was a complete failure. Saul built a monument *'in his own honour'* (v12). Like many today, Saul was full of his own self-esteem and self-importance. Yet God wants humility (Micah ch6 v8; James ch4 v10; 1 Peter ch5 v5). John Baptist, the greatest of the Old Testament prophets, could have had a good reason for boasting and pride. But he knew the recipe for walking with God. John said of Jesus (John ch3 v30): *'He must become greater: I must become less'.* That was God's will for John, and it is God's will for us too. Jesus himself is the complete definition and perfect example of humility.

Saul wanted a monument when he should have wanted abasement. How much does pride hinder our usefulness for the Lord? How much does loftiness and haughtiness nullify our effectiveness in God's service? Saul was seeking honour when he should have been seeking humility.

2 GOD WANTS OBEDIENCE, NOT SACRIFICE

God had told Saul to totally destroy everything that belonged to the Amalekites (v3) but *'they were unwilling to destroy completely'* (v9). Saul said that he had carried out the Lord's instructions (v13), but God said that he hadn't (v11). Saul tries to offload the blame onto his soldiers (v15), but Samuel didn't want to hear Saul's pathetic excuses. Some Christians excuse themselves from certain of God's instructions and expectations by

418

pointing to their commitment to their church, or to their giving, or even to their evangelism. But God demands obedience first and foremost.

3 GOD WANTS TRUTH NOT FALSEHOOD

Notice the development of Saul's falsehood in this narrative:

i] Making the Claim:

It was a blatant lie before God and his servant.

ii] Shifting the Blame:

Saul blamed his soldiers (v15) and his people (v24).

iii] Justifying the Aim:

(v21) He said that he had disobeyed for God's benefit anyway!

How often do we try and justify a sinful course of action or dereliction of Christian duty by claiming it's for God's work anyway? We may excuse the putting of service and sacrifice before obedience, yet God wants truth (Psalm 51 v6).

Jesus' life was characterised by humility, obedience and truth. His great humiliation began at his conception and concluded at his ascension. He came to do his Father's will (Hebrews ch10 vv5-7). No other consideration trumped this pre-eminent objective for Jesus. It was only 'what God wants'.

Saul had not bothered about what God wants but the divine sentence was carried out eventually (v33). The Lord always has the last word. He will forever have what he wants. Our preoccupation should be to know and to do what God wants.

JULY 22
1 SAMUEL Ch16.1-23

GOD'S CHOICE

When we consider the way in which the world chooses its leaders, it's not surprising that those choices are often seriously flawed. By contrast, we would expect God's choices to be perfect: that our sovereign and all-knowing God would choose according to his perfect knowledge, wisdom and power.

So what happened in Saul's case? Did God get it wrong? Of course not!

The whole of First Samuel is to do with the establishing of the kingship in Israel. They wanted a royal champion to head up their army and be a figurehead of unity and security within the nation. However, there was a great spiritual dimension to all of this. It wasn't just that Israel wanted a *human* king: they had rejected their *heavenly* King.

Israel's desire for a monarchy represented its denial of theocracy. They wanted a man instead of God.

God, in his grace and patience, had provided Israel with its first king, Saul. But Saul hadn't hoodwinked God, nor had God grudgingly conceded to Israel's wishes. God knew about Saul's weaknesses and failings from the start. He knew that Saul would abuse his office and disobey God's commands. For Samuel, it seemed that Saul had died (v1). The Lord *'was grieved that he had made Saul king over Israel'*, but not because he had made a mistake in his appointment. God was grieved over Saul's disobedience, yet he had not been shunted into 'Plan B'.

1 GOD CHOOSES ACCORDING TO HIS VISION

He certainly didn't choose according to physical stature or appearance. Jesse presented seven of his eight sons to Samuel, but God's appointee was not in the 'identity parade'. God was looking at hearts (v7) for a *'man's heart reflects the man'* (Proverbs ch27 v19). God sees behind our virtuous veneer and sees what we're really like. Our hearts deceive us (Jeremiah ch17 vv9-10), but God's gaze penetrates deep so that nothing is hidden from him (Psalm 44 v21). The piercing fire-like eyes of Jesus exposed the sinfulness of hearts and minds within the church of Thyatira (Revelation ch2 v23). Our hearts are the fount of pollution (Mark ch7 vv20-23) and God knows our hearts (Luke ch16 v15).

Yet we are encouraged to *'set (our) hearts on things above'* (Colossians ch3 v1). We must not act or think in the way that the ungodly acts and thinks.

2 GOD CHOOSES ACCORDING TO HIS MISSION

God had a mission for David to complete. That mission didn't require tall, handsome, strong young men who were looking for glory in Saul's army. At this point, God wasn't looking for a soldier but a shepherd. He didn't want a man who was in touch with Saul but a man who was in touch with God, *'a man after his own heart'* (ch13 v14). God found the qualities for Israel's kingship in the life of a humble shepherd boy whose heart was in tune with himself. David was the man of God's choice (v13). His first mission was to minister to the present king, Saul. One of the royal servants identified a suitable musician, *'a brave man and a warrior. He speaks well and is a fine-looking man. And the Lord is with him'* (v18). The Lord was with David, and that made all the difference! There may have been other brave, good-looking musicians but David possessed this superior qualification: the Lord was with him. That is still the first requirement for those engaging in a divine mission. We can do nothing apart from Jesus (John ch15 v5). There's a critical juncture in this narrative: v13 – the Spirit enters, v14 - the Spirit exits.

3 GOD CHOOSES ACCORDING TO HIS PROVISION

If you are energised by the Spirit of God then it is irrelevant whether you are weak, poor, uneducated or unpopular (1 Corinthians ch1 vv26-29). God provides all that is necessary for the chosen servant to be suitably equipped for service. Peter had been uneducated while Paul had severe afflictions (2 Corinthians ch12 v7), not to mention his violent background. William Wilberforce, who famously campaigned against the slave trade, was rather delicate and short-sighted. DL Moody, the nineteenth century American evangelist who saw hundreds of conversions through his preaching, was uneducated and couldn't spell. CT Studd, founder of the China Inland Mission, suffered frequent severe asthma attacks. Gladys Aylward, who rescued over a hundred Chinese children from the invading Japanese armies, had no training, no experience, and little education. But what was said of David could be said of each of these faithful trailblazers: 'The Lord is with him/her'.

God knows our hearts and chooses according to his vision, his mission, and his provision. *'My son, give me your heart...'* (Proverbs ch23 v26).

JULY 23
1 SAMUEL Ch17.1-58

THE BATTLE IS THE LORD'S

The names of David and Goliath have been used and misused to represent all kinds of nonsense about facing personal giants, discovering your real self, courage, conquering everything, and the ultimate triumph of the underdog. If our knowledge of this famous incident only comes from children's storybooks, then we need to examine the Biblical text. We quickly learn that this battle isn't David's, or Saul's, or Israel's: *'the battle is the Lord's'* (v47).

Goliath had defied the Lord and his armies, but the final truth which the giant heard was that it was the Lord's battle. David leaves us a wonderful example of faith in the living God. The one thing that leaps from these fifty-eight verses is that David trusted in a trustworthy God. David's example should be driven home to our hearts:

1 TRUST GOD WHEN OUR ENEMY LOOMS LARGE

Goliath checked in at over nine feet tall and he was immensely strong. His armoured coat alone weighed almost nine stone, without his javelin, sword, and spear, with its iron tip. Goliath was like a tank on legs, a mean fighting machine; the Philistines' not-too-secret weapon. The giant's daily challenge to single man-to-man combat would decide the outcome of the battle without resorting to carnage. Goliath's challenge (vv8-10) terrorised the Israelites, making them run away (vv23-24). This monster of a man, who had set himself up against God and his people, had thrown down the gauntlet. Goliath represents all those who defy God and his people in every generation, but behind the opposing human agencies and adversaries, there are the unseen powers of darkness that control them. Behind every 'Goliath' there is a devilish puppeteer pulling on the strings (Ephesians ch6 v12). Yet all such 'giants' are puny next to God.

2 TRUST GOD WHEN OUR FRIENDS GET ANGRY

David's oldest brother Eliab burned with anger when he heard David's conversation with the men (v28). His brothers had either misunderstood or ignored the surprising event of ch16 when Samuel had visited their home and had anointed David as the king-in-waiting. The Spirit of the Lord had come upon David in power, even in *'the presence of his brothers'* (ch16 v13), but jealousy, pride, ignorance, or ungodliness had clouded their understanding. Is it not the case that many of the believer's biggest battles are fought near home (Matthew ch10 v36)? The biggest disappointments and discouragements can come from the closest of friends and relatives. David's 'critical brothers' are still alive and well in many homes today with their undermining remarks, veiled criticisms, and lack of spirituality. But David trusted the Lord even when his nearest and dearest seemed to oppose him.

3 TRUST GOD WHEN OUR ARMOUR DOESN'T FIT

Saul also looked at David's *'outward appearance'* (ch16 v7) and compared David's youth to Goliath's military experience (v33). But David pointed out his experience of God, the experience that counts (v37)! Saul gave David his own armour (vv38-39), but the youth found them to be a hindrance. David had proved God in the most dangerous of personal situations, and he knew that he could depend on God's wisdom, grace, and power. Saul's poorly fitting armour would afford no protection. God's armour is the only spiritual protection that's effective. But even Paul doesn't say 'Be strong in the armour' but rather *'Be strong in the Lord and in his mighty power'* (Ephesians ch6 v10). The trimmings and trappings of Christianity are but an ill-fitting armour: our trust must be in the Lord.

4 TRUST GOD WHEN OUR WEAPONS SEEM SMALL

David trusted God to work through his human experience:

i] Knowledge:

He knew that an aerodynamic pebble could be slung more accurately.

ii] Skill:

David was able to use his sling and his strength to catapult a stone with deadly force.

iii] Experience:

David was also prepared for further use of the sling if God required (remember that he had five stones). David was ready for whatever use God had for him. The *'pouch of his shepherd's bag'* was full. Do we come to God with that expectancy and readiness to be used? David trusted in *'the name of the Lord Almighty'* (v45) and knew that on that very day Goliath would be delivered into his hand (v46) and *'the whole world will know'* as well.

David was a 'giant of faith' who was assured that it was the Lord's battle.

JULY 24
1 SAMUEL Ch18.1-30

THE JEALOUS EYE

It didn't take long for David's victory over Goliath to be broadcast across Israel (vv6-7). Saul's reaction was one of fury since the dancers' ditty had attributed greater victory to David than to Saul. *'From that time on Saul kept a jealous eye on David'* (v9).

Saul viewed David with jealousy. His sinful heart became the playground of an evil spirit. But the chronicler, who recorded these events under the hand of God, knows that nothing operates outside God's omnipotent control. If God is God then no evil spirit can operate autonomously or unilaterally. Although, like a pawn on a chess board, an evil spirit may be allowed to move within its own square, it's God's 'chess board' and he makes the moves. That's why the chronicler states that the evil spirit *'came from the Lord'* (ch16 vv14, 23; ch18 v10; ch19 v9). Far from causing us alarm, this should bring us assurance that each demonic agency only operates within God's framework. Saul's overwhelming jealousy was the vehicle the evil spirit used to take him further away from God. Envy, like a virulent cancer, was gnawing away at Saul's bones and his heart (Proverbs ch14 v30). His jealous eye was inflamed by David's:

1 CELEBRITY STATUS

David had become a celebrity in Israel, and his meteoric rise to national acclaim had turned Saul into 'a green-eyed monster' of bitterness and hatred. But Saul was also afraid (vv12, 15, 29). Envy and fear were a bitter concoction in his heart as he resented David's popularity (v30). Do we become jealous of those who are more popular, more outgoing, more gifted than we are? When someone becomes the centre of attention, do we secretly wish it were us? How many Christians are unhappy and fail to have peace in their heart because they envy the popularity of other believers?

2 SWEEPING SUCCESS

There's no doubt about it: David was successful (vv5, 14, 15, 30). Saul was consumed with an envy that erupted into unrestrained aggression. We must not *'fret when men succeed in their ways'* (Psalm 37 v7). It would have been easy for John Baptist to have suffered from a twinge of jealousy when his disciples spoke of Jesus' popularity (John ch3 v26). After all, John had led a simple and austere lifestyle. He had encountered enemies, and soon he would be imprisoned and beheaded. But John's humble response to the news of Jesus' popularity is a powerful lesson: *'He must become greater; I must become less'* (John ch3 v30). This is the antidote to all the selfish emotions that would overtake us: Christ must become greater, and we must become less.

3 SPIRITUAL STANDING

Even Saul recognised that the Lord was with David in all that he did (vv12, 14, 28). This was the secret of David's victories. David had seen the removal of God's Spirit from Saul and he was concerned that it should never happen to him, even when he had sinned (Psalm 51 vv11-12). It was not only in David's battle with the

Philistines that the Lord was with him, for he continued to consolidate David's position within the kingdom. The Lord had brought David from the life of an obscure shepherd to become the king's son-in-law. Michal loved David, which in itself fuelled Saul's hatred for David. Do we envy someone in the way Saul envied David because he had been used to bring great blessings to others?

In stark contrast to Saul, his own son Jonathan showed great spiritual qualities:

i] Humility:

As the 'crown prince', Jonathan was ready to submit himself to God's plan and surrender any right of succession in recognising that David was the Lord's 'anointed one'. Jonathan put David before himself (ch23 v17). There was no jealousy in his heart. Let us put others before ourselves and Christ before everything and everyone.

ii] Faith:

Jonathan trusted the Lord even when his own position seemed precarious. Did he also know that the Messiah would ultimately come from David's line and not Saul's? Jonathan's faith encouraged David's faith (ch23 v16).

iii] Love:

Jonathan loved the Lord, and he loved David (vv3-4). This was a solid and selfless love underpinned by a covenant and evidenced by a personal gift. This demonstrates that *'love is patient, love is kind. It does NOT ENVY...'* (1 Corinthians ch13 v4).

JULY 25
1 SAMUEL Ch19.1-24

GOD'S VARIOUS PROTECTION

God's protecting hand was upon his choice servant, David. Psalm 59 was probably written following this experience of ch19 when Saul sent men to put David's house under surveillance with the plan to eliminate him at first light. David calls out: *'Deliver me from my enemies, O God; protect me from those who rise up against me. Deliver me from evildoers and save me from bloodthirsty men'* (Psalm 59 vv1-2).

David trusted the Lord for his protection even in his younger days when a bear or a lion had attacked his flock (ch17 v37). It's not enough to know God's loving care and protection theoretically. We must rest daily upon God's omnipotence and sovereignty.

We may observe the different means which the Lord employs to protect his people:

1 GOD PROTECTS HIS PEOPLE WITH PERSUASIVE WORDS (vv4-5)

Jonathan warns David of Saul's determination to kill him. But Jonathan approaches his father and *'spoke well of David to Saul'* (v4). What a lovely phrase! Jonathan only had good words to say about David. What a lesson for Christians to learn in their everyday conversations. How often do we hear: *'You know, he's very faithful...she's very generous...BUT...'* There's always the 'but', the detractor, the negative, which undermines and subtracts from the virtues of that person. Let's be those of Jonathan's ilk, who speak well of one another, rather than be those who drip the poison of mischief and envy into our conversations. Jonathan spoke up for David (vv4-5) and, in a moment of sanity, Saul was persuaded. (Compare Gamaliel's persuasive speech in Acts ch5.)

2 GOD PROTECTS HIS PEOPLE WITH PHYSICAL AGILITY (vv9-10)

There are many occasions when the Lord uses ordinary human ability, agility, stamina, strength and fitness to protect his own people. David *'eluded'* Saul. He sidestepped the spear that had been aimed at him. It wasn't necessary for the Lord to paralyse Saul's spear-throwing arm or divert the spear's flight. Instead, he used David's sharp eye and nimble movement to avoid getting impaled on the wall. More often the Lord equips his people with perception, anticipation and strength to shield them.

3 GOD PROTECTS HIS PEOPLE WITH CUNNING ACTIONS (vv11-17)

David's wife, Michal, tricked her husband's would be murderers. The Lord gives his people wisdom and sharp-wittedness to evade danger. Believers throughout history have experienced God's prompting of the right reply at various times to escape harm.

4 GOD PROTECTS HIS PEOPLE WITH SPIRITUAL RESTRAINT (vv18-24)

There may be nothing supernatural about persuasive words, physical agility and cunning actions, but in vv18-24 we are told about the supernatural power of God to protect David when he sought refuge with Samuel at the prophets' 'theological college'.

As this group assembled to be taught the truth, God's Spirit would come upon them in such a way that they would be overwhelmed by the power of his presence and would respond in worship. The Hebrew word for *'prophecy'* is not just to do with predicting the future: it can also mean 'to sing songs of praise'. The Lord shielded David from the evil of Saul and his henchmen by subduing them through the direct operation of the Spirit. 'Prophesying' didn't make Saul a prophet, and also, we should note that:

i] Religious experiences don't make a Christian:

People can have 'spiritual happenings' in their lives without ever being truly converted. Coming under the 'spell' of a Christian gathering, being affected by the atmosphere, or being emotionally moved by what is heard, is not the same as being converted or 'born again'.

ii] Spiritual powers don't make a Christian:

Those within Christendom, who claim powers of healing, perception, prophecy and various shades of so-called 'white magic', are summed up by Jesus in Matthew ch7 vv21-23.

iii] Enthusiastic preaching doesn't make a Christian:

Included within the band of early preachers (Matthew ch10 vv7-8) was Judas, the betrayer, whom Jesus described as *'a devil'* (John ch6 v70). This preacher was spiritually unclean (John ch13 v11) and *'doomed to destruction'* (John ch17 v12). Being a public speaker, and even being an enthusiastic listenable preacher, doesn't necessarily prove the genuineness of conversion (John ch3 v3).

Don't underestimate the means God uses to protect his people. The weapons of men are but paper darts compared to the armoury of the Almighty (2 Corinthians ch10 v4). Is your confidence in the protective panoply of God's love, grace and power (Proverbs ch18 v10)?

JULY 26
1 SAMUEL Ch20.1-42

FAMOUS FRIENDSHIP

Throughout history and literature, there have been many celebrated friendships. But the friendship of David and Jonathan is probably the most famous of them all. It epitomises all the essential qualities of a genuine and enduring friendship – trust, loyalty, reliability, thoughtfulness, selflessness and love. The cement of genuine friendship may be stronger even than the blood of brotherhood (Proverbs ch18 v24; John ch15 v13). True friendship is a friendship to die for.

1 A COSTLY FRIENDSHIP

Commitment, dedication, selflessness, and sacrifice are all words that describe the costliness of friendship. For Jonathan, it meant suffering his father's venom for being David's best friend (vv30-33). Jonathan also gave himself unconditionally to David (v4). Jonathan was a friend of the highest calibre. Do we have an upper limit on the cost of our friendship, or is it unlimited and unconditional?

2 A KIND FRIENDSHIP

This wasn't just a formal friendship where an agreement had been established between two parties. Kindness was the hallmark of this friendship (v8). Paul refers to some of his closest friends who had proved '*a comfort to him*' (Colossians ch4 v11). The word for '*comfort*' in this verse means 'soothing' or 'solace'. The Greek word gives us our word 'paregoric', which is used to describe those medicines that soothe irritation and ease pain. Are we that kind of friend? Jonathan sought from David '*unfailing kindness like that of the Lord*' (v14), which would be exercised in perpetuity (v15). Our kindness should have a heavenly ring about it.

3 A COVENANT FRIENDSHIP

Underneath the kindness and cost of their friendship, there was the security of a covenant (vv8, 16, 17) to which the Lord was witness (vv23, 42). It was a covenant of love (ch18 v3). A covenant seals the agreement, binds the parties, and guarantees the promises. How much of our friendships fluctuate from year to year and are affected by differences and upsets?

Every believer has been brought into a covenant relationship with God. The covenants between men and women are bilateral and are only as good as the parties involved. But in our covenant of redemption, God is not an equal party. He is the Author of the covenant, he initiated it, he determined the conditions, he provided everything to make the covenant work and he ratified the covenant through the blood of Jesus, his Son. It's a unilateral covenant of grace. God is not only the major contributor to this covenant: he is the only contributor. If we had any part in this covenant, then that would be its weakness, and it would be doomed to fail. Our part is to believe it, to receive it, and to live by it. But just in case someone might think that an unfailing guarantee of God's friendship is a licence to live as they please, then that is proof that they are not the friend of God (John ch15 vv14-16). So how crucial was Jonathan's friendship to David?

i] This friendship represents the importance of David's life

To Saul, David was the worst of enemies. To Jonathan, David was the best of friends. Jonathan's friendship was the means of preserving David's life (v13). Jonathan's grief at Saul's shameful treatment prompted him to devise the plan that would signal David to escape (vv35-40). They wept, and David wept the most (v41).

ii] This friendship reflects the abundance of David's love

David reaffirmed his oath out of love for Jonathan (v17). He also showed kindness to Saul's family, even though Saul had only shown murderous intentions toward David. It reminds us of God's love to us when we were his enemies (Colossians ch1 v21). How amazing is God's great love and grace!

iii] This friendship reveals the significance of David's line

Jonathan wanted a guarantee of peace from David and his successors (v42), but the greatest guarantee of peace would come from the Prince of Peace himself, who would reign on David's throne (Isaiah ch9 v6). Joseph took his pregnant wife to Bethlehem because *'he belonged to the house and line of David'* (Luke ch2 v4). Jesus came from David's line to demonstrate a greater friendship than even David's.

Jesus came to be the Friend of sinners. But are we true friends of Jesus?

JULY 27
1 SAMUEL Ch21.1-15

WHICH WAY?

As David left Jonathan, he was beginning a difficult and dangerous exile which lasted up to ten years. David's first stop as a fugitive was in the town of Nob, just north of Jerusalem, which had become the centre of worship after the fall of Shiloh. David found sanctuary there among the remnants of the tabernacle. But here he was faced with a crossroads. Geographically, he would turn west to seek refuge among the Philistines at Gath. But what about the spiritual crossroads that confronted David? Would he make the right choice of direction?

We learn from ch22 v10 that the high priest *'enquired of the Lord for (David)'*. Neither was it the first time that Ahimelech had sought God's will for David (ch22 v15). In response to the high priest's questions in v1, David was faced with his first crossroads:

1 FACT OR FALSE?

Does he divulge to the high priest the real reason why he is alone, or does he make up some 'cock and bull' story about being on a 'royal secret mission'? Perhaps he justified his lie by thinking that he would be protecting the high priest by giving him minimal information and thus avoiding any recrimination from Saul. If that was David's excuse for lying, then it failed (see ch22 vv18-19). Sometimes we may be faced with a situation in which telling the truth will hurt the one with whom we are speaking or make them more accountable. The easy way out is to lie and justify the untruth on the grounds of compassion and consideration. As Christians, we must not be pressurised into selecting a sinful path, whatever the motives may be, for the justification. Of two evils, choose neither.

2 FOOD OR FAINT?

David was hungry and asked for bread, but the high priest didn't have *'ordinary bread'*, only *'consecrated bread'*, that is, bread that was placed before the Lord and renewed each week (Exodus ch25 v30). Only the priests were permitted to eat this bread when it had served its purpose. Here is the quandary: David was hungry, and the only bread available was consecrated bread. What should he do? Jesus provides a helpful commentary on this incident (Mark ch2 v25). The basic needs for food, water, shelter, emergency aid, and protection take priority over the ceremonial worship of God. The Lord graciously provides us with daily bread.

3 FIGHT OR FLIGHT?

David had fled from Jerusalem without a weapon. Ahimelech had just one sword: the sword which the young David had snatched from the hand of Goliath and with which he had cut off his head (ch17 v51). David said, *'There is none like it'* (v9). So with Goliath's sword, he flees to enemy territory, in fact, to Goliath's hometown, where there would have been many widows as a result of David's military campaigns. David must have been desperate and confused to flee to a Philistine king for refuge. Even Achish's servants recognised the

Hebrew hero and reminded the king that the 'pop song' among the Israelis at that time celebrated David's slaughter of tens of thousands (v11)! David had a powerful weapon and an all-powerful God, but we find him hiding among the heathen. Do we stand at a crossroads with the invincible weapon of the Spirit's sword (Ephesians ch6 v17; Hebrews ch4 v12), ready to face the enemy, or do we skulk away and try to be camouflaged within our evil society? Like David with Goliath's sword, we can believe in the effectiveness and uniqueness of the Bible but still suffer defeat in our lives.

4 FAITH OR FEAR?

Did David approach Goliath's city in the same way that he approached Goliath in ch17 v45? David is portrayed not as a warrior but as a wimp (v12). David's acting skills were convincing. The monarch was acting as a madman. Israel's leader had become Philistia's lunatic. What pathetic and humiliating behaviour for the Lord's anointed king over Israel! How easily we can drivel nonsense when gripped by the fear of men. How easily we succumb to acting like imbeciles in the presence of overwhelming paganism and secularism. But we have a mighty God who champions his people. The fear of men drove David to the fear of God (Psalm 34 was written at this time).

'Which way?' will not be so difficult when trusting in Jesus Christ, the Way (John ch14 v6).

JULY 28
1 SAMUEL Ch22.1-23

THE CAVE MEN

From a palace in Jerusalem, to a place for lunatics in Gath, to a cave in Adullam, David continues his humiliating descent. The anointed king of Israel is now living as an outlaw in a cave on the outskirts of the city of Adullam, along with four hundred of his loyal followers. David's band of fugitives included the distressed, the debtors and the discontented (v2).

Doeg the Edomite, Saul's head shepherd (ch21 v7), had witnessed the high priest's help to David. Now Doeg spills the beans, and Saul summons Ahimelech and his family. Though the royal guard refuses to execute the priests, Doeg seizes his moment of infamy and slaughters eighty-five captive priests and their families (v18). He also annihilated the town of Nob. One man, Abiathar (v20), escaped to report the news, and David felt responsible since he had suspected Doeg as a spy (v22). Psalm 52 is David's response. But there are many 'Doegs' around today – some who murder God's people, but others who take delight in vilifying evangelical, Bible-believing Christians. They occupy universities, schools, workplaces, councils, politics, media, scientific institutions, and even some denominational pulpits. *'Everlasting ruin'* will be their end (Psalm 52 v5). Your circumstances may be likened to David's cave. You may feel the darkness, coldness, and loneliness, but, like David, with God's help and direction, you can:

1 MAKE YOUR CAVE INTO A STRONGHOLD

The cave was a *'stronghold'* (v4) which reflected the level of security that the fugitives enjoyed. David had re-learned the truth that the Lord was his stronghold (Psalm 57 vv1-2). David also had written Psalm 142 in that cave and speaks of the Lord as *'my Refuge'* (v5). Furthermore, he pleads that he may be set free from his prison to praise the Lord (v6). How often do we pray something similar? For example, 'Set me free from my 'prison' –my 'cave', my circumstances - and I will praise you and serve you'? But God shields his people even in the most distressing of situations. David could see Satan's menacing shadow behind Saul and knew that his only refuge was in the Almighty. There are many who will swallow us up if they can, but we have a super-strong God, and the trusting believer can know that his or her 'cave' is a 'stronghold'.

2 MAKE YOUR CAVE INTO A SCHOOL

- or, more specifically, a place of learning. What a joy it is to know that our lowly cave is an academy in which we can learn about God – his Person, his purposes, his word, his friends, and even his enemies. David wanted to learn God's will (v3). He had come to learn that he must submit himself to God's purposes (Psalm 57 v2). The number one lesson in David's School of Adversity was 'The Knowledge of God'. How poor and weak we are for not making this lesson a priority. Jesus' great concern was that his followers might know God (John ch17 v3). Paul's chief quest was *'to know Christ and the power of his resurrection and the fellowship of sharing in his sufferings...'* (Philippians ch3 v10).

3 MAKE YOUR CAVE INTO A SANCTUARY

- the place where God is served and worshipped. We may not choose the circumstances or the environment that we are in, but there is no reason why that particular place shouldn't be a sanctuary devoted to the Lord. David's cave became a cathedral. He sings (Psalm 57 vv5, 7-11).

What does worship mean to us? Someone has said that many western Christians today are those who 'work at their play, play at their worship, and worship their work'. But worship is more than Sunday. Worship is all about the right attitude towards God and right acts for God. Every worshipper is a minister, ministering before the Lord with true worship. In David's time, sacrifice, priesthood, and tabernacle were central to worship. The writer to the Hebrews affirms that all of these have been fulfilled in Christ. He is our altar, lamb, and high priest. Jesus must be the object and motivation of our worship.

In our corporate worship, we may be 'led' in that worship, to help us focus and to encourage us to unite. But if we are to be a 'worshipper', then we must be a 'contributor'. A real worshipper is not dependent upon premises or circumstances. Our 'cave', wherever that may be, can become a sanctuary in which our Lord and Saviour is worshipped and served out of full and obedient hearts.

JULY 29
1 SAMUEL Ch23.1-29

HELPING ONE ANOTHER TO FIND STRENGTH IN GOD

We may be tempted to think that espionage is a modern operation associated with such names as Anthony Blunt, Guy Burgess, and James Bond, but espionage was an integral part of government administration and military activity at the time of Saul and David. Consider the intelligence that is obtained and exchanged in this chapter and the clandestine missions that were made to discover what was happening (Note the expressions: *'was told', 'learned', 'heard'* in vv1, 7, 9, 10, 13, 15, 19, 22, 23, 25). It seems that wherever Saul and David operated, there were spies ready to trade information. But David was able to keep one step ahead of Saul despite the soldiers, raiders, spies, and turncoats hunting him. They were unable to trap David, even at Keilah, where David and his men had delivered the city from the Philistines.

Although his enemies were prevented from detecting David's whereabouts, his friend Jonathan went straight to him and *'helped him to find strength in God'* (v16). This is a snapshot of what true godly friendship is all about.

The measure of Jonathan's friendship is summed up in this phrase. What else can we learn about Jonathan's friendship, and in what ways can we help someone to find strength in God? Notice four things about Jonathan in vv16-18:

1 HE IDENTIFIED NEED

Jonathan was perceptive enough to identify David's needs. His friend was in distress and danger. With a succession of physical, mental, and spiritual challenges, it's easy to feel low, hurt, and alone. These are times when self-pity can creep in. Christians believe that trials and difficulties excuse them from an active role in Christian ministry and the church. Other Christians can think that they need special attention and consideration because 'no one has experienced what I've experienced'! Self-pity focuses on the self and is frequently linked to worry. Jesus instructed his children not to worry, just as he instructed them not to be hypocritical, not to lust, not to lie, and not to store up treasure on earth. Fear, worry, and self-pity may have been the wolves that surrounded David's heart at this time. He knew something of the abyss of despair (Psalm 69 vv1-4), and Jonathan spotted his need.

2 HE PROVIDED ENCOURAGEMENT

Jonathan knew that David was not in Saul's hand but in God's hand (v14). 'Encouragement' is not just about being cuddly and whispering a few soothing, meaningless sentiments. 'Encouragement' is not only associated with 'comfort': it's to do with stimulating and driving one forward. It's about inspiring with courage and making one bold. 'Encouragement' is needed when a person has lost their courage. Gentle spiritual erosion can affect older Christians who may succumb to a sedentary life of ease. A person's age is often confused with spiritual maturity, and some older Christians can slip into a lifestyle where the local church and Christian ministry are only a second-hand experience for them. It was David's close friend (not his counsellor, his house group leader, his pastor, or his therapist) who saw the need for encouragement and came alongside him to *'help him find strength in God'*. We all could do with friends like that.

3 HE OFFERED ASSURANCE

'You shall be king over Israel' (v17). Jonathan delivered some rock-solid assurance. It wasn't some wishful thinking that would cheer up David temporarily. This was the assurance of God's word. God had clearly stated that David would be king over Israel. Everyone, including Saul (v17), seemed to know and believe God's word at that moment, except David. Someone who helps a friend to *'find strength in God'* will bring them the assurance of God's word. David lacked assurance because he doubted God's word and lacked faith in God's promises.

4 HE DEMONSTRATED HUMILITY

'...and I will be second to you' (v17). Humility is one of the great characteristics of true friendship (Romans ch12 v10; Philippians ch2 v3). Humility will cement Christian unity like nothing else. Arrogance always destroys it. Christians put their friends before themselves. Godly friendship will remind us of the self-sacrificing friendship of Jesus, who identified with need, provided encouragement, offered assurance, and demonstrated humility.

JULY 30
1 SAMUEL Ch24.1-22

WHAT KIND OF HANDS?

Saul had resumed his pursuit of David and was closing in on him as David and his men hid in a cave on the western side of the Dead Sea. Saul's soldiers outnumbered David's men five to one. So close were they that, when Saul wanted some personal privacy, he entered the precise cave in which David and his men were hiding (v3). There he was – David's greatest enemy – alone in a dark cave where David and his six hundred men were poised, ready to pounce. The men were excited at the situation which they believed God had arranged for them. This was the day of reckoning, they believed (v4). Their enemy had walked straight into their hands. But David restrains his hands and the hands of his men. Instead, he cuts off a corner of Saul's robe. More than anything else in this chapter, it's striking just how responsible David is for the right action he takes in the circumstances in which the Lord had placed him. Look at the maths! Out of three thousand six hundred and two men who were in that region of En Gedi at that time, three thousand and one were determined to kill David, six hundred were determined to kill Saul, but one man alone was sensitive to the Lord's purposes and responsible before God for his actions.

How much do we face up to the responsibility for the freedom and understanding God has given us? How do we put into practice those instructions, directions and warnings which are rooted in Biblical truth? Day by day, the Lord entrusts challenges, opportunities and missions into our hands. But what kind of hands do we have?

What kind of hands should they be? Look at this incident in the life of David.

1 FAITHFUL HANDS

God places his people in circumstances so that they will exercise faith in discharging their responsibilities. Notice this gigantic responsibility that God had placed into David's hands, even the life of King Saul (vv4, 10, 18). At times, we may be tempted to seize the moment and to vent our feelings and frustrations, but God wants his people to be faithful in every situation. He's looking for a 'safe pair of hands' to do his work. How many Christians pick up a task, run with it for a short time, and drop it again (Ecclesiastes ch9 v10)? Faithful hands will mean diligent hands, working hands, praying hands.

2 MERCIFUL HANDS

In contrast to Saul's murderous hands, observe David's merciful hands (vv6, 10, 12, 13, 17). The natural, worldly response is to take vengeance on an enemy and to retaliate. But the people of God will be different as they act according to the Lord's requirements, that is, *'to act justly, to love mercy and to walk humbly with (their) God'* (Micah ch6 v8). It's not going to be easy to show mercy when you have been ill-treated, maligned, and abused. It's not so easy to muster mercy when the opportunity comes. When you have been shamefully treated, despised, and attacked...when you have been misrepresented and unjustly criticised – it seems so natural to retaliate. The act of showing mercy defies explanation by our antitheist, evolutionist, unregenerate, secular society. But Jesus declares in the 'Manifesto of his Kingdom' that mercy is a characteristic of his family (Matthew ch5 v7). The single motivation for showing mercy is that we have been shown mercy by God (Ephesians ch2 v4; 1 Peter ch1 v3). Jesus' merciful hands were cruelly nailed to a Roman scaffold in a feeble attempt to halt his earthly mission. While it's *'a dreadful thing to fall into the hands of the living God'* (Hebrews ch10 v31), it's a wonderful thing to be held in the merciful hands of a loving Saviour.

3 POWERFUL HANDS

Even Saul had to admit to David that Israel's kingdom *'will be established in your hands'* (v20). The kingly power had been transferred to David. He had enjoyed power in numerous victories, but possibly one of the greatest displays of his power was there in the cave when he prevented Saul's destruction (Proverbs ch16 v32; ch29 v11). The followers of Jesus are required to exercise the power to refrain from sinful acts, the power to resist temptation, the power to subdue evil thoughts, the power to control their temper, and the power to serve Jesus in serving others. Yet it can never be a power or strength that comes from us because that would fail. It's the power from above. Paul prays that God's people will be strengthened with power through the Spirit (Ephesians ch3 vv16-17).

Saul's cut robe was a permanent reminder of David's faithful, merciful, powerful hands. How will others be reminded of *our* hands?

JULY 31
1 SAMUEL Ch25.1-44

THE GOOD, THE BAD, AND THE UGLY

'The good, the bad, and the ugly' may not only be the title for a spaghetti western, but it fits this passage too. The elements of goodness, badness, and downright ugliness appear in these verses. As a great chapter in Israel's history closes with the death of Samuel (v1), David encounters a married couple in Maon.

The Ugliness of Nabal

He was *'surly and mean in all his dealings'* (v3), which may have contributed to his wealth (v2). Nabal was insulting (v14) and contemptuous (v39), and who paid back *'evil for good'* (v21). His employee said that *'he is such a wicked man that no one can talk to him'* (v17), and his wife confirms that he was *'a fool'* (v25), as his name suggests. He was odious and ostentatious (v36): an unpleasant and disreputable wretch; 'a dog' (v3).

The Beauty of Abigail

Abigail is the 'good' contrasted with Nabal's 'bad and ugly'. But her beauty was not skin deep. Her attractiveness was not merely cosmetic. A person's beauty is in their godliness (Proverbs ch31 v30).

How attractive and winsome are we?

1 THE BEAUTY OF PENITENCE

Abigail was repentant, contrite, sorry for sin and ready to make amends (vv23, 28). We are impressed by her humility, and in her penitence, she identified herself with her husband's sin. She knew how wicked her husband was and that his life was a life of folly (v25). But to save Nabal's life, she assumed his guilt. In interceding for her husband, this noble lady bears his sin. In seeking to avert imminent judgement upon Nabal, she sacrificially identifies with his wickedness. Although Abigail could never fully atone for her husband's sin, we are reminded of the supreme Sin-bearer, Jesus the 'Good', who gave himself for the 'Bad and Ugly'. He didn't go to the cross in a blaze of stardom, but he suffered the ignominy of crucifixion *as* a guilty sinner to atone for sin. *'He had no beauty or majesty to attract us to him'* (Isaiah ch53 v2). The picture of Jesus on the cross is not a neat, sweet, sanitised death. But the believer sees in his death the stunning beauty of a loving, compassionate, and sinless Saviour.

There was an urgency about Abigail's penitence (vv18, 34). David was advancing in judgement upon Nabal and his household. If Abigail had hesitated, she would have been too late. There was no greater priority than to put things right with her king.

2 THE BEAUTY OF PRUDENCE

Abigail was intelligent (v3) and exercised *'good judgement'* (v33). David's exemplary restraint with Saul (ch24) seems to have evaporated in Nabal's case. Isn't it just like our flimsy, fluctuating humanity to show restraint in one situation, then to lose our temper in another? David was brought down to earth by Abigail's sensible and prudent action. Prudence means 'discretion and practical wisdom', that is, good judgement. Her prudence prompted generosity towards David and his men (v18) and saved Nabal. David's own son said that we mustn't let sound judgement and discernment out of our sight (Proverbs ch3 v21). Good judgements are formed upon a sound working knowledge and daily application of God's word. Abigail saw that David fought the Lord's battles (v28) and that he was secure in God's word since he was the appointed leader over Israel (v30).

3 THE BEAUTY OF PATIENCE

Abigail may have thought, 'What did I ever see in Nabal to marry him?' He was selfish, uncharitable, insulting, and embarrassing to the sweet and sensitive nature of his wife. But she didn't accuse him or nag him. She was wise and she got on and did what she believed was right (Proverbs ch19 v11). Our supreme example of patience is in Jesus, and we must exercise patience with everyone (1 Thessalonians ch5 v14). Love is patient (1 Corinthians ch13 v4) and that patience bears with one another in love (Ephesians ch4 v2). Abigail showed patience with her circumstances, but she didn't let those circumstances control her. We must be patient in our prayers, patient in developing gifts, patient in pursuing ministry, patient with brothers and sisters who frustrate us, patient with God (his timing and his ways).

God may not always free us from a hostile environment as he did with Abigail (v38).

Do we have a desire to be beautiful? Not the cosmetic, chocolate-box beauty which fades so quickly, but that inner beauty which increases with the knowledge of Jesus?

Abigail became the wife of the king (v42), and King Jesus' Bride will be most beautiful.

AUGUST 1
1 SAMUEL Ch26.1-25

THE VALUE OF A LIFE

David's incursion into the enemy camp at night, when he was able to penetrate security and stand over Saul's sleeping form, had all the hallmarks of an assassination attempt. Indeed, David's companion, Abishai, was eager to become the assassin. He boasted that he could kill Saul with only one blow from his spear (v8). Like the rest of David's men at En Gedi (ch24 v4), Abishai believed that it was the Lord who had delivered Saul into David's hands (vv9-11). But David left the camp with Saul's *'spear and water jug'* (v12) as evidence that once more he had allowed the king to live. He had chosen to spare Saul and not to spear Saul. On being told what had happened, the moody monarch launches into one of his sentimental speeches. He claims to have changed, and for this reason: *'Because you considered my life precious today...'* (v21).

David also responded: *'As surely as I valued your life today, so may the Lord value my life and deliver me from all trouble'* (v24).

We are directed to consider the worth of a life: its value and preciousness.

1 THE RESULT OF BELIEVING THAT LIFE IS VALUELESS

The dignity and value of a life is at odds with the notion that humanity is essentially no different from animal life; that we are just a part of the 'molecules to man' story; that we are no more than just a piece of over-developed slime. If it is believed that a child is no different from a chipmunk, or a man is no different from a monkey, then there is little significance to life, except the survival of the fittest. Once our secular evolutionist society has established that life has little or no meaning, then it's free to dispatch its unborn children, its elderly, its disabled, and sick, when and how it chooses. Abortion, euthanasia, assisted suicide, and eugenics have not only become approved but also legislated for. If you reject the Bible's teaching that every life has value and worth, then you will identify disabilities in the unborn child and provide the pregnant mother with the opportunity to destroy it. If God is eradicated from men's thinking and conscience, then life is regarded as having little or no real value.

We may also be brainwashed into equating 'quality' with 'value'. The medical and caring professions frequently refer to the 'quality' of one's life. Though we applaud therapies and treatments which stimulate and mobilise, we may not be aware that 'quality' has become a measurement of life itself. At what point does 'poor quality' equal 'valueless'? If life is perceived to be valueless, does it then become disposable?

2 THE RESULT OF BELIEVING THAT LIFE IS VALUED

A 'valued life' means that it is highly regarded and greatly esteemed. David regarded Saul's life as *'precious'* (v21). David knew that he had a huge responsibility towards God for the life of Saul (v23). To believe that we are created *'in the image of God'* (Genesis ch1 v27), and that *'you are not your own'* (1 Corinthians ch6 v19), clashes head-on with secular thinking. The secular worldview is always against the Biblical view that teaches God to be the Creator and Sustainer, the Giver and Controller of life. Those who love the Lord *'choose life'* (Deuteronomy ch30 vv19-20). Jesus, 'the Life' (John ch1 v4; ch14 v6), gave his own life (Mark ch10 v45) to bring life in all its fullness (John ch10 v10). How valued are those who follow Jesus? He calls them his *'friends'* (John ch15 v14). He regards them as his closest of family (Matthew ch12 v50). He has shed his own blood to save them.

Isn't it mind-blowing, therefore, that men and women, marred and scarred by the Fall, are still more like God than anything else in all creation?

3 THE RESULT OF BELIEVING THAT LIFE IS VALUABLE

We should not only have the highest regard for the life of everyone, irrespective of age, gender, ethnicity, social standing, health, and ability, but we should know that everyone who is living the life of Christ is valuable to the work of God. There is a glorious, preciousness about each disciple of Jesus. Though flawed and spoilt, God takes the clay and shapes it into something useful and therefore valuable (Jeremiah ch18 v6; Ephesians ch2 v10). Our lives are valuable, not because we have contributed to their worth, but because God has made us in his likeness. He has purchased us through the death of his Son, living within us by his Spirit and holding us in his hand as vessels and instruments to be used for his eternal purposes. If we really believe that, then we shall always try to be the best instrument and the best vessel that we can be.

AUGUST 2
1 SAMUEL Ch27.1-12

GIVING IN TO PRESSURE

One may sympathise with David after all the anguish that he had endured because of Saul. David had been pursued to within an inch of his life as Saul had threatened him, ridiculed him, and had deprived him of his 'home comforts'. David had been a fugitive from Saul while still fighting Israel's enemies. He had experienced several low points, and it appears from this chapter that David had succumbed to pressure.

1 HE SETTLED IN THE WRONG PLACE

David, with six hundred men and their families (perhaps two to three thousand altogether), *'settled in Gath'* (v3), living in Philistine territory for sixteen months (v7). This was Israel's anointed king, whom God had blessed with power and victory, now settled within his enemy's borders. David had *'thought to himself'* (v1). We don't read that he prayed about it, or that he sought spiritual counsel, or that he looked for divine guidance. His thinking led him to conclude that *'the best thing'* was *'to escape to the land of the Philistines'*. How quickly this Godly man's judgement had become unbalanced when he wallowed in self-pity and thought only of himself. David reckoned that his best option was to settle in a land that had been opposed to God and his kingdom. David the giant-killer made his home in the hometown of the giant he had killed (ch17 vv4, 50). For some, of course, settling in an alien land is their mission to reach the lost for Christ. But some Christians settle in 'Gath', away from a 'church family' and regular Christian fellowship, because God and his people are no longer their first concern.

2 HE ASSOCIATED WITH THE WRONG PEOPLE

David had become friends with the Philistines, the very ones who were opposed to God and his people. The reason why David was accepted among these godless people was that he gave every indication that he was one of them. We must be extremely careful if those who are declared enemies of God consider us to be their friends. Friendship with the world means hatred towards God (James ch4 v4). Believers have been 'called out' of the world (1 Corinthians ch6 vv14-17). The world should no longer enchant them. They should no longer be driven or dominated by the world. Christians are called to be distinctive from the world by the lives they live. Jesus is the greatest example of One who was able to interact with ungodly men and women but whose life remained untarnished and unpolluted. He wasn't ashamed to be in their company, but he wasn't 'one of the boys'! He wasn't there to show that you could be 'normal' and have a 'good time' like everyone else. His purpose in coming alongside sinners was to bring them the good news (Matthew ch9 v13). But association with sinners doesn't mean that believers should become polluted by them (James ch1 v27).

3 HE CHANGED TO THE WRONG PRIORITIES

Discouragement can provoke a despondency that may cause us to view our circumstances differently. We may not see God in those circumstances. David's priorities had changed to pleasing the Philistines (*'If I have found favour in your eyes...')* and becoming their *'servant'* (v5). David had temporarily forgotten God's promises to him, and he still entertained the notion of being killed by Saul (v1). Our priorities quickly change when we falter in our faith and when we question God's methods. The believer's priority should be to *'make the Most High (his) dwelling'* (Psalm 91 v1). Don't make an 'Achish' or a 'Gath' your priority!

4 HE ENGAGED IN THE WRONG PRACTICES

David had exterminated everyone in the villages that he raided to protect himself (*'And such was his practice as long as he lived in Philistine territory'* v11). David waged a campaign of annihilation against the Philistines' allies while lying to Achish that he had been destroying Israeli villages. We can't even excuse David's lies as a 'one-off': he kept it up for sixteen months. *'Keep falsehood and lies far from me'* (Proverbs 30 v8).

You may think that, after learning about David's godly life in the previous eleven chapters that David's actions here are out of character. But the Bible records 'warts and all' as one of the proofs of its own veracity and authenticity. David is no different in this respect from Christians today. He struggled with the pressures of living for God in a godless world. But it was the Lord Jesus who exemplified a righteous life under pressure, and he wanted his heavenly Father to receive all the glory (John ch12 vv27-28).

AUGUST 3
1 SAMUEL Ch28.1-25

DISASTER ALERT

It seems that disasters are reported from around the world on a weekly basis. Another headline about some earthquake, tsunami, flood, fire, epidemic, famine, or war quickly replaces the previous disaster headline. Without minimising the scale or seriousness of such calamities, there's even a greater disaster to an individual that is illustrated in the life of King Saul. Saul's disastrous situation in this chapter is summed up by Samuel's words (v16): *'The Lord has turned away from you and become your enemy'*.

1 THE GREATEST DISASTER: THE LORD TURNING AWAY

Saul had been on a slippery slope for some time. Inch by inch, he had slipped further from God's will and God's way. This solemn pronouncement on the penultimate day of Saul's life (v16) was in response to the obvious fact that he had turned away from the Lord. 'Crunch time' had come for Saul, and the Bible leaves us with the impression that Saul died without God. What greater disaster can there be? These last four chapters chart the final decline for the first king of Israel: fear (vv5, 20); distress (v15); spiritism (v8); weakness (v20); defeat (ch31); death (ch31). Because Saul had turned his back on God, God had turned his back on him. When Saul finally realised his desperate condition and the hopelessness of his situation, he turned to an agent of Satan for help. How low and desperate Saul had become!

Spiritism is alive and well today, with tens of millions of people fascinated with horoscopes, occult literature, séances, Ouija boards, clairvoyance, levitation, as well as the more extreme arts of black magic, witchcraft, and Satanism. Spiritism (referred to incorrectly as 'spiritualism' by the cult itself) has millions of priests and worshippers globally. Though some have respect for the Bible and honour Jesus, they don't believe the Bible to be infallible and they don't believe Jesus to be the Christ, the Son of God (ref 1 John ch4 vv2-3). Spiritism is full of the 'spirit of antichrist' because the whole 'spirit movement' is diametrically opposed to Jesus and his kingdom. The results of spiritism point to a trail of mental, spiritual, and physical destruction. Yoga and transcendental meditation have clear occultic roots. Ignorance of their origins in Hinduism and spiritism may not be a protection from their spell and influence.

We must be alert to that slippery slope of spiritual decline:

i] When the Bible is uninspiring: For Saul, communion with God had dried up. God wasn't talking to him in dreams, Urim, or prophecy. God's word is the way in which he speaks to us today, but if this word no longer appeals to us, look out for danger.

ii] When prayer is unanswered: (v6) Saul's complaint to Samuel was *'He no longer answers me'* (v15). Saul wouldn't pray the prayer of a penitent, and the door of heaven was shut to him. So he knocks on Satan's door. Watch out for a decline in prayer life!

iii] When Christian fellowship is unattractive: Saul didn't want to keep company with godly people. In fact, he had slaughtered eighty-five priests (ch22 v18). Saul sought solace from a medium instead. Spiritual rot sets in when people no longer want to be associated with the church family because the local church is the means of God's special blessing.

2 THE GREATEST URGENCY: TURNING TO THE LORD

Saul refused to turn to God in repentance and humility. He could have turned to the Lord and found mercy and pardon (Isaiah ch45 v22; ch55 vv6-7), but he had refused, and in this his destiny was sealed. Conversion to Christ means 'turning' – turning *from* sin and turning *to* Jesus. The Bible provides a vivid picture of godless sinners walking down the broad road that leads to destruction (Matthew ch7 v13). The direct route from cradle to grave follows that broad road. To access the narrow road that leads to life, there must be a change of direction, a different course: a turning.

It was far too late for Saul. God had sovereignly intervened in this séance to trump Satan's power and speak through the spirit of the dead Samuel (v17). The kingdom would be wrenched from Saul and given to David (v17); Israel and Saul would be handed over to their enemies; Saul and his sons were to be killed (v18). There was no longer any opportunity to turn, and Saul collapses in a pathetic heap (v20).

But in the gospel of God's grace, there is still the call to *'turn to God'* (Acts ch3 vv19-20) before it is too late. Through Christ's death on the cross, a way has been opened into the presence of God so that those who believe may be eternally saved.

AUGUST 4
1 SAMUEL Ch29.1-11

WHO IS MY LORD AND KING?

It was the fear of 'fifth columnist' activities which caused the Philistine generals to demand that David and his men didn't fight with them against Saul and the Israeli army (v4). Though Achish, the Philistine king of Gath, had been impressed with David and had *'trusted'* him (ch27 v12), he was outvoted by the other generals. David's pretend loyalty to the Philistines had convinced Achish completely, but the other generals weren't so gullible. The Philistines hadn't forgotten the lyrics of the 'pop song' of the day (v5), which praised David's victories, many of which had been victories over the Philistines!

When Achish urges David to *'do nothing to displease the Philistine rulers'* (v7), David protests (v8): *'Why can't I go out and fight against the enemies of my lord the king?'*

David was saying one thing to Achish, but did he mean something else? Who did David mean when he referred to *'my lord the king'*? This is a relevant question.

Was David referring to Saul as his lord and king because, after all, David had consistently shown the highest respect for Saul as *'the Lord's anointed'* (ch24 v6)? Did he not call to Saul from the cave: *'my lord the king'* (ch24 v8)?

Or was David referring to Achish as his lord and king? He had referred to himself as Achish's servant (ch27 v5), and he had been regarded as a permanent servant (ch27 v12).

Or was David speaking about a 'higher authority' in referring to Almighty God as his Lord and King? Who is *my* lord and king?

1 IS IT A POPULAR RELIGION REPRESENTED BY SAUL?

For many in Israel, Saul was identified with a nation and a government of their own making. God had acceded to their demands in appointing a king like the other pagan nations. They had been warned about the consequences, but they wouldn't listen (ch8 vv19-20). The Israelites downgraded the kingship of the Lord in favour of the kingship of a man. They wanted to be like everyone else. They wanted a man-centred government rather than a God-centred one. We are in danger today of replacing a God-centred, Bible-focused Christianity with a man-centred, church-focused orthodoxy. At the heart of this popular, organised religion is a deficient view of God, his people, his word, and his gospel. The popular religion of our day markets itself under a gospel of good feelings, good atmosphere, good music, good food, and good times, without reference to the good news that *'Christ Jesus came into the world to save sinners'* from judgement, sin, Satan, and an everlasting hell. Popular religion is more about 'peace with yourself' than 'peace with God'. It's more about works than faith; more about karma than Christ. Popular religion is not rooted and grounded in an unswerving allegiance to the authoritative word of God. Instead, it's a random collection of spiritual jingles and sound bites associated with post-modernism. Are we serving a lord and king that is merely a product of our twenty-first-century 'pop church'?

2 IS IT THE SECULAR WORLD REPRESENTED BY ACHISH?

Are we finding that, to a great degree, the world around us dominates our thinking, influences our feelings, and controls our behaviour? When was the last time you adjusted your lifestyle as a result of reading the Bible? We are instructed not to love this world (1 John ch2 vv15-17), which is opposed to God and his righteousness. The spiritual kingdom of this secular world is regularly skirmishing with the kingdom of Christ – in the media, in politics, in employment, in public funding, in law and order, and even in religion. Many professing Christians seem to have capitulated to our current secular society and are willing to be pressed and shaped by its mould.

3 IS IT THE ETERNAL GOD REVEALED IN JESUS?

Is David's reference to *'my lord the king'* really an allusion to *'the King of Glory'*, of whom he writes in Psalm 24? God had been merciful, gracious, and patient with David, despite his running away to settle in enemy territory. David had been living as one of the enemy, and the Philistines couldn't tell any difference! But the Lord hadn't deserted David even though he had settled in Philistia (Psalm 139 vv7-10), and David still had to be reminded that he was the anointed servant of his Lord and King. Rather than a servant of the enemy, David should have been an ambassador in an alien land, representing the *'King of Kings and Lord of Lords'*. Are we fulfilling that ambassadorial role here?

AUGUST 5
1 SAMUEL Ch30.1-31

SQUEEZED

How often do you manage to escape or recover from one distressing situation, only to be plunged quickly into another? David and his men had just been saved from being forced into battle against their own people. They wouldn't have relished fighting against Saul and the Israeli army. But on returning to Ziklag, they were faced with a shock. In their absence, the Amalekites had raided the town and had taken everyone captive. David and his men discovered the charred remains of their town, and everyone was gone. Imagine the shock, the grief, and the anger! Six hundred men wept and wailed at this disaster (v4), yet David is more *'greatly distressed'* (v6) because the men's anger was directed at him. But David *'found strength in the Lord his God'* (v6).

1 THE LORD'S STRENGTH FOR OUR DISTRESS (v6)

The word *'distress'* is the word used for 'squeezing' or 'placing under pressure'. We all know something about pressure, even distress, but the Lord Jesus experienced a depth of distress that we could never experience. At the place of the 'olive press' – Gethsemane – Jesus was squeezed spiritually and emotionally so that his sweat fell like drops of blood. He said, *'My soul is overwhelmed with sorrow to the point of death'* (Matthew ch26 v38). He was *'crushed for our iniquities'* (Isaiah ch53 v5). One of the reasons that we can find strength in the Lord (even as David did) is because he fully understands our sorrows and distresses (Hebrews ch2 v18). David suffered the:

i] Distress of Loss: (vv3-5) Their town had been plundered and burned by the raiders. Their wives and children had been seized. Everything they possessed had been snatched away. Everything they held dear had been taken from them. Rarely can we relate to someone who has had all their possessions suddenly destroyed, as in a house fire. But Jesus can! The Creator and King of everything experienced the poverty of the earth. He owned no cradle for his birth, no boat for his transport, no pillow for his head, no money for his taxes, no donkey for his entry into Jerusalem, and no tomb for his burial. Jesus suffered total loss to bring us total gain.

ii] Distress of Rejection: (v6) David was the obvious one on whom to dump their bitterness and blame. Christians, too, must be prepared to suffer rejection by their nearest and dearest. The hurt of rejection can be very deep, but it is the way the Master went (Isaiah ch53 v3). Often the Lord may lead us into and through our distresses:

- to bring us closer to the Lord (would David have found strength in the Lord if he hadn't been weakened by distress?).

- to move us to new situations (for David, this was the end of living with the Philistines).

- to prove real friendship (were some of David's friends merely 'fair weather friends'?).

2 THE LORD'S SUCCESS FOR OUR BATTLES (v17)

The nomadic, marauding Amalekites were already under God's judgement (Exodus ch17 vv14-16). God had rejected Saul because he had refused to wipe out the Amalekites and their possessions (ch15 v3). David had already enjoyed some successes against them (ch27 v8). The Lord tells David through Abiathar to pursue them (v8). For almost twenty-four hours, David and his men fought against them, and only four hundred young men escaped on camels (v17). Everything that had been taken was recovered (vv18-20). Though there are times of great loss on the way, the Lord will ultimately bring his people to complete victory. David's men suffered great grief, exhaustion, effort, and fighting on the way, but God brought them success in the end. Give thanks for the victory (1 Corinthians ch15 vv57-58).

3 THE LORD'S SUPPLY FOR OUR NEEDS (v23)

Sometimes we can be so overwhelmed by pressures that we miss God's provisions and so blinded by grief that we fail to see God's grace.

i] God's Protection: David's men and their families had been protected throughout.

ii] God's Direction: David sought guidance before embarking on his rescue mission.

The Lord had been gracious and generous to David. How did David respond?

- The Egyptian slave: They gave him food and drink despite their pressing operation.

- The two hundred exhausted soldiers: They were not disqualified from the blessings of victory.

- The Judean elders: David didn't forget his real friends (vv26-30) who had taken risks to protect him.

Let us not overlook those who have been used by the Lord to help us, supply us, and encourage us.

AUGUST 6
1 SAMUEL Ch31.1-13

WHEN GOD'S ENEMIES SEEM TO BE VICTORIOUS

We have been building up to this great battle since ch28. There was a huge difference in the size and 'firepower' of the two opposing armies. Saul was terrified at the sight of the Philistines' military might (ch28 v5). On previous occasions, when Israel had faced Philistia's superior strength, Israel had been victorious because God was on their side. In this final battle, however, between Saul and the Philistines, the Lord had turned away from him. It should have come as no surprise to Saul that the Philistines would be the victors (ch28 v19). The enemy had Saul 'in their sights' and they killed him and his three sons (v2). What can we salvage from this desperate chapter in Israel's history?

- King Saul, his armour-bearer, and three sons had been killed (v6).

- Many Israelite soldiers lay dead and brutalised on Mount Gilboa (v1).

- Hundreds of others had fled in terror (v1), and many had abandoned their towns (v7).

- Saul's armour was displayed in the pagan temple, and the corpses were impaled (v10).

- Saul's head would probably have been paraded through Philistia before it ended up in the temple of their pagan god Dagon (1 Chronicles ch10 v10).

Can you imagine the sound bites from the heathen 'evangelists' (v9) – 'Philistines triumph'...'Hebrew God failed to help his people'...'Ashtoreth –Queen of the gods'?

We may also think of where God's enemies seem to triumph today:

- Christians are massacred, executed, imprisoned, and exiled in various countries.

- False gods seem to reign, and Christianity is suppressed and oppressed.

- God's enemies win debates in Parliament, and laws are allowed onto the statute books which are contrary to God's word.

- Christians are penalised in the law courts, workplaces, and council chambers.

- God's enemies triumph in the media, schools, and hospitals (where unborn infants are massacred daily).

How can we be motivated today when it seems God's enemies are victorious?

1 GOD'S WORD IS ENDURING

It's not as bleak as it may seem. God has not abdicated control of history. Saul, his sons, and his army may be defeated, but God's word is not defeated. Chapter 31 is the fulfilment of God's word (1 Chronicles ch10 vv13-14). God's word will always have the last word (Matthew ch24 v35). Nothing can halt the word of God or deflect it from its purpose. The enemies of God are but pawns in his sovereign hand. When they appear to triumph, their powers have been permitted. But they are all outclassed, outgunned, outmanoeuvred, and outlasted by God's eternal word. The Bible is not only reliable: it's relevant. Every promise that we rightfully claim is fulfilled, and each one is 'Yes' in Christ (2 Corinthians ch1 v20).

2 GOD'S PEOPLE ARE SERVING

In vv11-13 the people of Jabesh Gilead showed their respect, faithfulness, and bravery. King Saul's first victory (ch11) was to rescue the town of Jabesh from the cruel Ammonites. The people of Jabesh were elated at this divine deliverance, and they couldn't forget it. Now they marched through the night, behind enemy lines, to respectfully remove the bodies of Saul and his sons. Let us not forget the kindnesses done to us. It was gratitude that moved the people of Jabesh to serve. One of the measurements of our gratitude to the Saviour for all that he has done for us is in our degree of service. The men of Jabesh risked their lives to do something that was unseen, unpleasant, and unrewarded. Much of our service may fall into a similar category.

3 GOD'S KING IS COMING

The rule of David is about to commence (read 2 Samuel). He will be anointed and enthroned in Jerusalem, and he will subdue his enemies. This points to David's greater Son, the Lord Jesus (Isaiah ch9 v7), who is on the throne of the universe and all his enemies will become his footstool (1 Corinthians ch15 v25; Hebrews ch10 v13). *The Root and Offspring of David'* (Revelation ch22 v16), who prayed for his enemies at the cross, will judge all his enemies at the throne. His example in praying for his enemies should encourage us to pray for our enemies, too. Jesus said that we are to love them and to pray for them (Matthew ch5 v44).

AUGUST 7
2 SAMUEL Ch1.1-27

SHOW RESPECT

1 and 2 Samuel were originally one book in the Hebrew Scriptures. We might call it *'a book of two halves'*. In this second half, the kingdom is expanded under Israel's second king, David. David's throne is a key theme in the Old Testament, for it is of David's line that the Messiah would come, and it is upon David's throne that the Messiah would sit. This book describes David's greatness and success, as well as his weaknesses and failures. Biblical history is a frank and true account without partiality. Above all, this book shows that God is on the throne of Israel. The secret to David's success or failure was his relationship with the Lord. Faith and obedience were not only essential to his boyhood victory over Goliath, but they were essential on every military, mental, and moral battlefield in King David's life. This first chapter gives us an insight into the wisdom, discernment, and respect which David showed. We must also learn to:

1 RESPECT GOD'S APPOINTMENTS

Saul and his three sons had been killed in a fierce battle with the Philistines (1 Samuel ch31). Though 1 Samuel ch31 and 1 Chronicles ch10 conclude that Saul's ultimate death was by his own hand, the Amalekite scavenger tells a slightly different story, crediting himself with Saul's final death (vv9-10). He had miscalculated that this would place him in good standing with the new king. By delivering Saul's crown and armband, the Amalekite hoped to secure honour and reward for claiming to have killed David's number one enemy. But he hadn't reckoned on the great outburst of grief from David and his valiant men (vv11-12). Though they had been fugitives from Saul for several years, they still saw Saul and his family as appointed by God (v14). The Amalekite was speechless. He hadn't expected David to react like this, nor did he see his own death coming (vv15-16). From his meteoric rise to Israel's first king, Saul had descended to rebellion, disobedience, jealousy, and hatred. But he was still God's appointed and anointed king, and David continued to respect his office. How much respect do we show for those God continues to appoint to office within the church and to service on his mission field?

2 RESPECT SPIRITUAL MATTERS

David was undoubtedly the composer of this lament (vv19-27) in which he sorrowed for Saul and Jonathan. Jonathan had been a skilled bowman who was brave in battle (v22), and perhaps it was for this reason that the poem was entitled 'Lament of the Bow' (v18). To David, it was a tragedy that Israel should have been defeated so conclusively by the Philistines and that this defeat had cost the lives of Saul and Jonathan. But if this heartbreaking news of defeat and death wasn't enough, David didn't want the Philistines to gloat and glory in Israel's humiliation (v20). The Philistine cities of Gath and Ashkelon should not be given further ammunition to humiliate the people of God: *'Tell it not in Gath!'* Christians should be careful not to provide the world with ammunition that can be used against them. How often are the internal workings of the church family gossiped among the world? How often are matters that concern the church family debated and criticised by unbelievers?

How often are the mistakes and failings of God's people used to further humiliate them by indiscreet comments and malicious gossip? If we love the Lord and his people, then we shall not say anything that can be used against them. The world doesn't appreciate the preciousness of spiritual matters just as pigs don't appreciate the value of pearls (Matthew ch7 v6). They only trample them underfoot. Beware! *'Tell it not in Gath!'*

3 RESPECT NOBLE VIRTUES

David still acknowledges Saul's virtues: graciousness (v23), might (vv19, 21, 25, 27), bravery (vv22-23), and that he was loved by many (v23). We see how the world despises noble virtues such as meekness, honesty, faithfulness, fairness, moral purity, and chivalry. We must guard against siding with the world in trashing these virtuous qualities. We must protect the noble virtues of marriage, motherhood, pure friendship, and children's 'childhood innocence'. Why should we be led by the world in making young children into adults by how they look, what they hear, what they see, and what they do? David showed respect for these precious qualities that he had seen in his soulmate, Jonathan, and even in his enemy, Saul.

AUGUST 8
2 SAMUEL Ch2.1-32

DON'T LOSE SIGHT OF THE ONE WE SERVE

The land of Canaan was now divided into two separate territories: the southern section of Judah (about fifty miles wide and one hundred miles long, roughly between the Dead Sea and the Mediterranean Sea) and the northern section of Israel (an irregular shaped territory extending from the north of the Dead Sea up to above and beyond Lake Galilee). Following Saul's death, it was Judah who anointed David as their king (v4).

In Israel, to the north, General Abner appears to be intensely loyal to Saul's dynasty and believes it's in his power to preserve Saul's line. While three of Saul's sons had been killed in battle, Abner appointed a fourth son, Ish-Bosheth, to succeed his father as king. So Israel and Judah had different kings. It wasn't God's will for Canaan (the Land of Promise) to be divided in this way. David was the divinely appointed king, and therefore, by trying to cling to plans that are not God's, this can only lead to disaster.

In the power struggle for Canaan, there was a concern for damage limitation. Victory may be decided by two representative teams of combatants. The twelve strongest and best warriors from each side were chosen to represent Judah and Israel. The team champions killed each other, and the stalemate ignited an all-out battle between the forces of David and Ish-Bosheth (v17). General Abner was in retreat and was being eagerly pursued by Asahel, one of David's elite warriors (v18). Asahel's bravery and tenacity ended in his death at the hands of Abner (v23). Israel had lost three hundred and sixty men while David had only lost twenty (vv30-31).

Notice three relevant points which seem to emerge from this chapter:

1 SEEKING GOD'S WILL MAY MEAN BIG CHANGE (vv1-4)

David wanted to know from the Lord where he should go next (v1). Although there could have been several options open to him, David was sent to Hebron.

i] Change in Attitude:

If you are serious about divine leading, then you should be prepared to do God's will before you even know what it is. Remember how Naaman had to surrender and be humbled before he experienced healing (2 Kings ch5).

ii] Change in Location:

For some Christians, the place to which God has sent them is never the 'right' place for them! Conversely, others may put their fingers in their spiritual ears when God speaks to them about changing their location.

iii] Change in Role:

For David, it was a seismic change in role as he was now the anointed King of Judah. Seven men in Acts ch6 were led by the Lord to take on new duties and new responsibilities within their own church. Sometimes the role to which we are called may not seem vital or glamorous, but God alone knows the bigger picture.

2 SHARING GOD'S GRACE MAY MEAN BIG DISAPPOINTMENT (vv4-7)

David appreciated the reverent way in which the men of Jabesh Gilead had buried the body of Saul (vv5-6). Jabesh was an Israeli town and a supporter of Saul in his enmity towards David, yet David is ready to be gracious. Although he wants them to be shown lovingkindness, there is no record that the men of Jabesh responded to the grace that David held out to them. They remained entrenched in their own loyalties and their past way of life. They would not yet surrender to another king: one of wisdom and grace. The men of Jabesh may remind us of those who refuse the grace and lovingkindness that God offers in the gospel. The word for *'love'*, or *'kindness'*, or *'lovingkindness'*, is used to describe a grace shown to those in desperate situations. It's a grace that's rooted in the loyalty and faithfulness of a covenant relationship. Jesus is the supreme expression of God's lovingkindness, but, alas, like the men of Jabesh, there are numberless hordes who spurn his grace.

3 SERVING GOD'S PEOPLE MAY MEAN BIG OPPOSITION (vv8-32)

David was called to lead and serve the whole united country, but for the moment, he had to deal with division and opposition. Sometimes, service for the Lord can mean big opposition from both inside and outside the church. A large enemy may seem to loom in our labours for the Lord. It may not be Islam or Communism, but it can take the form of family, friends, neighbours, and colleagues who can be subtle in their attacks and can be extremely wearing. Let's not lose sight of the One whom we serve. Jesus wasn't deflected in his selfless service.

'The Son of Man did not come to be served, but to serve, and to give his life as a ransom for many' (Matthew ch20 v28).

AUGUST 9
2 SAMUEL Ch3.1-39

THE POWER BEHIND THE THRONE

The French may not have wanted King Edward III to rule over them, and the northern territory of Israel didn't want David to rule over them. In the case of England and France, the Hundred Years' War began. In the case of Israel and Judah, *'The war between the house of Saul and the house of David lasted a long time'* (v1).

David was growing stronger while Saul's dynasty was becoming weaker. With God's grace, David was on track to sit on the throne over Judah and Israel.

Much of this chapter is devoted to Abner, who was Saul's cousin and who had been general over Saul's armies. Abner had been fiercely loyal to Saul and, following Saul's death, had put Saul's fourth son, Ish-Bosheth, on the throne of Israel. Abner was undoubtedly the power behind the throne.

1 HE HAD A SELF-CENTRED CAREER

Although Abner had been a faithful supporter of Saul, he had also been looking out for himself. There may be good reasons, but where had Abner been when Saul and his three sons had been killed in battle? Why hadn't Abner mounted a campaign to recover Saul's body from the battlefield instead of the men of Jabesh-Gilead? Abner had been strengthening his own position (v6). According to Ish-Bosheth's suspicions, Abner had been further consolidating his power (v7). Abner was aware of God's plan for David to be king, yet he opposed that plan for his own ends. How much control do some believers seek to retain for themselves? How much do they seek to improve their own standing in the eyes of fellow Christians, or so that they can advance their own credibility and eligibility within the church?

2 HE USED A MAN-MADE STRATEGY

Because he could manipulate Ish-Bosheth, Abner may have thought that he had some influence on God's plans and actions, too. Even when Abner eventually met with David, he still believed that it was his strategy that would achieve God's purposes for a united kingdom (v21). How much are we in danger of believing that God's purposes depend upon the success of our plans, our efforts, and our strategies? We may look upon disasters and defeats in the Christian life as being contrary to God's sovereign purposes, as if he were unable to stop them! But God is in full control, and even the judgement of earth's judges comes under the judgement of the Judge of all the earth.

3 HE KNEW A SHORT-TERM PEACE

'Peace' (referred to three times in vv21, 22, 23) was short-term and short-lived for Abner. David's own general, Joab, told the king that Abner was a spy (v25), probably because he regarded Abner as his brother's murderer (ch2 v23). Joab couldn't bear to think that Abner had been allowed to walk free, and so he devised a plan to get his revenge. Abner's peace didn't last very long as he met a violent end at the hands of Asahel's

avenger. Peace that's dependent upon men and nations is always short-term, while the long-term, everlasting peace can only come through David's greater son (Isaiah ch9 v7). Those who are justified receive peace *with* God (Romans ch5 v1), which is a guarantee of the peace *of* God. It's a peace that transcends understanding. It's a peace that the world can't provide and it can't take away.

A Prince and a Great Man

The final comment on Abner's life lies with King David (v38). Abner had many faults and failings, but it was the final estimation of the king that mattered. No doubt David was being particularly sensitive and politic in his words to the people. He wanted to unite the whole kingdom of Judah and Israel, but the assassination of Abner may have only served to divide the kingdom still further. So David distanced himself from Abner's murder. He even composed a lament for him (vv33-34) and demonstrated grief at his death (vv32,35). The king's final appraisal of Abner was that *'A prince and a great man has fallen this day in Israel'* (v38).

Those conducting funeral services for two thousand years have borrowed this eulogy. You may confess to living the kind of life that Abner lived with a self-centred career, man-made strategies, and short-term peace, but what matters ultimately is whether your relationship has been restored with your King. Abner had wanted the king to *'rule over all that (his) heart desires'*.

Is our concern to see the Lord ruling over every territory in our lives?

AUGUST 10
2 SAMUEL Ch4.1-12

RESPONDING TO NEWS

Sunday, 30th October 1938, was the day when millions of American radio listeners were shocked to hear a news bulletin alerting them to a Martian invasion. It was all part of the ground-breaking dramatisation of HG Wells' classic 'War of the Worlds'. Thousands of people panicked, police emergency phone lines were jammed, and city roads were gridlocked as thousands of people tried to escape. This reveals to us not only how convincing media deceptions may be, but also how various listeners respond to the news that they receive. We could entitle this chapter 'Responding to News'.

[i] Responding Fearfully

Though the 1938 radio broadcast was a spoof, the ensuing response of terror and panic was real enough. Fear swept through Israel when news of Abner's assassination filtered through. Ish-Bosheth had lost his right-hand man, the driving force in Israel.

[ii] Responding Carelessly

When news reached Saul's household of Saul's death, the nanny responsible for his grandson Mephibosheth, picked up her charge and was in the process of fleeing, when she dropped him. The fall was so severe that Mephibosheth became permanently *'crippled in both feet'* (ch9 v3). We may sympathise with the nanny's panic, but was it her primary concern for self-preservation that caused her to drop the child, which had been entrusted to her care?

[iii] Responding Selfishly

Recab and Baanah received news of Abner's death and wanted to take advantage of the situation. Perhaps they could curry favour with David if they assassinated his rival, Ish-Bosheth. Maybe they would earn a royal reward or honour. But their selfish and violent act in murdering Ish-Bosheth while he slept backfired on them.

[iv] Responding Righteously

David was shocked to receive news of Ish-Bosheth's murder. The death penalty was a righteous judgement upon these assassins who had killed Saul's son. Their severed heads, hands, and feet were exhibited for all to see. Here were the feet of those who brought bad news.

By contrast, Isaiah described *'the feet of those who bring good news'* as *'beautiful'* (Isaiah ch52 v7). Paul also speaks of 'gospel runners' who bring the good news of Jesus to those held captive by sin (Romans ch10 v15). From heaven's viewpoint, there are no more beautiful feet than those that take the good news about Jesus to a needy world.

But even the most beautiful feet of all the gospel messengers cannot compare with the feet of Jesus, who walked this sin-damaged world to bring life, freedom, and pardon to repenting sinners. In a desperate attempt to stifle the message and eliminate the Messenger, wicked men nailed those wonderful, beautiful feet to a cross.

How should we respond to the good news that Jesus brings?

1 IT SHOULD GIVE US PEACE

The good news of salvation should be the cause of the greatest assurance and deepest peace. Though we hear much news that agitates, disturbs, and shatters, yet the news of Jesus our King and Saviour should serve to reassure our doubting hearts.

2 IT SHOULD MAKE US PASS

Should not the gospel news that we have received encourage us to pass it on? We have no right to keep it to ourselves (2 Kings ch7 v9). Every day, the apostles didn't stop passing the news that Jesus is the Christ (Acts ch5 v42).

3 IT SHOULD TOUCH OUR PURSE

How do we think that this good news is able to be published, preached, and translated unless the Lord touches the hearts and the purses of his people? If this is really good news, then it should affect every part of us, including our bank accounts.

4 IT SHOULD PROMPT OUR PRAISE

News from God causes praising hearts (Daniel ch2 v19; Acts ch4 v24). News about Paul's conversion and ministry caused the Judean churches to respond with praise to God (Galatians ch1 v24).

What does the news about Jesus' life, death, and resurrection do for our hearts if our hearts don't overflow with joyful, thankful praise?

AUGUST 11
2 SAMUEL Ch5.1-25

UNITED KINGDOM

The flags of St George, St Patrick, and St Andrew represent the three kingdoms that make up the United Kingdom of Great Britain and Northern Ireland (since 1921). The first of three sections in this chapter centres on another United Kingdom:

1 DAVID'S UNITED KINGDOM (vv1-5)

At last, the kingdoms of Judah and Israel were united again. The twelve territories of the twelve tribes were once more united under David's sovereignty. He was accepted because of:

His Family Ties: (v1) Several hundred years earlier, Moses was told that any king must come from among the Hebrew people (Deuteronomy ch17 vv14-15).

His Military Prowess: (v2) They wanted a monarch with a proven track record of leading from the front. David was a successful warrior.

His Divine Approval: (v2) The people could see in David the fulfilment of the Shepherd-Ruler prophecy. It was David's role as shepherd that served as another Old Testament signpost pointing to David's greater son, Jesus – *'the Good Shepherd who (laid down) his life for the sheep* (John ch10 v11).

The United Kingdom of King David points to the United Kingdom of King Jesus over which he shall rule forever (Revelation ch11 v15). David prays for his royal successors, including his Messianic successor in Psalm 72 vv8, 11, 17). So David experiences his third anointing (ref 1 Samuel ch16; 2 Samuel ch2). David is better than Saul (1 Samuel ch15 v26), but in Jesus we have a king who is better than the best. His kingdom may appear fragmented and divided at times, but it cannot be shaken (Hebrews ch12 v28).

2 DAVID'S SIGNIFICANT CAPTURE (vv6-16)

David's throne had been in Hebron, where he had been reigning over Judah for seven and a half years from the age of thirty (v5). But Hebron had been linked specifically to Judah, and David needed a royal city that would inspire and unite his kingdom. Though the settlement of 'Salem' had been subdued by the men of Judah (Judges ch1 v8), they failed to live in that city. Consequently, the Jebusites built the city as a citadel for themselves. They were the last Canaanites to be ejected from the Promised Land. They were confident that their citadel city of Jebus was impregnable, but David captured the city, and thus it became *'the city of David'* (v7).

David's power came from the fact that *'the Lord God Almighty was with him'* (v10). The Jebusites' fortifications were no match for the man who had the power of God with him.

Aren't there times when we look at the citadels of God's enemies today and we think that they are invincible and impregnable? It may be the citadel of Parliament, or the citadel of the Charity Commission, or the citadel of the Planning Authority, or the citadel of 'Stonewall', or the citadel of Islam. But the man or woman who has the power of God with them is unstoppable and invulnerable.

3 DAVID'S SPIRITUAL CONQUEST (vv17-25)

The Phoenicians and the Philistines in this chapter reacted in opposite ways to David's kingship. The Philistines made an all-out push for the land of Palestine. But David used a formula that had been tried and tested by God's people over many years:

Prayer: *'David enquired of the Lord'* (vv19,23). David may have had an earthly priest, and the Urim and Thummim, but we have two supremely important resources that David didn't have in the same way – the complete written word of God and the indwelling Instructor, the Holy Spirit, the Divine Counsellor, to help us in our praying.

Obedience: When the Lord said *'Go'* (v19), *'David went'* (v20). To know God and to know the blessing of answered prayer is not about intellect, understanding, or even sacrifice. It's all about obedience. Do we have the same readiness to obey?

Divine Assistance: (v24) Listen to the sound of God at work as he moves out in front (v24). We shall always know that our Lord is in front of us if we are prepared to walk in his footsteps.

Success: (v25) For David, the success was obvious and measurable. It may not always be like that for us, but we can rest assured that God's design and purpose will always be successful. His will and his word never fail. The place was named 'Lord of the Breakthrough' (v20). When our way seems barred by 'impasses' or 'impossibilities', let us remember that he is still the 'Lord of the Breakthrough'.

AUGUST 12
2 SAMUEL Ch6.1-23

DON'T BE CASUAL WITH THE THINGS OF GOD

God provided his own set of instructions to build and assemble the special furniture for the tabernacle. The Most Holy section of the tabernacle contained the Ark of the Covenant (Exodus ch25). This was a wooden chest about the size of a small coffin (same word used for Joseph's mummy-case/coffin in Genesis ch50 v26). It was made of acacia wood and overlaid with pure gold inside and out. It had a lid of gold ('atonement cover' or 'mercy seat') with two golden cherubs with outstretched wings. This Ark had golden rings on each corner through which golden-covered poles were passed so that it could be carried by priests. The blood of the sacrificial lamb was sprinkled upon the lid of the Ark. It represented God's presence because it was at that precise location that he rendezvoused with his people through the high priest.

But the Ark had been captured by the Philistines after Eli's sons had taken it into battle as 'divine insurance'. It was sent back when the Philistines suffered a terrible plague, and the Ark of the Covenant remained under the guard of Eleazer in the house of Abinadab (1 Samuel ch7 v1) for up to a hundred years. Now David sought to recover it and bring it to the new *'City of David'* (ch5 v9). During the jubilant journey, the oxen slipped, the cart jolted, Uzzah reached out to steady the Ark, and God struck him dead (v7). The account underscores the absolute holiness of the Lord God Almighty and our responsibility not to trifle with him (Exodus ch15 v11; Job ch34 v10; Isaiah ch6 v3; Habakkuk ch1 v13; 1 John ch1 v5).

1 THE LORD MUST NOT BE ADDRESSED IRREVERENTLY

The Ark bore the Lord's name (v2). God's presence was represented by the Ark, and his name is awesome and not to be misused (Exodus ch20 v7; Psalm 111 v9). How much do you love and revere God's holy name? Are you hurt and feel 'cut to the quick' when his name is profaned or cheapened? How do you feel when God is ridiculed as the 'big brother who is watching you' or 'the man upstairs'? King Darius decreed *'that in every part of (the) kingdom people must fear and reverence the God of Daniel'* (Daniel ch6 v26).

2 THE SACRED MUST NOT BE TREATED CASUALLY

Uzzah's sudden death may be puzzling at first. Yet Uzzah and David and all Israel were well aware that the things belonging to God must be treated with great reverence and respect. God had spelt out the Ark's mode of transport (Numbers ch4 v15; 1 Chronicles ch15 vv13-15). God doesn't compromise his standards, nor does he permit his holiness to be violated. David had brought thirty thousand hand-picked men to escort the Ark. It was a brand new cart to carry the Ark, and the whole journey had been accompanied by music, singing, praise, and worship (v5). But though David had attempted to transport the Ark carefully, respectfully, prominently, and religiously, he had failed to obey God's word (1 Samuel ch15 v22). We may build our 'carts' today for our worship, evangelism, fellowship, and discipleship, but they may still supplant God's word. We dare not treat casually those things that God has made holy

3 THE END MAY NOT JUSTIFY THE MEANS

Some will say 'O, but they meant well!' Yet we should be aware that 'the road to hell is paved with good intentions'. The purpose of restoring the Ark to Jerusalem was to demonstrate the Lord's kingship. But here they were, transporting the very symbol of God's rule and authority in a way that completely disregarded his word. Paul's words in 1 Corinthians ch9 v22 have been used to justify all kinds of weird and perverted methods of evangelism. Paul was actually declaring his readiness to sacrifice personal desires and comforts to lead people to Jesus.

4 THE BLESSING IS NOT FOR THOSE WHO ACT ARROGANTLY

Because he was ready to accommodate the Ark, Obed-Edom's family received a great blessing (v11). David experienced a blessing when he transported the Ark obediently, sacrificially, and with humility. David disregarded the trappings of his regal position to worship the Lord. But David's wife, Michal, watched arrogantly from a distance (vv16, 20), and there are those on the periphery of the church who are shackled by their pride and self-esteem. They refuse to humble themselves and submit to the Lordship of Christ. Michal seriously missed out on the blessings of David's household and suffered the consequences (v23) because she was not prepared to fully surrender to the Lord. Are you most like Michal or David?

AUGUST 13
2 SAMUEL Ch7.1-29

LOVE FOREVER

Global events can occur so quickly and forcefully, emphasising the volatility of our planet. Even in our own comparatively stable nation, leaders can come and go, almost overnight. Throughout the First Book of Samuel and right up to this chapter in Second Samuel, we witness the turbulence and transience of Israel and its leadership. But here in this chapter, we view something that is sure and certain, immovable and unchangeable. For this to be so, it must emanate from Almighty God. David, who had scanned the night sky on numerous occasions while shepherding his sheep, needed to be reminded of the One Fixed Point of an ever-changing universe. The king had to be reminded of those things that don't change and decay.

1 A HOUSE FOREVER

David was living in a cedar palace while the Ark of God was still in a tent (v1; ch6 v17). David wanted to build a house for the Lord, but the Lord says that he is going to build a house for David, that is, a dynasty, a royal line from which Jesus would come (Luke ch2 v4).

2 A KINGDOM FOREVER

(vv13, 16) The throne of David is eternal in the sense that it is fulfilled in King Jesus. Though on the world's stage, in the drama of time, kingdoms constantly rise and fall, the Lord Jesus is king over an everlasting kingdom (Isaiah ch9 v7; Luke ch1 vv32-33).

3 A PEOPLE FOREVER

(v24) Just as Jesus is the 'forever King' of David's dynasty, so the Church is the 'forever people' of God's covenant (Hosea quoted in Romans ch9 vv25-26; 1 Peter ch2 v9).

4 A PROMISE FOREVER

(v25) The basis for David's prayer was the promise God had made. Do you approach God humbly, yet boldly, by laying claim to the 'forever promises' of his word? David had the courage to pray as he did (vv27, 28).

5 A NAME FOREVER

(vv25-26) The first page of the New Testament introduces us to Jesus as the descendant of David. The writers of the New Testament show conclusively that the eternal name of our living God is revealed in the Son of David. His name is the name above every name (Philippians ch2 vv9-10). It's a superior name (Hebrews ch1 vv3-4). It's the only name that matters, and it will last forever.

6 A BLESSING FOREVER

(v29) The blessing is linked to the promise that will be fulfilled in Jesus. All the good things that will come to the house and dynasty of David will come through David's greater son, the Lord Jesus.

7 A LOVE FOREVER

The Lord told the prophet Nathan that his love for David would never be reduced or removed (v15). The Hebrew word for God's 'covenant love' is a key theme of the Old Testament. This unconditional love is fulfilled in Jesus. To the spiritually thirsty and poor who come to Christ, God's *'faithful love'* is guaranteed (Isaiah ch55 vv1-3; 1 John ch4 v10). The greatest and deepest expression of God's covenant love is seen at the cross and, in the resurrection of Jesus, love's blessings are revealed (Acts 13.34).

You might say, 'If God took his love away from Saul, he might one day remove it from me?' But you can be sure that God's covenant love is secure in Jesus (Romans ch8 v38). It's infinite, eternal, unbreakable, and irrevocable. It comes to us with daily freshness and power (Lamentations ch3 vv22-23).

Do you respond to such covenant love as David did with a question and exclamation?

- **WHO AM I? (v18)**

Do you feel so wretched, ruined, sinful, and helpless? Do you wonder at how God has brought us *'this far'* – to know his word, to hear his gospel, to receive his love? Do you find yourself asking such a question as you consider his gracious dealings with you?

David was still amazed when he prayed at the end of his life (1 Chronicles ch29 v14).

- **HOW GREAT YOU ARE! (v22)**

If you are amazed at your own smallness, then you must be astounded at God's greatness. Does your daily praise and worship contain the unbridled exclamation of your heart *'How great you are!'*? David sang out in the 145th Psalm: *'Great is the Lord and most worthy of praise; his greatness no one can fathom'* (v3).

AUGUST 14
2 SAMUEL Ch8.1-18

RIGHTEOUS REIGNING

The kingdom of Jesus is an everlasting kingdom, without an army, navy, or air force. It's not limited to particular countries or continents, nor is it prone to a revolution or a coup. It's a kingdom over which Jesus Christ is its undoubted King.

The mighty warriors of King David declared their allegiance to him. We are told of one platoon leader (1 Chronicles ch12 v18) who said: *We are yours, O David! We are with you, O son of Jesse! Success, success to you, and success to those who help you, for your God will help you'*. It was this verse that prompted the Victorian poet Frances Ridley Havergal to ask the questions: *'Who is on the Lord's side? Who will serve the King? Who will be his helpers, other lives to bring? Who will leave the world's side? Who will face the foe? Who is on the Lord's side? Who for him will go?'*

David's reign was designed to be a picture/shadow/foretaste of Jesus' reign. Though David's reign was imperfect and deficient, we are assured that Jesus' reign will be perfect and sufficient in every respect.

1 DAVID REIGNED VICTORIOUSLY

Verses 1-14 reveal the scale of David's victory. *The Lord gave David victory wherever he went'* (vv6, 14). David's victory extended from Egypt in the southwest to the Euphrates in the northeast. This was precisely the territory that had been promised to Abraham (Genesis ch15 v18). From the Nile to the Euphrates, David was sovereign. He had comprehensively crushed any resistance. David was king over kings, and his reign points to the King of Kings who rules supremely. In a world that is rocked by earthquakes, tsunamis, volcanoes,, and nuclear explosions, our sovereign Saviour reigns victoriously. He who rebuked the wind and the waves from the stern of a Galilean fishing boat is able to subdue the most ferocious forces of earth and hell, time and space. The greatest victory of all is that of King Jesus, who crushed the serpent's head at the cross (Colossians ch2 v15). He is not a champion of particular causes or select groups like Spartacus, Che Guevara, or even Nelson Mandela. Jesus is king over all, and his victory means our victory too (1 Corinthians ch15 v57).

2 DAVID REIGNED FAMOUSLY

(v13) All the fame and honour which was accorded to David only came to him because God's hand was upon him (ch7 v9). David's greatness was all the more special because he had learned to serve. Joseph's fame and honour as Number Two in the whole Egyptian empire were after he had learned to serve. And Jesus, the Lord of Glory, came among us as the Servant-King (Matthew ch20 v28; Philippians ch2 vv7, 9). Yet many of the contemporary darlings of the small screen claw at and crave fame as an end in itself. They are not famous because they have achieved anything great. They are unknown individuals who have been suddenly propelled into stardom and celebrity status because they have sought fame for fame's sake. The path to true fame is through humble service, but there is One to whom all the glory is due (Isaiah ch42 v8). David attracted fame only because the Lord had exalted him. All the nations knew that he was great because he trusted in the Lord God Almighty.

3 DAVID REIGNED RIGHTEOUSLY

(vv15-18) David's righteous reign can be seen in:

His Equity:

David was fair to *'all his people'*, without discrimination or prejudice.

His Authority:

The people of Israel 'under David' were really 'under God'.

His Responsibility:

He established order and structure in his kingdom's administration.

David carefully appointed a private secretary, chief priests, a chief court administrator, a captain over the royal guard, and various royal advisors. All these individuals held responsible positions in David's righteous kingdom. Every post needed filling: every task had to be done. What post, what office, do we hold in the eternal kingdom of Jesus? Every member has an essential role in the body of Christ. Neither our prominence nor our age determines our significance, yet every member needs to be fully functioning in that body. Jesus' kingdom is upheld with righteousness, and it is God's zeal that will accomplish it (Isaiah ch9 v7). If the Lord is zealous about his righteous reign, then shouldn't we be enthusiastic about it too? It is his kingdom and righteousness that should be our number one priority (Matthew ch6 v33).

AUGUST 15
2 SAMUEL Ch9.1-13

Born in 1773, the Frenchman Stephen Grellet served as a missionary in Europe and South America. He said, *'Any kindness that I can show to any fellow-creature, let me do it now...for I shall not pass this way again'*. Grellet was gripped by the urgency to show God's kindness. It was this concern and urgency that gripped King David (v1).

SHOWING GOD'S KINDNESS

David and Saul's son, Jonathan, had made a covenant (1 Samuel ch20 vv13-15) based on the deep love they had for each other. David hadn't forgotten that pact, and he is prompted to consider whether Jonathan had any descendants left alive to whom he could show kindness. Jonathan's disabled son Mephibosheth (ch4 v4) was probably in his teens at this time, and he became the focus of the king's lovingkindness, which reflects the grace of God to sinners. Notice the huge changes with which we may identify:

1 FROM ENEMY TO FRIEND

Mephibosheth may have been the son of David's best friend, but he was more aware that he belonged to the family that had been at enmity with David for many years. David's contact with Saul's descendant was on the basis of grace. Mephibosheth could sleep easy knowing that David's lovingkindness was rooted in a covenant. That which held good for Mephibosheth holds good for every child of God who was once an enemy (Romans ch5 v10; Colossians ch1 v21). The sinner is God's would-be assassin, but in the gospel, God reaches out the hand of friendship to those who repent and trust in him (John ch15 v15).

2 FROM POVERTY TO PROSPERITY

Since Mephibosheth had been dispossessed of all his estate, and since he was disabled, it seems that he was totally dependent upon the gifts and support of others (for example, Makir, v4). In a magnanimous act of kindness, the king confers prosperity on him (v7). With one royal decree, Mephibosheth was transformed from a poor man to a rich man. Jesus came to bring eternal wealth to the spiritually poor (Luke ch4 v18; 2 Corinthians ch8 v9).

3 FROM WEAKNESS TO STRENGTH

Physically, Mephibosheth was dependent on others, but David gives him new power and authority (vv9-11). From a man who could do little, he was now in a position to command thirty-six stewards and servants. Though 'disabled by the fall' (ch4 v4) like us (Genesis ch3), he receives the new authority of the king himself (Colossians ch1 v11; Philippians ch4 v13).

4 FROM FAR OFF TO VERY NEAR

Perhaps it had suited Mephibosheth to be far away from Jerusalem and the king in Lo Debar on the other side of the Jordan. But now he who was far off is brought near (v5; compare Ephesians ch2 v13). The prodigal was *'still a long way off'* (Luke ch15 v20) when his father saw him and poured his grace upon him. *'It is good to be near God'* (Psalm 73 v28).

5 FROM A DOG TO A PRINCE

The fairy tales tell us about the transformation of a frog into a prince, but in Mephibosheth's case, it was from a dog (v8) to a prince (v9). The reference to himself as a dog was like saying 'I'm scum, I'm loathsome, I'm rotten and unworthy'. And that's the place where every sinner needs to come so that they can marvel at God's lovingkindness that reached them in their wretched condition. We must be stripped of all self-esteem and self-worth to appreciate properly the grace of God. Sin dehumanises. We are not the beings God made us to be, but he has expressed his great kindness in seating us *'with him in the heavenly realms in Christ Jesus'* (Ephesians ch2 vv4-7).

Do you always keep your promises?

David hadn't forgotten the promise he had made. The Lord was his witness (1 Samuel ch20 v42). Are you known as a person of your word whenever you promise to do something, to be somewhere, or to pray for someone?

How practical is your kindness?

David took his responsibilities seriously. David had the power to restore Mephibosheth's estate. He also provided transport for the disabled and a place at his table. What can we do within our limited resources?

How consistent is our Christianity?

He *'**always** ate at the king's table'* (v13). David's kindness wasn't a one-off, flash-in-the-pan action. How reliable are you?

How humble is your gratitude?

The last phrase of the chapter reminds us of his lameness. He wasn't at the king's table because he had earned it or bought it. He was there because of the king's lovingkindness. How grateful we should be for grace.

AUGUST 16
2 SAMUEL Ch10.1-19

Just imagine if our world were subject to the haphazard, unpredictable forces of nature and the uncontrolled aggression of man without any divine control or administration. Is there the remotest possibility that man or nature could cause its own suicide? Not if you believe the word of God (Psalm 33 vv6-11; Hebrews ch1 v3; Colossians ch1 v17). Doesn't it fill us with reassurance to know that Jesus Christ is actively governing this world; that our security is not dependent upon the accidents of nature or the whims of humanity but, instead, it is rooted eternally in the plans and counsels of our God? This was the truth that David and some of his men had learned. David's general, Joab, had declared (v12):

'THE LORD WILL DO WHAT IS GOOD IN HIS SIGHT'

This is not the fatalist's cry but the solid faith of the child of God. If this statement is incontestably true, then there are certain ways in which we should respond.

1 BE SENSITIVE WHEN YOU ARE EXALTED

David had been exalted from the unimportance of a Bethlehem shepherd to the prominence of an Israeli king. When someone is elevated to a position of power and prestige, there is the risk that they can become detached from the needs and feelings of others. It's significant that yet again King David reaches out with kindness and sympathy to Hanun, king of the Ammonites (vv1-2). David hadn't forgotten some help that Nahash had given him, and now he sought to show kindness to his son in return. It reminds us that we should never become too big, too important, too exalted, or too proud that we are prevented from coming alongside someone in sympathy. Jesus himself leads the way (Hebrews ch4 vv15-16). We have a Saviour in Glory who fully understands our weaknesses, our dilemmas, and our heartbreaks.

2 BE FAITHFUL WHEN YOU ARE REJECTED

David didn't overreact to the humiliating way in which Hanun treated David's men. It was only when the Ammonites assembled a huge army that David responded similarly (v7). At this stage, David was dependent on the Lord to do *what is good in his sight* (v12). There are times when our kindnesses and sympathies are rebuffed and rejected. How often are Christians measured by men's own selfish and mercenary motives? The world can't cope with godliness! But Jesus promised a special blessing to those who are *persecuted because of righteousness* (Matthew ch5 vv10-12).

3 BE PATIENT WHEN YOU ARE HUMILIATED

David's ambassadors to Hanun were greatly humiliated (v4). To be left half-naked and with half a beard was the deepest of disgrace and degradation. There have been many examples where the disciples of Jesus have reached out with compassion in the gospel, only to be greatly humiliated (2 Chronicles ch36 vv15-16). It's likely that you will have met that kind of response when you have tried to share the good news with someone. They may have got angry, or laughed in your face, or marched off in a huff. But it's nothing compared with the humiliation of Jesus (1 Peter ch2 vv23-24). If Jesus was patient in the midst of the most horrendous pain and humiliation, then we who claim to follow in his footsteps must also expect to be abused and ill-treated for his sake.

4 BE STRONG WHEN YOU ARE THREATENED

General Joab was sent to confront the Ammonite threat (vv9-12). He stayed calm in a crisis. He chose an elite detachment of special forces to deal with the Arameans while appointing his brother Abishai to be deployed against the Ammonites. He used the skill, knowledge, and experience that he had acquired, but he didn't depend on them. Joab trusted in the Lord and knew that he *'will do what is good in his sight'*.

Do we expect the Lord to do what is good in *our* sight? We may expect him to operate according to what *we* think is best in a given situation. That's why, at times, we become so disappointed, frustrated, and even disillusioned. It's *our* fault that we get like that because we thought that God would do what is good in *our* sight. We don't fully trust the Lord and therefore we are not prepared for his unexpected. But the call to *'be strong'* (v12) was not just for themselves. It was for *'our people and the cities of our God'*. It wasn't just a private battle or a personal fight. There were other things at stake, namely the Old Testament church, the people of God. Are we identified with *'our people'*? Do we stand together as the church of Jesus Christ, and are we strong for them?

AUGUST 17
2 SAMUEL Ch11.1-27

IN THE WRONG PLACE AT THE WRONG TIME

The Bible is unique because it's truth (John ch17 v17). Therefore, we shall expect to prove its honesty, integrity, and equity in what it tells us about individuals. It won't sidestep their embarrassing mistakes, or gloss over transgressions, or artificially reveal people in a 'good light'. In the case of David (Israel's greatest king, the composer of over seventy-three psalms, the Hebrew hero, the famous ancestor and type of Jesus), the Bible doesn't shy from proclaiming uncomfortable truth. David fell into sin as easily as anyone of us.

His weakness caused him to yield to temptation. What contributed to his downfall?

1 BEING IN THE WRONG PLACE

Joab and the entire Israelite army went off to fight God's enemies. All the *'king's men'* went into battle – but not their king. Those five words hold the key to David's downfall: *'But David remained in Jerusalem'* (v1). This was unusual because David had always led from the front. He was the 'action-man' king. But not this time! When the rest of his men were risking their lives, David was lolling around at home. When they were in battle, David was in bed. Being in 'the wrong place at the wrong time' left David exposed to temptation. How many Christians succumb to temptation when they are weak and vulnerable by being 'in the wrong place'?

2 LOOKING IN THE WRONG DIRECTION

(vv2-3) The first sight of such things should cause us to look away. If, with the first look, we don't learn, with the second look, we may lust. His eyes feasted on what they saw, and David planned to satisfy his eyes (Job ch31 v1). The glance became a gaze which became greed (Matthew ch5 v28).

3 STRIVING WITH THE WRONG MOTIVE

David should have been exercising his clever tactics and expending his considerable energies on the battlefield with his troops. Instead, he was deploying his powers to scheme and manipulate in getting Bathsheba (v4). Once he had achieved his short-term desire, it didn't stop there, for he had to cover his tracks. Bathsheba's husband, Uriah, had been where David should have been. Uriah was recalled, but his loyalty and faithfulness, as a converted pagan, wouldn't allow him to rest at home (vv9-11). Even David's 'Plan B' failed to provide David with the cover he needed. Only 'Plan C' – the premeditated murder of Uriah – could achieve David's goals.

4 SATISFIED FOR THE WRONG REASON

Uriah's death satisfied David (v25), but the Lord was dissatisfied. If David was pleased, the Lord was displeased (v27). The weak had been subdued; the pure had been violated; dignity had been shamed; authority had been compromised; the innocent had been killed, and the Almighty had been offended. The last statement sums up the whole chapter. The last word is always God's word.

How can we avoid our downfall and God's displeasure?

We must recognise the certainty of temptation:

If we believe that somehow we are immune to temptation, then this proves that we are not. Temptations affect everyone. Even the Lord Jesus here on earth was not exempt from temptation.

We must be alert to the power of temptation:

We must resist temptations firmly, but we cannot afford to dismiss temptations casually. Jesus said that we must *'watch and pray'* (Matthew ch26 v41). Neither asceticism nor monasticism is God's way of dealing with temptation. Isolation from the world is not the answer.

We must know how to overcome temptation:

We must learn early on that we cannot deal with temptations in our own strength. Jesus himself demonstrated in the midst of Satan's personal attack upon him that the word of God is an indispensable weapon when it comes to temptation. Let the Scriptures strengthen you and defend you. Let the Holy Spirit wield his sword. Frequently, it's the small, insignificant temptations that lead to the most damage. David's downfall began with being in the wrong place at the wrong time. It began with that 'second look'.

'So if you think you are standing firm, be careful that you don't fall. No temptation has seized you except what is common to man. And God is faithful; he will not let you be tempted beyond what you can bear. But when you are tempted, he will also provide a way out so that you can stand up under it' (1 Corinthians ch10 vv12-13).

May the Lord's uplift keep you from your downfall.

AUGUST 18
2 SAMUEL Ch12.1-31

The prophet Nathan uses a word-picture to bring a vital message to King David. David must have thought that all the 'dust had settled' after the incidents of the previous chapter. Maybe he had thought that he had covered his tracks and had got away with it. When Nathan appears, possibly twelve months later, David is a sitting duck for the parable that he delivers about the poor man with one little ewe lamb, which the rich man seized. David is enraged at the rich man's callousness, and Nathan's trap is sprung. David demands that judgement be passed on the rich man (vv5-6), and Nathan's punchline, his coup de grace, his finishing stroke was v7:

'YOU ARE THE MAN!'

David couldn't sidestep the ammunition that was aimed directly at him. As we consider God's message to David, let's consider God's message to us in the Bible.

1 IT'S GOD'S WORD FOR YOU

It couldn't be more personal, could it? *You are the man!* Many people would have fallen outside the scope of Lord Kitchener's iconic WWI poster: *'Your country needs you'*. Many others would have fallen outside the scope of the 1990s BT advert: *'It's for you'*. But in the case of God's word, it is for you! No one falls outside the scope of the Bible. God spoke to David, and he knew that unquestionably. The Bible is not for white, middle-class, middle-aged people exclusively. It's for everyone. Jesus said, *'He who has ears, let him hear'* (Matthew ch11 v15). Of course, the Christian reads the Bible differently because he is personally acquainted with the Author. How sweet are the Lord's words to your taste (Psalm 119 v103)? Do you read the Bible as a book written in the 'third person singular' for the 'third person plural' or do you read it as a letter written from God in the 'second person singular' for the 'first person singular'?

2 IT'S GOD'S WORD FOR NOW

If we believe that God's word is for humanity, and we are included in that collective term, then it's easy to sidestep the particular relevance of the Scriptures by convincing ourselves that it is more appropriate to another era, another generation, and another time. David might have hoped that Nathan's parable could have referred to someone else at another time, but the message from God caught David unawares. The word came like a 'guided missile' on a mission: *You are the man!* The word of God is both living and active (Hebrews ch4 vv12-13). It's a short step from believing that God's word is irrelevant and out of date to despising that word and rejecting it (v9). The message of the gospel is no less appropriate now than it has ever been (2 Corinthians ch6 v2). It is for now.

3 IT'S GOD'S WORD TO DO

God's word always demands a response. Jesus described people who hear his words but don't put them into practice as a man who builds a house without a foundation (Luke ch6 v49). David's response to God's word was *'I have sinned against the Lord'* (v3). He had no excuses; no mitigating circumstances. Around this time, David composed Psalm 51 in which he cried out for mercy, compassion, cleansing, and renewal. And it's at the place of penitence, repentance, and humility that we can experience the wonderful grace of God.

Notice the instances of God's grace to David in this chapter:

In giving everything:

(vv7-8) Nothing had been withheld from David. God said that he would have even given him more (v8).

In sending Nathan:

(vv1-6) Sure, he brought a word of condemnation, but it was delivered in grace so that David would repent. How often does God's word come to us through a messenger with a message finely tuned for our needy hearts?

In delivering judgement:

(vv7-12; 15-23) Even God's word of judgement upon David and his family is tempered by grace.

In removing sin:

(v14) David composed Psalm 32 in response to the personal experience of God's forgiveness.

In providing a blessing:

(vv24-25) David and Bathsheba had the son of their illicit relationship snatched from them. But in God's grace, he provides this couple with another son, Solomon. Can there be a greater comment than: *'The Lord loved him'*?

In achieving victory:

(vv26-31) Sin may cause defeat for a while, but repentance can restore victory through God's grace.

AUGUST 19
2 SAMUEL Ch13.1-39

FAMILY HEARTBREAK

Family heartbreaks can affect most people on one or more occasions in their lives. Indeed, for some people, they may feel as if they are in a lifetime of family heartbreak. *Jonathan Livingston Seagull,* a popular book in the 1970s, emphasised the independence and individuality that causes problems in a seagull society. Some of those same problems are reflected in a human family.

1 FAMILY HEARTBREAKS CAN BE INDISCRIMINATE

No particular family is totally exempt from suffering, tragedy, sorrow, and heartbreak:

Big People are not Exempt:

Who could have been greater, more prominent, or more influential than David? Even Queen Elizabeth II had her 'annus horribilis' in 1992.

Buoyant People are not Exempt:

You may think that wealthy people could buy themselves out of many of the troubles that less prosperous people face. David was extremely rich, but his riches couldn't come to his aid.

Beautiful People are not Exempt:

David was privileged and blessed with a family of 'beautiful people'. David had been handsome (1 Samuel ch16 v12), his wife Abigail was intelligent and beautiful (1 Samuel ch25 v3), his third son Absalom was the pin-up of his day (ch14 v25), and the subject of this chapter, Tamar, was also beautiful (v1). Absalom's own daughter (also called Tamar) was described as beautiful (ch14 v27). But beauty doesn't guarantee immunity from tragedy and heartbreak.

Believing People are not Exempt:

David was a believer. He had been a faithful follower of the Lord, especially during his youth. He was *'a man after (the Lord's) own heart'* (1 Samuel ch13 v14), but he was not exempt from suffering. The *'blameless and upright'* Job (Job ch1 v8) endured the worst of family heartbreaks. But he learned that our sovereign God has a purpose in our pain and a design in our distress. Believers have consistently proved the faithfulness and love of God in the most painful of heartaches.

2 FAMILY HEARTBREAKS CAN BE COMPLICATED

Sometimes, though not always, our heartbreaks can be caused by our own actions. David had been warned of the calamity that would befall his family (ch12 v11). Tamar was the victim of her half-brother's desire and obsession. He didn't love her (v15). This monstrous crime, perpetrated within David's own family, underlines to us the abuse and violation that continues behind the doors of some family homes. Tamar was crushed by her shame and disgrace. David failed her as her advocate, her king, and her father. He may have been *'furious'* (v21), but he was a failure to Tamar. His inaction compounded Tamar's ignominy. David's lust and murder are now reproduced in the next generation. How complicated family situations can become, and we must be sensitive to such convoluted relationships. Because the law had failed Tamar, Absalom exacts revenge by killing his half-brother, the 'crown prince'. Families continue to be the place where jealousies are spawned, greed is nurtured, pride is unchecked, and grudges are nursed. Sadly, few families remain untouched by disappointment, desertion, divorce, and death, which can bring misery and grief.

3 FAMILY HEARTBREAKS CAN BE REPAIRED

There is hope in the midst of despair: there is a solid ground in the quagmire of uncertainty. The gospel is the remedy for man's greatest problem: his sin. In the Lord Jesus, there is One who can save from the stranglehold of sin. *'Heartache crushes the spirit'* (Proverbs ch15 v13) but *'The Lord is close to the broken-hearted and saves those who are crushed in spirit'* (Psalm 34 v18). *'He heals the broken-hearted and binds up their wounds'* (Psalm 147 v3). Jesus declared that he had come to *'bind up the broken-hearted'* (Isaiah ch61 v1). Jesus is the only one who can mend broken hearts. He can forgive sin and overcome the power of sin. Our families need Jesus, and David's family needed Jesus. In a most singularly wonderful way, Jesus visited David's family as a member of that earthly family (Galatians ch4 v4, John ch1 v14). He made his dwelling among the descendants of David, and so he fully sympathises with heartbroken families (Hebrews ch4 v15). Jesus came to be a part of that sinful, tragic, heartbroken family, though remaining unblemished himself. We can approach him with the bitterest of family heartbreaks knowing *'that no one understands like Jesus'*.

AUGUST 20
2 SAMUEL Ch14.1-33

If glossy magazines had existed in 1000BC, then Absalom would have been on the front page of every one. He was the glamour model who required no airbrushing or cosmetic camouflaging. He enjoyed star status, not only as the Crown Prince, but as the 'pop pin-up' of image and fashion. His hair was a valuable asset (v26). But Absalom had not been so popular with his father (ref ch13). Following Amnon's murder, Absalom had escaped to Geshur and stayed there for three years (ch13 v38). But the royal advisers, especially Joab, knew that although David was furious with Absalom, he had a secret yearning to be reconciled with him (v1).

This chapter is dominated by Joab's plan of reconciliation, which is in marked contrast to God's way of reconciliation.

GOD'S WAY OF RECONCILIATION

'(God) devises ways so that a banished person may not remain estranged from him' (v14). Yet this woman from Tekoa, like many deceiving preachers of our day, was only telling part of the truth.

What must we know about God's way of reconciliation?

1 GOD'S WAY OF RECONCILIATION IS A DIVINE INITIATIVE NOT A HUMAN INITIATIVE

Joab had tried to engineer a reconciliation between the king and Absalom. The woman attempted to persuade the king to move on this issue. The scheming, acting, pretence, flattery, and inventiveness were all calculated to influence the king's mind. But by contrast, God's way of reconciliation is not prompted by human schemes or influence. Man has no inclination to be reconciled to God. He is a spiritual corpse. Romans ch3 vv12-18 portrays his perilous condition. However, Romans ch3 v21 continues, *But now a righteous from God...has been made known'.* It's from God! God has graciously acted to save those who believe. He has provided the Mediator and Saviour himself.

2 GOD'S WAY OF RECONCILIATION IS COMPLETE, NOT PARTIAL

When David agreed for Absalom to be brought back to Jerusalem (v21), he lived there for two years before he saw his father (vv24, 28). Maybe David was embarrassed about his treatment of Absalom, or perhaps he still harboured a little bitterness towards him. For whatever reason, Absalom was kept 'at arm's length'. By contrast, God's way of reconciliation is total, as seen in the parable of the prodigal (Luke ch15). The wayward son received the kiss that Absalom didn't receive for another two years. If you are really saved by God's grace, then the reconciliation is not provided in stages or increments. You are not made a 'son' and kept for two years at arm's length (Romans ch8 v17)!

3 GOD'S WAY OF RECONCILIATION IS REPENTANCE, NOT ARROGANCE

We glimpse something of Absalom's unrepentant heart (v32). Here was a plan of reconciliation without the vital ingredient of repentance. Absalom remained defiantly unrepentant of his sin, and any reconciliation was doomed to fail. The 'wise (?) woman's' message was a gospel without the need of repentance. Any restored communion between a holy God and sinful man must include confession of sin, admission of guilt, and acceptance of blame (Luke ch13 v3; Acts ch3 v19).

4 GOD'S WAY OF RECONCILIATION IS RIGHTEOUS, NOT ARBITRARY

David may have swallowed the woman's flattery (vv20-21), but God is not similarly influenced. His ways are *'just'* (Deuteronomy ch32 v4); *'holy'* (Psalm 77 v13); *'righteous'* (Psalm 145 v17; Hosea ch14 v9). His ways are not subject to pressure or are the product of a whim. His ways are full of justice.

5 GOD'S WAY OF RECONCILIATION IS A CROSS, NOT A KISS

Although the kiss brought David and Absalom face to face – literally (v33) – it didn't represent true reconciliation. The next dozen verses reveal Absalom's treachery. The reconciliation was just a sham. God's way, however, is sure and certain because of the death of his Son (Romans ch5 v10; Colossians ch1 vv21-22).

Do you feel that you are 'distant' from God; that there's a barrier between you and God? Does God seem remote and impersonal at the moment? Then come by God's way, through repentance, faith, and humility, trusting in the cross of the Lord Jesus. Realise that in this way your sins will not be counted against you (2 Corinthians ch5 v19). Indeed, *'we implore you on Christ's behalf: Be reconciled to God'* (2 Corinthians ch5 vv20-21).

AUGUST 21
2 SAMUEL Ch15.1-37

In a BBC interview on 20th November 1995, Princess Diana said, *'I'd like to be a queen in people's hearts'*. From this chapter, there are three kings who contend for that place.

A KING IN PEOPLE'S HEARTS

David's son and the Crown Prince, Absalom, wanted to be a king in people's hearts so that he could seize the throne from his father. Secondly, David was desperate to remain the king of people's hearts as he tried to protect them from Absalom. But the third king who wanted to reign in people's hearts was the Lord God Almighty.

We may recognise the struggle that existed in Israel being replayed in the kingdom of our own hearts. Who is the king that reigns in your heart? To which king are you loyal and committed? Who has the most influence on your life? Is it a king, like Absalom:

1 THE KING OF FRAUD

The kiss of reconciliation (ch14 v33) was just a sham. Absalom was not only unrepentant; he was now single-mindedly focused on toppling his father, David, from his throne. Absalom could market his own image to his best advantage and deceive the people:

His impressive bodyguard

(v1) Chariots, horses, and fifty personal protection officers served to demonstrate the success and power he had achieved.

His enthusiasm and hard work

(v2) He was out on the streets early in the morning, driving his own publicity campaign while others would be lying in their beds.

His listening ear

(vv2-3) He intercepted the complainants before they got to David, and he told them the things they wanted to hear. He was the 'nice Mr Absalom'!

He sowed seeds of rebellion

(v4) He tried to ingratiate himself with the people by suggesting that he would make a better king than his father. In this way, *'he stole the hearts of the men of Israel'* (v6). Over the course of four years, Absalom wages his 'charm offensive', sowing seeds of rebellion in the people's hearts. Similar seeds of discontent are often sown today: *'If only I...'* (v4). If only I were appointed...deacon, elder, youth leader, secretary, pastor...etc. Beware of the 'Absalom seeds'!

He showed generosity

(v11) Two hundred people were taken in by his charade. These prominent people were blissfully unaware that Absalom had been plotting a coup. How easily we can be 'sucked in' by someone's apparent generosity and charm.

His religious appearance

(vv8, 12) His speech to the king was so sanctimonious. Even our arch-fiend masquerades as *an angel of light* (2 Corinthians ch11 v14).

So it was reported that *'the hearts of the men of Israel are with Absalom'* (v13).

2 THE KING OF FEAR

(vv13-15) This fearful, fleeing king was the same man who, in his youth, had confronted a lion, a bear, the giant Goliath, thousands of Philistines, and even Saul and his army. But he's on the run from his son. How quickly we can become paralysed with fear when we lose contact with the Lord. Which fears intimidate us? Fear of men; fear of sickness and immobility; fear of unemployment and loss; fear of the unknown and the uncontrollable? This was the David who had said, *'Though an army besiege me, my heart will not fear'* (Psalm 27 vv1-3). Specific sins of activity or neglect can affect our relationship with the Lord and can cause us anxiety and fear.

3 THE KING OF FAITH

David's four loyal servants demonstrated faith in the Lord. Hushai is described as *'David's friend'* (v37). Are we known as a friend of King Jesus? While David's faithful supporters were bravely busy, David had crossed the Kidron Valley and had climbed the Mount of Olives in sorrow and humiliation. It cannot escape our attention that a thousand years later, Jesus took the same route on the eve of his death. As David had said, *'Let him do to me whatever seems good to him'* (v26), so Jesus prayed in the olive groves, *'Not as I will but as you will'* (Matthew ch26 v39). The triumph of the cross was achieved through Jesus' submission to his heavenly Father's plan. And for David, who had reached the nadir of humiliation and heartache, it seems that a note of victory had been sounded when he said, in effect, 'Your will be done'. If at the moment the Lord is taking you 'across the Kidron Valley and up the Mount of Olives', where you may be suffering the humiliation of sin and a broken relationship with God, then turn to trust in the wisdom and grace of God. Which king has stolen your heart?

AUGUST 22
2 SAMUEL Ch16.1-23

David was deserting Jerusalem to the east as Absalom approached from the south. Absalom was determined to seize the throne from his father as David fled from confrontation with his rebellious son. We are provided with three separate incidents in this chapter, two of them directly involving David.

HOW DO WE RESPOND?

Every day, we are confronted with a variety of situations, some of them very complicated and sensitive, but each of them demands a response from us. What kind of response should we give?

1 RESPONDING TO DECEITFUL ACCOUNTS

Ziba gives an account of why Saul's grandson Mephibosheth remained in Jerusalem after David and his followers had left (vv1-4). Ziba had been the one who had identified this disabled son of Jonathan (ch4 v4) so that David could show kindness to him (ch9 v3). David restored to him his grandfather's estate and appointed Ziba to serve him. Now Ziba meets David on the far side of the Mount of Olives and offers refreshment (v2). When asked about Mephibosheth, Ziba provides this account (v3). Like David, we may be appalled to learn that Mephibosheth had abandoned David, who had been so gracious towards him. Perhaps we may have reacted like David (v4). Ziba becomes wealthy with one fell swoop. But wouldn't you have investigated the veracity of Ziba's account? Was this story consistent with what you already knew? David had been duped by Ziba's account. How quickly people can become maligned by another's gossip. How skilled are some people in being selective about which facts to reveal while attaching their own spin? We are all guilty of making judgements on appearances alone. Unlike David, we should be humble enough to receive generosity but discerning enough to spot hypocrisy. David had not bothered to get the true picture. Instead, he made a judgement about a loyal and trusted believer based on someone else's deceitful account. Note David's own words (Psalm 15 vv1-3).

2 RESPONDING TO HURTFUL ABUSE

In the bizarre incident of vv5-14, David is subjected to a sustained attack by one man called Shimei. If David's response to Ziba is inadequate and regrettable, his response to Shimei is gracious and laudable. Shimei was Saul's relative (v5) and an enemy of David. His boldness was boosted as he viewed the king in retreat (v7). He continued to wage a single-handed attack with stones and dirt across the gorge (v13). But David showed restraint even when one of his bodyguards offered to go and decapitate him (v9). It's not hard to see the parallels today. How many 'Shimeis' persistently dog the feet of the saints? Is there a 'Shimei' who is verbally abusing you, slandering you and making your life a trial? But the Lord gives humility and grace to endure such persecution (Matthew ch5 vv11-12). He gives patience to those who rely wholly on him.

3 RESPONDING TO SINFUL ADVICE

Ahithophel had been David's trusted counsellor (v23), but he had defected to Absalom. Absalom esteemed Ahithophel's advice as greater than God's word. Here was a man who had the reputation of being in close contact with God, so that it was believed that he could direct people in the will of God.

History is littered with men and women who have held such a reputation: those who were believed to have held the key to special divine revelation outside of the Bible (Joseph Smith, Charles Taze Russell, Mary Baker Eddy, Herbert Armstrong, and a host of others). These are the 'Ahithophels' of modern history. Don't let an 'Ahithophel' come between you and your Bible! And don't make an 'Ahithophel' out of someone who isn't an 'Ahithophel'! Even in evangelical Bible-believing circles, there is the danger of supplanting the Bible with the commentaries of a John Calvin or a Matthew Henry; or with the sermons of a Spurgeon or Lloyd-Jones; or with the Bible notes of a Schofield or MacArthur! We must be aware that the good and godly advice of Christian notables is no substitute for God's inspired word.

David had known that he had been installed as God's king (Psalm 2 vv1-7), but his enthronement was a pale reflection of the One to whom the New Testament author applies Psalm 2 (compare Hebrews ch1 v5). Jesus is God's appointed King of Kings. He has revealed the perfect way to respond to selfish 'Zibas' (Luke ch9 v48); treacherous 'Ahithophels' (Matthew ch4 v10) and hurtful 'Shimeis' (1 Peter ch2 v23). As we focus on Jesus, our perfect Example, we shall learn the perfect way to respond.

AUGUST 23
2 SAMUEL Ch17.1-29

Double agents are not an invention of spy thriller writers or the secret service. In this chapter, we are introduced to the operation of a double agent named Hushai. He had presented himself to Absalom as a friend and adviser when he was actually working for David. Even when Hushai's advice conflicted with the advice of Absalom's long-term counsellor, Ahithophel, it was Hushai's counsel that was preferred *'for the Lord had determined to frustrate the good advice of Ahithophel in order to bring disaster on Absalom'* (v14).

THE LORD DETERMINES

The word *'determined'* may also be translated *'appointed'* or *'commanded'*. This is the same word used to describe God's powerful decrees in creation (Psalm 33 v9). Such are those authoritative commands that none can resist. It's impossible to imagine the stars resisting the Lord's marshalling (Isaiah ch45 v12).

1 THE LORD DETERMINES TO FRUSTRATE EVIL SCHEMES

To pursue David with twelve thousand men and crush him right away (v1) may have been a reasonable tactic. But the Lord had determined to frustrate Absalom's evil schemes, and he caused him to choose Hushai's advice in preference to Ahithophel's scheme. Where the Lord determines, nothing or no one can thwart his purposes. Even when the darkness of sin and unbelief holds the sinner captive, nothing can resist the effectual call of the gospel.

2 THE LORD DETERMINES TO HELP FAITHFUL MESSENGERS

Jonathan and Ahimaaz were acting as messengers between David and Hushai (vv17-22). Although they were keeping a low profile in En Rogel (v17), they were spotted and reported to Absalom. Would this frustrate God's plan? Of course not! The Lord had determined that these messengers would complete their mission. Security for the saints is provided, not by the absence of danger, but by the presence of God.

3 THE LORD DETERMINES TO UPHOLD DIVINE APPOINTMENTS

Despite David's faults and failings, he remained God's appointed king. God had determined that he would be on the throne of Israel (Psalm 2 vv4-6). But as God's appointed and anointed king (1 Samuel ch13 v14), he signposts the installation of King Jesus who *'will reign on David's throne'* (Isaiah ch9 v7). That divine appointment, like every other divine appointment, cannot be postponed or cancelled. *'The authorities that exist have been established by God'* (Romans ch13 v1). Even the great world emperor, Nebuchadnezzar, was brought to a point where he testified *'that the Most High is sovereign over the kingdoms of men and he gives them to anyone he wishes...'* (Daniel ch4 v17). Presidents, prime ministers, preachers, or pastors are all determined by God's sovereign appointments.

4 THE LORD DETERMINES TO ANSWER EARNEST PRAYERS

We must see this ch17 in the light of David's fervent prayer in ch15. Read ch15 v31 and then ch17 v14. Answers to prayer are in the divine domain. God determines to answer prayer in his particular way and according to his timetable. Therefore, we should try to never allow ourselves to become disappointed. Our 'disappointment' is a challenge to God's 'appointment'. The word 'disappoint' means 'to dispossess of an appointed office'. So our disappointment is in contradiction to his appointment, that is, his appointed times and methods. The Lord had all the circumstances under his perfect control, carefully regulating the degree of heartache and hardship that David experienced.

5 THE LORD DETERMINES TO PROVIDE NEEDY SUPPLIES

David and his people had been in desperate need (v29). But notice the generous and thoughtful gifts that were supplied through God's agents. Although the Lord supernaturally supplied his people with manna and quails in the Sinai desert and employed ravens to supply Elijah with bread and meat in the Kerith Ravine, in most cases God uses his people to supply his people. Shobi, Makir, and Barzillai identified a need and were prompted to supply that need. David and his followers received such a blessing because faithful, loving believers were prepared to give. Shouldn't we be looking for needs that we can supply, for while the Lord determines to supply, he most often supplies through us?

AUGUST 24
2 SAMUEL Ch18.1-33

The slogan of News International plc has been 'We believe in the power of news'. Certainly, this company's management has felt the crushing 'news power' as they have been subject to intense scrutiny and investigation following the charges of phone hacking. The narrative of these chapters in 2 Samuel is the stuff of newspapers with its schemes and scandals, deceivers and defectors, its political intrigue and espionage.

GOOD NEWS INTERNATIONAL

Absalom had listened to David's double-agent Hushai instead of listening to Ahithophel, and he suffered the consequences that God had determined. The battle between Absalom's forces and David's loyal troops took place in the Forest of Ephraim. David's army triumphed over the enemy, including the defeat of Absalom himself, who had been riding a mule when his head became caught in the branches of a large oak tree (v9). His fate was sealed. Although the soldier who found him recalled David's words about protecting the king's son, the commander Joab had no such compunction as he impaled Absalom on three javelins (v14). All of Absalom's followers were dead, or lost in the forest, or had fled to their homes. David was a victor, but he didn't yet know it. The news had to be relayed to the king by runners.

As we consider the way in which this news was transmitted, we may also think about the way in which we communicate the good news about Jesus. We must:

1 TREAT IT WITH RESPONSIBILITY

Ahimaaz was keen to run and take the good news to the king. But Joab was very perceptive (v20). He knew that the news that was 'good' to them was not necessarily 'good' to David. Ahimaaz's jubilant, enthusiastic, and euphoric announcement may not have been well received by David. So a Cushite was chosen to be the runner, although Joab eventually relented and permitted Ahimaaz to accompany him. The business of conveying news is a most responsible business, as it should be delivered faithfully and truthfully. The good news of Jesus is not a headline or a sound bite with our slant or spin upon it. We have the responsibility to proclaim Biblical truth (1 Corinthians ch15 vv1-4). We mustn't be guilty of only relaying particular bits of that message. Paul told the Ephesian elders that he hadn't hesitated to proclaim to them *'the whole will of God'*. He preached faithfully the whole plan of salvation.

2 TELL IT WITH URGENCY

Ten times in eight verses we are told that the messengers 'ran'. They did not hesitate or procrastinate: they were determined to ensure that others received the message. When Ahimaaz blurted out the message (v28) he was not prepared for David's response (v33). We may also meet with unexpected reactions to the gospel. Some may be challenged, convicted, shocked, affronted, embarrassed, or distressed, yet if we are faithful in conveying the message, we must not be alarmed.

3 TRUST IT WITH CERTAINTY

Ahimaaz knew that the message he carried was true. He knew the accuracy of that news because he had eye-witnessed Absalom swinging by his head in the oak tree, or he had seen Joab and ten of his armour-bearers strike the final blow, or he had observed his body buried in a large forest pit (v17). He could put his trust in the message because of personal involvement. If we have come to know the gospel for ourselves, and we have been forgiven, delivered, and saved personally, then we can trust it with certainty. Just as the message was entrusted to runners, so the gospel message has been entrusted to the church. There are heretics and religious bandits around who will hijack the gospel if they can. Timothy was told to *'Guard the good deposit that was entrusted to (him)'* (2 Timothy ch1 v14). Don't let this trustworthy message become tainted or corrupted. Preserve its purity in the way that this message is conveyed. This noble, priceless treasure has been entrusted to our charge, and we have no business tampering with it.

If we have experienced the wonder-working power of the cross to change our lives, then can't we trust it to change the lives of others? Shouldn't this be our motivation and confidence, that the effectiveness of the gospel is not in our eloquence, or how fast we can 'run', but in the power of this God-given international news?

AUGUST 25
2 SAMUEL Ch19.1-43

The banner that might be written over this chapter is:

COME, MEET THE KING!

For three specific characters, the royal invitation represented a break with the past and the incentive to begin a new life under the authority of a new king. Yet the first few verses of the chapter show David to be anything other than kingly. David's sorrow for Absalom made him neglect his own troops, who crept home like defeated casualties of war rather than being hailed as heroes. General Joab gave David such an ear-bashing (vv5-7) that the king responded by making himself available to his people (v8).

Winning the hearts of the men of Judah was surprisingly easy as they went to *'meet the king'* (v15). The men of Israel were rather more suspicious.

Yet among the welcoming party, there were three men who came to meet the king, providing us with three lessons to be learned:

1 Shimei – THE KING FORGIVES OUR ENMITY

Shimei hurried to meet the king (v16), crossing the Jordan to help David. He threw himself at the king's feet and pleaded to be forgiven. This is the same Shimei who had shouted curses at David as he left Jerusalem and had pelted him with stones and dirt (ch16). But now he confesses his wrong (v19), begging that the king would forget it. The place of humility and penitence at Jesus' feet is the place to which we all need to come. Shimei was contrite (from the Latin, meaning *'thoroughly crushed'*). King David forgave Shimei's enmity, and King Jesus can do the same for us (Romans ch5 v10; Colossians ch1 v21).

Unbelievers are at war with heaven in their attitudes, actions, and beliefs. They are opposed to God's purposes, adversaries of his truth, and enemies of his righteousness. But the king wants sinners as his friends and we must come 'just as we are', confessing our sinfulness and unworthiness. Shimei was given the word of the king as his assurance (v23). There were those who had wanted to exact revenge on Shimei, but he was protected by the king's word, and no one could touch him. David's grace to Shimei is a pale reflection of the grace of God to his enemies. In Christ, those who once were far off have been brought near.

2 Mephibosheth – THE KING UNDERSTANDS OUR DISABILITY

Mephibosheth's servant, Ziba, had slandered him by telling lies about the reason his master had remained in Jerusalem as Absalom had approached (ch16 v3). Now Mephibosheth, unkempt through mourning for David, had the opportunity to set the record straight (vv26-28). He comes to meet the king (v24) and explains that the reason he hadn't been able to leave Jerusalem was because he was lame and had been abandoned by his servant. David understood Mephibosheth's disability and limitations. You may feel that you have very few abilities and gifts for Christian service. You may lack academic achievement, or you may possess physical limitations and medical problems. Your spelling may be atrocious, and you may be artistically challenged. You may be a technophobe, get tongue-tied, or travel-sick. But the Lord understands your disabilities. He can equip you and resource you for his special 'kingdom service'. Just come, meet the king!

3 Barzillai – THE KING USES OUR AVAILABILITY

Our brief introduction to Barzillai in ch17 v27 is complemented by vv34-39. He is an octogenarian who has revealed his generosity and kindness in attending to David's needs. But he is now feeling the weakness of advanced years. He confesses that his taste is not so delicate; his hearing is not so sharp, and his judgement is not so perceptive (v35). Although he didn't want to be a burden to friends and family, the king hadn't given up on him. God still wants to use our availability. Others may be ready and able to do the job better (v37), but the king still wants his people to serve him and walk with him (v33). You may not feel as energetic as you once did, but your ministry and faithful service are still valuable. It may be praying *for* and praying *with* God's people. It may be encouraging people, writing a letter, sharing a coffee, or reading the Bible with someone who is young in the faith, or with someone who struggles to read.

There's a brilliant Day approaching when the Lord Jesus will return from Glory and every believer will be summoned: 'Come, meet the King!'

AUGUST 26
2 SAMUEL Ch20.1-26

David's kingdom was divided. Judah, a territory approximately a hundred miles by fifty miles, with its northern border just north of Jerusalem, was inhabited by the tribe of Judah and Simeon. Israel, further to the north, consisted of the remaining ten tribes led by Ephraim. We see the Old Testament church in the twelve tribes. At times, we glimpse something of her unity and oneness, but often we see her fragmented and pursuing personal, tribal, and party interests. There are two people in this chapter who have an impact on that 'Old Testament church situation'. One is a man, the other is a woman. One is named, the other is unnamed. One is a troublemaker, the other is a peacemaker.

TROUBLEMAKER OR PEACEMAKER?

Sheba is announced as a *'troublemaker'* (v1), and the unnamed woman from the city of Abel Beth Maacah testifies to being among *'the peaceful and faithful in Israel'* (v19). This *'wise woman'* is responsible for brokering peace and saving the city from disaster.

Sometimes the distinction between troublemakers and peacemakers is not so obvious.

Let's ask four supplementary questions from this chapter to make things clearer:

1 FOR OR AGAINST THE KING?

Sheba makes his position very clear from his trumpet call and rallying cry. He wants no share in the king or his reign (v1). Consequently, the split between Judah and Israel deepened. Israel *'deserted David'* while Judah *'stayed by their king'* (v2). At the heart of many controversies that divide Christendom, this fundamental question must be asked: Are you for or against the King? Are you a disciple or a rebel; are you a loyalist or a deserter? In Joshua's day, Israel had been presented with two stark choices. Joshua said, *'But as for me and my household, we will serve the Lord'* (Joshua ch24 v15).

2 UNDER OR ABOVE AUTHORITY?

Joab was a loyal supporter of David when it suited him, but he was not averse to criticising David or manipulating him. He could be treacherous too, as in his murder of Abner and also of Amasa (v10), who had been David's appointed replacement of Joab. Joab could be successful, but he was also a 'loose cannon', making unilateral decisions to achieve his own ends. At times, he believed he was outside, even above, David's authority. The church is also full of mavericks like Joab: men and women who have imbibed the 'spirit of the age', who don't want to be restricted by Biblical impositions, who don't want to be tied down to church membership. How much do we love the word of God? Is it a lamp to our feet, a wonder to our eyes, and honey to our taste? Sheba was a blatant insurrectionist, but in Joab, we see someone who professed to be loyal to the king but who, in practice, had a personal agenda to follow.

3 WITH OR WITHOUT SINCERE WORDS?

Joab's greeting *'My brother'* (v9), was immediately followed by a dagger into Amasa's stomach. By contrast, the *'wise woman'* provided *'wise advice'* to Joab and the citizens of her city (v22). The city had a reputation for peacefulness and faithfulness (v19). Of course, evangelical, Bible-believing Christians are accused of being troublemakers because they will not compromise Biblical truth, such as the infallibility of God's word, the true deity and humanity of Jesus, justification by faith alone, the reality of heaven and hell, and the eternal sonship of Christ. But we must strive to broker peace in proclaiming the gospel of *'peace through his blood shed on the cross'* (Colossians ch1 v21).

4 BATTERING OR BUILDING THE LORD'S INHERITANCE?

Joab had laid siege to the city in which Sheba had been hiding. They were trying to batter their way through the walls when the *'wise woman'* proposed a peace deal. The city and its citizens were part of *'the Lord's inheritance'* (v19). Joab was shown another way to achieve his objective without battering and beating the Lord's inheritance (see Psalm 33 v12). The church is immensely precious to the Lord Jesus. She is his bride and the apple of his eye. So who are those who dare to batter the Lord's inheritance, and beat the church, and undermine the local testimony of the church by their whispering and slander? Who are the troublemakers who continue to erect their 'siege-ramps' against the local church? Peacemakers are builders. There's no such thing as 'passive peacemaking'. Peacemakers are not 'peace-takers' who merely cherry-pick bits of the church they want. Truly, gospel people are peacemakers.

AUGUST 27
2 SAMUEL Ch21.1-26

George Müller is best remembered for establishing five large houses in Bristol to become the homes and Christian training centres for over two thousand orphans. His continual witness in his sermons, tracts, and books was to a God who hears and answers prayer. Müller said, 'I live in the spirit of prayer. I pray as I walk about, when I lie down, and when I rise up. And the answers are always coming'.

OUR PRAYER-ANSWERING GOD

The chapter begins with answered prayer. We can't imagine that it took three years of famine *before* David consulted the Lord about it. But the fact that *'David sought the face of the Lord'* suggests that David prayed to God with a specific request for God's grace and favour towards them. God's 'face' symbolised God's favour towards his people (for example, Numbers ch6 vv25-26), just as when he is displeased, he sets his face against them (Leviticus ch26 v17). Do we merely go through the old mechanical 'prayer routines' or do we actually 'seek God's face'? Is it a duty or a delight? Do we want God's grace without seeking his face? Famines were common in ancient times, just as they still ravage parts of the world today. When David prayed, the answer was not long in coming. The reason for the famine was something that had happened many years earlier.

Peace pact: The Gibeonites had deceived Joshua in obtaining a 'peace pact' from him so that they wouldn't be expelled or destroyed. They were protected by a treaty (Joshua ch9 vv19-20). But years later, King Saul had broken that treaty by trying to annihilate the Gibeonites. Saul's broken treaty was the cause of the famine.

Atonement: David asks how he can *'make amends'* (v3). The word is linked to 'expiation', 'propitiation', and 'atonement'. The sacrifice of seven male descendants of Saul was offered to satisfy the divine demands for atonement and reconciliation with God (v6). Some people struggle to understand God's holy requirements because they don't understand the utter wickedness of sin and the absolute holiness of God. This is another Old Testament signpost pointing to the perfect, once-and-for-all atonement that was achieved by Jesus. The 'peace pact' of Calvary remains fully intact for each believer.

One man, not seven men, achieved peace with God for repenting, trusting sinners. That's why we can be confident in our prayers (Hebrews ch4 v16). It's not a guarantee that God will answer our prayers in precisely the way we expect. It's a guarantee that God hears and answers prayer in his perfect though sometimes mysterious way.

What things should we specifically pray for, prompted by this narrative?

1 PRAY THAT THE LAW WON'T BE PUT ASIDE

We need good law and good governance in our country, but this can only be achieved when law and justice are founded upon Biblical principles. David had to re-learn the truth that the peace treaty between the Israelites and the Gibeonites, witnessed by God, could not be broken. God's law cannot be put aside or ignored without consequences. God's holiness can never be put 'on hold'.

2 PRAY THAT THE LAND WON'T BE PUT DOWN

When justice had been done and God's standards had been obeyed, then we read *'After that, God answered prayer on behalf of the land'* (v14). We may lament over our land today as Jeremiah once lamented over Jerusalem (Lamentations ch1 v1). We regret that our land, which has enjoyed so much of God's grace and has even been the agency for proclaiming the gospel throughout the world, has now turned its back on its God and Saviour. The healing of our land depends on prayer and repentance (2 Chronicles ch7 v14). Do we really want the Lord to answer prayer on behalf of our land?

3 PRAY THAT THE LAMP WON'T BE PUT OUT

David's champions – his 'pride of Israel' – are listed in vv15-22. David had been in mortal danger from a Philistine when Abishai rescued him. After that, David's men declared that their king should not go out to fight again *'so that the lamp of Israel will not be extinguished'* (v17). David's brave giant-killers were concerned for God's testimony in Israel. Do we have the same concern that God's testimony in our nation is not extinguished? Is it an urgent enough matter for our persistent prayers? The history of the church reveals that times of powerful prayer have brought spiritual revival to the church and a spiritual revolution to the nation. Would that answer *our* prayers?

AUGUST 28
2 SAMUEL Ch22.1-51

When the old Cornish lifeboats returned from a successful mission, the sound of the survivors' singing could sometimes be heard over the screaming of the wind and the crashing of the waves. Their songs of joy and gratitude were testimony to their salvation. In this chapter, and in Psalm 18, we have David's:

RESCUE SONG

It's a song which praises the Divine Rescuer after he had saved David from the hand of his enemies (v1). There are five elements to any rescue:

1 THE RESCUE SERVICE (vv1-3)

David speaks of his Rescuer as his Rock, his Fortress, his Deliverer, his Shield, his Stronghold, his Refuge, and his Saviour. Our God is secure and dependable. He is incomparably strong and impregnable. *'Horn'* (v3) implies strength and power, just as the horns of a ram and wild oxen represent might and conquest. To be de-horned meant defeat and humiliation. Jesus' death upon the cross proclaims him as a strong and capable Saviour. He is the only Rescuer (Acts ch4 v12). Jesus is the Final Word; the Word personified; the Word made flesh. If you are not saved by Jesus, you are not saved at all.

2 THE DISTRESS CALL (vv4-7)

David knew all about making a distress call to the Lord in an emergency. David sees himself drowning in the turbulent waves, just like Peter in Galilee (Matthew ch14 v30). Peter issued his 'Mayday' and was plucked from death by his Saviour. There is no one who has descended so low to lift us so high, and he is *'worthy of praise'* (v4). It's amazing to consider that Jesus, who is so deserving of eternal praise, should give himself in death for one so undeserving of eternal pardon. But he has!

3 THE EMERGENCY RESPONSE (vv8-20)

We are provided with fascinating images of the Lord's mighty response to the distress call. He harnesses creation's power to make his triumphant appearance. *'He parted the heavens and came down...he flew...he soared on the wings of the wind...he reached down...He rescued me'.* David's enemies are no match for the Sovereign Ruler of the universe, for whom the powers of lightning, thunder, rain, and fire rush to do his bidding. His response is timely (Romans ch5 v6). He is never too late, too inefficient, or too busy. He is also able to save completely (Hebrews ch7 v25).

4 THE URGENT TREATMENT (vv21-30)

Any change for the better that has occurred in David's life is only because of God's grace to him in the first place. Our acceptance by God – our justification – is not based upon our efforts at cleanliness and godliness but upon what God has done for us in Christ. Following the transformation of new birth (2 Corinthians ch5 v17), a continuing change will take place as the believer draws closer to the Lord, who is the *'lamp'* (v29), and the darkness is dispelled. There are often too many shadowy, murky, unlit areas in the darkened recesses of our hearts that keep us from experiencing the joy and security of the Lord, our Lamp. The light is the motivation to persevere. Such is the encouragement which the Lamp brings, that David feels he can take on the world (v30).

5 THE AFTER-CARE (vv31-51)

David asks *'Who is God besides the Lord?'* (v32) because our God is perfect, flawless, and our Shield (v31); our Rock (v32); our God and our Saviour (v47). Though he is unique and incomparable, he stooped even to the cross to lift us up and make us children of God (v36). The Christian life is a battle in a war which Jesus has already won. But he arms us (v33) and enables us (v34) and trains us (v35) and preserves us (v44) and gives us success (vv38-42). He attends to our welfare in our warfare. He's concerned about every detail, every threat, and every discomfort. Our great and awesome God, our Rescuer, is personally interested in our care and protection. He even makes the ground solid and smooth so that we don't twist our ankles (v37). His after-care is unparalleled, and he knows all about the way that we take (Job ch23 v10). And just in case someone may think that this God is the deity of some former era, the God of 'BC' only, we can declare three thousand years after David:

'The Lord lives! Praise be to my Rock! Exalted be God, the Rock, my Saviour' (v47).

DISEASE AND SICKNESS LIMITED

He reached down from on high and took hold of me; he drew me out of deep waters.

2 Samuel ch22 v17

Disease and sickness may invade these flimsy tents of ours,

Diminishing our faculties and weakening our powers.

We may discover with alarm the things we did with ease

Become frustratingly curtailed by sickness and disease.

They may cause apprehension as we face health's slippery slope,

They may attack assurance, but they cannot shatter hope.

They may assault our bodies as our sufferings increase:

They may exhaust our patience, but can never seize our peace.

Disease and sickness prey upon the things that we regret,

And prompt us to remember things we rather would forget.

Sometimes to Doubting Castle, we may find that we are driven,

But in the precious blood of Christ, we see our sins forgiven.

These rogue intruders work within the scheme that God has planned:

Their strength and scope is governed by a Providential Hand.

They sometimes cripple bodies but can never cripple love,

Nor dare prevent us soaring to our Father's home above.

Disease and sickness fail to cause our friendships to erode;

They cannot silence courage, nor can make our faith corrode.

They may invade our body, but will not purloin our soul,

Nor is one single hair outside omnipotent control.

They cannot sever fellowship or snap the three-fold cord,

Nor separate us from the love of Jesus Christ our Lord.

They cannot sap eternal life nor quench the Spirit's power,

Nor stop our resurrection at the last triumphant hour.

Disease and sickness may deprive our lives of many things,

But cannot thwart our access to our Saviour, King of Kings.

They cannot steal our heaven nor deny us sovereign grace,

And cannot barricade us from the sight of Jesus' face.

Geoff Fox

AUGUST 29
2 SAMUEL Ch23.1-39

REAL-LIFE SUPERHEROES

Many children from two or three generations have grown up around the comic book superheroes that can fly through the sky, lift cars, and combat ruthless villains. If such famous fictional figures have been so popular among impressionable people looking for champions, what impact did David's real-life superheroes have upon tenth-century BC Israel? In vv8-39 we are introduced to:

1 THE MIGHTY MEN OF DAVID

The success of David's many exploits and conquests had much to do with the bravery and competence of three elite groups of champions. Two groups of 'Special Forces' were made up of three superheroes, with a leader, and the other group of thirty-four men was referred to as 'The Thirty' (v23). They gave David's kingship *'strong support'* (1 Chronicles ch11 v10). God made ordinary men into champions and superheroes, for example:

JOSHEB-BASS HEBETH (v8), who was the leader of 'The Three' and who took on eight hundred men in a single encounter and dispatched them all with a spear.

ELEAZAR (v9) stood his ground with David in the middle of an exposed barley field when the rest of the army ran away, and gained a great victory.

SHAMMAH (v11) enjoyed a similar victory in the middle of a lentil field.

ABISHAI (vv18-19) became the leader of another Threesome and killed three hundred men with his spear. Abishai had personally rescued David when he was in danger of being killed.

Three of 'The Thirty' had entered the Philistine camp and drew Bethlehem spring water especially for David (v15). But the king considered the water too precious to be drunk by him. He offered it to the Lord instead (vv16-17).

BENAIAH (vv20-23) killed two of Moab's champions, disarmed an Egyptian giant, and killed a hungry, trapped lion. He became the leader of David's bodyguard (v23).

David's power increased because the Lord was with him (1 Chronicles ch11 v9) and because the Lord had surrounded him with men of faith and courage.

2 THE MIGHTY MAN OF GOD

David had been *'anointed'* and *'exalted'* by God (v1). His might and dominion were only in reference to his relationship with the Lord. We possess no inherent strength of our own and so we must recognise that our strength is *'in the Lord and his mighty power'* (Ephesians ch6 v10). The last words of a person are often accorded a certain poignancy and significance. David describes himself in his 'last words' as:

THE SON OF JESSE: He wasn't embarrassed about his humble origins.

THE MAN EXALTED BY THE MOST HIGH: God had exalted David by his grace.

THE MAN ANOINTED BY THE GOD OF JACOB: David had been handpicked by God for a specific role. David was a chosen vessel set apart for a special task. This reminds us of Jesus: 'the Anointed One' who was also set apart by his Father for the unique mission to save his people from their sins.

ISRAEL'S SINGER OF SONGS: Seventy-three of the one hundred and fifty Psalms are attributed to David.

GOD'S SPOKESMAN: He was the spokesman and penman of God's words recorded in Scripture, particularly the Psalms (v2, Psalm 139 v4, 2 Peter ch1 vv19-21).

3 THE MIGHTY GOD-MAN

David refers to the *'everlasting covenant'* (v5), which is more than just the occupation of an earthly throne. The *'everlasting covenant'* is to do with the redemption of sinners for which the purchase price was the death of the Son of God. The Mighty God-Man has sealed this covenant with his own blood. The *'fruition'* of our *'salvation'* is realised fully in him (v15). David's hope was in his greater Son, the *'Mighty God'* (Isaiah ch9 v6). Jesus is truly the mighty God and the mighty Man. The word *'mighty'* relates to 'excellence'. There's no one more excellent than Jesus, who perfectly radiates God's glory and who is *'the exact representation of his being'* (Hebrews ch1 v3).

In Conclusion:

David asks a question which we should all ask, if in a slightly different sense: *'Is not my house right with God?'* (v5). We may identify with David in all kinds of troubles, failures, sins, and disasters that rocked his house. How much would our spiritual checklist be similar to David's? What are those things in 'our house' and family, and life of which the Lord would approve or disapprove? Is my house right with God, and, more importantly, am I right with God?

AUGUST 30
2 SAMUEL Ch24.1-25

Every efficient administration will have systems of documenting, recording, counting, analysing, and census-taking. King David was no exception. Yet it was precisely this – a census, a count – which provoked divine anger and a great disaster that came to Israel. Despite Joab's protests, David ordered a count of his fighting men (v2). At first reading, this may seem sensible since any competent king taking his troops into battle needs to know the exact size of his army. However, there's much more to David's 'big census' than we may realise initially. Compare v1 and 1 Chronicles ch21 v1. Satan is the originator of sin, and so he is the agent that God uses to perform his sovereign plan. God is in control and so, in that sense, *'he incited David'* (v1). Yet God tempts no one to sin, but he permits Satan to act as David's adversary and, in that sense, *'Satan... incited David'*.

1 DAVID'S GREAT SIN

David didn't excuse his sin as just being 'a little mistake', nor did he shrug it off by saying 'Well, these things happen!' He was *'conscience-stricken'* and confessed: *'I have sinned greatly'* (v10). But what was his great sin? After all, taking a census cannot be a sin in itself. Such an exercise would usually be regarded as methodical and prudent. Even the Lord ordered a census in Numbers ch1. Joab's protest (v3) appears to lie at the heart of this answer. Joab seemed to imply that as long as the Lord is David's 'Rock' (ch23 v3), and has made an *'everlasting covenant'* with him (ch23 v5), then it doesn't depend on David's strength. It doesn't matter whether David has 1.3 million *'fighting men'* (v9) or a hundred times that amount (as Joab says: v3), it's the Lord's power and the Lord's strength by which David wins his battles and destroys his enemies (Zechariah ch4 v6). David's failure at this point was that he had taken his eyes off the Lord's provision and was ready to boast in his own resources rather than in his unfailing Rock.

Having made his protest, Joab and the army commanders set off on their mission to enumerate David's militia – a mission which ties them up for nearly ten months. Notice-

David's Guilt over the Counting:

David confesses his foolishness but realises that there are consequences to sin. Judgements must be endured; penalties must be paid. Out of three options, David chose the shortest period of judgement and one which seemed to be so obviously controlled by God directly (v14). David trusted himself to God's judgement and God's mercy. We must learn from David's folly that we mustn't pursue an innocent action (for example, census-taking) for a sinful reason (for example, pride or greed).

God's Grief over the Calamity:

(vv15-16) This has nothing to do with the Lord showing remorse or regret, but it does reveal that he is hurt by sin and the afflictions of his people as a consequence of sin (see Genesis ch6 v6). We mustn't think that because God is detached and untainted by sin that he is unaffected by it.

2 GOD'S GREAT MERCY

David had discovered the vastness of God's mercy (v14, Psalm 51 v1). In the middle of a terrifying plague sweeping across the country, God intercepts judgement with mercy at Araunah's threshing-floor (v16). This was near the spot that mercy intercepted Abraham's actions in sacrificing his son (Genesis ch22 v11). Later, David's son Solomon would build the temple here: a place where countless animal sacrifices were offered as God showed his mercy to sinners. But, ultimately, just a stone's throw from this site on Mt Moriah, *'the kindness and love of God our Saviour'* revealed his mercy at the cross (Titus ch3 v4). God withheld judgement on Isaac, and further judgement on Jerusalem, but he didn't withhold the judgement that should have fallen upon us from falling upon his Son (Romans ch8 v32). Jesus has borne the judgement in full so that every child of God may escape the judgement of God. David's response to God's mercy was to worship. He wanted to buy Araunah's threshing-floor as well as the oxen and wood for sacrifice. Araunah was keen to let David have it all for nothing (vv22-23), but David insisted on paying for it. His worship wasn't going to become a freebie (v24). He believed that his worship and service for the Lord shouldn't be merely a casual, cheap, cut-price exercise. Worship should cost us something in effort, time, commitment, preparation, and personal sacrifice. Paul urges *'living sacrifices'* (Romans ch12 v1). Let's not be among those who are only willing to give the dregs and leftovers of their time, efforts, abilities, and finances.

AUGUST 31
THE GOSPEL OF LUKE Ch1.1-25

The Author:

Although you won't find Luke's name in the Gospel that bears his name, most evidence supports the traditional view that Luke is the author. With a physician's attention to detail, a perceptive analysis of information, and a thirst for authenticity, *'Luke, the doctor'* (Colossians ch4 v14) compiles his Gospel account under the inspiration of the Holy Spirit.

The Recipient:

'most excellent Theophilus' (compare Acts ch24 v3; ch26 v25) suggests an official of rank, influence, and possibly wealth. Perhaps he had the power and resources to publish Luke's work.

Theophilus could be certain of the veracity of the narrative. In a forensically detailed inquiry, Luke had *'carefully investigated everything from the beginning'* (v3). With surgical accuracy, he had excised fable and fiction from the various reports, to leave the truth for all to read and believe. Just as a doctor must record his case notes in a precise and thorough manner, Luke tells Theophilus that *'it seemed good also to me to write an orderly account for you'* (v4). The seamless sequel to Luke's account of the Gospel is his Book of Acts.

The Introduction:

Side by side in this opening chapter, we are provided with the antenatal events concerning John, who would come *'in the spirit and power of Elijah'* (v17), and Jesus, who *'will be great and will be called the Son of the Most High'* (v32). These two figures would appear on the world stage just six months apart – John, the greatest of the prophets, and Jesus the Greatest of all.

Zechariah and his wife Elizabeth are portrayed as a godly couple (v6). Elizabeth could also prove her priestly pedigree as a direct descendant of Aaron, as well as sharing the name of Aaron's wife (Exodus ch6 v23). Zechariah was from one of the twenty-four priestly divisions associated with Abijah (v5). When Zechariah was performing his priestly duties in the Holy Place of the temple, God visited him through his angel, Gabriel. He reveals the character and calibre, the mission and the message of the son that would be born to them, even John Baptist. Zechariah responded to this amazing news with a question (v18).

HOW CAN I BE SURE OF THIS?

Do we also ask this question when confronted with some of God's words or his works? Maybe we need the assurances which Zechariah could have mused over during his nine months' enforced silence.

1 GOD'S PROVIDENCE OVERRULES CHANCE (vv8-9)

At that time, there could have been as many as eighteen thousand priests serving in shifts. To be chosen by lot for the special honour of burning incense was a once-in-a-lifetime privilege. Yet it was precisely at this time that God came to Zechariah. Every detail of life is controlled by an omnipotent God. God speaks to us neither through accidents nor flukes of fate but by his own carefully designed plans.

2 GOD'S PRESENCE OVERSEES PRAYER (v13)

Presumably, the godly couple had been praying hard about children for many years. It seemed it wasn't God's purpose for them to have this privilege. But God had been present in their prayers and had heard their cries. He doesn't always answer as we expect, but he honours with his presence those who honour him with their prayers.

3 GOD'S PROMISE OVERWHELMS DOUBT (v20)

The promise of the coming of John would be fulfilled at the proper time. Zechariah's muteness was God's judgement on his unbelief as well as a sign of God's promise. Do you doubt God's word? Christ is the unwavering affirmation of all of God's promises (2 Corinthians ch1 v20). No wonder the deity of Christ is constantly under attack!

4 GOD'S POWER OVERCOMES IMPOSSIBILITIES (vv7, 18)

That which was naturally impossible had become supernaturally possible (vv36-37). Is anything too hard for God (Genesis ch18 v14; Jeremiah ch32 v27)? Elizabeth had suffered years of disgrace and humiliation. People despised her, thinking that her barrenness was a result of some sin. But God's grace removes her disgrace (v25). You may have been made to feel unsuitable, handicapped, unqualified, or even inferior. But Jesus can make all the difference as he covers our weaknesses and embarrassments with his love and kindness. How can I be sure of this? Turn to Christ and prove him to be all-sufficient.

SEPTEMBER 1
THE GOSPEL OF LUKE Ch1.26-56

The doctrine of the Virgin Conception of Christ has been a fundamental teaching of traditional Christianity. This tenet of the faith declares that Jesus was conceived miraculously by the power of the Holy Spirit and that he was born to Mary, who had no sexual union with any man. But why is the Virgin Conception so important?

Because the Bible says so: We believe the full and final authority of God's Word.

Because history supports it: Luke records the facts from reliable witnesses (vv1-4).

Because it emphasises Christ's deity: The Holy One is the Son of God.

Because it affirms Christ's humanity: Jesus experienced humanity fully.

Because it reveals divine grace: God's favour is shown to Mary and to every believer.

The virgin conception of Christ identifies Jesus' uniqueness as the incomparable Christ:

His unique Name: (v31) 'Jesus' translates the Hebrew, 'Jehovah the

Saviour'.

His unique title: (vv32a, 35) Gabriel underlines both his greatness and his sonship.

His unique kingdom: (v33) His majestic 'Davidic' kingdom is eternal.

So this young, godly, peasant girl is visited by an angel who announces that she is to become the mother of Jesus, the Son of God. And what was her humble response?

'I am the Lord's servant…may it be to me as you have said' (v38).

THE LORD'S SERVANT

In a remarkably exemplary way, Mary surrenders herself to the will and purposes of God, despite the possible costs and consequences. We can note five aspects of this model of humility.

1 SHE BELIEVED GOD'S WORD

Mary yields herself entirely to the Lord as his servant, his bondslave. The assurance of her faith is the unshakeable promises of an Almighty God. Mary's consecration is without reservation.

2 SHE ACCEPTED GOD'S CONDITIONS

Mary would have realised quickly that becoming pregnant outside marriage would mean public disgrace, humiliation, and loss of reputation, not to mention the possibility that Joseph would break off the engagement. Also, if the strict Mosaic Law were invoked, she could face stoning (Deuteronomy ch22 vv23-24). The prospects were not rosy for an unmarried mother. But Mary accepted the conditions without a murmur of complaint. What a lesson for us! How ready are we to accept the consequences of surrendering to God's plan, not just because it's an act of his sovereign will, but because it's the outworking of his superior wisdom?

3 SHE TRUSTED GOD'S TIMING

Mary may have understood nine months of pregnancy, but she didn't know when Jesus would receive *'the throne of his father David'* (v32). Yet she knew something of her ancestor's testimony when the king said, *'My times are in your hands'* (Psalm 31 v15).

4 SHE AWAITED GOD'S SPIRIT

Mary accepted without question that the Holy Spirit would create this mysterious biological miracle within her own body. How is God's Spirit preparing us for service?

5 SHE GLORIFIED GOD'S NAME

In this song of praise (vv46-55), the Spirit-inspired girl exhibits her godliness and knowledge of Scripture. This exclamation of worship reveals her heart.

The Lord is Mindful:

(vv47-48a) He knows Mary is weak, young, vulnerable, and is a sinner. She still needs a Saviour (contrary to 'Immaculate Conception' teaching) and God looks on her with grace. He knows our weaknesses, vulnerabilities, and inadequacies too (Psalm 103 v14), and he is loving, kind, and compassionate towards us.

The Lord is Mighty:

(vv49,51) The 'virgin conception' may be an impossibility from a human perspective, but God specialises in impossibilities. Do we doubt God's power in a particular situation? Do our doubts affect our prayers?

The Lord is Merciful:

(vv50, 52-54) Mary exclaims that God has displayed his mercy to the holy (v50), the humble (v52), the hungry (v53), and the helpless (v54). He is *'rich in mercy'* (Ephesians ch2 v4) to those who repent and believe the gospel.

There may be many, like Mary, who may say *'I am the Lord's servant'*. But how many of those who talk about holiness and humility are fully prepared to stoop low enough and to pray earnestly enough: *'Do to me as you will'*.

SEPTEMBER 2
THE GOSPEL OF LUKE Ch1.57-80

The home of Zechariah and Elizabeth must have been very special because the Lord chose it as a sanctuary for Mary. He uses the simple tools of an open home and an open heart to provide spiritual care and nourishment (v56). Mary may have stayed until John was born. The birth of Elizabeth's newborn son came as a shock to her *'neighbours and relatives'* (v58), but they quickly rejoiced with her.

REJOICING

What did they rejoice in?

1 THE LORD SHOWED ELIZABETH GREAT MERCY (v58)

God's mercy is all about his loving and kind actions. Despite the advanced years of these parents, they were to be the mother and father of the last and greatest of the prophets, whose special role was to prepare the way for Jesus, Mary's son (v76). Though it was customary for a firstborn son to take the name of his father or grandfather, Elizabeth voiced her protest at the naming ceremony. The assembled witnesses may have thought that Elizabeth, as a woman, didn't have the authority to name the child. To depart from established custom and tradition was a serious issue. They may have thought that Elizabeth was taking advantage of her husband's handicap (being dumb)?

When Zechariah was asked for his verification of his son's name, he wrote, *'His name IS John'* (v63). Naming ceremony, or no naming ceremony, his name was already John. They had been referring to 'John' for the last nine months, and they had been calling the cooing, gurgling baby 'John' for the past eight days! Zechariah's enforced silence was immediately ended. Now it was the crowd's turn to be dumbstruck as they were *'all filled with awe'* (v65). The news spread like wildfire!

2 THE LORD SHOWED ISRAEL COVENANT MERCY (v72)

Zechariah's Spirit-filled prophecy declares how God had been faithful to their forefathers. Israel is undeserving, but God had covenanted with Abraham (Genesis ch22 vv16-18) to provide: numerous descendants to Abraham; the defeat of their enemies, and blessing to all the nations through Abraham's offspring. So, in Zechariah's 'Benedictus' (from the first word in Latin, meaning 'blessed'), he praises God for the redemption of his people, the rescue from enemies, and the blessing that would come through that specific 'offspring' of Abraham: the Messiah, the Christ.

3 THE LORD SHOWED HIS PEOPLE TENDER MERCY (v78)

Nobody accrues sufficient credit to deserve salvation (Romans ch3 v10). God's compassionate mercy is in the provision of what we don't deserve (Titus ch3 v4). He delights in showing mercy (Micah ch7 v18). Note Zechariah's descriptions of Christ:

A Horn of Salvation (v69) The horn represents might and strength. We need a super-strong Deliverer who can save us and redeem us.

The Rising Sun (v78) The dense darkness was giving way to the glow of the dawn. The blazing Light, appearing over time's horizon, would dispel the darkness (Isaiah ch9 v2; John ch8 v12). But what did Christ, God's saving Son, come to do?

i] Christ came to rescue us

(vv68, 74) Jesus didn't orchestrate a rescue from the security of heaven. He had to come himself and give himself. Our rescue involved the cross.

ii] Christ came to enable us

(vv74, 75) To do what? God rescues us for a purpose. He saves us so that we may serve him:

With fearlessness – with God 'on side', we should never be scared;

With holiness – we shouldn't compromise our service by aping the world;

With righteousness – a right relationship with God means behaving right.

iii] Christ came to forgive us

(v77) What a profound relief it is to hear from the lips of the Saviour that sweetest of words, 'Forgiven!' Jesus forgives those who repent and turn to him for deliverance.

iv] Christ came to guide us

(v79) There is a wonderful illumination for those in the shade and shadow of darkness and death. Throughout all of history, lights have been used to guide. But the rising sun outshines all other luminaries. John Baptist was to be the last and the brightest of those guiding lights that pointed to the glorious 'sunrise' in Jesus Christ, our Lord and Saviour.

SEPTEMBER 3
THE GOSPEL OF LUKE Ch2.1-20

If a national census in the UK continues to be a mammoth exercise, taking many months to collate and analyse, such a worldwide census as that conducted in the first century would have probably taken several years to complete. This may account for why history records the census as taking place in AD6, some time after Jesus' birth. It's likely that this date was associated with the conclusion of Caesar Augustus' imperial census. Octavian was the great-nephew of Julius Caesar, and he shared the rule of the empire after Julius' murder.

Octavian eventually defeated Mark Antony and Cleopatra of Egypt, and the Roman Senate gave him the prestigious title 'Caesar'. In addition, he claimed the title 'Augustus' (meaning 'worthy of reverence, even worship') for himself.

Caesar Augustus encouraged a period of stability, peace, and prosperity within the Roman Empire, known as the 'Pax Romana' (the Roman peace). It was against this background that the emperor issued a decree for the purpose of taxation (v1).

Here was an earthly ruler, who fancied himself as a god, issuing a decree that forced a humble peasant couple to travel eighty miles south to be in Bethlehem, just in time for the birth of their firstborn son, Jesus, the Son of God. All of this conforms to a superior decree issued seven hundred years earlier (Micah ch5 v2). We see how the scaffolding of history was perfectly poised to support the coming of Christ. Everything in God's timetable was complete.

THE SHEPHERD'S REACTION

The shepherds feature in the early moments of Christ's birth. Notice four aspects of their reaction:

1 HEARING ABOUT WHAT THEY FELT (vv9-12)

They felt fear initially (*'terrified'* v9). But the angelic messenger addressed their fear. Though they remained 'shell-shocked', the shepherds heard about the all-important reason for the angelic visitation (vv10-11). *'Good news'* and *'great joy'* go hand in hand. If the news really is *'good'*, then the joy will be really *'great'*. What better news can there be than the coming of the Saviour? The royal ensign flying over the castle of a believer's heart and life is joy—deep, durable joy.

2 SEEING ABOUT WHAT THEY HEARD (vv15-16)

It seems that the shepherds didn't need an invitation to visit the newborn Saviour. Although the angel hadn't specifically instructed them to go to Bethlehem, it was presumed that they would go. Who could keep them away now? The angel had proclaimed *'peace to men on whom his favour rests'*. It's not a peace or goodwill that is for all men. There's certainly no peace for the wicked (Isaiah ch48 v22). Rather, the good news of the gospel is a message of peace with God for those who repent and believe. This is at the heart of the gospel. It's peace for those upon whom God has elected to lavish his favour.

The urgency with which the shepherds sought and found Jesus is striking. It was far more important than their sheep, their businesses, and their livelihoods. Do we have that living, vibrant faith that puts 'discovering Christ' at the top of our list of priorities?

3 SPEAKING ABOUT WHAT THEY HAD SEEN (vv17-18)

Were these shepherds the first evangelists of the New Testament era? When they found the small, weak, newborn infant wrapped up in cloths, lying in an animals' feeding trough, attended by young, poor, inexperienced parents, the shepherds believed. Their faith triumphed! They didn't skulk away to keep their experience to themselves. With confidence and assurance *'they spread the word'*. Their limited abilities and limited understanding didn't hinder them from being faithful witnesses. They didn't use their inadequacies and weaknesses as an excuse. Their testimony caused amazement among everyone who heard.

4 BELIEVING ABOUT WHAT THEY HAD SPOKEN (vv19-20)

The shepherds had listened, had acted, and had believed. Their response was to glorify and to praise God for the truth of his word. God's words and his works were seen to be in perfect harmony. There was no discrepancy between the revelation and the reality. Such displays of divine grace and love should prompt us, with Mary, to treasure up all these things and ponder them in our hearts (v19). Where are the things that you value and esteem? What do you treasure above all else (Matthew ch6 v21)?

THE CHRISTMAS LAMB

And there were shepherds living out in the fields nearby,

keeping watch over their flocks at night.

Luke ch2 v8

In Bethlehem's fields with their storm-sculptured rocks,

Some Judean shepherds sat tending their flocks.

No changes since David, each decade the same.

The temple supply was their sole claim to fame.

For from their exclusive collection of beasts,

lambs went to the temple for slaughter by priests.

Forgiveness and favour from God they would win

by the blood of the sacrifice offered for sin.

As Days of Atonement rolled on year by year,

God's final solution was now drawing near.

The gloom and despair of eternity mocks

the short-lived salvation of Bethlehem's flocks.

Could ever a permanent answer be found

To the need of redemption and sin all around?

Good News is the theme of a sudden display-

'A Saviour is born in the city today!'

From the back of beyond, and much further too,

A herald from heaven had flashed into view.

The darkness was shattered, and day came so soon,

As midnight gave way to the brightness of noon.

These Bethlehem shepherds were first to receive,

This message from Glory, and came to believe.

The sacrifice lambs on the hills where they trod,

were now superseded by this Lamb of God.

Geoff Fox

SEPTEMBER 4
THE GOSPEL OF LUKE Ch2.21-40

Ancient Jewish culture attached certain rituals to the birth of a child and the naming of that child. Immediately following birth, the baby was wiped with salt, water, and oil, after which it was wrapped tightly in strips of cloth or clean rags (see v7). It had also become customary for the baby to be named at the circumcision ceremony on the eighth day. Childbirth was believed to make a woman ceremonially unclean. This meant that she couldn't participate in any religious observance or touch any sacred objects for forty days after the birth of a son; twice as long if a daughter (Leviticus ch12). At the end of this purification period, she would present the baby to the Lord and offer a sacrifice, which was usually a lamb. If a lamb couldn't be afforded, then poor people were permitted to sacrifice two doves or two young pigeons. Mary and Joseph's humble obedience is illustrated in v21:

'HE WAS NAMED JESUS'

It wasn't an ancestral name or a traditional family name. Neither was it a wacky name dreamt up by parents who wanted to be outrageously different.

1 A NAME TO HOPE WITH ('Consolation' v25)

Simeon is an ordinary man with an extraordinary faith. The Bible is concerned with his character, not his credentials. He was *'righteous and devout...the Holy Spirit was upon him'*. What's more, Simeon was *'waiting for the consolation of Israel'* (v25). The Greek word for *'consolation'* gives us our word 'paraclete', literally 'one called alongside'. It speaks of one who is called to bring help, perhaps as an advocate or an intercessor. There are two levels of comfort and consolation.

To speak about the coming of the Comforter gives a measure of comfort in itself. When an injured casualty is waiting for the paramedic to come alongside, it's important to give them reassurance. Some comfort is derived from knowing that help will soon arrive. It's that hope and consolation that the casualty needs.

The arrival of the one who is promised. Simeon was given that special promise that he would see the Messiah (v26). He firmly believed the promise and spent his life working and serving in anticipation of Christ's appearing.

Every year, Simeon may have thought, 'Is this going to be the year when the Messiah comes?' Isn't that the way we should live our lives – earnestly serving our Master in the expectation of his Second Coming?

2 A NAME TO TRUST IN ('Salvation' v30)

The one name that is associated with spiritual, eternal salvation is the lovely, fragrant, powerful name of Jesus. As Simeon took the infant Jesus in his arms and looked down into the baby face of his Creator and Saviour, he said (vv29-30), *'Sovereign Lord, as you have promised, you now dismiss your servant in peace. For my eyes have seen your salvation...'* Simeon was content that he had accomplished his life's vocation – to see his Saviour appear.

Your life's mission may not yet be at an end, but are you at the stage where you can say with confidence, 'Lord, you can dismiss your servant in peace any time you like, because I know your salvation'?

The second amazing encounter at the temple was with the elderly prophetess Anna (vv36-38). She spent every day being fully occupied with God. Anna had been trusting in the coming of God's redemption through Christ. She didn't doubt that God would provide One who would pay the ultimate price to redeem a people for himself.

3 A NAME TO LIVE FOR ('Revelation' vv32,35)

This light of revelation in Christ not only reveals men's hopes; it also reveals men's hearts. Some people will live and die by the name of Jesus, while others will want nothing to do with him. For some, Christ's coming means salvation, while for others it means condemnation. Some hearts will joyfully accept Christ while others will be firmly closed to him.

The examples of Simeon and Anna show us that Christ's coming was the focus of their lives. Even in old age, they were fully and faithfully engaged in the Lord's service. They weren't in the process of 'winding down' as if viewing their old age as a well-deserved holiday or reward for work and service in earlier life. No doubt old age brought restrictions, weaknesses, and even illnesses to Simeon and Anna. But they didn't give up. Instead, they actively lived for the name of their Saviour and Redeemer.

SEPTEMBER 5
THE GOSPEL OF LUKE Ch2.41-52

The central truth of evangelical Bible-believing theology is that when Jesus came to earth, he became fully human while remaining fully divine. Throughout history, that pivotal plank of faith has been challenged repeatedly.

ARIUS was a North African priest, probably born in Libya in AD256. As a popular preacher, he taught that the Father alone was God and that the Son (the Logos) was a created being, the first and greatest of God's creation. That teaching, under the name of Arianism, has infected history ever since. It denies the deity of our Lord and Saviour, Jesus Christ.

APOLLINARIS was a bishop in the church of Laodicea around AD 361. He taught that Christ had a fully human body but not a human mind or spirit. He argued that the mind and spirit of Christ were only from his divine nature.

NESTORIUS was a popular preacher from Antioch who became bishop of Constantinople in AD428. He came into conflict with other Christian leaders because he taught that Christ was really two separate persons – a human person and a divine person. There is no Biblical support for this Nestorianism.

EUTYCHES was the leader of a monastery in Constantinople at about the same time as Nestorius. Eutyches' claim to fame was that he taught the opposite of Nestorianism. Eutyches believed that the human nature and divine nature somehow got mixed together to form one new nature. The Greek for 'one' is 'monos' and the Greek for 'nature' is 'physis'. So this heresy has been called Monophysitism (that is, Christ had only one nature).

So how did the church respond to these erroneous teachings?

The CHALCEDONIAN DEFINITION was drawn up and agreed by a large church council in AD451. It has been the standard orthodox definition regarding the Bible's teaching on the Person of Christ ever since. It states that Jesus Christ is truly God and truly man with two distinct but inseparable natures. He is one Person, not divided into two persons, but one and the same Son, the only begotten of God, who is the Word, the Lord Jesus Christ.

The One who is said to *'grow'* (v40) is the unchanging and unchangeable One. The One who became *'strong'* (v40) is the omnipotent Lord of heaven and earth. The One who *'grew in wisdom'* (v52) is the omniscient, Fount of all wisdom.

The child who knew weakness is the One who sustains the worlds with his word. The twelve-year-old who sat among the temple teachers (v46)

is the Wonderful Counsellor who counselled the counsellors.

So the King of Kings yields to young, inexperienced human parents (v51).

THINKING HE WAS IN THEIR COMPANY (v44)

1 THEY BEGAN TRAVELLING WITH THE WRONG ATTITUDE

There's no criticism of Mary and Joseph in these verses. We may quickly identify with their frantic search when they realised that Jesus was missing. They were unaware that he had stayed behind in Jerusalem (v43). We must not be complacent in the 'journey of life', assuming that everything is fine and that Jesus is with us. We must know and be sure that Christ is with us in the whole of our lives.

2 THEY BEGAN LOOKING IN THE WRONG PLACE

We wouldn't have been any different, searching among family and friends first. But their missing son wasn't there. Jesus' parents were amazed at what they saw when they eventually found him in the temple courts (v46). He was competently questioning and answering the top religious experts of his day. Do we earnestly and passionately seek Christ in the right places of worship, prayer, and in the reading of God's word?

3 THEY BEGAN ASKING THE WRONG QUESTION

There's a hint of censure and blame in Mary's question (v48). She was focusing on her own feelings, her own desperate circumstances, and her own needs. Jesus' first recorded words, in response to Mary's comment (*'Your father and I have been...'*), were concerning his heavenly Father's will. In the difficult periods of life, we are also prone to asking the wrong questions, such as, 'Why does it happen to me?' We are quick to ask questions about our worry rather than our Father's will. Let our heavenly Father's purposes be our paramount thought throughout our Christian lives.

SEPTEMBER 6
THE GOSPEL OF LUKE Ch3.1-20

Luke pinpoints a particular year by referring to those who were in positions of rulership:

Tiberius Caesar – stepson of Caesar Augustus (ch2 v1);

Pontius Pilate – appointed governor of Judea in about AD26;

Herod Antipas – one of three sons of Herod the Great (Matthew ch2 v3), whose kingdom was divided into four when he died. Herod Archelaus ruled Judea and Samaria. He was cruel and tyrannical and was the reason why Joseph and Mary settled in Galilee (Matthew ch2 vv.22-23). Herod Philip ruled Iturea and Traconitis in the northeast. Lysanias ruled Abilene, a small kingdom in Lebanon. Herod Antipas was the tetrarch who ruled Galilee and Perea.

Annas had been high priest until AD15 when his son-in-law Caiaphas had taken over (though it seemed the real power behind the office continued to lie with Annas).

It's right in the middle of this complicated political and religious scene that John Baptist emerges as the messenger of the Messiah. It's at this precise time that *the word of God came to John...'* (vv2-3). John could have followed in his father's footsteps into the temple ministry. John, who was eligible to be a priest, was appointed a prophet in the calibre of Elijah. After four hundred years of Biblical silence, John comes to fulfil the final prophetic postscript of the Old Testament (Malachi ch4 vv5-6). The words of Isaiah (vv4-6) emphasise John's vocation to prepare the way for Jesus. The 'rescue road' was to be level, straight, and smooth, and along this blessed track would come the Deliverer, the Saviour of his people.

PREPARING THE WAY

John had been clearly set apart from his birth to be the preparatory preacher for Christ, and this *'great'* man *'in the sight of the Lord'* (ch1 v15) had an itinerant ministry around the Jordan (v3).

Four aspects of John's preaching that we can underline include:

1 THE FORGIVENESS OF SINS (v3)

Sometimes we may only think of John as a minister who baptizes rather than as a messenger who preaches. His primary call was to preach *'a baptism of repentance for the forgiveness of sins'*. We should not miss the point that there may be all kinds of media today in which God's word may be presented and proclaimed: many of them with significant validity. But none of them can replace preaching as God's primary method of communicating his word. While there may be some merit in the ancillary activities of the church, we must not be deflected from a right view of the primacy of preaching. The message of John and every faithful minister of God's word must include the uncomfortable truth that *'all have sinned'* (Romans ch3 v23) and that there is unconditional forgiveness for those who genuinely repent, confessing their sin and trusting in the Saviour.

2 THE FRUIT OF REPENTANCE (vv7-14)

John wasn't particularly polite or politically correct in addressing the crowds, and especially the Pharisees and Sadducees (reference Matthew ch3 v7) as *'You brood of vipers!'* (v7). Matthew also records that John said, *'Repent, for the kingdom of heaven is near'* (Matthew ch3 v2). True repentance will also be observable by its fruit:

Be kind, generous, and loving to the needy (v11);

Be honest, truthful, trustworthy, and fair (v13);

Be lawful and be content: don't abuse your authority (v14).

3 THE FORK OF SEPARATION (v17)

The picture of Christ with a winnowing fork in his hand illustrates that he will separate the wheat from the chaff. John wasn't talking about separating the Jews from the Gentiles, or the children of Abraham from the heathen. He was speaking of the believer and the unbeliever, repentant and unrepentant, saved and unsaved.

4 THE FIRE OF JUDGEMENT (vv9, 17)

Anything that is not the genuine wheat grain will ultimately be destroyed. There is no last-minute reprieve for the chaff. John's powerful and personal preaching had dire consequences for him (vv19-20; Mark ch6). But he had clearly signposted Jesus.

Jesus is more powerful

(v16) He isn't coming as John's successor or as his disciple but as the One with superior power, even the power to forgive sins.

Jesus is more worthy

(v16) We confess that we are nothing but he is everything.

SEPTEMBER 7
THE GOSPEL OF LUKE Ch3.21-38

Why was Jesus baptised (v21)? Was he responding to John's call to baptism for repentance? No, for Jesus is the sinless One (2 Corinthians ch5 v21; Hebrews ch4 v15) whose critics couldn't prove that he was guilty of sin (John ch8 v46).

Was Jesus another disciple of John Baptist who was being confirmed as his follower? There's no Biblical evidence to show that Jesus was a 'Baptist disciple'. The only sense that Jesus followed John was that he came after John (v16). John showed that Jesus was more powerful and more worthy.

If Jesus had to obey every command, was one of those commands to be baptised? Again, John's baptism was to do with repentance of sin, and Jesus had no sin.

Does Jesus' baptism anticipate 'believers' baptism' and point to the baptism for all Christians, in the same way that Jesus shared the Last Supper when he said, *Do this in remembrance of Me*? If that were so, the apostles (and especially Paul) would have drawn the parallel between Jesus' baptism and 'believers' baptism'.

So, why was Jesus baptised? Look at the accounts of Matthew and John as well.

Revelation

(John ch1 vv31-34) John couldn't be sure that Jesus was the Messiah until God confirmed it during Jesus' baptism.

Righteousness

(Matthew ch3 v15) All the righteous requirements of God's redemptive plan were to be fulfilled in Jesus. Jesus was not only committed to preaching the Gospel, but to being the Gospel.

So who is Jesus?

JESUS THE SON

1 JESUS IS THE SON OF GOD (v22)

The commending voice and the descending dove represent God the Father's ringing endorsement of his Son. In this great trinitarian demonstration, where the Godhead is revealed, God the Son prays, God the Spirit anoints, and God the Father speaks. God comes to this planet in the Person of his Son, Jesus Christ. The Son voluntarily surrenders himself to his Father's plan for the purpose of achieving the salvation of every sinful person who turns to Christ in repentance.

The Father's love for his Son:

Something of the Father's unfathomably deep and intimate relationship with his Son is revealed here. The indivisible and infinite unity is beyond our comprehension. Yet it is revealed in a way, and with an emotion, of which we do have limited experience, that is, love. Jesus reveals later that the Father loves his followers in a similar way (John ch17 v23). How wonderful!

The Father's satisfaction with his Son:

The pronouncement that he is *'well pleased'* is an authoritative seal upon Jesus' thirty years of holy living. It's the endorsement and the confirmation that Jesus is equal to the singular task of seeking and saving the lost.

2 JESUS IS THE SON OF JOSEPH (v23)

Joseph's fatherhood, bearing in mind the truth of the Virgin Conception, is not a deceit (that is, *'so it was thought'*). Rather, it reveals Jesus' status. Jesus could trace his lineal descent through David to Abraham, and so his Jewish pedigree and royal descent were not in question. Luke is not slow in pointing out Jesus' royal connection with the Davidic dynasty (ch1 vv27, 32; 69; ch2 vv4, 11).

Doesn't it thrill our souls to know that Jesus meets all the criteria of the promised Messiah? He is eligible in every way. The One who sits upon the throne of David is the eternal King whose government will never end.

3 JESUS IS THE SON OF ADAM (v38)

Jesus is identified with all mankind in tracing his genealogy to Adam (Hebrews ch2 vv16-17).

Imperfect kings (for example, David v31), deceitful patriarchs (for example, Jacob v34), inconsistent leaders (for example, Judah v33), wealthy businessmen (for example, Abraham and Boaz), elderly statesmen (for example, Methuselah v37) are included together with over eighty per cent of the characters in vv24-31 who are unknown. But Jesus is also *'the last Adam'* (1 Corinthians ch15 vv45 and 49). The first Adam brought sin; the last Adam brings salvation. Shouldn't it comfort us to know that Jesus has been this way before? The Son of Adam lived and ministered among Adam's descendants that he might become the Last Adam and the Saviour of his people. Our security depends on the *last* Adam, not the *first* Adam.

SEPTEMBER 8
THE GOSPEL OF LUKE Ch4.1-13

KNOW YOUR ENEMY

When the Lord seems particularly close to you, don't forget that the devil is lurking not far away. If that's our experience, we can take comfort in knowing that this was Jesus' experience too. The devil clashed with Jesus head-on. But Jesus knew his enemy very well, and there are important things that we need to know about our enemy.

1 KNOW YOUR ENEMY'S TIMING

Do you know the times when the devil is more likely to appear to you than at others?

When our joy is the greatest:

It's often when you are on a 'spiritual high', when you are replete with joy, that the devil puts in an appearance. Jesus had just experienced one of the 'high points' of his earthly life at his baptism. For Jesus, this would have been a joyful occasion. We must be alert to the possibility that our greatest joys in life may be followed quickly by our greatest temptations.

When our devotion is the choicest:

Jesus had just heard his Father's approval (v22). He had been led by the Spirit into the desert (v1). Jesus' communion with his Father was so perfect. Time spent alone in communion and meditation can be so wonderfully sweet as the Lord's presence is known in a real and personal way. But even such devotional sessions are not exempt from outside interference. The knock at the door, the phone ringing, something happening outside the window – can provide untimely distractions, even temptations. Jesus' time in the desert with his Father would have been perfect - without the devil.

When our resistance is the lowest:

It's not by accident that Satan's first temptation is directed at Jesus' physical weakness: his hunger. Like most temptations, this one is appealing and appropriate. The temptation is almost logical in relation to our feelings and circumstances. The devil comes to us when our resistance is low physically (when we're hungry, tired, suffering pain) or mentally and emotionally (when we feel dejected, unwanted, humiliated, and desperate). The devil tried to drive a wedge between the Father and the Son. He wanted Jesus to operate outside of the Father's will because he knew that the Son had been sent to demolish Satan's enterprises (1 John ch3 v8). He continues to try and drive a wedge between our relationship with God.

520

2 KNOW YOUR ENEMY'S TACTICS

The enemy's temptations frequently involve taking shortcuts. If we're provided with a 'quick fix' to our goal, then we may be tempted. The devil offered Jesus a shortcut:

To Personal Satisfaction:

Bread would have satisfied Jesus' hunger pangs. How easily do we succumb to the temptations to satisfy our personal demands for knowledge, popularity, wealth, success, and friendship?

To Personal Power:

In vv5-6 Jesus is tempted to gain instant world domination by worshipping the devil. He uses the same ploy: '*If you worship me* (by ignoring the Bible and common ethics), *all this can be yours!*'

To Personal Glory:

Such a temptation (v9) appeals to those who want to make a show of their position and authority. Jesus IS the Son of God, and this was not the divine plan to declare his deity. God's plan included the cross, the appointed means to victory and glory (ch24 v26). No bypass of the cross was possible.

3 KNOW YOUR ENEMY'S TENDER-SPOT

Be aware of the devil's weaknesses and vulnerability. The devil is not omniscient, omnipresent, or omnipotent. What's more, there is a warrior and a weapon that can seriously wound the enemy. Jesus resisted the tempter's suggestions-

Through the Holy Spirit:

v1 not only tells us about Jesus' movements but also his strength. We cannot stand in our own strength hoping to fend off the devil's fiendish attacks. We need the Spirit's daily power: his filling and his leading.

Through the Holy Scripture:

The Spirit's sword is the mighty weapon that cuts Satan down to size. Misappropriating Scripture is no defence (vv10-11). The very psalm that the devil quoted says that God will protect his faithful followers *from the fowler's snare'* (Psalm 91 v3). The headlines of the devil's ultimate defeat have already been written (Revelation ch20 v10).

Know your enemy well! Resist him by submitting to God (James ch4 v7).

SEPTEMBER 9
THE GOSPEL OF LUKE Ch4.14-30

SCRIPTURE FULFILLED

The Synagogue

'Synagogue' refers to an assembled company or to the building which they occupied.

From the time of the exile into Babylon, and perhaps even earlier, the synagogue was the place of worship when God's people were denied access to the temple. By the first century, synagogues were an important institution and could be found everywhere. The two principal officials in the synagogue were the Ruler of the Synagogue (responsible for supervision, property, and appointing persons to read or pray) and the Attendant (responsible for the care of the building, furniture, and scrolls of Scripture in particular). It was Jesus' home synagogue in Nazareth that was the background to these verses. We can't be sure whether Jesus had read in the synagogue prior to this occasion, but we do know that every Sabbath day, Jesus had attended this synagogue to hear the word of God and to worship.

Jesus' regular attendance

We can't imagine Jesus missing a service because he was tired, or because a customer was waiting for a carpentry task to be finished, or because the weather was inclement, or because he had taken too long over breakfast! Jesus didn't need to come up with any lame excuses for not being at the place of worship every week. He was there without fail because he loved his heavenly Father so much and because he wanted to be about his Father's business. Jesus wasn't a stranger in his local place of worship. Every week for thirty years, the synagogue Ruler never wondered whether Jesus would turn up. He was reliable, dependable, and enthusiastic.

After his baptism, Jesus began his itinerant ministry teaching in many different synagogues (vv14-15). But he returns to the Nazareth synagogue, and he is invited to read the Scriptures. The Attendant would have handed Jesus the particular scroll, and the 'Word from God' reads the 'word of God' with clarity and authority. Seven hundred years after Isaiah had written the words, Jesus announces to his stunned listeners, *'Today this scripture is fulfilled in your hearing'* (v21). He's saying that he is:

1 ANOINTED TO PREACH GOOD NEWS

The Good News in Isaiah's day referred to God graciously bringing the Jews home from captivity in Babylon. But Jesus applies Isaiah's gospel to himself. He comes to bring hope to those who are *'poor in spirit'* (Matthew ch5 v3; Luke ch6 v20). Jesus proclaims the life-giving message to those who have reached the end of themselves and their meager resources. The gospel is for the spiritually bankrupt who have nothing to offer.

2 ANOINTED TO PROCLAIM FREEDOM AND SIGHT

There is spiritual freedom and sight for all who turn from sin and trust in Christ. This radical transformation is life-changing for the blind and the bound.

3 ANOINTED TO RELEASE THE OPPRESSED

'Oppressed' means 'absolutely broken' and 'crushed by distress'. Jesus not only brings the message but, unlike Isaiah, he has the power to make the message happen.

4 ANOINTED TO PROCLAIM GOD'S GRACE

The year of God's favour' (v19) seems to refer to Israel's Jubilee Year (one in fifty). It was regarded as the year of freedom and forgiveness. The gospel announces 'the time of God's grace' – the 'Jubilee of freedom and forgiveness'. Charitable organisations may work with those they believe to be 'deserving cases'. But the truth of the gospel is that none of us is a 'deserving case'. We are all thoroughly undeserving, and we can only plead the undeserved, unmerited kindness of our God.

So how should we respond to this gospel? How did Jesus' hearers respond?

Everyone's tongues praised him

(vv15, 22) It wasn't just Jesus' message that was attractive; it was his manner. His style, personality, and authority were compelling and winsome.

Everyone's eyes fastened on him

(v20) They were 'glued' to Jesus as he emphasised examples from the Old Testament, showing that close proximity to God didn't guarantee forgiveness. The Gospel was for Gentiles too.

Everyone's hearts were furious with him

(v28) They wanted to kill Jesus, but now wasn't the time or the place.

SEPTEMBER 10
THE GOSPEL OF LUKE Ch4.31-44

Is a teacher only teaching when the student is learning? If a person is communicating with a group of people, at what point does he or she become the teacher? Surely a teacher is only a teacher when there are learners who are learning. An effective teacher must have authority in his or her subject as well as authority over the students. This is where we join Jesus at the start of his Galilean ministry – on a particular Sabbath, in a synagogue, at the fishing village of Capernaum – teaching the people (v31).

JESUS' AUTHORITY

We may observe four things about Jesus' authority.

1 AUTHORITY OVER STUDENTS

(v32) We can be sure that Jesus wasn't merely speaking to a congregation of synagogue worshippers. Jesus was teaching because his hearers were learning. His teaching was authoritative, *'not as the teachers of the law'* (Mark ch1 v22). Those law teachers were more than just scribes and copyists by the time of the New Testament. They had gained a higher status as 'legal experts' and 'doctors of the law'. But the rabbis based their teaching on the traditions and the interpretations of their predecessors, whereas Jesus' teaching carried a different authority altogether. The people couldn't help but note that Jesus' message carried his personal authority, the One who himself was the very embodiment of the message, the Word made flesh.

2 AUTHORITY OVER SPIRITS

(vv33-37, 41) The forces of evil couldn't hide from the presence of the Son of God. Neither could they operate effectively. Jesus had come to:

Defeat the spiritual forces of evil and darkness, death and sin (1 Corinthians ch15 v57).

Disarm *'the powers and authorities'* (Colossians ch2 v15).

Destroy *'the devil's work'* (1 John ch3 v8).

We therefore notice that the evil spirits:

Recognised the Person of Christ:

This was not just another carpenter from Galilee! This wasn't just another 'Jesus' among many called by that name. This is 'Jesus of Nazareth', *'the Holy One of God'* (v34)...*'the Son of God...the Christ'* (v41).

Recognised the Mission of Christ:

They knew Christ's purpose in coming into the world, and they trembled at his words. Would this clash between the power of Satan and the power of God signal the complete overthrow of the kingdom of darkness? Yes – but not yet! Demons fear and flee before Jesus' authority. As believers, we have no need to be intimidated by the powers of darkness just as long as we trust, not in ourselves, but in the strength and victory of a crucified and risen Saviour. *'The accuser of our brothers...has been hurled down'* through the *'power and the kingdom of our God, and the authority of his Christ'* (Revelation ch12 vv10-11).

3 AUTHORITY OVER SICKNESS

(vv38-40) Jesus responds to the request for help from Simon's family. Jesus visits the sick mother-in-law and draws close to her (*'bent over her'*). Jesus rebukes the fever, and there is immediate healing. Jesus heals completely. There's no convalescence. She *'got up at once and...'*

The Jewish day concluded at sunset. As soon as the Sabbath was over, at the very earliest opportunity, needy people sought Jesus. Jesus ministered to every need since no personal problem or affliction was outside the scope of his authority. It was Jesus' work at the cross that sealed the ultimate victory (see Matthew ch8 vv16-17).

Note too that those who were unable to come to Jesus for themselves were brought to Jesus by friends and relatives who had their best interests at heart. Similarly, let the friends and relatives of those who will not pray for themselves persevere in bringing them to God in prayer.

4 AUTHORITY OVER SINNERS

(vv42-44) There's a sense of urgency in Jesus' declaration: *'I must preach...'* Nothing could stand in his way as he visited the towns and synagogues of Judea, proclaiming *'the good news of the kingdom of God'*. How we need a similar conviction and motivation in our ministries and spheres of service today. It's all too easy for us to become casual, lethargic, and dispassionate regarding the desperate plight of men and women around us who live and die without Christ. Our ministry must 'have heart'.

SEPTEMBER 11
THE GOSPEL OF LUKE Ch5.1-26

The Jewish historian, Josephus, records that there were three hundred and thirty fishing boats working the freshwater lake, Galilee, during the New Testament period. It's this local industry that provides the background to much of Jesus' ministry. Jesus borrows Simon Peter's boat from which to teach the crowds that flocked to hear him. When he had finished, Jesus told Simon to *'put out into deep water, and let down the nets for a catch'* (v4). Simon may have wondered what a Nazareth carpenter knew about fishing. He may have been a little tired and frustrated at having an unsuccessful night's fishing, and he respectfully reminded Jesus that it had been a fruitless expedition. But, thankfully, Simon didn't stop there. He said, *'But at your word'* – or – *'Because you say so, I will let down the nets'* (v5). We talk about someone's 'say so', meaning one's personal statement or assertion; their final authority or command. We say that we'll do this or that 'according to someone's say-so', meaning 'with their permission and authority'

HIS SAY SO

1 BECAUSE YOU SAY SO, I'LL DO WHATEVER YOU TELL ME

Jesus told the fishermen, *'Let down your nets'* (v4).

What did Jesus know about fishing? Well, he knew everything since he had not only made each and every species of fish in the lake, but he had made the lake in which they swam. There's a hint of faith as well as obedience in Simon's heart as he casts his fishing nets on Jesus' say-so.

Jesus told the leper, *'Show yourself to the priest and offer sacrifices'* (v14).

To be a leper meant an end to normal living. It was the sentence of a 'living death' as the victim tried to exist for as long as possible in isolation while the 'uncleanness' of the disease covered him. This leper knew that Jesus was able to heal him, but was he willing? Jesus responded immediately with a thorough healing. The Mosaic Law required that certain rituals be observed before a leper could be pronounced clean. The ceremony (Leviticus ch14) involved examination by the priest, as well as washing and sacrifice. Though his recovery was complete, he was not exempt from following the Old Testament procedure that verified his healing. But he was ready to do whatever he was told.

Jesus told the paralytic, *'Take your mat'* (v24).

We notice the determination, effort, and faith of this paralytic and his friends. They wanted a personal encounter with Jesus, and wall-to-wall guests in the house wouldn't put them off. He was lowered right in front of Jesus (v19). The work in lifting, carrying, digging, and lowering would have been of little use unless they believed that Jesus could heal someone who was paralysed. The final test of faith was for the man to take up his mat and walk. He was prepared to do whatever Jesus told him.

2 BECAUSE YOU SAY SO, I'LL GO WHEREVER YOU SEND ME

To the paralytic, Jesus said *'Go home'*. To the leper, Jesus said *'Go…to the priest'*. In Simon's case, he was to go and *'catch men'*. Jesus would later tell him, *'Go into all the world and preach the Gospel'* (Mark ch16 v15). Countless men and women have stood where Isaiah stood, in the presence of our majestic God, and have responded, *'Here I am. Send me!'* (Isaiah ch6 v8). For some, it has meant going to other lands and speaking in another language. For some, it has meant going to religious people who are sceptical and suspicious of the transforming power of the gospel. For others, it has meant going home to be a witness to the truth in familiar surroundings with friends and family.

3 BECAUSE YOU SAY SO, I'LL BE WHATEVER YOU WANT ME

In these three separate accounts, we note that Simon Peter dropped to the ground at Jesus' knees (v8); the leper fell to the ground before Jesus (v12); the paralytic was lowered to the ground in front of Jesus (v19). In each case, there is the suggestion of humility and submission. Faith is also a common factor. Simon believed Jesus' power, the leper trusted Jesus' ability, and the paralytic had faith in Jesus' authority. Each one made a life-changing break with the past. They would never be the same again. The fishermen didn't know Jesus' resources, but they *'left everything'*, and neither did they know exactly where Jesus was going, but they *'followed him'* (v11).

The Lord wants those today who will *do* the work, *go* to the field of service, and *be* the faithful servant that he wants them to be – because of Jesus' say-so.

SEPTEMBER 12
THE GOSPEL OF LUKE Ch5.27-39

OUTREACH MEAL

At the time of Jesus' ministry, Palestine was under Roman occupation. Therefore, the Jewish tax collectors were working for the Romans and were consequently hated and despised. The average person wouldn't want a taxman as a neighbour. They wouldn't be seen talking to one, or travelling with one, much less eating with one. The taxman's job was to collect the levy as dictated by Rome, and he had the power and support of the Roman army behind him if this was refused. As long as they collected what Rome wanted, the tax collectors could add whatever percentage they felt like to line their own pockets. The teachings of the rabbis encouraged Jews to hate taxmen and their families, even to defraud them if possible! Taxmen were the pariahs of society – traitors, apostates, and outcasts.

It's therefore immensely significant that, when Jesus visited the Capernaum tax office, he said to Levi, the taxman, *'Follow Me...and (he) got up, left everything and followed him'* (vv27-28). Levi severed his ties with the past and openly declared his allegiance to Jesus. In fact, he *'held a banquet'* in Jesus' honour. It was a kind of 'outreach meal' to which all Levi's colleagues and friends were invited to meet Jesus. The critics' complaint (v30) prompted the first of two statements from Jesus:

1 THE DOCTOR CALLS (vv31-32)

Jesus' words convey two fundamental truths:

The Sinner's Condition. The sinners to whom Jesus came are not healthy in spiritual terms. Each one is in desperate need as sin's fatal disease overcomes little by little. Within the New Testament, the concept of sin is revealed in such words as fault, guilt, injustice, unrighteousness, offence, transgression, and evil. It's portrayed as rebellion, disobedience, and a conscious deviation from what is right. This debilitating disease has infected every single human being (Romans ch3 vv10, 23). The victims have no means of halting its advance. They are under sentence of death (Ezekiel ch18 v4, Romans ch6 v23).

The Saviour's Mission. Jesus makes one of his several 'mission statements' (v32). Mankind is utterly depraved, totally incapable, and unquestionably guilty. He has neither the power nor the will to heal himself of sin's terminal illness. Indeed, everything he touches he contaminates. Everything he tries to do is thoroughly condemned. But Jesus, the divine Doctor and faithful Physician, comes to call *'sinners to repentance'*. The will to change is only possible as a result of the Surgeon-Spirit operating on their hearts. Witness it in action in the life of Levi! Everything changed for him the day that Jesus called him. He abandoned his old way of life, his selfish ambitions, and his old priorities in favour of Jesus (compare Philippians ch3 vv7-9).

2 THE BRIDEGROOM DEPARTS (vv34-35)

The Pharisees and teachers of the law were complaining that Jesus' disciples ate and drank while John Baptist's disciples fasted and prayed. Jesus illustrated by pointing to a wedding where the accent was upon friendship, love, and closeness. But something dreadful happens at the wedding when the bridegroom is removed from the celebrations. He is 'lifted off'…'carried away'. Jesus hints at his own death, that is, *'taken away'* (Isaiah ch53 v8). For Jesus, the 'countdown to Calvary' had already begun. But while the glorious Bridegroom of God's grace is still among the wedding party, it's a time of feasting, not fasting.

Something Old, something New; something…

The parables of the patched clothes and the old wineskin bottles warn us about trying to mix the old and the new. Jesus is speaking about change. Though the old Jewish religion with its customs and practices had a role to fulfil, it cannot be harmonised with the new ways and teachings that Jesus was inaugurating. You can't mix and match, pick and patch! With the coming of Christ and his gospel, there was a new attitude, a new approach, a new spirit, and a new heart. 'New wine' is not about new media, new methods, new gimmicks, new technology – it's all about a right view of Jesus, which may mean a fresh and vibrant view of the Son of God our Saviour. How much do we want to know him (Psalm 42 v1; Philippians ch3 v10)? Some people are quite content to keep on sipping from the old wine, saying *'the old is better'* (v39), without tasting the 'new wine' of Jesus and his life-changing gospel.

SEPTEMBER 13
THE GOSPEL OF LUKE Ch6.1-26

BLESSINGS

ONE OF SEVEN

The Security Service, more commonly known as MI5, is the United Kingdom's secret intelligence agency. Its main objective is that of national security, which it pursues frequently by extensive surveillance. The Pharisees in Jesus' day, though less sophisticated in their approach, were constantly spying on the teacher from Nazareth 'in the interests of national security'. They were keen to prove that Jesus and his disciples were Sabbath-breakers and, therefore, to discredit them and to halt their work.

In the Pharisees' eyes, Jesus and his disciples were guilty of reaping, threshing, winnowing, and preparing food by plucking, rubbing, and eating the grain. This contravened the strict Jewish regulations.

Jesus was under close surveillance in the synagogue, too. He had infuriated the Pharisee spies by healing on the Sabbath, as this could undermine their authority.

But Jesus was not bound by man-made regulations attached to the Law of God. God's law regarding the Sabbath was clear in his provision of one day in seven that is set apart and uniquely special, free from the work and duties of everyday (Exodus ch20 vv8-11).

TWELVE OF MANY

Jesus' appointment of this select group was preceded by a night spent in prayer. When we are faced with important choices and far-reaching decisions, how much do we pray? Although this natural amphitheatre was bulging with eager listeners, it was to the twelve apostles that Jesus directly addressed his induction training.

FOUR OF NINE

Luke summaries Matthew's nine Beatitudes into four 'blessings' and corresponding 'woes':

1 BLESSING TO THE POOR BUT WOE TO THE RICH (vv20, 24)

No wonder everyone was hanging on Jesus' every word as he spoke about the poor, the hungry, the sorrowful, and the despised. These were conditions with which all the people could identify. But Jesus is speaking about more than just physical ailments and material privations. He is referring to those who are empty of themselves and who know that they possess nothing in spiritual terms. It's not a false demonstration of humility or piety, nor is it a show of self-sacrifice. Rather, it's in the recognition that I am a sinner and no one except the Saviour of sinners can help me. For those who come in the poverty of penitence, there is the promise of God's kingdom, while to those who boast in the riches of their self-sufficiency, their comfort is shallow and transient.

2 BLESSING TO THE HUNGRY BUT WOE TO THE WELL-FED (v21a, 25a)

Matthew's account elaborates on what this 'hungering' is all about (Matthew ch5 v6). It's a yearning for righteousness. This particular blessing is for those who are thoroughly dissatisfied with the diet of this world's recipes, and who hunger for food to meet their spiritual need. The real calamity today is in a spiritual starvation with no appetite for God's truth and no hunger for righteousness. The 'number one' priority must be the nutritional diet of holy living and Christlike behaviour (Matthew ch6 v33).

3 BLESSING TO THE SORROWFUL BUT WOE TO THE HAPPY (v21b, v25b)

'Being happy' is the elusive quest of a vast number of people every day. Genuine joy is not dependent upon food, mood, plenitude, or solitude, but upon a right relationship with God. The blessing to those who mourn is not for those who mourn over debt, disease, disadvantage, or death. It's for those who mourn over their sin. It's *'godly sorrow that leads to repentance'* (2 Corinthians ch7 v10). Developing a greater God-consciousness within our being will automatically produce a greater sensitivity to the loathsomeness and filthiness of our sin.

4 BLESSING TO THE PERSECUTED BUT WOE TO THE HONOURED (vv22, 26)

Jesus points out that to be identified with him, the Son of Man, is going to mean persecution, ostracism, insults, and rejection. The history of the Church is one of intense persecution. It's 'normal' in parts of our twenty-first-century world to be murdered as a Christian rather than to die naturally. Jesus' blessing is not for those who have been persecuted for opposing authorities, or for taking militant action, or for being religious activists, or for scoring political points. Jesus' blessing is specifically for those who are persecuted for living holy, Godly, Christ-centred lives (2 Timothy ch3 v12).

SEPTEMBER 14
THE GOSPEL OF LUKE Ch6.27-49

FRUIT AND FOUNDATIONS

Jesus emphasises three important points in this section of his famous sermon:

1 LOVE AT ITS BEST

This is the kind of love that is demonstrated towards enemies. To love your friends is natural. Doing good to those who do good to you, lending things to those who promptly return them, and in good condition, giving to those who give generously to you, is not a great love. Jesus asks, *'What credit is that to you?'* (v33). Unbelievers love each other with that kind of love. A follower of Jesus, however, will be displaying a love that is embossed with the hallmark of heaven. How should Christians treat their enemies?

Bless them (v28) – praise them, commend them, speak well of them.

Pray for them (v28) – like Jesus did (Luke ch23 v34; Romans ch5 v10).

Yield to them (v29) – no retaliation, no redress, no looking to get even.

Give to them (v30) – even lend without expecting to get anything back.

Do good to them (vv27,31,35) – this love has a heavenly quality about it.

2 MERCY AT ITS MOST

(vv36-38) You may struggle with the idea of showing mercy to someone who has hurt you or offended you. You say, 'But they don't deserve it!' -and that's just the point. Mercy is love to the undeserving, kindness to the unworthy, and forgiveness to the guilty. But any mercy that we can ever show is only a pale reflection of the mercy that has been shown to us in Christ (Titus ch3 v4). In showing us mercy, God has made us his friends.

3 CRITICISM AT ITS WORST

The illustration of the plank of wood and the speck of sawdust is very vivid. The word for *'hypocrite'* is the word for 'actor' – someone who is putting on a show. It doesn't mean that there is never a place for criticism, but it requires a person to deal with their own major problems before criticizing the minor problems of others.

These Christian characteristics of love, mercy, and forgiveness are exemplified by the men in the parables that Jesus told. He refers to two model men who represent the loving and faithful virtues of which Jesus is preaching.

The good person with the right fruit (vv43-45)

Jesus provides examples of how thornbushes don't produce figs and briers don't produce grapes. A tree cannot produce fruit that is out of character with its species.

The fruit of 'love for your enemies' and 'forgiveness for your critics' and 'mercy for your offenders' will only come from a heart that is made clean through the blood of Christ.

It's Jesus alone who can transform lives and change hearts. What's stored away in the treasury of your heart? How easily and how naturally do you speak words of criticism, accusation, bitterness, complaint, and anger? *'For out of the overflow of his heart his mouth speaks'* (v45). It's only by dealing with the source that we can control the quality of the supply. The output is directly linked to the input (James ch3 vv10-12). *'A wise man's heart guides his mouth'* (Proverbs ch18 v23).

The genuine person with the right foundations (vv46-49)

One man builds his house on a foundation of rock, while the other builds his house without any foundation. The person who is religiously courteous but scripturally disobedient is identified with the man who has no foundation. Merely saying *'Lord, Lord'* (v46) is nothing without obedience. The nominal Christians who quickly write 'Christian' when asked for their religion on a form, but who have no intention of putting Jesus' words into practice, are like those without foundation.

Foundation Principle No1:

Coming to Jesus is the first important requirement (v47). Salvation is found in no one else (Acts ch4 v12). If you need real, long-term rest, then come to Jesus (Matthew ch11 v28). If you're thirsty, come to Jesus (John ch7 v37).

Foundation Principle No2:

Hearing the message is more than just hearing the sound of Jesus' voice. It is to listen intently and to consider carefully the words spoken.

Foundation Principle No3:

It's no good coming to Jesus if there's no intention to obey him and to put his words into practice. We must be the doers of his words so that it may be said of our faith and practice, *'It was well built'* (v48).

SEPTEMBER 15
THE GOSPEL OF LUKE Ch7.1-17

Psalm 121 may well have been a song that the pilgrims sang as they made their way to the city of Jerusalem and the gates of the temple in particular. It begins with a question and answer: *'I lift up my eyes to the hills – where does my help come from? My help comes from the Lord, the Maker of heaven and earth'* (Psalm 121 vv1-2).

When Paul stood before King Herod Agrippa, the apostle acknowledged that the gospel of repentance and faith was not too popular among his fellow Jews. He admitted that they had tried to seize him in the temple courts and kill him. Paul says, *'But I have had God's help to this very day'* (Acts ch26 v22). Many of us can also testify to God's help being personally provided to us, not only in rare dramatic ways, but every day. What other god can say to his people, *'I will strengthen you and help you; I will uphold you with my righteous right hand'* (Isaiah ch41 v10)?

In these two incidents in Jesus' ministry, he is seen to provide divine help to the needy. So much so, that the crowd of people from Nain, who formed the cortege, *'were all filled with awe and praised God'* at the restoration to life of the young man in the coffin. They commented, *'A great prophet has appeared among us...God has come to help his people'* (v16).

The Jews had probably thought that they had been largely abandoned by God. They may have considered that they were on the outer fringe of his blessings, since they had called out for help constantly during the days of the Roman occupation. They had believed that they had been ignored by God, even forgotten by him, and as a consequence, they had suffered pain, hardship, humiliation, and loss. But there's clearly a joyful note of hope in the people's exclamation. There's light at the end of the tunnel. The night may be over, and the dawn is about to break. A great prophet has arrived and *'God has come to help his people'*.

GOD HAS COME TO HELP HIS PEOPLE

1 GOD COMES TO HELP IN BRINGING HOPE TO THE BELIEVING

The centurion's faith amazed Jesus (v9). He was:

Respectful and religious – he had won the hearts of the Jews (v5).

Wealthy and generous – donating to the building of a place of worship.

Kind and compassionate – showing great concern for his paralysed servant.

Humble and undeserving – not sufficiently worthy to receive Jesus.

Trusting and believing – he believed what he had learned about Jesus.

What have we learned about this outstanding Jesus of Nazareth? The Gentile military man of faith, who didn't want Jesus to enter his house, nor did he want his medicine, or his therapy, or even his touch, wanted his word (v7). Are we looking for the signs, the touch, the drama, the special visitations, the supernatural manifestations, or are we content with his powerful, life-changing, life-giving word?

2 GOD COMES TO HELP IN BRINGING LIFE TO THE DYING

One man was dying (v2), and the other young man was already dead (v12). But the coming of Jesus makes all the difference! In each case, the recovery was instantaneous. There was no protracted period of convalescence or physiotherapy, for the restoration was immediate and complete. These factual accounts of God coming to help the dead and dying illustrate to us that our only hope of salvation from our spiritual death in transgressions and sins is in Jesus Christ. From the inky, smelly darkness of the whale's belly, Jonah cried, *'From the depths of the grave I called for help, and you listened to my cry'* (Jonah ch2 vv1-2).

3 GOD COMES TO HELP IN BRINGING COMFORT TO THE GRIEVING

Not only is Jesus amazed at great faith (v9), but he is also affected by great grief (v13). Jesus steps into the middle of this woman's desperate grief and loss and he puts a stop to the funeral and puts a stop to her misery. *'His heart went out to her'*, which represents the meaning of the word, referring to an inward moving of the soul that is demonstrated in practical help. Jesus continues to provide heavenly help to his people in their time of misery, sorrow, and loss. He has authority over the grave and over grief. He is sensitive to his people's deepest needs and sympathetic to his people's darkest distresses.

SEPTEMBER 16
THE GOSPEL OF LUKE Ch7.18-35

The narrow, gloomy passages of the ruins of the Machaerus fortress, in the desert region of the Dead Sea, provide shelter from sudden storms for nomads and their flocks. But history records that it was here that Herod Antipas imprisoned John Baptist before beheading him. It must have been a lonely, depressing place for John to live out his last days on earth. But it seems that he had communication with his disciples, and they were reporting to him about Jesus.

Was John troubled with uncertainties and doubts at this time? Did things appear to be less clear than they were? After all, John had heralded Jesus' coming (v27), had declared him to be God's Lamb (John ch1 v29), and had testified to Jesus' commission (John ch1 vv32-34). But John needed assurance, and he knew precisely where to get it – from Jesus himself (v20). Jesus instructs John's disciples to report back with the evidence of their own eyes (v22). Jesus Christ, of course, is the issue. He is either our Rock of foundation and faith, or he has become a stone over which we stumble and fall (v23).

Our faith will only develop when we are prepared to acknowledge the rightness of God: that everything he does is right, without any hint of error.

THE RIGHTNESS OF GOD

1 GOD'S WAY IS RIGHT (v29)

This is Luke's comment on all the people's assessment of Jesus' words. It's in this sense that the people 'justified' God. They acknowledged that Jesus' testimony was right. It was the truth. But John may have been harbouring doubts:

Doubts about Christ's Person: Perhaps John saw Jesus' style in direct contrast to his own. The Jewish religious critics were saying that John *'has a demon'* because he abstained from bread and wine, and that Jesus was *'a glutton and a drunkard'* because he ate and drank with tax collectors and sinners. John had preached in the Jordan Valley while Jesus had preached in towns and villages. John had spent time baptising, while we have no record that Jesus baptised. So John's disciples posed the question (v19).

Doubts about Christ's Kingdom: Perhaps John had become influenced by the thinking that Jesus would champion the Jewish cause, vindicate their religion, and set the Hebrews free. Maybe he thought that Jesus could overthrow the Romans with supernatural powers and restore justice, faithfulness, and truth.

Doubts about God's Will: Had John thought that he may have been too critical of Herodias, or at least he shouldn't have criticised her publicly (ch3 v19)? Perhaps he reasoned that his incarceration was God's punishment upon him. Sometimes our circumstances can colour our rationale. There's a rightness in all of God's purposes – for each one of his people individually (Deuteronomy ch32 v3-4).

2 GOD'S WISDOM IS RIGHT (v35)

The second time the Greek word for 'justified' is used in this passage is in v35. The children of wisdom are those who had repented, believed, and were baptised (v29). The infantile way in which the critics tried to play off Jesus against John revealed their absence of wisdom. It's just as childish today as it was then (vv32-34). God's wisdom is revealed in the way in which he chooses difference and diversity for his purposes.

God's wisdom is seen to be right within his church as he uses –

Different Callings:

The roles of each church member are vital and valuable. John Baptist's primary role was as a messenger.

Different Characters:

A rich diversity of characters and personalities make up the 'ticklish all sorts' who are engaged in their various ministries.

Different Capabilities:

As well as supernatural gifts conferred on the church, God uses natural gifts in his service.

Different Conditions:

God's people are employed in all kinds of places and in myriad circumstances. Those conditions may not always be the most pleasant. Yet a place of safety outside of God's way and God's wisdom is too risky and too dangerous a place for any Christian to consider.

If you doubt your calling, dislike your character, underestimate your capabilities, or despise your present conditions, think again about the rightness of God's way and wisdom in everything.

SEPTEMBER 17
THE GOSPEL OF LUKE Ch7.36-50

The twentieth-century proverb, 'actions speak louder than words', could be written across this account of the woman who anointed Jesus.

Speaking about this unnamed, unknown woman who gatecrashed Simon's dinner party, Jesus said:

'SHE LOVED MUCH' (v47)

Whether it was out of a genuine interest in Jesus' ministry, or whether it was an attempt to trap Jesus, or whether he had hoped that Jesus would provide the cabaret in the form of miracles, Simon invited Jesus to dinner. The woman is not an invited guest, although she had access to the room without being intercepted. Perhaps she was among some who were invited as spectators or as one of the poor who may have been permitted to scavenge the leftovers.

If Simon were aware of her presence, he wouldn't have liked it since this woman had 'a reputation'. Simon thought that Jesus had failed the 'prophet test' too because if he were a prophet, he would have known *what kind of woman she is – that she is a sinner*' (v39). But Simon was in for a shock. Not only did Jesus know all about this woman, he knew all about Simon: his heart and his thoughts.

The stark bottom line is this: that however much we may 'dress up' or 'talk up' our sin, we are only sinners at best. But the test of those who are wonderfully forgiven by the grace of God will be in the lives of loving service that they live for him. This woman loved much because she had been forgiven much. She had a testimony to tell of God's love and God's kindness shown to her individually. Jesus had done a transforming work in her life, and she had come to Jesus to express her great love and deep appreciation for saving her. She loved much. How much?

1 MUCH GRATITUDE

It wasn't that Jesus had forgiven this woman after she had demonstrated sufficient love to him. It was the other way round. His love was unconditional, yet real forgiveness will evoke genuine appreciation and love. The love that this woman showed was as a result of the love God had shown to her in Christ (v48, 1 John ch4 vv10, 19). Any definition of true, sincere love must begin with God for *'God is love'* (1 John ch4 v16). A penitent, pardoned sinner loves God with the gift of love that God has given. As this woman wet Jesus' feet with her tears, her sorrow for sin and her gratitude for grace were self-evident. Here was not just a dampening of the eyes or a few tears trickling down her cheeks. Her tears were sufficient to wash the Lord's feet. Like the man in Jesus' parable (v41), who owed over a year and a half's wages to a moneylender, the woman was overwhelmed with gratitude when she learned that she had been forgiven.

2 MUCH HUMILITY

Not only did she wash Jesus' feet with her tears, but she also used her hair to wipe them dry (vv38, 44). A woman's hair was considered to be her glory (1 Corinthians ch11 v15), but this woman was willing to despise any vestiges of her own honour and glory to lay them, quite literally, at Jesus' feet. We are all guilty of hanging on to remnants of our pride. We want to 'maintain a degree of dignity'. We may stoop so low, but no further.

3 MUCH RESPECT

While Simon may have been polite to Jesus (*'Teacher'* v40) yet he had not extended to Jesus the traditional form of welcome, the kiss. Simon may have denied Jesus this respectful greeting, but the woman had not ceased to kiss Jesus' feet from the moment he had entered the room. Do we honour him with our lips and our lives?

4 MUCH GIVING

Simon hadn't even used inexpensive olive oil to anoint Jesus' head, but the woman liberally poured expensive perfume over his feet. Her love was:

Extravagant:

She loved much, and nothing would be too much for Jesus!

Fragrant:

Though there's no recorded word that she spoke, this woman's love was so obvious to everyone. The aroma of her actions and the presence of Jesus would have lingered in Simon's house for many weeks.

What impact do we leave on our surroundings?

What sweet fragrance of Christ is left behind when we depart?

SEPTEMBER 18
THE GOSPEL OF LUKE Ch8.1-15

MISSION SUPPORT TEAM

Mary Magdalene, Joanna, and Susanna were among the women who formed an essential support team that cared for the daily needs of Jesus and his disciples. Mary had experienced wonderful deliverance from demonic control. Susanna is unknown, but Joanna was the wife of King Herod's 'Lord Chamberlain'. She was an important lady, probably with wealth and status, yet she devoted herself to Jesus and his mission team in the spread of the Gospel. Though we may know little else about these women, their names are preserved forever in God's word as those who supported Jesus and his gospel preachers. What an accolade! The work of teaching the Bible and preaching the gospel still requires the invaluable support of those like Mary, Jo, Su, and the other women -faithful followers of Jesus who are identified by their humility, commitment, and sacrifice.

These women would have remained in the background as Jesus told this famous parable about a farmer, with a bag of seed slung over his shoulder, sowing in a field.

Where are the four places that the seed fell, and what happened to the seed?

1 SEED ON THE PATH – NO BELIEF

Some seed fell on the path where it was trampled and devoured by birds (vv5, 12). Jesus compares this seed to those who hear the word of God, but it is snatched away by the devil before it can take root in their hearts. There are numerous people who listen to the word preached occasionally or every week. They may listen attentively and may remember much of what is said, but something happens between the ear and the heart. The word is quickly snatched away so that they do not believe and do not become saved. The seed doesn't have time to germinate. It's trampled upon, and the devil snatches it away.

2 SEED ON THE ROCK – SHORT BELIEF

This kind of person receives the word with joy to begin with (vv6, 13). They are happy that they have had some religious experience, and things seem to go well for a while. But it's only a short-term faith, which is no faith at all. The type of soil in which this seed has fallen is only very shallow. There are professing Christians who claim to have an experience of God, and initially, there's a flush of faith and a surge of enthusiasm. They want to be identified with other believers. They attend all the services and may even pray in the prayer meeting. They want to be included on this rota, and in this venture, and on that working party. But eventually, after five weeks, five months, or five years, there's a withering and a falling away. When their faith is tested by adversity, opposition, or demands for consecration and perseverance, they are nowhere to be seen. The word for 'falling away' gives us our word 'apostasy'.

3 SEED IN THE THORNS – LITTLE BELIEF

Another cause of failing to grow and be fruitful is the 'choking effect' (vv7, 14) that the things of this life produce. The world is a strangler and will choke the very life out of a professing Christian. The word for *'worries'* suggests an excessive, even obsessive, concern for one's welfare and self-interest. A preoccupation with self is the very opposite of what the Bible teaches. We must learn to rest in God and to put our trust in him. Jesus taught this in his 'mountain sermon' (Matthew ch6 vv25, 32, 33).

4 SEED ON THE SOIL – REAL BELIEF

Hearing the word of God and responding with faith and obedience is the only way to be fruitful in God's estimation (vv8,15). There's no alternative way to be saved and to become a member of God's family. It's in hearing, believing, and doing God's word with perseverance. If you receive God's word casually, carelessly, superficially, and indifferently, then your classification, according to Jesus, is patently obvious. You are like the seed on the path, on the rock, and in the thorns. It's in the transforming power of the word of God that brings life, growth, and fruitfulness. This is produced in those hearts that have been made *'noble and good'*. These are hearts that have been changed by the grace of God; hearts that have been made clean through Jesus' blood; hearts that are consumed with love for God and undying devotion to his word.

May our hearts be the rich and ready soil to receive God's word today.

SEPTEMBER 19
THE GOSPEL OF LUKE Ch8.16-56

Among the world's recognised and respected works of reference is a book containing over thirty-three thousand potted biographies of living, noteworthy, and influential individuals. It's the famous *'Who's Who'*, which provides a ready answer to the question 'Who is this?' And this is the very question that the disciples asked one another when Jesus *'got up and rebuked the raging waters'*, when a squall hit Galilee just as Jesus' mission team was crossing the lake.

WHO IS THIS?

These four separate accounts of Jesus' power once more reveal his authority over natural phenomena, Satan's demonic forces, terminal illness, and death itself.

1 LORD OVER DISASTERS (vv22-25)

Cyclones, hurricanes, typhoons, and tornadoes, as well as tidal waves and tsunamis, regularly wreak havoc in some part of the world. Winds of huge strength and waves of towering height terrorise many communities. It's precisely the wind and the waves of which the disciples were petrified (vv22-25). Many of the disciples were hardened, professional fishermen who had experienced the Sea of Galilee in all its moods, and they knew that they were in great danger from the sudden squall. The cool air from the mountains colliding with the warm air above the lake produced fierce and sudden storms. Yet in the little fishing boat, tossed around by the waves, we see the greatest of contrasts. Outside the boat, the wind was whipping up the seas into powerful waves that swamped their vessel, while inside, Jesus was fast asleep in the stern. Outside, the forces of nature combined to display their awesome power, while inside, their Master and Maker was asleep. Who is this? This is our Creator Christ, who is Lord over wind and wave, tornado and tsunami (Colossians ch1 vv15-16). He is Lord over natural phenomena and supernatural forces. Of course, God is not the architect of sin and evil, but he chooses to use the background of this world's devastation and disaster, its sorrow and sin, to call people to himself.

2 LORD OVER DEMONS (vv26-39)

Jesus is met by a demon-possessed man on the shores of the Gentile territory of Gadara. He was naked, homeless, self-harming, and completely untamed. This poor man had not only become a playground for the demons, but he had also become a battleground for their encounter with Jesus. The demons may have outnumbered Jesus, but they couldn't outfight him or outmanoeuvre him. They were subject to his lordship. We view the man thoroughly transformed. The number one reason Christ had set his mind and heart on going to the cross and laying down his life as a sacrifice for sin was so that Satan's stranglehold upon humanity should be broken (1 John ch3 v8). The first enemy, the devil, has been crushed, and the last enemy, death, has been vanquished, and every enemy in between has been overcome. Jesus Christ is Lord over the world, the new world, and the underworld. Christians exceed the status of conqueror (Romans ch8 v37) for the Lord Jesus Christ has fought and won on their behalf.

3 LORD OVER DISEASES (vv43-48)

The woman with the incurable sickness would have been an 'untouchable' while she had been ceremonially unclean for twelve years. She was embarrassed, ashamed, and desperate. She believed that by touching Jesus she could be healed, and her faith saved her. But Jesus called her to public confession. Some believers think that they can remain secret and silent in their faith, but Paul makes it clear that, in addition to repentance and faith, a clear confession is required (Romans ch10 vv9-10). This woman's joy was complete as she heard the sweetest of words from the lips of her Saviour (v48).

4 LORD OVER DEATH (vv40-42, 49-56)

The messenger expressed the mood of everyone in revealing that all hope had gone (v49). But death is not the end, either for Jairus' daughter or for anyone else. A glimpse of Christ's resurrection victory is seen in this girl's restoration to life (v54). The spirit, previously separated from the body, was returned, and Jesus had the last word because he is 'the Last Word'. Death may be the greatest terrorist to stalk our world, but Jesus is Lord over every terror: He is the King of Kings. The cross *'takes its terror from the grave, And gilds the bed of death with light'* [Thomas Kelly].

SEPTEMBER 20
THE GOSPEL OF LUKE Ch9.1-17

THE BRIEFING

In calling and commissioning 'the Twelve', Jesus gave them specific instructions which we could summarise as four clear injunctions:

1 DO ANYTHING

Jesus' mother told the servants at the Cana wedding (John ch2 v5): *'Do whatever he says'*. At this Commissioning Service, we might encourage the Twelve, 'Do whatever he says'. In fact, Jesus sent them out *'to preach the kingdom of God and to heal the sick'* (v2). He didn't send them on an advertising campaign, or a fund-raising mission, or on a music tour, or even a political campaign. He sent them to preach the good news about God's kingdom, which would have included the call to repent and believe, and the declaration that the kingdom has arrived in Christ and that there's more to come. The preaching would also have included the warning that those who reject the message of grace must face God's judgement. In association with preaching the gospel, Christ's followers should attend to the physical needs of others. Whatever aspect of ministry and style of gift God has given you, be sure to be faithful and consistent in that service for him.

2 TAKE NOTHING

Jesus instructed his disciples to 'travel light'. They should not become cluttered or bogged down with unnecessary baggage. Jesus ordered *No staff, no bag, no bread, no money, no extra tunic'* (v3). Certainly, Jesus is not saying that these particular things are wrong in themselves, but he is training his followers to trust in him and not to be distracted by the cares and concerns of a materialistic world. They shouldn't be concerned about: a staff for protection against wild animals; a bag for personal comforts and knick-knacks; preparing food days in advance; building up a healthy reserve in a savings account; extra clothing for climate or comfort. And all of this 'just in case...'

What they needed was to rely on Jesus. God supplies our every need, and he frequently tests our faith in the way that he provides (Psalm 145 vv16, 18). God's 'open-handedness' is a wonderful picture of his gracious provision to all his people. *'Take nothing'*, Jesus said, but behind the instruction 'the Twelve' had to learn the all-important lesson that he is the supplier of everything. *'He gave them power and authority...'* (v1). Here was a special apostolic authority that was conferred upon the disciples, yet Jesus tells them at the end of his earthly ministry that *'All authority in heaven and earth has been given to me...Go and make disciples of all nations...and surely I am with you always...'* (Matthew ch28 vv18-20). Those who obey Christ in 'taking nothing' as they serve him are 'taking everything' as he goes with them.

Don't become 'weighed down' with unnecessary 'baggage' in your service for God, whether it's in the preaching of the gospel or in ministering to physical needs.

3 GIVE SOMETHING

As 'the Twelve' gave something (v13), Jesus multiplied their giving to bring blessing to everyone. The little that the disciples gave represented all that they had, yet giving to Christ never means a loss. Any giving that we do must be seen in perspective to the cross and all that God has given in Christ to save guilty sinners. The giant plus sign of the cross may remind us of the *'all things'* which accompany the giving of Jesus to be the Saviour (Romans ch8 v32).

3 BE EVERYTHING

Be everything that God wants you to be! Don't settle for a half-hearted, part-time, second-rate, underachieving for Christ. Jesus wanted disciples who would be his preachers and healers, witnesses and messengers, crowd marshals and stewards, bread distributors and collectors. One minute, the disciples were distributing spiritual bread; the next minute, they were distributing barley bread. But 'being everything' is not just about roles and responsibilities but about character and conduct too. A follower of Christ must live the life of Christ, as a reflection of Christ, in the power of Christ.

We must not succumb to the myth that believers are volunteers in Christ's work rather than his bondservants. We're not 'doing God a favour' by anything we do in our Christian service. Instead, we are called to be faithful and dependable, fully committed and fully involved in the ongoing work of the church of God.

SEPTEMBER 21
THE GOSPEL OF LUKE Ch9.18-36

The Quaker William Penn wrote in 1669 while imprisoned:

'No pain, no palm; no thorns, no throne; no gall, no glory; no cross, no crown'.

NO CROSS, NO CROWN

This title would fit both of these incidents, separated by eight days. In vv18-27 we are provided with a prefiguration of Christ's glory, and in vv28-36 we are given an account of a transfiguration of Christ's glory. In each case, the cross is not far from the Saviour's thoughts. Suffering is uppermost in his mind and heart. But Jesus could see beyond the pain and anguish, for he had in view the glorious objective of his mission.

As an introduction to the revelation about his death and resurrection, Jesus enquires of his disciples, *Who do the crowds say I am?'* (v22). The popular view, said the disciples, was that he was John Baptist, Elijah, or one of the other prophets. The majority of people were respectful of Jesus. While that is commendable, it is not to those who respect him that he gives *'the right to become children of God'* (John ch1 v12) but to those who receive him. In response to Jesus' pointed question, Peter answers, *The Christ of God'* (v20). All the profound Christological teachings are telescoped into this one concise pronouncement. Now Jesus begins to reveal further details to his disciples about the climax to his mission and the gateway to glory – the cross.

1 THE CROSS IS THE WAY IN

This is the first clear statement that Jesus makes regarding his death (v22). Jesus refers to the inescapable pathway of pain that would take him to resurrection glory via the cross. It was for the *'joy that was set before him (that he) endured the cross'* (Hebrews ch12 v2). Jesus' joy was his Father's total satisfaction, and the sudden sound of his Father's voice confirms that Jesus was still on course for the cross and the crown (v35). The cross also marks the 'way in' for everyone who wants to be free from the guilt and burden of their sin. The 'way in' to forgiveness, new life, peace with God, eternal hope, and glory is through the cross of Jesus, the Christ of God.

2 THE CROSS IS THE WAY THROUGH

The footsteps of faithfulness are never 'pain-free'. It's the Christian who is victimised; it's the disciple who is despised; it's the godly who are persecuted.

Denial:

(v23) The cross is not only a gruesome picture of one's death but also one's denial. Cross-bearing means a surrender of pride, dignity, and independence. Those who whine about some discomfort, sickness, or inconvenience, and talk about 'the cross that they have to bear', miss the whole point. Jesus is not talking about our gripes and grievances; he's speaking about self-denial. How often does 'self' get in the way of our close walk with God?

Day by Day:

This is not a once-in-a-lifetime cross-bearing exercise. Discipleship is about each day, every day. What's the point in gaining the whole world and losing your soul?

Direction:

Jesus' cross-bearing disciples will follow him. This is the only course available; this is the only direction in which to proceed.

The cost of living the Christian life is represented by a cross.

3 THE CROSS IS THE WAY OUT

The disciples hadn't expected to see a preview of the glory of Christ's kingdom just eight days after the promise. The dazzling glory of Christ's appearance is even eclipsed by the topic of conversation: Christ's *'departure'* (literally, his 'exodus'). Moses' greatest 'way out' experience was the Exodus from Egypt and from its slavery, suffering, and death. Elijah's 'way out' experience was his unique departure from earth in a whirlwind. But their 'exodus experiences' only pointed to Jesus' ultimate exodus and the fulfilment of God's great blueprint of redemption. The One who is greater than Moses leads his people through the blood-red sea of redemption and will eventually lead them to the far shore of freedom and glory. Jesus continues to lead the exodus out of this world. He is the Pioneer of faith, the Trailblazer of our hope, the Firstborn from among the dead, and the Firstfruits of those who have fallen asleep (1 Corinthians ch15 v20). The 'way out' is the way of separation, freedom, and victory. But if no cross, then no crown!

SEPTEMBER 22
THE GOSPEL OF LUKE Ch9.37-62

BEWARE PITFALLS

If we're honest, we can often see ourselves mirrored in the actions, opinions, and attitudes of The Twelve. Although we may criticise them for being so inattentive to Jesus' teaching, and so insensitive to Jesus' vocation, and so selfish about their own situations, we're not really a million miles from these disciples' experiences. Our powerless discipleship may be illustrated by the five pitfalls that may hinder our progress and jeopardize our pathway as believers:

1 TOO LITTLE FAITH (vv37-45)

From the glory of the 'New World', revealed to the disciples on the mountain-top, they descend to a confrontation with the underworld the very next day. From a glimpse of heaven in the transfiguration of Jesus (vv28-36), the disciples are given a glimpse of hell in the terrible transformation of this boy. This man's son is in a desperate condition. A demon possesses him so that he screams and is thrown into convulsions (v39), foaming at the mouth and gnashing his teeth (Mark ch9 vv17-18). He is often thrown into the fire or water (Matthew ch17 v15), and he is unable to speak. It's a terrifying experience for the boy and for his father, who can only look on helplessly. What compounds the problem is that Jesus' Mission Team was also powerless to exorcise the spirit because they had *'so little faith'* (Matthew ch17 vv19-20). Our powerlessness today is a result of too little faith. We trust our doctors, dentists, gas engineers, electricians, and car mechanics for our personal health and safety, but we fail to trust God sufficiently. Let's learn to develop a stronger, greater, deeper faith in God, the All-trustworthy.

2 TOO MUCH PRIDE (vv46-48)

After all that the disciples had witnessed in the previous few days, it's sad to read v46. They argued with each other about who would be the greatest. Prominence, preeminence, and pride continue to rob individual believers of a powerful discipleship. We measure greatness according to the 'household names' of gospel preachers, Bible teachers, authors, musicians, charity volunteers, relief workers, and missionaries, while Jesus measures 'greatness' on a different scale altogether. In fact, those who are humble enough to welcome the poor, the weak, the insignificant, the despised, and the young, like the child, are *'the greatest'*. Jesus said so!

3 TOO STRONG JEALOUSY (vv49-50)

We can't help noting the contrast between v40 and v49. The Twelve failed miserably to drive out a demon, while another man successfully evicted a demon in Jesus' name (v49). If you were one of The Twelve, wouldn't you be tempted to be just a little jealous? The disciples tried to prohibit this man from conducting his ministry because *'he is not one of us'* (v49). And how many petty jealousies continue to divide and subdivide the church today? How many times are Christians given the 'cold shoulder' in their various ministries because *'he is not one of us?* This stranger was another disciple of Jesus who trusted in Jesus' power and authority as the Christ of God. He was to be regarded as a fellow-labourer and partner in the gospel.

4 TOO QUICK TEMPER (vv51-55)

v51 marks the second section of Luke's Gospel where Jesus changes the focus of his ministry from Galilee to Jerusalem. His journey takes him through Samaria, where there was no welcome for him because the Samaritans were not sympathetic to the view that Jerusalem was the centre of worship. The *'Boanerges'* brothers (Mark ch3 v17), James and John, wanted to blast them all. How impatient or intolerant can we be?

5 TOO GREAT COST (vv57-62)

Although these declarations may at first glance appear reasonable, Jesus could see the half-heartedness of their hearts.

Too much demand on comforts (vv57-58)

He had not fully considered the sacrifice involved in becoming a follower of Jesus.

Too much demand on time (vv59-60)

He wanted to delay any commitment to an uncertain date, that is, after his father's death.

Too much demand on priorities (vv61-62)

'Me first' can hinder real discipleship. Even the demands of family are frequently believed to be a legitimate excuse for only a half-hearted commitment to God's work.

SEPTEMBER 23
THE GOSPEL OF LUKE Ch10.1-24

The Lord of the harvest is responsible for recruiting his harvesters, and Jesus' disciples in every age are required to pray and to ask. These seventy-two disciples are an illustration of the Lord's recruitment programme as he appoints and sends them in pairs to be:

Messengers (v1) – representing Jesus and announcing his arrival;

Harvesters (v2) – working in the most rewarding aspect of farming;

Lambs (v3) – there's an obvious contrast between the vulnerability of the lambs and the viciousness of the wolves. Being a disciple of Jesus is no picnic! The history of the church is a record of perpetual 'wolf attack'. The previous verses (ch9 vv57-62) show that there were three 'wannabe disciples' who were disqualified.

GO

But to these thirty-six small teams of disciples, Jesus says, 'Go' (Matthew ch28 v19; Mark ch16 v15).

1 GO – WITH JUDGEMENT

'Judgement' in the sense of discernment, perception, wisdom, and understanding. Go with your eyes open. Jesus provides helpful information that will help us to make sound judgements about:

Our Opposition – v3 puts our Christian service into perspective. Peter and the apostles told the 'wolfish' Sanhedrin, who were baying for their blood, *'We must obey God rather than men'* (Acts ch5 v29).

Our Urgency – v4. Again, Jesus' followers were to travel light, without unnecessary baggage. Some people spend their lives making contingencies for whatever they do, but in reality, they do very little.

Our Support – vv5-8 emphasise the importance of being supported by those who share our goals and with whom we are one in mind and purpose. Such support, whether in the form of food, hospitality, or wages, should be received graciously, recognising God's provision through the kindness of the giver. We shouldn't be picky about it either (v8).

Our Mission – v9 underlines the whole purpose of going. There's people to be reached and a gospel to be preached. We must not lose sight of this fundamental truth that the gospel is the good news about Jesus and his reign as our Redeemer and King.

Our Reception – vv10-16. Judgement needs to be exercised in respect to those who receive or reject the message.

2 GO – WITH JOY

As disciples of Christ, we have so much to be joyful about. We should:

Rejoice in divine authority (v19) – With Christ's power and authority, no enemy is too big or too dangerous for the servant of God.

Rejoice in divine security (v20) – The joy that's even greater than authority and power is that we can have the certain knowledge that, as a child of God, our name is written in heaven. It has been entered there as on a register or census, never to be transferred or erased.

Rejoice in divine sovereignty (vv21-22) – God works according to his *good pleasure*. God chooses to reveal his gospel, not to those who are intelligently superior, but to those who are *little children* in terms of maturity.

Jesus, too, is *full of joy* for God's sovereign revelation of salvation.

Rejoice in divine clarity (vv23-24) – There is great joy and blessing among those whose spiritual eyes are illumined. Disciples are uniquely privileged.

3 GO – WITH JESUS

These seventy-two disciples may have been *'sent...ahead of (Jesus)'*, but they had been sent *'to every town and place where he was about to go'* (v1). What's more, disciples then and now need to be regularly reminded that it's the Lord's harvest, the Lord's harvest field, and the Lord's harvesters (v2). What's the point in going if we don't go with Jesus? The church has always proclaimed the new Great Commandment to *'Love your neighbour'* as well as the new Great Commission to *'Go and make disciples'*. If we love, then we shall want to go – not always to the uttermost parts of the earth but sometimes to the guttermost parts of our towns and villages. But go with Jesus!

SEPTEMBER 24
THE GOSPEL OF LUKE Ch10.25-32

A lawyer sets out to *'test Jesus'* (v25). He was a scribe, a legal expert, who had a thorough knowledge of the Scriptures in his head, if not his heart. He may have wanted to test the veracity and authenticity of Jesus' teachings.

TESTING JESUS

He may have wanted to know how much of Jesus' instruction and preaching was founded in the orthodox Jewish faith. In one sense, we should all 'test' our preachers. Not that we want to turn a congregation into a jury and place the preacher 'on trial', but there is a need to test our preachers and their preaching against God's word. The Berean believers heard the greatest itinerant preacher in the world at that time – Paul the apostle. But they still checked him out against Scripture (Acts ch17 v11). If this lawyer's motives had been genuine, then that would have been commendable, but it was likely that he was just trying to catch Jesus out.

Jesus answers the lawyer's question with another question to which he gives a textbook answer, quoting Deuteronomy ch6 v5 and Leviticus ch19 v18.

1 ONE THING IS DEMANDED - LOVE

Being a true worshipper is all about love

It's a love for God and his glorious attributes. It's to love all that we know about God – his grace and kindness, his love and mercy, his patience and faithfulness, his power and greatness, his justice and holiness, his truth and righteousness. It's a love demonstrated in devotion – the devotion of the total self: heart, soul, mind, and strength. Love for God is not just about the devotion of mind and strength, but it's also about the heart and soul as well.

Being a true neighbour is all about love

The evidence of a deep love for God is in our love for our neighbour. In trying to vindicate his position, the lawyer wanted to prove that his daily customs and rituals, the repeating of phrases and tossing alms to the poor, met the demands of the law. But it's in response to his question, *'And who is my neighbour?'* (v29) that Jesus tells this well-known parable about the Samaritan who demonstrated neighbourly love.

A man was travelling the road from Jerusalem to Jericho – the road with a reputation! The seventeen mile journey, descending nearly three thousand five hundred feet, wended its way through bandit country. The traveller was attacked and left for dead. A glimmer of hope was seen in two passers-by – a priest and a Levite – pious, religious people. If this half-dead mugging victim could expect any help at all, it was likely to come from these 'hands-on, people-friendly, religious ministers'. But no help was forthcoming, and the dying man appeared doomed. Instead, a loathed and 'unclean' Samaritan stopped to assist.

He saw who he was:

The Samaritan would have recognised the victim as his traditional enemy. But true godly neighbourliness transcends man-made barriers.

He came where he was:

He got down from his donkey and stooped down to the dirt and degradation of where the man lay. Doesn't it remind us of Jesus' stoop?

He changed what he was:

Here was love in action (vv34, 35). He attended to his needs – transport, accommodation, finance, after-care, and a lasting concern.

How great is our love for the despised, the contemptible, the unsavoury, and the unlovely?

2 ONE THING IS NEEDED - JESUS

Martha's love was also a practical love, opening her home to Jesus. A home is a house plus a heart. But Martha's problem was not in her preparations but in her priorities. She had become distracted by valid, everyday concerns (v40) and had shunted Jesus' words into second place. Listening to God's word should take priority.

How many things conspire to distract us from *'sitting at Jesus' feet'* and listening to God's word? Perhaps it's our social calendar, the weather, our pets, sport, TV programmes, family visits, or even the odd headache that keeps us from listening to Jesus' word through his servants?

Mary's choice to listen to Jesus was *'the one thing that was needed';* the one thing that counts; the one thing that places everything else in perspective. Mary had chosen the better part. She enjoyed her time with Jesus, and we, too, must not neglect the one thing needed for a victorious Christian life – a daily communion with Christ.

SEPTEMBER 25
THE GOSPEL OF LUKE Ch11.1-13

Although it's one of the strong strands of the Bible, and a foundational slab of the Christian church, and a constant occupation of the Lord Jesus while here on earth, prayer suffers from a poor image; some people regard prayer as a weak alternative to practical activity. But while practical love is vital, prayer is not the least we can do but the most. Prayer should never be regarded as an excuse for doing nothing!

Of course, we are frequently intimidated by preachers who continually remind us of such prayer warriors as James the Righteous (Jesus' brother), John Hyde, Martin Luther, David Brainerd, and John Wesley. When we hear about their commitment to prayer, we are tempted to give up altogether. Yet although a few are called to the special ministry of prayer, every believer will be a person of prayer.

The disciples, who witnessed Jesus' commitment to prayer, were prompted to ask:

LORD, TEACH US TO PRAY

1 BE FOCUSED ABOUT PRAYER'S CONTENTS (vv1-4)

'The Lord's Prayer' could be entitled 'The Disciples' Prayer' as Jesus couldn't pray for forgiveness because he was *'holy, blameless, pure, set apart from sinners'* (Hebrews ch7 v26).

'Father'

Only God's true children can address him in this privileged and intimate way. The 'pass' that gives us instant access into the 'Throne Room' is *'Father'*.

'Hallowed be your Name'

Because God is our Father, we should never be casual or disrespectful in our praying. His name is holy and he demands our regard, our respect, and our reverence (Psalm 8 v1; 29 v2; Isaiah ch57 v15). Certainly, God's children are encouraged to come to him without any great formalities, without earthly intermediaries, and even without appointments. But we must come with awe and humility before the greatness of his majesty.

'Your kingdom come'

There's a longing for the ultimate visible reign of Christ. But there's a sense in which his kingdom is growing in the lives of his people. The expansion of the true Church worldwide is in anticipation of that victorious day when everything will be placed under the nail-pierced feet of our heavenly King (1 Corinthians ch15 v25).

'Give us each day our daily bread'

The first personal petition is for daily food. Prayer may 'move the hand that moves the world,' but it's the hand that supplies our daily needs. He provides all we need (1 Timothy ch6 v17).

'Forgive us our sins...'

One of the marks of true humility and penitence is the willingness to forgive others. It shows the right attitude to God and to one another.

'Lead us not into temptation'

We need to request spiritual protection. God knows our endurance limit and our pain threshold. He never leads us into a spiritual cul-de-sac. There's always an exit (1 Corinthians ch10 v13).

If you find it difficult to launch into prayer at an allotted time and place each day, prepare by reading and using a Psalm, a hymn, or even this prayer that Jesus taught.

2 BE BOLD ABOUT PRAYER'S PETITIONS (vv5-8)

Humility in prayer must be matched with boldness and persistence. We have a divine mandate (Hebrews ch4 v16). The friend banging on his neighbour's door at midnight had a nerve. *'Boldness'* implies 'shamelessness'. His tenacity and gall about the timing and the size of his petition produced a positive response. But Jesus didn't intend for us to compare the neighbour with God. Our heavenly Father doesn't respond grudgingly nor just for the sake of peace.

3 BE SURE ABOUT PRAYER'S ANSWERS (vv9-13)

Guaranteed Answers (vv9-10)

He will give, reveal, and open the door. This is the cast-iron statement in Jesus' teaching on prayer. God doesn't play 'cat and mouse' with his praying people. But note that even the praying disciple doesn't always get exactly *what* they want, nor always *when* they want it.

Gracious Answers (vv11-13)

Such a response to a child asking for a fish or an egg is unthinkable. If sinful human parents act with love, kindness, and wisdom, then *'how much more'* does God respond? The size and scope of his grace is immeasurable. The Holy Spirit – his presence, guidance, and protection – represents the most wonderful and most beautiful gift of God's grace to his praying people.

SEPTEMBER 26
THE GOSPEL OF LUKE Ch11.14-36

JESUS WITHOUT EQUAL

The Lord Jesus towers over the names of the world's greatest. His life transcends the bravest and the best. He is superior to all priests and prophets, prime ministers and presidents, kings and dictators, lords and leaders. Jesus Christ is unparalleled in his passion, unrivalled in his righteousness, unequalled in his qualities, inimitable in his sayings, and incomparable in his character. There's no one like Jesus!

1 JESUS IS STRONGER THAN SATAN – so we should trust him (vv14-28)

Jesus drives out demons

(vv14-20) Jesus knows that his critics were thinking that he was exorcising demons by the power of Beelzebub (v15), Prince of Demons. But Jesus declares that if that were the case, then Satan would be fighting against himself – a divided kingdom. But more conclusively, if Jesus is not driving out demons by Satan's power, then he must be doing it through God's power (*'the finger of God'* v20).

Jesus takes away defences

(vv21-22) We are given a vivid picture of a strong man, guarding his home, being overpowered by an even stronger man. Through the conquering mission of the cross, Jesus has invaded the 'strong man's castle' and has overpowered the Prince of Demons (Colossians ch2 v15).

Jesus shows up divisions

(v23) If you're not a true disciple of Christ and serving in his army, then you remain among the ranks of his enemies. You cannot fly the 'Swiss flag' over your heart and life, declaring it to be neutral territory! If you're not championing the cause of Christ – upholding Biblical truth, promoting his teachings, proclaiming his gospel – then you need to be saved.

Jesus points out the dangers

(vv24-28) A 'spiritual spring clean' in one's life may be good and necessary, but it's not enough. Reformation alone is insufficient. A transformation is required through the work of Christ by his Spirit. It's possible to 'do' all the right things and only to be engaged in 'spring cleaning'. The house must be occupied. God's Spirit must reside there (Romans ch8 v9).

2 JESUS IS WISER THAN SOLOMON – so we should listen to him (v31)

Solomon's wisdom was legendary even in his own lifetime. The Queen of Sheba may have made a two-thousand-mile round trip across the deserts to check out Solomon's wisdom. Jesus makes the point that if Sheba's queen went to such lengths to listen to the wisdom of Solomon, how much more should people listen to the wisdom of Jesus, who is greater than Solomon. If God's wisdom means that he always chooses what's best, then Jesus is seen as the Centre and Circumference of that wisdom (1 Corinthians ch1 vv24, 30).

We see God's wisdom in orderly creation

(Psalm 104 v24; Jeremiah ch10 v12) There's nothing random or chaotic about his orderly creation. It remains a singularly powerful testimony to God's breathtaking wisdom.

We see God's wisdom in his masterly control

Each difficulty and dilemma that crosses our path is not to be viewed as part of a haphazard barrage of assaults that dog our pilgrimage. Each one is appointed by God's masterly control.

We see God's wisdom in his Fatherly care

God's wisdom never has an 'off day'. God is not sharper at one time more than any other. It's with his loving wisdom that he guards us, leads us, and provides for our every need.

3 JESUS IS GREATER THAN JONAH – so we should respond to him (vv29-30, 32)

In response to this lone Jew preaching in a pagan enemy's capital, more than one hundred and twenty thousand believed. Even the King of Assyria himself was affected by this 'great awakening'. If these thousands of Assyrians responded to God's disobedient, runaway prophet Jonah, what's our response to the preaching of the One who is *greater than Jonah*?

Have you repented, turning from sin to trust in Christ? If you don't believe that you have sinned, or that you have failed God's standards, or that you have not loved God as you should, then you may not feel the need to repent. But as God opens your heart to show you the loathsomeness of your sin and the vast chasm that exists between your sin and his holiness, you may wonder whether there could ever be reconciliation. But the cross of Christ proves that reconciliation is possible for those who repent (2 Corinthians ch7 v10).

What a God who loves sinners! What a Saviour! Jesus without equal.

SEPTEMBER 27
THE GOSPEL OF LUKE Ch11.37-54

Jesus was invited to a dinner party at a Pharisee's house. At that time, Pharisees were the most influential of the three prominent Jewish groups. *'Pharisees'* means 'the separated ones'. Pharisees were separatists, and the greatest qualification to become a member of this exclusive sect was the strict adherence to the Law, including the particular tradition of interpretation that they had established. Pharisees were fiercely patriotic and were sticklers for ceremonial purity. They followed their traditions to the minutest detail. But their religion was all about externals rather than internals. It was all to do with appearance rather than the heart. Inevitably, the Pharisees bitterly opposed Jesus, and it's not surprising, therefore, that the host and his guest clashed before they sat down to eat.

The Pharisees' strict traditions meant that they followed a handwashing ritual prior to eating. This had nothing to do with health and hygiene, but it was supposed to indicate their holiness and purity before God. But Jesus confronts his host over his thoughts about cleanliness and godliness (vv39-41). Jesus is saying that you can be fanatical about cleaning your crockery (or tidying your kitchen, or bleaching your patio, or washing your car) and your heart can remain *'full of greed and wickedness'* (v39).

EXTERNAL OR INTERNAL?

So in vv42-52 Jesus pronounces six 'woes' upon the Pharisees and those who are like-minded. A 'woe' implies severe consequences, a pronouncement of judgement.

1 THE WOE OF INCONSISTENT BEHAVIOUR (v42)

Although Jesus didn't condemn them for their tithing, they were neglecting the most important truths of God's justice and love. The Pharisees were selective about which of God's laws they would obey. But that selectiveness is not limited to first-century Pharisees. It's common for Christians to be meticulous over certain details of behaviour or Church procedure, but also to misrepresent God's love and grace to neighbours and fellow believers.

2 THE WOE OF ARROGANT BEHAVIOUR (v43)

There are always those who crave the limelight and want the most prestigious jobs and the most important places. Humility is often in short supply in both the pulpits and the pews. There's no place in the kingdom of God for those wanting to attract attention to themselves.

3 THE WOE OF UNHELPFUL BEHAVIOUR (v44)

Jesus condemned the Pharisees for being a 'death-trap' to the ignorant. People looked up to the Pharisees and respected them as good teachers and interpreters of the Scriptures. But people trusted their support and fell into the spiritual death-trap. We should be on our guard and be certain of the ground on which we stand.

There are too many who claim to be trustworthy in religious and spiritual matters, but they are like *'unmarked graves'*. You must be sure that you are standing on Jesus and his word.

4 THE WOE OF HYPOCRITICAL BEHAVIOUR (v46)

Jesus accuses the *'experts in the law'* of weighing people down with the heavy weights of religious duties without lifting a finger to help them. Let us be among those who are a *'great help'* (like Apollos in Acts ch18 v27).

5 THE WOE OF VIOLENT BEHAVIOUR (vv47-51)

The Jewish forefathers had murdered several of the prophets because they couldn't bear to listen to their messages of righteousness. Both Abel and Zechariah (believed to be the first and the last of the Old Testament martyrs) had been killed by their fellows. Though the Jews had built tombs to honour such Old Testament messengers, they were complicit in their deaths. They may well have protested their innocence, but even vv53-54 reveal their brewing hatred of Jesus, which would culminate in their murder of him.

6 THE WOE OF DECEPTIVE BEHAVIOUR (v52)

The *'experts in the law'* had, in one sense, the key to the knowledge of God as custodians of the Scriptures. But they had held onto the key. The Bible is primarily a revelation of God. It's his own self-disclosure. The Bible is not a secret code to be broken (as some would have us think), but rather it is the key to the knowledge of God and to his kingdom. Let us encourage folk to open the Scriptures with faith and perseverance, that they may discover the truth about our great and gracious God.

SEPTEMBER 28
THE GOSPEL OF LUKE Ch12.1-21

One of the expressions that we use to indicate urgency and desperation is:

FOR DEAR LIFE

We talk about 'clinging on for dear life' or 'running for dear life'. It makes us concentrate on perspective and purpose, on vision and value. In this passage, Jesus brings life into sharp focus. He's concerned with veracity, not duplicity, faithful, not fake, fact, not facsimile. Jesus warns about hypocrisy that's like yeast affecting the whole batch of dough. Hypocrisy is all about being something that you are not. It's a word that comes from the Greek theatre, where actors would try to convince audiences that they were someone else. Jesus condemns those who live their lives as a 'pretend performance'. All will be brought out into the open in the end. Be genuine, both with God and yourself! Don't give the appearance of being something that you are not.

1 DON'T BE AFRAID – FOR YOUR LIFE! (vv1-12)

The fear of men is very powerful, and we can easily imagine how vicious threats can paralyse with panic. Jesus assures that the worst that men can do is only to kill the body, while our souls are in the safekeeping of Almighty God. But even in death, God lovingly clothes his servants with courage and serenity. We must fear God so that we shall reverence him and be filled with a holy dread of displeasing him. He is a loving God and he is a holy God who *'has the power to throw you into hell'* (v5). God's holiness is referred to in Scripture even more than his love.

Don't be afraid of your worth

If God cares for the cheap and lowly sparrow then you are much more valuable than they are. No sparrow flies or falls outside of the will of God (Matthew ch10 v29). God doesn't take his eyes off the righteous (Job ch36 v7). He guards his people day and night like a vineyard (Isaiah ch27 v3). His people are too precious to be trusted to anyone else (Deuteronomy ch33 v3). If God is well aware of the fluctuating number of hairs on your head, he is also perfectly aware of your fluctuating circumstances: your family problems, your job threats, your home insecurity, your health concerns, or your bank account difficulties.

Trust in God! By his grace, you are inestimably valuable to him!

Don't be afraid of your words

Words Forgiven (v10) Even blasphemies against the Son of Man are forgivable of those who are truly repentant. The unforgivable sin is blasphemy against the Spirit, which denies and rejects the Spirit's work in softening the conscience, bringing sorrow for sin, and leading to Christ as the Saviour.

Words Given (vv11-12) Don't despair about what you will say under trial and examination for being a Christian. The Holy Spirit himself will be your Instructor and the Prompter of your witness statement in the hour of crisis.

2 DON'T BE A FOOL – WITH YOUR LIFE! (vv13-21)

It's likely that the questioner's problem was 'greed' (v15). Real life is not possession-dependent. It's not conditional upon 'creature comforts' or the bottom line of your bank account. It's a sad fact that men and women in our own culture are willing to be eternally bankrupt and hopeless just so that they can enjoy their riches in these few fleeting moments of time. Real life and lasting riches are all about the understanding and knowledge of God (Jeremiah ch9 vv23-24). The rich man in Jesus' parable was:

Rich without God

In one sense, the farmer was wise and prudent in making provision to store his fruitful harvest. But the whole tenor of the parable points to a life without God and riches fly away so quickly, especially with the advent of death (Proverbs ch23 vv4-5). His self-indulgence and self-complacency were all snatched in an instant (Proverbs ch11 v28).

But Jesus makes the contrast with those who are:

Rich Towards God

The issue is not about making plans or even making money: it's about making priorities. Is it going to be 'self first' or 'God first'? What a privilege it is to live for God and be in the centre of his will and purposes; to be *'rich towards God'*. Don't let prosperity become a higher priority with you than eternity. Don't let obsessions with possessions become a hindrance to true fellowship with God.

SEPTEMBER 29
THE GOSPEL OF LUKE Ch12.1-21

If many of us are honest, we have to admit that worry and anxiety affects much of our lives. How often do we urge someone, *'Don't worry! I'll do that'* or *'Don't worry! I'm sure it'll be alright'*? Such an expression is easy to use, but it will be much more difficult to comply with.

DON'T WORRY!

For some people, worry is a permanent feature of their lives, and its effect can range from an uncomfortable hindrance to a paralysing phobia. In such a condition, it's not very helpful just to say to the sufferer, *'Don't worry!'* unless the solid ground for 'not worrying' is provided too. That's precisely what Jesus does in vv22-34.

1 WHAT'S YOUR TROUBLE?

He says to his disciples, *'Don't worry!'* and then he provides them with the rock-solid assurance of why they shouldn't worry. His supplies are always sufficient:

Sufficient Diet

(vv24-26) From the example of the sparrows (v6), Jesus uses the example of the ravens (v24) to emphasise our value to God. They live one day at a time, dependent upon their Maker to supply their daily food. Jesus states that if this despised, unclean bird, which neither works at producing its own food nor storing it, is provided with food each and every day, what about God's children? They are much more valuable.

Sufficient Dress

(vv27-28) God promises to supply all our needs, including clothing. We must remember that our 'need' doesn't include the necessity to mirror fashion, or to have umpteen alternative outfits. Lilies don't last very long, and they don't supply their own attire, but their beauty outshines the splendour of Solomon. So if God takes such particular care of his flowers, will he not take even greater care of his followers?

Sufficient Days

(v25) You can't add a day or even an hour to your life by worrying. Jesus is saying that we shouldn't worry about how long we are going to live.

What we eat, what we wear, and how long we live are all in God's providential hands. He is our personal 'Registered Carer'! We have stored away supplies for the future, contingencies for the unexpected, and pensions for our retirement. But our faith is in short supply when it comes to everyday necessities. We don't always trust in our heavenly Father who *'knows that you need them'* (v30). Our Father's care for our circumstances should be the greatest antidote to fear and anxiety. His commitment is to supply, and our commitment should be to seek (v31).

If we continue to wallow in worry, how does that reflect upon our caring Father who knows all things, plans and controls all things, and has the power to provide all things?

Jesus also connects the 'absence of worry and fear' to 'generosity towards others' (v33). Love for self produces constant anxiety. Focusing on others' needs takes our attention away from ourselves. Being absorbed with ourselves produces discontentment and despair. Being preoccupied with God (seeking his kingdom) and other people (helping them in their needs) is the remedy for unnecessary worry. In doing this, you will gain the best treasure of all.

2 WHERE'S YOUR TREASURE?

It's Invaluable

It's a treasure *'in heaven'* that will not depreciate or plummet on the Stock Market. Instead, this treasure is pegged to Christ, who is forever the Father's 'chief delight'.

It's Inexhaustible

It *'will not be exhausted'* (v33). Its supply will never dry up or run out. God's guarantees are totally dependable.

It's Indestructible

The efforts of thieves or moths reveal the transience and vulnerability of treasures on earth. Nothing can ever threaten heaven's secure treasure.

It's Interminable

There's no time limit imposed on this treasure. The *'purse'* or money bag (v33) *'will not wear out'*.

If you are a child of God – a member of his flock – then you have nothing to be anxious about as long as he is your heavenly Father.

SEPTEMBER 30
THE GOSPEL OF LUKE Ch12.35-59

ARE YOU READY?

1 ARE YOU READY TO SERVE DILIGENTLY? (vv35-48)

We are provided with the illustration of servants awaiting the return of their master from a wedding banquet. As servants, they need the:

Right Attire

Being dressed correctly indicates a readiness to serve (v35). The long, flowing clothes of Middle Eastern servants were generally tucked up into their belts when there was work to do or if speedy movements were necessary. The state and style of dress are indicators of just how ready a person is to serve. How often are we 'dressed' for other engagements but not to serve.

Right Attention

Preparation to serve is all about being alert. The Bible frequently refers to 'watching and waiting'. We must always be on the lookout for our Master's return, with the lamps lit (v35) and being ready to open the door (v36). In watching the master closely, the servant learns to think like him and learns to anticipate his moves. It doesn't matter if the master plans to return home in the middle of the night – when he is least expected and when everyone is least alert – *'it will be good for those servants whose master finds them ready'* (v38).

Right Attitude

Your attitude to Christian service reflects the genuineness of your heart. A true servant and a *'faithful and wise manager'* (v42) would not abuse his position. Such an abuser will be shown to be a fraud, an unfaithful servant. Judgement will be severe and reveal him to be an *'unbeliever'* (v46). It's the attitude of people who claim to be servants of Christ that betrays their real position. In addition to the unfaithful, unbelieving servants, there are those who know their Master's will but who are disobedient and unprepared. There are also those who haven't bothered to know their Master's will and who are disobedient through wilful ignorance. Servants of Christ will be assessed according to their knowledge. The more one knows, the more responsible that person is for their actions (v48).

2 ARE YOU READY TO SUFFER DIVISION? (vv49-53)

For Jesus, during his earthly ministry, the cross was never far away. The cross occupied Jesus' thoughts and dominated his preaching. The anticipation of the cross brought distress (v50). Jesus knew that his death would cause severe division (a *'sword'* - Matthew ch10 v34). That sword has cleaved communities, workforces, teams, and even the most fundamental unit, the family. Divisions occur on the basis of those who are disciples of Christ and those who are not; believers and unbelievers. Believers are cold-shouldered, scorned, ostracised, and discriminated against. Christian family members have been denied privileges and have been 'cut out of a will'.

In many cases, those divisions run deeper when believers are mentally and physically tormented, even killed, for their faith. Jesus came to bring reconciliation between God and men, but he hasn't promised to reconcile believers with unbelievers. Instead, it's not consent but dissent. It's not a sop but a sword.

3 ARE YOU READY TO SETTLE DISPUTE? (vv54-59)

Jesus issues a warning about putting things right before it's too late. If amateur weather forecasters can get it right by reading the signs (Matthew ch16 vv1-3), shouldn't people be able to read the signs of what God is doing in the gospel? They understand 'cumulus clouds' but not 'Christ's claims'. It's also important to settle disputes while you have time. But why are we not ready to settle disputes quickly?

Pride

We don't like to 'lose face' and so arguments continue (Proverbs ch13 v10).

Jealousy

Grudges are nursed, and lives are screwed up by jealousy.

Bitterness

Self-pity can develop into spite where love is absent (1 Corinthians ch13 v5).

If we are truly exhibiting the love of the Lord Jesus, then such love will ensure that disputes rarely arise and, when they do, they will be settled quickly. Are you ready for the return of your Lord and Master, Jesus Christ? Will he find you waiting and watching if he returns today? Or will he find the wrong attitudes, unsettled disputes, and his servants 'not properly dressed'?

OCTOBER 1
THE GOSPEL OF LUKE Ch13.1-17

The Jewish historian, Flavius Josephus, who was born in Jerusalem just four years after Jesus' crucifixion, documents a number of massacres perpetrated by both Jews and Romans. The particular massacre ordered by Pilate (v1) was reported to Jesus, maybe to provoke a political comment or even a condemnation of Roman occupation. But Jesus responds with a question of his own (vv2-3) and in a few words, Jesus alerts his hearers to the big issue, the greatest challenge of all:

REPENT OR PERISH

Jesus refers to two disaster examples: one occurred through violence (v1) and the other seems to have occurred through negligence (v4).

Disaster 1:

This was an attack by Pilate and his soldiers on those preparing to offer sacrifices in the temple.

Disaster 2:

This was the collapse of a tower at Siloam when eighteen people died.

There were two different kinds of disasters in which people suffered. The question raised in many peoples' minds is, 'Are people worse sinners because they suffer tragedy or disaster?' A theodicy (meaning 'justice of God') deals with answering the question: 'How can God be both good and Almighty when there is so much evil in the world?' Does it mean that God is powerless to act in situations, or that he abstains from an active role in the natural world? Is he morally culpable for not intervening in such disasters if he has the power to do something about them?

Of course, there are disturbing reports of tragedies every day. Our headlines are other peoples' worst heartaches. Our concern is someone else's catastrophe. But death and disaster are part of sin's evil legacy to the world (Romans ch5 v12). Instead of remaining detached or uncaring, God came to this world in the person of his Son to deal with the cause, not just the symptoms. He has endured our hunger, thirst, fatigue, loneliness, pain, and heartache to deal with sin (2 Corinthians ch5 v21). Jesus says that the manner and timing of our death are not indicators of more guilt or less guilt. The real issue is whether we are ready for eternity. In the context of eternity, it boils down to this fundamental option: repent or perish. The real preparation is by repenting of sin.

There are two aspects of the gospel that we can notice in vv6-17:

1 THE GOSPEL BEARS FRUIT (vv6-8)

For three years, a man checked out his fig tree, but it was fruitless. The useless tree may be sucking the life out of the rest of his vineyard, and so it was ordered to be chopped down. But the vineyard manager pleads for another twelve months of care and fertilising to prove the genuineness of its root. A genuine believer will produce fruit as a sign of life and growth. Jesus warned religious leaders, *'Produce fruit in keeping with repentance'* (Matthew ch3 v8). If you are a Christian believer, then we can expect the *'fruit of lips that confess his name'* (Hebrews ch13 v15); *'fruit of righteousness'* (Philippians ch1 v11) and the *'fruit of the Spirit'* (Galatians ch5 v22).

2 THE GOSPEL SETS FREE (vv10-16)

In great grace and compassion, the Lord intervenes in this crippled woman's life. He said, *'Woman, you are set free from your infirmity'* (v12). Jesus replied to the criticism of the synagogue ruler (vv15-16).

Freedom from Satan's crippling power

'Freedom' is one of the great themes of the Bible. In the gospel, Jesus brings freedom from sin, guilt, fear, hopelessness, death, and Satan. A true servant of God has been *'freed'* (Psalm 116 v16).

Freedom from men's crippling rules

The synagogue ruler was at odds with what Jesus had done on the Sabbath, even though God had obviously healed this woman. Jesus doesn't violate the fourth command. He is not advocating the breaking of God's Law. Much can be learned about individual Christians today from the casual way they treat the Lord's word, the Lord's people, the Lord's Name, and the Lord's Day. The right attitude to these issues is the fruit of Christianity. But the preaching of the gospel must not be restricted by men's rules as to when and where or to whom it should be preached. Are you one of those who are *'delighted with all the wonderful things'* (v17) that God has done for you in the gospel?

OCTOBER 2
THE GOSPEL OF LUKE Ch13.18-35

For many people, they live their lives without any real idea of what they are doing or where they are going. There's little sense of purpose or direction. They have no real aims or objectives. They stumble from one event to another without any goals.

GOALS WITH GOD

On the other hand, there are those who have very clear goals for their lives. They have everything carefully mapped out with long-term aims and short-term objectives. But in the majority of cases, they have goals without God.

These verses present us with two clear goals:

1 THE KINGDOM AS THE GOAL (vv22-30)

What is the kingdom like?

Jesus uses two parables to illustrate the kingdom of God.

Parable 1: The kingdom is compared to a *'mustard seed'* which is planted by a man in his garden. It grows and develops into a tree, providing a resting place for birds.

Parable 2: The kingdom is compared to *'yeast'* that is mixed into a *'large amount of flour'* and permeates the whole batch of dough.

In the first parable, we are taught that the kingdom is growing and developing. It's also a kingdom of strength and shelter since it's seen to give shade to the birds. Jesus Christ is building his church. The process is ongoing, but one day it will be completed. Every child of God will be saved and will find eternal shelter in the kingdom. At times, we may feel that the kingdom is small and weak, but Jesus assures us through the parable of the yeast that his kingdom will penetrate the whole earth. As Christians who are part of that kingdom, we should be like the yeast, influencing our society for truth and righteousness.

How do you enter that kingdom?

There is a sense of seriousness and urgency in Jesus' reference to the *'narrow door'*. Our goal must be that narrow door. Jesus said, *'make every effort'* (v24). There's no automatic right of entry through this door. But neither does it suggest that works will save anyone. The whole tenor of Scripture is that it is by faith alone that we are saved. But we must earnestly seek the Lord (2 Chronicles ch30 vv18-19; Psalm 119 v2; Hebrews ch11 v6). The Lord Jesus is the only door to the kingdom of God (John ch10 v9). The finality of the 'closed door' is a terrible prospect:

No Admission: Many will try and enter but will not get in (v24).

No Recognition: It's a tragic thing to hear Jesus' words, *'I don't know you'* (Matthew ch7 v23).

No Remission: Failing to enter means no pardon, no release, and no forgiveness.

Who will be in that kingdom?

They may have all come from different directions (north, south, east, and west, v29) to take *'their places'* in the kingdom, but they will have all come through the narrow door. Those who find their 'place cards' on the banqueting table are those who have made Christ and his kingdom their goal.

2 THE CROSS AS THE GOAL (vv31-35)

We might refer to this as the 'Fox and Chickens' passage! Jesus refers to the destructive King Herod as *'that fox'* (v32) and to the people of Jerusalem as *'chicks'* (v34). But Jesus reveals his own personal goal in v33. He has a mission to fulfil. Jesus would not be deflected from his goal by Herod's premature threat on his life.

Not only was Jerusalem the historic place of martyrdom for many of God's prophets, it was also the appointed place of Christ's death. Jerusalem was the object of God's love, even if Jerusalem was an unwilling object. God was ready to lavish his love upon them, but they refused. Is there a more distressing situation than for people to be lost because they were unwilling to be saved? Jesus' goal from Glory to Golgotha was the cross. In the gospel, we see God's 'wings' lifted, ready to embrace those who fly to him for refuge. But God will abandon Jerusalem, and all those who reject God's offer of mercy in the gospel (*'desolate'* v35).

To what goal are we committed in the context of the eternal kingdom of God?

May our Lord Jesus Christ, the King, be a great incentive and inspiration for achieving that goal.

Jesus said, *'I will reach my goal'* (v32). With his help, we can reach our goal too!

OCTOBER 3
THE GOSPEL OF LUKE Ch14.1-24

I SPY

Spying is ancient history (see, for example, Numbers ch13, 2 Samuel ch10, Galatians ch2 v4). So it doesn't come as too much of a surprise to learn that Jesus was regularly spied upon by his enemies. Even when Jesus is invited to dine with a *'prominent Pharisee'* (v1), he is kept under surveillance. So intense was the spying that some people believe that the sick man (v2) was a 'plant' and part of an elaborate plot to trap Jesus (reference ch11 v54).

There are four types of people in these verses, of whom we should take note so that we don't become like them.

1 I SPY THOSE WHO WANT TO BECOME EXPERT (vv1-6)

Expert critics, that is. The *'experts in the law'* (v3) couldn't, or wouldn't, provide a response to Jesus' question (v4). So Jesus heals this man who was suffering from *'dropsy'* – a serious accumulation of fluid, resulting in swollen limbs and tissue. The expert critics and expert deceivers had been reduced to silence by Jesus' act of grace and mercy. They had wanted to pick holes in Jesus' theology. How could Jesus be faithful to God and be a true Jew unless he complied with their established traditions and fabricated regulations? Jesus has not come to repeal the creation principle of one day's rest in seven. Nothing would deflect Jesus from worshipping and teaching on that day. We should beware of those who seek to be such experts in traditions and superstitions that they hinder the progress of God's people today.

2 I SPY THOSE WHO WANT TO BE EXALTED (vv7-11)

Those who wanted to grab the best seats at the Pharisee's dinner party prompted Jesus' parable about pride. There were those who were pushing to sit on the 'top table' and to sit as close as possible to the host. But what chagrin it was for the man who had plonked himself in the most prestigious place to be moved in favour of the distinguished guest. Pride is to do with the obsession to be better and to be treated better than others. The word for *'exalted'* was also used for hoisting a sail on a ship. We may imagine the sail filled out by the wind, stretched to its full size: prominent and unmissable. Pride is self-glorification and self-exaltation (Proverbs ch16 v5, Isaiah ch2 v12). Sometimes pride can show itself in refusing to do the menial tasks of the church. Sometimes people are too proud to talk with this person or sit with that person.

Sometimes we're too proud to have certain people in our home or our car. Note v11.

3 I SPY THOSE WHO WANT TO BE EXCLUSIVE (vv12-14)

They may appear generous and kind, but they have ulterior motives. They are looking to get something in return. This kind of host only invites those who can return the favour. He courts the rich and affluent, knowing that they can repay his kindness. But Jesus strikes at the corrupt motive and shows the better way (vv13-14).

It's Christlike to give of oneself without counting the cost or imposing conditions. This is at the very heart of the gospel, seen in the greatest act of grace humanity has ever known. In God's supreme grace, he 'spreads the table of the gospel' for those who are *'the poor, the crippled, the lame, the blind'*, in their sin. In the gospel, he invites sinners to repent and turn to God through Jesus Christ.

4 I SPY THOSE WHO WANT TO BE EXCUSED (vv15-24)

Jesus continues with the theme of the banquet. Although the invitation has been issued through the gospel, there are many who excuse themselves. They decline together, but their excuses are pathetic and lame (*'all alike'* means 'unanimously').

Excuse 1:

If the field already belonged to him, what's the urgency in viewing it?

Excuse 2:

If the farmer bought five yoke of oxen, wouldn't he have tested them first?

Excuse 3:

The recently married man didn't even ask to be excused: he just said that he wasn't coming.

The same old excuses are trotted out regularly – possession, occupation, or relation. Some Christians are too tired to serve the Lord, too tired to pray, too tired for Jesus, who spent all night in prayer for his people.

But the host is anxious that there is a full house, and if it takes outcasts to fill it, then let it be filled. Jesus is looking for outcasts still – those who are blinded by Satan, crippled by sin, and poor in spirit. By his grace, there's still room. It's *'to as many as receive him...'* (John ch1 vv11-12). Our excuses are inexcusable.

OCTOBER 4
THE GOSPEL OF LUKE Ch14.25-35

We may imagine Jesus on his journey from Galilee to Jerusalem with the crowds that followed him. Many people may have entertained thoughts of revolution and routing the Romans. They may have perceived their march on the capital, Jerusalem, as the opportunity to drive the Roman governor from his palace. We may even visualise these followers chanting songs of resistance and triumph. As the crowds increased, so did their enthusiasm and fervour. Most of them had no idea what Jesus' mission was about. How could they have ever contemplated ending the march with a cross?

THE CONDITIONS OF BEING JESUS' DISCIPLE

But Jesus stops the march. Everyone comes to a halt, and silence reigns. In the space of a few moments, Jesus spells out the conditions for being one of his true followers (vv25-27). Jesus doesn't mince his words as he hammers home the cost of discipleship.

1 YOU CANNOT BE JESUS' DISCIPLE IF YOU DON'T LOVE HIM FIRST (v26)

It's impossible to be Jesus' disciple and a disciple of fashion, fame, fortune, friends, or even family at the same time. You cannot be a disciple of Jesus unless you love him first and foremost. Loving God and loving our neighbours are the two all-time great commands. Therefore, hating our family (v26) is not to be taken literally here. The Bible teaches us to love unselfishly and unconditionally, including loving those who hate us. Jesus identifies his disciples as those who are prepared to put his name at the top of their 'priority list'. The word *'hate'* is also used rhetorically in John ch12 v25 to emphasise the contrast in priorities. If life is more precious than Christ, then any claim to discipleship is rather hollow.

2 YOU CANNOT BE JESUS' DISCIPLE IF YOU WON'T CARRY YOUR CROSS (v27)

Note that Jesus doesn't say, 'Anyone who is not crucified cannot be my disciple', for it's plain that not every disciple was crucified. Even in the first century of pain and persecution, there were disciples of Christ who died peacefully in their own beds. However, Jesus refers to his disciples as those who are willing to follow him; willing to go down the road with him, knowing that the road may lead to suffering and death. We must never trivialise the importance of the cross. It's nonsense to talk about some trouble or sickness as 'the cross that I bear'! For Jesus, the cross meant incomprehensible suffering, unprecedented spiritual affliction, and immeasurable isolation. For Jesus, the cross meant clashing with the powers of darkness head-on.

The Cross implies Calculation

No rational person engages in a building project unless he has first calculated whether he has enough money to finance it. In the same way, a careful assessment is needed before declaring total allegiance to Christ.

The Cross implies Completion

The builder must be able to complete his building (v29). Through lack of commitment, many professing Christians never finish. The greatest example of a completed work is in the cross of Christ (John ch17 v4; ch19 v30).

3 YOU CANNOT BE JESUS' DISCIPLE IF YOU WON'T SURRENDER EVERYTHING (v33)

Jesus illustrates with a king evaluating the prospect of victory (vv31-32). Will he blindly order his ten thousand men into a suicidal battle with his enemy's twenty thousand men, or will he first consider the likelihood of success? A shrewd commander assesses the cost first. The word for *'give up'* (v33) means 'farewell'. A genuine disciple will be ready to say 'goodbye' to everything for the cause of Christ. However, surrendering and renouncing our claims to possessions and people doesn't always mean the disposal of them. In his great grace and love, the Lord frequently makes us stewards of them.

But this consecrated life is not an empty life. It's a life of immense quality and supreme value, and it's compared with salt (vv34-35). If salt is not salty, it is worthless and useless. What a damning epitaph – 'fit for nothing!' It's no good as a preservative, or as a fertiliser, or even on food. A disciple of Jesus who is not living the 'Jesus life' is just as useless. Let us not lose our influence and 'saltiness' as disciples of Jesus.

OCTOBER 5
THE GOSPEL OF LUKE Ch15.1-32

SEEKING, SAVING, RESTORING

The critical *Pharisees and the teachers of the law* were correct in their muttering: *'This man welcomes sinners, and eats with them'* (v2). Jesus' business here on earth was to draw near to sinners so that they could draw near to him. If it weren't with sinners that Jesus associated, then he would have had a lonely time here on earth. This muttered remark of the Pharisees and Law-teachers prompted these three memorable parables of the sheep, silver, and son. Although myriad preachers and commentators have approached these parables from numerous helpful angles, we must not fail to glimpse the glorious character of God our Father as revealed in his zeal, his grace, and his joy.

1 WE SEE THE ZEAL OF GOD IN SEEKING

The shepherd searches for the lost sheep while the woman turns her house upside down to find the lost coin. The father, whose son left his home to squander *'his wealth in wild living'* (v13), has maintained a constant vigil. He is always on the lookout, scanning the distant horizon, searching for the familiar figure of his own lost son. In each case, the lost received special attention. God is personally interested in the lost. We should never underestimate the dire plight of those who are lost and not yet found (*'without hope and without God in the world'* Ephesians ch2 v12; *'still powerless'* Romans ch5 v6). Everything is desperate and hopeless except for the zeal of God in seeking the lost. In the case of the ever-watchful father of the prodigal, he spotted him long before he reached 'the garden gate'. It was while we were still a long way off (see v20) that God saw us and initiated our rescue. He came to us (Mark ch2 v17; 1 Timothy ch1 v15).

2 WE SEE THE GRACE OF GOD IN SAVING

The grace of God is not only unmerited favour but also de-merited favour. It's not that we have done something to qualify us for God's favour, but rather that we have done everything to disqualify us from receiving anything except God's judgement. Grace is all about demonstrating kindness and favour to the unworthy and undeserving. The son had demanded the fruit of his father's lifetime of hard work, and he hadn't been prepared to wait. He wanted it there and then. But he lived an undisciplined, profligate life far away. He became embroiled in *'wild living'* and, probably for the first time in his life, he had to seek employment. And what employment! We find this young Jew working for a Gentile, engaged in one of the most dishonourable jobs that any of his own race could do – a swineherd, a caretaker of unclean animals. He hit rock bottom. He was even worse off than the pigs since they had something to eat. He was undeserving, unworthy, unwanted – but not unloved. Far away, there was a loving heart beating for him and loving eyes that were constantly roving the horizon on the lookout for him. Eventually, this young man *'came to his senses'* (v17). He was repentant and ready to submit himself to his father's authority. He wanted the power to change and the opportunity to start again, and his father met him in great grace. We cannot excuse our sins or justify our past way of life, merely writing it off as 'an unfortunate experience'. We must call on God for his mercy and pardon.

3 WE SEE THE JOY OF GOD IN RESTORING

Restoration is an integral part of each of these parables. The lost sheep is restored to the shepherd's flock. The lost silver is restored to the woman's purse. The lost son is restored to the father's family. In each case, too, there is great rejoicing. Repentance is the key to restoration, and restoration is the springboard to rejoicing. But the elder brother refuses to join in the 'welcome home' party (v28). He had always enjoyed his father's presence, and everything his father owned belonged to him (v31). He might have demanded justice in the case of his younger brother, but the father demonstrated grace.

How much does our loving heavenly Father teach us?

If our Father is zealous in seeking lost sinners, shouldn't we also share his zeal and enthusiasm in reaching out with the gospel?

If our Father is gracious in saving lost sinners, shouldn't we be gracious, supporting, and encouraging to those who trust in Christ for salvation?

If our Father is joyful in restoring lost sinners, shouldn't we rejoice in the recovery and restoration of those who had once wandered far from God?

OCTOBER 6
THE GOSPEL OF LUKE Ch16.1-15

HOW WELL DO WE FULFILL OUR RESPONSIBILITIES?

'It is required that those who have been given a trust must prove faithful' (1 Corinthians ch4 v2). We all have responsibilities, individually or collectively, within our families, work situations, and circles of friends. But chiefly we are responsible to God. We look around at a world that is replete with vast resources. God, in his common grace, has lavished his good supplies upon us (Psalm 85 v12, 145 v9). Every good we enjoy comes from a divine source (John ch3 v27, James ch1 v17). The Lord, Designer and Creator of heaven and earth, has not been miserly in his wealth and possessions (Psalm 145 vv15-16). Even to a world that openly denies him, rejects him, blasphemes him, and constructs pathetic deities and ridiculous religions to replace him, yet he remains wonderfully patient and gracious.

But if God has been so kind and generous in providing us with so much.

How well do we look after all that he has entrusted to us?

How well do we manage the resources that He has given?

What kind of caretakers are we, of all the supplies he has provided?

1 OUR RESPONSIBILITY IN MANAGING GOD'S WORLD

'The art of management' is a favourite topic in business and commerce today. Jesus introduces a manager who works for a rich man. Someone has made an accusation that the manager has been wasting his employer's possessions. So the boss calls him in to give an account. There appears to be some truth in the allegation since the manager didn't protest. He had kept a list of his boss's debtors, which now he intended to put to his own benefit. This white-collar worker considered it to be too hard to do manual work, and it was too much of a disgrace to beg. So he devised a plan to make himself favourable to other potential employers (v4). With his delegated authority, he reduced the size of their debts with a pen stroke! It was the boss who recognised this as a shrewd move. In fact, he commended him for his prudence (v8). The whole of life is about stewardship. Man was originally given delegated sovereignty by the King of creation himself (Genesis ch1 v26, Psalm 8 vv5-6). He is God's steward to see that creation is not exploited, wasted, or ruined, and that food is distributed fairly. God's steward must ensure that the benefits of *'seedtime and harvest'* (Genesis ch8 v22) are managed shrewdly, sensibly, and selflessly.

2 OUR RESPONSIBILITY IN HELPING GOD'S PEOPLE

There's a contrast between the children of light and the children of darkness (vv8-9). It's an indictment of the followers of Christ that the *'children of the world'* may be more generous and supporting to fellow unbelievers than Christians are to the family of God. Giving should be regular, dependable, and generous. 'Giving' will be the overflow of the heart (2 Corinthians ch9 v7) and not an opportunity to flaunt generosity (Mattew ch6 vv3-4).

3 OUR RESPONSIBILITY IN MAINTAINING GOD'S VALUES

In our hearts, we have either a concern for God's values or the world's values. The 'Pharisees' of today, like those who sneered at Jesus (v14), consider themselves to be moral and decent but will also reject Christ and his gospel. The values of our society continually clash with the values of God's kingdom, for example:

The principle of 'remuneration for work' is threatened by incitements to gamble.

Personal standards of morality, health, and hygiene are despised by the lifestyles of those who put pleasure first.

God's values of family life and parenting are scorned by Parliament and the politically correct agenda of our humanist society.

4 OUR RESPONSIBILITY IN SERVING GOD'S WILL

(v13) Through the gospel, God calls people into his royal service. These servants have been delivered from sin's slavery and 'silver service' by the power of Christ's victorious atonement at the cross. The divine detergent of Christ's precious blood can effectively *'cleanse our consciences from acts that lead to death, so that we may serve the living God'* (Hebrews ch9 v14). If we're going to be servants of God, we must be made spotlessly clean. It's possible for the ugliest, foulest, and filthiest to be wonderfully forgiven and made clean for God.

OCTOBER 7
THE GOSPEL OF LUKE Ch16.16-31

FACING THE END

Jesus portrays something of the desperate hopelessness of an unbeliever in this account of the rich man and Lazarus. We can't be sure that it was a parable, but if it was, then it's the only parable in which Jesus gives a name to one of the characters. Lazarus shouldn't be confused with the Lazarus whom Jesus raised from the dead in John ch11. The name of the rich man is not provided, though traditionally he has been called 'Dives' from the Latin, meaning 'rich'.

Both men came to their end. Death is no respecter of persons. The humblest, poorest beggar and the wealthiest, loftiest millionaire must both face the end. Death is the greatest of all levellers. Each one of us is put in our place by death. But which place?

The Lord Jesus reveals enough about the end so that we may be suitably challenged, warned, assured, and comforted.

1 TROUBLES THAT WILL END

Lazarus' condition in life was far from comfortable. He appears to be severely handicapped and immobilised. Lazarus *'was laid'* at the rich man's gate (v20). Such was his immobility that he couldn't prevent the dogs from licking his sores (v21). He was obviously in great pain, and if you are completely plagued with sores and unable to obtain relief by moving, it's a miserable condition indeed. This is compounded with hunger (v21). But God cares for his people. He doesn't always provide the vast array of food that stocks the supermarkets and fills our deep freezes and larders. Yet God is faithful, and he is never uncaring of his children. For those Christians who may be suffering conditions like those of Lazarus – crippling immobility (either from physical handicap or incarceration) or whether they are suffering from various sores, aches and pains, or even experiencing hunger, homelessness, and loneliness – it's only for a short while. There's a day coming when the distresses of this life will become history and the glories of heaven will become an unending reality.

2 DEATH IS NOT THE END

For the believer like Lazarus, or for the unbeliever like the rich man, death is not merely extinction or annihilation. Lazarus was carried by the angels to *'Abraham's side'* (v22), representing the place of the faithful, where they may experience rest, joy, and peace. But though Abraham is identified with Glory, it is Glory that is identified with Christ. The security of God's covenant with Abraham will be our lasting inheritance, but it will be the Saviour who lived and died for us on the cross whom we shall long to see most of all. Lazarus entered the splendour of paradise and into the presence of his Saviour-King. He had an angelic escort into the throne-room of his Redeemer and Friend.

Jesus makes it clear that the rich man was imprisoned in an eternal hell, illustrated by unbearable heat and unquenchable thirst. There was no comfort for this man, not even in the knowledge that his five brothers would be deterred from following him.

3 HELL THAT WILL NEVER END

Although caricatured in numerous ways, the reality of hell is too horrific to imagine. The *'great chasm'* (v26) represents the desperate hopelessness of no reprieve, no release, and no escape. The 'everlastingness' of hell is too immense and too fearful to contemplate. If the unsaved sinner were sentenced to a million years in hell, or even a trillion years of judgement, at some point there would be the prospect of release. But the Bible provides no such glimmer of hope. The rich man and every unbeliever who refuses Christ and his gospel is eternally doomed.

4 PREPARATION TO MEET THE END

We must have a burning enthusiasm to seek God and to know his truth. We must have a 'forceful desire' to enter the kingdom of God (v16). You won't access heaven by a casual approach to religion or by a light-hearted attitude towards the gospel. You won't get to heaven by default! In fact, the default position is hell, and Jesus is the only One who can deliver us and give us eternal hope and assurance. In the gospel, the doom and gloom are removed. Jesus was One who returned from the dead, having defeated the powers of hell, yet there are many who refuse to listen to his testimony or his warning in the word of God (v31).

Be assured that, with Jesus as your Saviour, you can face the end with confidence and hope.

OCTOBER 8
THE GOSPEL OF LUKE Ch17.1-19

The patriarchs, and Abraham in particular, were characterised by their calibre of faith. Therefore, it may not surprise us to discover the apostles asking Jesus:

'INCREASE OUR FAITH' (v5)

To have an 'increased faith' is to grow as a Christian. The apostolic age was one of growth and development. Christians didn't stand still in spiritual terms. If you were not progressing, then you were regressing, and the consequences could be catastrophic.

Is this our request today – 'Lord, increase my faith'? There are four aspects of faith:

1 THE ATTITUDE OF FAITH (vv1-5)

The apostles' request for an increase in faith was in response to Jesus' instruction to watch ourselves and to forgive one another. We must have the right attitude towards sin and a right attitude towards sinners. In vv1-3 Jesus warns about those who are the agents of sin, and we must always be alert to the possibility that we could cause another believer to fall into sin. We must ever be vigilant to ensure that we don't put a *'millstone'* around the neck of a Christian young person, or a young Christian, by our disregard for their weakness and vulnerability. If we show contempt for the fragile faith of another believer, which destabilises them and causes them to sin, then we are better off *'to be thrown into the sea with a millstone tied around (our) neck'*. We may consider that we are 'strong' in our use of the World Wide Web, or playing computer games, or watching films, or attending concerts and parties, or drinking socially. We may think that we know where to draw the line. But the arrogant attitude of some Christians, which says 'what I do is between God and me', has been the downfall of vulnerable believers (1 Corinthians ch8 v9). The 'attitude of faith' also means showing a forgiving spirit to those who repent (Colossians ch3 v13). Forgiveness must be unconditional if the repentance is genuine, just as God forgives us (Isaiah ch43 v25).

2 THE MAGNITUDE OF FAITH (v6)

Jesus speaks of the extent of faith – its importance and its far-reaching effect. The mustard seed is very small, while the mulberry tree has a vast root system and can live for hundreds of years. Such a strong and secure tree was unmovable - except for faith (reference the faith compared to a mountain in Matthew ch17 v20). We may feel intimidated by the 'giants of faith' through Christian history. By comparison, our faith is pathetically minuscule. But Jesus' words should encourage us. Faith develops faith. Like some muscles that develop as they are used and shrink when they become inactive, so faith grows with its exercise. It's an everyday faith that's required – a faith to read God's word, a faith to pray, a faith to act in a Christian way. That 'faith' is great and powerful.

3 THE SERVITUDE OF FAITH (vv7-10)

A servant who obediently follows all his master's instructions is only doing his duty. The servants of Christ, who faithfully, loyally, and obediently serve their Master, are only doing their duty. 'Duty' means 'what is due' (what we 'owe' or 'ought'). Because the general norm in our society is incompetence, inefficiency, and misconduct, people now expect to be rewarded for just doing their duty. So we reward children in schools for dutiful behaviour, and we reward or tip employees for doing what they are only contracted to do. We compliment citizens for only doing what should be expected as common decency and acceptable behaviour. Paul refers to Greek Christians and their duty in helping the poor at Jerusalem (Romans ch15 v27). Are we doing our duty?

THE GRATITUDE OF FAITH (vv11-19)

To be a leper meant a 'living death'. The end of life would be miserable and lonely. This one grateful leper had been in a disastrous situation:

Outskirts of the Community

He was on the border and on the edge of the village (v11);

Outcast from Society

He *'stood at a distance'* (v12), shouting to be heard (v13);

Outside of the Nationality

He was a Samaritan, ostracised from the Jews.

But Jesus' mercy (v14) changed his life, and this leper was profoundly grateful (v16). He recognised that Jesus had been sent by God and he trusted him for healing and salvation. Once he had only stood at a distance: now he was prostrate at Jesus' feet.

Our hearts should also be bursting with thankfulness to God for all that he has done for us in Christ. But where are the nine? Where are those who should be grateful?

OCTOBER 9
THE GOSPEL OF LUKE Ch17.20-37

RED LETTER DAYS

There are three days that we can refer to in these verses.

1 REMEMBRANCE DAY

The day on which Jesus answered the Pharisees' question about the coming of the *'kingdom of God'* (v1) was a day on which he prompted his disciples' memories. Jesus wanted them to recall what they knew about the days of Noah and Lot. Right up to the day that Noah and his immediate family entered the ark, one week before the heavy rains began, people continued as normal (v27). It was also the same in Lot's day. Jesus drove home the point: *'Remember Lot's wife!'* (v32). She had more than a vested interest in Sodom. She resisted the command to flee, and she became *'a pillar of salt'* (Genesis ch19 v26). These two completely different situations, separated by hundreds of years, showed that people were unconcerned and indifferent to imminent judgement. They ignored the warnings, rejected the message, and refused to repent. Things went on as normal – business, commerce, socialising, industry, construction, relationships – until the very moment that God's judgement fell either by flood (on the whole earth) or by fire (on Sodom and Gomorrah). Jesus urges the people of his day to remember. Today should be a day of remembrance. The coming of Jesus Christ into the world for the second time will interrupt all the normal cycles of life, and so everyone should be completely ready for his return (v31).

2 REJECTION DAY

Before Jesus could appear in the splendour of his Second Coming, he had to *'suffer many things and be rejected by this generation'* (v25). His cross preceded his crown. His rejection preceded his return. Isaiah described the details of Christ's rejection (Isaiah ch53 vv3-5). Throughout the Old Testament, we learn how that the Jews had repeatedly rejected God's covenant (1 Kings ch19 v10), had rejected God's decrees (2 Kings ch17 v15), and had rejected God's word (Jeremiah ch8 v9). Now they had rejected God's one and only Son (Psalm 118 v22; 1 Peter ch2 v4; Luke ch10 v16; John ch3 v36). They rejected Jesus when he lived here on earth. They had no room in the inn for the baby; no room in their homes for him to lay his head; no room in their city for the King, and no room in their hearts for the Saviour.

3 REVELATION DAY

The days of Noah and Lot will be very similar to the day that Jesus comes again (v30). This Revelation Day will be unique for a number of reasons. Although it will be 'business as usual' prior to Christ's coming, the moment he appears will signal the end of time as we know it.

i] It will be Unforeseeable

Jesus' disciples have longed for his appearance all through history. Especially when the Church has suffered periods of intense persecution, God's people have cried out for the Lord's personal return (v22). There will be various false prophets and fake Messiahs (v23) who will try to deceive the saints. Some of the 'pretend Christs' are quite convincing with their Scripture-couched addresses and their heavenly-sounding messages. But we're not to go running after them! We must wait patiently for the Lord's appearance whenever that will take place (Matthew ch24 v36; Luke ch12 v40). Although we may be uninformed, we must not be unprepared.

ii] It will be Unmistakable

In complete contrast to some who believe that Jesus will return stealthily, silently, and secretly, we need to listen to Jesus' own words (v24).

The day of Christ's revelation will be more brilliant than lightning or the sun. It will be obvious, totally visible, and the most high-profile of any event in world history. It will be noisy too (1 Thessalonians ch4 v16). No one is going to miss it, although for many it will mark the beginning of unimaginable judgement. Such judgement will be quick and sudden, as emphasised by the separation (vv34-35). Close companionships or relationships do not guarantee the same eternal destiny. The only certainty is through faith in Christ.

iii] It will be Inescapable

Everyone will be there in one way or another. There will be no opting out of that day. But for the believer who is trusting fully in Jesus, it will be the day of all days (1 John ch3 vv2-3). We may not be privy to all the details of that future event, but we can be sure of one thing – we're going to see Jesus and be like him.

In marvellous, supernatural grace, he supplies us with his love, his wisdom, his Spirit, his word, his servants, and his Church, to help us to be ready for Revelation Day.

OCTOBER 10
THE GOSPEL OF LUKE Ch18.1-17

Some people tend to regard prayer in the same way that they take a couple of painkillers! A headache, a spell of discomfort or upset, and they reach for the paracetamol. For them, praying is the spiritual version of a couple of tablets with a glass of water. Now that doesn't mean that we cannot, or should not, pray about everything that concerns us. The Throne of Grace is not restricted to Sundays, 9 am - 9 pm. It is always open to the bold and needy who pray. Fundamentally, prayer is to do with access to God, the Almighty King. We enter his audience chamber with the authority and permission of Jesus, our Saviour, Redeemer, and Friend.

COMING TO GOD

In these verses, we are provided with three illustrations of those who came to God:

1 COMING TO GOD AND NOT GIVING UP (vv1-8)

Jesus explains that the reason for telling this parable was so that his disciples would be persistent in prayer. It's not by accident that the central character is a widow. In first-century Middle East society, as in many places today, a widow was the most helpless and vulnerable of adults. She had lost her protector and provider, and she was therefore exposed to all the charlatans, oppressors, and predators of that society. Furthermore, she was often despised and treated with contempt. But it was such a widow who persisted relentlessly in appealing to a careless, godless judge for justice in respect of her adversary, and who was successful in her appeal (v5). Jesus says that if such an unrighteous, insensitive judge responds to the persistent pleas of a powerless widow, how much more will our righteous heavenly Father respond to the prayers of his children? We are exhorted to come to God regularly and confidently. There's no doubt that when Jesus comes again in the power of his glory that he will bring justice (v8). God listens to the continual cries of his people who don't cave in or give up.

2 COMING TO GOD AND NOT BEING STUCK UP (vv9-14)

This next parable is told to *'some who were confident of their own righteousness and looked down on everybody else'* (v9). Two men, who were in the temple praying, had very different attitudes and approaches:

The Pharisee

He prayed to himself or about himself (v11). He was the subject of his own prayer – self-confident, self-righteous, and self-praising. Although Old Testament law required fasting once a year on the Day of Atonement, Pharisees made a show of fasting every Monday and Thursday. They even went out of their way to look sombre and to cover their heads with ashes and disfigure their faces so that people would think they were more serious. Neither did they limit their tithing to that required by Old Testament law. They made it obvious that they tithed everything.

The Tax Collector

By contrast, his prayer was a confession of sin. He didn't stand in a conspicuous part of the inner courts. He stood *'at a distance'* and wouldn't even lift his head heavenwards. He didn't try to justify himself before God as the Pharisee had done, but God justified him on the basis of Christ's redeeming sacrifice. The subject of the tax collector's prayer was God. He left the temple court knowing that he had been forgiven. Through justification, the tax collector and every believing sinner is declared righteous.

3 COMING TO GOD AND NOT BEING HELD UP (vv15-17)

Jesus was engaged in a very busy ministry where the pressure was becoming even more intense as he approached the cross. But he still had time for needy sinners and *'little children'* in particular. Children teach us about simple, uncomplicated, unreserved trust, and Jesus is ready to receive children and those who are childlike in faith. It is with that kind of wholehearted trust that we should approach God and let nothing hinder us or prevent us from coming. Being too busy, or too tired, or not feeling in the right mood may hold us up. Jesus summons people to himself (Matthew ch11 v28; John ch7 v37).

If God calls us to come to him, and Jesus represents us and intercedes for us, why are we so reluctant to come?

Let us come regularly, persistently and consistently, not giving up easily.

Let us come with humility and penitence, confessing our unworthiness and sin.

Let us come with childlike confidence, without being hindered or put off.

OCTOBER 11
THE GOSPEL OF LUKE Ch18.18-43

WANNABE FOLLOWERS

This wealthy ruler probably fits the modern description of a 'wannabe' – someone who wants to fit in with a particular group of people. He was a 'wannabe follower' of Jesus who, along with many like him today, misunderstood some basic facts about discipleship. There are:

1 WANNABE FOLLOWERS WHO MISUNDERSTAND THE CALL (vv18-27)

Jesus called this young, wealthy official to follow him. The one huge obstacle he had was his wealth. He addressed Jesus in a unique way (*'Good teacher...'*), and although it may have been offered as an expression of flattery, Jesus uses it to point out that God is the only One who is absolutely good. He is wholly good in the moral sense since our own condition is morally corrupt (Ecclesiastes ch7 v20; Romans ch3 v12). Even our so-called 'good works' are tainted by pride or self-righteousness. Such 'good works' can never save us (Ephesians ch2 vv8-9), although we have been *'created in Christ Jesus to do good works'* (Ephesians ch2 v10). To the rich man's question about obtaining eternal life and who boasted a string of 'good deeds', he said that he still lacked one thing (v22). He might have felt that he was almost there: he had only one box left to tick, until he heard Jesus' instruction to give away everything and to follow him. He had a great fortune but no faith. He was a doer but not a believer. Just as Naaman had to trust and obey (2 Kings ch5 v13), so this young man had to believe and to trust in Jesus. His riches couldn't get him into heaven any more than a camel could pass through a needle's eye (v25). This wannabe follower had misunderstood that it was faith, not works or riches, that would bring him eternal life.

2 WANNABE FOLLOWERS WHO MISUNDERSTAND THE COST (vv28-30)

The disciples were not particularly rich, but Peter reminded Jesus that they had left all they had to follow him (v28). But these wannabe followers didn't understand that whatever sacrifice they had made, it was never too much for Jesus. Have we ever questioned whether a cost for the sake of Christ and his gospel was a demand too much, a step too far? Jesus makes it clear that our eternal reward will infinitely outweigh any present sacrifices.

Today, Jesus' followers in many Muslim lands do not misunderstand the cost. Frequently, it means a permanent separation from all their relatives. They are ejected from their homes, rejected by their families, and forced to renounce any title to possessions or inheritance. They become 'non-citizens' and 'fair game' for all the abuse and ill treatment that evil hearts can conceive

3 WANNABE FOLLOWERS WHO MISUNDERSTAND THE CROSS (vv31-34)

The disciples were mystified about the implications of what Jesus was saying to them. It wasn't that Jesus' words were unintelligible, but rather they couldn't comprehend how the cross could fit into their idea of Jesus' messianic mission. Similarly, there are wannabe followers in countries without persecution who are willing to adopt the Sermon on the Mount as a Mission Statement. There are those who seek to emulate Jesus' ascetic life or view him as a celebrity supermodel in all kinds of weird and wacky cults. They misunderstand that the singular purpose of Christ's coming into the world included the cross (Mark ch10 v45).

But on the outskirts of Jericho, Jesus met a blind man who demonstrated what it takes to become a real follower of Jesus:

He heard what others didn't hear (the truth of the word of God);

He knew what others didn't know (he recognised Jesus as the promised Messiah);

He saw what others couldn't see (Jesus, *'Son of David'*, fulfilled Old Testament prophecies);

He cried what others didn't cry (*'Lord, have mercy on me'*);

He achieved what others didn't achieve (*'Jesus stopped'* for him – v40);

He received what others didn't receive (healing that came through faith in God);

He did what others didn't do (he *'followed Jesus, praising God'* –v43).

The first thing that he saw when his eyes were opened was the face of Jesus. Did he rush off to behold the wonderful vistas of the Judean countryside or coastline? No! He didn't want to let Jesus out of his sight, for he was determined to follow him.

A COST TOO GREAT

It is easier for a camel to go through the eye of a needle than for a rich man to enter the kingdom of God.

Luke ch18 v25

To be a real Christian,

The cost would be too great.

To give up each possession,

And forfeit my estate.

To turn my back on riches,

My friends, my fun, my fame;

To change my style of living,

Adopt a different name.

To leave behind the pleasures,

I sample every day,

As if with just a pen stroke,

I sign my life away.

To sacrifice all prospects,

Of living life for me;

Divorce the world I've married,

For Christianity.

To give up time and effort,

To yield my very best;

Submitting skill and talent,

Forsaking all the rest;

Surrendering the things I've held,

So tight within my clutch,

And give myself to Jesus?

No thanks! It costs too much.

And yet the Lord of glory,

Behind the starry sky.

Laid down a crown of splendour,

And passed the angels by.

He did not pause to barter,

Or haggle at the cost.

He left the courts of heaven,

Exchanged them for a cross.

And there, so empty-handed,

Except the nails, he died;

Not crowned with regal splendour,

But Jesus crucified.

He did not stop to question,

The worth of my estate;

When he gave his all to pay,

A cost that was so great.

Geoff Fox

OCTOBER 12
THE GOSPEL OF LUKE Ch19.1-10

Tax collectors have never enjoyed great popularity! Although Luke has referred to tax collectors previously, here we are introduced to Zacchaeus, who was *'a chief tax collector'*. Being a chief tax collector, or major tax collector, meant that he would have other tax collectors working for him in the district. He had probably tendered for the contract to run the 'local tax office'. If individual collectors made their profits on the percentages they extorted over and above the basic tax, then the chief tax collector would exact his own 'cut' from his collectors. Tax collection has often been a murky, non-transparent business in which the collectors have been despised, ostracised, and regarded as outcasts on a par with lepers and prostitutes.

AN OPENING

But we may state four commendable things about Zacchaeus:

1 HE HAD AN OPEN MIND (vv3-4)

He was curious to find out about this 'Jesus' whom people were talking about (v3). He may well have heard conflicting reports about this 'unusual man' from the Pharisees, the teachers of the law, and from the crowds which had witnessed his miracles and had heard his teachings. But it was the sheer size and volume of the Jericho crowd that prevented their local chief tax official from seeing Jesus. Yet he was determined to see Jesus. He may have been short, but he was athletic enough to run ahead of the crowds and to climb a sycamore-fig tree. We don't know how conspicuous Zacchaeus was as he sat perched in the tree, but he could definitely see Jesus, hear Jesus, and make up his own mind about who this popular figure was. Open-mindedness, however, must not be confused with faith, which Jesus demands of those who would sincerely follow him.

2 HE HAD AN OPEN HOUSE (vv5-7)

The account of Zacchaeus is wonderful and beautiful, not least because, however much he wanted to see Jesus, the greater fact is that Jesus wanted to see him. Despite our priority in seeking and determining to find God, he sought us first of all. It wasn't an accident that Jesus took that specific route and stopped at that one tree on that particular day. Zacchaeus was on Jesus' heart, and he came to where the needy sinner was, perched on a branch of that tree. Jesus' call had a note of urgency attached to it – *'immediately'* ... *'today'*. Jesus was not going to pass through Jericho again. The opportunity was right there and then to receive Jesus, and the chief collector responds positively (v6). We can't expect to know the blessing of Christ visiting us if we remain perched among the branches of self-righteousness and pride. We must come down from our haughty position so that we can welcome Jesus into our lives and homes. Once again, we see the divine 'must' (v5), which reminds us of the sovereign blueprint overlaying the twists and turns of men's circumstances and needs. Zacchaeus opened his house to Jesus. He had only set out to glimpse Jesus, but now Jesus wanted to stay with him and fellowship with him.

3 HE HAD AN OPEN PURSE (v8)

Restitution is an essential feature of conversion. This rich tax collector stands in stark contrast to the rich ruler of ch18. This is an example of a person who does pass through the proverbial *'eye of a needle'* (see ch18 v25) because he was willing to sacrifice his riches to follow Jesus. Can you imagine the queue at Zacchaeus' door when he announced that, to anyone he had cheated, he would repay four hundred per cent? But unlike the rich official of ch18, this rich official was ready to sacrifice everything to get right with God and to put things right with his fellow man. Conversion is not an alternative to restitution. It's not a 'get out of jail free' card! Though sin may be pardoned, there are often consequences that need to be addressed seriously.

4 HE HAD AN OPEN HEART (vv9-10)

The outward change in Zacchaeus was because of his inward transformation. Salvation had come to him (v9) and, though he was already a Jew, he had been made a true *'son of Abraham'* through believing God's word (that is, a son of faith - Romans ch4 v16). The fourteen monosyllabic words of v10 sum up the Saviour's 'search and rescue' mission so simply. The 'lost' Zacchaeus was a clear example of how Christ saves sinners - seeking them and finding them by his inescapable grace and wonderful love.

OCTOBER 13
THE GOSPEL OF LUKE Ch19.11-27

After Herod the Great died, his son Archelaus reigned in Judea (Matthew ch2 vv21-23). He was just as cruel and tyrannical as his father was. The Jews hated Archelaus, and Josephus, the Roman historian, reports that a delegation of fifty men was sent to Caesar in a bid to get him removed. It may have been this incident that Jesus' hearers called to mind as Jesus narrated this parable about a *'man of noble birth (who) went to a distant country to have himself appointed king'* (v12). Jesus explained that this king's subjects didn't want him to reign over them (v14). Jesus told the parable to those who expected that God's kingdom was going to appear immediately (v11). But they still had a lot to learn. The king needed to go away before the final kingdom would appear in all its global glory, and Jesus' disciples had to learn how to wait for the return of their King.

In the parable, the king distributes ten minas (each mina is calculated to be about four months' wages) to ten of his servants. His specific instruction was *'Put this money to work...until I come back'* (v13). The Greek words used are related to trade and business. He's saying, 'Engage in business'...'Make a profit'...'Do your trading' – or:

BE BUSY IN THE KING'S BUSINESS

The message of this parable concerns the duties we must perform and the service we must engage in while waiting for the return of our King. Three groups of people are spotlighted by this parable:

1 THOSE WHO REJECT THE KING TOTALLY

There is only the greatest of contrasts between Archelaus, who applied to Rome for kingship, and Jesus, who is King of Kings. But just as Jesus has 'gone away' temporarily and will return in the full power of his majestic reign, he is largely rejected and disowned, except for a small remnant of believers. Our anarchic world only acknowledges rulers of its own making. Jesus is rejected as King of the nations, the sovereign Ruler of heaven and earth. People resist his influence, resent his jurisdiction, and reject his authority (Isaiah ch53 v3, John ch1 v11, 1 Peter ch2 vv4-7). In the final analysis of final judgement, all those who reject Christ, hate Christ, spurn Christ, or merely ignore Christ and his offer in the gospel, will be eternally condemned (v27, John ch3 v36).

2 THOSE WHO SERVE THE KING FAITHFULLY

Unlike a similar parable in Matthew ch25, in which three servants are given five talents, two talents, and one talent, the ten servants of this parable are given the same amount –one mina. They were instructed to make this money work for them. The king entrusted his servants with the responsibility of making his money grow. One servant made his money increase 1,000% and another, 500%. Both servants had been faithful in discharging their responsibilities to the king, and they duly received their master's commendation: *'Well done, my good servant!'* They had been *'trustworthy in a very small matter'* (v17). All the Lord's servants are entrusted with something. Some Christians may hanker after large responsibilities, but each one is required to be faithful in the smaller matters too.

Are we trustworthy in our personal devotional times with God?

Are we trustworthy in our weekly commitment to our local church and fellowship?

Are we trustworthy in our use of freedom to worship and our freedom of speech?

Are we trustworthy in availing ourselves of opportunities to hear God's word?

Are we trustworthy in the use of our homes, our finances, and our resources?

Are we trustworthy in proclaiming the gospel and reaching people for Christ?

Are we trustworthy in employing our skills, abilities, intellect, and gifts for God?

3 THOSE WHO TREAT THE KING CASUALLY

One servant had no progress report to give because he had not invested his money. He had been unfaithful and negligent in the gift that the king had entrusted to him. But is he a true servant? He doesn't enjoy a right relationship with his king. He's paralysed with terror (v21). He doesn't know his king since he portrays him to be harsh and uncaring (vv17-19). Furthermore, he is described as a *'wicked servant'* (v22). The 'casual Christianity' which infects the twenty-first century church is not Biblical Christianity. It has no responsibility to God's word, God's service, or God's Church and is therefore untrustworthy. Let us invest in him those gifts which he has invested in us.

OCTOBER 14
THE GOSPEL OF LUKE Ch19.28-48

In AD70, Jerusalem suffered such a terrible calamity. The Romans under General Titus besieged the city and conducted a most vicious massacre. Christians within Jerusalem had miraculously escaped during a brief interval when the Romans withdrew their forces. But Titus regrouped his armies and surrounded the city, building huge embankments for the battering rams and demolishing the walls.

Jesus is now approaching Jerusalem for the last time. He weeps over it and describes the last days of the city in just over three decades (vv43-44). Jesus provides the reason why Jerusalem is going to be destroyed. They had rejected the coming of God in Jesus. He prefaced his prophecy with this lament (v42):

'IF YOU, EVEN YOU, HAD ONLY KNOWN ON THIS DAY WHAT WOULD BRING YOU PEACE...'

Jesus' triumphal entry into Jerusalem proclaims a message of peace.

Even in the way that the disciples appropriated the donkey colt, there could have been anything but peace with the owners, but Jesus had prepared the event (v31).

The colt was unbroken and unridden, but Jesus rides it peacefully.

Jesus enters with lowliness, meekness, and humility on a donkey rather than on a white charger symbolising might, victory, and supremacy.

The crowds spread their cloaks on the road and praised God (v36). Jesus, the Prince of Peace, demonstrates a heavenly peace:

1 PEACE IN HEAVEN

Every believer has a solid hope of experiencing peace in heaven one day. Though we live in a world of unspeakable evils, of endless conflicts, of perpetual disquiet and unrest, we are assured that heaven is the principality of peace. Here, we are threatened by the 'king of terrors', but there we are ruled by the Prince of Peace. Here we are surrounded by culprits that cause us to shed tears, or to mourn, or to sorrow, or to suffer pain, or to experience loss and death. But there, *He will wipe every tear from their eyes. There will be no more death or mourning or crying or pain, for the old order of things has passed away'* (Revelation ch21 v4). In simple terms, so simple that a child can understand, the New Testament portrays heaven as 'being with Jesus'. When Jesus provides comfort to his distressed disciples, he says he's going to return and take them to be with him (John ch14 v3). He prays that they may be with him, where he is (John ch17 v24). Even the penitent thief was promised Jesus' presence (Luke ch23 v43). Whatever unimaginable vistas and inexplicable pastimes heaven holds, there will be nothing to outshine this reality – it's about being with Jesus. Nothing will unsettle or disturb the peace in heaven because Jesus, the Prince of Peace, is there.

2 PEACE OF HEAVEN

However, it's possible to know the peace of heaven here upon earth. Jesus demonstrated that even the temple was not to be the place of lasting peace. Its present corruption (vv45-48) and its future destruction could not guarantee sanctuary. But just as heaven is all about Jesus, so the 'peace of heaven' here upon earth is all about Jesus. That's why it's possible to enjoy the incomparable peace of heaven in the midst of the most violent crisis or shocking drama. Like being in the 'eye of the storm', the believer can know the peace of heaven in the worst of life's conditions (Isaiah ch26 v3).

3 PEACE WITH HEAVEN

If only they had realised that here was the Christ, the Son of God, who had come on his 'seeking and saving' mission. Jesus had come to reconcile hostile humanity to a holy, sovereign God. It was on the battlefield of Calvary that our Saviour and Mediator secured peace for all who turn to God for salvation, by making peace through his blood (Colossians ch1 vv19-20). You cannot 'make your peace with God' either now or on your deathbed. Peace has already 'been made' for the believing sinner. The whole peace initiative has been conceived and executed by God himself through justification (Romans ch5 v1). The gospel we preach is the gospel of peace since it declares the purpose of Christ's coming into the world – to bring peace with God. Let us be among those who have known peace *with* heaven, and the peace *of* heaven, and who are looking forward to the peace *in* heaven because we are trusting in Jesus, our Prince of Peace.

OCTOBER 15
THE GOSPEL OF LUKE Ch20.1-19

Chapters 20-23 describe events that took place during the week that Christendom has described as 'Passion Week' or 'Holy Week'. Jesus is observed by the Gospel writers to spend much time in and around the temple. It's here that Jesus is *'preaching the Gospel'* (v1). Don't miss the significance of his preaching! Jesus was at the very place where hundreds of priests had been preparing the symbols and sacrifices that God had ordained as 'signposts'. These were not an end in themselves: they were pointing somewhere. Here was Jesus, to whom all the Old Testament signposts were pointing, positioned in the temple courts and proclaiming the good news. But what is this 'good news'? It is the truth that God has now sent his Christ to save his people: that in Jesus all the symbolism and sacrificing would be fulfilled. In Jesus, all the signposted routes of the Old Testament converge. But the people and their leaders failed to comprehend.

RESPECTING OR REJECTING?

Jesus tells a parable of a landowner who *'planted a vineyard'*, walling it in and building a tower for protection and a winepress for production (see Matthew ch21 v33). Then he rented out his ready-made business while he went away on a journey *'for a long time'* (v9). When harvest came, he sent a servant to collect his share of the fruit.

1 DO WE RESPECT OR REJECT GOD'S SHARE?

Allowing a tenant to use land in return for a share of the crop has a long history in many parts of the world. In one sense, we are all tenants in this world where God has placed us. We breathe God's air, drink his water, eat his food, and shelter with the materials he provides. But how much do we recognise God's provision in our lives? How much are we willing to give back to God? Do we respect or reject God's share?

God's Share of our Time

The principle is established in the opening pages of the Bible, where one day in seven is devoted to God. The Mosaic Law reinforced the importance of that one day. The New Testament church preserved that principle and called it 'the Lord's Day'. How much do we cut down on God's share, dismissing his day?

God's Share of our Possessions

Deuteronomy ch26 vv13-15 provides an oath of honesty that the Hebrews took when they had calculated and had offered the right share of their produce to God. Could we truthfully affirm that we have given to the Lord his rightful share of our possessions and our wealth?

God's Share of our Energies

What percentage of our ability, capability, and mobility does the Lord receive from us? God's service is not the forced labour of a slave but the loving devotion of a faithful child of God. So do we serve the Lord 'for love's sake'?

2 DO WE RESPECT OR REJECT GOD'S SERVANTS?

You might have thought that these servants would have been treated with respect (vv10-12). Instead, they were rejected. They were either beaten, stoned, or killed (Matthew ch21 v35). To a constantly wayward people, God had sent his servants, the prophets, to point to Jesus, the Messiah. People continue to have 'selective hearing' and frequently reject God's word that is preached exegetically, expositionally, and evangelically.

Do we share the eagerness and examination of the Bereans (Acts ch17 v11) who were willing to check out the Scriptures to make sure that Paul the apostle was preaching the truth? They didn't just search through a few pages to find something soothing and comforting: they studied and investigated the word thoroughly every day.

3 DO WE RESPECT OR REJECT GOD'S SON?

The landowner still had one final option, one trump card to play. He could send his son. The parable doesn't correspond with reality in every detail. It's not meant to! The sending of God's Son and Heir was planned from before the beginning. God wasn't hesitant or reluctant in sending Christ into the world. His representatives couldn't provide redemption, and so God had to come himself. On earth, he bore our frustrations, and he wore our flesh. Jesus came – the One adored by ranks of heaven's angelic beings and loved by his Father. The rejected stone has become the keystone. The stone that the builders discarded is essential to the whole building. Some break themselves upon him in their attacks. But upon all who reject him, he will fall in crushing judgement (v18).

OCTOBER 16
THE GOSPEL OF LUKE Ch20.20-26

Israel is a past master at spying. The Hebrew Biblical history records the missions of Moses' spies and Joshua's spies who conducted operations inside enemy territory. Even today, it's generally acknowledged that Israeli spying operations are among the most advanced in the world. It shouldn't come as a surprise to learn that the authorities regularly spied upon Jesus. Secret agents were sent to *'keep a close watch on Jesus'* (v20). The word for *'spies'* means 'those hired to lie in wait'. We may imagine them lurking in the shadows of the temple courts, on the edge of the crowds, mentally recording Jesus' conversations and addresses. But these spies were also agents provocateurs, eighteen hundred years before the term was coined. Their role was to provoke Jesus into saying something for which he could be punished.

The Herodians and Pharisees, who were opponents of each other, joined forces to lay a trap for Jesus. They came with their weasel words of duplicity and hypocrisy (v21). They posed their crucial question (v22) and waited for Jesus' answer. But he knew their hearts (Matthew ch22 v18) and called for a Roman denarius (v24) on which the image of Caesar was displayed. Responding to their answer (vv24-25) Jesus said (v25):

'GIVE TO CAESAR WHAT IS CAESAR'S, AND TO GOD WHAT IS GOD'S'

No wonder the agents provocateurs were totally astonished and dumbstruck. They hadn't allowed for this kind of answer. But then they hadn't allowed for Jesus. Several areas should be considered regarding our responsibilities to the state and to God.

1 TAXATION

This was the specific question (v22) behind the principle. By paying the poll tax, everyone was forced to acknowledge the emperor. The Pharisees and Herodians wanted to know whether Jesus believed that God's people (the Jews) were exempt from paying the poll tax. All human government is in the context of divine sovereignty (Romans ch13 vv1-2), and whether authorities recognise this, they are God's agents (Romans ch13 vv6-7). Rulers exist for the benefit of society. God appoints rulers who are even godless, corrupt, pagan, and brutal, though he doesn't condone their wickedness. Give to Caesar, Caesar's taxes. They may take the form of income tax, value-added tax, fuel tax, corporation tax, or National Insurance contributions. Our tax self-assessment must be completed honestly. We are required to give what is due lawfully, even if we disagree politically.

2 CITIZENSHIP

As Christians, we possess dual citizenship. We shall want to live according to the standards and ethics of our heavenly citizenship (Philippians ch3 v20) while living out our earthly citizenship. We shall not always agree with the government of the day. We may strongly oppose their policies and practices. One of the blessings of a democracy is that we can influence the election or the removal of a government through the ballot box. As

Christians, we have responsibilities for influencing our society for truth and righteousness, justice, and equity. Lives should be 'salty' and 'illuminating'.

3 LAW AND ORDER

This is a gift of God's common grace (Romans ch13 vv4-5). Remember that Paul is writing when Nero is on the throne and Rome ruled the world. Christians were good citizens and law-abiding up to the point where their allegiance to Christ would have been compromised by allegiance to the emperor. At that point, they followed the example and the principle of Peter and the apostles (Acts ch5 v29).

4 DEFENCE

Christians have differed over views of war in defence of the nation. Whether a pacifist or conscientious objector who finds war repugnant and inexcusable, or whether someone who believes that military action can achieve God's purposes, such deeply held views should be respected where conscience has been shaped by God's word.

5 EMPLOYMENT

How do we deal with issues of integrity at work – expense claims, timesheets, mileage forms, requisitions, overtime? How do we cope with workplace sweepstakes, staff binges, and company policies that compromise our honesty and faithfulness? How do we respond to rostering that interferes with our church commitments and our use of the Lord's Day? Does Caesar get what is Caesar's, and does God get what is God's?

OCTOBER 17
THE GOSPEL OF LUKE Ch20.27-47

BE SURE AND BEWARE!

Marrying a brother's widow, as a means of maintaining her welfare and ensuring the rights of an heir, can still be found in some African cultures. It was certainly a part of Judaism (Deuteronomy ch25 vv5-10) in which a brother was obliged to marry the widow of a childless deceased brother, with the firstborn child being treated as the child of the deceased brother. It was this matter of 'levirate marriage' that was on the Sadducees' minds when they approached Jesus with their question (vv28-33).

1 WHOSE WIFE?

The Sadducees were a Jewish sect that rivalled the Pharisees. They had been founded in the second century BC and followed the Hebrew Bible quite literally, rejecting the Pharisees' oral interpretations. But the Sadducees denied the existence of angels and spirits; neither did they believe in the immortality of the soul or a resurrection. That's why they asked Jesus this hypothetical question about levirate marriage to demonstrate the nonsense of belief in a resurrection. They imagined a woman who had seven husbands, six of them by levirate marriage. In a post-resurrection world, the monogamous wife is confronted with seven legal husbands. Presupposing that there is a resurrection, the Sadducees wanted to know: *'whose wife will she be...?'* (v33). They thought that they had set a clever trap for Jesus, but he spoke about:

Characteristics of the Resurrection

Unlike the people of this age who *'marry and are given in marriage'* (v34), this will not feature in the afterlife. Those who live life in the New Order will not be constrained by the characteristics of the Old Order, such as marriage and death.

Children of the Resurrection

'They are God's children...' (v36) These are the children who qualify for the resurrection to eternal life. We must not confuse *'considered worthy'* with anything we may have achieved or contributed. Access to heaven is all about the worthiness of Jesus and what he has achieved through his death and resurrection. We can only qualify through faith in Christ.

Evidence for the Resurrection

Jesus proves from the Old Testament Scriptures that the resurrection is not some new, wacky teaching. He could have cited Job ch19 v26 or Daniel ch12 v2, but, instead, he quotes from the Books of Moses that were held in the highest regard by the Sadducees (Exodus ch3 vv2-6). The living God uses the present tense to describe himself as the God of Abraham, Isaac, and Jacob. His divine title is proof that the patriarchs still exist, and therefore, there must be resurrection.

2 WHOSE SON?

Son of David

The Jews believed that Christ (the Messiah) would be the Son of David. But David himself refers to Christ as *'my Lord'* (Psalm 110 v1).

Son of God

Jesus challenged them to consider the deity of Christ. How could David refer to his future descendant as his Lord (the title of God) unless he was the Son of God? The enemies of the church have sought to undermine the deity and the humanity of Christ with their convoluted teachings:

APOLLINARIANISM – Christ had a human body and a divine mind.

NESTORIANISM – Christ was two separate persons – human and divine.

EUTYCHIANISM – Christ's human nature is absorbed into his divine nature.

The fifth-century church was prompted to set out a Biblical statement asserting that.

Jesus is perfectly man and perfectly God at the same time.

Jesus is equal with God the Father in terms of Godhood and equal with humanity in his Manhood, but without sin.

He is one Person, not two persons, with two natures *'inconfusedly, unchangeably, indivisibly, inseparably'* in one Person [Council of Chalcedon AD451].

He is the eternal Son of God, the only Begotten, the Word, the Lord Jesus Christ.

We should be encouraged to heed these injunctions:

BE SURE!

We must know that this competent, capable, and fully qualified Jesus is our Lord and Saviour. This priority should take precedence over all others.

BEWARE!

Be on guard against the theologians and churchmen who make a profession out of their religion (vv45-47) and who would deceive us about Christ, the Bible, the gospel, and about salvation by faith in Christ alone.

OCTOBER 18
THE GOSPEL OF LUKE Ch21.1-19

THE BEGINNING OF THE END

If you knew that you only had a week to go, how would you live it? Jesus is well into his final week before the cross. He spent each day at the temple, and he spent each night on the Mount of Olives (vv37-38). Every morning, Jesus would make his way to the temple courts where huge crowds assembled to hear him preach. On this occasion, Jesus was sitting opposite the treasury, which was situated in the Court of Women or in a room adjacent to it. Among the rich people who threw much money into the offertory boxes, a poor woman deposited two copper coins, equal to one hundredth of the average daily wage. She didn't give much in terms of value, but Jesus knew that she had given everything (v4) and therefore she had given the most. The important thing is not the amount we give but the percentage that we have left over.

The large ornately decorated blocks of the temple attracted comments from the disciples, but Jesus stuns them when he reveals that they will not be left located one upon another (v6). They will all be thrown down. This prompts the disciples' question: 'When?' (v7) The destruction of the temple in AD70 would be accompanied by the slaughter of hundreds of thousands of Jews. Such a historical event in the divine programme must not be overlooked. But AD70 would also mark the introduction of a new era – the beginning of the end. From that time until the moment when the Son of Man returns in great glory, there is going to be the fulfilment of Jesus' words.

1 DON'T BE SEDUCED! (v8)

The word for *'deceived'* means 'to go astray', 'to wander'. It gives us our English word 'planet' as it was considered to be a 'wandering star'. The word was frequently used by the early church fathers to describe the seductive words and activities of heretics, false teachers, and 'pretend Messiahs'. Jesus takes twenty-eight verses in Luke's Gospel to answer the disciples' questions about what will take place and when. But right at the top of Jesus' detailed answer, he warns clearly against being deceived. That warning is just as critical and timely today. Motley frauds, impostors, false Christs, and mock messiahs continue to strut the world stage with their seductive claims. We must not give credibility to men or women simply because they wear dog collars or religious fancy dress, or because they are good orators, or are very intelligent, or because they have good memories or siren voices. The key question is whether they are faithful in proclaiming unadulterated Biblical truth.

2 DON'T BE SCARED! (vv9-11)

God's people who genuinely trust in Him should not become terrified of events that happen around them in the world. There have been paranormal phenomena, inexplicable mysteries, and disturbing events in every generation. Demonic powers, astral apparitions, extra-terrestrial spectres, whether recorded on parchments or X-files, have spooked millions. Jesus said, *'Do not be frightened'*. Why shouldn't we be scared of strange and spooky happenings?

Because God is in control of this universe

To those who think that we live in a runaway world, with no one to steer the wheel or apply the brakes, the Bible tells us that God is in control (Hebrews ch1 v3; Colossians ch1 v17).

Because God is in control of our lives

There are no accidents in the life of a Christian (Romans ch8 v28). It's faith, not fear, that should guide and influence our lives.

3 DON'T BE SWAYED! (vv12-19)

Persecution will be conducted by civil governments and religious authorities, as well as by families and friends, but *'by standing firm you will gain life'* (v19). God will give us:

Unshakeable Witness (v13)

You may feel neither courageous nor eloquent, but be assured that God will supply all you need at precisely the right time.

Uncontradictable Words (v15)

During the judicial trials and subsequent sufferings of God's people through history, their testimony in the hour of gruelling interrogation has been compellingly truthful and eloquent (ch12 vv11-12).

Irresistible Wisdom (v15)

God's wisdom channelled through his people crushes the so-called wisdom of this world.

Jesus didn't go to the cross for us to be seduced, scared, or swayed by the deceptions and inventions of men's pride, greed, or anger.

OCTOBER 19
THE GOSPEL OF LUKE Ch21.20-38

IT'S NEAR!

For many years, evangelical Christians have been caricatured by the image of a 'doom and gloom' prophet, dressed like an undertaker, carrying a placard with the words, 'The end is nigh'. People have been able to comfortably evade the relevance of Jesus' words by pouring scorn and ridicule upon those who seem to fit those caricatures. But the church has not helped itself as it has been frequently discredited by self-styled self-appointed 'prophets' who have predicted with great conviction that the end of time would occur in a specific year or day, due to the way that they had interpreted current affairs. But all the false announcements of prophecy fanatics shouldn't mask the truth of Jesus' words concerning the signs of the times. He says:

1 THE DESOLATION IS NEAR (v20)

What is meant by *'desolation'*? *'Desolation'* means 'to lay waste'; 'to destroy utterly'. Its primary meaning is 'to make lonely'. So the destruction and devastation will be so comprehensive that there will be no inhabitants remaining. How can we know such *'desolation is near'*? There's no doubt that AD70 has been etched into Jewish history as a huge 'annus horribilis' – a year of disaster. Before the Roman general Titus, the emperor's son, besieged Jerusalem, the Christians had time to escape the city (vv20-23). Thereafter followed a bloodbath of gigantic proportions, with between one and two million Jewish people slaughtered and nearly a hundred thousand sold into slavery. The Jews were subdued and humiliated by the Gentiles (v24).

2 THE REDEMPTION IS NEAR (v28)

What's the connection between the fall of Jerusalem in AD 70 and the coming of the Son of Man in power and glory? These events mark the beginning and the ending of that period in history which Jesus refers to as *'the times of the Gentiles'* (v24). God uses the Gentiles to bring punishment on Israel for its faithlessness. The destruction of Jerusalem would mark a period in which the Gentiles would dominate; when the gospel would be preached throughout the Gentile nations; when those without a Hebrew history would turn to God through faith in Jesus, the Messiah and Mediator. *'Redemption'* implies 'restoration', in the wider context of being freed from a fallen world and the ultimate consequences of freedom from sin (Acts ch3 vv19-21; Romans ch8 v23).

3 THE KINGDOM OF GOD IS NEAR (v31)

Jesus tells another parable with a clear and simple lesson. Deciduous trees, like fig trees, lose their leaves in winter. When the branches and twigs become tinged with green as small shoots and leaves develop, summer is on the way. Jesus points out that the consummation of the kingdom of God – the spiritual rule and reign of Christ – will have its signs. The fall of Jerusalem was only the beginning, yet it indicated that Christ's coming was 'near' (see also James ch5 v8). But what should we do?

i] Lift up your Hopes (v27)

Jesus, who suffered humiliation and rejection in his first coming, will appear in all the magnificence of his majesty at his second coming. What a concrete hope for the believer! The coming of Christ doesn't depend on politics, economy, environment, or religion, but on the omnipotence of the sovereign Ruler of time and space, even Christ.

ii] Lift up your Heads (v28)

The believer has no need to be fearful or ashamed at Christ's coming. Godless nations will cower in terror and shame, but the Christian can stand up and lift up his head with confidence because his redemption is secure in Christ. God doesn't rescue us from Satan and redeem us from sin so that we can walk this earth apologetically, as if in disgrace. We can walk with heads held high because of what God has done (Leviticus ch26 v13) and what he's going to do in vindicating our faith at the coming of Christ.

iii] Lift up your Hearts (v34)

Jesus warns about hearts becoming weighed down by a careless attitude to righteous living and a casual regard for the Saviour's return. The Greek word for *'weighed down'* provides us with the prefix 'baro', as in barometer, meaning 'pressure' or 'weight'. The *'anxieties of life'* may prevent hearts from being lifted in worship, love, and adoration. Be careful about allowing our everyday burdens to make us cold and indifferent to the things of God and the coming of Christ.

OCTOBER 20
THE GOSPEL OF LUKE Ch22.1-38

THE FIRST AND LAST SUPPER

The Jews loved their feasts! They were an important part of their Old Testament religion, and, although they were sacred occasions, they were always observed with great joy and celebration. The first feast of the Jewish calendar, and the most important feast, was the Feast of Passover, which overlapped with the Feast of Unleavened Bread. In fact, the two feasts had become a double festival: a double celebration.

Feast of Passover

This commemorated the deliverance of the Jews from Egypt. The blood of the sacrificial lamb represented rescue and redemption.

Feast of Unleavened Bread

This began the day after Passover and lasted seven days.

Passover lambs were slaughtered during the afternoon, ready for the feast which began after sunset. The disciples were instructed to prepare the Passover meal in the appointed place (v12) and at the appointed time (v14). This was the beginning of a devilishly dark night of sorrow and suffering for Jesus as Satan's superpowers positioned themselves to do their worst. But as the disciples prepared the Passover lamb for the feast, Jesus, our Passover Lamb, was preparing himself for the cross. The Passover meal, with its lamb, bitter herbs, unleavened bread, and four cups of wine, was wonderfully poignant, but this was not the 'last supper'. Right at the end of this meal, Jesus takes some bread and one of the cups and introduces the 'love feast of the church', which was to represent the New Covenant to be sealed in his own blood (v20). The 'Last Supper' becomes the 'first supper' of the New Covenant – the 'Breaking of Bread', the Communion Service, the Eucharist (thanksgiving – v19). This is the most precious and privileged of all meals. It's the place where all true believers will want to be.

But there are a number of attitudes and conditions that may spoil this Communion.

1 INDIFFERENCE (vv3-6)

The life of Judas reveals that there are those who live close to Jesus and profess to work for him but who, in reality, may be indifferent and casual towards him, even to the point of treachery. Judas was just a 'hanger-on', yet through him, Satan makes his crucial move (v3). The indifference of Judas provides Satan with the opportunity he needed to checkmate Jesus, or so he thought!

606

2 PRECEDENCE (vv24-30)

Here at the Last Supper, where the Lord Jesus was the supreme central figure, the disciples were actually arguing over which of them was the most important! Jesus warned of two things:

Tyranny

Beware of those who *'lord it over them'* (v25), who flaunt power (1 Peter ch5 vv2-3).

Title

Beware of self-designations to improve rank or status, like *'Benefactor'* (v25).

The world vies with itself for academic recognition, skills' achievement and social status, but the church should have no truck with that – *'But you are not to be like that'* (v26). The communion of believers is characterised by meekness and servitude (v27).

3 ARROGANCE (vv31-34)

Jesus' disciples are also Satan's target. He wants to crush them and destroy them. Peter's confidence overestimated his own strength. To the one who boasted the loudest (see Mark ch14 v29), Jesus warned of categorical denial (v34). There's no place for self-importance or self-confidence at the Lord's Table. But Jesus' prayers for Peter were answered ultimately. There's a Man in the Glory who intercedes for his people and, though they may trip and fall at times, his consistent prayers will bring them through. However far they fall, or whatever mess they make of their lives, Jesus' prayers will always be effective for his own disciples.

4 IGNORANCE (vv35-38)

The disciples completely misunderstood what Jesus was telling them. He wasn't interested in their metal swords. It wasn't flesh and blood that they were up against, but spiritual forces of evil (Ephesians ch6 v12). They would need spiritual swords. But Jesus draws a line under their discussion: *'That is enough!'* (v38).

There is a real need for participants at the Lord's Table to understand the significance of Jesus' death: the reason why he died. There's no excuse for not reading the Bible and understanding the fundamental truth of the cross. Neither is there any excuse for being empty or hollow in our worship as we come to God at this 'family meal'.

OCTOBER 21
THE GOSPEL OF LUKE Ch22.39-53

Ephesians ch1 v11 speaks of *'the plan of him who works out everything in conformity with the purpose of His will...'* God's plan included the treachery of Judas and the tragedy of Jesus. Within the supreme scheme of God, he provided Satan with opportunity – the opportunity to do his most deadly and dastardly. Jesus announced this 'window of devilish opportunity': *'But this is your hour – when darkness reigns'* (v53).

THE REIGN OF DARKNESS

We may observe that there are four key characteristics that are not confined to this darkest of nights. We see them in some measure wherever we experience the oppression of darkness.

1 THE FALL OF TEMPTATION (vv40, 46)

Jesus prepared himself with prayer. But he also encouraged his disciples, not to pray for him, but to pray for themselves, and specifically that they would *'not fall into temptation'.* The fall of temptation is perilously close, and the real answer lies in prayer. Those who walk near to God and maintain a close relationship with him are shielded from the Tempter's snare.

2 THE SLEEP OF SORROW (v45)

Jesus and his disciples are on a cultivated part of the Mount of Olives called 'Gethsemane' (Matthew ch26 v36). The name means 'oil press' and suggests that this is where the olives were crushed under stone wheels to produce the profitable olive oil. The stone oil press is symbolic of that night of anguish that Jesus endured as he was crushed by suffering and sorrow (Matthew ch26 v38). Jesus was under unspeakable spiritual pressure as the grinding wheels were slowly crushing him to exhaustion. But what were his closest friends doing at this time? Sleeping (v45)! Despite Jesus' request that they should be vigilant, they had succumbed to sleep. It's possible for those who reckon themselves among Jesus' closest of friends and disciples to be indifferent and 'asleep' to God's real work and will. They may even be indifferent to Jesus' sufferings.

3 THE KISS OF BETRAYAL (vv47-48)

The posse that awaited Judas' pre-arranged signal of a kiss comprised of religious men. Is it not the case that Jesus continues to be betrayed by religious people who spurn his friendship and reject his word? Men and women enter pulpits week by week, holding in one hand the flickering 'torches and lanterns' of a pseudo-gospel, while in the other hand they hold 'swords and clubs' with which they attempt to destroy Biblical truth. They try to seize Jesus: to give him a makeover and relaunch him as acceptable to our society. They strip away his deity; deny his miracles; cast doubts on his claims; undermine his teachings, and vilify his true disciples.

4 THE SWORD OF VIOLENCE (vv49-51)

From v38 we know that the disciples had two swords between them, though they completely misunderstood Jesus' teaching in v36. Just a short while afterwards, one of these swords appears in the hand of Simon Peter. All the Gospel writers refer to the attack on Malchus, the high priest's servant, but only Dr. Luke mentions his healing. Jesus is never too preoccupied to notice personal immediate need. It reminds us that though we may be violently opposed to Jesus, he can touch our 'ears' so that they become attuned to his word.

Yet, however dark the night we may be called upon to pass through, we must

Pray for God's Strength

Jesus, the Son of Man, is strengthened by an angel he had created. What a picture of humanity and humility! For Jesus, prayer was his daily routine. We should also learn to pray continually, about our joys and sorrows, in the day and the night, about great things and small things.

Submit to God's Will

Jesus' request for an alternative was only if it were his Father's will. He didn't make any demands outside of God's purposes. God's will meant the cross with its suffering, humiliation, judgement, and sacrifice to bring rebel, repentant sinners to him. We praise God for our Saviour's heart, brimming with compassion and love, so that he could pray, *'Not my will, but yours be done'*. Do we readily come to the place of complete surrender, or do we try and manipulate God in our prayers?

OCTOBER 22
THE GOSPEL OF LUKE Ch22.54-71

Among the list of the famous trials of history, both lawyers and historians have included the first-century trial of Jesus. But in these verses, we witness two parallel trials being heard simultaneously:

THE TALE OF TWO TRIALS

The first trial focused on the Accused, the Lord Jesus Christ. It was held in six stages over the space of just a few hours. Jesus was examined by:

1] ANNAS (John ch18 v13) – the previous high priest, who quizzed Jesus about his teaching and his disciples (John ch18 v19).

2] CAIAPHAS – the current high priest. He wanted the charge of blasphemy brought against Jesus so that he could be executed. He permitted his soldiers to ill-treat him.

3] THE SANHEDRIN (v66) – the highest Jewish Court. This Court could pass a death sentence, but it had to be ratified by the Roman governor.

4] PILATE – the Roman proconsul who was in his city house for the Passover (ch23 v1).

5] HEROD – the king was also staying in Jerusalem for the feast. Although he ill-treated Jesus, he wouldn't pronounce judgement on him (ch23 vv6-12).

6] PILATE – eventually Pilate is pressured into permitting Jesus to be crucified (ch23 v25).

But it was a travesty of a trial for, even by their own laws, the Jewish authorities had made the court's jurisdiction null and void on several counts.

VENUE: It was in the high priest's house when it should have been the temple.

DATE: It was forbidden to try anyone on a feast day.

TIME: The first part of the examination took place at night, which was prohibited.

NO DEFENCE: Jesus was tried without a proper legal defence.

TESTIMONY: There was contradictory testimony (Mark ch14 v56) which nullifies the evidence.

CHARGE: Technically, Jesus didn't pronounce the divine name.

PRONOUNCEMENT OF GUILT: The least senior members should decide first.

VERDICT: Conviction and sentence couldn't take place on the same day.

INCRIMINATION: Jesus was forced to incriminate himself under oath.

TREATMENT: Jesus was beaten before his trial and struck in the face in court (John ch18 v22).

Jesus had been denied the most basic of rights, which were accorded to the lowliest of citizens. But this is another indicator of the depths to which Jesus descended to become the Saviour of his people. He who possessed all divine rights was stripped of all human rights. He who was and is everything was made as nothing (2 Corinthians ch8 v9).

The One who is the righteous Judge of all the earth, and who sits in the Supreme Court of the universe, willingly subjected himself to the false verdict of a corrupt judiciary.

But another trial was taking place. While Jesus was on trial for his deity, Peter was on trial for his loyalty. Jesus affirmed he was the Christ but denied himself. Peter saved himself but denied Christ.

1st DENIAL- PETER DENIED AWARENESS OF JESUS (v57)

Peter claimed not to know the One who had been his most loyal, faithful, and loving Friend over the last three years. Sharper than the sword that sliced Malchus' ear was the sword that pierced Jesus' heart. How much do our lives deny awareness of Jesus?

2nd DENIAL- PETER DENIED ALLEGIANCE TO JESUS (v58)

He denies being one of Jesus' disciples (John ch18 v25). Are we among those who claim to follow Jesus in church and among other followers, but out in the day-to-day world of work and business, we talk and act as if we have no allegiance to Christ? Are we always ready to uphold the laws, honour the name, promote the business, and 'fly the flag' of Jesus, our King and Saviour? What does discipleship mean to us?

3rd DENIAL- PETER DENIED ASSOCIATION WITH JESUS (vv59-60)

The third specific accuser was a relative of Malchus (John ch18 v26). The Galilean accent was conspicuous even in cosmopolitan Jerusalem (Matthew ch26 v73). Peter flatly refutes any connection with Christ and uses oaths and cursing to enforce his denial. But as he was protesting any link with Jesus, the 'alarm cock' went off! Jesus' penetrating gaze of love and concern (v61) reduced Peter to floods of bitter tears. If only he could have lived the last couple of hours again! But Jesus is a great forgiver to those who are sincerely sorry. The way back to God is through regret, remorse, and repentance.

OCTOBER 23
THE GOSPEL OF LUKE Ch23.1-25

Pontius Pilate had travelled to Jerusalem from his headquarters at Caesarea. Along with King Herod and thousands of Jews and proselytes, Pilate attended the Feast of Passover. But the central figure in this passage is Jesus. Despised and humiliated, the Lord commands our full attention as we read these final minutes before the cross.

1 NO GUILT

In his three previous examinations before Annas (John ch18 v22), Caiaphas and the Sanhedrin (Matthew ch26 vv59-60), there is no hint of any guilt which can be attributed to Jesus. Now, neither Pilate nor Herod finds any basis for a charge against him (vv4, 14, 15). Pilate confronts the crowd for the third time (v22) and declares that he finds no grounds for the death penalty. Pilate's own wife referred to Jesus as *'that innocent man'* (Matthew ch27 v19). The Jews had brought three specific charges against Jesus (v2):

Subversion

They were suggesting that Jesus was a religious agitator or a militant activist;

Secession

Their claim that Jesus had opposed taxes was ludicrous (see ch20 v25);

Sedition

They tried to portray Jesus as a king who would overthrow the government.

But Jesus, the sinless Saviour, was innocent of all charges. Yet theologians in many centuries have argued that Jesus' sinlessness was neither possible nor necessary.

If Jesus is not the Son of God, then it was impossible for him not to sin. But if Jesus is the Son of God, then it was impossible for him to sin. Jesus asked his enemies, *'Can any of you prove me guilty of sin?'* (John ch8 v46). No answer! But in Jesus there was no sin (1 John ch3 v5). *'He committed no sin'* (1 Peter ch2 v22) and he *'had no sin'* (2 Corinthians ch5 v21).

Matthew reports Pilate's famous hand-washing incident (Matthew ch27 v24), but, far from any innocence on Pilate's part, he permitted Jesus to be crucified and Barabbas to be released.

2 NO ANSWER

Pilate thought he could 'pass the buck' to King Herod when he realised that Jesus was Galilean. Herod wanted to see Jesus (v8), hoping that he would put on a 'miracle show'. But *Jesus gave him no answer* (v9). Jesus didn't retaliate to their insults, nor did he make any threats (1 Peter ch2 v23). What glorious, good news is this, that Christ didn't argue his way out of court, or debate his way out of death, but he surrendered himself to the masterplan of God: to save sinners through the cross. It teaches us, too, that when we are ridiculed, ill-treated, and condemned for being a follower of Jesus, there comes a point when silence is the best answer to give. Certainly, there is a place for discussion, debate, and even defence, but there is a point at which the believer should follow the Master's example and remain silent in the face of criticism and slander.

3 NO RETREAT

Pilate has special mention in the Apostles' Creed (*'crucified under Pontius Pilate...'*) which accords with vv23-25. Pilate wasn't the innocent third party that he claimed. The One who had surrendered himself to his Father's will (ch22 v42) was surrendered by Pilate to the people's will (v25). Jesus would not retreat from suffering and death. Although at any time Jesus could have summoned twelve legions of angels (Matthew ch26 v53), he knew that the pathway of redemption led straight to the cross.

Friendship

Notice how a most dubious friendship had been forged that day between Herod and Pilate (v12). Up until that time, relationships between the Judean king and the Roman governor had been strained at best and hostile at worst. Pilate was neither politically nor religiously sensitive in the massacre of Herod's citizens while they were worshipping and sacrificing (Luke ch13 v1). But now all that has been put behind them. How many more traditional enemies have been united in their opposition to Jesus? It comes as no surprise that the Herods and Pilates of our day are locked in all kinds of unholy partnerships with the aim of doing away with Jesus and his followers. But a friendship forged by opposition to Christ is no friendship at all.

The one friendship that really matters is Jesus, the Friend of sinners (Matthew ch11 v19). Pilate made a wrong choice that day in choosing Herod's friendship; in choosing political expediency; in choosing Barabbas instead of Jesus.

THE SILENCE OF THE LAMB

(Herod) plied him with many questions, but Jesus gave him no answer.

Luke ch23 v9

With threatening sounds like baying hounds,

Religious leaders screamed for blood.

Ignoring hints of innocence,

They prosecute the Son of God.

Those scenes appal in Pilate's hall,

Where men, their God, interrogate.

The robe, the reed, and crown, indeed,

But crown of thorns and wreathed in hate.

No lying quips had passed his lips,

His reputation stood intact.

Though men would slur his character,

They could not change this changeless fact.

That God's own Son, the sinless One,

Would not and could not be defiled.

Yet for our gain, he bore the pain

That sinners might be reconciled.

His life refused, he stood accused

Without a shred of evidence.

With none to plead or intercede,

No friend to speak in his defence.

But make amends: you are his friends,

If you obey the Lord's commands.

And for a start, make clean your heart,

But not of Jesus, wash your hands.

Geoff Fox

OCTOBER 24
THE GOSPEL OF LUKE Ch23.26-43

SHARING, BEARING, AND CARING

Calvary had come! The focal point of the whole of time and space, heaven and earth, had arrived. The cross marks the spot! Never had there been a day like this one. This is the time and the place at which all the lines of history, prophecy, and theology converge. All the Old Testament signposts pointed to this specific date and event. This was *'the place called the Skull'* (v33)...*'Golgotha'* in Aramaic (Mark ch15 v22)... 'Calvaria' in the Latin...Calvary. It's likely that this place was so named because the ground at that point was skull-shaped. This was the climax to the divine plan so that *'Christ (could redeem) us from the curse of the law by becoming a curse for us'* (Galatians ch3 v13). Three different people in five verses taunted Jesus with the words *'save yourself'* (vv35, 37, 39). Certainly, Jesus could have saved himself. But he couldn't save himself and his people at the same time. He willingly gave himself to rescue his children from their sin. He suffered alone as the Substitute and Sin-bearer. What do these verses tell us about 'sharing'?

1 NONE TO SHARE HIS CROSS

None to bear its burden

Simon from Cyrene, father of Alexander and Rufus (Mark ch15 v21), was suddenly plucked from the crowd and conscripted to carry Jesus' cross. But he couldn't bear its shame, its curse, its judgement, or even its pain.

None to ease its sorrow

A group of women who *'mourned and wailed'* (v27) were told that their sorrow was misdirected since they should have been mourning for the calamity that would befall Jerusalem and which would affect their children. These women may have been sympathetic towards Jesus, but he wasn't looking for sympathy. Many millions have expressed sympathy for the dying Christ. But it's not sorrow for the Sin-bearer that God requires, but sorrow for sin.

None to stop its pain

The soldiers taunted Jesus with *'wine vinegar'* and Jesus later refused the drugged wine that was offered to deaden the pain (Matthew ch27 v34). In response to Jesus' cry, *'I thirst'* (John ch19 v28), he took a drop of wine on a sponge so that he would be able to declare his final triumphant cry with loudness and strength (Mark ch15 v37). But there was none to share in the sacrificial sufferings of the Lamb of God.

2 TWO TO SHARE HIS CONDEMNATION

Two others were crucified that morning (v32). Here were three men suffering the same condemnation: the same sentence of crucifixion. But any similarity ends there. The two criminals were receiving their just desserts. They were *'punished justly'* (v41). They got what their *'deeds deserve(d)'* (v41). The criminals had done much that had been wrong, whereas Jesus had done *'nothing wrong'* (v41). They were guilty, but Jesus was innocent. As Jesus stooped lower and lower, he shared the same sentence, the same verdict, and the same condemnation as the worst of criminals.

3 FOUR TO SHARE HIS CLOTHING

The final act of derision against the dying Christ was to share out all his clothes in front of him (v34). Four soldiers of the execution squad gambled for Jesus' garments (John ch19 v23). This lottery fulfilled David's Messianic prophecy a thousand years earlier (Psalm 22 v18). But Luke alone includes Jesus' prayer of forgiveness for them (v34). One of the great characteristics of God's family is forgiveness. If Jesus could forgive those who had caused him the most sorrow, and inflicted the most pain, and provoked the worst humiliation, and forced the worst blasphemy, is there anyone that we couldn't forgive?

4 ONE TO SHARE HIS KINGDOM

In the last recorded words of this criminal, which he gasped in agony through parched lips, there is great truth and great faith revealed (vv40-43).

The fear of God

This is the beginning of wisdom for the believer (Psalm 111 v10; Isaiah ch33 v6).

The rightness of the sentence

We have no pretended goodness to hide behind.

The belief in Christ

We must trust in a sinless, fully competent Saviour (v41; Romans ch10 v13).

The certainty of eternal life

What comfort there is in '...*the truth...today...with Me*'. Does that assurance thrill you, encourage you, and motivate you to reach out to others with the gospel? Have you learned to forgive those who trespass against you for the sake of Jesus, who died the death of the cross to bring rescue and reconciliation?

HOW WILL THEY REMEMBER ME?

Then he said, 'Jesus, remember me when you come into your kingdom.'

Luke ch23 v42

Some, remembered for their beauty,

Some, for personality:

Joyful, gracious, warm, and winsome,

How will they remember me?

Some, remembered as artistic,

Some, for their ability,

Others known for their achievements.

How will they remember me?

Some, remembered for commitment,

And their strong tenacity,

Never wavering in duty.

How will they remember me?

Some, remembered for their courage,

Undeterred by threat or plea,

Faithful, even in death's valley.

How will they remember me?

Some, remembered just as critics,

Some, for their disunity.

And their mission to discourage.

How will they remember me?

John, remembered for compassion,

Thomas, for uncertainty,

Peter, for his forthright manner.

How will they remember me?

Luke, remembered for his writings,

Judas, for his treachery,

Paul, for publishing the gospel;

How will they remember me?

Saviour, help me to remember,

Everything you mean to me.

And, when coming to your kingdom,

Jesus, do remember me.

Geoff Fox

OCTOBER 25
THE GOSPEL OF LUKE Ch23.44-56

Many people, including Basil the Great, Jan Huss, Lady Jane Grey, Nicholas Ridley, and even the Genoese explorer Christopher Columbus, have uttered with dying lips the same words that Jesus uttered: *'Father, into Your hands I commit My spirit'*. But Jesus didn't whisper these words with his last, shallow, fleeting breath. Instead, he cries out with a powerful, authoritative voice: a voice that cuts through the midday darkness. Neither does Jesus rush to say something before life finally ebbs. He is in full control of life and death (John ch10 vv17-18). Jesus chose the precise moment when he breathed his last. He deliberately entrusted his spirit into the hands of his heavenly Father. His head didn't flop as the last gasps were squeezed from him. It's as if our precious Saviour consciously laid his head on the pillow of his Father's hands. It was in victory that he died. He had taken on Satan and death on their own territory: he had fought and won conclusively. Christ's death was as decisive and precise as any other act he had performed. Here, in the nadir of humiliation and suffering, the Son of God had the power to lay down his life just how and when he wanted.

What a sun-stopping, curtain-tearing, earth-shattering moment that was! Literally! Reading the Gospels in parallel, four phenomena occurred when Jesus died:

Darkness

(vv44-45) This was used to veil Christ's deepest agonies, as he became the curse for sin. It's appropriate that creation bows in deference to its Creator;

Temple curtain torn

(v45) The ripping of this huge curtain in front of the Most Holy Place symbolised the *'new and living way opened for us...'* (Hebrews ch10 vv19-20);

Earthquake

(Matthew ch27 v51) The earth trembles at the death of the Son of God;

Appearance of dead saints made alive

(Matthew ch27 vv52-53) These godly people enjoyed a temporary resurrection of their old bodies, which was a foretaste of the eternal resurrection in new bodies.

RESPONDING TO JESUS' DEATH

But how do we respond to the death of Jesus? There are four responses here:

1 A SINCERE RESPONSE (v47)

We can't be sure what this centurion believed, or whether he became a Christian, but his testimony convinces us he believed in Jesus' innocence. In the midst of lies and falsehood, it's refreshing to discover this ray of sincerity. We must begin with sincerity, though sincerity alone cannot make us a Christian. There are many noble, moral, likeable, charitable people who are very sincere. But sincere hearts must be accompanied by faith (Hebrews ch10 v22).

2 A REGRETFUL RESPONSE (v48)

Calvary's spectators had a profound mood change. Jesus' death had such an impact upon them that they were in anguish over his death. They beat their breasts, as did the tax collector in the temple (ch18 v13), though we can't be sure that this Calvary crowd was contrite or penitent. They wished they could have reversed the outcome, though. Repentance, rather than regret, is the key element to conversion.

3 A LOVING RESPONSE (vv49, 55, 56)

This group of faithful women had followed Jesus from Galilee. They knew Jesus and had kept watch during those last distressing hours. Now they swung into action, preparing burial spices and perfumes, as Jesus' body was taken down from the cross and laid in the tomb. These women would have remained in the background while the Twelve were more prominent in Jesus' ministry. But whereas the disciples were noticeably absent here, the women were not so easily intimidated and demonstrated loyalty, diligence, commitment, and obedience (v56). You may not be prominent in your Christian ministry, but are you serving Christ with faithfulness and love?

4 A COURAGEOUS RESPONSE (vv50-54)

Joseph of Arimathea was a member of the Sanhedrin who did not vote with them over Jesus' death. He was a secret disciple who had previously feared the Jews (John ch19 v38). But in response to Jesus' death, he puts everything on the line: his membership of the Jewish Council, his reputation, his faith, and his life. Up to this point, Joseph had an unused tongue and an unused tomb. But God was able to use both. He boldly went to Pilate requesting Jesus' body, and his courage ensured that Jesus was not buried in dishonour. How often do we dishonour Christ through our cowardice and fear?

OCTOBER 26
THE GOSPEL OF LUKE Ch24.1-12

Never has there been a greater fraud perpetrated in the name of religion; never has there been a greater waste of time, energy, health and life; never has there been a greater deception foisted upon humanity IF Jesus Christ is not risen from the dead; IF he is not the Victor over sin, Satan and the sepulchre; IF Jesus Christ is not the living, reigning Son of God.

This chapter begins with a new day and a new dawn for humanity. As the women returned to the tomb with their prepared spices (v1), they were shocked to find the stone rolled away and two angels *'in clothes that gleamed like lightning'* (v4). The angels' question challenges the women and every other stumbling seeker:

WHY DO YOU LOOK FOR THE LIVING AMONG THE DEAD?

We must ensure that we search for Christ in the right places.

1 JESUS IS NOT AMONG DEAD BODIES

The women found the right tomb, but they were in the wrong place that morning. They had remembered where Jesus' body had been laid, but they had forgotten his words (vv6-8). They were still looking for the Living One among the dead. Many people are searching in vain for a living faith in a living God, but they have forgotten or ignored his word (Romans ch10 v17).

2 JESUS IS NOT AMONG DEAD ISSUES

We refer to 'dead issues' as those matters that are no longer current, relevant, or important. But the truths and claims of Jesus are eternally relevant and crucially important. We cannot easily sidestep the issues of Christ's life, death, and resurrection. Whether men choose to loathe or to love the Saviour, his power and influence continue to challenge the contemporary mindset from Whitehall to the White House, from the high court to the high church.

3 JESUS IS NOT AMONG DEAD RELIGIONS

The fabric of human society is built upon religion. It may be the religion of the pagans and polytheists, or the religion of the humanists and the secularists, but generally, the world is tolerant of most faiths. But the risen Christ challenges every dead belief system.

4 JESUS IS NOT AMONG DEAD WORKS

There's a widespread rumour that 'pardon for sin', 'entrance to heaven', and 'peace with God' can all be earned by works. This is despite the Bible's clear statement in Ephesians ch2 vv8-9. *'Dead works'* or *'acts that lead to death'* are those works that are ineffective and whose consequences include death. Personal efforts and achievements will not secure salvation. It's Christ's finished work alone that saves.

Jesus lives never to die again. The Lord of Life has fatally wounded the Prince of Death. Jesus comes to us personally and powerfully in our individual lives:

Jesus lives in the hopes of earnest seekers

If you are genuine about seeking God, he will be faithful to you. *'If you seek Him, He will be found by you'* (1 Chronicles ch28 v9). He rewards those who seek him by faith (Hebrews ch11 v6).

Jesus lives in the homes of faithful disciples

A home that has been established by a Christian couple is a beacon proclaiming the reality and relevance of a living Saviour. What a privilege to bring up children to know the Lord Jesus! But even in a home where only one partner is a Christian, there is a special influence and blessing that the believer has in that home (1 Corinthians ch7 v14). God appoints such chosen individuals to that important role for his glorious purposes.

Jesus lives in the hearts of loving believers

When Christ's Spirit is in our hearts, he calls out *'Abba, Father'* (Galatians ch4 v6). The Greek word for *'calls out'* is a word of deep, intense emotion. Interestingly, it's the same word used to describe Jesus' cry from the cross when he committed himself into his Father's hands (Matthew ch27 v50). If you have come to know God as your heavenly Father because you have trusted in his crucified and risen Son, then your worship will not be the shallow repetitions of a casual acquaintance but the deep, meaningful praise of a loving heart.

OCTOBER 27
THE GOSPEL OF LUKE Ch24.13-35

Many roads are historic, scenic, romantic, or fantastic for a number of reasons, but the seven-mile road from Jerusalem to the village of Emmaus became the site of a unique encounter. Unlike the road to Damascus, which saw another divine encounter, the road to Emmaus is not so easily located. Several suggestions have been made, with the most popular location being to the northwest of Jerusalem. But if the physical road is unknown, it is possible to know something of the experience of walking with Jesus. We frequently refer to our lives as a 'walk' and the Bible is no stranger to this theme (for example, Deuteronomy ch5 v33; Joshua ch22 v5; Psalm 23 v4; Isaiah ch2 v5; Micah ch6 v8; John ch8 v12; 2 John v6).

WALKING THE ROAD

For Cleopas and his companion, the walk was literal. They were returning home from Jerusalem, where they had experienced the Passover festivities and celebrations of the last few days. There are lessons we can learn from their walk along this particular road.

1 AVOIDING ROAD BLOCKS (vv13-16)

There wasn't a physical roadblock, but there seems to have been a spiritual one (vv15-16). Their recognition of Jesus was blocked. The two travellers had 'Jesus' on their lips, but they didn't recognise him with their eyes. God had concealed Jesus' identity from them, and the answer may be found in part in v25 where Jesus rebukes them for being *'slow of heart to believe all that the prophets have spoken'*. They were prevented from recognising Jesus because they failed to believe their Bibles. These walkers were well versed in Scripture, but reciting or quoting it wasn't enough. They had to believe it. Recognition of Jesus wasn't just about seeing with the eyes but seeing with the heart, that is, by faith (compare Matthew ch28 v16; John ch20 v14; ch21 v4). We may be 'moved' or 'affected' by reading or hearing the word of God, but it is faith that opens the eyes of our understanding.

2 PASSING ROAD TESTS (vv17-24)

Jesus conducts his 'road test' of Cleopas and his companion. Jesus' question (v17) stopped them dead in their tracks. They could hardly believe that he hadn't heard what had been going on, and so they began to tell Jesus about:

THE PROPHET – but not an ordinary prophet (v19). Jesus was different, extraordinary, and unique. He was a man of God, a servant of God, a messenger of God, and a representative of God.

THE MESSIAH – They had pinned their hopes on Jesus, that he would reign over them and establish a material, political kingdom. But for these travellers, their future had come to an abrupt end at the cross. They couldn't see beyond Calvary, even though their friends and companions were already testifying to the empty tomb (vv22-24). They still had a deficient view of Jesus, believing him to be a prophet, leader, rabbi, and champion, but stopping short of believing that he was the eternal Son of God.

3 OBSERVING ROAD SIGNS (vv25-27)

Jesus points out to them that the path to glory was via Golgotha. So Jesus proceeds in taking them on a conducted tour through the Scriptures, *'beginning with Moses and all the prophets'* (v27). But Jesus' special Bible study was to point out what was said in Scripture *'concerning himself'*. Here was Jesus, the divine Author, taking his listeners through a detailed study of his word and revealing himself. How we need to approach the Bible studiously and prayerfully so that we don't miss the pre-eminent theme, namely Christ.

4 SHOWING ROAD SENSE (vv28-35)

It was at the meal table when Jesus had given thanks for the bread that they had their eyes opened to recognise him. Whether it was the way in which he prayed, or the nail scars in his hands, the Spirit of God unlocked their understanding (v32). Suddenly, everything made sense. Do you still enjoy that regular wonder and excitement of discovering truth in the Bible, when the Holy Spirit unlocks your understanding? Christ-centredness is directly or indirectly on every page of Scripture. We desperately need the Lord Jesus to be uppermost and centremost in our preaching, evangelism, conversations, meditations, and our Christian work, witness, and walk. We have nothing unless we have Christ. What a privilege to walk life's road with Jesus and to know his communion and fellowship in every step.

OCTOBER 28
THE GOSPEL OF LUKE Ch24.36-49

It is regretted that some people have just enough religion to make themselves comfortable and complacent in their own sins. Yet the heart of the message that Jesus reveals to his disciples is that *'the Christ will suffer and rise from the dead on the third day'* – a clear message of *'repentance and forgiveness of sins'* (vv46-47). This is also the message that the disciples would preach to *'all nations, beginning at Jerusalem'* (v47). When we seek God, pleading that he would save us from our sin, we must be prepared for the changing of our will, and the willing of that change.

But how much did the disciples believe in the evening of Christ's resurrection? How great was their faith?

WHAT IS BELIEVING?

1 SEEING IS NOT BELIEVING

The Galilean women, Peter, and John had already witnessed the empty tomb at least. Mary Magdalene had also met the risen Jesus. The two Emmaus Road travellers had rushed back to Jerusalem to proclaim that Jesus was alive; that he had actually walked and talked with them. It was while they discussed Jesus' appearances that he came and *'stood among them'* (v36). They saw the living Lord Jesus in the very room in which they were assembled, but they thought that they were seeing a ghost (v37). How many people have commented over the last two thousand years, 'If only I could see Jesus, I would believe in him'? But here were Jesus' eleven closest followers doubting their own eyes. Even with the physical presence of Jesus among them, they were still reluctant to believe. But they didn't need a change of eyes: they needed a change of heart!

2 HEARING IS NOT BELIEVING

The first words Jesus spoke when he appeared in the presence of his disciples were *'Peace be with you'* (v36). They were alarmed, troubled, and disturbed. The familiar sound of Jesus' voice and the soothing assurance of his tones should have allayed their fears and doubts. Jesus asked why they were so anxious (v38). The fact that we hear the truth is not faith in itself. Hearing is very important as a channel to believing (Romans ch10 v17), but hearing is not believing. Jesus spoke in his 'Parable of the Sower' about those who hear and who do not believe (Luke ch8 v12). There will always be a 'pick 'n mix' collection of churches that will tell you all the things you want to hear if you don't want to hear the word of God.

3 TOUCHING IS NOT BELIEVING

(vv39-40) Presumably this is a reference to the marks of crucifixion – the nail wounds – in Jesus' hands and feet (John ch20 vv19-31). Thomas had the opportunity to hear, to see, and to touch, although that didn't automatically mean that he believed. However, Thomas did believe as a consequence. But Jesus reserves a special blessing for the vast majority of true believers who have never seen or touched. Our faith is not dependent upon the tangible. We don't need to touch some relic like a shroud or a splinter of wood reported to have been taken from the cross. We don't need to touch an image of Christ or cling to a crucifix. We don't need to finger the stone flag on which Jesus stood in Pilate's Hall, or plant our feet on the same pathway that he took to Calvary, or caress the rock from which the sepulchre was hewn. Faith transcends feeling. Faith is not about touching the possessions of a visible god but trusting the word of an invisible God.

4 UNDERSTANDING IS NOT BELIEVING

It's frequently the case that understanding coincides with believing. As the veil is removed from the mind, so faith grasps those things that are understood. But understanding alone is not believing. Understanding leaves men without excuse (Romans ch1 v20). It's possible to apprehend the meaning of God's word, to comprehend its message, to understand its truth, even to understand the implications of rejecting that truth – and yet not to believe. But John the apostle sought to proclaim the word of life, so that others would believe in the One whom they had seen and touched (1 John ch1 vv1-3). Peter assures fellow believers that though they have not seen Jesus, it doesn't mean that they believe in him less or love him less (1 Peter ch1 vv8-9). We don't share Thomas's touch of Jesus, or Peter's gaze upon Jesus, but we can experience the same faith and joy.

OCTOBER 29
THE GOSPEL OF LUKE Ch24.50-53

The two volumes authored by Luke (his Gospel and the book of Acts) are joined almost seamlessly. Luke begins Acts: *'In my former book, Theophilus, I wrote about all that Jesus began to do and to teach until the day he was taken up into heaven'* (ch1 vv1-2).

It's precisely that day, forty days after Jesus' resurrection, *'the day he was taken up into heaven'*, which is the day that overlaps the final verses of Luke's Gospel and the first verses of Acts. The ascension of Jesus marks the end of Jesus' earthly ministry and the resumption of his heavenly ministry.

THE RELEVANCE OF JESUS' ASCENSION

In his ascension, Jesus is exalted and enthroned at the highest pinnacle of time and space.

He was exalted in *'glory'* (1 Timothy ch3 v16) and *'higher than all the heavens'* (Ephesians ch4 v10).

He is now *'crowned with glory and honour'* (Hebrews ch2 v9) with all *'angels, authorities and powers in submission to him* (1 Peter ch3 v22) and with *'everything under His feet'* (1 Corinthians ch15 v27).

He sits *'far above all rule and authority, power and dominion, and every title that can be given, not only in the present age but also in the one to come'* (Ephesians ch1 v21).

'God exalted him to the highest place and gave him the name that is above every name' (Philippians ch2 v9) so that he might be honoured as *'Lord of all'* (Acts ch10 v36).

There can be no doubt that Christ has been raised to the very zenith of power, majesty, and glory. But what has Jesus done for us in his ascension?

1 HIS ASCENSION UNDERLINES THE PAST

This is shown in two ways:

Completion

Jesus' mission is accomplished. The completeness of Christ's ministry on earth is often portrayed in reference to him sitting down. A priest had to perform his service while standing because that service was never completed (Hebrews ch10 vv11-12). But Jesus dealt with sin at the cross in a final way (Hebrews ch1 v3) and so he sits down (Hebrews ch8 v1);

Continuation

We must never make the gross mistake of thinking that Jesus *became* God's Son, or *became* Lord, or *became* the divine Sovereign. Christ has been the Son of God forever, and he continues *'to sustain all things by his powerful word'* (Hebrews ch1 v3). Jesus is the eternal Son whose status is uniquely divine. He is the One who created all things and was *'before all things'* (Colossians ch1 vv15-17). It's only those who would seek to undermine Christ's work or cast doubts on his character who would deny his pre-existence or his pre-incarnation.

2 HIS ASCENSION UNDERWRITES THE PRESENT

Because Jesus is risen and has ascended, we are provided with:

Assurance

He gives the guarantee against every risk that we are likely to encounter. We have a Man who represents us in heaven, One who agrees to personally support his people in every way. Jesus assured his apprehensive disciples of his unfailing presence (Matthew ch28 v20). Although each and every day may be unknown circumstances and unexplored territory for us, we can possess an unshakeable assurance in our ascended, ever-present Saviour.

Assistance

One of the great themes of Hebrews is the high priestly ministry of the Lord Jesus (Hebrews ch4 vv14-16). Because Jesus has lived here among us as a Man, he is able to lavish upon us immediate and sympathetic assistance. He knows our human limitations and human temptations. He has firsthand experience of our stresses and strains, and he knows our detailed needs.

3 HIS ASCENSION UNDERPINS THE FUTURE

Christ's ascension and exaltation paves the way for his glorious return and future kingdom (John ch14 v3). Jesus ascends so that one day he may descend (1 Thessalonians ch4 v16).

The final two verses of Luke's Gospel reveal the disciples' response to Jesus' ascension.

Obedience

They obeyed his word and stayed in the city (vv49, 52, 53).

Joy

They knew that Jesus had promised to return. The angels confirmed this (Acts ch1 v11).

Worship

The natural response of hearts overwhelmed by God's majesty is to worship.

Expectancy

They waited eagerly for the promised Gift (Acts ch1 v4). These transformed apostles would become the channels for the Holy Spirit's power.

OCTOBER 30
ECCLESIASTES ch1.1-18

We all love good teachers. The positive memories that we have from our schooldays often surround good teachers. The words of a good teacher may be remembered indefinitely. The Book of Ecclesiastes is the words of *'the Teacher'* (v1), who is not mentioned by name, but some passages may point to King Solomon (for example, ch1 vv1,12,16; ch2 vv8-9). Solomon, or Jedidiah, was a great man whom the Lord loved (2 Samuel ch12 v24). He was an intelligent and efficient administrator through whose reign Israel and Judah enjoyed peace and prosperity. Solomon's legendary wisdom was God-given. He was divinely commissioned to build the first great temple. He was also a great writer with three thousand proverbs and one thousand songs to his credit (1 Kings ch4 v32) as well as two psalms (72 and 127), together with, possibly, the books of Ecclesiastes and Song of Songs. But Solomon's great weakness was his seven hundred wives and three hundred concubines, which *'turned his heart after other gods'* (1 Kings ch11 v4) and which led to his decline and the division of his kingdom. While a degree of pessimism may pervade this book from the opening cry of *'Meaningless! Meaningless!'* We may get a better perspective by reading ch12 vv13-14. The writer reveals that true devotion to God is the design purpose of mankind. Without this vital component, life is meaningless and mankind is useless.

CHASING AFTER THE WIND

This phrase is used nine times in the first five chapters. Unlike God, who controls the wind (Psalm 104 v4; Nahum ch1 v3; Mark ch4 v41), mankind is powerless, and chasing the wind is futile.

1 WORKING WITHOUT GOD IS POINTLESS

(v3) Frustrations and futilities are universal (*'under the sun'* is used twenty-nine times). This 'meaninglessness' is common to everyone, that is, everyone without God. The labour of life is ultimately all in vain if they are not in the service of our Lord and King. Giving ourselves *fully to the work of the Lord'* will ensure that our *'labour in the Lord is not in vain'* (1 Corinthians ch15 v58).

2 FAMILY WITHOUT GOD IS FRUITLESS

(v4) Human history continues from generation to generation in its perpetual cycle of birth-life-death. Although families may appear fruitful in all kinds of ways, yet, they will only really be fruitful when God is at the centre. Huge inheritances may be passed from one generation to the next, but the only inheritance which is lasting is that one that can *'never perish, spoil or fade'* (1 Peter ch1 vv3-4).

3 CREATION WITHOUT GOD IS SENSELESS

In vv5-7 the Teacher refers to the clockwork motions of the sun, the wind, the streams, and the sea. These repetitive phenomena are testimony to the order and structure within a created universe. If nature and the cosmos were haphazard and unpredictable, then it would make no sense at all. But a creation of order stands as testimony to a Creator of order. All scientists base their assumptions on the fact that the universe is orderly, predictable, and uniform. Today's scientists speak of 'optimum design', yet they are blinkered to the fact that for every design there has to be a designer and to every creation there has to be a creator. Cue the Creator Christ (Hebrews ch1 v3; Colossians ch1 vv16-17). One thousand years BC, the wise Teacher of Ecclesiastes makes the point that creation without God is senseless.

4 LIFE WITHOUT GOD IS HOPELESS

(vv8-11) There is nothing new or valuable if you remove the divine component. History repeats itself. Novelties and innovations come and go, but there is nothing new in something new! Without God, your whole life can be summarised as a dash between the dates of your birth and your death. Living without God and, ultimately, dying without God is the deepest, darkest, hellish hole of helplessness (John ch3 v36). Those who are not saved are *'separate from Christ'* and *'without hope and without God in the world'* (Ephesians ch2 v12). By contrast, those whose hope is in Jesus have an immovable *'anchor for the soul'* (Hebrews ch6 v19).

5 WISDOM WITHOUT GOD IS MEANINGLESS

(vv12-18) The Teacher claims to have devoted himself to study and to exploring the meaning of life (v13). People may increase their intellect and capacity for knowledge, but the application of all this is meaningless without the divine dimension. The wisdom of men is folly if disconnected from God. Even those who have some 'God awareness', and claim to be wise, are mere fools in exchanging God for gods (Romans ch1 vv21-23). But *'the fear of the Lord is the beginning of wisdom'* (Psalm 111 v10). Man's wisdom may be measured in degrees and doctorates. His wisdom may be honoured by professorships and knighthoods. Without God, it is just *'chasing after the wind'*.

OCTOBER 31
ECCLESIASTES ch2 vv1-26

We are all subjected to tests of various descriptions, but have we taken the test that Solomon took:

THE PLEASURE TEST

(v1) What pleasures do we live for? What joys do we derive from life? Are they meaningful? Are they eternal? Solomon eventually analysed the results of his 'pleasure test' and there seems to be three clear results:

1 PLEASING OURSELVES IS FUTILE

Solomon's 'pleasure test' to determine *'what is good...proved to be meaningless'* (v1). His greatness was universally known, and therefore, he could please himself with:

Great Pastimes (vv2-3)

Just like millions of folk today, Solomon may have thought that the more you are able to laugh, the greater the pleasure you will enjoy. But he quickly concluded that *'laughter is foolish'* (v2). Another pastime he tried was alcohol (v3), but concluded that he was merely *'embracing folly'*.

Great Projects (vv4-6)

This included building the first temple, several palaces for himself, planting vineyards, building parks, gardens, and reservoirs. People embark on great projects today – climbing mountains, rowing across oceans, founding humanitarian organisations – but these only provide temporary pleasure.

Great Possessions (vv7-8)

There was no one like Solomon in his accumulation of wealth. He had incomparable buying power. Everything in his palace was made of pure gold (1 Kings ch10 v21) and in Jerusalem he *'made silver as common... as stones'* (1 Kings ch10 v27). The exotic Queen of Sheba went to see for herself and commented that *'not even the half was told me'* (1 Kings ch10 v7).

Great Prestige (v9)

Solomon became the greatest man that Jerusalem had ever seen. He had all the fame, success, and adulation that anyone could have wished for in their wildest dreams. People constantly long for that 'big break' that will propel them into celebrity status with all its popularity and wealth.

But even with all Solomon's inestimable greatness, Jesus revealed that in himself, *'one greater than Solomon is here'* (Matthew ch12 v42). Jesus is the 'X Factor' that can transform the person who comes in humble repentance and simple faith to trust in his wonderful salvation.

2 PLEASING OUR SUCCESSOR IS FRUSTRATING

(vv12-23) Solomon loathes the idea that everything he has worked for, everything he has created, everything he has acquired must, in the end, be left to someone else (vv18-19). All power and wealth that has been accumulated must ultimately be passed on to another. That 'someone' may be a wise or a foolish person. In one sense, it will make little difference.

Wise and Foolish both Fail

A wise person is not exempt from making mistakes, some of which may be catastrophic.

Wise and Foolish both Die

(vv14-15) Death is indiscriminate, and death is the great leveller. Death removes the distinction between king and commoner, rich and poor, wise and foolish. If death is the outcome for both, the Teacher thought: *'What then do I gain for being wise?'* (v15)

Wise and Foolish will both be Forgotten

(v16) The cemeteries of our land are full of both wise men and women and foolish men and women. They lie side by side in death, with rarely an indication of the difference. Except for close relatives and friends, virtually all memory of the deceased could be erased within a generation.

3 PLEASING OUR GOD IS FULFILLING

True meaning and satisfaction in life will only be found in pleasing the Lord. To ignore our spiritual dimension is folly. Paul warns Timothy to have nothing to do with those who are *'lovers of pleasure rather than lovers of God'* (2 Timothy ch3 v4). *'Eternal pleasures'* are at God's *'right hand'* (Psalm 16 v11). It's not the transient short-term thrills that matter, but those things that are eternal.

Satisfaction is found in God's Work

(v24) We should serve even our employers as if we were serving the Lord (Ephesians ch6 vv5-7).

Satisfaction is found in God's Gifts

The reason why such divine gifts (v26) are satisfying is that an individual may find eternal satisfaction in the greatest gift of God's Son. Jesus and his cross make sense of an otherwise senseless existence. Give thanks for that Gift (2 Corinthians ch9 v15).

Satisfaction is found in God's Pleasure

God rewards the *'one who pleases God'* (v26). It is *'to the man who pleases him'* that he *'gives wisdom, knowledge and happiness'* (v26). Paul emphasises that we should please God in all that we do (1 Corinthians ch10 v31).

'Pleasing God' will mean trusting him in the good times and the bad times. Great satisfaction can be found in living a meaningful life in a world full of meaninglessness. How successful are you in 'the pleasure test'?

NOVEMBER 1
ECCLESIASTES ch3 vv1-22

While outside of God there is disorder, chaos, fruitlessness, and meaninglessness, with God at the centre of your life, everything takes on meaning and purpose. The teacher of this book is taking his readers on a conducted tour of time and space, showing them that everything is meaningless and repetitive unless it is in the context of the 'grand design'. Until the Master Designer is revered and trusted for what he is doing, life will seem purposeless and invalid.

This chapter begins with the famous passage that is read at all kinds of poignant occasions.

GODLY LIVES ARE MEANINGFUL

1 EVERYTHING GOD PLANS IS TIMELY (vv1-8)

This poetic passage teaches us that God's design plan for time and eternity is firmly under the control of his sovereignty (v1). Not only is this true in our natural world, where life cycles and productivity follow seasonal patterns, but this is true for all of us in our personal world. However, if we are no more than *'blobs of inanimate matter'* or *'computers made of meat'* (as someone has referred to humanity), then what's the point? Indeed, if everything is just a huge game of chance, and life is just *'millions of mindless accidents'*, then life is meaningless. Life is nothing more than a fantastic fluke. Yet the Bible student needs to venture no further than the opening verse of God's word to discover exactly why the universe is exactly the way it is (Genesis ch1 v1). Therefore, everything God plans is timely. There is order, structure, and purpose in God's creation. This is the very opposite of the godless secularist who only sees chaos, accident, chance, and fluke in the world around. In the fourteen statements (vv2-8), we can be assured that there is an overruling providence. The Christian, who is trusting in Jesus, can be certain that the memorable and momentous milestones of life are under the ultimate control and direction of God. He is never the author of evil, yet, within this fallen world, he presently permits evil to survive. Among the joys and sorrows, blessings and heartaches that we encounter, we should see the hand of a gracious and loving God.

2 EVERYTHING GOD MAKES IS BEAUTIFUL (v11)

Young people may moan that life is boring, and workers may complain that life is a grind. Even old people can comment that life is tedious. Each of these remarks underscores the theme of Ecclesiastes, that is, that life without God is meaningless. It's a grind! It's tedious! It's boring! But to the discerning eye, there is a wonderful beauty in this world, despite the invasion of sin and evil. We are captivated by the awesome beauty of God's handiwork. But the teacher here is referring to something more than the beauty of God's design and craftsmanship in the natural world. He's pointing out the exquisite beauty that there is in God's sovereign control over our lives. There's a wonderful symmetry in God's order and design for each one of us – if only we could acknowledge that. God has a beautiful design purpose for every child of his. Every Christian is a work in progress and an integral component of God's beautiful master plan.

3 EVERYTHING GOD GIVES IS SATISFYING (vv12-13)

'Job satisfaction' is still a vital part, if not the most important part, of our work. Sadly, today, people are not only dissatisfied with their work but they are dissatisfied with their home, marriage, car, health, neighbours, income, teachers, doctors, politicians, and even the quality of life in general. Solomon had been given by God all that he could possibly have wished for – wealth and wisdom – but he was dissatisfied. Some folk are naive enough to think that if they win a few million on the lottery, then they will be completely satisfied. Solomon had the equivalent of several lottery wins, and he was dissatisfied (ch2 v11). True satisfaction is being content with God's gifts and the circumstances of life that he provides for us.

4 EVERYTHING GOD DOES IS ENDURING (v14)

There's a precious permanence about God's work. The reason is *'so that men will revere him'*. God is still seeking to recover men and women to himself, so that they will turn to him in repentance and faith. But they must come on God's terms. There's no room for 'special deals' or 'privately negotiated settlements'. *'God will call the past to account,'* but his plan of salvation is enduring and the saving work of his Spirit is enduring and eternal. Jesus' atoning death and its effectiveness for believing, trusting sinners is enduring. There will never come a point in eternity when Jesus' justifying work will become invalid or irrelevant. God's word is enduring, and his promises are enduring. He will never leave or forsake his people (Hebrews ch13 v5). The powerful crosswork of Jesus is enduring, and therefore we shall never *'exchange it one day for a crown'* [reference George Bennard's 1912 gospel song] because it remains the eternal guarantee to our security.

True satisfaction and freedom from the spiral of a meaningless mentality will only be found in Jesus, our Saviour.

NOVEMBER 2
ECCLESIASTES ch4 vv1-16

We live in a world dominated by oppression in one form or another. This ranges from child labour, where two hundred and fifty million of the world's children work for a living in squalid, dangerous conditions, to domestic violence, which is the greatest form of oppression against women today. It also includes the recruitment of children, some as young as three, to fight in the world's armed conflicts, as well as the estimated forty million street children of Latin America. While these are only some examples of 21st-century oppression, the author of Ecclesiastes had seen it all before (v1). He had witnessed the oppressors':

Power (v2)

The oppressed are the weak and the vulnerable who become victims of exploitation and injustice. The only thing that has changed in three thousand years is the scale of the suffering which the oppressed are forced to endure. This can occur in the workplace, the home, and even the church. Bullying and oppression can be conducted by powerful leaders, dogmatic individuals, and strong personalities. We must guard against such manipulation and even exploitation.

Envy (v4)

While competition and rivalry can be healthy (in school, in sport, in business), it is often the case that competition, covetousness, and envy are interlocked. Envy consumes more people than is realised. Healthy competition can lead to unhealthy envy, which leads to bitterness and anger. Friendship built on true love does not entertain envy (1 Corinthians ch13 v4). Envy can even infiltrate our churches and can be the stranglehold upon some folk who have a fixation about the role, responsibilities, gifts, experiences, and opportunities of others. Even *'some preach Christ out of envy and rivalry...'* (Philippians ch1 v15). We are confronted then with two extremes: those who want everything and the *'fool'* who wants to do nothing (v5; Proverbs ch6 vv9-11).

But in the remaining verses, we can learn some important things about:

THE VALUE OF FRIENDSHIP

1 THE LONELINESS OF ONE (vv7-8)

Here is the picture of the man all alone in the world. He is without relatives (v8), and he is without God. To fill the void of friendship, he works night and day, yet he is not satisfied. His 'obsession with possession' is like a roundabout from which he can't get off. It's a *'miserable business'* indeed. That's a fair description of a man or woman without God. You can be lonely in the middle of a very busy life. Your friends may be a job, a career, income, investments, pension, but if this is all you have, then you are very lonely. The friendship of God can transform such a lonely life.

2 THE FRIENDSHIP OF TWO (vv9-12a)

Three benefits of friendship are listed:

Wealth (v9)

Good partnerships built on solid relationships can be very profitable.

Welfare (v10)

Friends are invaluable when in need, whether that need is falling, failing, or floundering.

Warmth (v11)

As well as physical warmth, there is spiritual warmth in true friendship.

'A friend loves at all times' (Proverbs ch17 v17). David and Jonathan built a lasting friendship which could not be destroyed by family hostility, envy, intimidation, treachery, or force. Jonathan and David stuck closer together than brothers (Proverbs ch18 v24). Such a relationship proves that friends are often closer than relations (Proverbs ch27 v10). Of course, the best way to get a friend is to be one! Jesus referred to his obedient servants as his *'friends'*. These were those for whom he would lay down his life (John ch15 vv13-15). To be a friend of Jesus means renouncing the world's claims, values, and attractions (James ch4 v4). God spoke with Moses as a friend (Exodus ch33 v11). A wonderful tribute to Abraham's faithfulness was that he was widely known as the friend of God (2 Chronicles ch20 v7). What an inscription for a person's headstone: 'Friend of God'.

3 THE SECURITY OF THREE (v12b)

Three strands in a rope are better than two strands. It is a fact that in friendships, marriages, and churches, the third strand – the Person of Jesus Christ – ensures security. The Lord's beloved can rest securely between his divine shoulders (Deuteronomy ch33 v12). Such a secure place is the place of power for the *'government will be on his shoulders'* (Isaiah ch9 v6). It's also the place of eternal salvation. The shepherd put the sheep on his shoulders to take it home (Luke ch15 vv5-6). With Jesus in our three-stranded cord, it will never be broken. It is forever secure. But it not only needs the three strands for security, it also needs them tightly and neatly woven together for unity. That may be an illustration of the life of our church and fellowship. We need to be knitted together as one. If there is no unity, no common purpose or objective, no overlap and underlay of God's love through his people, then that cord is in danger of parting altogether. Real unity as friends is to be united in the Person of Jesus, *'making every effort to keep the unity of the Spirit through the bond of peace'* (Ephesians ch4 vv2-3).

NOVEMBER 3
ECCLESIASTES ch5.1-20

Solomon had been chosen by God to build the first magnificent temple in Jerusalem (1 Chronicles ch28 v6). It was a huge construction project that took seven years to complete, employing tens of thousands of builders. The temple was patterned on the tabernacle, and both were places where God chose to represent his presence in a powerful way. When the temple had been completed, 1 Kings ch8 v11 informs us that *'the glory of the Lord filled his temple'*. Such a place cannot, therefore, be entered casually or lightly. So the Preacher warns:

WATCH YOUR STEP!

Or: *'Guard your steps when you go to the house of God'* (v1). The instructions and principles emphasised here are just as important for us today. We may talk about 'family worship' or 'contemporary worship' (whatever is meant by that), but unless it is humble, respectful, reverent worship, it's not 'worship' at all! So we must be careful to:

1 PRAY REVERENTLY (vv1-3)

Listening is more important than speaking (vv1,2). The effectiveness of our prayers is not measured by eloquence but by reverence. The story Jesus told (Luke ch18) about the proud, boastful Pharisee and the humble, penitent tax collector shows the folly of much speaking, especially when it's self-centred. One pleaded his merits while the other pleaded God's mercy. The Pharisee may have sounded eloquent, religious, and super-spiritual, but his prayer didn't even hit the temple ceiling. The tax collector, however, who prayed with heartfelt repentance and faith, gained an audience with the Almighty. We cannot approach God full of ourselves. We must be filled with his Spirit. We are not ordered to be silent in God's presence but rather to be thoughtful about the words we use. It doesn't mean that we must compile a speech, or be poetic, or that our prayers should be liberally sprinkled with Bible quotations or packed full of hackneyed clichés. But we must be sincere and reverent.

2 COMMIT SINCERELY (vv4-7)

Our mouths can lead us into sin if we are too hasty or too careless in the promises we make (v6).

'It is better not to vow than to make a vow and not fulfil it' (v5). One of the classic Biblical examples is Jephthah (Judges ch11 vv29-40). His thoughtless vow was immensely costly and shows the misery that can ensue. Ananias and Sapphira were deliberately deceptive in the vows they made about giving (Acts 5). They didn't have to give a hundred per cent of the proceeds of the sale of their property, but they announced that they would. Yet they retained a percentage for themselves. Those vows were costly, too. Their commitment was insincere and hypocritical. We cannot afford to treat holy things casually. *'Stand in awe of God'* (v7).

3 WORK DILIGENTLY (vv8-17)

It's man's *'lot'* to *'find satisfaction in his toilsome labour'* (v18). If money is the only driving force, then the earning of money can become a 'drug' that quickly produces its addicts. The acquisition of wealth is the lifelong obsession of many people, bringing with it the injustice that is created by ridiculous bureaucracy (vv8-9). If life is only viewed in terms of income and expenditure, then life is *'meaningless'*. Man has no buying power or bartering leverage in exchanging his soul (Matthew ch16 v26). Only One has the purchasing power to redeem a desperately lost soul (Mark ch10 v45). Jesus forfeited the riches of glory to endure the poverty of earth so that he might become the ransom for those who trust him for salvation. It is therefore in God's service that we work diligently and productively for his kingdom.

4 PERSEVERE JOYFULLY (vv18-20)

There is satisfaction and joy in our wealth and possessions when (a) they are seen as God's gracious and loving gifts, and (b) when they can be offered back to God for use in his service and in his honour. The difference between the meaninglessness of life and the meaningfulness of life is the difference in our priorities and perspectives. If we leave Jesus out of the big equation, then there is a large negative result. But if Jesus is foremost and centremost, then we shall experience the joy that he brings so that we can *'be happy in (our) work – this is a gift of God'* (v19). *'God keeps him occupied with gladness of heart'* (v20). If we are serving the Lord where he wants us to be, then it makes no difference as to whether the work is ground-breaking or back-breaking, rousing or routine – we shall be able to persevere with joy. Solomon realised that during the monotonous cycles of work and sleep, life and death, that it is possible for a man *'to find satisfaction in his toilsome labour under the sun during the few days of life God has given to him'* (v18). It's possible to know that deep-seated joy in every mundane, regular routine of our daily lives: in all our repetitive jobs and strenuous efforts, when Jesus Christ is the focal point and our ultimate objective.

NOVEMBER 4
ECCLESIASTES ch6.1-12

Winnie the Pooh wished to live until he was a hundred minus one day. A Cambridge geneticist has predicted that life expectancy could be dramatically extended to 1000 years within a generation. The Preacher of Ecclesiastes talks about living to 2000 years old ('...*even if he lives a thousand years twice over...*' v6). This Preacher drives home the point, which is consistent with the theme of this entire book, that life without God is meaningless.

IF WE LIVE FOR 2000 YEARS

Unless we are saved, changed, and reoriented by God's grace, our existence is just a monotonous cycle of work and sleep, gain and loss, life and death.

1 IF WE LIVE FOR 2000 YEARS, OUR WEALTH WILL NOT BRING LASTING JOY

(vv1-2) King Solomon's own experience is reflected here. Real, enduring joy does not come as part of the *'wealth, possessions and honour'* package. God invited Solomon to ask for whatever he wanted (2 Chronicles ch1 v7) and Solomon asked for wisdom (2 Chronicles ch1 v10). Because of Solomon's creditable request, God added incomparable wealth, riches, and honour to the gift of wisdom and knowledge. Ultimately, the king discovered that his unparalleled riches and prosperity did not guarantee happiness. It's not huge wealth but true wisdom, which brings lasting joy, and the Bible equates true wisdom with a personal relationship with God through Jesus Christ. The Bible is the key to wisdom that leads to salvation (2 Timothy ch3 v15).

2 IF WE LIVE FOR 2000 YEARS, OUR DESCENDANTS WILL NOT BRING LASTING PROSPERITY

(vv3-6) You can live to be as old as Methuselah, but unless there is a godly meaning to your life, you are no better off than a stillborn child (v3). It's no good adding prosperity to your life unless you add life to your prosperity. Jesus not only brings purpose to life but life with purpose (John ch10 v10). It's a 'full life' for which we were designed by our Maker – a life lived in the knowledge, experience, and service of God. A 'full life' is not just a 'busy life'! Even if you live to see your two thousandth birthday and have 100 children, there must come a day when you leave it all. Any prosperity is only short-term. Even a man with a hundred children can experience loneliness in death. None of them cares about him, and he doesn't receive a *'proper burial'* (v3). Such a man is no different from the unknown child who is buried without a name (v4). Throughout Scripture, children are described as a blessing from the Lord. Yet the meaninglessness of life without God is compounded in our generation, in which children are legally killed (abortion) and in which fierce debates are taking place about the killing of the elderly (euthanasia). Life in our so-called 'civilised, caring society' is cheap as well as meaningless. What hope can there be without God?

3 IF WE LIVE FOR 2000 YEARS, OUR EFFORTS WILL NOT BRING LASTING SATISFACTION

(vv7-9) A wealthy man may make much effort with his money, and a poor man may make much effort with his muscles, but neither will achieve lasting satisfaction: *'his appetite is never satisfied'*. If life is only about appetite, then it's meaningless because appetite is never fully satisfied. We may 'eat to live', but if we only 'live to eat', we are only *'chasing after the wind'* (v9). But if our lives are lived for God; if he is the reason for our work and the focus of our efforts, then there is deep satisfaction (Psalm 103 v5). The effort that brings lasting satisfaction is *'doing the will of God from your heart'* (Ephesians ch6 v6). Jesus himself demonstrated supreme effort, resulting in eternal satisfaction (John ch4 v34). Jesus applied consistent, constant, one hundred percent effort in fulfilling his heavenly Father's mission and, in that, he has blazed a trail for us. Our effort should be directed towards that which satisfies the Lord. We don't have to live to be two thousand years old to achieve that!

4 IF WE LIVE FOR 2000 YEARS, OUR WORDS WILL NOT BRING LASTING CHANGE

(vv10-11) Neither the millions of written words nor the billions of spoken words can bring a fundamental change to the problem of man's sin. There's only one Word that can make an eternal difference: the Word made flesh, the Lord Jesus (John ch1 v14). Jesus is the first Word and the last Word. He is the Alpha and the Omega. *'In the beginning was the Word, and the Word was with God, and the Word was God'* (John ch1 vv1-2). We may be excited or depressed at the prospect of living for two thousand years, but we don't know what's going to happen in the next hour (v12). Although some people have always tried to discern the future, the future is not our business. The future is the exclusive domain of our sovereign, all-knowing God. If we are not trusting in God, then we become anxious about the future (Matthew ch6 v27). The antidote to anxiety is faith: faith in our Lord Jesus Christ. The Guarantor of eternal salvation, the Mediator between God and humanity, and the Anchor for the soul is Jesus. Whether we live for two thousand minutes or two thousand years, life without God is meaningless.

NOVEMBER 5
ECCLESIASTES ch7.1-29

One of the key themes, to which the Preacher returns frequently, is 'wisdom'. The word is used twenty-eight times throughout the book. Wisdom is evident in words, actions, and attitudes.

BE WISE

The fool, without wisdom, is condemned repeatedly for his folly.

1 BE WISE ABOUT THE PRESENT (vv1-9)

In considering the present, the Preacher says that we must be wise about:

Our Reputation:(v1) Men may have a problem buying the right perfume for the one woman in their lives, but imagine Solomon with seven hundred women in his life (1 Kings ch11 v3)! Where would he begin to shop for enough distinctive perfumes for each of his 'special women'? But his point is that *'a good name'* excels even the most expensive and the most distinctive of perfumes. It will continue to linger even when the fragrance of those perfumes has evaporated. As *'death is the destiny of every man'* (v2), we should all consider the reputation that we leave behind. Will it be a delightful scent or a horrible stench? We are urged to take life seriously because there are eternal consequences. Although life can be full of laughter, life is not a joke. Life has been given by God to be lived for him. If life is only dependent upon laughter, then it is meaningless.

Our Humility: (v5) The *'song of fools'* may be 'flattery'. The 'cackling of fools' is compared to the 'crackling of thorns', which are burning under a cooking pot (v6). We must be humble enough *'to heed a wise man's rebuke'*.

Our Temptations: We must be alert to the temptations which can lead to extortion or bribery (v7). Your reputation, like *'fine perfume'* (v1), may disappear in an instant if you become corrupted by bribery and extortion. In its simplest form, it can be something like: 'If you do this for me, then I'll do this for you'. See how easily we can become manipulated, even when we believe that we have the right motives. We can become ensnared by temptations. Jesus knows about our temptations (Hebrews ch4 v15) and he is best placed to provide help (Hebrews ch2 v8) because he never succumbed.

Our Patience: Patience trumps pride every time! The wisdom of being patient will always outmanoeuvre the temptations that appeal to our pride. On careful and honest examination, we can find our hearts corrupted by pride even in the smallest of things.

William Plumer [Bible teacher and commentator]: *'The greatest wisdom on earth is holiness'*.

2 BE WISE ABOUT THE PAST (vv10-13)

How many people do you hear commenting that the old days were the best? The Preacher states: *'Do not say 'Why were the old days better than these?'. For it is not wise to ask such questions.'* (v10). The older we get, the greater tendency there is to live in the past. We may become nostalgic, and that nostalgia is like a drug for which we may crave regular doses. While our memories may be skewed to remembering only the best of the past, the good times and the 'sunny days', the preacher is instructing us to *'consider what God has done'* (v13). Both the good times and the bad times are under God's providence: *'God has made the one as well as the other'* (v14). While God is never the Author of sin, yet he permits sin for his purposes. Considering what God has done for us in the past is a profitable exercise (v11). It is often said that history is 'his story'. Considering God's activity in Bible history and in our nation's history, as well as what he has done for us individually, is both a sobering reflection and a joyful memory.

3 BE WISE ABOUT THE FUTURE (v14)

All the future is in God's control and planning. Some Christians are so obsessed with trying to discern God's programme for their future that they have almost abdicated responsibility for living the life God intends them to live in the present. If our trust is truly in God, then our future is secure. We need genuine, Jesus-focused faith. Paul told his protégé Timothy that it is the Bible which is *'able to make you wise for salvation through faith in Christ Jesus'* (2 Timothy ch3 v15).

Observe the four 'prohibition notices' positioned throughout the chapter:

Do not become quickly provoked (v9)

Don't jump to conclusions and don't assume the worst.

Do not live in the past (v10)

Don't get hooked on nostalgia and miss out on serving God now.

Do not be unbalanced (vv16-17)

Extremism can be avoided by fearing and following God.

Do not be oversensitive (v21)

Don't get 'prickly' with people because you might be like them.

There's a shortage of real wisdom: the wisdom of knowing God. Though traps had been set for the Preacher (v26), he claims to have found only one wise man. Was this a comment on where he was looking? If only he had found that one wise woman to have kept him faithful (1 Kings ch11 vv3-6)! We all need to be reminded that humility is one of the clearest evidence of a person's wisdom (James ch3 v13). Wise humility means putting others first.

NOVEMBER 6
ECCLESIASTES ch8.1-17

Does your attitude towards situations define who you actually are? For example, if you were David facing the giant Goliath, would you say: 'He's so big I'm not staying here!' or 'Wow! He's so big I can't miss!' The Teacher of Ecclesiastes was learning to put things into perspective and apply the right attitude to what he saw. He says (v9), *'All this I saw, as I applied my mind to everything done under the sun'*. In David's situation, faced with Goliath, he applied his mind to the situation. You may protest, 'But surely it was David's *faith* which made him the victor?' Sure! David had great faith. But it was not a mindless faith. David applied his mind to the situation. Here's his logic: 'I have proved God to be my protection in saving me from both a lion attack and a bear attack, therefore, he will protect me from this giant attack!' Certainly, it was faith. But it was faith with logic. He *'applied (his) mind'*, like the Teacher (v9). And wisdom is all about faith with logic. If logic tells me that any God who is truly God must be all-knowing, all-powerful, and all-present, then nothing is too hard for him. My mind tells me that this is the truth, but I must exercise faith to trust him daily. Four types of power are revealed in this chapter, and our response to them.

1 OBEYING THE POWER OF THE KING (vv1-6)

A courtier would swear an oath of allegiance to the king. Kings could be very powerful in Old Testament days – *'a king's word is supreme'* (v4). A king's word could mean life or death. Such a tyrannical, unelected leader could do virtually whatever he pleased. The humble courtier couldn't expect to contradict the king's views or orders. Such extreme conditions could be overwhelming. But the Teacher explains that wisdom is the answer to working in such a depressing atmosphere (v1). Tactics and strategies for dealing with the king will come through wisdom (vv5-6). In our society, with its comparative freedom, Christians should be campaigning for better laws and fairer statutes. This can be done with the wisdom of logic and faith that God supplies.

2 OBSERVING THE POWER OF CREATION (vv7-8)

In these two verses, the Teacher suggests three powers of creation over which man has no control or influence:

Power over the Future

(v7) We are not given any powers to know or discern the future. Our times are in God's hands (Psalm 31 v15). Because we don't know what is going to happen tomorrow, we are urged to say, *'If it is the Lord's will, we will live and do this or that'* (James ch4 vv14-15).

Power over Nature

(v8) The movement of the wind, waves, stars, and planets; the timing of volcanic eruptions; the power of earthquakes – are all ultimately controlled by the Creator himself.

Power over our Departure

(v8) The breath that we breathe is in the hand of God. God is in control of the day of our death. That is immensely reassuring to the believer. Don't be duped by popular comedy or television images showing that our death is in the hands of some 'grim reaper'. The keys of death are firmly in Jesus' hands.

3 OBSTRUCTING THE POWER OF THE COURT (vv9-13)

Injustice can occur even when justice is delayed. The cynic would say that today's UK justice system has a vested interest in seeing justice delayed for as long as possible, often with tragic and unjust consequences. Christians will not always be spared injustice in the court of men, but the Teacher says: *'I know that it will go better with God-fearing men, who are reverent before God'* (v12). They will always receive justice in the court of God – justice tempered with mercy. Life can appear to be so unfair (v4), but God remembers and honours the lives that are lived for him.

4 OBTAINING THE POWER OF CONTENTMENT (vv14-17)

The instruction to *'eat and drink and be glad'* (v15) is not the arrogance of the rich fool in Luke ch12 v19. Instead, this is the contentment of those whose faith is in God. They aren't trusting in their newly built barns for tomorrow's supplies: they are trusting in God and his provision for their needs every day. To be totally satisfied with God is a power of its own that controls every aspect of our lives. Lasting contentment comes from knowing God and experiencing peace with him (Philippians ch4 vv11-12).

'Thou, O Christ, art all I want: More than all I find in thee' [Charles Wesley]. King Solomon had all the power and wealth that anyone could wish for, but still, he yearned to be satisfied. He says, *'Then I saw all that God has done'* (v17). As our eyes are opened to see all that God has done for us - the provision of food, drink, shelter, friends, work, and especially a Saviour – then we can begin to experience real and lasting contentment. Our riches should not be measured by the greatness of our possessions but rather by the fewness of our wants.

Jesus should be all I want, for he is all that I need.

NOVEMBER 7
ECCLESIASTES ch9.1-18

Life may be full of different enemies that may be encountered or avoided in numerous ways. But the Last Enemy – death – cannot be circumvented. We may try to soften the impact of death by variously referring to it as 'passing on'; 'leaving us'; 'going into the next room'; 'final relief from suffering', and so on, but the reality is this: one out of one dies. Sometimes we may describe death as an 'accident'. But death is never an 'accident' for, in God's terms, death is an 'appointment' (Hebrews ch9 v27). It's an appointment with the Last Enemy that none of us will miss, except for the intervention of Jesus' Second Coming. *'The last enemy to be destroyed is death'* (1 Corinthians ch15 v26). For the Christian, there is nothing to fear from this Last Enemy. Sometimes the 'dying' part can be uncomfortable, and sickness can be painful, but death itself holds no terrors for the believer. *'Death is swallowed up in victory'* (1 Corinthians ch15 v54). The sting of death has been removed because of Jesus' cross. Death stung itself to death when it stung Jesus! From a human perspective, believer and unbeliever share *'a common destiny'* (v2). While men may try to blot from their minds the reality of their own mortality, they cannot avoid the inevitable (v12). But for the child of God, who is immovably secure in his love, the Last Enemy is not a foe to be feared. The precise moment of death is *'in God's hands'* (v1). Death is a door to which Jesus holds the only key (Revelation ch1 v18). Believers are not dragged to the grave, nor are they driven to the grave. Death is the appointed route to heaven for the believer. Death is not a terminus: it's a transition. Death is not the end: it's a corridor that takes a believer into the throne-room of our King and Saviour. We may not have an enthusiasm for death because death is the Last Enemy, the final frontier. But the believer's enthusiasm is to be with Jesus: to be released from the presence of sin and to share in the glory of heaven. How should we be ready to meet the Last Enemy?

READY TO MEET THE LAST ENEMY

1 BE HOPEFUL (vv4-6)

We hear the expression: 'where there's life, there's hope'. The Teacher says that a *'live dog'* is better off than a *'dead lion'* (v4). Certainly, it's when we are alive that we are urged to get right with God and to be assured that we are in his family. Death spells the end of the opportunity to be saved. We must all be ready. 'Hope' for the Christian is the opposite of 'uncertainty'. Hope is solid, firm, and secure. It has been said that hope is faith in the future tense. The Christian, who peers through the thickest clouds of death and sees heaven on the other side, is not clinging to some slim expectation. He's not grasping 'hope against hope', as the expression goes. Rather, he is saying, *'My hope is built on nothing less than Jesus' blood and righteousness...On Christ the solid Rock I stand'* [E Mote].

2 BE THANKFUL (vv7-8)

The food, drink, shelter, family, friends, income, security, and peace are all gifts from our gracious God. This should make us thankful. Our lives should be lived in gratitude to God for his continuing love and grace. The best 'Thanksgiving' is 'thanks-living'. If we learn to be grateful to God, instead of taking everything for granted, then we shall also learn to be appreciative of what other people do and say. It can change our perspective on life. One of the antidotes to grumbling is gratitude.

3 BE JOYFUL (vv8-9)

Rather than make every day a day of mourning and misery, we are encouraged to make every day a festive occasion (v8). Life, which is lived to the full, with God as the focal point, brings lasting joy and deep satisfaction. Happiness, which people generally experience, is conditional upon circumstances, possessions, status, or reward. The joy which a Christian experiences surpasses these things even when the Last Enemy may be near.

4 BE FRUITFUL (v10)

Faithfulness and fruitfulness go hand in hand. We are to work while it is day (John ch9 v4) and we are to work conscientiously because we are working for the Lord (Colossians ch3 v23). All our tasks and duties should be performed as if the Lord were our employer. Everything should be done to his standards to please him. That doesn't mean that we shall necessarily be the fastest, strongest, wisest, shrewdest, or cleverest (v11). But we must be faithful.

The believing Christian can be assured of the divine Shepherd's care all the way through the shadowy valley of death (Psalm 23 vv1,4). The shadow will not hurt, and the Last Enemy is powerless in the presence of Jesus, our Shepherd. Death is merely the place that we cross to get Home.

NOVEMBER 8
ECCLESIASTES ch10.1-20

The expression we use to describe a folly, which can hinder or tarnish the outcome of something larger and much more important, is taken from v1:

THERE'S A FLY IN THE OINTMENT!

One mistake can affect a person's whole life. One folly can colour a person's reputation. Such 'flies' underline the need for wisdom. It's the single folly that is remembered rather than a lifetime of wisdom. The Teacher concludes that wise words are much better than war weapons (ch9 v18). So what does this ch10 further teach us about wisdom?

1 WISDOM LEADS TO CORRECT DECISIONS (vv2-3)

In the not-too-distant past, right was believed to be right and left was believed to be wrong! Some left-handed folk will testify to being forced to use their right hands because it was believed, erroneously, that left-handedness was somehow unnatural and even perverse! The Latin word for 'left' gives us our English word 'sinister'. By contrast, the Latin word for 'right' gives us our word 'dextrous', that is, skilled, capable, and clever. Even in Solomon's day, the 'right' direction represented wise thoughts, wise actions, and wise speech, whereas the perverse heart of a fool is inclined to the 'left' (v2). There's an in-built bias to folly and corruption. Though *'the fool has said in his heart, 'There is no God'* (Psalm 14 v1), Paul told Timothy that the holy Scriptures *'are able to make you wise for salvation through faith in Christ Jesus'* (2 Timothy ch3 v15). The wisdom of knowing God through a saving relationship with Jesus will help to keep us on track and not veer off in folly's direction.

2 WISDOM LEADS TO CALM RESTRAINT (v4)

Wisdom will ensure that we have control over the direction we take. It will also help us to have control over ourselves. To avoid our hearts becoming battlegrounds, we must exercise calm restraint, even when provoked and baited. *'Do not leave your post'*. Stay calm and remain focused, even when the storms rage (Proverbs ch16 v32). *'Like a city whose walls are broken down is a man who lacks self-control'* (Proverbs ch25 v28). One of those tasty segments in *'the fruit of the Spirit'* (Galatians ch5 v22) is *'self-control'*. Some people will always argue that they are being open and transparent in acting however they feel or saying whatever they think. But if the presence of royalty or dignitaries enforces self-control, then why shouldn't there always be self-control in the omnipresence of the King of Kings? God's grace is the restraining influence (Titus ch2 vv11-12).

3 WISDOM LEADS TO SAFE CONDITIONS (vv5-11)

A number of dangerous situations are identified in these verses. As with any risk assessment, the hazard is first identified, followed by the degree of the risk associated with that hazard.

Hazard: Ruling people (vv5-7). **Risk:** Foolish decisions (for example, the power to the wrong people).

Hazard: Digging pits (v8). **Risk:** Falling in.

Hazard: Demolishing walls (v8). **Risk:** Snake bite.

Hazard: Quarrying stone (v9). **Risk:** Struck by falling stones.

Hazard: Splitting logs (v9). **Risk:** Struck by flying logs or hurt by a blunt axe head.

Hazard: Charming snakes (v11). **Risk:** Snake bites.

A wise person will evaluate the risks and do something about them. If this is true at a physical level, it is also true at a spiritual level. Identifying the hazards in our lives, such as pride and jealousy, will enable us to assess the risks and to concentrate on 'Spirit-control measures' such as love (1 Corinthians ch13 v14). This godly wisdom not only produces practical sense but spiritual sensitivity.

4 WISDOM LEADS TO GRACIOUS WORDS (vv12-15)

The gossip thrives on information (Proverbs ch11 v13), but wisdom always ensures discretion. Wisdom leads to words that do not threaten anyone or breach their confidentiality and privacy. Those words are never harsh, or bitter, or cutting. He never speaks with 'forked tongue'! That tongue can be a *restless evil, full of deadly poison'* (James ch3 v8), but the Christian who is truly converted is the possessor of a converted tongue too (Proverbs ch22 v11). Knowing Jesus will help our speech to be seasoned with grace, our lips smothered with love, and our tongues animated by wisdom.

5 WISDOM LEADS TO GOOD GOVERNMENT (vv16-20)

The *'king'* may represent any leader, ruler, or governor, appointed by *'noble birth'* (v17) or by fellow *'princes'* or by wealth (v19). But wisdom will be the key characteristic. Folly is noticeable by:

1 Lack of Responsibility

v16 suggests the partying prince's priorities are wrong. Such immaturity may lead to laziness (v18) and other foolishness.

2 Lack of Respectability

(v20) Though respect for an office may be demanded, respect for an office-bearer is earned. That applies in government, business, and in the church. One folly can outweigh wisdom (v1). If we lack wisdom, then ask God (James ch1 v5) so that we may avoid folly's flies.

NOVEMBER 9
ECCLESIASTES ch11.1-10

The Teacher uses the word for 'emptiness and futility' thirty-eight times to describe 'life'. A summary of Ecclesiastes' teaching emphasises that 'life is meaningless – without God!' Without God, life is a cul-de-sac. It's going nowhere except in a cycle of existence which ends with death (ch9 v2). It all seems so futile. One person can work hard and conscientiously, and another person does nothing – and they both die. One person can amass a fortune while his neighbour may not have a penny to his name – and they both die. One person may be extremely famous as a celebrity; the next person may be a 'nobody' – and they both die. One person may live a moral, upright life, and the next person may live an evil, corrupt, selfish, and godless life – and they both die. All are equal in death. So what's the real difference that matters? The difference is in a personal knowledge of, and personal relationship with, God. It is only God who provides point and purpose to life by offering a family relationship with him, through his Son, the Saviour Jesus. This is quality life with significance and substance. This is life that has been liberated from the humdrum monotonies and ever-decreasing circles which end in emptiness and death. This is living as God intends for us to live.

This chapter speaks of investing in the future: living today in the light of tomorrow.

LIVING TODAY IN THE LIGHT OF TOMORROW

Without being too simplistic, we can summarise the three sections with three words:

1 LAUNCH (vv1-2)

These verses teach us some important points about vision and venture. In a thousand years BC, businessmen may have recognised the phrase used in v1. If you have the vision to increase trade, then you must venture. Venturing meant launching ships that would sail to distant shores, laden with cargoes of grain and other commodities, eventually expecting those same ships to return laden with new cargoes purchased from exotic ports. The launching of the ship was part of the vision to progress and develop. Of course, prudent entrepreneurs will also make contingencies (v2). We don't know what each day has in store, but the wise person will trust in God, who controls the future. Maybe God has given us a vision of some task or service that we can launch with him. Like Peter, we may protest that our efforts are fruitless to date, but Jesus told Peter to launch the boat to find fish: *'Put out into the deep water, and let down the nets for a catch'* (Luke ch5 v4). Because he obeyed (launched the boat and shot the nets), he was hugely rewarded.

2 LEAP (vv3-6)

We may be required to take a leap of faith. If we sit around awaiting the ideal conditions, the right factors, and the best weather, then we may never see results (vv4-5). Traditionally, farmers and fishermen have had to take a 'leap' with their work even when the conditions are less than ideal. Trees are predictable (v3). They stay in one place and, even when they fall, they remain where they have fallen. But the wind and clouds are harder to forecast (v4). The moods and movements of creation are in the hands of the Creator (v5), and it's in knowing this that we can take a leap of faith, freeing us from idleness (v6). Don't be lazy: leap! The Christian believer who leaps with God is not trusting in the whim of creation but in the will of the Creator. We may not be able to see the 'full picture' and the conditions may be less than ideal, but we can have total faith in our Heavenly Father.

3 LIVE (vv7-10)

We may talk about fairytale conditions and perfect characteristics as being 'all sweetness and light'. The Teacher says that *'light is sweet'* (v7). Light is particularly sweet to those who have been deliberately or accidentally incarcerated in darkness. *'In him was life and that life was the light of men'* (John ch1 v4). There may be some happiness in youthfulness (v9), but real, deep, lasting joy cannot be discovered without reference to God. This is the joy that surpasses the temporary thrills of life and survives the throes of death. The health and vigour of youth (v10) are meaningless and transient unless life is lived for God. We may recall our youth with nostalgia, remembering the things we were once able to do. Our energies seemed endless. But time takes its toll, and the realities of ageing and death are inescapable (v9). The secular humanist tells us that religion is just a drug to bring some relief to the pain of life, and yet the Christian knows that Jesus is the exclusive source of a meaningful and eternal life (John ch10 v10). The believer has a new identity because he or she belongs to God. Just as soldiers in an army, or players in a football team, or employees in a business may all be identified by the uniform or colours that they wear, so each Christian is called to be identified with Christ. Jesus identified with them in his humanity, and they are called to identify themselves with him in their humility, living life in him and for him (Galatians ch2 v20).

NOVEMBER 10
ECCLESIASTES ch12.1-14

The Teacher compares life to the humdrum monotony of a production line. We clock in at birth and clock out at death, leaving everything to appear to be just a repetitive cycle of meaningless activity. Just as the presence of a royal guest can give meaning and purpose to a factory production line, so the presence of God gives meaning and purpose to life. Once again, the realities of life and death are brought into sharp focus. The Teacher gives such warnings as:

Don't ignore the opportunities of youth; don't underestimate the frailty of old age; don't forget the inevitability of death, and don't overlook the duty of life.

REMEMBER!

Notice that God, who gives meaning to life, is referred to as the One who creates (v1), shepherds (v11), and judges (v14)

1 REMEMBER YOUR CREATOR URGENTLY

Due to the inevitability of the ageing process, with its eventual limitations on ability, and its various diminishing of faculties, and its possible restrictions on mobility, it's essential to enter into a relationship with God earlier rather than later (v1). To accomplish the most meaningful life, we must start early. The earlier the better! 'Remembering' is not just simply saying 'O, I remember God, our Creator' in the same way that we might say, 'O, I remember Harold Wilson' or 'I remember Margaret Thatcher'. The 'remembering' of the Old Testament Hebrew vocabulary always precipitates action. Because we remember, we must do! This is not the remembering of 'passive nostalgia', but it is the remembering of 'active response'. We are called to remember our Creator God and to do something about it. The One who has made us has a design purpose for our lives, which he reveals to us in the Bible. God, our Maker, provides an 'operating manual' of instructions for us, showing us how we can come to know him and to live life in the way the Divine Manufacturer intended. In vv1-7, the Teacher uses wonderful poetry to describe the ageing process and the toll that it takes on our lives:

v1 – describes old age as *'days of trouble'* when the pleasures of health and youth may be past.

v2 – we may recall our youth with delight, but age may bring *'darkness'* and *'rain clouds'*.

v3 – arms and legs get weaker, teeth present problems, and eyes become dim.

v4 – walking is not the same; hearing is affected, sleep is shorter, and the voice grows weaker.

v5 – fear of heights increases, and hair becomes white; senses and desires are not the same.

v6 – a picture of finality where things are severed, broken, shattered, and no longer work.

Remembering our Creator, the One who made us, is vitally important (Psalm 139 v13). Yet it suits folk not to remember their Creator because remembering demands accountability (v7). While their Creator is ignored, people are free to live lives as they please, according to their own values.

2 REMEMBER YOUR SHEPHERD DILIGENTLY

The wise Teacher taught clear truth in a systematic and structured way, searching *'to find just the right words'* (v10) and carefully presenting the message in proverbs and preaching. *'Much study'* (especially of error, nonsense, and unprofitable knowledge) *'wearies the body'* (v12). But the words of *'one Shepherd'* (v11) are to be heeded and obeyed. There is much false teaching and dangerous shepherding in the billions of words published every year. The word of God is to be used for correcting and rebuking (as *'goads'* v11) and for teaching and training (like *'firmly embedded nails'* v11). Such nails are robust and dependable. They will not bend with weight, or loosen with use, or corrode with age. The one book of God's word is not tested by the *'many books'* (v12) of man's word. The Shepherd's word is reliable just as the Shepherd's voice is recognisable (John ch10 vv4-5). There are many pseudo-shepherds around who neglect their flocks and don't provide the right sort of food. Such shepherds are *'worthless'* (Zechariah ch11 v17).

3 REMEMBER YOUR JUDGE REVERENTLY

(vv13-14) The design purpose for human life is given in v13. Life lived without God is meaningless, and life lived for anything other than its design purpose is pointless. To *'fear God'* is not just the terror which makes little children hide behind the sofa, but it's an attitude of reverence and deep respect. Such a fear will not allow us to be casual or flippant with God. We should forever be in awe of his holiness and greatness. We must remember that ultimately we are accountable to him. Our fear of God will bring us to that point of submission where everything is stacked in second place behind and beneath God. The *'whole duty of man'* is to put him first in our priorities, our affections, our attitudes, our skills, and our possessions. Our awe of God should not freeze us with fear but free us to love. When you really love someone, you can't do enough for them. Loving God and worshipping him is the whole point of our life on earth.

NOVEMBER 11
1 THESSALONIANS ch1.1-3

In Paul's tour of the Aegean coastline, he ventures into Europe after visiting Troas (north-west Turkey). After establishing founder members in the church at Philippi, he made his way through Macedonia in response to the vision of the Macedonian asking for help (Acts ch16 vv6-10). Paul and his mission team (at least Timothy and Silas) arrived at Thessalonica. Here Paul preached in the synagogue on three consecutive Sabbaths (Acts ch17 vv1-9). Folks were converted, and a young church, shortly to be tested by persecution, was established. Christian friends provided safe passage for Paul and his team after things turned nasty in Thessalonica. But these young Thessalonian believers were not just another 'notch on Paul's preaching belt'! Their love and faith had made a deep impression upon him. He had witnessed the power of God's Spirit transforming their lives so much so that Paul remembered them continually (v3).

HOW WILL WE BE REMEMBERED?

If we were to move to another country, not to be seen again by friends here, how would they remember us? If, as a believer, the Lord calls you home to himself, how will you be remembered? Paul gives three clear qualities for which the new believers at Thessalonica were remembered.

1 THEIR WORK PRODUCED BY FAITH

These Thessalonian Christians had been wonderfully saved by faith as they listened to Paul preaching in the synagogue. They were Jews, plus a large number of religious locals, including a good number of respected women in society. They had been saved by faith, not works (Ephesians ch2 vv8-9). But while our work cannot produce salvation, our faith can, and should, produce work. The faith by which we are saved is the faith that should be the engine for a life lived in the power of God each day. Our life lived for Jesus should continually be reformed and transformed by an ever-increasing, ever-developing faith. The more you get to know someone's true, dependable, righteous character, the more you will trust them. How much more will you trust in God as you get to know him better each day? The evidence for that trust will be seen in our work of faith.

We shall want to share the Good News with others. Our work of faith will mean reaching out to our families and into our communities with the gospel of Jesus.

2 THEIR LABOUR PROMPTED BY LOVE

While the word 'work' refers specifically to the job that's done, the word 'labour' emphasises the way in which that job is done, that is, with 'exceptional effort and determination'. The 'oil' which lubricates this labour is love. The supreme example of 'labour prompted by love' is God's incomparable effort to 'save his people from their sins' (Matthew ch1 v21). His love prompted him to give – his only Son (John ch3 v16). Such was the size and scope of that love that it didn't make any difference how sinful the sinner was, or how far away he was. Love reached the sinner in the person of Jesus. God's love, unlike human love, is not dependent upon the object of that love. It was while we were still ugly, vile, rebellious sinners that 'Christ died for us' (Romans ch5 v8). God's labour prompted by love should encourage us to be motivated by love in our labour. Sometimes our labour may be prompted by the desire for recognition and honour. Sometimes it is influenced by greed or even the expectation of getting something in return. But if it's real love, then there can be no hint of selfishness.

3 THEIR ENDURANCE INSPIRED BY HOPE

Paul specifies that it is *'hope in our Lord Jesus Christ'* (v3). You may notice that this concludes a succinct introduction to three principal Christian graces – faith, love, and hope. Faith is rooted in the past; love is active in the present, and hope is secure in the future. The Thessalonians' hope was not merely a vain or vague expectation. It was an unshakeable belief in the solid and certain return of Jesus. Paul had only witnessed this quality in the lives of the young Thessalonian converts during the two or three weeks he had been with them. But what he had witnessed was a hope in Jesus' second coming, which spurred them on to endure all kinds of pressures, threats, losses, and persecutions. In a sense, they regarded whatever happened to them in this life as of no consequence compared to their rock-solid hope in Jesus' coming. The Christian's hope is not teetering unsteadily on future uncertainties but is founded on God's unchangeable truth.

Will you be remembered as someone who had eagerly awaited Jesus' return?...someone whose work was faith-driven?...someone whose endurance (of all the pains, problems, and heartaches of this life) was inspired by a firm hope in Jesus, your Lord and your Saviour?

NOVEMBER 12
1 THESSALONIANS ch1.4-6

When Eileen Nearne died in 2010 in Torquay, it was discovered that she had been a secret agent with SOE in France during the Second World War, who had escaped from the Nazis on three occasions. For years, she had kept this secret from her relatives and closest friends. Yet it was a secret that affected her attitude to life and the many choices she made. There are many people who harbour secrets which, consciously or unconsciously, have a bearing on the choices and decisions they make throughout their lives. Friends and relatives may wonder why a particular choice has been made. But it had been made according to a personal secret or specific knowledge which had remained undisclosed. If we accept that this happens among us as human beings, why are some people so reluctant to accept the Biblical truth that God makes choices and decisions based upon his own secret knowledge and divine wisdom? The Bible's teaching about election is a case in point. So when Paul writes (v4) *'For we know, brothers, loved by God, that he has chosen you...'* – it shouldn't throw the church into a flat spin, or polarise Christians between the followers of Pelagius and the followers of Calvin. Instead, we should be ready to accept that God's choice is made based on his superior wisdom and according to a secret known only to him. Why should that pose an insurmountable problem for some Christians? God chooses because he loves, and God loves because he loves (Deuteronomy ch7 vv6-8). The pivotal plank of election truth is not hushed up by Paul for fear of upsetting some church members!

These chosen Thessalonian believers wanted to live faithful and holy lives. They had the written instructions of the Scriptures, but they wanted a visual aid, a pattern to copy. So they looked to the pattern of Paul's life, the lives of the apostles, and, principally, the life of Jesus (v6). The Greek word for *'imitators'* gives us our English word 'mime'. They wanted to mimic character, conversation, and conduct. We may often think of a mimic or impressionist using their skill in a derisory or mocking form. But miming and imitating are also used positively. We teach babies to imitate the actions and attitudes of their parents. Pupils may imitate their teachers. Apprentices were taught to imitate their masters. The Thessalonian Christians became copycats, which is a nineteenth-century expression referring to kittens learning by imitating their mother.

COPYCAT CHRISTIANS

They had every opportunity to observe Paul, Silas, and Timothy up close (v5). It begs the question as to what sort of life would emerge from someone who lived with us 24/7 and, not only watched us closely, but copied us? The transforming agent is the gospel.

1 IT'S A GOSPEL OF WORDS

It came to the Thessalonians *'not simply with words'* (v5) – but it did come with words. Literally, it came *'in word'*. The history of the Bible is that *'the word of the Lord came to...'* individuals. It is the word of God. It may be supported with visual images, pictures, dramas, or even model lives, but essentially it is a gospel of words.

2 IT'S A GOSPEL OF POWER

The Good News about Jesus Christ, the Son of God, the Lord of Glory, the Saviour of sinners, is a powerful message (Romans ch1 v16; 1 Corinthians ch1 v18).

3 IT'S A GOSPEL OF THE HOLY SPIRIT

It is only God's Spirit who makes the gospel message powerfully effective. For the words to get past the ears and to affect the mind and heart, the Holy Spirit must be operational.

Note that Paul makes a distinction between *'power'* and the *'Holy Spirit'*. The Holy Spirit is not merely a force, an energy, or a power. Jesus introduced the Spirit as the *'Counsellor'* or *'Comforter'* (John chs14-16). He is active in our conversion (John ch3 v5) and he becomes resident in our lives (Romans ch8 v9). The only real way that we can have any hope of imitating Spirit-filled Christians and imitating Jesus is to be filled and controlled by the Spirit.

4 IT'S A GOSPEL OF DEEP CONVICTION

It was a *'deep conviction'*, not of sin, but rather a confidence about the rightness and the relevance of the Good News message. Their assurance of its truth made them brave and bold. We don't need to shout or be aggressive in our confidence. 'Calm assurers' are always more convincing than 'shouting asserters'. To be a 'copycat Christian' we should:

Watch Closely

Our eyes should be glued upon Jesus (Hebrews ch12 v2).

Listen Carefully

Listen to Jesus' words and remember them (Matthew ch11 v15; Mark ch12 v37; John ch6 v68).

Copy Clearly

After listing some of the ways we should copy Jesus (Ephesians ch4 vv23-29), Paul adds: *'Be imitators of God'* (Ephesians ch5 v1). Believers will be like Jesus (1 John ch3 v2).

NOVEMBER 13
1 THESSALONIANS ch1.7-10

MODEL BELIEVERS

If a printer had wanted to make good copies of printed material with his old letterpress printing machine, he would need to ensure that all the type was set level, even, and clean, with nothing broken or damaged. He would need to confirm that the type was secure in its chase so that none of the letters dropped out. He would also ensure that the ink was mixed well and evenly applied to the rollers, which, in turn, inked the type. The Greek word for *'model'* (v7) gives us our English word 'type'. Just as the lead type contacts the paper and leaves an exact reproduction, so the Thessalonian believers, coming into contact with new converts across Greece, resulted in other reproductions or copies.

Because the Thessalonian Christians had been careful *'imitators'* of Jesus and his apostles (v6), they had now become the *'model'* (v7) for all believers in *'Macedonia and Achaia'*. So what should the Thessalonian believers and the Christians of today need to remember about those who monitor them as they live their lives in a pagan community?

1 THEY KNOW YOUR FAITH (v8)

'The Lord's message' was heard clearly in the testimony of the new converts. The Good News was *'echoed'* (taken from a Greek word) in the witness that the Thessalonian Christians gave. *'The Lord's message'* is God's word and, specifically, concerning his Son, Jesus. This is the message that was trumpeted forth for all to hear. This is precisely the same message that we proclaim today. Our faith in God cannot be separated from the word of God. We believe what he has said in the Bible. This message echoed around first-century Greece because the Thessalonian believers gossiped the gospel. Paul told them that *'your faith has become known everywhere'* (v8). While we may have many forms of media to communicate the message, the easiest, quickest, cheapest, and, probably, the most effective means is to gossip the gospel, whether it's in the supermarket queue, on the beach, in the street, or over the garden fence. If we live out the life of the Lord Jesus clearly, then folk will want to know what we believe and what we stand for. Our overflowing heart should then find its satisfaction in speaking of Jesus. *'My heart is full of Christ and longs its glorious matter to declare'* [Charles Wesley].

2 THEY NOTE YOUR ATTITUDE (v9)

When Paul, Silas, and Timothy arrived in Thessalonica, they were welcomed by those who became Christians in response to the preaching of the gospel. Their attitude was warm and receptive to the things of God. It should challenge us as to the way in which unbelievers, whom we know and with whom we mix daily, note our attitudes as much as our words. In some cases they may not hear our words because our attitudes are shouting so loudly. How often do we show bitterness, anger, jealousy, pride, and selfishness – not in our words, but in our attitudes? How often does our attitude undermine our word or our deed? We may appear disinterested, grumpy, sullen, unsociable, and ungracious, and that attitude may be remembered long after our words.

3 THEY SEE YOUR CHANGE (v9)

The *'turning'* is crucial. There must always be a *'turning'* in becoming a Christian. Conversion is fundamentally a one-hundred-and-eighty-degree turn. They had been serving and worshipping idols, but now they were serving and worshipping *'the living and true God'*. Twenty-first-century Westerners may smile at those who worship carved images and sculpted idols, but they fail to see that they are also guilty of such paganism. If 'worship' may be defined as 'giving honour' and 'showing reverence', then most unbelievers give honour or show reverence to someone or something in the place of God. It may be work or a hobby, a personality or a celebrity, a fashion or trend, a possession or an achievement, a belief or a fantasy. That modern-day idol holds people in its vice-like grip, preventing them from serving *'the living and true God'* with all their heart, mind, and soul.

4 THEY WATCH YOUR LIFE (v10)

Christians are being watched closely as they wait for Jesus patiently and with confident expectancy. Christians in every century and generation have clung to the promise of Jesus' return, expecting that his coming would be imminent. Christians in every age since the first century have pointed to extraordinary signs and indications that the Lord's coming has been very near. But every believer is required to wait with patience and confident expectancy, busy about their Master's business, until he comes. Paul emphasises that the returning Jesus is the rescuing Jesus. God has raised him from the dead to be the invincible Rescuer of all who trust in him. But Jesus hasn't merely rescued us from unhappiness, friendlessness, monotony, inferiority, or loneliness. He rescues us *'from the coming wrath'* and from sin, death, and judgement.

NOVEMBER 14
1 THESSALONIANS ch2.1-5

In some of our contemplative, more honest moments, we may become keenly aware of our weaknesses and our failures. We may not have been the successful parents that we could have been. We are not as gifted and talented as we thought we were. Occupationally, we find it difficult to do the things we used to do. Physically, we are declining. Emotionally, we are more fragile. But our weaknesses need not contribute to our failure. For the Christian who is trusting in God's word, weakness is the opportunity to experience God's strength (2 Corinthians ch12 v9; Hebrews ch11 v34). When Paul visited Philippi and Thessalonica (Acts chs16-17), he had experienced *'strong opposition'* (v2). This is a sporting term to suggest a contest or a struggle. Paul and his associates had been insulted, unjustly treated, flogged, and imprisoned while in the city of Philippi (Acts ch16). When they arrived in Thessalonica, they had been threatened and pursued by a riotous mob, so much so that they had to leave the city under cover of darkness (Acts ch17). So now Paul realises that some of his opponents are trying to capitalise on his speedy exit. The missionaries are being accused of heresy, and their evangelistic visit is a failure. So Paul asserts (v1) that his visit was not a failure.

NOT A FAILURE

The word *'failure'* refers to an emptiness, a waste of time, even a falseness and insincerity. How many of God's faithful followers today have been similarly accused? Why do they bother to spend time with such a small church when they could fulfil their potential elsewhere? Why put up with people who are always complaining or accusing? Why devote every Sunday to worshipping God when you could be enjoying yourself with friends and family? Why do you bother to attend two services on a Sunday in this day and age when one should be enough? Why struggle to attend the prayer meeting when you can pray in the comfort of your own home? But in these verses, Paul addresses the accusation of being a failure by showing that he is genuine:

1 A GENUINE APPEAL IN THE GOSPEL (v3)

The message of the Good News about Jesus – his coming into the world, his perfect life, his atoning death, his powerful resurrection – is not a fairy story. The persuasive appeal to turn from sin and to turn to Jesus, believing he can save you and change you, is not emotional blackmail. The warning of judgement to come and everlasting condemnation is not a scare tactic to boost church membership. There is a reality about this message, and the appeal of the gospel is genuine. We shouldn't be ashamed about being enthusiastic about the gospel when folk can be enthusiastic about their sports, their hobbies, their fashions, their celebrities and their achievements. There should be a fervour and a zeal in pointing the way to heaven. How easily we can become cool and clinical in our religion! Paul wouldn't be intimidated, even when he was accused of *'error and impure motives'* (v3). Our inviting, urging, entreating in the gospel should never be for ulterior or devious motives but rather because we have a great love for the unsaved.

2 A GENUINE APPROVAL BY GOD (v4)

Paul's approval by God was based on the testing of his heart and mind. With a supernatural X-ray vision, God could see the state of Paul's heart, and he knew that he could be *'entrusted with the gospel'*. Paul was awarded the divine stamp of approval. His mission had been approved and accredited by none less than Almighty God! Sadly, there are too many 'people-pleasers' in the Christian ministry today. They want to do those things that give them the most popularity, the largest following, and the loudest applause. But such motives are alien to Paul. He didn't use *'flattery'*, nor was he *'greedy'* (v5), nor was he *'looking for praise from men'* (v6). The 'marketing machine' of contemporary evangelicalism would have branded the apostle a failure! Yet his claim, which trumped every criticism and accusation of his opponents, was that he was *'approved of God'*.

3 A GENUINE APPLICATION OF GRACE (v5)

The conversion of the Thessalonians had been a testimony to the marvellous grace of God. Paul knew that he could rely on God's witness (v5), but the Thessalonian believers themselves were living witnesses to God's majestic grace. The evidence to counter Paul's opponents could be seen in the lives of these new Greek Christians. Paul was not using a religious *'mask'* to cover up his ulterior motive or hidden agenda. Paul was just as you 'see it on the tin'! It was not about greed but grace. So many within Christendom today are using a 'religious mask' to disguise an unconverted heart. A skin-deep holiness is no holiness at all. Profit was not Paul's priority. Tent-making and money-making didn't dominate his life. Paul was a transparent, twenty-four-carat, one-hundred-percent committed follower of Jesus. Do we share his faith, his commitment, and his genuineness, or are we masking some insincerity?

NOVEMBER 15
1 THESSALONIANS ch2.6-12

When the two major shareholders of the billion-dollar company, Kingston Technology Corporation, sold their shares, they divided their windfall among all their employees. The benefactors said that sharing their success brought them the most joy. Or, to quote v8, they were

DELIGHTED TO SHARE

Those Thessalonian believers, who had been converted when Paul and his mission team had visited their city, were very special. Paul says, *'We loved you so much...You had become so dear to us'* (v8). A deep bond had been cemented between Paul and his Greek converts. As far as Paul was concerned, they were 'family'. God's family! Paul told Ephesian Christians that he knelt before the Father *'from whom his whole family in heaven and on earth derives its name'* (Ephesians ch3 vv14-15). Paul prized the family relationship that is in Jesus. It's this relationship – this bond – which is even stronger, closer, and deeper than any other human relationship. The 'cement' that bonds each believer together is the love of God, which glues us inseparably to our heavenly Father (Romans ch8 v39). But the Christian's love for his brothers and sisters is not an optional extra (1 John ch4 v21). In some human relationships, it is said that 'blood is thicker than water'. But it's the blood of Jesus that unites and binds God's family together because it's faith in Jesus and his sacrifice upon the cross. So we are required to love all of God's children with all their faults, weaknesses, moodiness and personality traits. We must learn to love each member of our church indistinguishably and unconditionally. Paul provides three lovely illustrations of what practical love in the family of God is really like.

1 CARING LIKE A MOTHER (vv6-7)

The apostle admits that his team could have been a *'burden'* to the new converts. The word *'burden'* implies a weight. The apostles could have thrown their weight around. They could have been very authoritative and overbearing, imposing codes of conduct, flexing their apostolic muscles, and demanding that the new converts conform to new practices, procedures, and disciplines. But they didn't! They responded with a mother's care, which is revealed in 2 ways:

They were gentle

The 'motherly' apostles were sensitive and gentle with these 'baby Christians'. As a mother often becomes childlike (not necessarily childish) to relate to her children, so the apostles were quick to relate to the young Christians by interacting with them at their level. A mother's gentle approach to her offspring includes stooping down to their level, listening patiently to their unintelligible sounds; providing words of comfort and assurance, protecting them when they could injure themselves; feeding them regularly, even though some of the food has been spilled and wasted, and holding them when all they want is their mother's presence. Gentleness is one of the characteristics of a mature Christian as listed in the fruit of the Spirit (Galatians ch5 vv22-23).

They were sacrificial

They wanted to share not only the gospel, but their lives as well. The missionaries were ready to put their lives on the line so that pagans would come to know the Saviour. The passion and power of preaching become more important than life itself.

2 HELPING LIKE A BROTHER (v9)

Paul refers to them as *'brothers'*. Paul had no intention of sponging off these believers as an itinerant preacher. Paul paid his own way. The evangelists suffered *'toil and hardship'* so that the poverty of the Macedonian churches wouldn't be made worse. As a tentmaker, Paul knew all about hard work (Acts ch18 v3; ch20 v34) and he knew about the dangers and difficulties encountered in spreading the gospel (2 Corinthians ch11 vv23-28). He endured it for the sake of Jesus and because he eagerly wanted to help his brothers and sisters in the church. How much toil and hardship are we prepared to put up with to help our church family? Where do we draw the line and say, 'That's enough! I'm not going to help them anymore'?

3 ENCOURAGING LIKE A FATHER (vv11-12)

By this illustration, Paul is not suggesting that a father is not caring or that a mother is not encouraging. His metaphors illustrate the closeness of family relationships, which reflect the family of God. If it is true that we all want believers *'to live lives worthy of God'* (v12), how best can that be achieved? Some try to achieve it by threatening and scaring folk into living godly lives. Paul knew the value of encouragement by *'comforting and urging'* (v12), leading and guiding, enthusing and motivating. Real blessing and spiritual health are frequently produced by the tonic of encouragement. But encouragement should not merely make us feel better. It should spur us on to live lives worthy of God. We must learn to be humble enough to accept the encouragement and, sometimes, the admonishment of fellow believers. But we must also be generous enough to give such encouragement and support to God's family members.

NOVEMBER 16
1 THESSALONIANS ch2.13-16

If we advertised that our Sovereign had a personal, pertinent message for our village or community, which was to be delivered at our church at 11 am today, then we might reasonably expect the place to be filled to capacity with many people unable to get in. Yet when we announce that we're going to bring a personal, pertinent message from Almighty God, most people don't want to know. So we ought to address the question:

HOW DO WE RESPOND TO GOD'S MESSAGE?

In this passage, we may note four ways in which the Thessalonian believers responded.

1 ACCEPT GOD'S WORD

Paul and his colleagues were very thankful that the discerning Thessalonians recognised Paul's preaching as the message from God. It wasn't merely 'the word of a man' or *'the word of men, but as it actually is, the word of God...'* (v13). When we come to worship, we have no particular interest in the word of a man or the word of men. We should want to be thoroughly Biblical because this is the living, active word of God (Hebrews ch4 v12). We're not interested in a preacher's personal theories, or hypothetical fancies, or corrupted hermeneutics. We want to hear what God has to say. We have no need to be clever: we have every need to be clear! As preachers, we are frequently guilty of muddying the waters; of making understanding far murkier and making truth far more complicated. We should forever hold Jesus, the Prince of Preachers, before our gaze. Every day, down-to-earth, non-intellectual folk listened eagerly to Jesus' preaching and accepted God's word. We don't need to disguise God's word or dress it up. We don't have to make God's word more presentable, more attractive, or more palatable. We just need to preach it – consistently, transparently, faithfully. We can accept God's word for two reasons:

Because it's Authoritative

It wasn't merely the words of men but *'as it actually is, the word of God'* (v13). Paul claimed to write according to the Lord's command (1 Corinthians ch14 v37). Some critics will try to make the point that to claim the Bible is the word of God, because it says it is the word of God, is to argue in circles. But if the Bible is the very word of God, to which higher authority could we appeal to authenticate its credentials? There is none! God's word is the final word. His word is the highest authority (Psalm 119 v89).

Because it's Active

'...the word of God, which is at work in you who believe' (v13). One good reason for believing in something is that it works! Millions of believers through history have known that it works. Tens of thousands of people across the UK today can testify that it works.

2 LEARN FROM GOD'S PEOPLE

The Thessalonian Christians looked to their Judean brothers and sisters, and they copied them (v14). It should make us more careful about how we act and behave if there are people watching us so closely that they can copy us. Parents need to be very careful around their children. Such children are not able to distinguish between Dad's gratitude and his greed; between Mum's dignity and her vanity. What happens at home is also reflected in the church. Why are we so surprised that children show contempt for the Lord's Day when their parents treat it much like any other day? Why are we so surprised that children have a low regard for the Bible when parents are not eager to hear God's word taught? Why do we get upset when local communities are not affected by the gospel when, in some places, the church is doing its best to copy the world?

As Christians, we should be the living, dynamic, faithful witnesses to the truth in the lives we live.

3 SUFFER AS GOD'S SERVANT

(v14) Both the Jews and the Greeks were opposed to the gospel. Paul says that Jews were complicit in Jesus' crucifixion, as were the Romans. The son came to his vineyard but was ejected and killed (Matthew ch21 vv35-39). Jesus had come *'to that which was his own, but his own did not receive him'* (John ch1 v11). Along with every nation on earth, the Jews are in darkness. Darkness neither understands nor likes the light (John ch1 v5). If you live as a Christian, then you must expect resentment, ridicule, discrimination, and even hostility. Family members may be frosty.

4 SHARE GOD'S GOSPEL

(vv15-16) Although Jews in particular are reported as attempting to prevent the spread of the gospel, it's true that both Jews and Gentiles, religious people and secularists, share a mission to muzzle the proclamation of the gospel. Yet our response is to share that message. We won't be muzzled or censored. The sentence has been passed on those who reject Jesus and his message (v16). So the Good News of Jesus' bridge-building, sin-atoning, life-transforming death on the cross is the news that people need to hear today.

NOVEMBER 17
1 THESSALONIANS ch2.17-ch3.5

If we have been parted from loved ones for any length of time, we may understand the *'intense longing'* which Paul had to see the Thessalonian believers again. The Greek word for *'torn away'* (v17) contains the word-element 'orphan'. This may give us a clue as to the severity and enormity of Paul's separation from the Thessalonians. He had already illustrated his relationship to them as *'mother'* (v7) and *'father'* (v11). Now he compares his entire enforced separation as children who have been made orphans. The apostle hadn't planned to leave Thessalonica so suddenly. He had agonised over his departure and was desperate for news of his young converts. He ached to see them again (v18). So what was the reason that he hadn't sailed the couple of hundred miles up the coast to be reunited with them? He said: *'Satan stopped us'* (v18). It's easy for us to blame the devil for our faults, weaknesses and failures. It sounds so spiritual to blame him for our errors and inadequacies. It appears to get us off the hook as if everything were out of our hands! But we know too that the Prince of Darkness is subject to the Lord's supreme authority (Matthew ch28 v18). So if Satan's plans clash with God's purposes, Satan loses every time. It's also true that God uses Satan's schemes within his own overarching plan. God is never the author of evil, but he permits evil and sin to operate within his divine purposes and parameters.

SATAN'S STRATEGIES

Four such strategies may suggest themselves from these verses.

1 TO HINDER OUR FELLOWSHIP (ch2 vv17-18)

Regular fellowship with our brothers and sisters in Christ is the oxygen of our Christian lives. God wants us to share and contribute to this fellowship. It's through the body of the church that we grow and develop. So if Satan can thwart or prevent such fellowship, then he reckons to have scored significantly. Satan wants to isolate us because it's then that he can inflict the most damage. He doesn't always use earth-shattering techniques to stop our fellowship, but he uses his tried and tested methods of tiredness, friction between individuals, business priorities, family commitments, social events, among other things. How do we view *'the tie that binds our hearts in Christian love'*? Do we look upon our fellowship as an anchorage or as a bondage? According to what we view, our Christian fellowship will determine how easily Satan will hinder it. If we believe it to be the family of God, into which we have been born by his marvellous, matchless grace, then we shall esteem that fellowship to be above every earthly relationship. As the hymnwriter and pastor John Fawcett wrote: *'The fellowship of kindred minds is like to that above'*.

2 TO STEAL OUR JOY (ch2 vv19-20)

Paul is stating that on that day, when Jesus returns in his majesty and power, when he will judge and assess every believer's works, his heart's delight will be that the Thessalonian believers will be there too. That great event will prove the greatness of God's grace to sinners. The joy of the crown will forever complement the justice of the cross. Paul anticipates the joy that these believers will bring him when they are all ultimately gathered together with Jesus. But future joy is only a part of it. There is present joy too. One of Satan's strategies is to deprive believers of that joy. He can make our thinking so self-centred and self-pitying that we lose sight of God's grace in our lives and in the lives of others, causing us to be sad and joyless.

3 TO DISTURB OUR PEACE (ch3 vv3-4)

If Satan can unsettle you, disturb you, or unnerve you, then he believes that he has achieved a minor victory. As a Christian, you can know that you have peace *with* God because of Jesus' death on the cross (Colossians ch1 v20). But while the peace *with* God is final and guaranteed, the peace *of* God may be more fragile and elusive, especially when Satan is deploying his devilish strategies. Paul was concerned that the trials of persecution might unsettle the young Christians. He sent Timothy to *'strengthen and encourage'* them. But persecutions are not the only weapons that Satan uses. Sometimes it's criticism and the hurt caused. Sometimes it's simmering jealousy over the successes of friends. Sometimes it's sickness or bereavement; impatience at life's circumstances, or worry about a situation that gives sleepless nights. With God's help, we can overcome his devious tricks by keeping our eyes on Jesus (Romans ch8 v37). We must trust ourselves to God's perfect plan for our lives, with its prosperity and its adversity.

4 TO WEAKEN OUR FAITH (ch3 vv2&5)

Satan will do his best to disable our faith, even if he can't destroy our faith. The Christian life is the life of faith. We resist the prowling lion by *'standing firm in the faith'* (1 Peter ch5 v9). Timothy went to encourage them and strengthen them in their faith. Our faith is Satan's number one target, and we need to encourage each other and support each other so that our faith may grow deeper roots.

NOVEMBER 18
1 THESSALONIANS ch3.6-13

The famous eighteenth-century painter, Benjamin West, used to testify that, when he was a small boy, his mother's kiss of encouragement propelled him to develop his great skills and an illustrious career in art. Paul is seeking to encourage his young converts. But far from being a one-way street, the news that Timothy brings from Thessalonica is a terrific boost of encouragement for Paul. In the absence of any other information, Paul had to wait for his 'special agent' Timothy to return with good news about the Thessalonian believers' *'faith and love'* (v6). Paul had encouraged these Greek Christians, and they had encouraged Paul.

MUTUAL ENCOURAGEMENT

'The faintest whisper of support and encouragement uttered by a Christian in the ears of his fellow believer is heard in heaven' [John Murray, Scottish Presbyterian theologian]. We need encouragement:

1 IN GROWING FAITH (vv7-8)

The only way to be grounded in faith is to be grounded in the Bible. Why do we preach from the Bible, discuss the Bible, and arrange Bible studies? It's because we want our faith to grow. We need to encourage each other in knowing God's word, for in getting to know God's word, we come to know God. We may be shocked at the images of undernourished child refugees, but we are not shocked and appalled that someone who claims to have been a Christian for many years is so undernourished in their faith. Their limited excursions into the Bible are compared with those who are always 'snacking': living on crisps, chocolate, and fizzy drinks. They never sit down to a good, square meal in Bible terms.

2 IN ABOUNDING JOY (v9)

If we're really honest, it may be easier to say to some people, 'You are my sadness, my heartache, my pain in the neck' rather than to say, *'You are (my)...joy'* (ch2 v20). It's God who is the source of true joy, and his children should be one of the main channels through which we receive such joy (compare 3 John vv3-4). Christians should bring joy to each other. To know that God's children – our brothers and sisters – are walking with God and walking in truth, should give us immense joy.

3 IN UNCEASING PRAYER (v10)

We may be tempted to think that *'night and day'* refers to a morning prayer and an evening prayer, or maybe it refers to the impossible goal of praying 24/7. In reality, Paul's experience reminds us that our praying should be both fervent and frequent. While it's important to have a daily routine of prayer, our praying should not be restricted to those times. We should learn to live, work, and breathe in an atmosphere of a prayerful relationship with God. Paul prayed for two things:

To see them

This was Paul's burden (ch2 v18; ch3 v6). Paul's young fellow-believers were his legitimate concern. How enthusiastically do we pray for our fellow-believers? Paul wanted to see these Christians again. He wasn't praying about a reunion party or a celebration dinner or anything like that. He wanted to see them. But why?

To supply them

He wanted to make up for any deficiencies in their faith (v10). A daily walk with Jesus means increasing our faith and dependence upon him. We can motivate and encourage each other to trust God.

4 IN INCREASING LOVE (v12)

Love between believers needs to be nurtured so that it grows and overflows. We talk, preach, and write about 'Christian love,' but do we foster it and encourage it? What changes could we expect to take place if we really learned to encourage one another in love, by loving them? If anything will change a person, it's warm, genuine, practical love. This is the love that's patient and kind. It's neither self-centred nor self-seeking. It's not easily angered and keeps no record of wrongs. It always protects, trusts, hopes, and perseveres. It never fails. It's the stuff of 1 Corinthians ch13.

5 IN STRENGTHENING HEARTS (v13)

Christian conduct is inseparable from Christian character, and therefore, 'strong hearts' lead to blamelessness and holiness. The final day of accounting will take place at Jesus' coming when believers' character and conduct will be assessed. This final accounting should focus our minds as we try to live blamelessly in anticipating Jesus' return. Paul's prayer for strengthening is important, just as we need to support and strengthen one another. The word for 'strengthen' is the word for 'buttress'. We must 'buttress' each other. The front row forwards in a rugby scrum can only face the opposition if they are fully 'buttressed' by the players behind them. Each of us needs to be locked into each other – supporting, strengthening, motivating, encouraging (Romans ch1 vv11-12). At the heart of a successful church will be a core of faithful and loving encouragers.

NOVEMBER 19
1 THESSALONIANS ch4.1-12

Paul has already encouraged the believers in their faith, joy, prayer, love, and in living a blameless and holy life for God. Now he continues to urge these believers, as a matter of priority, to *'live in order to please God'* (v1).

LIVING A GOD-PLEASING LIFE

'Now we ask you and urge you in the Lord Jesus to do this more and more'. Not only was Paul 'asking' them: he was 'urging' them. We may see an athlete running in the race of their life. All the practice and all the training have come together at that moment, and they are being cheered and encouraged by their coach, who is shouting enthusiastically in the stands. Then there's Derek Redmond in the four hundred metres semi-final in the Barcelona Olympics, who pulls a hamstring at the first turn. After hobbling to within a hundred metres of the finishing line after all the runners had finished, he felt he would have to give up. But then his father steps onto the track and, to the cheers of sixty-five thousand spectators, he helps him over the finish line. In both races, the athletes were being supported and encouraged, but it was Mr Redmond Sr. who actually urged his son by coming alongside him, putting his arms around him, bearing his weight, and sharing his pain. This is what the word *'urge'* means in this context, and, in living God-pleasing lives, we need to urge and support each other.

1 LIVING A HOLY LIFE (vv2-8)

The Greek converts were living in a culture and living by recognised standards that were pagan and immoral. They had grown up in this environment and hadn't known anything different. *'Sexual immorality'* (v3) was the norm. As in our Western society, there is little in the way of a 'moral compass'. Anything is acceptable, providing it is consensual, so we're told. The Greek word for *'sexual immorality'* gives us our word 'pornography'. Paul had to be firm with these Greek Christians. He had to show them that the acceptable behaviour within their society was unacceptable behaviour in God's new society. Christians must be different in the way that they behave. When we become believers through personal faith in Jesus to pardon and to purify us, we now belong to a community with different values – higher values. We no longer live our lives to please ourselves but to please God. Our vision of the cross should constantly remind us that Jesus didn't merely die to make us happy but to make us holy.

2 LIVING A LOVING LIFE (vv9-10)

This love is the kind that's found in families. In the family of God, we have one Heavenly Father, and therefore, we should be showing brotherly/sisterly love to each other. The nearer we live to God, the dearer our brothers and sisters will become. Jesus gave a new command with a new standard and a new characteristic (John ch13 vv34-35). The livery of Jesus that we wear includes active, practical, demonstrated love, which is not just the product of words (1 John ch3 v18). But these acts of love don't need to be dramatic, expensive, or time-consuming. A regular sprinkling of such expressions of love will spread the fragrance of heaven. It's learning to think about and have regard for others that should prompt 'love in action'.

3 LIVING A QUIET LIFE (v11)

There are many things that can disrupt the quiet unity of believers and suddenly plunge them into the stormy seas of strained relationships. Paul addresses two of those things:

Don't be Nosy!

'Make it your ambition....to mind your own business...' Something that can disturb church life is for someone to take an interest in other people for all the wrong reasons. To disturb a believer's peace by prodding, prying, and poking is to violate their space. Kindliness is not nosiness. Nosiness is rarely an innocent pursuit because it quickly fuels gossip and can further lead to criticism, passing judgement, and even control or manipulation.

Don't be Lazy!

'Work with your hands,' said Paul. In Greek society, manual work was despised, as this was the work of slaves. Manual work and all kinds of other work should never be regarded as inferior in the family of God. We should never be ashamed of getting our hands dirty or be afraid of hard work. Paul was a tentmaker, and he followed in the footsteps of Jesus, who had been a carpenter. Laziness is not an option for a believer, whether at home or in the church.

4 LIVING A RESPECTABLE LIFE (v12)

Christians have a responsibility to be decent and respectable. While we must never compromise with a perverse, selfish, politically correct, multi-faith society, we must show a sense of moral and social responsibility within our community. It may be very difficult to *'win the respect of outsiders,',* but with God's help, we can live to his standards in a world that is constantly seeking to remove those standards. We must display the living reality of our faith in lives that are pleasing to God by their holiness, love, quietness, and respectability.

NOVEMBER 20
1 THESSALONIANS ch4.13-18

While Paul has talked much about encouragement and being encouraged, he now provides a further reason for encouraging each other. As those who live in a Christ-less society, we shall stand out because of the clear differences that there will be in the attitudes we display, the language we use, the actions we demonstrate, the values we hold, and the standards we keep. The church, which has a mural on its walls of a single fish swimming in the opposite direction to the shoal, is a graphic illustration of Christians who are living out the life of Jesus in our present culture.

CHRISTIANS ARE DIFFERENT

We may notice three clear differences in this passage.

1 WE GRIEVE DIFFERENTLY (v13)

It has always puzzled me, from an early age, why those who have no time for God, who despise his laws, who reject his word, who ridicule his people, and who blaspheme his name, choose to have their funeral in a church building with a religious ceremony. For some, the only time they will enter a church building will be in a coffin. To me, it is the height of hypocrisy! Often, the service itself, with its universalist message and hollow comfort, only serves to compound that hypocrisy. What comfort can you give to the family of someone who has consistently rejected the love of God and spurned the eternal salvation of God? If they die without Jesus, they die heavenless and hopeless. Yet a Christian's funeral should be so radically different. Of course, there is sadness, sorrow, heartache, and grief. But all of that is bathed in the light of a glorious hope. Their hope is not some flimsy, wispy sentiment. The hope of eternity with Jesus is built on God's word, his promises, and the blood and righteousness of Jesus, who is an anchor for our souls (Hebrews ch6 v19). If we belong to Jesus, the day of our death is the dawning of our glorious hope when we shall see the King in his beauty. When the crematorium curtain is drawn, or when the coffin is lowered to its final resting place, when those last words are spoken, *'earth to earth, ashes to ashes, dust to dust'*, the believer's believing family need not *'grieve like the rest of men who have no hope'*. As Christians, we should be different in life and different in death. Our hope is in a wonderful Saviour who brings us to Glory.

2 WE BELIEVE DIFFERENTLY (vv14-15)

We believe differently from the world because we trust what God has to say to us in the Bible. Paul touches on three things that we believe differently:

The Redemption

'We believe that Jesus died...' Death is painful: death separates. That's why we grieve. Yet Jesus voluntarily entered death (John ch10 vv17-18) so that repentant sinners may be redeemed, purchased, and set free. In his decisive, deliberate act of death, he brings eternal redemption (Hebrews ch9 v12) and he brings us into his kingdom (Colossians ch1 vv13-14).

672

The Resurrection

'...*and rose again...*' Jesus' powerful emergence from death on the third day, not only seals the victory of the cross, but it guarantees to those who have *'fallen asleep'* in Jesus (v13) that they will awake in their new sin-free, stain-free, Satan-free home. In his own resurrection, Jesus has blazed a trail for every believer (1 Corinthians ch15 vv17-20).

The Reunion

'...*and so we believe that God will bring with Jesus those who have fallen asleep in him.*' There's going to be a great reunion when those who have fallen asleep and those still alive will be united around Jesus. Believers who are 'asleep' and believers who are 'awake' are equal, and none shall precede the other. For both groups, the last enemy, 'death', has been neutralised. Death fails to intern believers who are asleep, and it fails to intercept believers who are awake.

3 WE LEAVE DIFFERENTLY (vv16-17)

Jesus' coming will signal the greatest separation in history: the separation of believer and unbeliever, of tares and wheat. Believers alive at Jesus' coming will be *'caught up'* together with believers who have previously died. For unbelievers, it will be a great day of unimaginable tragedy as their only prospect will be the eternal, unquenchable judgement of God. For the believer, it will be the greatest wedding day of all.

Note that Jesus will return:

Personally: He doesn't send an angel or an archangel. He comes in person. The first time he came, he met us at the cross. The second time he comes, he will meet us in the clouds. Every eye will see him; every knee will bow to him, and every tongue will confess his name.

Noisily: This verse doesn't convey a silent, secret, stealthy, or almost sneaky return. The heavens will reverberate to the sounds of his coming – the command, the voice, the trumpet call.

Orderly: Far from being a time of chaos, there will be perfect divine order. It will be a day that will be carefully orchestrated by our sovereign God. Such glimpses of our Saviour's coming should be enough to encourage each other.

NOVEMBER 21
1 THESSALONIANS ch5.1-7

Following on from the end of ch4, Paul proceeds to give further details about the momentous day of the Lord's second advent. He compares that day to a thief in the night.

A THIEF IN THE NIGHT

Paul uses the illustration of the night-time burglar in the same way that Jesus did (Luke ch12 vv39-40). The thief comes suddenly and unexpectedly, and therefore, we must be ready. We must also note very carefully that Jesus did not compare himself to a thief. Neither did Paul (v2) nor Peter (2 Peter ch3 v10) compare Jesus to a thief. What they said was that *'the day of the Lord will come as a thief in the night'*. We cannot subscribe to the deficient theology that compares Jesus to a thief, returning to earth silently and stealthily, snatching Christians away under the cover of darkness without anyone knowing what has happened. Jesus is not a thief, and he's not taking anything that doesn't belong to him. This notion is ridiculous and is a grotesque misrepresentation of what the Bible teaches. On the contrary, he collects his possessions, purchased through the cross (Acts ch20 v28), publicly and palpably. The truth is that Jesus is certainly coming again, and we must all be ready. There are three things implied here that could hinder our preparation.

1 THE TIMES AND DATES OF SPECULATION (vv1-2)

For hundreds of years, various groups of people have speculated as to the date and time of Jesus' coming. Some have claimed to have broken codes, while others have concocted elaborate theories as to the precise time of Jesus' coming. It seems that Paul's converts were not so preoccupied (vv1-2). They had learned to expect the unexpected. Jesus confirmed that the hour of his coming has not been disclosed (Matthew ch24 vv36&44). Our Christian lives must not be lived in date-setting, clock-watching, or sign-seeking. We must live every day as if that day were the day of the Lord.

2 THE PEACE AND SAFETY OF COMPLACENCY (v3)

The world around us, and especially folk in our cosy communities, are largely indifferent to the stark warnings of God's word. They are content to roll themselves up in the 'cotton wool' of 'peace and safety' with no thought for the reality of Jesus' coming. They believe that the references to destruction, judgement, and an eternal hell are only 'mythical' or allegorical at best. The gospel message is reduced to *peace and safety* without any rebuke, warning, or challenge. Providing we get lots of 'peace and safety' in our lives, providing we're cosy and comfortable, unthreatened and unchallenged, then we enjoy 'church' and the 'Christian society'. But it's *'while people are saying 'Peace and safety' destruction will come on them suddenly, as labour pains on a pregnant woman, and they will not escape'* (v3). Where the house owner is aware of the thief and the thief enters his house, then that's inexcusable. Where a pregnant woman begins her labour pains, then that's inescapable. For those who complacently reject the glorious gospel of God's saving grace, the destruction that follows is inexcusable and inescapable. Don't harden your hearts (Hebrews ch3 v15)!

3 THE NIGHT AND DARKNESS OF IGNORANCE (vv4-7)

The light of understanding is in stark contrast to the night of ignorance. Even though Jesus, the Light of the world, *'shines in the darkness...the darkness has not understood it'* (John ch1 v5). People prefer darkness to light (John ch3 v19). Such night-lovers are allergic to the light, and they fail to appreciate that they have been blinded from seeing the light of the gospel (2 Corinthians ch4 v4). But as ignorance is no defence in law, so ignorance is no excuse for being lost (Hebrews ch2 v3). If we want to be ready for the burglar who is due at our house, we shall be *'alert and self-controlled'*. To be ready for Jesus' return, we must also be *'alert and self-controlled'*

Alert not Asleep

We must be wide awake to the work of God and to the coming of Jesus. As a believer, you're a 'day child', not a 'night child'. It's no good trying to cope with the day if you hanker after the night. We must not cling to the clothing and the conduct of the night. The 'drunkenness' of nighttime (v7) is just an illustration of those things which may have enlivened our sociableness but deadened our senses prior to becoming a Christian. We may have lived for our clubs, sports, socials, earnings, careers, idols, and superstars, but now we live for Jesus. *'The old has gone: the new has come'* (2 Corinthians ch5 v17). The night has gone: the day has come. We belong to the day, and therefore we must be alert and not asleep.

Self-Controlled not Self-Centred

In contrast to those who become 'out of control' through drink, or other addictions or perversions, Christians are taught to be 'in control', temperate, self-controlled. Our society today is much like the Greek society of the first century, in which people can do what they like just as long as they don't hurt anyone else. Our unprincipled lawmakers have been decriminalising bad things and are poised to criminalise good things. Yet believers must be the opposite of the self-centred and self-promoting world around. Let's be the children of the day!

NOVEMBER 22
1 THESSALONIANS ch5.8-11

If you met Savanna Fulkerson at home, you would think that she is a normal nine-year-old girl. But if you met her outside in the street or the park, you would realise that there's something very different about her. Savanna has a rare condition that affects her blood cells. In short, Savanna is allergic to sunlight. Everything she does needs to be done under cover, indoors, or after dark. Savanna is a 'child of the night'. There's nothing she can do about it, and, sadly, at the moment, the doctors have no cure. In the opening verses of this chapter, Paul says that believers shouldn't be surprised at Jesus' second advent because they are *'sons of the light and sons of the day'* (v5). Christians are no longer those who skulk around in spiritual darkness because they are allergic to the Light. Peter tells us that we should declare *'the praises of him who called you out of darkness into his wonderful light'* (1 Peter ch2 v9). Paul says: *'We belong to the day'* (v8). We are therefore:

CHILDREN OF THE DAY

We are no longer part of the 'spiritual nightlife'. Just like plants arcing and twisting to get the most of the sunlight, we become determined to live and stretch for God's Son-Light. We want more of Jesus. We want to live for him, and Paul reminds us of three actions in which we shall be engaged.

1 PUTTING ON (v8)

Paul moves the analogy from sons to soldiers. We would expect good soldiers to be fine examples of those virtues which have been described earlier: alertness, self-control (v6), and sobriety (v7). The Christian soldier will also be dressed in the right armour:

Putting on the Breastplate

King Uzziah was the first Israeli king to equip his entire army with helmets and breastplates (2 Chronicles ch26 v14). In Paul's day, it was the Roman soldiers who wore breastplates, and the apostle describes the *'putting on'* of *'faith and love as a breastplate'*. Paul uses the image of a soldier on several occasions to illustrate the Christian's responsibilities and duties (Romans ch13 v12; 2 Corinthians ch6 v7; ch10 v4; Ephesians ch6 vv11-17). British soldiers have at times complained of being sent into battle under-equipped. But that can never be said of the Christian soldier. All the equipment and body armour necessary for the fight are available from our divine Quartermaster. Paul had proved that the Quartermaster's stores are always open to the believing Christian (Philippians ch4 v19). It's often true that Christians suffer more from minor skirmishes than big battles. We need breastplates constructed of the resilient alloy of *'faith and love'*. Some may have the faith 'to move mountains' but may still be deficient in love.

Putting on the Helmet

Together with faith and love, hope completes the triad of virtues that are listed in ch1 v3. The security of our salvation is in Jesus. If we are concerned about venturing onto a construction site, or down a mine, or riding a cycle, or climbing mountains, or riding horses without wearing head protection, how much more should we be adequately protected in this life, and in the next, with the great salvation which is only found in Jesus (Acts ch4 v12)?

2 LIVING WITH (vv9-10)

As a Christian, I can be unshakably assured that I am going to *'live together with (Jesus)'* (v10). I can be confident that my previous appointment with eternal death, judgement, condemnation, and hell has been cancelled. I have a new appointment! It's to live with Jesus. But while Paul has been directing our thoughts to the future dimension of our living with Jesus, for the Christian, that relationship begins in the 'here and now'. Whether we're dead or alive at Jesus' coming (*'awake or asleep'* v10), we are going to *'live together with him'*. But we are also learning to live and walk with him now. Solomon showed his love for the Lord *'by walking according to the statutes of his father David'* (1 Kings ch3 v3), and Paul quotes God's words to his Old Testament people: *'I will live with them and walk among them, and I will be their God, and they will be my people'* (2 Corinthians ch6 v16). Living and walking close to Jesus each day is the surest way of breaking sin's dominion and influence in our lives. Spend time listening to him in the Bible. Spend time conversing with him in prayer. Spend time considering his priorities, values, and standards.

3 BUILDING UP (v11)

When it comes to the church, Christians are good at building walls – separating walls, partition walls, dividing walls – but not so good at building bridges. While walls are important to the whole structure, we should not be looking to build internal walls in our churches. We want them to be 'open plan'. However, we do need to *'build each other up'*. We are given gifts and ministries to build each other up (Ephesians ch4 v12), including the ministry of encouragement. While we should not lose sight of the truth that Jesus is the Architect and Builder of his church (Matthew ch16 v18), there is a sense in which we as believers play an important part in the construction programme. If we want to be members of God's church, are we going to join the 'construction team' or the 'demolition gang'?

NOVEMBER 23
1 THESSALONIANS ch5.12-18

The apostle has made it clear in this epistle that we are not only 'children of the day', we are also 'children of the family of God'. We have to be born into that family by being converted. The local expression of this family is in the local church. In natural families, it's rather tragic when families would rather live apart than live together. This is also true of the spiritual family when family members choose not to share in the responsibilities and duties of the local family, the church. In this section, Paul deals with a list of essentials for the smooth functioning of the local church family.

CHURCH FAMILY ESSENTIALS

1 BE RESPECTFUL (v12)

Church families are encouraged to:

Show Acknowledgement

While some see a division between the clergy and laity, between paid and voluntary workers, we must acknowledge all those who serve faithfully according to their gift, ability, and ministry. The focus of any church should be the lifting up of its Head and the building up of its members. Remember v11.

Show Acceptance

Paul underlines the importance of accepting the authority of church leadership. Such leaders should never be dictatorial or autocratic in any way. Neither should they be overbearing or monopolising. Their role includes guidance, care, support, and teaching.

Show Affection

Leaders should never be regarded with suspicion, doubt, fear, jealousy, or even condescension. We must love those whom God has called to whatever office or service.

2 BE PEACEFUL (v13)

Peace is achieved when there is mutual respect, loyalty, and love within the church family. As soon as these virtues become corrupted or compromised, there is dissension, discord, and division. Christians should be the children of peace – peaceable, peace-loving, and peace-making. There are two prominent reasons for discord in churches: [i] people are not prepared to put God's word first, and [ii] they are not prepared to put themselves last.

3 BE HELPFUL (v14)

This 'helpfulness' in the church included stirring the lazy ones for everyone's benefit. It also means providing support for the vulnerable – the nervous, the shy, and the weak. If patience is needed in copious quantities to support *some* people, then Paul argues that we must *'be patient with everyone'*. Giving help often means the necessity of getting alongside someone to give practical support in their struggle.

4 BE CAREFUL (v15)

We are called to show care for each other in forgiveness and kindness. Our instinct to retaliate should be resisted with all the spiritual grace we can muster. While we may feel good at resisting the temptation to pay back wrong for wrong, that's only half the requirement. We are called to positively show kindness (Matthew ch5 vv38-41). The suppression of the desire to retaliate is one of the clearest signs of a Christian's maturity. For the believer, 'pay-back time' means kindness – in our actions, in our speech, and in our thoughts as well.

5 BE JOYFUL (v16)

Happiness, though welcome, may often be rather superficial and elusive. A Christian's joy, by contrast, is neither circumstantial nor emotional. It is completely independent of circumstances. Paul, with Silas, proved that this is possible, even in a Philippian gaol (Acts ch16 v25). This joy is unaffected by sorrow, suffering, and loss. We are to *'Rejoice in the Lord always'* (Philippians ch4 v4).

6 BE PRAYERFUL (v17)

Jesus made the point in his parable (Luke ch18) that if a godless judge will respond to a plaintiff's unyielding pleas, will not the righteous Judge of all the earth hear the cries of those who persist in prayer? 'Praying continually' is not so much perpetual prayer as persistent prayer. It's not so much the 'non-stop' speaking but the 'non-quit' pleading. If we're going to be real in our praying, we must be earnest in our praying. God delights in our prayers, and the more earnest we are and the more determined we are, the more delighted he is!

7 BE THANKFUL (v18)

There is real victory in the Christian life when a believer learns to be thankful *'in all circumstances'*. It's easier to be more thankful in the sunshine than in the storms; in our gains than in our losses; in our health than in our sickness; in our comforts than in our pains. It's easier to give thanks when we are light-hearted than when we are broken-hearted. But if we really believe in the practical outworking of Romans ch8 v28, that God works for our good *'in all things'*, then we shall be thankful for those *'all things'* and we shall *'give thanks in all circumstances'*.

NOVEMBER 24
1 THESSALONIANS ch5.19-28

Although Paul had been greatly thrilled to learn of the Thessalonian believers' *'faith and love'* (ch3 v6), there were areas in which they had needed direction, correction, and instruction. These issues had been covered in this letter. However, just in case those various commands and conditions had been likely to stifle their enthusiasm and reduce their Christian faith to something cold, clinical, dry, and even mechanical, Paul warns: *'Don't put out the Spirit's fire!'* (v19). The Holy Spirit has been associated with fire (for example, Matthew ch3 v11; Acts ch2 vv2-4). Depicted as the wind, the dew, or the fire, the sovereign Spirit is unstoppable and unquenchable. We shall never be able to diminish him or extinguish him in any way, for he is God Almighty. Paul's concern, however, is that those believers who are 'caught alight' by the Spirit are not extinguished in terms of their commitment, enthusiasm, Christ-centredness, and love. Paul told Timothy to fan into flame God's gift (2 Timothy ch1 v6), and he told the Ephesian believers not to grieve the Spirit (Ephesians ch4 v30). Fire is used both for heat and light. It is used for illumination and destruction. It can both energise and sterilise. If you are ignited by the Spirit in your service, your prayers, your ministry, your gift, or your worship, be sure not to extinguish that flame.

NO FIRE EXTINGUISHERS!

What kinds of spiritual fire extinguishers could Paul be suggesting? What agents could neutralise the Spirit's fire in your life? What could pour cold water on the Spirit's flame in your heart?

1 PREACHING THAT IS NOT BIBLE-BASED

(vv19-20) Paul was writing to a first-century church that had God's word in the Old Testament Scriptures and in the prophecies and letters of the New Testament writers, whose work at that time was incomplete. They were not yet in possession of the complete canon of the Bible that we have today. It would be another three hundred years before all the authoritative word of God would be collated into the books of the Bible, which we know and love today. Our preaching and teaching must therefore be Scripture-centred. We cannot afford to deviate from the truth of God's word, which is relevant for every age. The Bible writers wrote as moved by God (2 Peter ch1 v21). So it's the reading and preaching of that word which is capable of igniting hearts and lives spiritually. Conversely, it's the teaching of cosy homilies and moral fables which may pour water on flickering flames. Just because a speaker may be dynamic, charismatic, and contemporary, it's no guarantee that he's not going to be a 'fire extinguisher'. A fanatic can extinguish fires as easily as a formalist.

2 WORSHIP THAT IS NOT CHRIST-CENTRED

(vv21-22) The word *'good'* is the word that is the opposite of 'false' or 'counterfeit'. Worship in all its forms and shapes, even within the context of Christianity and the church, can be fake and lifeless. God would rather that his temple were shut than for false worship to be offered there (Malachi ch3 v10). The useless fire of meaningless sacrifice can extinguish the tireless fire of meaningful service. God seeks true worshippers (John ch4 v24). We can have popular music, infectious singing, emotional praying, and dynamic preaching, but unless

God's word is heard most, and the Spirit is stirring most, and Jesus is centre-most, then it will not be worthy worship.

3 LIVES THAT ARE NOT SIN-FREE

(v23) Paul is praying for the believers' purifying and persevering. He prays that they may be fully set apart and fully focused on living for Jesus faultlessly and blamelessly. Believers are made holy for God. But if we continue to embrace sin rather than evict sin, we shall find that it puts out the Spirit's fire. We need God's power to overcome the temptation to fall into sin and, when we do fall, we should seek his forgiveness (1 John ch1 v9).

4 FELLOWSHIP THAT IS NOT HEART-FELT

(vv25-28) By contrast, Paul exemplifies a fellowship that is both heartfelt and heart-warming. He believes in the family relationship of believers. Three times in these last few words, he uses the endearing term *'brothers'*. It is a word of inclusivity, for it embraces all brothers and sisters in God's family. In this respect, Paul ranks himself equal with other family members, suggesting no discrimination. There's no discrimination in praying (v25), greeting (v26), or hearing the word (v27). This message from the Lord was to be read to all believers, whatever their country, colour, or culture. How inclusive is that! It consists of all who love Jesus and who are committed to gospel work in their local church. If our fellowship and bond of communion are only half-hearted, then it's likely to extinguish the Spirit's fire. If our idea of fellowship is just the occasional, casual associations – the 'coffee and chit-chat' sort – then it's likely to pour cold water on the Spirit's fire. The New Testament believers understood true fellowship to be the unconditional sharing of their lives with their brothers and sisters within their church. Don't put out the Spirit's fire!

NOVEMBER 25
2 THESSALONIANS ch1.1-4

There may have only been a few months between Paul's first and second letters to the Thessalonian church (circa AD50-52). Along with his mission team, Silas and Timothy (v1), Paul is both encouraged and concerned about this young church. He was encouraged because of their growth and because of their perseverance under pressure. But he was concerned about the escalation of their persecution; the intensity and persuasiveness of false teaching (especially regarding end times), and he was concerned that some believers were close to giving up their Christian responsibilities because they believed that Jesus' Second Coming was imminent. However, he begins by telling them that he had reason to *'always to thank God for (them)'* (v3) and he provides three good reasons why he was so thankful to God for the Thessalonian church.

THANKING GOD FOR ONE ANOTHER

We can examine our own church and ask ourselves whether we ought to be thankful to God for three similar virtues in our fellow brothers and sisters.

1 THANKS THAT THEY WERE GROWING IN FAITH (v3)

It's always exciting to witness growth, especially when it's spiritual growth. We are obviously encouraged to see numerical growth, but spiritual growth is very different and far more important. What may be the marks of spiritual growth?

Thirst for God's Word

If we are growing spiritually, we shall have a thirst for the Bible and for learning what God has to teach us. We may not be naturally great readers, but we shall be avid seekers of what God thinks about issues and circumstances. We won't necessarily be interested in what the populist view may be, or indeed what a particular author or theologian says. We shall want to know what God says.

Call to God's Work

Every child of God has a ministry to perform and a role to fulfil in God's gospel programme. God's call to sonship is not distinct from his call to servanthood. Every single believer is recruited into God's service.

Stand for God's Truth

Taking a stand will always cost. We might call it the 'FT Index' of our resilience. We may suffer 'loss of Face' for the truth (that is, loss of prestige or promotion). We may suffer the loss of friends for the truth, or the loss of family, or the loss of finance, or even the loss of freedom for the truth.

Share in God's Church

Our gifts and ministries are not to be used in isolation. They are for the benefit of believers in the context of the local church. Every believer is a stone ('*living stones*' 1 Peter ch2 v5). They are not ornamental stones, monumental stones, millstones, hailstones, or kidney stones to cause pain! They are stones shaped and fit for a building: the temple of God.

Joy in God's Fellowship

A growing believer will love to spend time with God, getting closer to his Lord and Saviour. They will enjoy quality time with the Friend who gave his life for them.

Love for God's People

This brings us to the second virtue for which we can thank God:

2 THANKS THAT THEY WERE INCREASING IN LOVE (v3)

(see 1 Thessalonians ch3 v12; ch4 v10) As Christians, we have the responsibility to be both loving and lovable. Love grows when it is trained and nurtured. Like any cultivated plant, it needs the right climate and the right conditions. Jesus said, '*Love each other as I have loved you*' (John ch15 v12). John himself must have been so riveted by Jesus' specific teaching on love that he followed it up years later: '*This is how we know what love is: Jesus Christ laid down his life for us. And we ought to lay down our lives for our brothers*' (1 John ch3 v16). We may find it a little easier to lay down our lives for the most loving and lovable of believers, but what about the most difficult, the most disruptive, and the most disagreeable of our brothers and sisters? We are called to love unconditionally. We are not to be 'choosey' with our Christian love. What if Jesus had been 'choosey' with his love for us?

3 THANKS THAT THEY WERE ENDURING IN TRIALS (v4)

The Thessalonian Christians were not having an easy time. They were 'being put through the mill' in terms of persecution and trials. Nothing would budge them from their loyalty to Jesus. Their faithfulness would not buckle under spiritual pressure. We may feel at times that we have been taken right to our limits, but '*God is faithful; he will not let you be tempted beyond what you can bear.*' (1 Corinthians ch10 v13). But Paul could not only thank God for the Thessalonian believers' endurance, he could actually boast about it to other churches. Paul was able to hold them up as a clear example of perseverance and endurance: Christians who would not buckle under pressure. Whether we may be called to endure the '*trials*' of health, finance, business, legal matters, domestic issues, or natural phenomena, or whether we are called to endure persecutions on account of our faith in Jesus, we can prove the faithfulness of our God in all adversity.

NOVEMBER 26
2 THESSALONIANS ch1.5-10

There's a huge difference between knowing about God and knowing God. There are countless millions who know about God. Many will attend churches, read Bibles, recite creeds, say prayers, take part in church events, do Christian things, and even share Christian sacraments. They know all about God, but they have never come to know God personally, closely, experientially, or savingly.

KNOWING GOD

In v8 Paul refers to those who *'do not know God'* as those who *'do not obey the gospel of our Lord Jesus'*. By contrast, those who do know God will obey the gospel, which issues a divine summons to repent and believe (Acts ch2 v38; ch16 v31). It's through the good news truth of the gospel that we are introduced to God, and we are given the opportunity to come to know him in the person of Jesus, our Saviour and our King. As we deepen and develop our relationship with God, there are endless truths that we discover. Notice three in these verses:

1 WE CAN KNOW THAT GOD'S JUDGEMENT IS RIGHT (vv4-5)

Paul knows that the Thessalonian Christians have been persecuted because of their faith in Jesus and their trust in God's word. In that respect, nothing has changed in two thousand years of church history. Yet Paul sees in the Thessalonians' suffering the *'evidence that God's judgement is right'* (v5). How can that be? Isn't God a loving, caring, and compassionate God? Then how can it be said that allowing his faithful followers to suffer is evidence of his righteous judgement? Paul sees clearly that the Thessalonians' *'perseverance and faith'* (v4) is God-given, not man-made. Their ability to endure the suffering is not merely stoicism but grace: the grace of God. Jesus had told Paul, *'My grace is sufficient for you; for my power is made perfect in weakness'* (2 Corinthians ch12 v9). Do you think that you could ever put up with physical or mental persecution? Do you think that you would be so weak and frail that you could never endure pressures from hostile unbelievers? Then those are the precise conditions in which God's grace triumphs. Our human weakness is the stage on which divine power is displayed. Yet not only is the grace to endure a part of the evidence, but the suffering itself is part of God's plan. Over and over again, we are told that suffering is a prelude to glory (for example, Romans ch8 v17). The whole of Paul's Christian life was a catalogue of variegated sufferings (2 Corinthians ch11 vv23-29). But he said that all those sufferings couldn't compare with the glory that he would share one day (Romans ch8 v18).

2 WE CAN KNOW THAT GOD'S JUSTICE IS RELIEF (vv6-7)

God's justice ensures that two things will happen: [i] persecutors will receive retribution and [ii] the persecuted will receive relief. God has placed a strict time limit on our present troubles. They will not last indefinitely. In the context of eternity, our troubles are just the blink of an eye. At the time, our tribulations may seem relentless and unending, but *'rejoicing comes in the morning'* (Psalm 30 v5). Relief will be the reward for those who endure. Presently, it seems that evil triumphs and wicked people are in control. Persecutors, tormentors, and all the church's enemies seem to get away with anything, including murder, but a final day of reckoning is guaranteed (Galatians ch6 v7). Our world is full of injustice, and it would be easy to compile a list of believers who have suffered miscarriages of justice. But it's God's justice that will ultimately triumph *'when the Lord Jesus is revealed from heaven in blazing fire with his powerful angels'* (v7). On that day, there will be retribution for the trouble-makers and relief for the troubled (v6). As a believer, on what can you depend for eternal rest and relief? Of course, we hope in God's grace and mercy. But the underlying guarantee of security in Jesus' salvation is in God's justice. God's justice ensures that the pardon and new life procured through the cross can never be revoked or repealed.

3 WE CAN KNOW THAT GOD'S SON IS REVEALED (v7)

The day on which Jesus returns (the day he spoke about in 1 Thessalonians ch4 vv16-17) is going to be an awesome day. All eyes will be on Jesus, and everyone who knows God through Jesus, our Mediator and Saviour, will be eternally secure. But what about those who don't know him and who have rejected his offer of mercy in the Gospel?

His Punishment is Forever

We can't 'cherry-pick' the most palatable bits of the Bible. While some may excise or expunge parts of their Bible copies, God's word is unalterable.

His Presence is Forfeit

To be eternally excluded from God's loving and gracious presence is incomprehensible. But lest we should think that a vacuum has been created in God's omnipresence, we should remember that he will be present in justice and judgement.

His Power is Final

His majestic power will overwhelm and crush every power of humanity and every force of Satan. Once revealed in meekness (2 Corinthians ch8 v9), he will then be revealed in majesty.

Do you only know 'about God', or do you know him personally?

NOVEMBER 27
2 THESSALONIANS ch1.11-12

How often do we pray for our missionaries? We receive their regular newsletters, and we are assured that they pray for us. Paul and his mission team were missionaries whom the Thessalonian Christians prayed for. Paul, Silas, and Timothy promised prayer for them, too. Paul said, *'With this in mind, we constantly pray for you...'* (v11). What did Paul have *'in mind'*? He had in mind the suffering and persecution which the believers were enduring, so that on the day of the Lord they would be *'counted worthy of the kingdom of God'* (v5).

COUNTED WORTHY

Prayer was important in the first century. Prayer is just as important now in the twenty-first century. The church today doesn't need more strategies, more visions, or more techniques. It needs more prayer. It doesn't need more programmes. It needs more prayer. It doesn't need more organisations or more novel methods or more 'every-Christian-must-attend' seminars. It needs men and women of prayer. God, the Holy Spirit doesn't flow through plans. He flows through people – people of prayer. Even preaching without prayer is lifeless. We may notice three petitions which form the substance of Paul's prayers that they may be counted worthy.

1 HE PRAYS THAT GOD'S CALLING WILL BE EVIDENT (v11)

We should carefully note that this is God's calling. It's not their calling or, indeed, our calling, in the sense that it's our vocation, our ministry, or our service. This is God's effectual call of sinners through the gospel. When we preach the gospel, we don't know those whom God will save. So we proclaim the message to everyone, summoning them to repent, believe, and be saved. We must preach the gospel without distinction or discrimination, without fear or favour. As this message is preached, there are those to whom God specifically grants the gift of faith to believe. God calls them effectively. This is often referred to as the 'effectual call'. All those who are chosen by God – predestined to eternal life – will be called effectually (Romans ch8 v30). Therefore, we must conclude that God saves every single one of his children, his church, his flock, and his people. Not one of them will be lost if they are the elect of God. There's a very important verse in Acts ch13 v48. It tells us that as the Gentiles listened respectfully and attentively to Paul's preaching, *'all who were appointed for eternal life believed'*. Notice that it's not the other way round, that is, 'those who believed were appointed to eternal life'. The Bible is clear that they were not appointed to eternal life because they believed. Rather, they believed because they were appointed to eternal life. So this is the *'calling'* to which Paul refers. He prays that *'our God may count you worthy of his calling'*. He prays that believers will live lives that are consistent with their calling. If you and I are Christians, we must live the life of Christ. Our *'calling'* must be evident in the way we speak and behave. Paul is praying for this consistency.

2 HE PRAYS THAT GOD'S POWER WILL BE EFFECTIVE (v11)

Praying that God's power may be effective may seem like praying that the sea will be wet. God is omnipotent and almighty. God's power is majestic (Exodus ch15 v6) and awesome (Psalm 68 vv34-35). History is the record of God answering the prayers of his people. Paul was praying directly in line with God's will. His desire was that we share in his 'good purposes' and that faith would be the driving force of our actions. God's good purposes and our faithful acts identify God's people. As believers, we have been elected to God's 'church team' by grace and not by merit. We are not worthy of that privileged position. We are unworthy of God's selection. However, we are called to live our lives as faithful followers of Jesus. We are called to live holy lives: lives devoted to Christ and his kingdom. We need God's power for this to be effective in his *good purpose* and our *act of faith*. We must pray for it. A righteous person (James ch5 v16) will not be praying with selfish motives. A righteous prayer warrior will be putting God's glory first in their prayers.

3 HE PRAYS THAT GOD'S SON WILL BE EXALTED (v12)

Is there a greater reason for being *counted worthy* other than that Jesus may be glorified in our lives? Is there a better objective, a nobler aim? Will Jesus be exalted in our lives if the answer to our prayer request is not answered in the way we would like? Will we still honour him if his answer is 'No'? Will we still submit to him if his answer is 'Not now'? Paul prays for two further things:

Jesus Glorified in You

Jesus prayed for this prior to his death (John ch17 vv10, 22-23). When the union and unity with Jesus is obvious in our lives, then Jesus will be glorified in us. Jesus glorified in me? It's unthinkable – except for God's grace! But this truth is equally awesome:

You Glorified in Jesus

Where is the evidence that you have been counted worthy of your calling? The evidence (not just a testimony) is a life lived for God every day in our community.

NOVEMBER 28
2 THESSALONIANS ch2.1-12

This is the main section of Paul's letter. This is the primary reason for his writing. It's clear that the believers' enemies took the form of persecutors. But if you thought that these were the most dangerous enemies, then or now, you would be wrong! The church's most dangerous enemies are the false teachers who propagate lies and deceptions.

DON'T BE DUPED!

Deceivers can sound so convincing. Their survival depends on how successful they are in selling a fake as being genuine: whether that 'fake' is a product, a service, an ideology, or a teaching.

1 A WARNING ABOUT THE FAKE

We are being plagued by the false and the fake as never before, and religion is certainly not exempt. Paul's warning about the fake consisted of three aspects:

The Day of the Lord

There have been those cults and false teachers, like Charles Russell of the 'Jehovah's Witnesses', who taught that the Day of the Lord and the end of the world would occur on a specific date. Such fake news has duped thousands of people. That is precisely the issue which Paul confronts here. Apparently, there had been a fake *'prophecy, report, or letter'* which had supposedly come from the apostles. Paul kills that rumour. He refutes that 'fake news' (vv1-2). Paul tells the Thessalonian believers, and us, that we mustn't be duped by such fake news. The Day of the Lord is still future, and it will come. Far from being invisible and unnoticeable (as some have claimed), Paul has already described the Day of the Lord as highly visible and absolutely unmissable (1 Thessalonians ch4 vv16-17; Philippians ch2 vv10-11).

The Deception of the Lawless One

Paul indicates that the glorious coming of Jesus will be preceded by the appearance of someone who puts himself in the place of God and demands worship as God. He will be opposed to Jesus: anti-Jesus and anti-Christ. Throughout history, there have been many who have deserved the title 'Antichrist', as John reveals (1 John ch2). The period between Jesus' first and second comings is referred to variously as *'the last hour'* (v18) or *'the last days'* (Acts ch2 v17; Hebrews ch1 v2; 2 Peter ch3 v3). It's during this time that 'antichrists' appear. The emperor Nero may seem to have fitted the description at the time of the apostles. Paul had obviously spoken about a *'man of lawlessness'* (vv5,7). In every century through the last two thousand years of church history, there have been those who have set themselves up in the place of God and have demanded worship. Christians at various times have identified Domitian, the Vandals, Mohammed, the pope, the papacy, Napoleon, Kaiser Wilhelm, Hitler, Stalin, Mussolini, Idi Amin, Pol Pot, and others as being 'antichrist'. That *'secret power of lawlessness (was) already at work'*. But Paul also indicates that there will be a Lawless One immediately prior to Jesus' second coming. Paul refers to the restraining power that has prevented the worst atrocities and blasphemies (vv5-7). A sovereign God is in full control, whether he uses a government or the gospel as a tool.

The Delusion of the Lie

(vv10-11) The 'lie', which has been around since Satan's deception in the garden (Genesis ch3 v5), is *'You will be like God!'* And that 'god' is not God. God's *'powerful delusion'* makes them believe their own lie. They have convinced themselves, and God has sealed that conviction, that Satan's lie is the truth.

2 A PROMPTING ABOUT THE GENUINE

The best way to be alert to fakes is to be sure about what is genuine: the truth. How do we respond to the truth of God?

Love the Truth

Unbelievers perish because they refuse to love the truth (v10). Those who are wonderfully forgiven of their sin and saved by God's grace learn to love the truth. They have an appetite for God's word and God's truth. They yearn to read it, study it, and discuss it.

Believe the Truth

The condemned don't believe the truth (v12). They have not trusted the truth or committed themselves to it. They have no inclination to live by the truth.

Expect the Truth

By referring to a future day when *'the lawless one will be revealed'*, Paul declares (v8) that *'the Lord Jesus will overthrow (him) with the breath of his mouth...'* The *'lawless one'* may be powerful and influential, but he will be easily defeated by our almighty King Jesus. He will be 'blown away' by his breath. No one can resist the omnipotence of our Lord and Saviour, Jesus Christ. We can expect this revelation of truth in Jesus, who crushes all that's fake, false, and counterfeit on the day of his glorious appearing. We should examine ourselves to confirm whether our faith is genuine or fake. Do we merely put on a 'religious appearance' for 'respectability purposes' or have we personally come to know the truth in Jesus who declared *'I am...the Truth...'* (John ch14 v6). Our faith cannot be 'second-hand' or a 'hand-me-down'! It must be genuinely ours. We must *'live by the truth'* with that truth residing within us (1 John ch1 vv6,8).

NOVEMBER 29
2 THESSALONIANS ch2.13-17

We may have heard a lot from MPs, prospective MPs, government ministers, and the prime minister about 'strong and stable' leadership. It is a desirable feature of government, the economy, health, families, businesses, and homes that they remain stable. We also regard stability as a primary feature of structures, buildings, transport, and materials handling equipment.

But spiritual stability is an essential feature of the Christian life. One of Paul's main concerns in writing both letters to the young church in the Macedonian city of Thessalonica was that they should remain stable: stable in their faith and in their understanding of the apostles' teaching. There were threatening factors that could destabilize them in their faith:

Constant persecution

This came from religious people as well as from pagans (1 Thessalonians ch2 vv2,14).

Insidious lies

Some were spreading gossip that Paul couldn't be trusted (1 Thessalonians ch2 vv3-6).

Infectious laziness

Some stopped work altogether in view of Jesus' coming (1 Thessalonians ch5 v14).

False teaching

This was Paul's greatest concern in writing this second letter (v3).

Paul is anxious that his readers are not destabilized by fake news, false doctrines, and counterfeit phenomena. So he urges: '...*stand firm and hold to the teachings we passed on to you, whether by word or mouth or letter*' (v15).

HOW GOOD ARE YOUR STABILIZERS?

We all look for stability in various forms, and spiritually, we need the stability of building on the Rock, which is Jesus. In this passage, Paul rehearses the ingredients of that spiritual stability which is essential for our security and to enable us to grow in our faith. The Bible is our sure and stable foundation.

What do the Scriptures tell us about how we are stabilized in our faith?

1 YOU ARE LOVED (vv13,16)

Millions of aching hearts, lonely souls, abandoned friends, and dysfunctional family members yearn to be loved. They need to hear and know that someone loves them and cares for them. Yet we persist in our rebellion and waywardness without realising the glorious truth that God actively and practically loves us (Romans ch5 v8; 1 John ch4 v10).

2 YOU ARE CHOSEN (v13)

Some Christians will testify to the day when they first chose Jesus. Yet any choice of theirs is preceded by God's choice of them. Their 'decision' to repent and believe can only be because of God's decision to rescue them. We may think that our choice of Jesus was the pivotal factor, just as the disciples did. But Jesus spelt it out to them and to us: *'You did not choose me, but I chose you'* (John ch15 v16). Stability is not dependent upon fickle, flawed, fluctuating choices. Our eternal security sits solidly upon divine choice, which was made *'from the beginning'* (Ephesians ch1 v4).

3 YOU ARE CALLED (v14)

Romans ch8 v30 tells us that *'those he predestined, he also called...'* God calls through the gospel. This is why it's so important to preach, to read, to study, to transmit, to proclaim, and to live the gospel. It is God's authorised channel for calling believers to himself as he calls effectively, so God's flock, God's church, God's people respond positively to that call.

4 YOU ARE ENCOURAGED (vv16-17)

We can only be kept and preserved by God's encouragement. That encouragement, through *'love'* and *'grace'* (v16), gives hope and strength for *'every good deed and word'* (v17). The clear evidence of our spiritual stabilizers (God's love, choice, calling, and encouragement) is in our good deeds and good words. God's Spirit is God's personal Encourager (Counsellor, Comforter). We need the help and power of God's Spirit in every department of our lives so that we may live the life of Jesus. So how must we respond as we recognise these spiritual stabilizers?

Believe the Truth

(v13) Paul thanks God that the Thessalonian Christians have been saved and sanctified *'through belief in the truth'* (v13). God summons us to believe the truth, to confess sin, to turn from sin, and to trust in Jesus for his grace and forgiveness. We may have lots of puzzles, as yet unresolved. We may have lots of questions, as yet unanswered. But getting right with God is not about being able to solve every puzzle or to answer every question. It's about taking God at his word and believing the truth. Paul told the suicidal gaoler at Philippi: *'Believe in the Lord, and you will be saved'* (Acts 16.31). The gaoler and his entire family believed for the first time that night and were baptized.

Hold the Teachings

(v15) The word for *'teachings'* means those messages of truth which have been passed on by the apostles. They are the foundational principles of our faith and practice. We shall only get real stability when we build on the Bible and trust its truth.

NOVEMBER 30
2 THESSALONIANS ch3.1-5

When the Welsh revival of 1904 was in progress, some Welsh missionaries in Africa, hearing of the spiritual awakening, wrote to friends back home saying, 'Pray for us'. They wanted the revival to touch them, too. In a few weeks, they also experienced God's reviving power. They could have written with Paul: *'Brothers, pray for us that the message of the Lord may spread rapidly and be honoured, just as it was with you'* (v1).

PRAY FOR US

As believers' prayers ascended, God's power descended. God's word spread rapidly, and God's Spirit did his convicting, converting, and reviving work. Both Paul and the Thessalonian Christians could pray for each other in regard to specific requests:

1 THEIR RESPECTED MESSAGE (v1)

It was a message to be *'honoured'*. There's a hint here of a runner running a race and receiving an award for reaching the finishing post. The 'runner' is the gospel message, which is *'spread rapidly'* and which is *'honoured'* on achieving its goal. This is not 'any old message'. This is *'the message of the Lord'* which is to be respected and revered. Paul has witnessed the triumph of the gospel in the city of Thessalonica, and now he wants that powerful message to impact the rest of the Roman Empire. Shouldn't we be praying that the gospel will be respected and revered throughout our community? We want the gospel to flourish and, while we hear frequently about its opposition, we are thrilled to learn about those places where it is received joyfully.

2 THEIR EFFECTED DELIVERANCE (v2)

Paul seeks prayer that his deliverance from dangerous men will be effective. He is well aware that there are *'wicked and evil men'* who are religious and persuasive, but who are not believers. He says that *'not everyone has faith'*. Their hostility to the gospel is evidence that they have not been subdued by the gospel and, therefore, not saved by the gospel. Wherever the gospel is proclaimed, there will be opposition to it, more often from religious people. Paul had written this letter from Corinth, where he had been taken to court by fellow religious Jews. They had accused Paul of *'persuading people to worship God in ways contrary to the law'* (Acts ch18 v13). While Judaism had a dispensation from Roman authorities to continue its religion, Jews were claiming that Paul's 'new Christianity' had no such dispensation. They wanted the gospel to be made illegal. Fake religion continues to clash with real Christianity today. In some countries, Christianity is illegal, and if Jesus' opponents had their way, it would be illegal in many other countries, too.

3 THEIR PROTECTED FAITH (v3)

The *'wicked and evil men'* (v2) were faithless, but *'the Lord is faithful'* (v3). Our security is in the hands of an ever-faithful God who constantly watches over his people. He stands guard like a sentry, ready to defend against *'the Evil One'*. The Greek word for *'protect'* is a military word.

When the Israelites left Egypt, God is said to have protected them from attack from behind as well as in front – '...*the Lord will go before you, the God of Israel will be your rear guard*' (Isaiah ch52 v12). We should learn from the doubting, despairing Israeli refugees from Egypt that we need faith in God's all-round defence of his people. In our conflict with Satan, we must trust in the equipment which God provides. Paul describes personal protective equipment as '*the full armour of God*' (Ephesians ch6 v11). However, the key instruction is 'Put it on!' (Ephesians ch6 v13).

4 THEIR EXPECTED OBEDIENCE (v4)

Paul is confident and prayerful that the Thessalonian believers will do what is right. He is not confident in human nature, or human strength, or human wisdom, but he is confident '*in the Lord*'. Men and women can be unreliable and unpredictable. They fluctuate and vacillate like leaves in the wind. Promises are broken; commitments are false; moods vary; friendships are threatened, and relationships can become unstable. If obedience to God relied on human effort, we should have no confidence. We can pray for one another optimistically because '*we have confidence in the Lord*'.

5 THEIR DIRECTED HEARTS (v5)

If ever there were motivations for obedience and compliance, they are these.

God's Love

This is the dominant theme of the Bible, which is defined by the nature of God himself (1 John ch4 v8). Despite Adam's wretched sin, God's perfect Masterplan, drawn with the ink of divine love, determines not to exterminate Adam but to re-establish a relationship with him. God's love spans the gulf by building a bridge at the cross (Romans ch5 v8).

Christ's Perseverance

Jesus is the perfect pattern for perseverance (Hebrews ch12 vv1-3). He endured everything that everyone could throw at him. We must never give in to sin.

DECEMBER 1
2 THESSALONIANS ch3.6-18

We are often told that the ant is a model worker. Basically, the ant's life, which can be anything up to seven years, is spent working. Ants gather food and bring it back to the nest. They store food for the winter. They are also good gardeners, using organic material to grow mushrooms. Some ants are dairy farmers, herding and milking aphids and plant lice. Therefore, it should not come as a surprise to us to read in Proverbs ch6 v6: *'Go to the ant, you sluggard; consider its ways and be wise'*. A 'sluggard' is a habitually lazy person. Idleness and laziness were problems that Paul confronted head-on in the church. In effect, he's saying:

DON'T BE A LOAFER!

Paul specifically identifies fellow-Christians (*'brothers'* v6) whose lives were lived in idleness. They could be lazy because they sponged off the generosity of others. This message was something that the Thessalonian believers needed to hear, as well as believers everywhere today.

1 A PERSON TO AVOID (v6)

Paul is concerned for the church's unity and purity. He doesn't want them to be disrupted or destabilised by folk in the church who are too lazy to contribute to the fellowship. Such folk are idle and unreliable. Neither does he want the church to be corrupted by those who choose to live in such a way that is contrary to the apostles' teaching. Such threats to church unity and church purity are always lurking. Paul is not advocating at this stage that these loafers be excommunicated, but he is flagging up the threat that such Christians can be to the church fellowship. The word for *'idleness'* means 'disorderly'. This can result in the disruption and undermining of the church. Being idle means imposing more work on others. It means not facing up to the responsibilities of membership within a church. It means not using God-given abilities for the benefit of members. Idleness can also foster:

Temptation

This seems to come more easily to those who have time on their hands. Greed, jealousy, desire, and pride may be much harder to resist from a position of idleness.

Gossip

Gossip can be so damaging to relationships and fellowship (Proverbs ch11 v13; ch16 v28; ch26 v20).

Criticism

Criticism is often excused and disguised as 'discerning observations'!

'Avoiding such loafers' is not one of several options. It's a command issued with the authority of Jesus' name.

2 A MODEL TO FOLLOW (vv7-9)

The best way to learn any new skill is not by reading a book or by studying a diagram but by copying an example. Paul is a model of industriousness and faithful service. He wasn't idle, and neither did he rely on the handouts of others. He was able to pay his way. Now Paul acknowledges his entitlement to 'church support' as an apostle and a minister. He could have demanded food, accommodation, and all reasonable living expenses. But he didn't! He was prepared to give up his rights and privileges so that he could be a good model. In this, he was reflecting the supreme Model, who is Jesus. God the Son was prepared to give up all his rights and privileges to be the Sin-bearer of his people at the cross (Philippians ch2 vv6-8). Jesus is the perfect example to follow (1 Peter ch2 v21) in terms of commitment, perseverance, patient endurance, and hard work. His mission was to complete his Father's work *'as long as it is day'* (John ch9 v4; ch17 v4). Our mission is to complete the work which our heavenly Father has given us to do (Colossians ch3 v23).

3 A RULE TO OBEY (vv10-13)

Note that it's not being unable to work that's the vice; rather, it's the refusal to work. There are some who live for the church, who live by the church, and who live through the church. But there are others who clearly live off the church. Some direct their efforts at meddling in the efforts of workers. They should stop annoying people and get on with the work they should be doing. That work may be rather repetitive, and they may jump at the chance to do something novel, dynamic, and exciting. But the chief requirement is *'doing what is right'*.

4 A WARNING TO HEED (vv14-15)

There were those who ignored the apostles' instructions. They weren't false teachers, peddling lies and falsehoods, and neither were they to be regarded as enemies who were hostile to the gospel. Paul still calls them *'brothers'*, but he hopes that they will feel shame and repent. Such people should be avoided. Close fellowship is not possible based on serious disagreement regarding God's word through the apostles. Yet while they had forsaken their duty, they hadn't forsaken their faith. He hopes that the disobedient minority will soon be reconciled to the church.

He longs for a united church in every respect. His blessing of peace pronounced upon the church is for all believers, at all times and in all circumstances (v16), and God's grace is for all (v18).

DECEMBER 2
GALATIANS ch1.1-5

AD596 is a significant year in British history. It was the year that Pope Gregory I sent an Italian missionary called Augustine (not to be confused with the great theologian and Early Church father with the same name) to England to convert the English to Christianity. At first, Augustine's mission seemed to be successful. King Ethelbert I of Kent was one of the first converts, and a couple of years later, Augustine was enthroned as the first Archbishop of Canterbury.

But although Augustine's mission was successful among the Anglo-Saxon tribes of Southern and Eastern Britain, he found fierce resistance from Western Britain: in particular, the Celtic nations of Wales and Cornwall. These nations had already been influenced by Christianity, although it was often mixed with superstition and even some relics of paganism. The word 'Celt' comes from a Greek word meaning 'barbarian' and was generally associated with the Gauls, who migrated north-westwards across Europe. There was also a migration of Gallic tribes eastwards into Asia Minor (modern Turkey). These Gallic people, or Gauls, settled in an area which became known as 'Gal-atia'.

THE GOSPEL TO GALATIA

Paul had evangelised Galatia, especially the southern part (Acts chs13-14). Paul had witnessed the whole city of Antioch assemble to hear the gospel (Acts ch13 v44). The Gauls were *'glad and honoured the word of the Lord'* (Acts ch13 v48). *'The word of the Lord spread through the whole region'* of Galatia (Acts ch13 v49). How could Paul forget the way in which the Galatian druids had believed that the two apostles were Zeus and Hermes – gods appearing as humans? How could Paul forget the way in which crowds had stoned him or the way in which *'a large number of disciples'* were won through the preaching of the gospel (Acts ch14 v21)?

So Paul, the apostle (one who was recognised as carrying the supreme authority of the Lord who sent him) wrote (ch1 v1) to the *'churches in Galatia'* (ch1 v2), probably around AD48 or AD49.

He begins by directing them to Jesus, and he emphasises 2 points.

1 THE RESURRECTION OF JESUS

(v1) The resurrection of Jesus is one of the best attested events in history, with over five hundred and fifteen individuals witnessing the risen Christ on a dozen different occasions over a period of about six weeks. Who or what could have stopped the feared persecutor Saul dead in his tracks and changed him into one of the despised, persecuted believers, except the risen Jesus? But every day there are eloquent testimonies and vivid illustrations of *'the old has gone, the new has come'* by being *'in Christ'* (2 Corinthians ch5 v17). As a Christian, Christ's resurrection is:

-

Your Ground of Hope

The resurrection is the one solid guarantee that all God's redeemed people will also be raised. It's a *'living hope'* (1 Peter ch1 v3).

Your Power to Live

A living union to the risen Christ is essential to living the Christian life (Philippians ch3 v10).

Your Authority to Serve

The risen Jesus not only intervened dramatically on the Damascus Road and transformed Paul, but it was the risen Jesus who sent him as an apostle. His commission and appointment were from heaven.

2 THE RESCUE OF JESUS

(vv3-5) The word *'rescue'* or *'deliver'* means 'to take out' or 'pluck out' from dangerous, hostile conditions that would threaten to overwhelm. The gospel is presented as a Rescue Plan to lift sinners from the inevitable death and destruction of *'the present evil age'*. Christ died when sinners *'were still powerless'* (Romans ch5 v6).

He Gave Himself for our Sins

Jesus gave his life voluntarily: he laid down his life (John ch10 vv11, 17-18). Our sins enslave us, isolate us, and condemn us, but Jesus gave himself so that we may receive freedom, fellowship, and forgiveness. Theologians use the word 'vicarious' in referring to Christ's saving work, that is, taking the place of another (as in the word 'vicar'). He became the substitute at the cross for everyone who believes in him.

He Gave Himself to His Father's Will

The divine rescue wasn't a last-minute, last-ditch attempt to save sinners. It was a mission prepared before the inception of time and before the creation of the universe. The ultimate way of showing that God has saved you is to give yourself wholly to your heavenly Father's will.

DECEMBER 3
GALATIANS ch1.6-10

For the ancient Gauls who had settled in Western Europe, including Cornwall, the gospel became mixed with pagan superstitions. For the Gauls in Galatia, the gospel had become mixed with Judaistic superstition and tradition. Instead of the pure gospel of faith in Jesus Christ, the Galatian Judaizers had imposed additional requirements, including the rite of circumcision. They were teaching the gospel plus other conditions. Paul set out to reassert the purity of the gospel.

THE GOSPEL PLUS NOTHING

1 THERE IS NO OTHER GOSPEL MESSAGE (vv6-7)

The gospel is fundamentally the good news about the grace of God in Jesus Christ. 'Gospel' comes from the Old English word 'godspell' ('god' equals 'good' and 'spell' equals 'word'). The word 'gospel' translates the Greek word which Paul uses, from which we get our words 'evangelist' and 'evangelism'. This 'good word' is the truth about Jesus Christ, God's Son, and the wonderful grace in providing an efficient and all-sufficient Saviour. The heart of this gospel concerns salvation through faith in Jesus – his life, death, burial, resurrection, and ascension. John Mark introduces the second book of the New Testament with the opening line: *'The beginning of the gospel about Jesus Christ, the Son of God'* (Mark ch1 v1). When Paul had given his 'mission report' to the Church Council at Jerusalem after he had visited Galatia, there were those who insisted that those Galatian converts should add Judaistic tradition to the gospel. Peter sprang to the defence of these Gentile converts (Acts ch15 vv7-11). It's the same gospel for Jew and Gentile, for rich and poor, for the educated and uneducated. There is only one true gospel message that fits all, and it's still *'the power of God for the salvation of everyone who believes'* (Romans ch1 v16). There were two urgent issues about some:

Deserting the Gospel (v6)

The word *'desert'* implies that they were in the process of changing their position. They were turning away from the truth of God's word and the teaching of the apostles. They had become dissatisfied with the true gospel.

Perverting the Gospel (v7)

They were trying to distort/corrupt/pervert the gospel. They were not content to proclaim God's saving grace in Jesus: they wanted to introduce a requirement to do other things as well. It was not 'by faith alone'.

2 THERE IS NO OTHER GOSPEL PREACHER (vv8-9)

The calibre of the preacher doesn't guarantee the truth of the gospel. You can have eloquent, popular preachers, even *'an angel from heaven'*, but if he preaches a different gospel, he is a false teacher, an enemy of God, and he is *'eternally condemned'* (vv8,9). The true gospel preacher is not just a 'deliverer of a sermon': he is a 'deliverer of a message'. God referred to John Baptist, one of the greatest preachers of all time, as *'my messenger'*

(Malachi ch3 v1; Matthew ch11 v10). Paul never boasted eloquence or superior wisdom (1 Corinthians ch2 vv1-2), only a mandate to share the crucified Saviour. Preachers of a 'false gospel' are:

Causing Confusion (v7)

Unbiblical nonsense, peddled by celebrity speakers and preaching personalities, agitates people and sows disorder and bewilderment.

Earning Condemnation (vv8,9)

Paul doesn't mince words. He's not saying that if preachers are not preaching the Biblical gospel, then they are 'misguided' or 'mistaken'. He says that they are doomed.

3 THERE IS NO OTHER GOSPEL RESPONSE (v9)

Acceptance (v9)

The word 'acceptance' or 'received' means that it was taken from someone alongside them, that is, Paul. The apostle preached the gospel, and they accepted it by faith (Romans ch10 v17). They turned from their sin and trusted in the completed work of Jesus in his redemptive mission.

But the 'acceptance' of the gospel is proved by:

Allegiance (v6)

Paul wouldn't be referring to their 'desertion' unless they had already declared their allegiance to Christ. They were both believers (Acts ch13 v48; ch14 v1) and disciples (Acts ch14 v21). They could testify to the grace of God that had saved them. Their baptisms and their identification with local Galatian churches proved their allegiance to Christ. How do you show your allegiance to Christ?

Perhaps you sense that you have failed the Lord. Maybe you can admit to deserting him for 'another gospel' with 'another preacher' demanding 'another response'.

There is forgiveness for those who repent and return (1 John ch1 v9).

DECEMBER 4
GALATIANS ch1.11-24

Following Paul's successful preaching tour in Galatia, some Jewish Christians were insisting that the new Galatian converts must conform to certain Old Testament rites, including circumcision. Paul's critics were arguing that the gospel which Paul had been preaching was 'incomplete'. In fact, they were saying that Paul wasn't a proper apostle anyway! Cynically, they were suggesting that the only reason Paul had been successful in his Galatian mission was that he had removed the legal requirements. Many people had professed conversion, they argued, because Paul had made conversion too easy. Paul had come to realise the discovery that Martin Luther made fifteen hundred years later, that men and women are not justified before God by the works of the law, but they are justified by faith through the grace of God in Christ. For Paul, it was a *'revelation'* of seismic proportions. It was mind-blowing, soul-stirring, and life-changing. Paul received a revelation *from* Jesus, but it was also the revelation *of* Jesus.

Do we have the burden that Paul had, that is, to reveal Jesus?

SEISMIC REVELATION

1 REVEALING JESUS IN THE GOSPEL

It's not Man-Made

'*…the gospel I preached is not something man made up*' (v11).

The Good News is not some fable or fairy story that has been concocted by the church. It's not a set of ethics dreamt up by philosophers, nor is it a set of doctrines formulated by theologians. The gospel was neither an invention by the Early Church Fathers nor was it thrashed out by some Church Council.

It's not Man-Given

'*I did not receive it from any man*' (v12). The gospel wasn't a tradition handed down from generation to generation. Paul didn't receive it from his parents or his grandparents.

It's not Man-Taught

'*...nor was I taught it*' (v12). The Jewish rabbis were in the habit of passing their rabbinic traditions on to their students. In a similar way, craftsmen would not only teach skills and knowledge, but they would also transmit customs, traditions, and superstitions to their apprentices. Paul insists that the gospel concerning Jesus came directly to him from Jesus (Romans ch1 vv1-3).

2 REVEALING JESUS IN OUR PREACHING

Paul explains that there was a clear purpose of God in revealing Jesus *to* him and *in* him (vv15-16). Though Paul had been at war with God – despising God's gospel, attacking God's followers, and even persecuting God's Son – yet God had earmarked this brutal fanatic to be a preacher of the gospel. He had been '*set apart from birth'* and *'called...by his grace'* (v15). God had revealed Jesus to Paul so that Paul could reveal Jesus to the Gentiles. That must be the core objective of our preaching: to reveal Jesus. His preaching was occupied with Jesus (1 Corinthians ch1 vv22-23). The centre and the circumference of our preaching must be Christ. The glorious theme and dependable anchor to our preaching must be Christ. The overwhelming power and lifeblood of our preaching must be Christ.

The gospel brings hope, assurance, forgiveness, peace, joy, and life itself. What miserable failures we become if we don't preach the true gospel of God's grace!

3 REVEALING JESUS IN OUR LIVES

His Way of Life Before – Persecuting

Paul had been a fanatical enemy of the church (v13; Acts ch8 v3; ch26 vv9-10). Paul's obsession with traditions had turned him into one mean, destructive machine. He was fixed on exterminating the church.

His Way of Life After Preaching

After his conversion, he immediately started preaching (Acts ch9 v20). For three years God shaped, moulded, and taught his apostle.

Our Way of Life Always – Praising

(v24) *'They praised God because of me'.* Paul wasn't boasting: the believers weren't praising *him*. Yet they recognised God's gracious and merciful work in Paul's life. They looked upon Paul and saw the reflection of Jesus in his life. Let's cultivate the habit of looking out for God's footprints (where he has been) and his fingerprints (what he has done). Let's spot the evidence for the work of God, particularly in individual lives, that will be the springboard for our praise. It's easy to focus only upon the ugliness of sin in our churches – the infighting and backbiting, the complaints and criticisms, the idleness and irresponsibility. But let's learn to identify where God is wonderfully at work so that our lives will be lived in praising him constantly.

DECEMBER 5
GALATIANS ch2.1-10

In the history of the world and the narrative of the Bible, we need to understand how deplorably bad the 'bad news' is before we can appreciate how wonderfully good the 'good news' is. The bad news of man's desperate plight without God; his thorough contamination by sin; his total helplessness and hopelessness is the bleakest, blackest backdrop of all (Rom ch3 v10; ch5 v12; ch6 v23; Hebrews ch9 v27). Man can offer no excuse, and he can manufacture no escape. Sin leads to death, judgement, and the destruction of hell in all its final, awful, eternal reality. In this penitentiary, there is no reprieve, no parole, and no time off for good behaviour. The abject hopelessness is unimaginable. That's the bad news – the worst news ever! But in the gospel of God's grace, there is good news – the best news ever!

THE BEST NEWS EVER!

There is a Saviour, a Rescuer, who provides a way out by making the sinner righteous (Romans ch3 vv22-24). No wonder Paul says, *'Woe to me if I do not preach the gospel'* (1 Corinthians ch9 v16). Every believer is a living witness to the transforming power of the gospel. But there are other blessings and benefits too:

1 THE GOSPEL BRINGS FAITHFULNESS

One of the marks of a disciple of Jesus is their faithfulness to God's call, God's service, and God's people (the church). They remain loyal, unyielding, stable, and resolute despite the inevitable pressures. Paul knew all about pressures!

He didn't give in to the Pressure of Work

He had already been preaching the gospel for fourteen years (v1) and knew all about hardships and dangers (2 Corinthians ch11 vv24-28). Paul may have heard the insidious talk that we may hear today, such as 'Why don't you give up/pack it in?' ... 'You don't need to endure that kind of pressure as a church officer/Sunday School teacher/church caretaker. Give it up! Let someone else do it!' 'You can justify your actions by saying you have other responsibilities!' But Paul wasn't distracted by intimidation, threats, injuries, or malnutrition.

He didn't give in to the Pressure of Criticism

There were *'false brothers'* (v4) who were trying to make them slaves of Jewish rites and ceremonies. But Paul didn't *'give in to them'* (v5). Frequently, critics *'who (seem) to be important'* (v9) may try to negate the effectiveness of a person's ministry by unjust criticism, behind their back if not to their face.

He didn't give in to the Pressure of Prosperity

He didn't succumb to the desire to be rich, prosperous, and gain a more affluent lifestyle. Paul had a deep concern for Poor Relief (v10). He was sympathetic to the believers who were disadvantaged and in need. Paul's love and faithfulness didn't prevent him from giving too much!

2 THE GOSPEL BRINGS FREEDOM

The Judaizer legalists wanted all Gentile converts to be bound by ceremonies and rituals that had been binding on Old Testament Jews. They believed that to become a 'child of God' you had to become a 'child of Abraham' by being circumcised. Paul insisted that the signs of the Old Covenant could not be forced upon the children of the New Covenant. Paul's courageous and resourceful friend Titus may have been a 'test case' in this dispute (v3). Paul refers to *'the freedom we have in Christ Jesus'* (v4). We don't earn salvation by ticking off a checklist of 'must-dos'. We are justified by faith, not by conforming to a set of laws. Yet true gospel freedom makes us the slaves of Jesus. The freedom of faith produces devoted disciples.

3 THE GOSPEL BRINGS FELLOWSHIP

Although the apostles and early church leaders had been called to separate ministries, they knew the blessing of fellowship which the gospel brings (v9). Clasped right hands were the seal of trust, friendship, belonging, and identification. It was a sign of partnership in the gospel. But true unity can only be experienced in the Biblical gospel of God's grace. Solidarity and fellowship in the gospel can only be found among those who are *'justified by faith'*. Here is a fellowship that surpasses all other human friendships. The church suffers today from too many mavericks and 'lone rangers' who want to do their own thing, separate from the church. We need each other in the work of the gospel (1 Corinthians ch12 vv13-23). We need the partnership of service, outreach, mission, and prayer. What contribution are you and I making to the fellowship of the gospel?

DECEMBER 6
GALATIANS ch2.11-21

THE NEED TO STRAIGHTEN OUT

If 'orthopaedics' refers to that branch of medicine which deals with the correction or straightening of bones and muscles, the similar word 'orthopodeo' is to do with the straightening or correcting of feet. This is the word that Paul uses in v14 when he speaks of *'not acting in line with the truth of the gospel'*. Paul is accusing Peter of being 'out of step' with *'the truth of the gospel'*. But what had caused him to become out of rhythm and not march in line with the good news about Jesus? Peter had been influenced by certain Jews who believed that following Jewish customs and traditions was essential to becoming a Christian. In the light of the very gospel of grace which Peter himself had been preaching, Peter *'was clearly in the wrong'* (v11). It was almost as if Peter had forgotten what had happened in Cornelius' house (Acts ch10). But Paul had to jolt Peter and his friends back 'into step'. He didn't apologise for being confrontational, nor did he rebuke him in private. There were vital, fundamental issues of gospel purity at stake, and Paul challenged Peter as to his thinking (v14).

Paul underlines three important truths for us as well as for Peter

1 WE ARE UNIFIED BY GRACE (vv11-14)

The real unifying adhesive that holds the Church together is God's grace to each one of us. Paul emphasises that our unity is not because we are all members of the *'circumcision group'* (v12) or that we all continue to follow *Jewish customs'* (v14). Christians are not all united because they are Baptists, Methodists, Pentecostals, or any other denominational or non-denominational grouping. Neither are they united because they all use the same hymn book, the same Bible version, or the same edition of the Book of Common Prayer. They are not welded together in the Church because they have been christened, confirmed, or baptised. The unifying work is God's grace. Each individual Christian can point to the saving grace of God in their life. It was grace that brought the Saviour all the way to our perilous condition so that he could rescue us and bring us to God. Gravity may draw us to earth, but it's grace that draws us to heaven and unites us with each other.

2 WE ARE JUSTIFIED BY FAITH (vv15-19)

Although the Jews had been a privileged people and were not *'Gentile sinners'*, yet they were 'sinners' and just as much in need to be made right before God (*'justify'*). We are not justified based on what we DO (however great, noble, or sacrificial), but we are justified on the basis of what God has DONE in the life, death, and resurrection of Jesus. Justification is the very opposite of condemnation. 'To condemn' means 'to declare guilty': 'to justify' means 'to declare not guilty'. It's impossible for us to make ourselves acceptable to God or to make ourselves right or righteous. We must be 'made right and righteous'. Faith is the trusting, open hand that receives the righteousness of Jesus. By believing in him, we receive from God the verdict that Christ's obedience and sacrifice have obtained. All the righteous demands of the law have not been repealed or rescinded, but they have all been fulfilled in Christ. Therefore, we are justified by faith in Christ, not by faith in our efforts to keep the law.

3 WE ARE CRUCIFIED WITH CHRIST (vv20-21)

Faith is the key to living the life of Christ. Although Paul proclaims the cross as the place where Christ was crucified for him, it's also the place where he has been *'crucified with Christ'*. He is united with him in his death. The phrase refers to a past event (Christ's crucifixion) that has a controlling influence upon the present. Because Jesus died *for* sin, we must die *to* sin. The believer's life must be lived differently because of the cross. If we trust Christ to save us, then we can't live the same way anymore. We become dead to the law and to sin. If you are *'crucified with Christ'* then you will have discovered that the Son of God loves you and has given himself for you. Jesus has laid down his life for his sheep (John ch10 v11), his friends (John ch15 vv13-14). If we are his friends, then we must *'remain in his love'* and *'do the things he commands'*. Paul argues that if we could get right with God by our law-keeping, then the cross was a waste of time (v21). It has taken nothing less than the Son of the eternal God and his substitutionary death upon a blood-stained cross to make us righteous, so that we can be unified by grace, justified by faith, and crucified with Christ.

DECEMBER 7
GALATIANS ch3.1-14

GOSPEL PURITY

There are three spiritual states to which Paul alludes in this next part of his argument for the purity of the gospel.

1 UNDER THE SPELL

Paul wants to know who has *'bewitched'* these gullible Galatians (v1). Who has hypnotised them or captured them under a spell? They may feel helplessly under the influence of Jewish Lawkeepers who were trying to pervert the gospel, but it was their foolishness that had brought them under that 'spell' in the first place. Their powers of judgement had been neutralised. The gospel, that had so transformed the lives of these believers, had been received by faith. The Judaisers were now adding extra criteria for salvation. Their 'gospel' was 'believe in Jesus' plus 'behave as Jews'. So now the Galatians were in danger of being held in a trance, unable to think sensibly and Biblically. Paul tries to 'break the spell' by reminding them of the *'righteousness'* that is credited to those who believe. He uses Abraham as the supreme example of faith. Abraham was not 'made righteous' before God because he kept the law (that didn't come until four-hundred-and-thirty years later), nor because he was circumcised (that happened later too). He was 'made righteous' because of his faith (Romans ch4 vv13-25). Consider Abraham then (v6). Both Jews and Muslims claim Abraham as their father, but Paul, a Jew, says that Abraham is the spiritual father of everyone who believes in Jesus. Paul hammers home the point that just because you may be a Jew with a long Hebrew ancestry and a proven track record in keeping the law and conforming to all the traditional customs and practices, Abraham may not be your father! Abraham is the father of believing Jews and believing Gentiles (vv8-9; Romans ch4 v11).

If you have come to Jesus Christ in repentance and faith, then you are a 'child of faith' and Abraham is the 'father of the faithful'.

2 UNDER THE CURSE

If you refuse to repent of your sin and trust in Jesus but choose to comply with the law instead, then you are doomed from the start (v10; Deuteronomy ch27 v26). There's only one man who stands alone as the only one to have kept and fulfilled God's law perfectly in every microscopic detail. Jesus *'continue(d) to do everything written in the Book of the Law'* (v10). Jesus achieved the impossible. But for everyone else who chooses to use the law as their passport to righteousness, they are cursed by that law because they are unable to keep it. Even the tiniest of errors ruins everything. Everyone except Jesus has failed to keep the law and therefore cannot be made right with God by law-keeping (v11). Law and faith are mutually exclusive in salvation.

3 UNDER THE BLOOD

(vv13-14) Jesus came to redeem (buy back or buy out) those who could never make themselves right before God by law-keeping. Jesus endured the cross, became a curse, and shed his blood. The Redeemer paid the prescribed fee in blood so that the believing sinner may be released from his obligations to the law. Jesus' blood is the sum of the payment made to secure the believer's discharge from the law. Jesus became *'a curse for us'* (v13), suffering the judgement of the law to release us from the curse of the law. Transgressors of the law were humiliated in death by having their bodies exhibited for all to see. 'Strung up on a tree' demonstrated the depths of guilt and shame. For Jesus to be 'nailed to a cross' was equivalent to being 'hung on a tree' (Acts ch5 v30; 1 Peter ch2 v24). The blessing that comes to us because of Christ becoming a curse is *'the promise of the Spirit'*. It's the Holy Spirit who brings about the new birth and makes us children of God, and, if the Spirit lives within us, then we must show the evidence of that spirit-life. Although Paul's great debate in these verses focuses on our inability to satisfy God's justice by keeping the law, the evidence for 'faith in Jesus' is 'following Jesus'. The evidence for having *'receive(d) the promise of the Spirit'* (v14) is to live the life of the Spirit. Walking in the Spirit is to walk as Jesus walked, bearing the Spirit's fruit (ch5 v22). This is the distinguishing mark of a true child of Abraham.

So are you living 'under the spell' of a 'faith plus works gospel'? Are you still 'under the curse' of the law because you are not yet saved? Or are you 'under the blood' because you have been justified by faith and know Jesus as your Redeemer?

DECEMBER 8
GALATIANS ch3.15-25

THE ANSWER DOESN'T LIE IN THE LAW

A significant percentage of us fail to wear seat belts, so we're told. Before 1983, most people resisted the moral calls from government, medical authorities, and road safety organisations, despite overwhelming evidence that the wearing of seat belts saved lives and injuries. But in January 1983, the law was added. This became a defining date in 'seat belt history' because the law made it a transgression, and there could be no dispute as to the rights and wrongs, whether you agree or not.

That is precisely the point Paul is making in this passage.

1 THE PURPOSE OF THE LAW (vv19-21)

The main purpose of the law was to show up sin for what it is. The law made sin into a transgression because failing to comply was an offence. If a man's own conscience failed to underline the sinfulness of sin, the law would show it to be so (Romans ch4 v15). Before seat belt legislation, a person not wearing a belt didn't consider themselves to be a transgressor or a lawbreaker. But now, since the law, the sight of a police car will send drivers grasping for their seat belts (Romans ch3 v20). *'The law was added so that the trespass might increase'* (Romans ch5 v20). Paul certainly refuted any criticism of the law for doing its job. He said, *'I would not have known what sin was except through the law'* (Romans ch7 v7). The law was introduced to make wrongdoing a legal offence. The law wasn't a failure insofar as it went (v21). In fact, *'the law is holy, and the commandment is holy, righteous and good'* (Romans ch7 v12). But the law couldn't do what it hadn't been designed to do, just like a lighthouse that has no power to save those in peril because its job is to show the danger. You can't blame a lighthouse for not rescuing those who have come to grief on its rocks. Nor can you blame the law for not rescuing sinners. The law underlines man's need for a Saviour. The answer doesn't lie in law but in grace. Our right relationship with God is not dependent upon a conditional law but upon an unconditional promise (v18). The *'inheritance'* of salvation is not based upon the law of God's righteousness but upon the promise of God's grace. The law was a temporary arrangement from Moses to Jesus, for in him God's grace is fully realised.

2 THE PRISONERS TO THE LAW (vv22-25)

The law had its purpose, but it had its prisoners, too. Two images of the law are given:

The Law as a Gaoler

(vv22-23) The story of the Old Testament is the history of man locked up in a dungeon of sin. Since Genesis ch3 the world has been held in custody under sentence of death. Incarcerated in sin's penitentiary, there is no parole, no reprieve, and no escape. Liberty can never be gained by demolishing the walls, picking a lock, digging a tunnel, or bribing an official. There's no way out. But if sin's prison appears in Genesis ch3 where mankind is taken into custody, the gaoler appears in Exodus ch20 where the law is given to Moses. The law's role is to stand guard, enforcing the restraint that sin imposes. But for how long? – *'until faith should be revealed'* (v23). There is hope and *'freedom for the prisoners'* (Luke ch4 v18).

The Law as a Supervisor

(v24) The law held the temporary role of a guardian – a nanny – to exercise guidance and discipline until Christ came. As believers, our standard of behaviour is not merely complying with a checklist of 'dos and don'ts'. We ought to live to meet the approval of our Saviour, whom we love and serve.

3 THE PROMISE BEFORE THE LAW (vv15-18)

The law given to Moses has not superseded the promise given to Abraham.

The Inheritance

If a human covenant, like a will, cannot be amended, how much more so with a divine covenant. Nothing can change our eternal inheritance as a true child of Abraham through faith. That inheritance is ring-fenced from any dishonesty, damage, or depreciation. Should we therefore not be afraid to step forward, to act, to engage in spiritual battles on the secure foundation of God's promise?

The Seed

(v16) God's promise to Abraham (Genesis ch12 v3) is ultimately fulfilled in Jesus Christ and the power of the gospel of his grace. This should encourage us and challenge us to know that God has planned to bless the world through Jesus Christ, the Saviour of the world, the Seed of Abraham, the Son of God.

Is there a greater power than the life-changing power of the gospel?

Is there a firmer promise than in the inheritance that is ours in the one Seed, which is Christ?

DECEMBER 9
GALATIANS ch3.26-ch4.7

ADOPTING ADULTS

These verses tell us something about the wonderful truth of adoption. Every believer is adopted into the family of God. God is not the universal father of everyone. Certainly, he is the Creator of everyone, but he is not their father. Jesus declared in explicit terms to unbelievers concerning their parentage. Jesus told them that they belong to their father, the devil (John ch8 vv41-44). There is no doctrine of God's universal fatherhood. We are sinners from conception (Romans ch3 vv10, 23), and the devil is the father of each and every sinner. But the Good News about Jesus proclaims that in God's perfect timing *'God sent his Son, born of a woman, born under law, to redeem those under law, that we might receive the full rights* (or *'the adoption')* *of sons'*. Adoption involves an irrefutable legal transaction. Adoption is when God places believers into his family, not as infants, but as adult children with all the rights and responsibilities of adulthood.

What are the blessings of being adopted by God?

1 NEW FATHER

'Abba, Father' (ch4 v6) represents the closeness between a father and son (*'Father, dear Father'* – JB Phillips' translation). *'Abba'* is Aramaic for 'father'. It emphasises the awesome relationship that we as rebellious sinners can have with the sovereign Creator and Sustainer of the universe. This is the same intimate expression that Jesus used during his deepest sorrows (Mark ch14 v36). We may love to use that special term of endearment, *'Abba, Father'*, but can we add just as Jesus did: *'yet not what I will, but what you will'*? Our heavenly Father's will and desire being fulfilled on earth just as in heaven (Matthew ch6 vv9-10) must include obedience in the lives of his children. Our adoption means that we have a new Father – a wonderful Father who perfectly cares and provides for us. He never fails us and never lets us down. He never causes us to wait because he's too busy, though often he makes us wait for our good.

2 NEW CLOTHES

(v27) Two images are used to illustrate the change that has taken place. Both images (immersed in water and putting on new clothes) show that there is a separation from the old and an identification with the new. *'In Christ'* is repeated in vv26-29 to show the new, amazing union and unshakable security that a believer enjoys.

3 NEW FAMILY

(vv28-29) There is unity and equality in God's family.

No Racial Distinction

The promise to Abraham is not exclusively to Jews. In Abraham, all the families of the earth would receive blessing, irrespective of colour, race, or language.

No Class Distinction

Despite the many class systems in the twenty-first-century societies, no one has greater entitlement than any other in God's family. There's an equality in the way we access the grace of God. There's no front door for nobility and a back door for tradesmen. There is but one door, even Jesus.

No Gender Distinction

What a revolutionary statement for a society in which women were second-class citizens! Yet there are many differences. Christianity is not like some gender-neutral, sci-fi society where everyone looks and behaves the same! But in Christ, there is no distinction based on those differences.

4 NEW RIGHTS

Redemption

(ch4 v5) This is directly linked to a price paid for deliverance (a ransom). The blood of Jesus is sufficient to secure our freedom.

Adoption

A believer is not liberated to be an orphan or a vagrant. God accepts the justified sinner into his family and confers on him the full rights of sonship. Adopted sons have the title-deeds to Glory (1 Peter ch1 v4).

5 NEW IMAGE

(v7) We are no longer slaves but God's sons and heirs. The adopted son is provided with a new nature and a new image – *'a new creation'* (2 Corinthians ch5 v17), *'the new self'* (Colossians ch3 vv9-10). But we must rid ourselves of the old nature. There's so much that's associated with the old self and the old way of life that must be forsaken.

What image of God's family do you portray to other believers...to unbelievers?

What identifies you as an adopted son of God? Are your brothers and sisters in Christ embarrassed by the poor image you demonstrate to a watching world?

DECEMBER 10
GALATIANS ch4.8-20

We all know what it is to be hurt physically, psychologically, emotionally, and even spiritually. Paul knew only too well what it meant to be hurt. Physically, he had been hurt by floggings, beatings, stoning, and shipwrecks (2 Corinthians ch11). However, he had been severely hurt by the legalistic Judaizers who had tried to undermine his teaching and who had made many derogatory remarks about his credibility. Paul is particularly sensitive to the hurts that the Galatian church had also suffered because of his Jewish critics.

IT HURTS!

There are three causes of hurt that show up in these verses.

1 LAW HURTS (vv8-11)

The Galatian believers had formerly been slaves to their pagan influence (v8). They were in bondage to the pagan interpretation of what they knew in their hearts (Romans ch1 vv21-23). But God in his grace had revealed his wonderful Son to them in the gospel. The Galatians had come to 'know God' through the Lord Jesus or, as Paul says in v9, they are 'known by God'. He knows his people in an amazingly loving and saving way (2 Timothy ch2 v19; John ch10 vv14-15). So how hurtful it must have been to see these Galatians abandoning the gospel of grace and returning to 'those weak and miserable principles' (v9). How much had the law hurt these Galatians who had once been released from its clutches! So great was their slavery that they were shackled to a calendar all over again (v10). Their religion had degenerated to just a formal observance. Their lives had become unfruitful because they had wriggled into a straitjacket of joyless legalism. The legal stranglehold hurt severely.

2 TRUTH HURTS (vv12-16)

During the early days of Paul's ministry among the Galatians, he had suffered a particular illness. But they had given Paul a 'royal welcome' (v14) and they would have made great sacrifices if that had helped him (v15). But now they looked upon Paul as an enemy because he had told the truth. Where had all that love for Paul gone? How had it evaporated so easily? We shall experience similar reactions for telling the truth. But we must be careful that the truth we proclaim is the truth of God's word and not just a church foible, a denominational dogma, or a personal opinion. As a spiritual physician, the apostle couldn't avoid this frank diagnosis and prognosis, yet he delivers it with great love and concern.

3 LOVE HURTS (vv17-20)

At the time of their conversion, the Galatians had caused Paul to suffer like a woman in labour. Now he was suffering these 'birth pangs' again as they turned back, preferring slavery to sonship. Initially, the Galatian converts had been thrilled with the joy of their relationship within the church family. They had shown practical love (v15) and Paul had been regarded as a messenger (even an 'angel' – v14). But these professing believers had lost their love for their brothers and sisters in Christ; they had lost their esteem for the apostle, and they had lost their joy (v15). We may identify with Paul, who had suffered such physical injuries and was now being 'kicked in the teeth' by those who had once loved him, praised him, and fellowshipped with him. Though he had been abused and abandoned, he still loved them, and that love hurt. He still longed that Christ may be formed in them (v19). Paul seemed to be at his 'wits end' (v20). He couldn't understand the rationale that put the work of the gospel and the family of the church in second place to individual whims and warped beliefs.

We can learn from how Paul reacted to the abrasions of love:

He showed concern

He wanted them to think again and to know that he wasn't going to hold a grudge against them for their antagonistic behaviour (v12).

He showed understanding

His love for them hadn't cooled despite their hurtful and potentially destructive criticisms. He recognised the need to be *'zealous'*, but it had to be a zeal for all the right issues. Often, we may devote disproportionate time and energies to 'straining gnats' when we are in serious danger of 'swallowing camels'.

He showed patience

Paul hoped and prayed that Christlikeness would be seen in them soon. Labour pains will always come to an end.

He showed Christ

Paul represented and reflected the Saviour he loved as a faithful servant. He demonstrated the Christlike, practical love of 1 Corinthians ch13 vv4-7.

DECEMBER 11
GALATIANS ch4.21-31

Arab-Jew tensions have simmered for nearly four thousand years. The history of antipathy between Israel and all the Arab nations dates from one family: two brothers, in fact, Isaac and Ishmael. These were brothers who had different mothers but the same father, Abraham. God had promised Abraham that his offspring would be as numerous as the stars in the night sky (Genesis ch15 v5). His wife, Sarah, grew impatient and arranged for her Egyptian servant, Hagar, to be a surrogate mother. So the eighty-six-year-old Abraham had a son by Hagar, and he was named Ishmael. But God kept his promise to the ninety-year-old Sarah, and she gave birth to Isaac. Yet it seemed impossible for Sarah and her son to live together with Hagar and her son, and so Ishmael and his mother were sent away, much to Abraham's distress. Today, following Mohammed's example, all Arabs claim that they have descended from Ishmael and are therefore implacably opposed to Israel, the descendants of Isaac.

ISAAC'S SPIRITUAL LINEAGE

Paul points to this ancient enmity to illustrate another point. He uses the historical fact of Ishmael and Isaac to reveal a theological truth. He refers to the roots of Judaism to show the spiritual conflict that existed within the churches of Galatia.

What were the contrasts between Isaac and Ishmael?

Birth

Ishmael's birth was natural: Isaac's birth was supernatural, for his mother was well past childbearing age. Yet nothing is too hard for the Lord (Genesis ch18 v14).

Status

Ishmael was the son of a slave woman, and Isaac was the son of a free woman (v22). The distinction is between professing Christians who think they are saved by keeping the law and those who are saved and freed through faith in Christ.

Representation

(vv24-26) Hagar represents the Old Covenant of Moses based on law, and Sarah represents the New Covenant of Christ based on promise. The earthly Jerusalem stands for legal Judaism, and the heavenly Jerusalem represents the free Christian church.

Where do we fit into all this as believers? We are the true spiritual sons of Abraham through Isaac, not Ishmael (ch3 vv7,29;v28). We are:

1 CHILDREN OF PROMISE (v28)

God's promise to Abraham not only included Isaac but also a numberless multitude of descendants. Every spiritual child of Abraham and a child of God is an heir. The conditions of inheritance are strictly defined (v30). The 'narrow-mindedness' that some Bible-believing Christians are accused of as to their definition of a Christian is to do with the *'narrow gate'* of entry (Matthew ch7 vv13-14). The gospel is for all (John ch3 v16; Romans ch10 v13), but the wideness of God's mercy is contrasted with the narrowness of the gate (Acts ch4 v12). Hagar and Ishmael had no part in the inheritance of the children of promise. The inclusiveness of the gospel proclaims 'many people', but the exclusiveness of the gospel proclaims 'one way'.

2 PEOPLE OF THE SPIRIT (v29)

Both Jews and Arabs point to Abraham as their father, but the true children are 'Spirit-born'. Christians are brought to God through the supernatural new birth (John ch3 vv6-7). Such children have the *'right to become children of God'* (John ch1 vv12-13). What is impossible with men is possible with God. That's why we can trust the Lord to save those for whom we earnestly pray, however 'unlikely' it may seem that they can be saved. If it's a 'spirit-induced' birth, then we can be confident that *'The vilest offender who truly believes, That moment from Jesus a pardon receives'* [Frances Van Alstyne].

3 VICTIMS OF PERSECUTION (v29)

Isaac was victimised by Ishmael from the start. We must expect nothing less, not only as the true children of Abraham, but the disciples of Jesus. The bitterest enemies of Jesus were the Jews. The fiercest opponents of Paul were the Judaizers. The greatest opponents to the work of the church and the spread of the gospel are not the secularists and atheists but those within evangelicalism, the modern-day Judaizers. But the Lord is kind and gracious, giving us the strength to endure the hardships of today as Paul did yesterday. Persecution is the reaction of natural religion to supernatural Christianity. Persecution is the reaction of nominal, orthodox Christians to born-again believers. We may suffer hardship and heartache, persecution and victimisation, but don't be disheartened or discouraged.

DECEMBER 12
GALATIANS ch5.1-6

THE CHARACTER OF FAITH

Some people have come to regret the 'improvements' that they have made to certain artefacts on discovering later that the piece was worth thousands or even millions of pounds. By their own efforts, they had devalued the priceless work of art.

Paul is accusing some Christians of trying to 'make improvements' to the gospel of Jesus. By adding Jewish laws and customs, they are devaluing the priceless message of God's grace (v2). If we add anything to the gospel's requirements, then it is tantamount to subtracting from the work of Christ. The 'Faith Plus' religion has numerous examples in today's religious scene.

The Judaizers believed that faith plus works brings salvation.

Many religious people believe that works bring salvation, plus faith.

But the Bible teaches consistently that faith brings salvation plus works.

These six verses tell us four things about the character of this faith.

1 THE FAITH TO BE FREE (v1)

If our faith is a genuine saving faith in Jesus, then it will be a 'stand-alone' kind of faith. Imagine a judge setting a prisoner free but then informing him that he must wear handcuffs for the rest of his life! Would the 'released' prisoner consider himself to be free? The believer's conscience has been set free from guilt through knowing that Jesus has paid the penalty for sin at the cross. The believer is also free from the desperate struggle to keep the law to please God. The gospel is a message of God's grace, not because we have kept the law, but because Jesus has kept the law and has offered himself in our place (see James ch1 v25). He has paid the ransom to release us and set us free (1 Timothy ch2 vv5-6). If you are free, Paul is saying, then live as if you are free.

2 THE FAITH TO STAND (vv1-4)

'Stand firm...' (v1). Paul calls upon those who have been set free to be resilient, to persevere, and to resist re-enslavement. Do not yield; do not give in; do not be overwhelmed by the pressure to become enmeshed by man-made regulations.

Sometimes in evangelicalism, we can be accused of being unfriendly or ungracious because we have taken a stand on what we believe the Bible is saying. Some 'churches' preach a different gospel altogether (ch1 vv6-7). They are making Christ worth nothing, and they are devaluing his work and his mission. They are relegating his life and sacrificial death to the 'rubbish tip', and they are making the cross powerless and a waste of time. How can we, therefore, formally align ourselves with those who devalue our precious Saviour and negate his cross?

Stand firm, even when the tide of popular religion flows against you.

3 THE FAITH TO WAIT (v5)

Our salvation and security are a wonderful work of the Spirit. He gives us the faith to believe, and he seals that belief by his abiding presence. As Christians, we can be confident that we are *'justified by faith'* (Romans ch5 v1) and not *'justified by law'* (v4). If our faith is in the Lord, and not in the law, then we *'eagerly await'* that glorious day at our Saviour's coming when we shall be made perfect forever (Philippians ch3 vv20-21; Jude v24). We are changed and united to Christ by the Spirit. He is the Motivator and the Mainspring of our faith. The exercise of that faith is the evidence of the Spirit's work in our lives. How much are we living our lives in the eager expectation of that momentous occasion? Is the development of our faith learning to *'eagerly await'*?

4 THE FAITH TO LOVE (v6)

True faith is not a cold, lifeless, academic theory. True faith is warm, animated, and fruitful. The law of the Judaizers commands love, whereas the faith of the gospel produces love. Paul told the immature Corinthians: *'If I have the faith that can move mountains, but have not love, I am nothing'* (1 Corinthians ch13 v2). The young, fresh faith of the Early Church believers expressed itself in the selling of *'their possessions and goods'*, giving *'to anyone as he had need'* (Acts ch2 v45). The Christians in Philippi expressed their faith by demonstrating love for Paul in sending gifts *'again and again when (he) was in need'* (Philippians ch4 v16). If we claim to be men and women of faith, how is that faith expressed in terms of practical, everyday love?

DECEMBER 13
GALATIANS ch5.7-15

Even in the first century of athletics' competitions, with which Paul was familiar, there were basic rules, the contravention of which could mean disqualification. *'Running a good race'* (v7) is a classic illustration that Paul uses several times in his epistles to illustrate different aspects of the Christian life.

DON'T BE ELBOWED OFF THE TRACK!

Paul knows about some athletes who had been prevented from finishing the race because another runner had *'cut in'* on them. This unsportsmanlike action is a picture of what the Judaizers were doing in hindering/jostling/obstructing other runners in the Christian race. The Galatians had started well and were running fine up to the point where other 'runners' had cut in on them. The Galatians had been knocked off balance by the false teaching of 'gospel plus Judaism'. They had stumbled and had been deflected from the course.

1 HINDRANCES TO OBEDIENCE (vv7-12)

The freedom which Jesus brings to those who are set free from the shackles of the world and the handcuffs of a works' religion is obedience to the truth. Here is belief and behaviour married together: creed plus conduct. This is faith plus works, not as the Judaizers taught, as a means to salvation, but a saving faith which proves itself by its godly deeds. The words for *'obeying'* (v7) and *'persuasion'* (v8) are linked closely together as they both represent a change of mind and heart that is the result of influence. *'Obeying the truth'* suggests the persuasion of the grace of God revealed in the gospel. We are 'won over' by the love of the Lord Jesus so that we only want to serve him and comply with the truth. The kind of *'persuasion'* (v8) which comes from the false teachers had enchanted these Galatians in such a way as to be 'elbowed off' the track. Yet Paul is confident that the Galatians would come to their senses (v10) and see the way in which the false teaching is permeating the Christian community like yeast in dough (v9).

The word for *'confusion'* (v10) means to stir up and to agitate (see John ch5 v7). Those who stir up trouble in the church will be held accountable. Professing Christians should not expect to cause trouble, division, upset, and heartache and walk away 'scot-free'. Paul says that there is still a debt outstanding: there's a penalty still to pay.

2 HINDRANCES TO SERVICE (vv13-15)

There are two distinct dangers to which Paul alerts us.

The Danger of Self-Indulgence

Paul warns about the abuse of the freedom that we enjoy in Christ. Freedom is not 'Christian anarchy', in which believers can do what they like and when they like, without consideration for the word of God or the church family and its missions and disciplines. That is a self-focused freedom. Like the first century, there are too many Christians who are wrapped up in themselves, where their needs, wants, aspirations, benefits, and opportunities are their chief concern. The Jewish legalists who were obsessed with fine-tuning their own spin on God's law had missed the fundamental point that *'the entire law is summed up in a single command: Love your neighbour as yourself'* (v14).

The Danger of Self-Destruction

It seemed that Paul was experiencing the kind of behaviour that's more associated with feral cats. Those who are continually expressing their bitterness, anger, and frustrations will eventually be consumed by them. Those who are forever dominated by a critical spirit will be crushed by that spirit. Those who let 'self' off the leash will be savaged by that animal in the end. In spiritual terms, many Christians sit together with a hand grenade in their laps: fingering the pin, pulling it out, and putting it back in again. Jesus spoke to his own disciples about service just after he had demonstrated humility in washing their feet (John ch13 vv14-16). Our service to each other should be unconditional and of pure motive. We shouldn't serve to attract praise or plaudits; nor so that people will think highly of us and speak well of us; nor so that people will reward us. Does our self-centredness force us to limit our giving, to ration our compassion, to reduce our availability, and to count the cost?

Let us learn to be those who serve selflessly with love. That will doubtlessly take its toll in all kinds of ways, but is it any more than Christ's supreme service to us?

DECEMBER 14
GALATIANS ch5.16-26

For the Christians who have trusted in Jesus to save them from sin, death, and hell, there is a long process that will make them more and more like Jesus. It doesn't happen overnight! Yet the believer has been *'predestined to be conformed to the likeness of his Son'* (Romans ch8 v29). The Holy Spirit's work and ministry are to make the believer more like Jesus. As Christians, we may gaze into the mirror of God's word and despair that we are not more like Jesus. But we can be assured that one day *'we shall be like him'* (1 John ch3 v2). All the long process of a struggling, battling, suffering life will be over, and the Holy Spirit will produce the finished article.

A WORK IN PROGRESS

We are urged to *'stand firm'* (v1); to express our faith through love (v6); to withstand jostling from false teachers in the race (v7); to show love to each other and to serve one another (v13); to avoid destroying one another (v15). But how can this be done?

1 LIVE THE LIFE OF THE SPIRIT (vv16-21)

When a person is born again through repentance and faith, by the work of the Spirit, that person is set apart for Jesus. The Holy Spirit stamps and seals that brand new Christian by his own divine presence. As far as the myriad hosts of heaven and hell are concerned, the ownership of this new Christian is not in doubt. We can be confident of our security in Christ because of the Spirit's testimony (Romans ch8 v16; 1 John ch4 v13). But we are called to face up to the reality of our sinful nature.

The Facts of Our Sinful Nature

The sinful nature is very real and is at war with the new spiritual nature. The sinful nature is opposed to the Spirit (v17). We can't win the war on our own strength. There is a continual conflict between the old bias to sin and the new nature of the Spirit. Paul explains this well in Romans ch7 vv14-20. This is the tension that all Christians will recognise to a greater or lesser degree.

The Acts of Our Sinful Nature

The old nature may be compared to a deadly assassin working secretly and invisibly, yet with the trademarks of his activities for all to see. *'The acts of the sinful nature are obvious'* (v19). It can be guaranteed that tomorrow's headlines will be made up of these fifteen activities and *'the like'* (vv19-21).

2 BEAR THE FRUIT OF THE SPIRIT (vv22-23)

In complete contrast to the harvest of sinful disgraces, there is a harvest of spiritual graces. The fruit of the Spirit differs from the gifts of the Spirit since it is given to each and every Christian. Here is one fruit with nine segments. Every believer must produce this fruit because this is the evidence that a person belongs to Christ. It's not usual to produce instant, full-sized, fully-developed fruit, but rather it appears as life is lived in the Spirit. A Spirit-produced 'love/joy/peace' is rooted in God and transcends circumstances and stretches across huge gulfs to touch adversaries. It's not easily upset or squashed, nor is it quickly bruised or becomes rotten. It's of a divine quality. If it's the fruit of the Spirit, patience will be self-effacing, kindness will be self-denying, and goodness will be self-sacrificing. The goal will be God, and the motive will be 'love for the Saviour'. Faithfulness is seen in commitment to God and his people. Gentleness is the manner in which it is revealed. Self-control comes from the word for 'strength': the power to control the will, through the Spirit.

3 KEEP IN STEP WITH THE SPIRIT (vv24-26)

Walking orderly or in line with someone is the meaning of the phrase *'in step with the Spirit'*. If you *'belong to Christ Jesus'* (v24), then you are no longer your own master or Satan's slave. You were *'bought at a price'* (1 Corinthians ch6 v20). Keeping in step with the Spirit means that drastic action has been taken regarding the *'sinful nature'*. The crucifixion of the sinful nature has already taken place, but sadly, too many Christians want to revisit their sinful nature, to caress it, and even to revive it! Paul's implication is 'Don't touch it! Leave it there – nailed to the cross!' There's a war going on between the *'sinful nature'* and the producing of *'the fruit of the Spirit'*. At times, it may seem impossible to win the war, but the secret of victory lies in keeping *'in step with the Spirit'*. A dancer may have poise, presence, patience, and appearance, but if he or she is out of step, then it can look clumsy and unsynchronized. Such 'out of step' under pressure can sometimes lead to a fall!

DECEMBER 15
GALATIANS ch6.1-10

As we read of the great organisations and institutions that have been a tremendous benefit to our society in the last one hundred to two hundred years, it is impossible to avoid the fact that the majority of their founders were Bible-believing Christians. Here were believers who had left an indelible imprint upon our nation because they had been doing good. Although Paul had gone to great lengths in this epistle to emphasise that a person doesn't become a Christian by 'doing good', yet it is by 'doing good' that Christians will be recognised. 'Doing good' accrues no credit towards salvation, but 'doing good' is the badge of the believer.

THE AGE OF THE DO-GOODERS

Some Christians are called to a ministry of preaching, pastoring, writing, or evangelising, but all Christians are called to a lifetime ministry of 'doing good'.

1 DOING GOOD BY REPAIRING (v1)

The word used for *'restore'* is the same word used for mending or preparing nets (Matthew ch4 v21). The word was also used by the medical profession when referring to bones that had to be set following a fracture or dislocation. As believers, we should be in the 'repair business'. There are many broken ministries, broken homes, and broken hearts that are not irreparable. None of us may be exempt from the damage that sin causes. This restoration and repair call for specialist treatment. For the repenting, returning sinner who has received the forgiveness of God, the church must strive for gentle restoration. But watch out! Don't become damaged and broken as the one you are trying to repair.

2 DOING GOOD BY BEARING (vv2-5)

'Carry each other's burdens...' (v2) Burden-bearing is all about love in action. This is not the exclusive responsibility of the pastor/elder/church leader. This is the ministry of every believer. Thinking too much about your own burdens can prevent you from looking out for someone else. The ministry of the Church Family is to bear each other's burdens. The Galatian Judaizers had been concerned about strict law-keeping in respect to the Law of Moses and the laws of the Pharisees. But in reaching out to believers and in bearing their heavy loads, you *fulfil the law of Christ* (v2). Jesus made it clear that obedience to his pre-eminent command identified his followers (John ch13 vv34-35).

3 DOING GOOD BY SHARING (vv6-9)

A Bible teacher is entitled to receive the material and financial support of the church. Those in the family of believers who are the beneficiaries of *'instruction'* must be ready to *'share all good things with (their) instructor'* (v6). Like all principles, this one has been abused extensively.

Some preachers/teachers/pastors, employed by the church, are not conscientious in their role. They can be lazy, disorganised, and time-wasters with little discipline or structure to their position. They are easily distracted and underproductive.

Some teachers are abused or neglected by the church where they are expected to give of themselves without proper remuneration or even reimbursement of expenses (1 Timothy ch5 vv17-18).

Some churches try to control and manipulate the pulpit through the offerings. People give according to what they like to hear, so that when they are dissatisfied with some teaching, they adjust their tithes and offerings accordingly. We reap what we sow if we excuse ourselves from not *'shar(ing) all things'*.

4 DOING GOOD BY CARING (v10)

Just as we are exhorted to be persistent in doing good (v9), so we are encouraged to be opportunistic (v10). In the broader sense, the whole of the Christian life provides the opportunity for doing good. 'Doing good' embraces everyone – enemies, neighbours, friends, and especially those *'who belong to the family of believers'*. There should be no discrimination in 'doing good' for God is pleased with this (Hebrews ch13 v16). We must also prompt other Christians to demonstrate goodness and generosity (Hebrews ch10 v24). Far from being a naive, idealistic, interfering busy body, a godly do-gooder will be the backbone of our nation, the salt of society, the fabric of the church, and the copy of Jesus who spent his life doing good (Acts ch10 v38).

DECEMBER 16
GALATIANS ch6.11-18

LARGE LETTERS

Whatever reason Paul has for writing in *'large letters'* (v11), we can be sure that it is not because he is semi-literate. He may have been suffering from partial sight, or he may be using the same method we employ to emphasise important points. We use capital letters or larger print to highlight keynote facts. There have been several vitally important points that Paul has drawn attention to in this epistle. The danger of a different gospel, the fundamental truth of justification by faith, the call to live by the Spirit, and membership in the true Israel of God are but some of the major teachings that Paul could have written in larger letters for emphasis.

In this final section, Paul ties together the themes that he has already developed:

1 MAKING A GOOD IMPRESSION

Everyone wants to make a good impression at some time or other, even if it is little more than hypocrisy. Circumcision had become, for the Galatian Judaizers, a 'badge of identity'. More than that, it had become a 'medal of honour and distinction' to boast about.

It was this Judaistic rite, along with other ceremonies and traditions, which the Judaizers were insisting upon as of great importance. They maintained that a person could not become a Christian believer without the whole Judaistic package. On the other hand, Paul contended that it is by faith alone that you are saved.

Jesus frequently referred to the Pharisees, who were forever trying to make a good impression. They would stand and pray in public places, and they would make a show of any gift that they gave to the poor. Jesus spoke of the Pharisees as *'whitewashed tombs'* (Matthew ch23 vv25-28), which may have looked good on the outside but were full of death and decay inside. All the Christian ceremonies and traditions just contribute to 'whitewashing the tomb'. The death and decay in the heart can only be addressed by the saving work of Christ.

How much of our lives are just for making good impressions?

2 BOASTING A GREAT CRUCIFIXION

If the Judaizers were boasting about their circumcision, Paul could have boasted about his 'uncircumcision'. But he doesn't! He boasts in the power and the effect of the cross of Jesus. If anyone had reason to boast in success and aspiration, Paul had (Philippians ch3 vv5-6). Ironically, the one thing that he was entitled to boast about was the cause of his humility – the cross of Jesus. There are three clear crucifixions in v14:

The Crucifixion of Jesus

It was divinely planned that Christ should become a curse to liberate his people from the curse of sin (Deuteronomy ch21 v23; Acts ch5 v30; 1 Peter ch2 v24). Jesus was crucified on an accursed tree to bring glory to God by becoming the sin-bearer of his people. He has become the effective substitute of every single person who is justified by faith. Nothing less and nothing other than that cross will suffice.

The Crucifixion of the World

As far as the believer is concerned, the world has been put to death, crucified. The world's standards, values, mindset, and lifestyles are all dead. To the Christian, they are but a corpse.

The Crucifixion of Self

This further emphasises the separation between worldliness and godliness. As far as the believer is concerned, the world is dead. As far as the world is concerned, the believer is dead. Jesus prayed for his disciples in John ch17 v15, not that his disciples should be taken out of the world, but that the world should be taken out of his disciples.

3 BECOMING A NEW CREATION

Paul argues that conforming to the old regulation of circumcision counts for nothing. He states that even reforming to a doctrine of uncircumcision counts for nothing. What counts is transforming to *'a new creation'* (v15; 2 Corinthians ch5 v17). In connection with discipleship, Paul refers to two experiences:

Following the Rule (v16)

This fundamental principle ('canon' or 'measure') is the undiluted gospel by which a person is saved. It is the doctrine of the apostles and the word of God. Everything must be measured against that.

Bearing the Marks (v17)

Paul had suffered much on account of his love for the Lord Jesus (2 Corinthians ch11 vv23-28). The hideous wounds, ugly scars, and medical conditions that he must have borne were testimony to his faithfulness and affection for Christ.

What 'love marks' are we prepared to bear for Jesus?

DECEMBER 17
JOEL ch1 vv1-20

AUTHOR

He was one of fifteen people in the Bible called 'Joel'. This Joel was the *'son of Pethuel'* (v1). *'Joel'* means *'Jehovah is God'*

DATE

We can't be too specific about the time Joel lived and ministered. The balance of evidence favours the eighth century BC, although this has no effect upon the message.

MESSAGE

The message is specifically to Judah. The theme and thrust of this message is the warning of God's judgement and the call to repent. Joel points out that the 'locust disaster' that has enveloped Judah is just a shadow of the judgement that would fall on the people if they failed to repent.

JUDGEMENT OF LOCUSTS

1 THE WORD OF THE LORD THAT CAME (v1)

Joel is God's man with the message for the moment. This message is not some sentimental thought, or a rambling monologue, or even a moral homily – it's *'the word of the Lord'* (v1). The Lord has spoken to this humble servant, and his burden will only be relieved when he has discharged his responsibility to declare that message. This message brings with it a question, as they faced the destruction caused by locusts:

'Has anything like this ever happened in your days or the days of your forefathers?' (v2). The scale of suffering and devastation is described by the barren sight of no vegetation (v4). The locusts are an invading army – innumerable and unstoppable (v6).

Religious ceremonies and sacrifices are curtailed (v9). Crops are wiped out totally, and the harvest is destroyed (vv10-12). The barns and granaries are depleted (v17). The livestock are suffering terribly because there is no food (v18). Everyone is thoroughly miserable, overshadowed by feelings of joylessness and the blackest despair (v12).

As we read of the destruction and desperation in Judah, we can't help but compare the disasters that are familiar to us and to our world over the last few years.

Disasters remind us of past sin

Instead of asking *'Why should this disaster hit us?'* we should be asking *'Why SHOULDN'T such a disaster hit us?'* Have we forgotten how sinful we are? Disasters may not be the result of specific sins but because of sin. It's sin that has blighted God's creation, polluted our planet, and infected our hearts. The curse of Genesis ch3 is in direct response to sin. But note in Luke ch13 vv4-5, Jesus made it clear that the 'tower disaster' didn't mean that the victims were more guilty. Neither was the man's blindness in John ch9 attributed to specific sins. We are part of a frustrated creation riddled with sin.

Disasters speak of future judgement

They serve as an alarm, a wake-up call (vv5, 14,15). The locust invasion was a signpost pointing to a future judgement.

Disasters call for present penitence

Calamities should prompt a spontaneous expression of humility before God. Joel calls for mourning and sorrow for sin

2 THE DAY OF THE LORD TO COME (v15)

What does *'the day of the Lord'* represent?

The triumph of God in historical judgement

Many of the prophets proclaimed God's decisive actions against Babylon, Assyria, and even Jerusalem. Such divine interventions, frequently referred to as *'the day of the Lord'*, reveals God's overthrow of his enemies and the preservation of his people. It's about destruction and deliverance, retribution and redemption, vengeance and victory. Throughout history, God has used disasters and plagues, wars and invasions to punish sin and to vindicate his believing people.

The triumph of God in the final judgement

'The day of the Lord' is closely identified with the Second Coming of Christ (1 Corinthians ch1 v8; 1 Thessalonians ch5 v2). All the successive interventions of God in history will reach an awesome climax in the great and final day of the Lord. This will mean eternal destruction for the unbeliever and eternal deliverance for the believer. Any hope in the *day* of the Lord must be anchored in the *name* of the Lord. *'To You, O Lord, I call'* (v19).

DECEMBER 18
JOEL ch2.1-17

The land of Judah is under siege. A huge, unstoppable army has invaded the land. Its soldiers are everywhere. All the crops have been destroyed, leaving the people and their livestock starving. Resistance is a waste of time. Nothing can be done about this vast 'invasion force', because the Lord is at the head of this army, and his troops are locusts. God sends a vast cloud of locusts to envelop the whole land.

It's not surprising that everyone should tremble at the coming of this particular *'day of the Lord'* (ch1 v1). When the swarm arrives, it's just as if the sun has been extinguished (v2). Lush green gardens are transformed into desert wastes (v3).

God is the 'Lord of Hosts' or the 'Lord of Armies'. All armies are subject to his sovereign control – whether it's the Israeli armies, or the inhabitants of heaven (1 Kings ch22 v19), or the stars and planets (Psalm 33 v6). He is also Lord of the armies of frogs, gnats, and flies that invaded Egypt (Exodus ch8). He is the Lord of the army of worms that attacked King Herod Agrippa (Acts ch12 v23). He is also Lord of the army of locusts (vv2, 4-11). This 'invasion' is not a random disaster or a chance occurrence. The Lord is at the head of this army!

ABOUT TURN

The message of Joel to Judah and Jerusalem was not that God was 'behind the scenes', moving and manipulating. He is *'at the head of his army'*. The Lord is the General who directs the troops. He is leading and controlling his great invincible force. So is there a glimmer of hope for these defeated people? Is there any possible escape from crushing judgement? Is there any action that can be taken to avert an even greater disaster? Yes, there is! *'Even now, declares the Lord, Return to me with all your heart...'* (v12). So how must we return?

1 RETURN WITH SINCERITY AND HUMILITY

(vv12,13a) It's easy to tear clothes in a show of emotion – a graphic gesture of emotion or sorrow. But true humility will mean sorrow for sin. True repentance is more than an expression of regret or remorse: it involves a change of feeling, attitude, and will. The hungry wayward son had a change of feeling (*'he came to his senses'* – Luke ch15 v17). He had a change of attitude (*'I will set out and go back to my father and say to him, Father, I have sinned against heaven and against you...'* Luke ch15 v18v18). He also had a change of will (*'So he got up and went to his father...'* Luke ch15 v20).

Repentance will not take place unless the Holy Spirit performs his convicting ministry. But we are justified in looking for repentance as evidence of the work of God's grace.

2 RETURN WITH ASSURANCE AND CONFIDENCE

(v13b) The one solid, immovable foundation of a returning sinner's faith is in the unchangeable nature of our God. If there were the slightest fluctuation in God's Person, perfections, promises, or purposes, then how could we believe in him or trust him? The reason we can confidently return to God is because we know that he hasn't changed. Of course, God reacts to genuine penitence. He *'relents'* (v13). *'He may turn'* (v14). But it doesn't prove that he changes. He has an unchanging attitude toward sin. He never gets used to it, nor can he overlook it. But his compassion, grace, and abounding love do not waver either (Exodus ch34 vv6-7).

3 RETURN WITH EXPECTANCY AND URGENCY

(vv14-16) On the basis of his nature and covenant promises, we can expect God to turn to us if we return to him (v14). A hallmark of true repentance is the desire to bring to God our offerings of consecration and commitment. But this should not be delayed. Repentance calls for prompt action – *'Blow the trumpet!'* ... *'Sound the alarm!'*

4 RETURN WITH FERVOUR AND VIGOUR

(v17) As the ministering priests made their way to the place of sacrifice, from the porch to the altar, they were to call the people to mourn. No one was exempt – even babies and brides were summoned (v16). From the sinner's misery to the Saviour's Calvary, there is always a place for tears of contrition and penitence. From the time our hearts are prodded by the Spirit's conviction to the point where our burden is lifted, should we not be weeping tears of repentance? Sometimes the distance from our 'porch' to 'altar' may be a long one! What prevents us from returning to him today?

DECEMBER 19
JOEL ch2.18-32

'Destruction' grabs the headlines better than 'construction'. 'Devastation' sells more newspapers than 'restoration'. But throughout the world, there are many examples of reconstruction, reinstatement, and renovation. The magnitude of the disaster recorded for us by Joel cannot be fully understood. As countless millions of locusts shut out the sun as they moved across the land, consuming all vegetation in their path, the prophet describes this as the great day of the Lord – '...*it is dreadful. Who can endure it?*' (v11).

And the most common question asked in the wake of any disaster is 'Why?' Joel's message from the Lord is that the Lord Almighty has designed this calamity. It is punishment for unfaithfulness and disobedience.

GOD'S RECONSTRUCTION PROGRAMME

But there is hope for the decimated Judah. These verses tell us about God's reconstruction and restoration programme.

1 REJOICING AT THE GREAT THINGS GOD HAS DONE (vv18-24)

These *'great things'* are 'great' in terms of size and importance. God is great in his acts of judgement as well as in his acts of grace. The Lord, who is *'at the head of his army'* (ch2 v11), is seen at the rear of his army (v20) – driving them and pushing them away from Judah, to perish in the Dead Sea and the Mediterranean Sea.

But the *'great things'* of God are not confined to the provision of a solution to the 'locust problem' – mercy in response to repentance, deliverance in response to humility. There is also the provision of satisfaction (*'enough to satisfy you fully'* v19). The supply of *'grain, new wine and oil'* (v19) would fully satisfy. We too can be confident in the Lord's abundant provisions (Psalm 145 v16). The record of history is a register of the great things God has done for his people. In every age and generation, believers have been able to testify to God's 'greatness' to them. But the supreme example of God's greatness is not in the solving of problems, or in the supplying of provisions, but in the sending of a Saviour. Jesus satisfies fully.

2 RESTORATION FOR THE GREAT ARMY GOD HAS SENT (vv25-27).

In the aftermath of disaster, when the heaven-sent troops have accomplished their mission, God may begin his reconstruction programme, providing repayment and restoration. What 'army' may God deploy to bring you and me to repentance?

'Repayment' or 'restoration' is a derivative from the Hebrew word 'Shalom', meaning 'peace'. It represents more than just 'absence of war'. Rather, it means 'wholeness', 'completeness', even 'harmony'. How will God effect such wholeness?

You will have God's plenty

'... *plenty to eat until you are full*' (v26).

You will offer God's praise

'You will praise the Name of the Lord...' (v26).

You will be God's people

Restored in your covenant relationship with the Lord, you will be assured that he is the One and Only God and, as his people, you need never experience shame again (vv26,27).

We may feel ashamed that we have wasted so many years in barrenness and fruitlessness, like vegetation stripped bare. We have made mistakes in our relationships, priorities, families, marriages, churches, transactions, studies, and employment. How we would love to turn back the clock and start again! God says to the genuine penitent, *'I will restore (reimburse/repay) to you the years the locusts have eaten...'* Doesn't that thrill your soul and lift you from despondency and shame? What amazing grace!

3 REVIVAL BEFORE THE GREAT DAY GOD HAS APPOINTED (vv28-32)

These familiar verses form part of Peter's Pentecostal sermon in Acts ch2. The climactic event would begin at Mount Zion/Jerusalem and spread to all the earth.

God will pour out the Spirit

(vv28-31) This prophecy is clear: its fulfilment came on the fiftieth day after Jesus' death, at precisely 9 am (Acts ch2 v16). God's Spirit has been outpoured on men and women without discrimination. Sons and daughters, old and young, men-servants and maidservants have experienced the mighty moving and empowering of God.

God will call out the Saved

(v32) Notice that 'everyone who calls' is in fact 'everyone whom God calls'. Jesus came to call sinners to repentance (Matthew ch9 v13). Repentance is one of the first stones laid in the rebuilding of a wasted, ruined life. Praise God: He's still in the restoration business!

DECEMBER 20
JOEL ch3.1-21

The word of God through Joel not only pronounced judgement but also provided comfort and assurance. The future is not all bleak! The Day of the Lord will mean retribution for God's enemies but restoration for God's people.

FOR EVERY VALLEY THERE'S A HILL

1 THE VALLEY OF JUDGEMENT FOR THE ENEMIES OF GOD (vv1-16a)

The *'Valley of Jehoshaphat'* or the *'Valley of Decision'* is representative of the Supreme Court of the Universe in which the divine Judge will pronounce judgement on his enemies. This symbolic valley is given the name of *Jehoshaphat'* for possibly two reasons (see 1 Kings ch22 and 2 Chronicles ch20). We learn something about the nature of judgement on that awful day.

Total

(v2) There will be no escape: no evasion on that Final Judgement. No nation will be missing. Even the United Kingdom will be represented there. We may imagine that states and regimes will be present that have openly persecuted God's people and defied God's laws. But the UK? Will the nation that once led the world in social and moral reform, in the upholding of Biblical principles, in charitable services, in technological achievements, in ethical standards, in judicial integrity, in missionary enterprise, in examples of prudent administration, heroism, loyalty and good government ... a nation where the gospel rang out from its shores and where evil was condemned ... will such a nation be present on that Day? The virtues of the past cannot save us from the sins of the present. Pagan England, along with every other heathen nation, will be summoned to appear in the Valley of Jehoshaphat.

Just

(vv4-8) We cannot talk about the absolutes of justice and truth unless we refer to God (Deuteronomy ch32 v4; Isaiah ch45 v19). As believers, we are forever grateful for the grace and kindness God has demonstrated to us. But our eternal security is dependent upon God's justice and righteousness.

Severe

(vv9-13) Here is the portrayal of the Great War. It's the opposite of peace (Isaiah ch2 v4). The sickle is wielded and the grapes are trampled as a sign of final harvest and universal judgement. What kind of future are you anticipating? Are you looking for the garner of the fire? Is it 'barn' or 'burn'?

Decisive

(vv14-16) The 'decision' that gave its name to this valley is a reference to the Judge's pronouncement. A judicial decree will be made. The court's decision is final. There will be no appeals, no last-minute plea bargaining, no 'stay of execution'. How awesome is God's solemn and irreversible decision!

2 THE HILL OF BLESSING FOR THE PEOPLE OF GOD (vv16b-21)

There are numerous blessings for the redeemed of the Lord.

Sinless Separation

(v17) The hill is holy. Jerusalem is holy. They are set apart, consecrated, separated to the Lord. This city is free from evil. It's Sinless City (compare Revelation ch21 v27). Only those who have been made holy through the righteousness of Christ will be admitted into this city.

Endless Safety

(v17) *Never again will foreigners invade her'*. This has nothing to do with some 'political immigration policy'. The scope of Heaven's Admission Policy is clearly seen in ch2 v32. The old enemies, depicted by Egypt and Edom, will never be a threat again. Heaven will never be invaded by enemy forces.

Boundless Supply

(v18) Wine, milk, and water are symbols of generous provision. In Christ, there is always a boundless supply. The refreshing, sustaining water flows from God's very presence.

Timeless Citizenship

(v20) Many 'expat' societies have been formed in faraway places to refresh memory, foster fellowship, publish news, and promote the culture of the homeland. Believers have the right of citizenship to the land of New Birth. Its everlasting citizenship can never be cancelled (Philippians ch3 vv20-21).

Changeless Security

(v21) For the penitent, there is free, unmerited pardon. 'Hands full of blood' speak of guilt. But the final demands of the law have been met in the redeeming death of a fully competent Saviour.

Joel signs off his prophecy: *The Lord dwells in Zion!'* Shekinah. In Christ, God in glory has come to live with his people, and his people will live with God in Glory.

DECEMBER 21
MICAH ch1.1-16

AUTHOR

'Micah of Moresheth' (a small country town about 25m SW of Jerusalem). Little is known about the prophet except that he was a man of courage, faithfulness, and had a passion for justice.

DATE

The prophecy took place during the reigns of *'Jotham, Ahaz, and Hezekiah'*, which dates it between about 740BC and 690BC.

MESSAGE

Interwoven within this stark word of doom, there is a ray of hope.

The message of Micah is also revealed in his own name, meaning *'Who is like the Lord?'* It was a difficult message to evade wherever Micah appeared and ministered.

Micah's contemporary, Isaiah, asked, *'To whom then will you compare God? What image will you compare him to?'* (Isaiah ch40 v18). The Lord also challenges, *'To whom will you compare me? Or who is my equal?'* (Isaiah ch40 v25). The title of this chapter could be:

WHO IS LIKE THE LORD IN HIS POWER?

The Sovereign Lord stamps his authority upon the opening lines of this prophecy.

1 THE POWER OF HIS WORD (v1)

We are in danger of skipping this great statement and its significance (compare the opening lines of Joel and Jonah). Here is majesty, mastery, superiority, authority, and power! The great impassioned speeches of history may stir or challenge, but nothing will *'penetrate to dividing soul and spirit, joints and marrow; (judging) the thoughts and attitudes of the heart'* like the living, active, double-edged sword of the word of God (Hebrews ch4 v12)

2 THE POWER OF HIS WITNESS (v2)

In the courtroom scene of this verse, silence is called for across the whole earth as the Sovereign Lord from *'his holy temple'* takes the witness stand. Has there ever been a witness like this Witness? Who is able to refute his testimony or discredit his evidence? This is the One who does no wrong (Deuteronomy ch32 v4)...*'the God of truth'* (Isaiah ch65 v16)...*'the only true God'* (John ch17 v3) whose *'word is truth'* (John ch17 v17).

His evidence is thoroughly reliable and absolutely unshakeable.

His testimony cannot be challenged on the grounds that he was not present (Psalm 139) or that he did not see (2 Chronicles ch16 v9). Nothing is concealed from him.

And if such a powerful Witness is the security and hope of his people, how terrifying it will be to have this Witness *against* us (as in v2)! We cannot begin to imagine the power of his testimony to compound and intensify our guilt and shame.

3 THE POWER OF HIS WRATH (vv3-16)

God descends in the execution of his judicial power, not upon barbaric Assyrians, but upon Israel. God's people had been unfaithful, and they could no longer be smug in the security of their covenant or heritage. They had become indifferent to God's holy laws, and they were totally unprepared for the judgement to come.

How easy it is to become used to our sin! How quickly we can regard our sin to be petty and insignificant!

Sin is enticing

(v7) God's people had been lured away from the one true God to worship false gods.

Sin is infectious

(v9) Israel's *'incurable wound'* originated in the gangrenous north and now had infected even Judah and Jerusalem.

Sin is shameful

(vv10-11) Are we concerned for God's honour? Are we concerned that a pagan world is ready to pounce upon our mistakes and misdemeanours?

Sin is destructive

(vv12-16) The names of twelve towns, and the meanings of those names, are used to emphasise their calamity.

The Lord's power *against* sin is to be feared, but his power to *deliver* from sin is to be sought.

The power to cleanse from sin

The cross and the blood of Christ have the power to save and purge from sin. The cross divides mankind into the saved and unsaved, the lost and the found, the spiritually dead and the spiritually alive.

The power to keep from sin

It's God's power alone that can keep from sin's enticement, infection, shame, and destruction (2 Peter ch1 v3). It's this power that is *'able to keep us from falling'* (Jude 24) and the power that can shield us from sin.

Let us earnestly seek *'a heart from sin set free'* [Charles Wesley].

DECEMBER 22
MICAH ch2.1-13

There are many who are obsessed with comparing themselves with other people. But the ultimate comparison is the comparison with God, with whom there is no comparison. *'Among the gods there is none like you, O Lord, no deeds can compare with yours'* (Psalm 86 v8).

WHO IS LIKE THE LORD IN HIS PROMISES?

Israel was not only divided politically and religiously, but also socially. There was an arrogant, greedy, and powerful group in the land who were exploiting and defrauding the poor (v2). Such was their obsession to acquire wealth that they lay awake at night plotting and scheming evil (v1). As soon as they rose in the morning, they had the power to implement their wicked plans. But as men plan iniquity, God plans calamity (v3). The Sovereign God wo gives is the same God who takes. Have you noticed that when particular sins are highlighted and discussed, there will always be religious people who will defend and support those sins? When the word of God is preached faithfully, condemning the sins of arrogance, greed, idolatry, drunkenness, gambling, dishonouring parents, dishonouring the Lord's Day, homosexuality, abortion, and euthanasia, there will always be religious representatives and church leaders who will seek to excuse and defend such violations of God's law.

1 THE POPULAR PROMISES OF A PROPHET (vv6-11)

The false prophets attempted to gain popularity in three ways.

False prophecy about peace

(v6) God had declared judgement upon Judah (ch1 vv3-7), but what did the 'popular prophets' say (v6)? Compare Jeremiah ch8 vv8-12.

False preaching about providence

(v7) 'God is love' is the recurring text of false preachers who neither interpret it accurately nor understand it correctly. God is never a 'soft touch'. He never turns a blind eye towards sin. He cannot overlook transgressions. There's not the tiniest stain on God's character nor even the slightest suggestion of a blemish in his thoughts or motives. Our holy God hates sin with a perfect hatred (Habakkuk ch1 v13). To suggest that God doesn't get angry with sin, that he doesn't judge sin; that he doesn't *'do such things'* is a lie. But *'This is how God showed his love among us...'* (1 John ch4 vv9-10).

False prediction about prosperity

(v11) A popular prophet today is still the *'wine and beer'* prophet – one who says what the people want to hear and one who makes a prediction that is pleasing to them. That's why the 'health and wealth gospel' of the Word-Faith Movement has been so popular. The recipe is simple: mix up a blend of faith and fantasy; fold in a measure of selected anecdotes; add sweetener and a pinch of heresy; leave to prove for a few days, then cook in a moderate church. The smell and taste will be irresistible. Spiritual hunger will be temporarily relieved! Beware those like the 'profit prophet' Balaam, who is condemned as a 'greed-monger' (Jude 11; 2 Peter ch2 v15).

2 THE CERTAIN PROMISES OF GOD (vv12-13)

A Shepherd who will gather

Three times God says, *'I will'*. We must not doubt God's promise to bring his chosen sheep into the safety of his enclosure. The Good Shepherd has given his life to provide:

Fortification

The word for *'pen'* and *'enclosure'* is connected to a word for 'fortification' – a place of protection and impregnability.

Food

'A flock in its pasture'. Every resource for spiritual nourishment.

Fellowship

'The place will throng with people' who know their God.

A Conqueror who will break

He breaks through obstacles and forges a way. This reference is generally accepted as referring to the Messiah, who is revealed as the One who has opened a way through the curtain (Hebrews ch10 vv19-20). Jesus the Victor has defeated every last obstruction (Satan, sin, hell, and death too). Because he has broken through, we may follow where he leads.

A King who will lead

The people who experience the calamity of defeat and exile will be delivered. The King of the Ages sits on the throne of the universe and will march in triumph at the head of his people. Are we following closely?

DECEMBER 23
MICAH ch3.1-12

The first three verses of this chapter provide a snapshot of those 'pretend pastors' of the *'house of Israel'* who were not pastoring the flock but butchering the flock. These were prophets, preachers, and leaders who claimed to be speaking God's word and delivering God's message, but they were impostors, charlatans, and spiritual conmen. Their objective was to defraud and exploit the flock, even to the point of butchering them.

So how can we identify genuine messengers? They can be identified by the presence of God with them (Deuteronomy ch18 vv20-22). There are tests that prove God's presence with his prophets.

The Theological Test

Do they have a right view of Almighty God: his being and his glory?

The Factual Test

How faithful is the message? Does it come true?

The Moral Test

Are their lives consistent with their lips (see Jeremiah ch23)?

If a prophet enjoys the presence of the Lord and the exquisite privilege of communion with him on a daily basis, then he will speak the word of God truthfully. The Lord condemns those engaged in a sham ministry (Psalm 89 v15; Jeremiah ch23 vv18-22).

WHO IS LIKE THE LORD IN HIS PRESENCE?

What fellowship can be compared to fellowship with God? Moses needed to be assured of God's constant presence before he would agree to be sent (Exodus ch33 v14-17). Our burning quest should be to know and experience the presence of God in each department of our lives. False leaders will not have that special relationship with the Lord (v4). God's true messenger, Micah, could testify to the sign of authenticity, the hallmark of genuineness (v8) –

1 THE POWER OF HIS PRESENCE

The word *'power'* means 'the capacity to act or do something'. It means the ability to produce, to cope, to endure, and to implement. It's the word translated *'strength'* in Isaiah ch40 v31: *'...those who hope in the Lord will renew their strength.'*

As the Lord's people who hope in him and trust in him, we may know the capacity to do everything he wants us to do. We may not become 'supermen' or 'superwomen', in the sense that we shall be able to travel at the speed of light or scale the sides of skyscrapers or catch trucks (!), but we shall be able to say (with Paul), *'I can do everything through him who gives me strength'* (Philippians ch4 v13).

2 THE SPIRIT OF HIS PRESENCE

In contrast to his adversaries, Micah was a Spirit-filled preacher. See what the Lord has to say about the crooked preachers who vie for a hearing (vv5,11).

Deceptive ministers

God says that they *'lead my people astray'*.

False messages

They can even be paid to give the message that is palatable: *'if one feeds them, they proclaim 'peace'.*

Corrupt motives

They preach their messages for remuneration and reward.

How can we minister, preach, or teach unless the Spirit of God is present? Any true person of God would be riveted with fear if they believed that they entered the pulpit, or any other aspect of ministry, without the presence of God's Spirit. But we may be in danger of waking up from our sleep of lethargy, just like Samson who *'did not know that the Lord had left him'* (Judges ch16 v20). We desperately need God's Spirit in our hearts, our ministries, our preaching, our churches, and in the whole of our lives.

3 THE JUSTICE OF HIS PRESENCE

Every child of God has 'a duty of care' towards others (Isaiah ch1 v17; Jeremiah ch5 v28; ch7 v5; James ch1 v27). The presence of God in a believer's life will be characterised by a practical consideration for the needs of others. Micah had an 'eye' for the needs of others, unlike the *'rulers of the house of Israel who despise justice'* (v9).

4 THE MIGHT OF HIS PRESENCE

'Might' is connected to 'valour' and 'moral courage'. Micah took a clear stand against his nation's evil and wickedness. Those who live in the presence of God will influence the society in which they live. They will be ready to stand against the evils of their day and, with the Bible in hand, identify sin and the need to repent.

Many brag, *'Is not the Lord among us?'* (v11) when, in fact, the Lord's presence is not evidenced in power, Spirit, justice, or might. Mary and Joseph thought that Jesus was in their company, but he was not (Luke ch2 v44). Let's be certain of God's presence with us.

DECEMBER 24
MICAH ch4.1-13

The decline and demise of Israel had been unthinkable to the Hebrew people of Micah's day. They found it incredible that their future could include exile in Babylon (v10). They didn't believe that Israel's enemies, who were closing in for the kill, could ever be successful. Surely God would defend his own people from impending defeat and shame. But v12 proclaims this 'telling statement': *'But they do not know the thoughts of the Lord; they do not understand his plan'*.

WHO IS LIKE THE LORD IN HIS PLANS?

God has a mighty plan for his kingdom, which includes the two objectives: [1] the glory of his Person, and [2] the good of his people. Although quick to acknowledge the former, we may be slow to recognise the latter. *Our* plans would be very different. We wouldn't plan sorrow to bring joy, or plan loss to achieve gain, or plan suffering to produce godliness. But God's providential planning is governed by his perfect wisdom, his glorious sovereignty, and his unfailing love (Proverbs ch19 v21; Job ch42 v2).

'In the last days' (v1) is a phrase that generally refers to a period between the first coming and the second coming of Christ. It identifies the 'period of the Messiah' when Jesus would reveal the Kingdom of God and show what it was like. It's the Age of the Church and includes the time we're now living in. God had a plan to establish *'the mountain of the Lord's temple'* as *'chief among the mountains'* (v1). God's plan was for a temple inhabited by his Spirit (1 Corinthians ch3 vv16-17). This is the glorious, glistening, blood-bought Church of Christ (1 Peter ch2 v9; Revelation ch5 v9). Certainly *'peoples will stream to it'* (v1). What a majestic plan! What a mighty Planner! So what does God's plan entail?

1 TEACHING FROM HIS WORD (v2)

God's word is the training manual *'to teach us his ways'*. It is the mapbook *'so that we may walk in his paths'*. It is the statute book for *'the law will go out from Zion'*. The Scripture elsewhere describes itself as the lamp, the light, honey, and the Spirit's sword (Ephesians ch6 v17). In defeating Satan, Jesus didn't choose to use his blazing majesty and glory, or even his divine logic and masterful rhetoric. He could have easily defeated every argument and won every debate, leaving Satan as a gibbering imbecile. But our Master selected the best weapon, the one weapon that's available to every believer today: the sword of the Spirit (Matthew ch4 vv1-11). How can we expect to use that weapon by declaring, 'It is written!' unless we can honestly say, 'It is read!'?

2 SHELTERING UNDER HIS PEACE (vv3-4)

The Kingdom of God is a kingdom of peace ruled by the Prince of Peace. Jesus spelt it out to the war-worn governor Pilate in John ch18 v36. The character and conditions of Christ's kingdom are radically different from the power-crazed, sabre-rattling kingdoms of earth. Jesus promised peace to his disciples (John ch14 v27).

3 WALKING IN HIS NAME (v5)

Every citizen of Christ's kingdom is called upon to walk differently from those who have devised their own belief systems and who *'walk in the name of their gods'*. We are called to walk in the light (1 John ch1 v7)... to walk in love and in obedience (2 John v6). Those who claim *'to live in him must walk as Jesus did'* (1 John ch2 v6).

4 SUBMITTING TO HIS KINGSHIP (vv6-8)

Jesus Christ is on the throne, and the wonder of his kingship should thrill every believer's heart to know the eternal benefits of his reign.

His Remnant

(vv6-7) They will eventually be made into a *'strong nation'*.

His Rule

(v7) The Lord is King: Christ is Head of his Church.

His Restoration

(v8) As for Judah, they would be restored to their land following the painful Exile (vv9-10). But a more significant restoration of all God's people will mean that they will be rescued, redeemed, and ruled by 'David's greater Son'.

Perhaps we can identify with Judah in their defeat, loss, humiliation, and separation. Maybe we have endured the attacks of the ungodly who, like the pagan nations, gloat over us (v11). Praise God for his perfect plan (Psalm 40 v5)! He plans for *'something better'* (Hebrews ch11 vv39-40). Whether the circumstances of the present include ecstatic joys or traumatic sorrows, as a Christian, you can be sure that there is a carefully devised plan with a glorious objective in view.

Submitting to his kingship means accepting that God plans with perfect wisdom. It means acknowledging his plan is best and cannot be improved upon. It also means conforming humbly to that plan, even when some of its details seem painful or unpleasant.

DECEMBER 25
MICAH ch5.1-15

Politics has all to do with governing and government. Perfect politics implies a government that is good, holy, and righteous. Contrasted with Israel's dynasty of rulers, who were weak and vulnerable, Micah declares that there is great hope. In God's politics, He has appointed the King of Kings (Psalm 2 v6). The royal Messianic Ruler would appear from the line of Judah and would be the Lion of Judah.

WHO IS LIKE THE LORD IN HIS POLITICS?

There's an introduction to God's exalted Governor, his Supreme Sovereign, his Royal Ruler. This King would come from Bethlehem (specifically *'Ephrathah'*, also known as 'Bethlehem Judah'). It was precisely this document that the chief priests and teachers of the law quoted to the disturbed King Herod (Matthew ch2 vv5-6). There would be none like this Lion-King of Judah. No one else could bear his titles or wear his crown. So what do these verses inform us about the kingly Governor of God's politics?

1 PERSONAL KING

(v2) This is no maverick monarch or self-appointed sovereign. This is God's personal King who would *'come for me'*. He had been enthroned by God's power, and he would always find his supreme delight in doing his Father's will and fulfilling his purpose. The holy harmony of the Godhead is glimpsed when God the Son says to God the Father, when he came into the world, *'Here I am – it is written about me in the scroll – I have come to do your will, O God'* (Hebrews ch10 v7). Jesus' principal concern was to do his Father's will (Luke ch22 v42; John ch4 v34). And the 'coming for him' and the 'coming to do his will' meant that the Lion-King had to become the Lamb-Servant. From 'the highest place that heaven affords' to 'the lowest place that earth afflicts', the Lord Jesus descends to become the obedient suffering Servant. Certainly God could say that he would *'come for me'*, but in that other sense, can you say, 'He came for me'?

2 PERPETUAL KING

(v2) In God's politics, his King is an everlasting King. There's no fear that his empire will decline or fall (Psalm 45 v6; Isaiah ch9 v6). This King has not just descended from an ancient lineage. He is the eternal Son of God whose rule extends from eternity to eternity. His dynasty will never be truncated, his throne will never be vacated, and his sovereignty will never be abdicated. Jesus Christ is the everlasting Monarch (Psalm 10 v16).

3 PASTORAL KING

(v4) He is the Shepherd King who will lead and protect his flock. Israel as a nation would be *'abandoned'* for a time (v3). But the birth of the New Testament Church is in view. Eventually, all God's people would be united in Christ. Jesus spoke of this united flock in John ch10 vv14-16. Those who belong to the one flock and the one Shepherd will not be charmed by the voices of strangers. There are strange shepherds who come with their strange philosophy, strange theology, and strange ethics. Jesus said that his own sheep will recognise the stranger's voice and run away, not through cowardice, but because they have a wonderfully faithful Shepherd whose way is trustworthy and whose word is truth. The Great Shepherd will *'equip you with everything good for doing his will'* (Hebrews ch13 v21).

4 POWERFUL KING

The Lord's greatness (v4) is revealed in his mighty power that causes all weapons and fortresses to crumble before him (vv10-11); destroys all Satanic belief systems (v12) and eradicates all paganism and idolatry (vv13-14). We worry about circumstances, and we are concerned about dilemmas and disasters. We are confronted constantly with hostility, but *'his greatness will reach to the ends of the earth'*.

5 PEACEFUL KING

(v5) The world (represented by Assyria) is against Israel, and there seems to be anything but peace. But the message of the gospel will triumph, and one day the Church will be seen as a *'lion among the beasts of the forest'*. It will be victorious and will ultimately enjoy an eternal peace under the kingship of Christ, who is *'the Prince of Peace'* (Isaiah ch9 v6). For each of us who is a saved citizen of the heavenly kingdom, *'He himself is our peace'* (Ephesians ch2 v14). The reign of King Jesus in a believer's life, by the power of his Spirit, means that there is peace because he is our peace and he has reconciled us to God.

'Peace on earth and mercy mild, God and sinners reconciled.' [Charles Wesley].

DECEMBER 26
MICAH ch6.1-16

In this chapter, a courtroom scene is presented for us with the Lord as the Chief Prosecutor. With reference to the meaning of Micah's own name, we may further ask:

WHO IS LIKE THE LORD IN HIS PROSECUTION?

The court that sits here is a court of absolute justice, and there are seven features:

1 THE PROSECUTOR IS POWERFUL (v1)

The defendants cannot hope for error, inefficiency, forgetfulness, maladministration, or weakness in the prosecution if the Lord is the prosecutor.

His knowledge is perfect

There are no gaps in his knowledge. There is nothing left for him to research or discover (Job ch37 v16).

His wisdom is infinite

His wisdom is boundless, everlasting, unchanging, and *'profound'* (Job ch9 v4). Such divine wisdom is displayed in his creation, providence, and redemption.

His truth is absolute

The unalterable, unshakeable foundation of the universe and the core of eternity is the truth of God (Psalm 33 v4, John ch17 vv3,17).

2 THE WITNESSES ARE UNWAVERING (vv1-2)

The Lord calls the mountains, hills, and everlasting foundations of the earth to give testimony against Israel. They have witnessed all of Israel's history, and they cannot be discredited. The mountains would proclaim God's faithfulness to his covenant:

Mt Ararat witnessed God's covenant with Noah.

Mt Moriah witnessed God's covenant with Abraham.

Mt Sinai witnessed God's covenant with Moses.

Mt Zion witnessed God's faithfulness to David.

Mt Carmel witnessed God's faithfulness to Elijah.

3 THE EVIDENCE IS OVERWHELMING (vv4-5)

The Lord's *'righteous acts'* were emphasised in his deliverance from Egypt (v4 - redeemed from slavery and given great leaders) and his deliverance to Canaan (v5 - brought safely across the River Jordan from Shittim to Gilgal). How easily we can forget the Lord's *'righteous acts'* in our experiences and his blessings in our lives! (Psalm 103 v2).

4 THE GUILT IS OBVIOUS (v3)

The Lord makes an impassioned plea to Israel to testify against him. When has God failed them? When did he break his promise to them? When did he neglect his people or cause them harm? Israel have been given golden opportunity to testify in open court, to show that God is the cause of their sin and that the charge of ingratitude is unfounded. *'Answer me,'* says the Lord. But the most damning answer of all is Israel's silence. There's no evidence to offer against God. Israel is guilty.

5 THE LAW IS CLEAR (v8)

The desires and requirements of God are clear for all to see. His law and his standards are abundantly plain. This is one of the most all-embracing statements in the Old Testament.

6 THE CHARGES ARE SERIOUS (vv9-16)

They were dishonest in their actions

(v10) All of their gains are *'ill-gotten'*.

They were deceitful in their speech

(v12) They couldn't be trusted to tell the truth.

They were disobedient in their worship

(v16) They were engaging in the corrupt Baal-worship of Omri's evil dynasty (1 Kings ch16 vv25, 30). Every generation seemed worse than the one before.

7 THE PUNISHMENT IS SEVERE (vv9-16)

The punishment had been divinely appointed. Judgement is described as destruction and ruin (v13) as well as loss and fruitlessness (vv14-15). Israel would save and store, plant and press, but their hard work would count for nothing as the Babylonians would seize their land and plunder the fruit. So what does the Lord require? (v8)

Act Justly

Temporary appeasements (vv6-7) are not acceptable. God desires that his people act in accordance with divine standards.

Love Mercy

We must learn to love kindness, to show compassion and to be tender-hearted (Nehemiah ch9 vv30, 31; Matthew ch9 v13; Luke ch6 v36).

Walk Humbly

God's chosen people have nothing to boast about. Salvation is by grace and the matchless love and mercy of the Lord. We should not seek to be prominent or prestigious in our ministry, but to demonstrate a humble walk with God every day.

DECEMBER 27
MICAH ch7.1-20

The courtroom scene of ch6 reminds us that the charge, verdict and sentence against sinners is overwhelming. But a royal pardon has been issued to every believer. The citation on that pardon is clear: *'Therefore there is now no condemnation for those who are in Christ Jesus'* (Romans ch8 v1). We come to the climactic question of Micah's prophecy:

WHO IS LIKE THE LORD IN HIS PARDON?

1 THE GREAT DEPTH OF MISERY (vv1-6)

Micah begins this concluding section in v1 with a woe: *'What misery is mine!'* The prophet identifies himself with the sorry state of Judah and Jerusalem. He sees himself at the end of summer, looking to harvest fruit, but there is none to harvest. There are no grapes and no figs. We may relate to Micah's sorrow as he considers the fruitlessness of the land. His heart is grieved, and his mood is melancholy.

Breakdown in Society

(v2b): *'All men lie in wait to...'* This simple sentence provides a plain description of our own society with its greed, violence, deception, exploitation, selfishness, self-centredness, immorality and recklessness.

Breakdown in Authority

(vv3,4) Notice the conspiracy between the rulers and the rich. Politicians, judges and wealthy men conspire to defraud the country of its moral values and godly standards. History repeats itself.

Breakdown in Family

(vv5,6) Members of families can become enemies. Respect for parents is eroded, compounded by schools, celebrities and legislators.

Breakdown in the Church

(v2a) The nation is in a desperate situation when *'the godly have been swept from the land; no one upright man remains'*. What happens to a nation when the professing church is devoid of godly people and ceases to have an impact upon it? We can be part of a social church, a community church, a progressive church, an active church – but unless we are a Godly church, then we lose our credibility, our authority and our power.

2 THE GREAT DEPTH OF MERCY (vv7-20)

The Lord is merciful, and vv18 and 20 confirm that he is delighted to *'show mercy'*. Like Micah, we could become dejected and miserable if we focused on our ungodly land. But Micah knows better (v7). God wouldn't fail him or betray his trust. Satan and our enemies may gloat over us (v8), but there is hope (v11). God had blessed them *'in days long ago'* (v14) and God promises to *'show them (his) wonders'* (v15). What a loving and gracious

God he is. In spite of our worst transgressions, there is mercy. Where else could we find such depth of mercy or such breadth of pardon?

'Pardon' is to do with *'carrying'* or *'carrying/taking away'*. The goat of the sin offering was provided *'to take away the guilt of the community'* (Leviticus ch10 v17), and the scapegoat would *'carry on itself all their sins to a solitary place'* (Leviticus ch16 v22). However, Cain's punishment for killing his brother was *'more than (he) could bear/carry'* (Genesis ch4 v13). But what was too great for Cain to bear was not too great for Christ to bear. *'Surely he **took up** our infirmities and **carried** our sorrows'* (Isaiah ch53 vv4, 12). God's pardon is free and absolute for those who turn to him (Isaiah ch55 vv6-7). How can we be sure that our sin is dealt with and will not rear its ugly head to haunt us or intimidate us?

It's out of sight!

'You will tread our sins underfoot' (v19). Just as the Tempter himself would be trodden underfoot and whose head would be crushed by the Saviour (Genesis ch3 v15), so we can be assured that *'the God of peace will soon crush Satan under your feet'* (Romans ch16 v20). In the Calvary conquest of Jesus, our victorious Redeemer, both Satan and sin have been trodden underfoot. The slate is wiped clean. Every blot, spot, and stain is removed.

It's out of reach!

'...the depths of the sea' (v19). Our sins won't remain on the surface, bobbing around for all to see or even recover. They have been removed far away (Psalm 103 v12; Isaiah ch38 v17).

It's out of mind!

'You do not stay angry forever...' (v18). 'Forgetfulness' is a weakness, but God doesn't 'forget' our sins. He chooses not to remember them anymore (Isaiah ch43 v25; Jeremiah ch31 v34).

Are there sins from the past threatening you and harassing you? Seek God's mercy!

'Who is a pardoning God like thee, or who has grace so rich and free?' [Samuel Davies].

DECEMBER 28
MALACHI ch1.1-14

AUTHOR

'Malachi', whose name means 'My messenger'. The author is so unknown that some believe 'Malachi' refers to the title of his office rather than to his personal name.

DATE

The most popular opinion places Malachi in the last half of the fifth century BC, about a hundred years after Haggai and Zechariah.

MESSAGE

God's people were engaged in a faithless and heartless religion. This prophet brought another 'wake-up' call to stir them from their hardness and indifference.

There is a sense in which this strategically placed prophecy links the sunset of the Old Testament with the sunrise of the New Testament. This book is a type of bridge joining the antiquity of the Old Testament to the necessity of the New Testament. It shows the connection between God selecting Jacob (vv1-2) and God sending Jesus (ch3 v1). Here is the link that spans the gulf between the messengers of the Old Covenant and the Messenger of the New Covenant.

But there is a timely message for these wayward people whose work had become boring, whose love had become cold, and whose religion had become meaningless.

DON'T LIGHT USELESS FIRES ON GOD'S ALTAR!

The altar in the rebuilt temple would have been made of bronze and measured about thirty feet square and about fifteen high (9m x 4.5m). Sacrifices were offered here each day in the morning and evening. Significant days, feast days, and special events in family life were reasons for offering. Usually, the offering consisted of a goat or sheep, but the wealthy may offer a bull, and the poor may offer a pigeon or dove. In each case, the animal had to be healthy and free from injury or defect. The sacrificing was to be continual (Exodus ch29 v42) and provided atonement (Leviticus ch1 v4).

Lighting the altar's fires and making sacrifices demonstrated love for God, commitment to his laws and purposes, and a desire to lead a holy life. But v10 indicates that they had only been 'going through the motions' of offering endless sacrifices that meant nothing. Their actions were *'useless'*. Perhaps we have been lighting 'useless fires' on God's altar?

1 BY DARING TO DOUBT WITHOUT GRATITUDE (vv1-5)

Is there a greater message to humanity, from the heart of the Almighty, than, *'I have loved you'* (v2)? The history of Israel is a detailed record of God's love towards his people. Yet they dare to ask, *'How have you loved us?'* God had chosen Jacob instead of Esau (vv2-4) and had lavished his love upon him and upon his privileged descendants. Yet they doubted his kindness and compassion to them, just as men and women today doubt the provision of a Saviour in the Lord Jesus Christ.

2 BY ATTEMPTING TO WORSHIP WITHOUT REVERENCE (vv6-11)

We worship a great Lord (v5), a great name (v11), and a great King (v14). The respect/reverence/fear comes from a recognition of who God is. A son shows respect for his father, and a servant shows respect for his master (v6). Should not professing worshippers show respect for their God? The Lord God carefully guards the way we worship him. We don't need to resort to mimicking the world or to employing its entertainment in our worship.

3 BY SEEKING TO SERVE WITHOUT WILLINGNESS (vv12-13)

Not only was the worship of God heartless and meaningless, but their service to God had become a burden to them. Their delight had turned to drudgery; cheer had given way to chore! *'And you say, 'What a burden!' and you sniff at it contemptuously...'* (v13). Sometimes our particular service for God may appear dull, uninteresting, repetitive, and too much of a hassle. Do we complain of the burden?

4 BY PRETENDING TO SACRIFICE WITHOUT COST (vv8-9, 13-14)

The animals didn't constitute a real sacrifice – they were the worst and the weakest of the flocks and herds. God referred to those who brought them as *'cheats'* (v14). Do we try to appear as if we are making sacrifices when it costs us nothing (2 Samuel ch24 v24)? Do we try to get away with less than our best? The genuine sacrifices of God *'are a broken spirit; a broken and contrite heart...'* (Psalm 51 v17). Let his altar be ablaze with that kind of sacrifice.

DECEMBER 29
MALACHI ch2.1-17

Malachi – 'My messenger' – is on His Majesty's Service. His task was [i] to represent God before the people, [ii] to deliver the very solemn and urgent message to those people, and [iii] to act for God and to work on his behalf. Put simply, Malachi was to be an ambassador, an announcer and an agent.

But the message of this prophecy, and especially the thrust of this chapter, is to condemn those others who should have been acting as ambassadors, announcers and agents, that is, the priests.

ON HIS MAJESTY'S SERVICE

This singular text declares that the priest was *'the messenger of the Lord Almighty'* (v7). We can imagine how the authority of the messenger is undermined and how the importance of the message is underestimated if the messenger fails to act as the ambassador and representative of the one who has sent him

- Imagine listening to a message of health and hygiene from a hygienist who smokes and who stinks of body odour! How seriously would you heed their message?

- Consider listening to a message of road safety from a lecturer whose car displays dents and scratches, a bald tyre and large, furry dice dangling inside the windscreen! How seriously would you heed his message?

- So imagine a preacher who lives a dishonest life, who is casual about God and flippant about his standards. Would you take his message seriously?

There must be nothing about the messenger that compromises or paralyses the message he is delivering. Some seem to regard the preacher as a kind of 'sermon factory'. Feed in an amount of diverse ingredients between Monday and Saturday, and you will produce a tailor-made, standard-size sermon on Sunday! The preacher is not a teacher with a lesson, or a lecturer with a paper, or even a parson with a sermon – he is a messenger with a message! A preacher, like the Old Testament prophets, should have the burden of the Lord's message upon his heart. That burden is only ever relieved, and that duty is only ever discharged, when he has delivered that message faithfully.

What qualities should we expect from such messengers?

1 A HEART FOR GOD'S HONOUR (vv1-5)

A curse would be sent if the ministers would not listen and if they did not set their hearts to honour God's name. God's people are identified as *'those who love his name'* (for example, Psalm 69 v36). His name is majestic (Psalm 8 v1), glorious (Psalm 29 v2) and of great renown (Hosea ch12 v5). It's a name that we can trust in, hope in and rejoice in. How much concern and zeal for God's honour do we have in our nation, our home or our church? Are we prepared to deal decisively with sin and every attack upon God's honour?

2 A LOVE FOR GOD'S TRUTH (vv6-7)

The faithful priests, like Levi before them, had *'true instruction'* in their mouths, and *'nothing false'* upon their lips. The people of God should love the word of God (Psalm 119 v47). Do we find something real, vital and personal about the Bible? Can we say *'Oh, how I love your law! I meditate on it all day long'* (Psalm 119 v97)?

3 A DESIRE FOR GOD'S WAY (vv8-9)

The priests had *'turned from the way'* (v8) and had *'not followed (God's) ways'* (v9). They had failed in their priestly function. They were not faithful, not following and not fair! How much do we want to walk with Jesus?

4 A LOYALTY TO GOD'S COVENANT (vv10-17)

Each of verses 10, 11, 14, 15 and 16 refers to *'breaking faith'* or *'dealing treacherously'*. God's people are bound together in a family, which is protected by a marriage covenant. Just as the marriage covenant is formal, legal, public, sacred and binding, so God's covenant with Judah is formal, legal, public, sacred and binding. God's likes and dislikes are obvious. He loves all that is separated for him (v11), but he hates all that is separated from him (v16). This lesson about the prominence and permanence of marriage illustrates the greatest of all relationships: the relationship between a believer and Christ, the heavenly Bridegroom.

No wonder God hates divorce, because it represents opposition to everything that God, in his grace, has done for his covenant people who are redeemed through Christ.

DECEMBER 30
MALACHI ch3.1-18

In Proverbs ch25 v13 a trustworthy messenger is compared to the cool, quenching waters of melted snow that refresh the hot harvesters in their dry and dusty work. Compared with such cool and invigorating waters, Malachi delivers God's message about another messenger – the coming of God's Messenger-Messiah. In fact, Malachi speaks first about a messenger (John Baptist) who would prepare the way for the supreme Messenger, the Lord Jesus Christ (v1). Each of the four Gospel writers identifies John as the one Malachi refers to as the forerunner of Jesus, *'the Messenger of the covenant'*. John would preach righteousness and repentance in such a way that many people would come to realise that pardon and reconciliation with God can only be obtained ultimately through Jesus, the Messenger of the covenant. Jesus is referred to in v1 as the One *'whom you desire (are seeking)'*. Is he the One whom you desire and pursue?

THE DISTINCTION BETWEEN THOSE WHO SERVE GOD AND THOSE WHO DON'T

Verse 18 emphasises that such a distinction will be seen. Those who belong to God will be purged and tested. The image of a refiner occurs many times (for example, Isaiah ch48 vv10-11). When God allows his people to pass through the fires of adversity, it's not the same as the consuming fires of his wrath. The fire of vv2-3 is specifically designed and carefully controlled. This fire is not for total destruction. The whole purpose of this fire is to bring out the best: it's a quality-producing fire that will only yield pure gold and pure silver. The Lord is said *'to sit as a refiner and purifier of silver'* (v3). He carefully monitors the pressure in the furnace. He controls the temperature: never too cool to be ineffective or never too hot to irreparably damage. The Lord's eye is on the 'finished product'. He wants his people to be the:

Right Shape

They need to be moulded and fashioned into his instruments.

Right Strength

They must be capable of resisting adverse forces and tough pressures.

Right Standard

They need to be purged and purified from all impurities and pollutants.

God's laws and requirements do not change. God doesn't change (v6). He is faithful to all his promises, and he is gracious, calling wanderers to return (v7). Even though his people 'answer him back' (as in ch1 vv2, 6, 7; ch2 v17; ch3 vv7, 8, 13). The distinction between those who serve God and those who don't is emphasised again in vv8-17.

1 OFFERING OF WHOLE TITHES (vv8-12)

'Tithing' represents willing obedience, loving devotion and genuine gratitude to God for his grace. Withholding of such tithes is looked upon as *'robbing God'*. Every believer is responsible for giving back to God a percentage of what is received. Every church member has a responsibility to give back to God through the church – the storehouse of God's blessing – just as Israel was instructed to *'bring the whole tithe into the storehouse'* (v10). There are too many robbers in the church today. But you cannot beat God when it comes to 'giving'. Giving to God means serious investment. Are you prepared to *'test'* God in this?

2 ENGAGING IN WHOLSOME TALK (vv16-17)

Their Fellowship is Observed (v16)

The Lord listens to and hears the sanctified talk of faithful believers. In contrast to the sarcasm and cynicism which the Lord hears from the unfaithful, there are the holy conversations between those who *'fear the Lord and honour his name'* (v16). Do we derive mutual benefit from every conversation with the Lord's people? Is he glorified by our talk?

Their Relationship is Recorded (v16)

To think that God should keep a book of remembrance with regard to our conduct and conversation! As Christians, we may not always be able to see eye to-eye, but we should always be able to speak heart-to-heart and walk arm-in-arm. What has the Lord entered in his diary about you and me today?

Their Ownership is Guaranteed (v17)

There's no doubt about it! On the day that the Lord conducts his final accountancy and does a stock-take of his *'treasured possessions'*, the faithful and fearful believer belongs to him. Each one is marked out for God, and he says, *'They will be mine!'* A day is coming when the final distinction will be made.

THE MASTER PREACHER

'Then suddenly the Lord you are seeking will come to his temple;

the messenger of the covenant, whom you desire, will come,'

says the Lord Almighty.

Malachi ch3 v1

If you come to church one Sunday and the preacher isn't there,

And his unexpected absence gives no time to then prepare;

And the congregation's chatter throws the deacons in a spin,

And the vestry door swings open, and then Jesus Christ walks in.

Would there be a holy silence as he climbs the pulpit stairs?

Would the normal chat continue over trite mundane affairs?

Would you talk about his dress sense and his style of hair or beard?

Would things be any different from the moment he appeared?

When he introduced the singing, would you sing with heart and lung?

Would you sing the hymns and anthems in the way they're always sung?

Would you quickly be distracted when he calls the church to prayer?

Would your mind relax as usual, and your thoughts flit everywhere?

Would you miss the 'entertainment' – dances, musicals and mimes –

All the things that pass as worship in the church at other times?

Would you stick with all your customs that for decades have sufficed

And deny yourself the blessing just to concentrate on Christ?

Would you want the church announcements to provide their half-time break?

With their lists of sports engagements – all for which you stay awake?

Would you feel your conscience prick you as you pass the offering plate?

And that, in the circumstances, would you raise the 'giving rate'?

Would you listen to the lesson or react with yawns and smirks?

Would you criticise his accent and pronunciation quirks?

Would you moan about the passage – 'Far too long…made you confused'?

And would you loathe the version that the Saviour chose to use?

Would you moan about his preaching as you do on other weeks?

Disapprove of lengthy sermons and the way in which he speaks?

Would you like more illustrations, funny stories now and then?

And for style and presentation, would you mark him out of ten?

Would you sigh when Jesus finished and the last 'Amen' is said?

Would you rush to leave the building or remain at prayer instead?

Would your conversation focus on the message you had heard?

Or would you try to carry on as if nothing had occurred?

So now, when you come on Sunday, will you listen for the voice

of Christ, the Master Preacher, through the servant of his choice?

Will you long to know his Spirit breathe the message of God's word,

and give your rapt attention as if *JESUS*' voice is heard?

Geoff Fox

DECEMBER 31
MALACHI ch4.1-6

In these closing verses of the Book of Malachi, as well as the concluding paragraphs of the Prophets and all of the Old Covenant writings, the Lord warns, *'Surely the day is coming'* (v1). In Jewish thinking, important and significant events were given the title that began *'The Day of...'*. So specific historical events, such as 'the Day of Jerusalem's Destruction', or more general happenings such as 'The Day of Trouble', were described in this way.

LOOKING FORWARD TO THE DAY OF THE LORD

Among Israel's prophets, the title 'The Day' described a future climactic day of God's visitation that would be characterised by cursing and blessing; by calamity and security; by horror and hope. The 'Day of the Lord' would be both near and far. It was imminent yet distant. God would visit His people within history, but there was also the expectation of God's visit at the ultimate end of history. The New Testament identifies this 'Day of the Lord' as the 'Day of Christ' and points to the Second Coming of Christ.

1 UNBELIEVERS WILL FEAR THE DOOM OF THAT DAY

The period of Christ's coming, beginning with his incarnation, was a time when notice was served on those who reject the Saviour (for example, John ch3 vv18, 36). For all those entrenched in their opposition to Christ and his cross, the coming of the Messiah means judgement and doom. The final word of the Old Testament is one of the harshest words in the whole of Scripture: *'curse'* (v6). This word means 'utter destruction'; 'total ruin'; 'final doom'. For the unbeliever, the Day of the Lord's coming will *'burn like a furnace'* (v1). We can't begin to imagine the utter hopelessness of such judgement. It will be an awesome day... *'a great and dreadful day'* (v5). That day will be preceded by 'Elijah' (v5). It's speaking of John Baptist who would conduct his ministry *'in the spirit and power of Elijah'* (Luke ch1 v17; Matthew ch11 vv11-14). John was the last and greatest of all the Old Testament prophets, and this last prophetic writer (Malachi) points to the last prophet (John) who points to the supreme prophet (Jesus). John's business, as messenger and forerunner, was to prepare the way for Jesus. John knew his role precisely (John ch3 vv28-30).

John's illustrious Successor would be seen as a Harvester with a threshing fork, separating the wheat for the barn and the chaff for the fire.

2 BELIEVERS WILL LOVE THE DAWN OF THAT DAY

The day that is inaugurated by the coming of Christ is the day of God's glory. Although opinions may be divided over whether v2 refers directly to Jesus as *'the sun of righteousness'*, nevertheless, in the context of John Baptist's birth, he is described as *'the rising sun'* (Luke ch1 vv78-79). The glorious dawn of the new age is marked by the appearance of the Lord Jesus Christ on the stage of history. This is the 'epiphany': 'light shining forth'...'light appearing, as over the horizon'...'a beautiful sunrise'.

This appearance (epiphany) is seen in *'salvation'* (Titus ch2 v11) and in *'the kindness and love of God'* (Titus ch3 v4). To those believers who love the dawn of this day, they must:

Revere the Name

Believers are referred to as those who *'revere my name'* (v2) and *'those who fear the Lord'* and who *'honour his name'* (ch3 v16). Worship must be with *'reverence and awe'* (Hebrews ch12 v28).

Resist the Wicked

To *'trample the wicked'*, or to 'tread the wicked underfoot' (v3), denotes the total victory of the righteous over the unrighteous. This is not possible in the believer's own strength, but it is possible through Christ. Resisting the influences of the wicked means resisting the devil. This can only be done by submitting to God (James ch4 v7) and *'standing firm in the faith'* (1 Peter ch5 v9).

Remember the Law

This final admonition of the Old Testament is a fitting reminder, as one era draws to a close and another dawns, that the word of God is central to our faith and practice. The 'remembering' is not to be in a passive sense, but in the active sense of recalling the law, applying the law and keeping the law. How should we prepare for the day of the Lord's coming? By remembering the law of God and by obeying his word.

At this major milestone, right at the end of the Old Testament, it's a timely opportunity to reassess our commitment to, and our love for, the word of God.

As we anticipate the possibility of the Day of the Lord occurring in this next year's calendar, may our response here at the end of the Old Testament be the same as at the end of the New Testament:

'Amen. Come, Lord Jesus' (Revelation ch22 v20).